T0141425

# Perspectives on the Computer Revolution

## Second Edition

*Edited*
*with commentaries*
*by*

**Zenon W. Pylyshyn**
University of Western Ontario, London, Canada

*and*

**Liam J. Bannon**
Aarhus University, Aarhus, Denmark

 ABLEX PUBLISHING CORPORATION
NORWOOD, NEW JERSEY

Library of Congress Cataloging-in-Publication Data

Perspectives on the computer revolution / edited by Zenon W. Pylyshyn
  and Liam J. Bannon. — Rev. ed.
    p.  cm.
  Includes bibliographies and index.
  ISBN 0-89391-369-3 (cloth); 0-89391-591-2 (ppk)
    1. Electronic data processing.  2. Electronic digital computers.
  I. Pylyshyn, Zenon W., 1937–    II. Bannon, Liam.
  QA76.P429  1989
  004—dc19                           89-30213
                                           CIP

Ablex Publishing Corporation
355 Chestnut St.
Norwood, NJ 07648

*To Bill and Monica,*
*for their patience and understanding;*
*and to Linda, still.*

# TABLE OF CONTENTS

# Acknowledgments

Special thanks to the following authors who provided additional material for inclusion in this volume: John Carroll, Rob Kling, Jim Levin, Steve Miller, and Donald Norman.

Much of the work on the second edition of this book was done while Liam Bannon was on a postdoctoral fellowship at the Institute for Cognitive Science, University of California, San Diego. The fellowship was supported by funds from the System Development Foundation. Support facilities have also been provided by the Centre for Cognitive Science, University of Western Ontario, Canada, the Department of Computer Science, University College, Dublin, Ireland, and the Department of Computer Science, Aarhus University, Aarhus, Denmark.

Both editors wish to thank Roy Eagleson for constructing the subject index and for additional proofreading and Lisa Nadeau for her help in ensuring the project's final completion.

"Of the Analytical Engine" by Charles Babbage. Adapted from *Passages from the Life of a Philosopher* (London: Longmans Green & Co. Ltd., 1864). By permission of the publisher.

"Proposed Automatic Calculating Machine" by Howard Aiken. Adapted from *IEEE Spectrum,* Vol. 1, No. 8, 1964. By permission of the Institute of Electrical and Electronics Engineers Inc., Anthony G. Oettinger, and the author.

"Preliminary Discussion of the Logical Design of an Electronic Computing Instrument" by Arthur W. Burks, Herman H. Goldstine, and John von Neumann. Adapted from *John von Neumann, Collected Works,* ed. A.H. Taub (New York: The Macmillan Company Publishers, 1963), Vol. 5. By permission of the authors and the estate of John von Neumann.

"As We May Think" by Vannevar Bush. Reprinted from *The Atlantic Monthly,* Vol. 176, 1945. Copyright © 1945 by the Atlantic Monthly Company, Boston, Massachusetts 02116. By permission of the publisher and the author.

"The Destruction of Machines in Erewhon" by Samuel Butler. Adapted from *Erewhon* (New York: The New American Library Inc., 1961). Reprinted with permission of the publisher.

"The Fourth Discontinuity" by Bruce Mazlish. Reprinted from *Technology and Culture,* January, 1967, by permission of the University of Chicago Press, the Society for the History of Technology, and the author. Copyright © 1967 by the Society for the History of Technology.

ing Machinery, Inc., reprinted with permission of the publisher and the author.

"Engineers and the Work that People Do" by H.H. Rosenbrock. Reprinted with permission from *IEEE Control Systems Magazine*, Vol. 1(3), pp. 4–8, September, 1981, Copyright © 1981 IEEE. This paper also appears in IEEE *Technology and Society* (newsletter), Vol. 9(3), pp. 14–18, September 1981.

"Training Wheels in a User Interface" by John M. Carroll and Caroline Carrithers. Reprinted from *Communications of the ACM*, Vol. 27(8), 1984. Copyright © 1984 Association for Computing Machinery Inc. With permission of John M. Carroll.

"Algorithms" by B.A. Trakhtenbrot. Adapted from *Algorithms and Automatic Computing Machines*. Copyright © 1963 by University of Chicago Press. Published by D.C. Heath and Company, A division of Raytheon Education Co., Boston, Massachusetts. Reprinted with permission of the publisher, the University of Chicago, Alfred L. Putnam, and Izaak Wirszup.

"Computers, Knowledge, and the Human Mind" by Zenon W. Pylyshyn. Adapted from *Creativity and Liberal Learning: Problems and Possibilities in American Education*, David G. Tuerck (Ed.). Copyright © 1987 by Ablex Publishing Corporation: Norwood, New Jersey. By permission of the publisher and the author.

"Artificial Intelligence?" by Z.W. Pylyshyn, W.W. Bledsoe, E.A. Feigenbaum, A. Newell, N. Nilsson, D. Raj Reddy, A. Rosenfeld, T. Winograd, and P. Winston (Panel on Artificial Intelligence). Adapted from the chapter "Artificial Intelligence," in *What Can Be Automated? The Computer Science and Engineering Research Study*, Bruce W. Arden (Ed.). Copyright © 1980 by The Massachusetts Institute of Technology Press: Cambridge, Massachusetts. Reprinted with permission of the publisher.

"The Pioneering Work of Douglas C. Engelbart" by Liam J. Bannon. Adapted from *Extending the Design Boundaries of Human-Computer Interaction*, Institute for Cognitive Science Technical Report 8505, University of California, San Diego, May 1985. Copyright © 1985 by Liam J. Bannon. Reprinted with permission of the author.

"Personal Computers and Education" by James A. Levin and Yaakov Kareev. Adapted from *Personal Computers and Education: The Challenge to Schools*, Center for Human Information Processing Technical Report 98, University of California, San Diego, November 1980. Reprinted with permission of the authors.

The editors also wish to acknowledge the following sources from which quotations were drawn.

The Society of Authors (London). For permission to quote from *Man and Superman: A Comedy and a Philosophy* by George Bernard Shaw.

The Macmillan Company, Publishers (New York). For permission to quote from *Science and the Modern World* by Alfred North Whitehead, published in 1925.

Houghton Mifflin Company (Boston). For permission to quote from *Human Use of Human Beings* by Norbert Wiener, published in 1950.

Harcourt, Brace & World, Inc. (New York). For permission to quote from *The Physicist's Conception of Nature* by Werner Heisenberg, published in 1958.

Simon & Schuster, Inc. (New York). For permission to quote from *Unpopular Essays* by Bertrand Russell, published in 1950.

S. G. Phillips, Inc., Publishers (New York), and Bloud et Gay Librarie (Paris). For permission to quote from *Reflections sur la Science des Machines: Cahiers de Nouvelle Journee* No. 21 by Jacques Lafitte.

Porcupine Press, Ltd. For permission to quote from *The Soul of Man Under Socialism* by Oscar Wilde, published in 1948.

Prentice-Hall, Inc., and the author. For permission to quote from *Computation: Finite and Infinite Machines* by Marvin L. Minsky. Copyright © 1967 by Prentice-Hall, Inc., Englewood Cliffs, NJ.

Little, Brown and Company (Boston), and Curtis Brown Ltd. (London). For permission to quote "A Caution to Everybody" from *Verses from 1929 On* by Ogden Nash. Copyright © 1931 by Ogden Nash.

# Introduction to the Second Edition

Since the initial appearance of this book in 1970, there have been major developments in computing technology, specifically the emergence of micro-electronics technology and the commercialization of artificial intelligence, which have done much to further the spread of computers and computer-based technologies into society. This development has been accompanied by increased discussion in all sectors of exactly what the social effects of these new information technologies are, and whether the societal changes observed are beneficial or not. In this revision of the book, we have replaced more than half of the readings, have updated others, and have rewritten much of the introductory material. We hope that this new collection will reflect issues that have recently become more pertinent but our focus remains on the fundamental issues, rather than solely on technological developments. We felt that this book should reflect a concern about the nature and uses of computers, and offer some ''perspectives,'' as signified by the book's title.

Zenon Pylyshyn was primarily responsible for the selection and commentaries in Sections I, II, and VI. Liam Bannon was primarily responsible for Sections III, IV, and V.

The book retains much of the historical material on the development of computing (Section I). There is now also a major section on machine intelligence (Section II), containing much new material which discusses the issue from both a technical and philosophical stance. The growing importance of human-computer interaction research is reflected in the contents of Section III, which is devoted exclusively to this topic.

Sections IV and V focus on uses of computing in various environments and the technological choices that must be faced. It can be extremely difficult to develop an understanding of the issues involved in the use of new technology, as authors espouse different value frameworks that often affect the questions they raise concerning the social effects of technology. The commentary to Section V discusses this issue, and the ensuing articles allow the reader to observe some of these alternative views on current changes.

The articles selected for inclusion in this volume vary considerably in style and amount of detail. Our intention has been to offer a readable insightful text that does not require high-level mathematical knowledge. We hope to interest readers from a variety of backgrounds. The book should be of particular use in introducing computer science students to some of the broader issues concerning the development and use of computers in society. A number of the articles are reproduced in their original form in order to preserve their historical context and stylistic integrity. The sexist language employed by some of the authors may offend, but reflects the attitudes then prevalent, and may serve as a useful reminder of how times have changed. We expect most readers to browse, rather than read the book from start to finish in a single sitting. Given the public interest in computers and the social policy decisions being made about their use in many aspects of our lives, an informed public is vital. We hope that the contents of this volume will assist in this process. For those readers who wish to pursue a topic in more detail, there are extensive guides to further reading.

*Liam J. Bannon*                                                    *Zenon W. Pylyshyn*
*Aarhus, Denmark*                                                 *London, Ontario*

# About the Editors

ZENON W. PYLYSHYN is Professor of Psychology and of Computer Science, and Director of the Centre for Cognitive Science at the University of Western Ontario, London, Ontario, Canada. He is also national director of the program in Artificial Intelligence and Robotics of the Canadian Institute for Advanced Research. Professor Pylyshyn is past president of the Society for Philosophy and Psychology and the Cognitive Science Society and has acted as consultant on science policy and on Artificial Intelligence to government and industry.

LIAM J. BANNON is currently Visiting Associate Professor in the Computer Science Department at Aarhus University in Denmark. He was educated in psychology and computer science at University College Dublin, Trinity College, Dublin, Ireland and the University of Western Ontario, Canada. He has worked with Honeywell Inc. in Minneapolis, USA on human factors issues, was technical consultant to the European Community FAST Programme on Social Issues in Information Technology, and spent three years as a post-doctoral fellow on human-computer interaction at the Institute for Cognitive Science, University of California, San Diego. His interests focus on designing technology to enhance, rather than supplant, human skill and knowledge.

# Section I

# Some Landmarks in the History of Computers

The reasonable man adapts himself to the world; the unreasonable one persists in trying to adapt the world to himself. Therefore all progress depends on the unreasonable man.

G. Bernard Shaw
*Man and Superman*

God hath made man upright; but they have sought out many inventions.
*Ecclesiastes VIII: 29*

There is properly no history; only biography.

Ralph Waldo Emerson
*Essays: History*

Man is a tool-using animal. . . . Without tools he is nothing, with tools he is all.
Thomas Carlyle
*Sartor Resartus, Book 1, Chapter 4*

The greatest invention of the nineteenth century was the invention of the method of invention. A new method entered into life. In order to understand our epoch, we can neglect all the details of change, such as railways, telegraphs, radios, spinning machines, synthetic dyes. We must concentrate on the method itself; that is the real novelty, which has broken up the foundations of the old civilization. The prophecy of Francis Bacon has now been fulfilled; a man, who at times dreamt of himself as a little lower than the angels, has submitted to become the servant and the minister of nature. It still remains to be seen whether the same actor can play both parts.

A. N. Whitehead
*Science and the Modern World*

No human achievement is born in a vacuum. A long intellectual heritage provides the techniques as well as a comprehension of how they can be used. A combination of many circumstances provides a need—or at least an awareness of a need. A spectrum of diverse activities, interests, and recollections in a society sets up a background against which the need and the body of technique is

1

perceived. There is, as E. G. Boring[1] would put it, a *Zeitgeist*—a spirit of the times—which prepares a society for certain achievements. And finally, there is the vision in the mind of the right person at the right time which juxtaposes ideas in a novel combination and sees the significance of the new arrangement.

The history of computers and of the emerging computer and information sciences is the story of these visionaries—from the inventor of the abacus, the builders of Stonehenge,[2] and the designer of the Antikythera Mechanism[3] to many people whose names appear as authors in this collection. An appreciation of the fires in which the instruments of the Computer Revolution were forged must take account of some of this heritage.

Many excellent books and chapters have been written on the history of computers. The selections in this chapter have been chosen because they present material not usually contained in the introductory or historical chapters of computer books. Furthermore, several of them are documents which themselves were important landmarks in the history of computers and computer science. Consequently they help to give a picture of the spirit in which these developments took place. The papers by Charles Babbage, by Howard Aiken, by Arthur Burks, Herman Goldstine, and John von Neumann, and by Vannevar Bush are in this category.

The opening paper by Thomas M. Smith accurately sets the tone for the entire book. This essay, written especially for this volume, introduces the reader to the broad historical context within which the modern computer was developed. It is an eloquent description of the intellectual heritage which spawned a long line of marvelous devices, of which the modern digital computer is a contemporary example. It also introduces the reader to a remarkable person—Charles Babbage. Babbage's insights on the design and the implications of a self-sequencing calculating device—known as the Analytical Engine—were a century ahead of his time. In fact, when the British journal *Nature* published an account of one of the modern electronic computers, it titled the article, "Babbage's Dream Comes True." Some idea of the nature of both the Analytical Engine (which was never constructed for a number of technical as well as personal and financial reasons) and of its designer may be obtained from the selection by Babbage himself, taken from his autobiography. Babbage's discussion of the Analytical Engine is full of incidental details and shows something of the temperament of this eccentric genius.[4]

Nothing approaching the grand design of the Analytical Engine was attempted for over a hundred years after Babbage's ideas were developed in the early nineteenth century. Not until the Second World War did automatic calculators of various kinds begin to be developed, although in 1930 Bush developed a mechanical device, called a differential analyzer, for solving differential equations. During the war devices such as this were used to solve military problems. They were members of a species of computer called *analogue computers*. These have important engineering and control applications but do not have the wide applicability of the other species—the digital computers. Some of the first digital computers were developed by Bell Telephone Laboratories and used telephone switching relays.

The real dawn of the computer age arrived, however, with the construction of a machine which—like Babbage's Analytical Engine—could control the entire sequence of its calculations, reading in data and instructions at one point and printing results at another. The credit for the first such machine is usually given to Howard Aiken for his Automatic Sequence Controlled Calculator, or Harvard Mark I, completed in May 1944. Recently a copy of a memorandum written by Aiken, in which he proposed the construction of such a machine, was discovered in his Harvard files. The memorandum was undated, but an unknown recipient annotated it as "Prospectus of Howard Aiken, November 4, 1937." The entire memorandum, except the section describing how various mathematical functions could be calculated in terms of the simpler operations of addition, subtraction, multiplication, and division, is reproduced herein. The construction of the Mark I began in 1939, and the machine was retired in 1959 after a distinguished career.

Another memorandum which marked a turning point in the history of computers is one originally written for a U. S. Army contract in 1946 by Arthur Burks, Herman Goldstine, and John von Neumann. In it the authors propose a set of guidelines for the logical design of a computer. Many of these were radical departures at the time, although they accurately describe the features present in contemporary computers. One of the most important of their proposals was that of storing data and programs in a common memory. All modern digital computers incorporate this stored-program concept, first implemented on the Cambridge University machine EDSAC in 1949. The report also calls for the use of the binary number system for carrying out arithmetic operations and of a floating-point form for storing numbers to automatically keep track of the location of the decimal point. Burks, Goldstine, and von Neumann also introduced the idea of special memory registers to serve special sequence control functions and to perform arithmetic operations, and they worked out many details for carrying out arithmetic operations in the binary number system.

This report was part of a program of research at the Institute of Advanced Studies at Princeton University. The research eventually led to the construction, under von Neumann's direction, of a machine which incorporated the proposals described in the report. The machine was called the IAS Machine (or sometimes the von Neumann Machine or the Princeton Machine). It became the design standard for computers and was copied by such machines as the AVIDAC at the Argonne National Laboratory, the ORDVAC at Aberdeen, the ORACLE at Oak Ridge, the SILLIAC at the University of Sydney (Australia), the ILLIAC at the University of Illinois, the MANIAC at Los Alamos, and the JOHNNIAC (named after von Neumann) at RAND Corporation. It was also combined with the punched-card handling equipment developed by IBM to form the IBM-701. About half of the original report is reproduced herein. A description of the

Control Organ has been omitted for brevity because it goes into a number of technical details at considerable length.

The last paper in this section does not deal with computing machines directly but with the wider phenomena that paralleled the development of computers. It is an essay by Vannevar Bush which appeared at the close of World War II in the magazine *Atlantic Monthly*. We have already noted Bush's contribution to analogue computers with his electromechanical device, which became known as the Bush Differential Analyzer. While still serving as director of the Office of Scientific Research and Development, which coordinated applications of science to warfare, Bush wrote this impassioned essay. In it he urges the dedication of scientific instruments to give everyone access to the knowledge accumulated by society so that it may be used to better their lives. The essay is reproduced here because the insights which it contains, about how we are to deal with the explosive growth of knowledge, have had an important influence on current attempts to apply modern digital computers to the processing and retrieving of information.[5]

ZWP
*(For notes see page 63.)*

# 1

# Some Perspectives on the Early History of Computers

## 1970

### *Thomas M. Smith*

Present-day books about computers offer intriguing views of what passes for history, even the recent history of computers, and these views are, for the most part, erroneous. When one considers the nature of modern science and technology, however, the curious, plausible distortions of the past that the computer experts offer can be accounted for reasonably. For one thing, the scientific enterprise has a way of annihilating its past and changing its character. For another, today's experts are too busy working out tomorrow's solutions to today's technical problems to give yesterday's events the attention they require in order to be understood.

It is because of the way science buries its past that no one pays attention these days to the nonatomic theories of the structure of matter which, like atomism, have been around for centuries. Similarly, in our infatuation with the traditional private automobile, few have considered seriously and illuminatingly what modern, comfortable, carefree mass transportation could be like, and even fewer have paid serious attention to the possible configurations of an up-to-date Stanley Steamer or electric auto. It is in this respect that science and technology annihilate their past, because the past is unseemly since progress is their most important product.

The writers of computer textbooks reveal their commitment to progress and their misunderstanding of the past when they write so-called historical introductions and historical-review chapters. They are presumably experts on computers, and this fact encourages the reader to so very easily assume that they are experts about the past as well, that he forgets they do not have the time to study the past in its own right.

It is not that these scientific and technological experts are stupid; they are simply ignorant—ignorant of the past and ignorant of their own ignorance. Their plight is illustrated in the tale of the obstetrician who was being shown through a fine research library in the history of medicine. The obstetrician finally remarked that he was thinking seriously of taking up the history of medicine when he retired. "A fine idea," responded the professional historian in charge, without blinking an eye. "I'm thinking of taking up obstetrics myself."

The truth of the matter is, most experts on today's problems are ignorant of the past, both with respect to the data of the past and with respect to the techniques and theoretical apparatus for organizing those data. Instead, what they present in their "historical" introductions is the kind of appraisal of the past they picked up when they were schoolboys. Their views of the history of computers, for example, consist of an unorganized collection of tidbits and myths about who was the first to design which machine, and who came next, all strung together on a chronicled thread, like beads on a string—as though the relation of the past to the present were really that simple and linear in its nature. If it were, then our schoolboy acquaintance with history and with the problems of interpreting the past would suffice. The attractive idea that an historical introduction is an appropriate way to open up a subject (it really is, of course) could then be acted upon, because anyone possessing reasonable intelligence could interpret the past competently and forthwith, without first acquiring special skills and without even waiting with that well-meaning obstetrician to retire.

As a matter of fact, the past is nonlinear and reticulate. It is a fabric of events complicatedly, unexpectedly, and not always rationally, interwoven and interrelated. In consequence, the historical phenomenon of "convergence" is far more significant than the schoolboy question of who was first to invent the computer or who first provided the pegged counter so useful in simple adders and automobile odometers. (Computer experts commonly assert that Blaise Pascal did, in 1642, a date that accords well with the standard presumptions which abound concerning the nature of modern science and technology. But, alas, they are wrong.)

By historical convergence is meant the coming together of two or more traditions that have had separate pasts of their own. Their coming together sets in motion a new sequence of events. These new events become themselves traditional with the passage of time and participate in the converging network of occurrences that shape the present out of the past.

The appearance of computers late in the long history of counting and calculating provides a classic illustration of the phenomenon of convergence. Both historically and logically, computers owe their existence to many prior traditions. Among these are counting and reckoning, writing and the written record, the concept of quantity, the engineering tradition, and many more. Before there were computers there were calculators, before calculators there were adders, and before adders there were counters. Before all of these there occurred to men whose names are lost to history notions of quantity. Probably before abstract ideas of quantity emerged there was already an ages-old tradition of enumerating. The origins of this presumed tradition, too, are shrouded in prehistory.

Of early significance is the rise of the tradition of reckoning. It grew out of the convergence of the separate traditions of counting and of using symbolic designators for real things. Symbolic designators call to mind the systematic presentation of symbols called "writing." Writing dates back to the fourth millennium B.C.; it had achieved efficient form by the end of the second millennium B.C. in the Middle East.

History begins with the written record, but long before records began to be made, men had developed the concept of quantity in both its denumerable and its continuous forms. Arithmetic techniques and geometric techniques of dealing with quantities were already well developed for practical uses over 5,000 years ago, as surviving monuments and ruins demonstrate.

Just when, in the measurement of quantities, men began to use devices to assist their reckoning is not known. Nor do we know what the earliest counters looked like. The logic of numbers was applied in its rudimentary form probably before the dawn of civilization, in the activity of counting. Counting appears to have been well developed by the time writing was perfected during the second millennium B.C.

Although enumerating had become an accomplished fact long before 2,000 B.C., the *recording* of enumerations opened up a new and extensive range of possibilities. Thus, one primitive way to record a count was to employ scratch marks: 1, 11, 111, 1111, etc. Another early way was to vary the signs: 1 for "one," > for "ten." Then "twelve" becomes > 11, and so forth. A more sophisticated technique, practiced by Babylonian scribes in the time of Hammurabi (*ca.* 1800 B.C.), was to use 1 for "one" and to return to the same symbol when designating "sixty" or power of sixty or roots of sixty. The value of the symbol depends not only on the context of the problem but also on the position, or place, of the symbol alongside other symbols. This place-value notation characterizes our Hindu-Arabic numerical tradition: 1 for "one," 11 for "eleven," and so on.

One of the attractive features of place-value notation is the economy of symbols and spaces it uses; whereas "eight" requires four symbols in Roman-numeral designation, it requires only one symbol in our system. Large numbers can be denoted simply, and the systematic patterning of our decimal system allows us to perform the simple arithmetic operations with ease. Important to the ease of such calculating are the numerical symbols that have emerged as part of the generalized tool of writing.

Nonwriting apparatus is also commonly used to assist counting and reckoning. This apparatus came into being and developed independently of the written tradition. Whether the earliest forms of this apparatus were notches in a stick, scratches on a rock, knots in a length of vegetable fiber, or some other such device, they helped to make calculating more rapid, more accurate. They provided a more elaborate and powerful technique. No one knows how long small stones, or pebbles (Latin *calculi*), have been in use. Small sticks or rods do just as well. All these lend themselves to a more sophisticated level of distinctive identification when they are colored, notched, or otherwise shaped. (None of these primitive items is represented by Napier's "bones," however, for the latter represent far more advanced concepts.)

A board, slate, or slab (Greek *abax*) that can be marked or used as a platform to place counters on is another sort of instrument for simple counting and calculating. It, too, should not be confused with calculational techniques involving writing, for although these techniques intermingle in their use, they do not lose their identity as distinct techniques resting upon different principles.

In our habitual manner of speaking we are reluctant to call these devices from ancient history machines or machinelike instruments, perhaps because rods or pebbles on a counter don't form any kind of interconnected physical mechanism. But how about beads on a wire, especially several beads systematically arranged on several wires in a frame? This modern form of the abacus had a late-Roman predecessor consisting of "buttons" that slid in slots. Earlier, in the fifth century B.C., Herodotus referred to Egyptian and Greek reckoning techniques involving the systematic movement of pebbles on boards. Possibly they were lined boards that would perform similarly to the slotted Roman abacus of late antiquity.

The name *abacus* appears to have been applied as early as the sixth century B.C. to a bag of rods to be laid out on a board. By the twelfth century A.D.—a mere millennium and three-quarters later—the *suanpan* was in use in China; this is the bead-and-wire abacus still in use today.

The pebbles-on-lines, buttons-in-slots, beads-on-wires types of abacus all make use of the principle of place-value notation.

So does the odometer, the mechanism of which is described in detail in a treatise by Heron of Alexandria in Roman times. It incorporates the pegged counter-wheel principle, which Blaise Pascal mistakenly is often credited with inventing in the seventeenth century. A later writer of late antiquity possibly may have inserted the odometer description in Heron's treatise, but in any case the machine was described centuries before Pascal was born. The pegged counter-wheel is an earlier form of the single-tooth gear wheel that must revolve once for every time its tooth engages the teeth on an adjacent wheel. Heron employed this device in his odometer as part of a train of gears linked to a carriage or wagon wheel to measure the distance traveled.

Pascal's historical significance in building a train of pegged counter-wheels and using them to tot up sums is that he demonstrates the historical phenomenon of convergence. For he brought together briefly, in a special and novel way, the gear-trains design tradition stemming from antiquity and the arithmetical calculating tradition, also separately descended from antiquity.

Pascal saw that the number of teeth on the adjacent wheel would determine the number of times the single-tooth gear must revolve in order to impel the adjacent wheel through a complete revolution of its own, and if the adjacent wheel possessed a single peg that would engage the teeth of a third wheel, the third wheel would revolve as a function of the rotation of the second wheel.

Numbers placed on the wheels (in a fashion similar to that of present-day automobile mileage meters) would then indicate the sum of two or more quantities cranked into the wheels. In this way the arithmetic tradition could make use of the gear-train tradition and obtain with gear teeth a *mechanical* answer that would agree with the *logical* answer the human brain obtains through logical thought processes involving the addition of integers. In short, the machine would "add" automatically as a function of its rotational motions. Like the abacus in all its forms, Pascal's adder is a calculator that provides meaningful sums by the application of the principle of place-value notation.

Since the principles of arithmetic have endowed numbers with properties that render the product of multiplication equivalent to a soon tedious number of additions, any adder can add its way to an answer equivalent to the product of any two numbers, provided the adder has wheels enough.

Knowing this, Leibniz nearly thirty years after Pascal (1671) designed an adder that would multiply—or nearly so, for its products apparently were not always reliable, as a consequence of some mechanical defect in the machine.

*Did* Leibniz make the first multiplier? If it doesn't work reliably it could still be first, couldn't it? If so, one wonders what would qualify as the first airplane. Not the Wright brothers' 1903 model, nor Langley's either. But if we want to cling stubbornly to our linear schoolboy notions about how the past becomes the present, then we single out Pascal and Leibniz, and we ignore Morland and Mahon and Roth and Leupold and Gersten and Hahn and many others—and we no longer are talking about how the past became the present.

The past became the present without the kind of spectacular, mythical, heroic contributions from a Pascal or a Leibniz that computer experts refer to. The past became the present through the improvements and modifications contributed by many men. As it turns out, the bright ideas of the Pascals and the Leibnizes of this world have to be rendered practical before they become historically significant. Thus, progress in the design of machine tools did more for the emergence and perfection of calculators between the seventeenth and twentieth centuries than anything Pascal or Leibniz ever did, but the reader is hard put to it to find computer experts talking about machine-tool history because they uncritically regard the past as linear. In their linear past, machine tools are not worthy of mention until they reach the nineteenth century and explain why Charles Babbage's machines were never completed.

So Pascal and Leibniz emerge as the victims of historical distortion, well-intentioned distortion, but distortion nonetheless. Contrary to popular myth, they did not make the historically important advances. The historically important advances consisted of the evolutionary emergence of practical, working calculators, brought to pass through the efforts and small contributions of *many* men, including Pascal and Leibniz. As builders of reliable, practical, working calculators, Pascal and Leibniz were flops. As idea men they were superb and necessary, but as engineers and builders, they could not compete.

To rivet this historical judgment home once and for all would require a chapter-and-verse history of calculators and detailed examination of the mathematical and engineering contributions of dozens of men in the eighteenth, nineteenth, and twentieth centuries. For our purposes here, let it suffice that engineering and machine-tool efforts, especially during the nineteenth century, produced a complex technical tradition, that of the desk calculator. This tradition made possible the sophisticated desk calculators of the present. These are not computers, and I propose to say no more about their history, for although they produced a great deal of valuable engineering know-how and competence, they did not sire the computer. Instead, they provided experience and a tradition of working in the broad area of mechanical analogy and mechanical correspondence to logical thought processes that were to prove useful later.

In this tradition we encounter many original minds. A spectacular innovator and another engineering flop—this time germane to the birth of the computer—was the British misanthrope, Charles Babbage (1792—1871). He is a fascinating curmudgeon to read about, a monumental ego that his world ignored and, by doing so, turned him into a bitter old man.

He had reason to be bitter, for he was right. He was a creative genius, genuinely, and he knew it. So he could only conclude, since the world of his time ignored his brilliant insights, that it was the world's fault. It is perhaps worth reflecting that he never understood the world. A beleaguered idealist, he never understood people or what he was doing to them. He knew only that they were ungrateful, unappreciative, and unworthy of his approbation. Now that his difficult personality is laid to rest, we can afford to praise him. Had we been his contemporaries, most of us would have dismissed him as a crank and a "nut" about building super-fancy adding machines.

We would have been right at the time, to all appearances, for the machines he wanted to build could not be built. They were beyond the engineering and machine-tool state of the art.

Just what did Babbage do? He started to build one kind of calculator—a complicated adder—that he called a Difference Engine because it would calculate cubes of numbers by adding existing terms to get new numbers and adding the new numbers to get newer numbers, and so on—technically, the "Method of Differences."

While the Difference Engine was failing to be built, Babbage made matters worse by dreaming up a new engine—his Analytical Engine—that was so preposterously elaborate in prospect that anyone who had been worried about the £22,000 of government money he'd already spent on his uncompleted (never to be completed) Difference Engine could only conclude the chap was an impractical dreamer, not to be taken seriously.

He proposed an engine, a mechanical engine, that would get its information (its data) *and* its instructions from punched cards of the type devised for Jacquard looms. This machine would add, it would calculate, it would obtain results that it could store on fresh cards and then use. It would ring a bell to tell the operator to feed it the next card or batch of cards and if he fed it the wrong card it would ring a louder bell, according to Babbage.

But it posed truly formidable problems of construction, of minute tolerances, of power requirements to move all the cogged wheels and levers. . . . And above all it was the idea of a man who by that time was a demonstrated impractical dreamer.

It wasn't built. It was a premature concept. And it did not provoke the emergence of the digital computer, any more than Mendel established the science of genetics. Instead, analogy engines and radar were to do more to bring about the birth of the digital computer.

The tradition of analogy engines is as complicated an historical development as that of the desk calculators. Slide rules appeared in the seventeenth century. Their history is fully as involved as that of the abacus and can only be mentioned here.

If the slide rule is not a machine, the analogue computer is, and the differential analyzer Vannevar Bush built at the Massachusetts Institute of Technology in the 1930s, for example, was one that worked, in contrast to Babbage's numerical analyzer that never got off the drawing board.

Before the end of the Second World War the analog computer was accepted both as a practical mathematical approximator and as a practical mechanism for the control and simulation of physical movements and physical forces, whether the computer was mechanical in form, with cams and wheels, or electrical in form, with modulated electronic circuits, or a mixture of both.

Even before the war began, it was possible for a student to take mathematics courses and engineering courses at the Massachusetts Institute of Technology, for instance, that would put him in a position to learn both about differential analyzers and Eccles-Jordan flip-flops possessing bistable states. It was possible to explore the logical properties of binary arithmetic and point out, as one student did in his master's thesis at MIT, for example, how these abstract properties of binary arithmetic, alias yes-no logic, could be embodied in electronic circuits using radio tubes or relays.

It was possible, as Howard Aiken began to do at Harvard, to set up an electromechanical numerical machine, the "Harvard Mark I," that would perform arithmetic computations using punched cards to feed it data, feed it orders, and store results. It was possible, as George R. Stibitz began to do with relay machines at the Bell Telephone Laboratories, to set up independently of Aiken another type of electromechanical computer. It was possible, as J. Presper Eckert and John W. Mauchly began to do in the 1940s, to construct a logic machine, the digital "ENIAC," using vacuum tubes and electronic circuits for Electronic Research Associates to undertake similar work independently in Minneapolis. It was possible for Robert R. Everett by 1946 to undertake an exploratory engineering project at MIT that would culminate—unknown to them at the start—in the

production of a high-speed computer essential to tracking and intercepting potential air attacks on the United States.

By the mid-1940s, it was also possible for a logician-mathematician to make a
crucial public contribution. Familiarizing himself with some of these pioneering
efforts, reading that student's master's thesis and similar works, he pointed out
the desirability of mixing orders and data in a large storage center inside the
machine. As a result the computer would require a degree of flexibility and a
generality of purpose that would enable it to handle prodigious numerical problems in a surprisingly short time.

The only people who were interested in these ideas of John von Neumann's at
the time were a few fellow mathematicians, a few physicists, and even fewer
engineers. Most of them do not seem to have realized that they were participating
in the gestation of what would one day become a hundred-billion dollar industry.

Instead, some physicists and mathematicians thought about the mathematical
chores such a general-purpose machine might do, a few engineers thought about
appropriate circuits and components, still fewer began to explore the implications of using the electronic digital computer for practical control functions in
real-time situations, such as confront a military command-and-control center. As
for system-integration techniques, these lay still in the future.

Seen in historical perspective, these events of the decade of the 1940s mark
the close of the early history of the computer. This close is marked by a special
type of convergence that produced what I shall call (following the late A. P.
Usher's lead) an invention of strategic importance, namely, the high-speed general-purpose electronic digital computer, of which several examples were being
built by 1950.

This special type of convergence involved the contributions of mathematicians, radar engineers, telephone engineers, physicists, industrial manufacturers,
institutions of higher education, the Department of Defense, the National Security Council, and the outpouring of millions of dollars by an informed but
unsuspecting Congress.

This special type of strategic convergence brought together the conceptual
traditions of mathematics, electronic physics and engineering, practical politics,
fiscal policy, the logics of analogue and digital computation, and the complex
empirical philosophies of government-industry-higher education relationships.
The new tradition being generated by this amalgam is still without a name.
Automation is one of the products, cybernation another, systems engineering still
another, but none of these is what I have in mind, for each is too small, too
specialized, too fragmental.

Once man had an agricultural economy. About 200 years ago that which had
been a slow drift became a rapid shift to a power economy. Now, in addition, we
have discovered we can process information in so new and spectacular a way that
some call it the Information Revolution. Will future historians call this the dawn
of the computer economy? It is too soon to say. But agriculture grew from a
convergence of insignificant beginnings. So did our power and fuel economy. So

have our computers. Whatever the future, the early histories have followed the same patterns: for food, separate husbanding traditions coming together; for power and energy, separate scientific and technological activities drawing together; for integrated information processing, separate logical and technical traditions drawing together in a pattern whose form is too near and close for us to discern.

Curiously, all three are heavily pragmatically-oriented, materialistic enterprises. None draws directly from our ethical traditions or our religious traditions although all have interacted with these traditions. The last two, the power economy and the new information revolution, are busy coupling scientific inquiry and understanding with the control and exploitation of nature, relating theory and practice in new, powerful ways that remold our physical environment. It has become clear that the information revolution will permit us to remold our social environment with unprecedented deliberation, so we will do that.

And while these great adventures are afoot, somewhere the abacus inventors and the Pascals and the von Neumanns of other separate traditions will be bringing those traditions together to form new patterns, new traditions. Presumably this sort of convergence and cumulative synthesis will go on as obscurely and randomly as ever, and, presumably, it will continue to produce new worlds as yet undreamt of in our present philosophy. Such is the fabric of history.

# 2

# Of the Analytical Engine

## 1864

### Charles Babbage

*In an earlier section Babbage describes the development of his Difference Engine, which used a mathematical technique known as the Method of Differences to evaluate functions. It was intended as a tool to construct more accurate mathematical tables. Eds.*

The circular arrangement of the axes of the Difference Engine round large central wheels led to the most extended prospects. The whole of arithmetic now appeared within the grasp of mechanism. A vague glimpse even of an Analytical Engine at length opened out, and I pursued with enthusiasm the shadowy vision. The drawings and the experiments were of the most costly kind. Draftsmen of the highest order were necessary to economize the labor of my own head; whilst workmen were required to execute the experimental machinery to which I was obliged constantly to have recourse.

In order to carry out my pursuits successfully, I had purchased a house with above a quarter of an acre of ground in a very quiet locality. My coach house was now converted into a forge and a foundry, whilst my stables were transformed into a workshop. I built other extensive workshops myself, and had fireproof building for my drawings and draftsmen. Having myself worked with a variety of tools and having studied the art of constructing each of them, I at length laid it down as a principle—that, except in rare cases, I would never do anything myself if I could afford to hire another person who could do it for me.

The complicated relations which then arose amongst the various parts of the machinery would have baffled the most tenacious memory. I overcame that difficulty by improving and extending a language of signs, the Mechanical Notation, which in 1826 I had explained in a paper printed in the "Phil. Trans." By such means I succeeded in mastering trains of investigation so vast in extent that no length of years ever allotted to one individual could otherwise have enabled me to control. By the aid of the Mechanical Notation, the Analytical Engine became a reality: for it became susceptible of demonstration.

Such works could not be carried on without great expenditure. The fluctuations in the demand and supply of skilled labor were considerable. The railroad mania withdrew from other pursuits the most intellectual and skillful draftsmen. One who had for some years been my chief assistant was tempted by an offer so advantageous that in justice to his own family he could scarcely have declined it. Under these circumstances I took into consideration the plan of advancing his salary to one guinea per day. Whilst this was in abeyance, I consulted my venerable surviving parent. When I had fully explained the circumstances, my excellent mother replied: "My dear son, you have advanced far in the accomplishment of a great object, which is worthy of your ambition. You are capable of completing it. My advice is—pursue it, even if it should oblige you to live on bread and cheese."

This advice entirely accorded with my own feelings. I therefore retained my chief assistant at his advanced salary.

The most important part of the Analytical Engine was undoubtedly the mechanical method of carrying the tens. On this I labored incessantly, each succeeding improvement advancing me a step or two. The difficulty did not consist so much in the more or less complexity of the contrivance as in the reduction of the *time* required to effect the carriage. Twenty or thirty different plans and modifications had been drawn. At last I came to the conclusion that I had exhausted the principle of successive carriage. I concluded also that nothing but teaching the Engine to foresee and then to act upon that foresight could ever lead me to the object I desired, namely, to make the whole of any unlimited number of carriages in one unit of time. One morning, after I had spent many hours in the drawing office in endeavoring to improve the system of successive carriages, I mentioned these views to my chief assistant and added that I should retire to my library and endeavor to work out the new principle. He gently expressed a doubt whether the plan was *possible,* to which I replied that, not being able to prove its impossibility, I should follow out a slight glimmering of light which I thought I perceived.

After about three hours' examination, I returned to the drawing office with much more definite ideas upon the subject. I had discovered a principle that proved the possibility, and I had contrived mechanism which, I thought, would accomplish my object.

I now commenced the explanation of my views, which I soon found were but little understood by my assistant; nor was this surprising, since in the course of my own attempt at explanation, I found several defects in my plan, and was also led by his questions to perceive others. All these I removed one after another and ultimately terminated at a late hour my morning's work with the conviction that *anticipating* carriage was not only within my power, but that I had devised one mechanism at least by which it might be accomplished.

Many years after, my assistant, on his return from a long residence abroad, called upon me, and we talked over the progress of the Analytical Engine. I referred back to the day on which I had made that most important step and asked him if he recollected it. His reply was that he perfectly remembered the circumstance; for that on retiring to my library, he seriously thought that my intellect was beginning to become deranged. The reader may perhaps be curious to know how I spent the rest of that remarkable day.

After working, as I constantly did, for ten or eleven hours a day, I had arrived at this satisfactory conclusion and was revising the rough sketches of the new contrivance, when my servant entered the drawing office and announced that it was seven o'clock—that I dined in Park Lane—and that it was time to dress. I usually arrived at the house of my friend about a quarter of an hour before the appointed time, in order that we might have a short conversation on subjects on which we were both much interested. Having mentioned my recent success, in which my host thoroughly sympathized, I remarked that it had produced an exhilaration of the spirits which not even his excellent champagne could rival. Having enjoyed the society of Hallam, of Rogers, and of some few others of that delightful circle, I retired and joined one or perhaps two much more extensive reunions. Having thus forgotten science and enjoyed society for four or five hours, I returned home. About one o'clock I was asleep in my bed and thus continued for the next five hours.

This new and rapid system of carrying the tens when two numbers are added together reduced the actual time of the addition of any number of digits, however large, to nine units of time for the addition and one unit for the carriage. Thus in ten's units of time, any two numbers, however large, might be added together. A few more units of time, perhaps five or six, were required for making the requisite previous arrangements.

Having thus advanced as nearly as seemed possible to the minimum of time requisite for arithmetical operations, I felt renewed power and increased energy to pursue the far higher object I had in view.

To describe the successive improvements of the Analytical Engine would require many volumes. I only propose here to indicate a few of its more important functions and to give to those whose minds are duly prepared for it some information which will remove those vague notions of wonder, and even of its impossibility, with which it is surrounded in the minds of some of the most enlightened.

To those who are acquainted with the principles of the Jacquard loom and who are also familiar with analytical formulas, a general idea of the means by which the Engine executes its operations may be obtained without much difficulty. In the Exhibition of 1862 there were many splendid examples of such looms.

It is known as a fact that the Jacquard loom is capable of weaving any design which the imagination of man may conceive. It is also the constant practice for skilled artists to be employed by manufacturers in designing patterns. These patterns are then sent to a peculiar artist, who, by means of a certain machine, punches holes in a set of pasteboard cards in such a manner that when those cards are placed in a Jacquard loom, it will then weave upon its produce the exact pattern designed by the artist.

Now the manufacturer may use, for the warp and weft of his work, threads which are all of the same color; let us suppose them to be unbleached or white threads. In this case the cloth will be woven all of one color; but there will be a damask pattern upon it such as the artist designed.

But the manufacturer might use the same cards and put into the warp threads of any other color. Every thread might even be of a different color or of a different shade of color; but in all these cases the *form* of the pattern will be precisely the same—the colors only will differ.

The analogy of the Analytical Engine with this well-known process is nearly perfect.

The Analytical Engine consists of two parts:—

*First.* The store in which all the variables to be operated upon, as well as all those quantities which have arisen from the result of other operations, are placed.

*Second.* The mill into which the quantities about to be operated upon are always brought.

Every formula which the Analytical Engine can be required to compute consists of certain algebraical operations to be performed upon given letters and of certain other modifications depending on the numerical value assigned to those letters.

There are therefore two sets of cards, the first to direct the nature of the operations to be performed—these are called operation cards: the other to direct the particular variables on which those cards are required to operate—these latter are called variable cards. Now the symbol of each variable or constant is placed at the top of a column capable of containing any required number of digits.

Under this arrangement, when any formula is required to be computed, a set of operation cards must be strung together, which contain the series of operations in the order in which they occur. Another set of cards must then be strung together, to call in the variables into the mill, [in] the order in which they are required to be acted upon. Each operation card will require three other cards, two to represent the variables and constants and their numerical values upon which the previous operation card is to act, and one to indicate the variable on which the arithmetical result of this operation is to be placed.

But each variable has below it, on the same axis, a certain number of figure-wheels marked on their edges with the ten digits: Upon these any number the machine is capable of holding can be placed. Whenever variables are ordered into the mill, these figures will be brought in, and the operation indicated by the preceding card will be performed upon them. The result of this operation will then be replaced in the store.

The Analytical Engine is therefore a machine of the most general nature. Whatever formula it is required to develop, the law of its development must be communicated to it by two sets of cards. When these have been placed, the engine is special for that particular formula. The numerical value of its constants must then be put on the columns of wheels below them, and on setting the Engine in motion it will calculate and print the numerical results of that formula.

Every set of cards made for any formula will at any future time recalculate that formula with whatever constants may be required.

Thus the Analytical Engine will possess a library of its own. Every set of cards once made will at any future time reproduce the calculations for which it was first arranged. The numerical value of its constants may then be inserted.

It is perhaps difficult to apprehend these descriptions without a familiarity both with analytical forms and mechanical structures. I will now, therefore, confine myself to the mathematical view of the Analytical Engine and illustrate by example some of its supposed difficulties.

An excellent friend of mine, the late Professor MacCullagh, of Dublin, was discussing with me, at breakfast, the various powers of the Analytical Engine. After a long conversation on the subject, he inquired what the machine could do if, in the midst of algebraic operations, it was required to perform logarithmic or trigonometric operations.

My answer was, that whenever the Analytical Engine should exist, all the developments of formula would be directed by this condition—that the machine should be able to compute their numerical value in the shortest possible time. I then added that if this answer were not satisfactory, I had provided means by which, with equal accuracy, it might compute by logarithmic or other tables.

I explained that the tables to be used must, of course, be computed and punched on cards by the machine, in which case they would undoubtedly be correct. I then added that when the machine wanted a tabular number, say the logarithm of a given number, that it would ring a bell and then stop itself. On this, the attendant would look at a certain part of the machine and find that it wanted the logarithm of a given number, say of 2,303. The attendant would then go to the drawer containing the pasteboard cards representing its table of logarithms. From amongst these he would take the required logarithmic card and place it in the machine. Upon this the engine would first ascertain whether the assistant had or had not given him the correct logarithm of the number; if so, it would use it and continue its work. But if the engine found the attendant had given him a wrong logarithm, it would then ring a louder bell and stop itself. On the attendant again examining the engine, he would observe the words, "Wrong tabular number," and then discover that he really had given the wrong logarithm, and of course he would have to replace it by the right one.

Upon this, Professor MacCullagh naturally asked why, if the machine could tell whether the logarithm was the right one, it should have asked the attendant at all? I told him that the means employed were so ridiculously simple that I would not at that moment explain them; but that if he would come again in the course of a few days, I should be ready to explain it. Three or four days after, Bessel and Jacobi, who had just arrived in England, were sitting with me, inquiring about the Analytical Engine, when fortunately my friend MacCullagh was announced. The meeting was equally agreeable to us all, and we continued our conversation. After some time Bessel put to me the very same question which MacCullagh had previously asked. On this Jacobi remarked that he, too, was about to make the same inquiry when Bessel had asked the question. I then explained to them the following very simple means by which that verification was accomplished.

Besides the sets of cards which direct the nature of the operations to be performed and the variables or constants which are to be operated upon, there is another class of cards called number cards. These are much less general in their uses than the others, although they are necessarily of much larger size.

Any number which the Analytical Engine is capable of using or of producing can, if required, be expressed by a card with certain holes in it (Fig. 2-1).

The . . . card contains eleven vertical rows for holes, each row having nine or any less number of holes. In this example the tabular number is 3 6 2 2 9 3 9, whilst its number in the order of the table is 2 3 0 3. In fact, the former number is the logarithm of the latter.

The Analytical Engine will contain,

*First.* Apparatus for printing on paper, one, or, if required, two copies of its results.

*Second.* Means for producing a stereotype mold of the tables or results it computes.

*Third.* Mechanism for punching on blank pasteboard cards or metal plates the numerical results of any of its computations.

Of course the Engine will compute all the tables which it may itself be required to use. These cards will therefore be entirely free from error. Now when the Engine requires a tabular number, it will stop, ring a bell, and ask for such number. In the case we have assumed, it asks for the logarithm of 2 3 0 3.

When the attendant has placed a tabular card in the Engine, the first step taken by it will be to verify the *number* of the card given it by subtracting its number from 2 3 0 3, the number whose logarithm it asked for. If the remainder is zero,

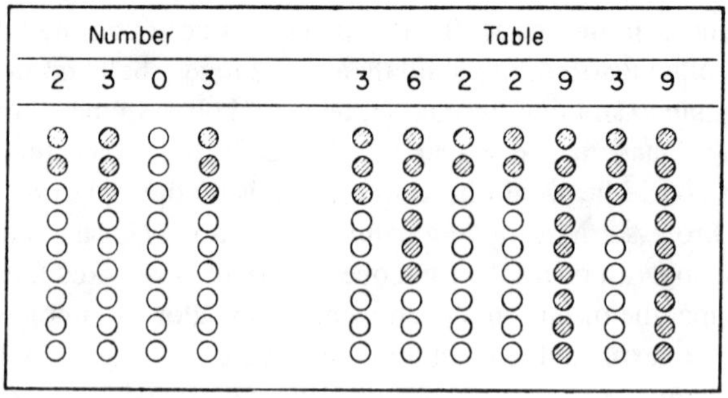

**Figure 2-1**

then the engine is certain that the logarithm must be the right one, since it was computed and punched by itself.

Thus the Analytical Engine first computes and punches on cards its own tabular numbers. These are brought to it by its attendant when demanded. But the engine itself takes care that the *right* card is brought to it by verifying the *number* of that card by the number of the card which it demanded. The Engine will always reject a wrong card by continually ringing a loud bell and stopping itself until supplied with the precise intellectual food it demands.

It will be an interesting question, which time only can solve, to know whether such tables of cards will ever be required for the Engine. Tables are used for saving the time of continually computing individual numbers. But the computations to be made by the Engine are so rapid that it seems most probable that it will make shorter work by computing directly from proper formulas than by having recourse even to its own tables.

The Analytical Engine I propose will have the power of expressing every number it uses to 50 places of figures. It will multiply any two such numbers together and then, if required, will divide the product of 100 figures by number of 50 places of figures.

Supposing the velocity of the moving parts of the Engine to be not greater than 40 feet per minute, I have no doubt that:

- Sixty additions or subtractions may be completed and printed in one minute.
- One multiplication of two numbers, each of 50 figures, in one minute.
- One division of a number having 100 places of figures by another of 50 in one minute.

In the various sets of drawings of the modifications of the mechanical structure of the Analytical Engines, already numbering upward of 30, two great principles were embodied to an unlimited extent.

*First.* The entire control over *arithmetical* operations, however large, and whatever might be the number of their digits.

*Second.* The entire control over the *combinations* of algebraic symbols, however lengthened those processes may be required. The possibility of fulfilling these two conditions might reasonably be doubted by the most accomplished mathematician as well as by the most ingenious mechanician.

The difficulties which naturally occur to those capable of examining the question, as far as they relate to arithmetic, are these:

*a.* The number of digits in *each constant* inserted in the Engine must be without limit.

*b.* The number of constants to be inserted in the Engine must also be without limit.

*c.* The number of operations necessary for arithmetic is only four, but these four may be repeated an *unlimited* number of times.

*d.* These operations may occur in any order or follow an *unlimited* number of laws.

The following conditions relate to the algebraic portion of the Analytical Engine:

*e.* The number of *literal* constants must be *unlimited*.

*f.* The number of *variables* must be *without limit*.

*g.* The combinations of the algebraic signs must be *unlimited*.

*h.* The number of *functions* to be employed must be *without limit*.

This enumeration includes eight conditions, each of which is absolutely *unlimited* as to the number of its combinations.

Now it is obvious that no *finite* machine can include infinity. It is also certain that no question *necessarily* involving infinity can ever be converted into any other in which the idea of infinity under some shape or other does not enter.

It is impossible to construct machinery occupying unlimited space; but it is possible to construct finite machinery and to use it through unlimited time. It is this substitution of the *infinity of time* for the *infinity of space* which I have made use of, to limit the size of the engine and yet to retain its unlimited power.

*a.* I shall now proceed briefly to point out the means by which I have effected this change.

Since every calculating machine must be constructed for the calculation of a definite number of figures, the first datum must be to fix upon that number. In order to be somewhat in advance of the greatest number that may ever be required, I chose 50 places of figures as the standard for the Analytical Engine, the intention being that in such a machine two numbers, each of 50 places of figures, might be multiplied together and the resultant product of 100 places might then be divided by another number of 50 places. It seems to me probable that a long period must elapse before the demands of science will exceed this limit. To this it may be added that the addition and subtraction of numbers in an engine constructed for $n$ places of figures would be equally rapid whether $n$ were equal to 5 or 5,000 digits. With respect to multiplication and division, the time required is greater:—

Thus if $a \cdot 10^{50} + b$ and $a' \cdot 10^{50} + b'$ are two numbers each of less than 100 places of figures, then each can be expressed upon two columns of 50 figures, and $a, b, a', b'$ are each less than 50 places of figures: They can therefore be added and subtracted upon any column holding fifty places of figures.

The product of two such numbers is:

$$aa' 10^{100} + (ab' + a'b) 10^{50} + bb'$$

This expression contains four pair of factors, $aa'$, $ab'$, $a'b$, $bb'$, each factor of which has less than 50 places of figures. Each multiplication can therefore be executed in the Engine. The time, however, of multiplying two numbers, each consisting of any number of digits between 50 and 100, will be nearly four times as long as that of two such numbers of less than 50 places of figures.

The same reasoning will show that if the numbers of digits of each factor are between 100 and 150, then the time required for the operation will be nearly nine times that of a pair of factors having only 50 digits.

Thus it appears that whatever may be the number of digits the Analytical Engine is capable of holding, if it is required to make all the computations with $k$ times that number of digits, then it can be executed by the same Engine, but in an amount of time equal to $k^2$ times the former. Hence the condition ($a$), or the unlimited number of digits contained in each constant employed, is fulfilled.

It must, however, be admitted that this advantage is gained at the expense of diminishing the number of constants the Engine can hold. An engine of 50 digits, when used as one of 100 digits, can only contain half the number of variables. An engine containing $m$ columns, each holding $n$ digits, if used for computations requiring $kn$ digits, can only hold $m/k$ constants or variables.

$b$. The next step is therefore to prove ($b$), $viz.$: to show that a finite engine can be used as if it contained an unlimited number of constants. The method of punching cards for tabular numbers has already been alluded to. Each Analytical Engine will contain one or more apparatus for printing any numbers put into it and also an apparatus for punching on pasteboard cards the holes corresponding to those numbers. At another part of the machine a series of number cards, resembling those of Jacquard, but delivered to and computed by the machine itself, can be placed. These can be called for by the Engine itself in any order in which they may be placed or according to *any law* the Engine may be directed to use. Hence the condition ($b$) is fulfilled, namely: An *unlimited number of constants* can be inserted in the machine in an *unlimited* time.

I propose in the Engine I am constructing to have places for only 1,000 constants, because I think it will be more sufficient. But if it were required to have 10, or even 100 times that number, it would be quite possible to make it, such is the simplicity of its structure of that portion of the Engine.

$c$. The next stage in the arithmetic is the number of times the four processes of addition, subtraction, multiplication, and division can be repeated. It is obvious that four different cards thus punched (Figure 2-2) would give the orders for the four rules of arithmetic.

Now there is no limit to the number of such cards which may be strung together according to the nature of the operations required. Consequently the condition ($c$) is fulfilled.

$d$. The fourth arithmetical condition ($d$), that the order of succession in which these operations can be varied, is itself *unlimited*, follows as a matter of course.

The four remaining conditions which must be fulfilled, in order to render the

Figure 2-2

Analytical Engine as general as the science of which it is the powerful executive, relate to algebraic quantities with which it operates.

The thousand columns, each capable of holding any number of less than 51 places of figures, may each represent a constant or a variable quantity. These quantities I have called by the comprehensive title of variables and have denoted them by $V_n$, with an index below. In the machine I have designed, $n$ may vary from 0 to 999. But after any one or more columns have been used for variables, if those variables are not required afterward, they may be printed upon paper, and the columns themselves again used for other variables. In such cases the variables must have a new index; thus, $V_{mn}$. I propose to make $m$ vary from 0 to 99. If more variables are required, these may be supplied by Variable Cards, which may follow each other in unlimited succession. Each card will cause its symbol to be printed with its proper indices.

For the sake of uniformity, I have used $V$ with as many indices as may be required throughout the Engine. This, however, does not prevent the printed result of a development from being represented by any letters which may be thought to be more convenient. In that part in which the results are printed, type of any form may be used, according to the taste of the proposer of the question.

It thus appears that the two conditions, ($e$) and ($f$), which require that the number of constants and of variables should be unlimited, are both fulfilled.

The condition ($g$), requiring that the number of combinations of the four algebraic signs shall be unlimited, is easily fulfilled by placing them on cards in any order of succession the problem may require.

The last condition ($h$), namely, that the number of functions to be employed must be without limit, might seem at first sight to be difficult to fulfill. But when it is considered that any function of any number of operations performed upon any variables is but a combination of the four simple signs of operation with various quantities, it becomes apparent that any function whatever may be represented by two groups of cards, the first being signs of operation, placed in the order in which they succeed each other, and the second group of cards representing the variables and constants placed in the order of succession in which they are acted upon by the former.

Thus it appears that the whole of the conditions which enable a *finite* machine to make calculations of *unlimited* extent are fulfilled in the Analytical Engine. The means I have adopted are uniform. I have converted the infinity of space, which was required by the conditions of the problem, into the infinity of time. The means I have employed are in daily use in the art of weaving patterns. It is accomplished by systems of cards punched with various holes strung together to any extent which may be demanded. Two large boxes, the one empty and the other filled with perforated cards, are placed before and behind a polygonal prism, which revolves at intervals upon its axis and advances through a short space, after which it immediately returns.

A card passes over the prism just before each stroke of the shuttle; the cards that have passed hang down until they reach the empty box placed to receive them, into which they arrange themselves one over the other. When the box is full, another empty box is placed to receive the coming cards, and a new full box on the opposite side replaces the one just emptied. As the suspended cards on the entering side are exactly equal to those on the side at which the others are delivered, they are perfectly balanced so that whether the formulas to be computed be excessively complicated or very simply, the force to be exerted always remains nearly the same.

Now at a very early period of the inquiry I had found it necessary to teach the engine to know when any numbers it might be computing passed through zero or infinity.

The passage through zero can be easily ascertained, thus: Let the continually decreasing number which is being computed be placed upon a column of wheels in connection with a carrying apparatus. After each process this number will be diminished, until at last a number is subtracted from it which is greater than the number expressed on those wheels.

Thus let it be......

$$00000,00000,00000,00423$$

Subtract ..

$$00000,00000,00000,00511$$
$$99999,99999,99999,99912$$

Now in every case of a carriage becoming due, a certain lever is transferred from one position to another in the cage next above it.

Consequently in the highest cage of all (say the fiftieth in the Analytical Engine), an arm will be moved or not moved accordingly as the carriages do or do not run up beyond the highest wheel.

This arm can, of course, make any change which has previously been decided upon. In the instance we have been considering it would order the cards to be turned on to the next set.

If we wish to find when any number, which is increasing, exceeds in the number of its digits the number of wheels on the columns of the machine, the same carrying arm can be employed. Hence any directions may be given which the circumstances require.

It will be remarked that this does not actually prove, even in the Analytical Engine of 50 figures, that the number computed has passed through infinity, but only that it has become greater than any number of 50 places of figures.

There are, however, methods by which any machine made for a given number of figures may be made to compute the same formulas with double or any multiple of its original number. But the nature of this work prevents me from explaining that method.

It may here be remarked that in the process, the cards employed to make the substitutions of the powers of ten are *operation* cards. They are, therefore, quite independent of the numerical values substituted. Hence the same set of operation cards which order the substitutions $1 \times 10^n$ will, if backed, order the substitution of $2 \times 10^n$, etc. We may, therefore, avail ourselves of mechanism for backing these cards and call it into action whenever the circumstances themselves require it.

The explanation of M. Mosotti's difficulty is this: Mechanical means have been provided for backing or advancing the operation cards to any extent. There exist means of expressing the conditions under which these various processes are required to be called into play. It is not even necessary that two courses only should be possible. Any number of courses may be possible at the same time; and the choice of each may depend upon any number of conditions.

It was during these meetings that my highly valued friend, M. Menabrea, collected the materials for that lucid and admirable description which he subsequently published in the Bibli. Univ. de Genève, t. xli. Oct. 1842.

The elementary principles on which the Analytical Engine rests were thus in the first instance brought before the public by General Menabrea.

Some time after the appearance of his memoir on the subject in the "Bibliothèque Universelle de Genève," the late Countess of Lovelace* informed me that she had translated the memoir of Menabrea. I asked why she had not herself written an original paper on a subject with which she was so intimately acquainted? To this Lady Lovelace replied that the thought had not occurred to her. I then suggested that she should add some notes to Menabrea's memoir, an idea which was immediately adopted.

We discussed together the various illustrations that might be introduced: I suggested several, but the selection was entirely her own. So also was the algebraic working out of the different problems, except, indeed, that relating to the numbers of Bernouilli, which I had offered to do to save Lady Lovelace the trouble. This she sent back to me for an amendment, having detected a grave mistake which I had made in the process.

The notes of the Countess of Lovelace extend to about three times the length of the original memoir. Their author has entered fully into almost all the very difficult and abstract questions connected with the subject.

These two memoirs taken together furnish, to those who are capable of understanding the reasoning, a complete demonstration *that the whole of the developments and operations of analysis are now capable of being executed by machinery.*

There are various methods by which these developments are arrived at: (a) By the aid of the differential and integral calculus; (b) by the combinatorial analysis of Hindenburg; (c) by the calculus of derivations of Arbogast.

Each of these systems professes to expand any function according to any laws. Theoretically each method may be admitted to be perfect; but practically

---

*Ada Augusta, Countess of Lovelace, only child of the Poet Byron.

the time and attention required are, in the greater number of cases, more than the human mind is able to bestow. Consequently, upon several highly interesting questions relative to the lunar theory, some of the ablest and most indefatigable of existing analysts are at variance.

The Analytical Engine is capable of executing the laws prescribed by each of these methods. At one period I examined the combinatorial analysis and also took some pains to ascertain from several of my German friends, who had had far more experience of it than myself, whether it could be used with greater facility than the differential system. They seemed to think that it was more readily applicable to all the usual wants of analysis.

I have myself worked with the system of Arbogast, and if I were to decide from my own limited use of the three methods, I should, for the purposes of the Analytical Engine, prefer the *calcul des derivations.*

As soon as an Analytical Engine exists, it will necessarily guide the future course of the science. Whenever any result is sought by its aid, the question will then arise: By what course of calculation can these results be arrived at by the machine in the *shortest time?*

In the drawings I have prepared I proposed to have 1,000 variables, upon each of which any number not having more than 50 figures can be placed. This machine would multiply 50 figures by other 50 and print the product of 100 figures. Or it would divide any number having 100 hundred figures by any other of 50 figures and print the quotient of 50 figures. Allowing but a moderate velocity for the machine, the time occupied by either of these operations would be about one minute.

The whole of the *numerical* constants throughout the works of Laplace, Plana, Le Verrier, Hansen, and other eminent men whose indefatigable labors have brought astronomy to its present advanced state, might easily be recomputed. They are but the numerical coefficients of the various terms of functions developed according to certain series. In all cases in which these numerical constants can be calculated by more than one method, it might be desirable to compute them by several processes until frequent practice shall have confirmed our belief in the infallibility of mechanism.

The great importance of having accurate tables is admitted by all who understand their uses; but the multitude of errors really occurring is comparatively little known. Dr. Lardner, in the ''Edinburgh Review,'' has made some very instructive remarks on this subject.

I shall mention two within my own experience: These are selected because they occurred in works where neither care nor expense were spared on the part of the Government to ensure perfect accuracy. It is, however, but just to the eminent men who presided over the preparation of these works for the press to observe that the real fault lay not in them but in *the nature of things.*

In 1828 I lent the Government an original manuscript of the table of logarithmic sines, cosines, and so on, computed to every second of the quadrant, in order that they might have it compared with Taylor's logarithms, 4to., 1792, of which they possessed a considerable number of copies. Nineteen errors were thus detected, and a list of these errata was published in the Nautical Almanac for 1832: These may be called

Nineteen errata of the first order. . . . . . 1832

An error being detected in one of these errata, in the following Nautical Almanac we find an

Erratum of the errata in N. Alm. 1832. . . . . . 1833

But in this very erratum of the second order a new mistake was introduced larger than any of the original mistakes. In the year next following there ought to have been found

1832. . . . . . . . . . . 1834

In the "Tables de la Lune," by M. P. A. Hansen, 4to, 1857, published at the expense of the English Government, under the direction of the Astronomer Royal, is to be found a list of errata amounting to 155. In the twenty-first of these original errata there have been found *three* mistakes. These are duly noted in a newly printed list of errata discovered during computations made with them in the "Nautical Almanac"; so that we now have the errata of an erratum of the original work.

This list of errata from the office of the "Nautical Almanac" is larger than the original list. The total number of errors at present (1862) discovered in Hansen's "Tables of the Moon" amounts to above 350. In making these remarks I have no intention of imputing the slightest blame to the Astronomer Royal, who, like other men, cannot avoid submitting to inevitable fate. The only circumstance which is really extraordinary is that when it was demonstrated that all tables are capable of being computed by machinery and even when a machine existed which computed certain tables, the Astronomer Royal did not become the most enthusiastic supporter of an instrument which could render such invaluable service to his own science.

# 3

# Proposed Automatic Calculating Machine

## 1937

## *Howard Aiken*

The desire to economize time and mental effort in arithmetical computations and to eliminate human liability to error is probably as old as the science of arithmetic itself. This desire has led to the design and construction of a variety of aids to calculation, beginning with groups of small objects, such as pebbles, first used loosely, later as counters on ruled boards, and later still as beads mounted on wires fixed in a frame, as in the abacus. This instrument was probably invented by the Semitic races and later adopted in India, whence it spread westward throughout Europe and eastward to China and Japan.

After the development of the abacus, no further advances were made until John Napier devised his numbering rods, or Napier's Bones, in 1617. Various forms of the Bones appeared, some approaching the beginning of mechanical computation, but it was not until 1642 that Blaise Pascal gave us the first mechanical calculating machine in the sense that the term is used today. The application of his machine was restricted to addition and subtraction, but in 1666 Samuel Moreland adapted it to multiplication by repeated additions.

The next advance was made by Leibnitz, who conceived a multiplying machine in 1671 and finished its construction in 1694. In the process of designing this machine Leibnitz invented two important devices which still occur as components of modern calculating machines today: the stepped reckoner and the pin wheel.

Meanwhile, following the invention of logarithms by Napier, the slide rule was being developed by Oughtred, John Brown, Coggeshall, Everard, and others. Owing to its low cost and ease of construction, the slide rule received wide recognition from scientific men as early as 1700. Further development has continued to up to the present time, with ever increasing application to the solution of scientific problems requiring an accuracy of not more than three or four significant figures and when the total bulk of the computation is not too great. Particularly in engineering design has the slide rule proved to be an invaluable instrument.

Though the slide rule was widely accepted, at no time, however, did it act as a deterrent to the development of the more precise methods of mechanical computation. Thus we find the names of some of the greatest mathematicians and physicists of all time associated with the development of calculating machinery. Naturally enough, in an effort to devise means of scientific advancement, these men considered mechanical calculation largely from their own point of view. A notable exception was Pascal, who invented his calculating machine for the purpose of assisting his father in computations with sums of money. Despite this widespread scientific interest, the development of modern calculating machinery proceeded slowly, until the growth of commercial enterprises and the increasing complexity of accounting made mechanical computation an economic necessity. Thus the ideas of the physicists and mathematicians, who foresaw the possibilities and gave the fundamentals, have been turned to excellent purposes, but differing greatly from those for which they were originally intended.

Few calculating machines have been designed strictly for application to scientific investigations, the notable exceptions being those of Charles Babbage and others who followed him. In 1812 Babbage conceived the idea of a calculating machine of a higher type than those previously constructed, to be used for calculating and printing tables of mathematical functions. This machine worked by the method of differences and was known as a Difference Engine. Babbage's first model was made in 1822, and in 1823 the construction of the machine was begun with the aid of a grant from the British government. The construction was continued until 1833, when state aid was withdrawn after an expenditure of nearly £20,000. At present the machine is in the collection of the Science Museum, South Kensington.

In 1834 George Scheutz of Stockholm read the description of Babbage's Difference Engine and started the construction of a similar machine with the aid of a governmental grant. This machine was completed and utilized for printing mathematical tables. Then followed several other difference engines constructed and designed by Martin Wiberg in Sweden, G. B. Grant in the United States, Leon Bolleé in France, and Percy Ludgate in Ireland. The last two, however, were never constructed.

After abandoning the Difference Engine, Babbage devoted his energy to the design and construction of an Analytical Engine of far higher powers than the Difference Engine. This machine, intended to evaluate any algebraic formulas by the method of differences, was never completed, being too ambitious for the time. It pointed the way, however, to the modern punched-card type of calculating machine since it was intended to use perforated cards for its control, similar to those used in the Jacquard loom.

Since the time of Babbage, the development of calculating machinery has continued at an increasing rate. Key-driven calculators, designed for single arithmetical operations such as addition, subtraction, multiplication, and division, have been brought to a high degree of perfection. In large commercial enterprises, however, the volume of accounting work is so great that these machines are no longer adequate in scope.

Hollerith, therefore, returned to the punched card first employed in calculating machinery by Babbage and with it laid the groundwork for the development of tabulating, counting, sorting, and arithmetical machinery such as is now widely utilized in industry. The development of electrical apparatus and technique found application in these machines as manufactured by the International Business Machines Company, until today of the things Babbage wished to accomplish are being done daily in the accounting offices of industrial enterprises all over the world.

As previously stated, these machines are all designed with a view to special applications to accounting. In every case they are concerned with the four fundamental operations of arithmetic, and not with operations of algebraic character. Their existence, however, makes possible the construction of an automatic calculating machine specially designed for the purposes of the mathematical sciences.

## THE NEED FOR MORE POWERFUL CALCULATING METHODS IN THE MATHEMATICAL AND PHYSICAL SCIENCES

It has already been indicated that the need for mechanical assistance in computation has been felt from the beginning of science, but at present this need is greater than ever before. The intensive development of the mathematical and physical sciences in recent years has included the definition of many new and useful functions, nearly all of which are defined by infinite series or other infinite processes. Most of these are inadequately tabulated, and their application to scientific problems is thereby retarded.

The increased accuracy of physical measurement has made necessary more accurate computation in physical theory, and experience has shown that small differences between computed theoretical and experimental results may lead to the discovery of a new physical effect, sometimes of the greatest scientific and industrial importance.

Many of the most recent scientific developments, including such devices as the thermionic vacuum tube, are based on nonlinear effects. Only too often the differential equations designed to represent these physical effects correspond to no previously studied forms and thus defy all methods available for their integration. The only methods of solution available in such cases are expansions in infinite series and numerical integration. Both these methods involve enormous amounts of computational labor.

The present development of theoretical physics through wave mechanics is based entirely on mathematical concepts and clearly indicates that the future of the physical sciences rests in mathematical reasoning directed by experiment. At present there exist problems beyond our ability to solve, not because of theoretical difficulties, but because of insufficient means of mechanical computation.

In some fields of investigation in the physical sciences, as, for instance, in the study of the ionosphere, the mathematical expressions required to represent the phenomena are too long and complicated to write in several lines across a printed page, yet the numerical investigation of such expressions is an absolute necessity to our study of the physics of the upper atmosphere, and on this type of research rests the future of radio communication and television.

These are but a few examples of the computational difficulties with which the physical and mathematical sciences are faced, and to these may be added many others taken from astronomy, the theory of relativity, and even the rapidly growing science of mathematical economy. All these computational difficulties can be removed by the design of suitable automatic calculating machinery.

## POINTS OF DIFFERENCE BETWEEN PUNCHED-CARD ACCOUNTING MACHINERY AND CALCULATING MACHINERY AS REQUIRED IN THE SCIENCES

The features to be incorporated in calculating machinery specifically designed for rapid work on scientific problems, and not to be found in calculating machines as manufactured for accounting purposes, are the following:

1. Ordinary accounting machines are concerned almost entirely with problems of positive numbers, while machines designed for mathematical purposes must be able to handle both positive and negative quantities.

2. For mathematical purposes, calculating machinery should be able to supply and utilize a wide variety of transcendental functions, as the trigonometric functions—elliptic, Bessel, and probability functions—and many others. Fortunately, not all these functions occur in a single computation; therefore a means of changing from one function to another may be designed and the proper flexibility provided.

3. Most of the computations of mathematics, as the calculation of a function by series, the evaluation of a formula, the solution of a differential equation by numerical integration, and so on consist of repetitive processes. Once a process is established it may continue indefinitely until the range of the independent variables is covered, and usually the range of the independent variables may be covered by successive equal steps. For this reason calculating machinery designed for application to the mathematical sciences should be fully automatic in its operation once a process is established.

4. Existing calculating machinery is capable of calculating $\phi(x)$ as a function of $x$ by steps. Thus, if $x$ is defined in the interval $a < x < b$ and $\phi(x)$ is

obtained from $x$ by a series of arithmetical operations, the existing procedure is to compute step (1) for all values of $x$ in the interval $a < x < b$. Then step (2) is accomplished for all values of the result of step (1), and so on until $\phi(x)$ is reached. This process, however, is the reverse of that required in many mathematical operations. Calculating machinery designed for application to the mathematical sciences should be capable of computing lines instead of columns, for very often, as in the numerical solution of a differential equation, the computation of the second value in the computed table of a function depends on the preceding value or values.

Fundamentally, these four features are all that are required to convert existing punched-card calculating machines, such as those manufactured by the International Business Machines Company, into machines specially adapted to scientific purposes. Because of the greater complexity of scientific problems as compared to accounting problems, the number of arithmetical elements involved would have to be greatly increased.

## MATHEMATICAL OPERATIONS WHICH SHOULD BE INCLUDED

The mathematical operations which should be included in an automatic calculating machine are:

1. The fundamental operations of arithmetic: addition, subtraction, multiplication, and division
2. Positive and negative numbers
3. Parenthesis and brackets: $( ) + ( )$, $[( ) + ( )] \cdot [( ) + ( )]$, etc.
4. Powers of numbers: integral, fractional
5. Logarithms: base 10 and all other bases by multiplication
6. Antilogarithms or exponential functions: base 10 and other bases
7. Trigonometric functions
8. Antitrigonometric functions
9. Hyperbolic functions
10. Antihyperbolic functions
11. Superior transcendentals: probability integral, elliptic function, and Bessel function

With the aid of these functions, the processes to be carried out should be:

12. Evaluation of formulas and tabulation of results
13. Computation of series
14. Solution of ordinary differential equations of the first and second order
15. Numerical integration of empirical data
16. Numberical differentiation of empirical data

## THE MATHEMATICAL MEANS OF ACCOMPLISHING THE OPERATIONS

The following mathematical processes may be made the basis of design of an automatic calculating machine:

1.  The fundamental arithmetical operations require no comment, as they are already available, save that all the other operations must eventually be reduced to these in order that a mechanical device may be utilized.

2.  Fortunately the algebra of positive and negative signs is extremely simple. In any case only two possibilities are offered. Later on it will be shown that these signs may be treated as numbers for the purposes of mechanical calculation.

3.  The use of parentheses and brackets in writing a formula requires that the computation must proceed piecewise. Thus, a portion of the result is obtained and must be held pending the determination of some other portion, and so on. This means that a calculating machine must be equipped with means of temporarily storing numbers until they are required for further use. Such means are available in counters.

4.  Integral powers of numbers may be obtained by successive multiplication and fractional powers by the method of iteration. . . .

## MECHANICAL CONSIDERATIONS

In the last section it was shown that even complicated mathematical operations may be reduced to a repetitive process involving the fundamental rules of arithmetic. At present the calculating machines of the International Business Machines Company are capable of carrying out such operations as:

$$A + B = F$$
$$A - B = F$$
$$AB + C = F$$
$$\text{(a)} \quad AB + C + D = F$$
$$A + B + C = F$$
$$A - B - C = F$$
$$A + B - C = F$$

In these equations $A, B, C, D$ are tabulations of numbers on punched cards, and $F$, the result, is also obtained through punched cards. The $F$ cards may then be put through another machine and printed or utilized as $A, B, . . .$ cards in another computation.

Changing a given machine form any of the operations (a) to any other is accomplished by means of electrical wiring on a plug board. In the hands of a skilled operator such changes can be made in a few minutes.

No further effort will be made here to describe the mechanism of the IBM machines. Suffice it to say that all the operations described in the last section can be accomplished by these existing machines when equipped with suitable controls and assembled in sufficient number. The whole problem of design of an automatic calculating machine suitable for mathematical operations is thus reduced to a problem of suitable control design, and even this problem has been solved for simple arithmetical operations.

The main features of the specialized controls are machine switching and replacement of the punched cards by continuous perforated tapes. In order that the switching sequence can be changed quickly to any possible sequence, the switching mechanism should itself utilize a paper tape control in which mathematical formulas may be represented by suitably disposed perforations.

## PRESENT CONCEPTIONS OF THE APPARATUS

At present the automatic calculator is visualized as a switchboard on which are mounted various pieces of calculating-machine apparatus. Each panel of the switchboard is given over to definite mathematical operations. The following is a rough outline of the apparatus required:

1.  IBM machines utilize two electric potentials: 120 volts ac for motor operation and 32 volts dc for relay operation. A main power supply panel would have to be provided, including control for a 100-volt-ac/32 volt-dc motor generator and adequate fuse protection for all circuits.

2.  Master control panel: The purpose of this control is to route the flow of numbers through the machines and to start operation. The processes involved are (a) deliver the number in position $(x)$ to position $(y)$; and (b) start the operation for which position $(y)$ is intended. The master control must itself be subject to interlocking to prevent the attempt to remove a number before its value is determined or to begin a second operation in position $(y)$ before a previous operation is finished.

It would be desirable to have four such master controls, each capable of controlling the entire machine or any of its parts. Thus, for complicated problems the entire resources could be thrown together; if simpler problems fewer resources are required and several problems could be in progress at the same time.

3.  The progress of the independent variable in any calculation would go forward by equal steps subject to manual readjustment for change in the increment. The easiest way to obtain such an arithmetical sequence is to supply a first value $x_0$ to an adding machine, together with an increment $\Delta x$. Then successive additions of $\Delta x$ will give the sequence desired.

There should be four such independent variable devices in order to (a) calculate formulas involving four variables; and (b) operate four master controls independently.

4.  Certain constants: Many mathematical formulas involve certain constants such as $\epsilon$, $\pi$, $log_{10}\epsilon$, and so forth. These constants should be permanently installed and available at all times.

5.  Mathematical formulas nearly always involve constant quantities. In the computation of a formula as a function of an independent variable these constants are used over and over again. Hence the machine should be supplied with 24 adjustable number positions for these constants.

6.  In the evaluation of infinitè series, the number 24 might be greatly exceeded. To take care of this case, it should be possible to introduce specific values by means of a perforated tape, the successive values being supplied by moving the tape ahead one position. Two such devices should be supplied.

7.  The introduction of empirical data for nonrepetitive operations can be accomplished best by standard punched-card magazine feed. One such device should be supplied.

8.  At various stages of a computation involving parentheses and brackets it may be necessary to hold a part of the result pending the computation of some other part. If results are held in the calculating units, these elements are not available for carrying out succeeding steps. Therefore it is necessary that numbers may be removed from the calculating units and temporarily stored in storage positions. Twelve such positions should be available.

9.  The fundamental operations of arithmetic may be carried on three machines: addition and subtraction, multiplication, and division. Four units of each should be supplied in addition to those directly associated with the transcendental functions.

10.  The permanently installed mathematical functions should include logarithms, antilogarithms, sines, cosines, inverse sines, and inverse tangents.

11.  Two units for MacLauren series expansion of other functions as needed.

12.  In order to carry out the process of differentiation and integration on empirical data, adding and subtracting accumulators should be provided sufficient to compute out to fifth differences.

13.  All results should be printed, punched in paper tapes or in cards at will. Final results would be printed. Intermediate results would be punched in preparation for further calculations.

It is believed that the apparatus just enumerated, controlled by automatic switching, should care for most of the problems encountered.

## PROBABLE SPEED OF COMPUTATION

An idea of the speed attained by the IBM machines can be had from the following tabulation of multiplication in which $2 \times 8$ refers to the multiplication of an eight significant-figure number by a two significant-figure number, zeros not counted.

|       | Products per Hour |
|-------|-------------------|
| 2 × 8 | 1,500 |
| 3 × 8 | 1,285 |
| 4 × 8 | 1,125 |
| 5 × 8 | 1,000 |
| 6 × 8 | 900 |
| 7 × 8 | 818 |
| 8 × 8 | 750 |

In the computation of ten-place logarithms the average speed would be about 90 per hour. If all the ten-place logarithms of the natural numbers from 1,000 to 100,000 were required, the time of computation would be approximately 1,100 hours, or 50 days, allowing no time for addition or printing. This is justified since these operations are extremely rapid and can be carried out during the multiplying time.

## SUGGESTED ACCURACY

Ten significant figures have been used in the above examples. If all numbers were to be given to this accuracy, it would be necessary to provide 23 number positions on most of the computing components, ten to the left of the decimal point, 12 to the right, and one for plus and minus. Of the twelve to the right, two would be guard places and thrown away.

## EASE OF PUBLICATION OF RESULTS

As already mentioned, all computed results would be printed in tabular form. By means of photolithography these results could be printed directly without type-setting or proofreading. Not only does this indicate a great saving in the publishing of mathematical functions, but it also eliminates many possibilities of error.

*dated by unknown recipient:*
*"Prospectus of Howard Aiken*
*Nov. 4, 1937*

# 4

# Preliminary Discussion of the Logical Design of an Electronic Computing Instrument

## 1946

### *Arthur W. Burks, Herman H. Goldstine, and John von Neumann*

## 1. PRINCIPAL COMPONENTS OF THE MACHINE

1.1. Inasmuch as the completed device will be a general-purpose computing machine, it should contain certain main organs relating to arithmetic, memory storage, control, and connection with the human operator. It is intended that the machine be fully automatic in character, i.e., independent of the human operator after the computation starts.

1.2. It is evident that the machine must be capable of storing in some manner not only the digital information needed in a given computation such as boundary values, tables of functions (such as the equation of state of a fluid), and also the intermediate results of the computation (which may be wanted for varying lengths of time), but also the instructions which govern the actual routine to be performed on the numerical data. In a special-purpose machine, these instructions are an integral part of the device and constitute a part of its design structure. For an all-purpose machine, it must be possible to instruct the device to carry out any computation that can be formulated in numerical terms. Hence, there must be some organ capable of storing these program orders. There must, moreover, be a unit which can understand these instructions and order their execution.

1.3. Conceptually we have discussed above two different forms of memory: storage of numbers and storage of orders. If, however, the orders to the machine are reduced to a numerical code and if the machine can in some fashion distinguish a number from an order, the memory organ can be used to store both numbers and orders.

1.4. If the memory for orders is merely a storage organ, there must exist an organ which can automatically execute the orders stored in the memory. We shall call this organ the *control*.

1.5. Inasmuch as the device is to be a computing machine, there must be an arithmetic organ in it which can perform certain of the elementary arithmetic operations. There will be, therefore, a unit capable of adding, subtracting, multiplying and dividing. It will be seen . . . that it can also perform additional operations that occur quite frequently.

The operations that the machine will view as elementary are clearly those which are wired into the machine. To illustrate, the operation of multiplication could be eliminated from the device as an elementary process if one were willing to view it as a properly ordered series of additions. Similar remarks apply to division. In general, the inner economy of the arithmetic unit is determined by a compromise between the desire for speed of operation—a nonelementary operation will generally take a long time to perform since it is constituted of a series of orders given by the control—and the desire for simplicity, or cheapness, of the machine.

1.6. Lastly there must exist devices, the input and output organ, whereby the human operator and the machine can communicate with each other. This organ will be seen . . . to constitute a secondary form of automatic memory.


## 2. FIRST REMARKS ON THE MEMORY


2.1. It is clear that the size of the memory is a critical consideration in the design of a satisfactory general-purpose computing machine. We proceed to discuss what quantities the memory should store for various types of computations.

2.2. In the solution of partial differential equations, the storage requirements are likely to be quite extensive. In general, one must remember not only the initial and boundary conditions and any arbitrary functions that enter the problem but also an extensive number of intermediate results.

2.3. It is reasonable at this time to build a machine that can conveniently handle problems several orders of magnitude more complex than are now handled by existing machines, electronic or electromechanical. We consequently plan on a fully automatic electronic storage facility of about 4,000 numbers of 40 binary digits each. This corresponds to a precision of $2^{-40} \sim 0.9 \times 10^{-12}$, i.e., of about 12 decimals. We believe that this memory capacity exceeds the capacities required for most problems that one deals with at present by a factor of about 10. The precision is also safely higher than what is required for the great majority of present-day problems. In addition, we propose that we have a subsidiary memory of much larger capacity, which is also fully automatic, on some medium such as magnetic wire or tape.

## 3. FIRST REMARKS ON THE CONTROL AND CODE

3.1. It is easy to see by formal-logical methods that there exist codes that are *in abstracto* adequate to control and cause the execution of any sequence of operations which are individually available in the machine and which are, in their entirety, conceivable by the problem planner. The really decisive considerations from the present point of view, in selecting a code, are more of a practical nature: simplicity of the equipment demanded by the code and the clarity of its application to the actually important problems together with the speed of its handling of those problems. It would take us much too far afield to discuss these questions at all generally or from first principles. We will therefore restrict ourselves to analyzing only the type of code which we now envisage for our machine.

3.2. There must certainly be instructions for performing the fundamental arithmetic operations. The specifications for these orders will not be completely given until the arithmetic unit is described in a little more detail.

3.3. It must be possible to transfer data from the memory to the arithmetic organ and back again. In transferring information from the arithmetic organ back into the memory there are two types we must distinguish: transfers of numbers as such and transfers of numbers which are parts of orders. The first case is quite obvious and needs no further explication. The second case is more subtle and serves to illustrate the generality and simplicity of the system. Consider, by way of illustration, the problem of interpolation in the system. Let us suppose that we have formulated the necessary instructions for performing an interpolation of order $n$ in a sequence of data. The exact location in the memory of the $(n + 1)$ quantities that bracket the desired functional value is, of course, a function of the argument. This argument probably is found as the result of a computation in the machine. We thus need an order which can substitute a number into a given order—in the case of interpolation the location of the argument or the group of arguments that is nearest in our table to the desired value. By means of such an order, the results of a computation can be introduced into the instructions governing that or a different computation. This makes it possible for a sequence of instructions to be used with different sets of numbers located in different parts of the memory.

To summarize, transfers into the memory will be of two sorts: *total substitutions,* whereby the quantity previously stored is cleared out and replaced by a new number; *partial substitutions* in which that part of an order containing a *memory location number*—we assume the various positions in the memory are enumerated serially by memory location numbers—is replaced by a new memory location number.

3.4. It is clear that one must be able to get numbers from any part of the memory at any time. The treatment in the case of orders can, however, be more methodical since one can at least partially arrange the control instructions in a linear sequence. Consequently, the control will be so constructed that it will normally proceed from place $n$ in the memory to place $(n + 1)$ for its next instruction.

3.5. The utility of an automatic computer lies in the possibility of using a given sequence of instructions repeatedly, the number of times it is iterated being either preassigned or dependent upon the results of the computation. When the iteration is completed a different sequence of orders is to be followed, so we must, in most cases, give two parallel trains of orders preceded by an instruction as to which routine is to be followed. This choice can be made to depend upon the sign of a number (zero being reckoned as plus for machine purposes). Consequently, we introduce an order (*the conditional transfer order*) which will, depending on the sign of a given number, cause the proper one of two routines to be executed.

Frequently two parallel trains of orders terminate in a common routine. It is desirable, therefore, to order the control in either case to proceed to the beginning point of the common routine. This *unconditional transfer* can be achieved either by the artificial use of a conditional transfer or by the introduction of an explicit order for such a transfer.

3.6. Finally, we need orders which will integrate the input-output devices with the machine. . . .

3.7. We proceed now to a more detailed discussion of the machine. Inasmuch as our experience has shown that the moment one chooses a given component as the elementary memory unit, one has also more or less determined upon much of the balance of the machine, we start by a consideration of the memory organ. In attempting an exposition of a highly integrated device like a computing machine we do not find it possible, however, to give an exhaustive discussion of each organ before completing its description. It is only in the final block diagrams that anything approaching a complete unit can be achieved.

The time units to be used in what follows will be:

$$1 \text{ } \mu\text{sec} = 1 \text{ microsecond}$$
$$= 10^{-6} \text{ seconds}$$
$$1 \text{ msec} = 1 \text{ millisecond}$$
$$= 10^{-3} \text{ seconds}$$

## 4. THE MEMORY ORGAN

4.1. Ideally one would desire an indefinitely large memory capacity such that any particular aggregate of forty binary digits, or *word* (cf. 2.3), would be immediately available—i.e., in a time which is somewhat or considerably shorter than the operation time of a fast electronic multiplier. This may be assumed to be practical at the level of about 100 $\mu$sec. Hence the availability time for a word in the memory should be 5 to 50 μsec. It is equally desirable that words may be replaced with new words at about the same rate. It does not seem possible physically to achieve such a capacity. We are therefore forced to recognize the possibility of constructing a hierarchy of memories, each of which has greater capacity than the preceding but which is less quickly accessible.

The most common forms of storage in electrical circuits are the flip-flop or trigger circuit, the gas tube, and the electromechanical relay. To achieve a memory of $n$ words would, of course, require about $40n$ such elements, exclusive of the switching elements. We saw earlier (cf. 2.2) that a fast memory of several thousand words is not at all unreasonable for an all-purpose instrument. Hence, about $10^5$ flip-flops or analogous elements would be required! This would, of course, be entirely impractical.

We must, therefore, seek out some more fundamental method of storing electrical information than has been suggested above. One criterion for such a storage medium is that the individual storage organs, which accommodate only one binary digit each, should not be macroscopic components but rather microscopic elements of some suitable organ. They would then, of course, not be identified and switched to by the usual macroscopic wire connections but by some functional procedure in manipulating that organ.

One device which displays this property to a marked degree is the iconoscope tube. In its conventional form it possesses a linear resolution of about one part in 500. This would correspond to a (two-dimensional) memory capacity of $500 \times 500 = 2.5 \times 10^5$. One is accordingly led to consider the possibility of storing electrical charges on a dielectric plate inside a cathode-ray tube. Effectively such a tube is nothing more than a myriad of electrical capacitors which can be connected into the circuit by means of an electron beam.

Actually, the above-mentioned high resolution and concomitant memory capacity are only realistic under the conditions of television-image storage, which are much less exigent with respect to the reliability of individual markings than what one can accept in the storage for a computer. In this latter case, resolutions of one part in 20 to 100, i.e. memory capacities of 400 to 10,000, would seem to be more reasonable in terms of equipment built essentially along familiar lines.

At the present time the Princeton Laboratories of the Radio Corporation of America are engaged in the development of a storage tube, the *Selectron*, of the type we have mentioned above. This tube is also planned to have a non-amplitude-sensitive switching system whereby the electron beam can be directed to a given spot on the plate within a quite small fraction of a millisecond. Inasmuch as the storage tube is the key component of the machine envisaged in this report, we are extremely fortunate in having secured the cooperation of the RCA group in this as well as in various other developments.

An alternate form of rapid memory organ is the acoustic feedback delay line described in various reports on the EDVAC. (This is an electronic computing machine being developed for the Ordnance Department, U.S. Army, by the

University of Pennsylvania, Moore School of Electrical Engineering). Inasmuch as that device has been so clearly reported in those papers we give no further discussion. There are still other physical and chemical properties of matter in the presence of electrons or photons that might be considered, but since none is yet beyond the early discussion stage we shall not make further mention of them.

4.2. We shall accordingly assume throughout the balance of this report that the Selectron is the modus for storage of words at electronic speeds. As now planned, this tube will have a capacity of $2^{12} = 4,096 \approx 4,000$ binary digits. To achieve a total electronic storage of about 4,000 words, we propose to use 40 Selectrons, thereby achieving a memory of $2^{12}$ words of forty binary digits each. (Cf. again 2.3.)

4.3. There are two possible means for storing a particular word in the Selectron memory—or, in fact, in either a delay-line memory or in an storage tube with amplitude-sensitive deflection. One method is to store the entire word in a given tube and then to get the word out by picking out its respective digits in a serial fashion. The other method is to store in corresponding places in each of the 40 tubes one digit of the word. To get a word from the memory in this scheme requires, then, one switching mechanism to which all 40 tubes are connected in parallel. Such a switching scheme seems to us to be simpler than the technique needed in the serial system and is, of course, 40 times faster. We accordingly adopt the parallel procedure and thus are led to consider a so-called *parallel machine,* as contrasted with the serial principles being considered for the ED-VAC. (In the EDVAC for the peculiar characteristics of the acoustic delay line, as well as various other considerations, seem to justify a serial procedure. For more details, cf. the reports referred to in 4.1.) The essential different between these two systems lies in the method of performing an addition; in a parallel machine all corresponding pairs of digits are added simultaneously, whereas in a serial one these pairs are added serially in time.

4.4. To summarize, we assume that the fast electronic memory consists of 40 Selectrons which are switched in parallel by a common switching arrangement. The inputs of the switch are controlled by the control.

4.5. Inasmuch as a great many highly important classes of problems require a far greater total memory than $2^{12}$ words, we now consider the next stage in our storage hierarchy. Although the solution of partial differential equations frequently involves the manipulation of many thousands of words, these data are generally required only in blocks which are well within the $2^{12}$ capacity of the electronic memory. Our second form of storage must therefore be a medium which feeds these blocks of words to the electronic memory. It should be controlled by the control of the computer and is thus an integral part of the system, not requiring human intervention.

There are evidently two distinct problems raised above. One can choose a given medium for storage, such as teletype tapes, magnetic wire or tapes, movie film, or similar media. There still remains the problem of automatic integration of this storage medium with the machine. This integration is achieved logically by introducing appropriate orders into the code, which can instruct the machine to read or write on the medium or to move it by a given amount or to a place with given characteristics.

Let us return now to the question of what properties the secondary storage medium should have. It clearly should be able to store information for periods of time long enough so that only a small percentage of the total computing time is spent in reregistering information that is "fading off." It is certainly desirable, although not imperative, that information can be erased and replaced by new data. The medium should be such that it can be controlled, i.e., moved forward and backward, automatically. This consideration makes certain media, such as punched cards, undesirable. While cards can, of course, be printed or read by appropriate orders from some machine, they are not well adapted to problems in which the output data are fed directly back into the machine and are required in a sequence which is nonmonotone with respect to the order of the cards. The medium should be capable of remembering very large numbers of data at a much smaller price than electronic devices. It must be fast enough so that, even when it has to be used frequently in a problem, a large percentage of the total solution time is not spent in getting data into and out of this medium and achieving the desired positioning on it. If this condition is not reasonably well met, the advantages of the high electronic speeds of the machine will be largely lost.

Both light- or electron-sensitive film and magnetic wires or tapes, whose motions are controlled by servomechanisms integrated with the control, would seem to fulfill our needs reasonably well. We have tentatively decided to use magnetic wires since we have achieved reliable performance with them at pulse rates of the order of 25,000 per second and beyond.

4.6. Lastly, our memory hierarchy requires a vast quantity of dead storage, i.e., storage not integrated with the machine. This storage requirement may be satisfied by a library of wires that can be introduced into the machine when desired and at that time become automatically controlled. Thus our dead storage is really nothing but an extension of our secondary storage medium. It differs from the latter only in its availability to the machine.

4.7. We impose one additional requirement on our secondary memory. It must be possible for a human to put words onto the wire or other substance used and to read the words put on by the machine. In this manner the human can control the machine's functions. It is now clear that the secondary storage medium is really nothing other than a part of our input-output system.

4.8. There is another highly important part of the input-output which we merely mention at this time, namely, some mechanism for viewing graphically the results of a given computation. This can, of course, be achieved by a Selectron-like tube which causes its screen to fluoresce when data are put on it by an electron beam.

4.9. For definiteness in the subsequent discussions we assume that associated with the output of each Selectron is a flip-flop. This assemblage of forty flip-flops we term the *Selectron register*.

## 5. THE ARITHMETIC ORGAN

5.1. In this chapter we discuss the features we now consider desirable for the arithmetic part of our machine. We give our tentative conclusions as to which of the arithmetic operations should be built into the machine and which should be programmed. Finally, a schematic of the arithmetic unit is described.

5.2. In a discussion of the arithmetical organs of a computing machine, one is naturally led to a consideration of the number system to be adopted. In spite of the longstanding tradition of building digital machines in the decimal system, we feel strongly in favor of the binary system for our device. Our fundamental unit of memory is naturally adapted to the binary system since we do not attempt to measure gradations of charge at a particular point in the Selectron but are content to distinguish two states. The flip-flop again is truly a binary device. On magnetic wires or tapes and in acoustic delay-line memories, one is also content to recognize the presence or absence of a pulse or (if a carrier frequency is used) of a pulse train or the sign of a pulse. (We will not discuss here the ternary possibilities of a positive-or-negative-or-no-pulse system and their relationship to questions of reliability and checking nor the very interesting possibilities of carrier frequency modulation.) Hence, if one contemplates using a decimal system with either the iconoscope or delay-line memory, one is forced into a binary coding of the decimal system—each decimal digit being represented by at least a tetrad of binary digits. Thus an accuracy of ten decimal digits requires at least 40 binary digits. In a true binary representation of numbers, however, about 33 digits suffice to achieve a precision of $10^{10}$. The use of the binary system is therefore somewhat more economical of equipment than is the decimal.

The main virtue of the binary system as against the decimal is, however, the greater simplicity and speed with which the elementary operations can be performed. To illustrate, consider multiplication by repeated addition. In binary multiplication, the product of a particular digit of the multiplier by the multiplicand is either the multiplicand or null according as the multiplier digit is 1 or 0. In the decimal system, however, this product has 10 possible values between null and nine times the multiplicand, inclusive. Of course, a decimal number has only $\log_{10} 2 \sim 0.3$ times as many digits as a binary number of the same accuracy, but even so multiplication in the decimal system is considerably longer than in the binary system. One can accelerate decimal multiplication by complicating the circuits, but this act is irrelevant to the point just made since binary multiplication can likewise be accelerated by adding to the equipment. Similar remarks may be made about the other operations.

An additional point that deserves emphasis is this: An important part of the machine is not arithmetical but logical in nature. Now logics, being a yes-no system, is fundamentally binary. Therefore, a binary arrangement of the arithmetical organs contributes very significantly toward producing a more homogenous machine, which can be better integrated and is more efficient.

The one disadvantage of the binary system from the human point of view is the conversion problem. Since, however, it is completely known how to convert numbers from one base to another and since this conversion can be effected solely by the use of the usual arithmetic processes, there is no reason why the computer itself cannot carry out this conversion. It might be argued that this is a time-consuming operation. This, however, is not the case. . . .

Indeed a general-purpose computer, used as a scientific research tool, is called upon to do a very great number of multiplications upon a relatively small amount of input data, and hence the time consumed in the decimal to binary conversion is only a trivial percentage of the total computing time. A similar remark is applicable to the output data.

In the preceeding discussion we have tacitly assumed the desirability of introducing and withdrawing data in the decimal system. We feel, however, that the base 10 may not even be a permanent feature in a scientific instrument and consequently will probably attempt to train ourselves to use numbers base 2 or 8 or 16. The reason for the bases 8 or 16 is this: Since 8 and 16 are powers of 2, the conversion to binary is trivial; since both are about the size of 10, they violate many of our habits less badly than base 2. . . .

5.3. Several of the digital computers being built or planned in this country and England are to contain a so-called "floating decimal point." This is a mechanism for expressing each word as a characteristic and a mantissa—e.g., 123.45 would be carried in the machine as (0.12345,03), where the 3 is the exponent of 10 associated with the number. There appear to be two major purposes in a "floating" decimal-point system, both of which arise from the fact that the number of digits in a word is a constant, fixed by design considerations for each particular machine. The first of these purposes is to retain in a sum or product as many significant digits as possible, and the second of these is to free the human operator from the burden of estimating and inserting into a problem "scale factors"—multiplicative constants which serve to keep numbers within the limits of the machine.

There is, of course, no denying the fact that human time is consumed in arranging for the introduction of suitable scale factors. We only argue that the time so consumed is a very small percentage of the total time we will spend in preparing an interesting problem for our machine. The first advantage of the floating point is, we feel, somewhat illusory. In order to have such a floating point one must waste memory capacity which could otherwise be used for carrying more digits per word. It would therefore seem to us not at all clear whether the modest advantages of a floating binary point offset the loss of memory capacity and the increased complexity of the arithmetic and control circuits.

There are certainly some problems within the scope of our device which really require more than $2^{-40}$ precision. To handle such problems we wish to plan in terms of words whose lengths are some fixed integral multiple of 40 and program the machine in such a manner as to give the corresponding aggregates of 40-digit words the proper treatment. We must then consider an addition or multiplication as a complex operation programmed from a number of primitive additions or multiplications. . . . There would seem to be considerable extra difficulties in the way of such a procedure in an instrument with a floating binary point.

The reader may remark upon our alternate spells of radicalism and conservatism in deciding upon various possible features for our mechanism. We hope, however, that he will agree, on closer inspection, that we are guided by a consistent and sound principle in judging the merits of any idea. We wish to incorporate into the machine—in the form of circuits—only such logical concepts as are either necessary to have a complete system or highly convenient because of the frequency with which they occur and the influence they exert in the relevant mathematical situations.

*The authors then go on to discuss the details of how addition, subtraction, multiplication, division, and round-off may be performed most efficiently in the proposed machine. This is followed by a concluding section on the control organ, "which can automatically execute orders stored in the Selectrons." This section considers the types of circuits which would be required for retrieving information from memory and for actually carrying out the operations stored in coded form in memory. Questions of timing and of error detection are considered as well as the relative merits of building certain functions into the machine as opposed to having them performed by a stored program (e.g., decimal-to-binary conversion). The report concludes by proposing the inclusion of an instruction which makes the machine reminiscent of Babbage's Analytical Engine. It is a facility which is not found in modern machines (except in some science-fiction films) but which gave the early computers a certain charm. Eds.*

There is one further order that the control needs to execute. There should be some means by which the computer can signal to the operator when a computation has been concluded, or when the computation has reached a previously determined point. Hence an order is needed which will tell the computer to stop and to flash a light or ring a bell.

# 5

# As We May Think

## 1945

### Vannevar Bush

*Readers are forewarned that this article is reproduced in its original form. A number of the views expressed herein may offend sensibilities today, particularly the sexist language, but the Editors have refrained from modernizing the text because of its historical importance. Eds.*

This has not been a scientist's war; it has been a war in which all have had a part. The scientists, burying their old professional competition in the demand of a common cause, have shared greatly and learned much. It has been exhilarating to work in effective partnership. Now, for many, this appears to be approaching an end. What are the scientists to do next?

For the biologists, and particularly for the medical scientists, there can be little indecision, for their war work has hardly required them to leave the old paths. Many indeed have been able to carry on their war research in their familiar peacetime laboratories. Their objectives remain much the same.

It is the physicists who have been thrown most violently off stride, who have left academic pusuits for the making of strange destructive gadgets, who have had to devise new methods for their unanticipated assignments. They have done their part on the devices that made it possible to turn back the enemy. They have worked in combined effort with the physicists of our allies. They have felt within themselves the stir of achievement. They have been part of a great team. Now, as peace approaches, one asks where they will find objectives worthy of their best.

## 1

Of what lasting benefit has been man's use of science and of the new instruments which his research brought into existence? First, they have increased his control of his material environment. They have improved his food, his clothing, his shelter; they have increased his security and released him partly from the bondage of bare existence. They have given him increased knowledge of his own biological processes so that he has had a progressive freedom from disease and an increased span of life. They are illuminating the interactions of his physiological and psychological functions, giving the promise of an improved mental health.

Science has provided the swiftest communication between individuals; it has provided a record of ideas and has enabled man to manipulate and to make extracts from that record so that knowledge evolves and endures throughout the life of a race rather than that of an individual.

There is a growing mountain of research. But there is increased evidence that we are being bogged down today as specialization extends. The investigator is staggered by the findings and conclusions of thousands of other workers— conclusions which he cannot find time to grasp, much less to remember, as they appear. Yet specialization becomes increasingly necessary for progress, and the effort to bridge between disciplines is correspondingly superficial.

Professionally our methods of transmitting and reviewing the results of research are generations old and by now are totally inadequate for their purpose. If the aggregate time spent in writing scholarly works and in reading them could be evaluated, the ratio between these amounts of time might well be startling. Those who conscientiously attempt to keep abreast of current thought, even in restricted fields, by close and continuous reading might well shy away from an examination calculated to show how much of the previous month's efforts could be produced on call. Mendel's concept of the laws of genetics was lost to the world for a generation because his publication did not reach the few who were capable of grasping and extending it; and this sort of catastrophe is undoubtedly being repeated all about us, as truly significant attainments become lost in the mass of the inconsequential.

The difficulty seems to be not so much that we publish unduly in view of the extent and variety of present-day interests but rather that publication has been extended far beyond our present ability to make real use of the record. The summation of human experience is being expanded at a prodigious rate, and the means we use for threading through the consequent maze to the momentarily important item is the same as was used in the days of square-rigged ships.

But there are signs of a change as new and powerful instrumentalities come into use. Photocells capable of seeing things in a physical sense, advanced photography which can record what is seen or even what is not, thermionic tubes capable of controlling potent forces under the guidance of less power than a mosquito uses to vibrate his wings, cathode-ray tubes rendering visible an occurrence so brief that by comparison a microsecond is a long time, relay combinations which will carry out involved sequences of movements more reliably than any human operator and thousands of times as fast—there are plenty of mechanical aids with which to effect a transformation in scientific records.

Two centuries ago Leibnitz invented a calculating machine which embodied most of the essential features of recent keyboard devices, but it could not then come into use. The economics of the situation were against it: The labor involved in constructing it, before the days of mass production, exceeded the labor to be saved by its use, since all it could accomplish could be duplicated by sufficient use of pencil and paper. Moreover, it would have been subject to frequent breakdown, so that it could not have been depended upon; for at that time and long after, complexity and unreliability were synonymous.

Babbage, even with remarkably generous support for his time, could not produce his great arithmetical machine. His idea was sound enough, but construction and maintenance costs were then too heavy. Had a Pharaoh been given detailed and explicit designs of an automobile, and had he understood them completely, it would have taxed the resources of his kingdom to have fashioned the thousands of parts for a single car, and that car would have broken down on the first trip to Giza.

Machines with interchangeable parts can now be constructed with great economy of effort. In spite of much complexity, they perform reliably. Witness the humble type-writer or the movie camera or the automobile. Electrical contacts have ceased to stick when thoroughly understood. Note the automatic telephone exchange, which has hundreds of thousands of such contacts, and yet is reliable. A spider web of metal, sealed in a thin glass container, a wire heated to brilliant glow, in short, the thermionic tube of radio sets, is made by the hundred million, tossed about in packages, plugged into sockets—and it works! Its gossamer parts, the precise location and alignment involved in its construction, would have occupied a master craftsman of the guild for months; now it is built for thirty cents. The world has arrived at an age of cheap complex devices of great reliability; and something is bound to come of it. . . .

## 2

To make the record, we now push a pencil or tap a typewriter. Then comes the process of digestion and correction, followed by an intricate process of typesetting, printing, and distribution. To consider the first stage of the procedure, will the author of the future cease writing by hand or typewriter and talk directly to the record? He does so indirectly, by talking to a stenographer or a wax cylinder; but the elements are all present if he wishes to have his talk directly produce a typed record. All he needs to do is to take advantage of existing mechanisms and to alter his language.

At a recent World Fair, a machine called a Voder was shown. A girl stroked its keys and it emitted recognizable speech. No human vocal chords entered into the procedure at any point; the keys simply combined some electrically produced vibrations and passed these on to a loudspeaker. In the Bell Laboratories there is the converse of this machine, called a Vocoder. The loudspeaker is replaced by a microphone, which picks up sound. Speak to it, and the corresponding keys move. This may be one element of the postulated system.

The other element is found in the stenotype, that somewhat disconcerting device encountered usually at public meetings. A girl strokes its keys languidly and looks about the room and sometimes at the speaker with a disquieting gaze. From it emerges a typed strip which records in a phonetically simplified language a record of what the speaker is supposed to have said. Later this strip is retyped into ordinary language, for in its nascent form it is intelligible only to the initiated. Combine these two elements, let the Vocoder run the stenotype, and the result is a machine which types when talked to.

Our present languages are not especially adapted to this sort of mechanization, it is true. It is strange that the inventors of universal languages have not seized upon the idea of producing one which better fitted the technique for transmitting and recording speech. Mechanization may yet force the issue, especially in the scientific field; where-upon scientific jargon would become still less intelligible to the layman.

One can now picture a future investigator in his laboratory. His hands are free, and he is not anchored. As he moves about and observes, he photographs and comments. Time is automatically recorded to tie the two records together. If he goes into the field, he may be connected by radio to his recorder. As he ponders over his notes in the evening, he again talks his comments into the record. His typed record, as well as his photographs, may both be in miniature, so that he projects them for examination.

Much needs to occur, however, between the collection of data and observations, the extraction of parallel material from the existing record, and the final insertion of new material into the general body of the common record. For mature thought there is no mechanical substitute. But creative thought and essentially repetitive thought are very different things. For the latter there are, and may be, powerful mechanical aids.

Adding a column of figures is a repetitive thought process, and it was long ago properly relegated to the machine. True, the machine is sometimes controlled by a keyboard, and thought of a sort enters in reading the figures and poking the corresponding keys, but even this is avoidable. Machines have been made which will read typed figures by photocells and then depress the corresponding keys; these are combinations of photocells for scanning the type, electric circuits for sorting the consequent variations, and relay circuits for interpreting the result into the action of solenoids to pull the keys down.

All this complication is needed because of the clumsy way in which we have learned to write figures. If we recorded them positionally, simply by the configuration of a set of dots on a card, the automatic reading mechanism would become comparatively simple. In fact, if the dots are holes, we have the punched-card machine long ago produced by Hollorith for the purposes of the census and now used throughout business. Some types of complex businesses could hardly operate without these machines.

Adding is only one operation. To perform arithmetical computation involves also subtraction, multiplication, and division, and in addition some method for temporary storage of results, removal from storage for further manipulation, and recording of final results by printing. Machines for these purposes are now of two types: keyboard machines for accounting and the like, manually controlled for the insertion of data, and usually automatically controlled as far as the sequence of operations is concerned; and punched-card machines in which separate operations are usually delegated to a series of machines and the cards then transferred bodily from one to another. Both forms are very useful; but as far as complex computations are concerned, both are still in embryo.

Rapid electrical counting appeared soon after the physicists found it desirable to count cosmic rays. For their own purposes the physicists promptly constructed thermionic-tube equipment capable of counting electrical impuses at the rate of 100,000 a second. The advanced arithmetical machines of the future will be electrical in nature, and they will perform at 100 times present speeds, or more.

Moreover, they will be far more versatile than present commercial machines, so that they may readily be adapted for a wide variety of operations. They will be controlled by a control card or film, they will select their own data and manipulate it in accordance with the instructions thus inserted, they will perform complex arithmetical computations at exceedingly high speeds, and they will record results in such form as to be readily available for distribution or for later further manipulation. Such machines will have enormous appetites. One of them will take instructions and data from a whole roomful of girls armed with simple keyboard punches and will deliver sheets of computed results every few minutes. There will always be plenty of things to compute in the detailed affairs of millions of people doing complicated things.

### 3

The repetitive processes of thought are not confined, however, to matters of arithmetic and statistics. In fact, every time one combines and records facts in accordance with established logical processes, the creative aspect of thinking is concerned only with the selection of the data and the process to be employed, and the manipulation thereafter is repetitive in nature and hence a fit matter to be relegated to the machines. Not so much has been done along these lines, beyond the bounds of arithmetic, as might be done, primarily because of the economics of the situation. The needs of business, and the extensive market obviously waiting, assured the advent of mass-produced arithmetic machines just as soon as production methods were sufficiently advanced.

With machines for advanced analysis no such situation existed, for there was and is no extensive market; the users of advanced methods of manipulating data are a very small part of the population. There are, however, machines for solving differential equations—and functional and integral equations, for that matter.

There are many special machines, such as the harmonic synthesizer which predicts the tides. There will be many more, appearing certainly first in the hands of the scientist and in small numbers.

If scientific reasoning were limited to the logical processes of arithmetic, we should not get far in our understanding of the physical world. One might as well attempt to grasp the game of poker entirely by the use of the mathematics of probability. The abacus, with its beads strung on parallel wires, led the Arabs to positional numeration and the concept of zero many centuries before the rest of the world; and it was a useful tool—so useful that it still exists.

It is a far cry from the abacus to the modern keyboard accounting machine. It will be an equal step to the arithmetical machine of the future. But even this new machine will not take the scientist where he needs to go. Relief must be secured from laborious detailed manipulation of higher mathematics as well, if the users of it are to free their brains for something more than repetitive detailed transformations in accordance with established rules. A mathematician is not a man who can readily manipulate figures; often he cannot. He is not even a man who can readily perform the transformations of equations by the use of calculus. He is primarily an individual who is skilled in the use of symbolic logic on a high plane, and especially he is a man of intuitive judgment in the choice of the manipulative processes he employs.

All else he should be able to turn over to his mechanism, just as confidently as he turns over the propelling of his car to the intricate mechanism under the hood. Only then will mathematics be practically effective in bringing the growing knowledge of atomistics to the useful solution of the advanced problems of chemistry, metallurgy, and biology. For this reason there will come more machines to handle advanced mathematics for the scientist. Some of them will be sufficiently bizarre to suit the most fastidious connoisseur of the present artifacts of civilization.

# 4

The scientist, however, is not the only person who manipulates data and examines the world about him by the use of logical processes, although he sometimes preserves this appearance by adopting into the fold anyone who becomes logical, much in the manner in which a British labor leader is elevated to knighthood. Whenever logical processes of thought are employed—that is, whenever thought for a time runs along an accepted groove—there is an opportunity for the machine. Formal logic used to be a keen instrument in the hands of the teacher in his trying of students' souls. It is readily possible to construct a machine which will manipulate premises in accordance with formal logic, simply by the clever use of relay circuits. Put a set of premises into such a device and turn the crank, and it will readily pass out conclusion after conclusion, all in accordance with logical law and with no more slips than would be expected of a keyboard adding machine.

Logic can become enormously difficult, and it would undoubtedly be well to produce more assurance in its use. The machines for higher analysis have usually been equation solvers. Ideas are beginning to appear for equation transformers, which will rearrange the relationship expressed by an equation in accordance with strict and rather advanced logic. Progress is inhibited by the exceedingly crude way in which mathematicians express their relationships. They employ a symbolism which grew like Topsy and has little consistency, a strange fact in that most logical field.

A new symbolism, probably positional, must apparently precede the reduction of mathematical transformations to machine processes. Then, on beyond the strict logic of the mathematician lies the application of logic in everyday affairs. We may some day click off arguments on a machine with the same assurance that we now enter sales on a cash register. But the machine of logic will not look like a cash register, even of the streamlined model.

So much for the manipulation of ideas and their insertion into the record. Thus far we seem to be worse off than before—for we can enormously extend the record; yet even in its present bulk we can hardly consult it. This is a much larger matter than merely the extraction of data for the purposes of scientific research; it involves the entire process by which man profits by his inheritance of acquired knowledge. The prime action of use is selection, and here we are halting indeed. There may be millions of fine thoughts and the account of the experience on which they are based, all encased within stone walls of acceptable architectural form; but if the scholar can get at only one a week by diligent search, his syntheses are not likely to keep up with the current scene.

Selection, in this broad sense, is a stone adze in the hands of a cabinetmaker. Yet, in a narrow sense and in other areas, something has already been done mechanically on selection. The personnel officer of a factory drops a stack of a few thousand employee cards into a selecting machine, sets a code in accordance with an established convention, and produces in a short time a list of all employees who live in Trenton and know Spanish. Even such devices are much too slow when it comes, for example, to matching a set of fingerprints with one of five million on file. Selection devices of this sort will soon be speeded up from their present rate of reviewing data at a few hundred a minute. By the use of photocells and microfilm they will survey items at the rate of a thousand a second and will print out duplicates of those selected.

This process, however, is simple selection: It proceeds by examining in turn every one of a large set of items and by picking out those which have certain specified characteristics. There is another form of selection best illustrated by the automatic telephone exchange. You dial a number, and the machine selects and connects just one of a million possible stations. It does not run over them all. It pays attention only to a class given by a first digit, then only to a subclass of this given by the second digit, and so on; and thus proceeds rapidly and almost unerringly to the selected station. It requires a few seconds to make the selection, although the process could be speeded up if increased speed were economically warranted. If necessary, it could be made extremely fast by substituting thermionic-tube switching for mechanical switching, so that the full selection could be made in one one-hundredth of a second. No one would wish to spend the money necessary to make this change in the telephone system, but the general idea is applicable elsewhere.

Take the prosaic problem of the great department store. Every time a charge sale is made, there are a number of things to be done. The inventory needs to be revised, the salesman needs to be given credit for the sale, the general accounts need an entry, and most important, the customer needs to be charged. A central records device has been developed in which much of this work is done conveniently. The salesman places on a stand the customer's identification card, his own card, and the card taken from the article sold—all punched cards. When he pulls a lever, contacts are made through the holes, machinery at a central point makes the necessary computations and entries, and the proper receipt is printed for the salesman to pass to the customer.

But there may be 10,000 charge customers doing business with the store, and before the full operation can be completed someone has to select the right card and insert it at the central office. Now rapid selection can slide just the proper card into position in an instant or two and return it afterward. Another difficulty occurs, however. Someone must read a total on the card, so that the machine can add its computed item to it. Conceivably the cards might be of the dry photography type I have described. Existing totals could then be read by photocell, and the new total entered by an electron beam.

The cards may be in miniature, so that they occupy little space. They must move quickly. They need not be transferred far but merely into position so that the photocell and recorder can operate on them. Positional dots can enter the data. At the end of the month a machine can readily be made to read these and to print an ordinary bill. With tube selection, in which no mechanical parts are involved in the switches, little time need be occupied in bringing the correct card into use —a second should suffice for the entire operation. The whole record on the card may be made by magnetic dots on a steel sheet if desired, instead of dots to be observed optically, following the scheme by which Poulsen long ago put speech on a magnetic wire. This method has the advantage of simplicity and ease of erasure. By using photography, however, one can arrange to project the record in enlarged form and at a distance by using the process common in television equipment.

One can consider rapid selection of this form and distant projection for other purposes. To be able to key one sheet of a million before an operator in a second or two, with the possibility of them adding notes thereto, is suggestive in many ways. It might even be of use in libraries, but that is another story. At any rate, there are now some interesting combinations possible. One might, for example, speak to a microphone, in the manner described in connection with the speech-controlled typewriter, and thus make his selections. It would certainly beat the usual file clerk.

5

The real heart of the matter of selection, however, goes deeper than a lag in the adoption of mechanisms by libraries or a lack of development of devices for their use. Our ineptitude in getting at the record is largely caused by the artificiality of systems of indexing. When data of any sort are placed in storage, they are filed alphabetically or numerically, and information is found (when it is) by tracing it down from subclass to subclass. It can be in only one place, unless duplicates are used; one has to have rules as to which path will locate it, and the rules are cumbersome. Having found one item, moreover, one has to emerge from the system and reenter on a new path.

The human mind does not work that way. It operates by association. With one item in its grasp, it snaps instantly to the next that is suggested by the association of thoughts, in accordance with some intricate web of trials carried by the cells of the brain. It has other characteristics, of course; trials that are not frequently followed are prone to fade, items are not fully permanent, memory is transitory. Yet the speed of action, the intricacy of trials, the detail of mental pictures are awe inspiring beyond all else in nature.

Man cannot hope fully to duplicate this mental process artifically, but he certainly ought to be able to learn from it. In minor ways he may even improve, for his records have relative permanency. The first idea, however, to be drawn from the analogy concerns selection. Selection by association, rather than by indexing, may yet be mechanized. One cannot hope thus to equal the speed and flexibility with which the mind follows an associative trail, but it should be possible to beat the mind decisively in regard to the permanence and clarity of the items resurrected from storage.

Consider a future device for individual use which is a sort of mechanized private file and library. It needs a name, and, to coin one at random, "MEMEX" will do. A MEMEX is a device in which an individual stores all his books, records, and communications, and which is mechanized so that it may be consulted with exceeding speed and flexibility. It is an enlarged intimate supplement to his memory.

It consists of a desk, and while it can presumably be operated from a distance, it is primarily the piece of furniture at which he works. On the top are slanting translucent screens, on which material can be projected for convenient reading. There is a keyboard and sets of buttons and levers. Otherwise it looks like an ordinary desk.

In one end is the stored material. The matter of bulk is well taken care of by improved microfilm. Only a small part of the interior of the MEMEX is devoted to storage, the rest to mechanism. Yet if the user inserted 5,000 pages of material a day it would take him hundreds of years to fill the repository, so he can be profligate and enter material freely.

Most of the MEMEX contents are purchased on microfilm ready for insertion. Books of all sorts, pictures, current periodicals, newspapers, are thus obtained and dropped into place. Business correspondence takes the same path. And there is provision for direct entry. On the top of the MEMEX is a transparent platen. On this are placed longhand notes, photographs, memoranda, all sorts of things. When one is in place, the depression of a lever causes it to be photographed onto the next blank space in a section of the MEMEX film, dry photography being employed.

There is, of course, provision for consultation of the record by the usual scheme of indexing. If the user wishes to consult a certain book, he taps its code on the keyboard, and the title page of the book promptly appears before him, projected onto one of his viewing positions. Frequently used codes are mnemonic, so that he seldom consults his code book; but when he does, a single tap of a key projects it for his use. Moreover, he has supplemental levers. On deflecting one of these levers to the right he runs through the book before him, each page in turn being projected at a speed which just allows a recognizing glance at each. If he deflects it further to the right, he steps through the book 10 pages at a time; still further at 100 pages at a time. Deflection to the left gives him the same control backward.

A special button transfers him immediately to the first page of the index. Any given book of his library can thus be called up and consulted with far greater facility than if it were taken from a shelf. As he has several projection positions, he can leave one item in position while he calls up another. He can add marginal notes and comments, taking advantage of one possible type of dry photography, and it could even be arranged so that he can do this by a stylus scheme, such as is now employed in the telautograph seen in railroad waiting rooms, just as though he had the physical page before him.

## 6

All this is conventional, except for the projection forward of present-day mechanisms and gadgetry. It affords an immediate step, however, to associative indexing, the basic idea of which is a provision whereby any item may be caused at will to select immediately and automatically another. This is the essential feature of the MEMEX. The process of tying two items together is the important thing.

When the user is building a trail, he names it, inserts the name in his code book, and taps it out on his keyboard. Before him are the two items to be joined, projected onto adjacent viewing positions. At the bottom of each there are a number of blank code spaces, and a pointer is set to indicate one of these on each item. The user taps a single key, and the items are permanently joined. In each code space appears the code word. Out of view, but also in the code space, is inserted a set of dots for photocell viewing; and on each item these dots by their positions designate the index number of the other item.

Thereafter, at any time when one of these items is in view, the other can be instantly recalled merely by tapping a button below the corresponding code space. Moreover, when numerous items have been thus joined together to form a trail, they can be reviewed in turn, rapidly or slowly, by deflecting a lever like that used for turning the pages of a book. It is exactly as though the physical items had been gathered together from widely separated sources and bound together to form a new book. It is more than this, for any item can be joined into numerous trails.

The owner of the MEMEX, let us say, is interested in the origin and properties of the bow and arrow. Specifically he is studying why the short Turkish bow was apparently superior to the English long bow in the skirmishes of the Crusaders. He has dozens of possibly pertinent books and articles in his MEMEX. First he runs through an encyclopedia, funds an interesting but sketchy article, leaves it projected. Next, in a history, he finds another pertinent item and ties the two together. Thus he goes, building a trail of many items. Occasionally he inserts a comment of his own, either linking it into the main trial or joining it by a side trail to a particular item. When it becomes evident that the elastic properties of available materials had a great deal to do with the bow, he branches off on a side trail which takes him through textbooks on elasticity and tables of physical constants. He inserts a page of longhand analysis of his own. Thus he builds a trail of his interest through the maze of materials available to him.

And his trails do not fade. Several years later, his talk with a friend turns to the queer ways in which a people resist innovations, even of vital interest. He has an example, in the fact that the outranged Europeans still failed to adopt the Turkish bow. In fact he has a trail on it. A touch brings up the code book. Tapping a few keys projects the head of the trail. A lever runs through it at will, stopping at interesting items, going off on side excursions. It is an interesting trail, pertinent to the discussion. So he sets a reproducer in action, photographs the whole trail out, and passes it to his friend for insertion in his own MEMEX, there to be linked into the more general trail.

## 7

Wholly new forms of encyclopedias will appear, ready-made with a mesh of associative trails running through them, ready to be dropped into the MEMEX and there amplified. The lawyer has at his touch the associated opinions and decisions of his whole experience and of the experience of friends and authorities. The patent attorney has on call the millions of issued patents, with familiar trails to every point of his client's interest. The physician, puzzled by a patient's reactions, strikes the trail established in studying an earlier similar case and runs rapidly through analogous case histories, with side references to the classics for the pertinent anatomy and histology. The chemist, struggling with the synthesis of an organic compound, has all the chemical literature before him in his laboratory, with trails following the analogies of compounds and side trails to their physical and chemical behavior.

The historian, with a vast chronological account of a people, parallels it with a skip trail which stops only on the salient items, and can follow at any time contemporary trails which lead him all over civilization at a particular epoch. There is a new profession of trail blazers, those who find delight in the task of establishing useful trails through the enormous mass of the common record. The inheritance from the master becomes, not only his additions to the world's record, but for his disciples the entire scaffolding by which they were erected.

Thus science may implement the ways in which man produces, stores, and consults the record of the race. It might be striking to outline the instrumentalities of the future more spectacularly, rather than to stick closely to methods and elements now known and undergoing rapid development, as has been done here. Technical difficulties of all sorts have been ignored, certainly, but also ignored are means as yet unknown which may come any day to accelerate technical progress as violently as did the advent of the thermionic tube. In order that the picture may not be too commonplace, by reason of sticking to present-day patterns, it may be well to mention one such possibility, not to prophesy but merely to suggest, for prophecy based on extension of the known has substance, while prophecy founded on the unknown is only a doubly involved guess.

All our steps in creating or absorbing material of the record proceed through one of the senses—the tactile when we touch keys, the oral when we speak or listen, the visual when we read. It is not possible that some day the path may be established more directly?

We know that when the eye sees, all the consequent information is transmitted to the brain by means of electrical vibrations in the channel of the optic nerve. This is an exact analogy with the electrical vibrations which occur in the cable of a television set: They convey the picture from the photocells which see it to the radio transmitter from which it is broadcast. We know further that if we can approach that cable with the proper instruments, we do not need to touch it; we can pick up those vibrations by electrical induction and thus discover and reproduce the scene which is being transmitted, just as a telephone wire may be tapped for its message.

The impulses which flow in the arm nerves of a typist convey to her fingers the translated information which reaches her eye or ear, in order that the fingers may be caused to strike the proper keys. Might not these currents be intercepted, either in the original form in which information is conveyed to the brain or in the marvelously metamorphosed form in which they then proceed to the hand?

By bone conduction we already introduce sounds into the nerve channels of the deaf in order that they may hear. Is it not possible that we may learn to introduce them without the present cumbersomeness of first transforming electrical vibrations to mechanical ones, which the human mechanism promptly transforms back to the electrical form? With a couple of electrodes on the skull the encephalograph now produces pen-and-ink traces which bear some relation to the electrical phenomena going on in the brain itself. True, the record is unintelligible, except as it points out certain gross misfunctioning of the cerebral mechanism; but who would now place bounds on where such a thing may lead?

In the outside world, all forms of intelligence, whether of sound or sight, have been reduced to the form of varying currents in an electric circuit in order that they may be transmitted. Inside the human frame exactly the same sort of process occurs. Must we always transform to mechanical movements in order to proceed from one electrical phenomenon to another? It is a suggestive thought, but it hardly warrants prediction without losing touch with reality and immediateness.

Presumably man's spirit should be elevated if he can better review his shady past and analyze more completely and objectively his present problems. He has built a civilization so complex that he needs to mechanize his records more fully if he is to push his experiment to its logical conclusion and not merely become bogged down part way there by overtaxing his limited memory. His excursions may be more enjoyable if he can reacquire the privilege of forgetting the manifold things he does not need to have immediately at hand, with some assurance that he can find them again if they prove important.

The applications of science have built man a well supplied house and are teaching him to live healthily therein. They have enabled him to throw masses of people against one another with cruel weapons. They may yet allow him truly to encompass the great record and to grow in the wisdom of race experience. He may perish in conflict before he learns to wield that record for his true good. Yet, in the application of science to the needs and desires of man, it would seem to be a singularly unfortunate stage at which to terminate the process or to lose hope as to the outcome.

# Notes and Suggestions for Further Reading—Section I
## Some Landmarks in the History of Computers

*Numbers refer to footnotes in the commentary for this Section, not to footnotes within the readings themselves:*

1. For Boring's views on the role of "the great man" as opposed to "the spirit of the times" in history see

    Boring, E. G., "Great Men and Scientific Progress." *Proceedings of the American Philosophical Society,* 94 (1950), 339–51.

2. Stonehenge is perhaps one of the earliest computers if "computer" is taken in its broad sense, having been begun nearly 4,000 years ago. As in most early computational aids it was used for making astronomical predictions. The deciphering of its function is described in

    Hawkins, G. S., in collaboration with J. B. White, *Stonehenge Decoded.* Garden City, New York: Doubleday & Company, Inc. 1965.

3. The Antikythera Mechanism is a 2,000 year old clocklike device used by the Greeks for calculating the motions of stars and planets. It is described in the delightful article,

    Price, D. J. de S., "An Ancient Greek Computer," *Scientific American,* 200 (1959), 60–67.

4. Many articles and books have been written about Charles Babbage, few more colorful than his autobiography,

    Babbage, C., *Passages from the Life of a Philosopher.* London: Longmans, Green, Longmans, Roberts and Green, 1864.

    Other books about him are

    Morrison, P., and E. Morrison, *Charles Babbage and His Calculating Engines.* New York: Dover Publications, Inc., 1961.

    See also papers by Charles Babbage and his son Major General H. P. Babbage reproduced in

    Bowden, B. V., ed., *Faster Than Thought.* London: Sir Isaac Pitman & Sons, Ltd., 1953.

    and an old article on Babbage,

    Morrison, P., and E. Morrison, "The Strange Life of Charles Babbage," *Scientific American,* 186 (1952), 66–71.

    Critics have noted how Babbage's discourses on the uses of machinery in society have contributed to the subordination of labor to the machine. Braverman (1974) quotes a piece from Babbage's *On the Economy of Machinery and Manufactures* (1832): "One great advantage which we may derive from machinery is from the check which it affords against the inattention, the idleness, or the dishonesty of human agents". (Braverman, H. (1974). *Labor and monopoly capital*. New York: Monthly Review Press.)

5.  Bush's paper has been acknowledged as a key influence on the thinking of many researchers over the years, including Douglas Engelbart, developer of the pioneering NLS system (Engelbart & English, 1968), and Ted Nelson, author of the engaging and idiosyncratic works: *Literary Machines* (1981) and *Dream Machines and Computer Lib* (1974). They both expand on the possibilities of linking "chunks" of text together in a variety of ways—producing what Nelson calls "hypertext," and providing facilities for users to peruse the resulting network complexes. See Chapter 15 in this volume for further information on Engelbart's work. (Engelbart, D. C., & English, W. K. A Research Center for Augmenting Human Intellect. *AFIPS Proceedings—Fall Joint Computer Conference*, Vol. 33, pp. 395–410, 1968. Nelson, T. H. *Literary Machines*, 1981 and Nelson, T. H. *Dream Machines and Computer Lib*, 1974 both available from the author, Box 128, Swarthmore, PA 19081.

Further historical information can be found in the following books

Goldstine, H. H. *The Computer from Pascal to von Neumann*. Princeton, N.J.: Prentice-Hall, 1985.

Williams, M. R. *A History of Computing Technology*. Englewood-Cliffs, N.J.: Prentice-Hall, 1985.

The AFIPS Annals of the History of Computing is an interesting quarterly publication for more serious readers.

# Section II
# Thinking Machines and Intelligence

Because we are their makers, we have too often deluded ourselves into believing that we knew all there was to know about machines. Although the study and construction of machines of all sorts owes much to advances in mechanics, physics, and chemistry, nevertheless mechanology—the science of machines as such, the science of the organized constructions of man—is not a branch of these sciences. Its place is elsewhere in the ranks of scientific disciplines.

Jacques Lafitte
*Réflexions sur la science des machines*

An unintellectual labor, all monotonous, dull labor, all labor that deals with dreadful things and involves unpleasant conditions must be done by machinery. Machinery must work for us in coal mines and do all sanitary services and be the stoker of steamers and clean the streets and run messages on wet days and do anything that is tedious or distressing. At present machinery competes against man. Under proper conditions machinery will serve man. There is no doubt at all that this is the future of machinery; and just as trees grow while the country gentleman is asleep, so while humanity will be amusing itself or enjoying cultivated leisure—which, and not labor, is the aim of man—or making beautiful things or reading beautiful things or simply contemplating the world with admiration and delight, machinery will be doing all the necessary and unpleasant work. The fact is, that civilization requires slaves. The Greeks were quite right there. Unless there are slaves to do the ugly, horrible, uninteresting work, culture and contemplation become almost impossible. Human slavery is wrong, insecure, and demoralizing. On mechanical slavery, on the slavery of the machine, the future of the world depends.

Oscar Wilde
*The Soul of Man Under Socialism*

Aristotle, so far as I know, was the first man to proclaim explicitly that man is a rational animal. His reason for this view was one which does not now seem very impressive; it was that some people can do sums. He thought that there are three kinds of soul: the vegetable soul, possessed by all living things, both plants and animals, and concerned only with nourishment and growth; the animal soul concerned with locomotion, and shared by man with the lower animals; and finally the rational soul, or intellect, which is the Divine mind, but in which men participate to a greater or less degree in proportion to their wisdom. It is in virtue of the intellect that man is a rational animal. The intellect is shown in various ways, but most emphatically by mastery of arithmetic. The Greek system of numerals was very bad, so that the multiplication table was quite difficult and complicated calculations could only be made by very clever people. Nowadays, however, calculating machines do sums better than even the cleverest people, yet no one contends that these useful instruments are immortal or work by divine inspiration. As arithmetic has grown easier, it has come to be less respected. The consequence is that though many philosophers continue to tell us what fine fellows we are, it is no longer on account of our arithmetical skill that they praise us.

Bertrand Russell
*Unpopular Essays*

The possibility of imitating life by a mechanism or an artifact has intrigued people throughout history (see note 1). But it is only in the second half of the century that the possibility of using the special type of artifact we call a computer has been considered seriously as a means of understanding mental phenomena. What is different about this latest interest is that the focus is not primarily on the imitation of movements (as was the case with early clockwork mechanisms) but on the imitation of certain unobservable internal "mental" processes. This idea only became conceivable with the gradual emergence, in several disparate areas of intellectual development, of a certain way of understanding *mechanism*.

The term "mechanism", or the adjective "mechanical" (as in a "mechanical mouse"), is usually assumed to mean something that (a) works by itself without human intervention and (b) works by the movement of elements such as wheels and levers which push and pull on other components. However, the new idea of mechanism that developed, initially within mathematics and later in computer science and communication and control theory (a discipline sometimes called "cybernetics"), was a more general one that still retained the first sense of mechanism (i.e., something that works without human intervention), but dropped the "contact mechanics" sense of wheels and levers and other moving parts. This was a revolutionary idea which parted, for the first time, with a way of thinking about how intelligence could be realized that went back as far as Descartes's speculations in the seventeenth century. This new and more abstract notion of mechanism is concerned only with operations such as storing and retrieving information—or writing and reading symbols or codes—regardless of how this was carried out.

## WHAT CAN BE MECHANIZED?

The new idea of what constitutes a mechanism developed out of the attempt to understand the nature of mathematics and of the puzzling idea of a "proof." The mathematician Hilbert wanted to show that the concept of a proof, or of mathematical truth, could be mechanized, or defined entirely in a self-contained way independent of the activities of mathematicians. Hilbert and other "formalists" believed that the idea of a mathematical "proof" could be completely expressed in terms of certain rules that specified the way that one was allowed to write or delete or move around certain symbols written on pieces of paper. Those who have come across the idea of a proof in geometry or symbolic logic will recognize that a proof is a sequence of lines on which symbols are written in such a way that each line is derived from previous lines by the "blind" application of such rules of logic. To make this idea of "blind application of rules" precise, Hilbert and his fellow mathematicians needed a precise definition of a *mechanism,* or of a device that operates without human intervention. But they were not interested in exactly how it was to be built (e.g. what materials it would be built out of, etc), so the definition was not supposed to be concerned with its physical properties—so long as there was some assurance that a mechanism that had the required properties could somehow be built, that is, that it was not incompatible with the laws of physics.

A number of such mechanisms were proposed, the best known of which was the one proposed by Alan Turing, which is now known as the Turing Machine. The idea of such a mechanism, and the discovery that there were certain things that such a mechanism could and could not do in principle, was one of the major intellectual achievements of this century. Some of these ideas are discussed in the reading by the Russian mathematician B. A. Trakhtenbrot, one of the few readable discussions of these important, though technical, ideas (see note 2) (some of these ideas also appear in Turing's paper reproduced here as well). This reading is included here not only because the abstract study of algorithms and computation represents an important milestone in our intellectual history, but also because understanding what computing is in a way that is independent of particular electronic gadgets is important for the appreciation of how computers are different from other kinds of equally complex machines or systems (see note 3).

Computers are different from other machines because they process information. But information is an abstraction; what information is does not depend on what material stuff is used to encode and store it. It has turned out to be possible to study information processing without concern for the particulars of particular physical devices. It is possible to study *information processing* or *algorithms* or even the art of *designing software* without once asking what kind or what brand of computer will carry out the process. A computer is what Newell and Simon (in the article reproduced here) call a "physical symbol system." Newell and Simon's discussion of the deeper significance of the development of computer science (which they presented as part of the ceremony marking their receipt of the "Turing Award," the highest award given for contribution to the field of computing), gives a tantalizing glimpse of where we stand today in terms of the historical significance of the set of ideas that many of us take for granted as part of the science of computing.

## COMPUTERS + KNOWLEDGE = ARTIFICIAL INTELLIGENCE

Even before actual computers were available, people like Alan Turing and others working on the mathematical ideas of information and algorithms felt that such information processing mechanisms might be designed to reproduce aspects of human intelligence. The papers by Turing, Newell and Simon, and Pylyshyn, all explore the implications of computing for the understanding of what intelligence is (see note 4). A segment of a report on *Artificial Intelligence,* prepared by a panel of experts for a survey sponsored by the National Science Foundation, called the *Computer Science and Engineering Research Study* (COSERS), is also reproduced in this chapter. Although the examples cited in that report are already a few years old, they nonetheless give a good flavor of the kinds of systems being designed in the field of artificial intelligence, as well as of the kinds of problems that preoccupy research scientists who work in that field (see note 5).

From the earliest studies of computing, by people like Alan Turing, it was clear to scientists that computing and the exercise of intelligence were closely related. The reason the two are closely related, however, was not always clearly understood. In the reading by Pylyshyn, some of the reasons are discussed in terms of the claim that what computers and people have in common is that both are physical systems whose behavior is (or can be) governed by knowledge. This rather outlandish-sounding suggestion is becoming widely accepted within that segment of the computer science community who call their field of study *artificial intelligence.* This idea is also raised in Newell and Simon's essay, as well as some of the books and essays cited in the ''Notes and Suggestions for Further Reading—Section II''. (see, in particular, Notes 4, 5, and 7).

Whatever the reason that computers are closely related to human intelligence, it is clear that they are encroaching more and more on areas of performance heretofore believed to be the sole prerogative of humans. This has created both excitement and concern. There have been two kinds of concerns; one is with our self-image as unique creatures of creation, the other with the social effects of increased automation of human intellectual functions. The second of these is part of the general concern with the consequences of automation and increased technological infiltration of our lives. These issues are discussed elsewhere in this book, especially in Section V (see note 6). The first of these—the concern for what the advent of artificial intelligence will do to our conception of human nature—is raised in the essays by Pylyshyn and by Mazlish (see note 7). Mazlish points out that the worry about our self-image is not unique to the development of computers, and that humans have had to revise their views about what is uniquely human several times in the past. Whether this ''fourth discontinuity'' will be as traumatic as the first three remains for history to determine. Whatever the conclusion, there is no doubt that we are in the midst of some important changes that will be wrought by the application of computers to emulating aspects of human intellectual skills in artificial intelligence.

ZWP
*(For notes, see page 239.)*

# 6
# The Fourth Discontinuity

## 1967

### Bruce Mazlish

A famous cartoon in *The New Yorker* magazine shows a large computer with two scientists standing excitedly beside it. One of them holds in his hand the tape just produced by the machine, while the other gapes at the message printed on it. In clear letters, it says, *"Cogito, ergo sum,"* the famous Cartesian phrase, "I think, therefore I am."

My next cartoon has not yet been drawn. It is a fantasy on my part. In it, a patient, wild of eye and hair on end, is lying on a couch in a psychiatrist's office talking to an analyst who is obviously a machine. The analyst-machine is saying, "Of course I'm human—aren't you?"[1]

These two cartoons are a way of suggesting the threat which the increasingly perceived continuity between man and the machine poses to us today. It is with this topic that I wish to deal now, approaching it in terms of what I shall call the "fourth discontinuity." In order, however, to explain what I mean by the "fourth discontinuity," I must first place the term in a historical context.

---

[1]After finishing the early drafts of this article, I secured unexpected confirmation of my "fantasy" concerning an analyst-machine (which is not, in itself, critical to my thesis). A story in the *New York Times*, March 12, 1965, reports that "a computerized typewriter has been credited with remarkable success at a hospital here in radically improving the condition of several children suffering an extremely severe form of childhood schizophrenia. . . . What has particularly amazed a number of psychiatrists is that the children's improvement occurred without psychotherapy; only the machine was involved. It is almost as much human as it is machine. It talks, it listens, it responds to being touched, it makes pictures or charts, it comments and explains, it gives information and can be set up to do all this in any order. In short, the machine attempts to combine in a sort of science-fiction instrument all the best of two worlds—human and machine. It is called an Edison Responsive Environment Learning System. It is an extremely sophisticated 'talking' typewriter (a cross between an analogue and digital computer) that can teach children how to read and write. . . . Dr. Campbell Goodwin speculates that the machine was able to bring the autistic children to respond because it eliminated humans as communication factors. Once the children were able to communicate, something seemed to unlock in their minds, apparently enabling them to carry out further normal mental activities that had eluded them earlier."

In the eighteenth lecture of his *General Introduction to Psychoanalysis,* originally delivered at the University of Vienna between 1915 and 1917, Freud suggested his own place among the great thinkers of the past who had outraged man's naïve self-love. First in the line was Copernicus, who taught that our earth "was not the center of the universe, but only a tiny speck in a world system of a magnitude hardly conceivable." Second was Darwin, who "robbed man of his peculiar privilege of having been specially created and relegated him to a descent from the animal world." Third, now, was Freud himself. On his own account, Freud admitted, or claimed, that psychoanalysis was "endeavoring to prove to the 'ego' of each one of us that he is not even master in his own house, but that he must remain content with the veriest scraps of information about what is going on unconsciously in his own mind."

A little later in 1917, Freud repeated his sketch concerning the three great shocks to man's ego. In his short essay, "A Difficulty in the Path of Psychoanalysis," he again discussed the cosmological, biological, and now psychological blows to human pride and, when challenged by his friend Karl Abraham, admitted, "You are right in saying that the enumeration of my last paper may give the impression of claiming a place beside Copernicus and Darwin."[2]

There is some reason to believe that Freud may have derived his conviction from Ernst Haeckel, the German exponent of Darwinism, who in his book *Natürliche Schöpfungsgeschichte* (1889) compared Darwin's achievement with that of Copernicus and concluded that together they had helped remove the last traces of anthropomorphism from science.[3] Whatever the origin of Freud's vision of himself as the last in the line of ego shatterers, his assertion has been generally accepted by those, like Ernest Jones, who refer to him as the "Darwin of the Mind."[4]

The most interesting extension of Freud's self-view, however, has come from the American psychologist Jerome Bruner. Bruner's version of what Freud called his "transvaluation" is in terms of the elimination of discontinuities, where discontinuity means an emphasis on breaks or gaps in the phenomena of nature—for example, a stress on the sharp differences between physical bodies in the heavens or on earth or between one form of animal matter and another—instead of an emphasis on its continuity. Put the other way, the elimination of discontinuity, that is, the establishment of a belief in a continuum of nature, can be seen as the creation of continuities, and this is the way Bruner phrases it. According to Bruner, the first continuity was established by the Greek physicist-philosophers

---

[2]Ernest Jones, *The Life and Work of Sigmund Freud* (three vols.) (New York: Basic Books, Inc., Publishers, 1953–57), II, 224–26.

[3]Ernst Cassirer, *The Problem of Knowledge: Philosophy, Science, and History since Hegel,* trans. William H. Woglom and Charles W. Hendel (New Haven, CT.: Yale University Press 1950), p. 160.

[4]Jones, *op. cit.,* III, 304.

of the sixth century, rather than by Copernicus. Thus, thinkers like Anaximander conceived of the phenomena of the physical worlds as "continuous and monistic, as governed by the common laws of matter."[5] The creating of the second continuity, that between man and the animal kingdom, was, of course, Darwin's contribution, a necessary condition for Freud's work. With Freud, according to Bruner, the following continuities were established: the continuity of organic lawfulness, so that "accident in human affairs was no more to be brooked as 'explanation' than accident in nature"; the continuity of the primitive, infantile, and archaic as coexisting with the civilized and evolved; and the continuity between mental illness and mental health.

In this version of the three historic egosmashings, man is placed on a continuous spectrum in relation to the universe, to the rest of the animal kingdom, and to himself. He is no longer discontinuous with the world around him. In an important sense, it can be contended, once man is able to accept this situation, he is in harmony with the rest of existence. Indeed, the longing of the early nineteenth-century romantics and of all "alienated" beings since for a sense of "connection" is fulfilled in an unexpected manner.

Yet, to use Bruner's phraseology, though not his idea, a fourth and major discontinuity, or dichotomy, still exists in our time. It is the discontinuity between man and machine. In fact, my thesis is that this fourth discontinuity must now be eliminated—indeed, we have started on the task—and that in the process man's ego will have to undergo another rude shock, similar to those administered by Copernicus (or Galileo), Darwin, and Freud. To put it bluntly, we are now coming to realize that man and the machines he creates are continuous and that the same conceptual schemes, for example, that help explain the workings of his brain also explain the workings of a "thinking machine." Man's pride, and his refusal to acknowledge this continuity, is the substratum upon which the distrust of technology and an industrialized society has been reared. Ultimately, I believe, this last rests on man's refusal to understand and accept his own nature— as a being continuous with the tools and machines he constructs. Let me now try to explain what is involved in this fourth discontinuity.

The evidence seems strong today that man evolved from the other animals into humanity through a continuous interaction of tool, physical, and mental-

---

[5]For Bruner's views, see his "Freud and the Image of Man," *Partisan Review,* XXIII, No. 3 (Summer 1956), 340–47. In place of both Bruner's sixth-century Greek physicists and Freud's Copernicus, I would place Galileo as the breaker of the discontinuity that was thought to exist in the material world. It was Galileo, after all, who first demonstrated that the heavenly bodies are of the same substance as the "imperfect" earth and subject to the same mechanical laws. In his *Dialogue on the Two Principal World Systems* (1632), he not only supported the "world system" of Copernicus against Ptolemy but established that our "world," i.e., the earth, is a natural part of the other "world," i.e., the solar system. Hence, the universe at large is one "continuous" system, a view at best only implied in Copernicus. Whatever the correct attribution—Greek physicists, Copernicus, or Galileo—Freud's point is not in principle affected.

emotional changes. The old view that early man arrived on the evolutionary scene, fully formed, and then proceeded to discover tools and the new ways of life which they made possible is no longer acceptable. As Sherwood L. Washburn, professor of anthropology at the University of California, puts it, "From the rapidly accumulating evidence it is now possible to speculate with some confidence on the manner in which the way of life made possible by tools changed the pressures of natural selection and so changed the structure of man." The details of Washburn's argument are fascinating, with its linking of tools with such physical traits as pelvic structure, bipedalism, brain structure, and so on, as well as with the organization of men in cooperative societies and the substitution of morality for hormonal control of sexual and other "social" activities. Washburn's conclusion is that "it was the success of the simplest tools that started the whole trend of human evolution and led to the civilizations of today."[6]

Darwin of course, had had a glimpse of the role of tools in man's evolution.[7] It was Karl Marx, however, who first placed the subject in a new light. Accepting Benjamin Franklin's definition of man as a "tool-making animal," Marx suggested in *Das Kapital* that "the relics of the instruments of labor are of no less importance in the study of vanished socioeconomic forms than fossil bones are in the study of the organization of extinct species." As we know, Marx wished to dedicate his great work to Darwin—a dedication rejected by the cautious biologist—and we can see part of Marx's reason for this desire in the following revealing passage:

> Darwin has aroused our interest in the history of *natural technology*, that is to say in the origin of the organs of plants and animals as productive instruments utilized for the life purposes of those creatures. Does not the history of the origin of the productive organs of men in society, the organs which form the material basis of every kind of social organization, deserve equal attention? Since, as Vico [in the *New Science* (1725)] says, the essence of the distinction between human history and natural history is that the former is the work of man and the latter is not, would not the history of *human technology* be easier to write than the history of natural technology? Technology reveals man's dealings with nature, discloses the direct productive activities of his life, thus throwing light upon social relations and the resultant mental conceptions.[8]

Only a dogmatic anti-Marxist could deny that Marx's brilliant imagination had led him to perceive a part of the continuity between man and his tools. Drawn off the track, perhaps, by Vico's distinction between human and natural history as man-made and God-made, Marx might almost be given a place in the

---

[6]"Tools and Human Evolution," *Scientific American*, CCIII, No. 3 (September 1960), 63–75.

[7]E.g., see Charles Darwin, *The Descent of Man* (New York: D. Appleton; Co., 1872), pp. 431–32, 458.

[8]Italics mine; Karl Marx, *Capital*, trans. Eden and Cedar Paul (2 vols.) (London, 1951), I, 392–93, note 2.

pantheon of Copernicus, Darwin, and Freud as a destroyer of man's discontinuities with the world about him. Before our present-day anthropologists, Marx had sensed the unbreakable connection between man's evolution as a social being and his development of tools. He did not sense, however, the second part of our subject, that man and his tools, especially in the form of modern, complicated machines, are part of a theoretical continuum.

The *locus classicus* of the modern insistence on the fourth discontinuity is, as is well known, the work of Descartes. In his *Discourse on Method,* for example, he sets up God and the soul on one side, as without spatial location or extension, and the material-mechanical world in all its aspects, on the other side. Insofar as man's mind or soul participates in reason—which means God's reason—man knows this division or dualism of mind and matter, for, as Descartes points out, man could not know this fact from his mere understanding, which is based solely on his senses, "a location where it is clearly evident that the ideas of God and the soul have never been."[9]

Once having established his God and man's participation through reason in God, Descartes could advance daringly to the very precipice of a world without God. He conjures up a world in imaginary space and shows that it must run according to known natural laws. Similarly, he imagines that "God formed the body of a man just like our own, both in the external configuration of its members and in the internal configuration of its organs, without using in its composition any matter but that which I had described [i.e., physical matter]. I also assumed that God did not put into this body any rational soul [defined by Descartes as "that part of us distinct from the body whose essence . . . is only to think"]."

Analyzing this purely mechanical man, Descartes boasts of how he has shown "what changes must take place in the brain to cause wakefulness, sleep, and dreams; how light, sounds, odors, taste, heat, and all the other qualities of external objects can implant various ideas through the medium of the senses, . . . I explained what must be understood by that animal sense which receives these ideas, by memory which retains them, and by imagination which can change them in various ways and build new ones from them." In what way, then, does such a figure differ from real man? Descartes confronts his own created "man" forthrightly; it is worth quoting the whole of his statement:

> Here I paused to show that if there were any machines which had the organs and appearance of a monkey or of some other unreasoning animal, we would have no way of telling that it was not of the same nature as these animals. But if there were a machine which had such a resemblance to our bodies and imitated our actions as far as possible, there would always be two absolutely certain methods of recognizing

---

[9]René Descartes, *Discourse on Method,* trans. Laurence J. Lafleur (Indianapolis, IN.: The Bobbs-Merrill Co., Inc., 1956), p. 24. The rest of the quotations are also from this translation, pp. 29, 35–36, and 36–37.

that it was still not truly a man. The first is that it could never use words or other signs for the purpose of communicating its thoughts to others, as we do. It indeed is conceivable that a machine could be so made that it would utter words and even words appropriate to physical acts which cause some change in its organs; as, for example, if it was touched in some spot that it would ask what you wanted to say to it; if in another, that it would cry that it was hurt, and so on for similar thing. But it could never modify its phrases to reply to the sense of whatever was said in its presence, as even the most stupid men can do. The second method of recognition is that although such machines could do many things as well as, or perhaps even better than men, they would infallibly fail in certain others, by which we would discover that they did not act by understanding, but only by the disposition of their organs. For while reason is a universal instrument which can be used in all sorts of situations, the organs have to be arranged in a particular way for each particular action. From this it follows that it is morally impossible that there should be enough different devices in a machine to make it behave in all the occurrences of life as our reason makes us behave.

Put in its simplest terms, Descartes' two criteria for discriminating between man and the machine are that the latter has (a) no feedback mechanism ("it could never modify it phrases") and (b) no generalizing reason ("reason is a universal instrument which can be used in all sorts of situations"). But it is exactly in these points that, today, we are no longer able so surely to sustain the dichotomy. The work of Norbert Wiener and his followers, in cybernetics, indicates what can be done on the problem of feedback. Investigations into the way the brain itself forms concepts are basic to the attempt to build computers that can do the same, and the two efforts are going forward simultaneously, as in the work of Dr. W. K. Taylor of University College, London, and of others. As G. Rattray Taylor sums up the matter: "One can't therefore be quite as confident that computers will one day equal or surpass man in concept-forming ability as one can about memory, since the trick hasn't yet been done; but the possibilities point that way."[10] In short, the gap between man's thinking and that of his thinking machines has been greatly narrowed by recent research.

Descartes, of course, would not have been happy to see such a development realized. To eliminate the dichotomy or discontinuity between man and machines would be, in effect, to banish God from the universe. The rational soul, Descartes insisted, "could not possibly be derived from the powers of matter . . . but must have been specially created." Special creation requires God, for Descartes' reasoning is circular. The shock to man's ego, of learning the Darwinian lesson that he was not "specially created," is, in this light, only an outlying tremor of the great earthquake that threatened man's view of God as well as of himself. The obstacles to removing not only the first three but also the fourth discontinuity are, clearly, deeply imbedded in man's pride of place.

---

[10]See G. Rattray Taylor, "The Age of the Androids," *Encounter* (November, 1963), p. 43. On p. 40 Taylor gives some of the details of the work of W. K. Taylor and others.

How threatening these developments were can be seen in the case of Descartes' younger contemporary, Blaise Pascal. Aware that man is "a thinking reed," Pascal also realized that he was "engulfed in the infinite immensity of spaces whereof I know nothing and which knows nothing of me." "I am terrified," he confessed. To escape his feeling of terror, Pascal fled from reason to faith, convinced that reason could not bring him to God. Was he haunted by his own construction, at age nineteen, of a calculating machine which, in principle, anticipated the modern digital computer? By his own remark that "the arithmetical machine produces effects which approach nearer to thought than all the actions of animals"? Ultimately, to escape the anxiety that filled his soul, Pascal commanded, "On thy knees, powerless reason."[11]

Others, of course, walked where angels feared to tread. Thus, sensationalist psychologists and epistemologists, like Locke, Hume, or Condillac, without confronting the problem head on, treated the contents of man's reason as being formed by his sense impressions. Daring thinkers, like La Mettrie in his *L'Homme machine* (1747) and Holbach, went all the way to a pure materialism. As La Mettrie put it in an anticipatory transcendence of the fourth discontinuity, "I believe thought to be so little incompatible with organized matter that it seems to be a property of it, like electricity, motive force, impenetrability, extension, etc."[12]

On the practical front, largely leaving aside the metaphysical aspects of the problem, Pascal's work on calculating machines was taken up by those like the eccentric nineteenth-century mathematician Charles Babbage, whose brilliant designs outran the technology available to him.[13] Thus it remained for another century, the twentieth, to bring the matter to a head and to provide the combination of mathematics, experimental physics, and modern technology that created the machines that now confront us and that reawaken the metaphysical question.

The implications of the metaphysical question are clear. Man feels threatened by the machine, that is, by his tools writ large, and feels out of harmony with himself because he is out of harmony—what I have called discontinuous—with the machines that are part of himself. Today, it is fashionable to describe such a state by the term "alienation." In the Marxist phraseology, we are alienated from ourselves when we place false gods or economies over us and then behave as if they had a life of their own, eternal and independent of ourselves, and, indeed, in control of our lives. My point, while contact can be established between it and the notion of alienation, is a different one. It is in the tradition of

---

[11]For details, see J. Bronowski and Bruce Mazlish, *The Western Intellectual Tradition: From Leonardo to Hegel* (New York: Harper & Row, Publishers, 1960), pp. 233–41.

[12]See Stephen Toulmin, "The Importance of Norbert Wiener," *New York Review of Books*, September 24, 1964, p. 4, for an indication of La Mettrie's importance in this development. While Toulmin does not put his material in the context of the fourth discontinuity, I find we are in fundamental agreement about what is afoot in this matter.

[13]See Philip and Emily Morrison, eds., *Charles Babbage and His Calculating Engines* (New York: Dover Publications, Inc., 1961).

Darwin and Freud, rather than of Marx, and is concerned more with man's ego than with his sense of alienation.

A brief glimpse at two "myths" concerning the machine may illuminate what I have in mind. The first is Samuel Butler's negative utopia, *Erewhon*, and the second is Mary Shelley's story of Frankenstein. In Butler's novel, published in 1872, we are presented with Luddism carried to its final point. The story of the Erewhonian revolution against the machines is told in terms of a purported translation from a manuscript, "The Book of the Machines," urging men on to the revolt and supposedly written just before the long civil war between the machinists and the antimachinists, in which half the population was destroyed. The prescient flavor of the revolutionary author's fears can be caught in such passages as follows:[14]

> "There is no security"—to quote his own words—"against the ultimate develop-
> ment of mechanical consciousness, in the fact of machines' possessing little con-
> sciousness now. A mollusk has not much consciousness. Reflect upon the extraor-
> dinary advance which machines have made during the last few hundred years, and
> note how slowly the animal and vegetable kingdoms are advancing. The more
> highly organized machines are creatures not so much of yesterday as of the last five
> minutes, so to speak, in comparison with past time. Assume for the sake of
> argument that conscious beings have existed for some twenty million years: See
> what strides machines have made in the last thousand! May not the world last
> twenty million years longer? If so, what will they not in the end become? Is it not
> safer to nip the mischief in the bud and to forbid them further progress?
>
> "But who can say that the vapor engine has not a kind of consciousness? Where
> does consciousness begin and where end? Who can draw the line? Who can draw
> any line? Is not everything interwoven with everything? Is not machinery linked
> with animal life in an infinite variety of ways? The shell of a hen's egg is made of a
> delicate white ware and is a machine as much as an egg cup is; the shell is a device
> for holding the egg as much as the egg cup for holding the shell: Both are phases of
> the same function; the hen makes the shell in her inside, but it is pure pottery. She
> makes her nest outside of herself for convenience' sake, but the nest is not more of
> a machine than the egg shell is. A 'machine' is only a 'device.'"

Then he continues:

> "Do not let me be misunderstood as living in fear of any actual existing machine;
> there is probably no known machine which is more than a prototype of future
> mechanical life. The present machines are to the future as the early Saurians to
> man. The largest of them will probably greatly diminish in size. Some of the lowest
> vertebrata attained a much greater bulk than has descended to their more highly
> organized living representatives, and in like manner a diminution in the size of
> machines has often attended their development and progress."

---

[14]The quotations that follow are from Samuel Butler, *Erewhon* (Baltimore, 1954), pp. 161, 164, 167–68, and 171. [See also 161 of this book. *Ed.*]

Answering the argument that the machine, even when more fully developed, is merely man's servant, the writer contends:

"But the servant glides by imperceptible approaches into the master; and we have come to such a pass that, even now, man must suffer terribly on ceasing to benefit the machines. . . . Man's very soul is due to the machines; it is a machine-made thing; he thinks as he thinks and feels as he feels through the work that machines have wrought upon him, and their existence is quite as much a *sine qua non* for his as his for theirs. This fact precludes us from proposing the complete annihilation of machinery, but surely it indicates that we should destroy as many of them as we can possibly dispense with, lest they should tyrannize over us even more completely."

And, finally, the latent sexual threat is dealt with:

"It is said by some with whom I have conversed upon this subject, that the machines can never be developed into animate or quasi-animate existences, inasmuch as they have no reproductive systems nor seem ever likely to possess one. If this be taken to mean that they cannot marry and that we are never likely to see a fertile union between two vapor engines with the young ones playing about the door of the shed, however greatly we might desire to do so, I will readily grant it. But the objection is not a very profound one. No one expects that all the features of the now existing organizations will be absolutely repeated in an entirely new class of life. The reproductive system of animals differs widely from that of plants, but both are reproductive systems. Has nature exhausted her phases of this power?"

Inspired by fears such as these, which sound like our present realities, the Erewhonians rise up and destroy almost all their machines. It is only years after this supposed event that they are sufficiently at ease so as to collect the fragmentary remains, the "fossils," of the now defunct machines and place them in a museum. At this point, the reader is never sure whether Butler's satire is against Darwin or the anti-Darwinist—probably both—but there is no question of the satire when he tells us how machines were divided into "their genera, subgenera, species, varieties, subvarieties, and so forth" and how the Erewhonians "proved the existence of connecting links between machines that seemed to have very little in common and showed that many more such links had existed, but had now perished." It is as if Butler had taken Marx's point about *human technology* and stood it on its head!

Going even further, Butler foresaw the threatened ending of the fourth discontinuity, just as he saw Darwin's work menacing the third of the discontinuities we have discussed. Thus, we find Butler declaring, in the guise of his Erewhonian author, "I shrink with as much horror from believing that my race ever be superseded or surpassed as I should do from believing that even at the remotest period my ancestors were other than human beings. Could I believe that ten hundred thousand years ago a single one of my ancestors was another kind of being to myself, I should lose all self-respect and take no further pleasure or interest in life. I have the same feeling with regard to my descendants and believe it to be one that will be felt so generally that the country will resolve upon putting an immediate stop to all further mechanical progress and upon destroying all improvements that have been made for the last 300 years." The counter argument, that "machines were to be regarded as a part of man's own physical nature, being really nothing but extracorporeal limbs. Man [is] a machinate mammal," is dismissed out of hand.

Many of these same themes—the servant-machine rising against its master, the fear of the machine reproducing itself (fundamentally, a sexual fear, as Caliban illustrates and as our next example will show), the terror, finally, of man realizing that he is at one with the machine—can be found attached to an earlier myth, that of Frankenstein. Now passed into our folklore, people frequently give little attention to the actual details of the novel. First, the name Frankenstein is often given to the monster created, rather than to its creator; yet, in the book, Frankenstein is often given to the monster created, rather than to its creator; yet, in the book, Frankenstein is the name of the scientist, and his abortion *has no name*. Second, the monster is *not* a machine but a "flesh and blood" product; even so informed a student as Oscar Handlin makes the typical quick shift, in an echo of Butler's fears, when he says, "The monster, however, quickly proves himself the superior. In the confrontation, the machine gives the orders."[15] Third, and last, it is usually forgotten or overlooked that the monster turns to murder *because* his creator, horrified at his production, refuses him human love and kindness. Let us look at a few of the details.

In writing her "Gothic" novel in 1816–17, Mary Shelley gave it the subtitle "The Modern Prometheus."[16] We can see why if we remember that Prometheus defied the gods and gave fire to man. Writing in the typical early nineteenth-century romantic vein, Mary Shelley offers Frankenstein as an example of "how dangerous is the acquirement of knowledge"; in this case, specifically, the capability of "bestowing animation upon lifeless matter." In the novel we are told of how, having collected his materials from "the dissecting room and the slaughterhouse" (as Wordsworth has said of modern science, "We murder to dissect"), Frankenstein eventually completes his loathsome task when he infuses "a spark of being into the lifeless thing that lay at my feet." Then, as he tells us, "now that I had finished, the beauty of the dream vanished, and breathless horror and disgust filled my heart." Rushing from the room. Frankenstein goes to his bedchamber, where he has a most odd dream concerning the corpse of his dead mother—the whole book as well as this passage cries out for psycho-

15"Science and Technology in Popular Culture," *Daedalus* (Winter 1965), 156–70.
16The quotations that follow are from Mary Shelley, *Frankenstein* (New York: Dell Publishing Company, 1953), pp. 30–33, 36–37, 85, and 160–61.

analytic interpretation—from which he is awakened by "the wretch—the miserable monster whom I had created." Aghast at the countenance of what he has created, Frankenstein escapes from the room and out into the open. Upon finally returning to his room with a friend, he is relieved to find the monster gone.

To understand the myth, we need to recite a few further details in this weird, and rather badly written, story. Frankenstein's monster eventually finds his way to a hovel attached to a cottage occupied by a blind father and his son and daughter. Unperceived by them, he learns the elements of social life (the fortuitous ways in which this is made to occur may strain the demanding reader's credulity), even to the point of reading *Paradise Lost*. Resolved to end his unbearable solitude, the monster, convinced that his virtues of the heart will win over the cottagers, makes his presence known. The result is predictable: Horrified by his appearance, they duplicate the behavior of his creator and flee. In wrath, the monster turns against the heartless world. He kills, and his first victim, by accident, is Frankenstein's young brother.

Pursued by Frankenstein, a confrontation between creator and created takes place, and the monster explains his road to murder. He appeals to Frankenstein in a torrential address:

> "I entreat you to hear me, before you give vent to your hatred on my devoted head. Have I not suffered enough that you seek to increase my misery? Life, although it may only be an accumulation of anguish, is dear to me, and I will defend it. Remember, thou hast made me more powerful than thyself; my height is superior to thine; my joints more supple. But I will not be tempted to set myself in opposition to thee. I am thy creature, and I will be even mild and docile to my natural lord and king, if thou wilt also perform thy part, the which thou owest me. Oh, Frankenstein, be not equitable to every other and trample upon me alone, to whom thy justice, and even thy clemency and affection, is most due. Remember, that I am thy creature; I ought to be thy Adam; but I am rather the fallen angel, whom thou drives from joy for no misdeed. Everywhere I see bliss, from which I alone am irrevocably excluded. I was benevolent and good; misery made me a fiend. Make me happy, and I shall again be virtuous."

Eventually, the monster extracts from Frankenstein a promise to create a partner for him "of another sex," with whom he will then retire into the vast wilds of South America, away from the world of men. But Frankenstein's "compassion" does not last long. In his laboratory again, Frankenstein indulges in a long soliloquy:

> "I was now about to form another being, of whose dispositions I was alike ignorant; she might become 10,000 times more malignant than her mate, and delight, for its own sake, in murder and wretchedness. He had sworn to quit the neighborhood of man and hide himself in deserts; but she had not; and she, who in all probability was to become a thinking and reasoning animal, might refuse to

comply with a compact made before her creation. They might even hate each other; the creature who already lived loathed his own deformity, and might he not conceive a greater abhorrence for it when it came before his eyes in the female form? She also might turn with disgust from him to the superior beauty of man; she might quit him, and he be again alone, exasperated by the fresh provocation of being deserted by one of his own species.

"Even if they were to leave Europe and inhabit the deserts of the new world, yet one of the first results of those sympathies for which the demon thirsted would be children, and a race of devils would be propagated upon the earth who might make the very existence of the species of man a condition precarious and full of terror. Had I right, for my own benefit, to inflict this curse upon everlasting generations?"

With the monster observing him through the window, Frankenstein destroys the female companion on whom he had been working. With this, the novel relentlessly winds its way to its end. In despair and out of revenge, the monster kills Frankenstein's best friend, Clerval, then Frankenstein's new bride, Elizabeth. Fleeing to the frozen north, the monster is tracked down by Frankenstein (shades of Moby Dick?), who dies, however, before he can destroy him. But it does not matter; the monster wishes his own death and promises to place himself on a funeral pyre and thus at last secure the spiritual peace for which he has yearned.

I have summarized the book because I suspect that few readers will actually be acquainted with the myth of Frankenstein *as written* by Mary Shelley. For most of us, Frankenstein is Boris Karloff, clumping around stiff, automatic, and threatening: a machine of sorts. We shall have forgotten completely, if ever we knew, that the monster, *cum* machine, is evil, or rather, becomes evil, only because it is spurned by man.

My thesis has been that man is on the threshold of breaking past the discontinuity between himself and machines. In one part, this is because man now can perceive his own evolution as inextricably interwoven with his use and development of tools, of which the modern machine is only the furthest extrapolation. We cannot think any longer of man without a machine. In another part, this is because modern man perceives that the same scientific concepts help explain the workings of himself and of his machines and that the evolution of matter—from the basic building blocks of hydrogen turning into helium in the distant stars, then fusing into carbon nuclei and on up to iron, and then exploding into space, which has resulted in our solar system—continues on earth in terms of the same carbon atoms and their intricate patterns into the structure of organic life, and now into the architecture of our thinking machines.

It would be absurd, of course, to contend that there are no differences between man and machines. This would be the same *reductio ad absurdum* as involved in claiming that because he is an animal, there is no difference between man and the other animals. The matter, of course, is one of degree.[17] What is claimed here is

---

[17]In semifacetious fashion, I have argued with some of my more literal-minded friends that what

that the sharp discontinuity between man and machines is no longer tenable, in spite of the shock to our egos. Scientists, today, know this; the public at large does not, *New Yorker* cartoons to the contrary.[18]

Moreover, this change in our metaphysical awareness, this transcendence of the fourth discontinuity, is essential to our harmonious acceptance of an industrialized world. The alternatives are either a frightened rejection of the "Frankensteins" we have created or a blind belief in their "superhuman virtues" and a touching faith that they can solve all our human problems. Alas, in the perspective I have suggested, machines are "mechanical, all too mechanical," to paraphrase Nietzsche. But, in saying this, I have already also said that they are "all too human" as well. The question, then, is whether we are to repeat the real Frankenstein story and, turning from the "monsters" we have created, turn aside at the same time from our own humanity, or, alternatively, whether we are to accept the blow to our egos and enter into a world beyond the fourth discontinuity?

---

distinguishes man from existing machines and probably will always so distinguish him is an *effective* Oedipus complex: *vive la différence!* For an excellent and informed philosophical treatment of the difference between man and machines, see J. Bronowski, *The Identity of Man* (Garden City, NY: Doubleday & Company, Inc., 1965).

[18]As in so much else, children "know" what their parents have forgotten. As O. Mannoni tells us, in the course of explaining totemism, "children, instead of treating animals as machines, treat machines as living things, the more highly prized because they are easier to appropriate. Children's appropriation is a virtual identification, and they play at being machines (steam engines, motor cars, an planes) just as 'primitive' people play at being the totem [animal]" (*Prospero and Caliban, The Psychology of Colonization,* trans. Pamela Powesland [New York: Frederick A. Praeger, Inc., Publish, 1964], p. 82). In *Huckleberry Finn,* Mark Twain put this "identification" to work in describing Tom Sawyer's friend Ben Rogers: "He was eating an apple and giving a long, melodious whoop, at intervals, followed by a deep-toned ding-dong-dong, ding-dong-dong, for he was personating a steamboat. As he drew near, he slackened speed, took the middle of the street, leaned far over to starboard, and rounded to ponderously and with laborious pomp and circumstance—for he was personating the *Big Missouri* and considered himself to be drawing nine feet of water. He was boat and captain and enginebells combined, so he had to imagine himself standing on his own hurricane deck giving the orders and executing them! . . . 'Stop the stabboard! Ting-a-ling-ling! Stop the labboard! Come ahead on the stabboard! Stop her! Let your outside turn over slow! Ting-a-ling! Chow-ow-aw! Get out that headline! *Lively* now! Come—out with your springline—what're you about there! Take a turn round that stump with the bight of it! Stand by that stage, now—let her go! Done with the engines, sir! Ting-a-ling! *sh't! sh't! sh't!*'" See the analysis of this passage in Erik H. Erikson, *Childhood and Society* (2nd ed.) (New York: W. H. Norton & Company, Inc., Publishers, 1963), pp. 209ff.

# 7

# Computing Machinery and Intelligence

## 1950

## A. M. Turing

### 1. THE IMITATION GAME

I propose to consider the question "Can machines think?" This should begin
with definitions of the meaning of the terms *machine* and *think*. The definitions
might be framed so as to reflect so far as possible the normal use of the words,
but this attitude is dangerous. If the meaning of the words *machine* and *think* are
to be found by examining how they are commonly used, it is difficult to escape
the conclusion that the meaning and the answer to the question "Can machines
think?" is to be sought in a statistical survey such as a Gallup poll. But this is
absurd. Instead of attempting such a definition I shall replace the question by
another, which is closely related to it and is expressed in relatively unambiguous
words.

The new form of the problem can be described in terms of a game which we
call the "imitation game." It is played with three people, a man (A), a woman
(B), and an interrogator (C) who may be of either sex. The interrogator stays in a
room apart from the other two. The object of the game for the interrogator is to
determine which of the other two is the man and which is the woman. He knows
them by labels X and Y, and at the end of the game he says either "X is A and Y
is B" or "X is B and Y is A." The interrogator is allowed to put questions to A
and B thus:

C: Will X please tell me the length of his or her hair?

Now suppose X is actually A, then A must answer. It is A's object in the
game to try and cause C to make the wrong identification. His answer might
therefore be "My hair is shingled, and the longest strands are about nine inches
long."

In order that tones of voice may not help the interrogator, the answers should
be written or better still, typewritten. The ideal arrangement is to have a tele-
printer communicating between the two rooms. Alternatively the question and
answers can be repeated by an intermediary. The object of the game for the third

player (B) is to help the interrogator. The best strategy for her is probably to give truthful answers. She can add such things as "I am the woman, don't listen to him!" to her answers, but it will avail nothing as the man can make similar remarks.

We now ask the question, "What will happen when a machine takes the part of A in this game?" Will the interrogator decide wrongly as often when the game is played like this as he does when the game is played between a man and a woman? These questions replace our original "Can machines think?"

## 2. CRITIQUE OF THE NEW PROBLEM

As well as asking "What is the answer to this new form of the question," one may ask "Is this new question a worthy one to investigate?" This latter question we investigate without further ado, there by cutting short an infinite regress.

The new problem has the advantage of drawing a fairly sharp line between the physical and the intellectual capacities of a man. No engineer or chemist claims to be able to produce a material which is indistinguishable from the human skin. It is possible that at some time this might be done, but even supposing this invention available we should feel there was little point in trying to make a "thinking machine" more human by dressing it up in such artificial flesh. The form in which we have set the problem reflects this fact in the condition which prevents the interrogator from setting or touching the other competitors or hearing their voices. Some other advantages of the proposed criterion may be shown up by specimen questions and answers. Thus:

Q: Please write me a sonnet on the subject of the Fourth Bridge.
A: Count me out on this one. I never could write poetry.
Q: Add 34957 to 70764
A: (pause about 30 seconds and then give as answer): 105621.
Q: Do you play chess?
A: Yes.
Q: I have K at my K1 and no other pieces. You have only K at K6 and R at R1. It is your move. What do you play?
A  (after a pause of 15 seconds): R-R8 mate.

The question and answer method seems to be suitable for introducing almost any one of the fields of human endeavor that we wish to include. We do not wish to penalize the machine for its inability to shine in beauty competitions nor to penalize a man for losing in a race against an airplane. The conditions of our game make these disabilities irrelevant. The "witnesses" can brag, if they consider it advisable, as much as they please about their charms, strength, or heroism, but the interrogator cannot demand practical demonstrations.

The game may perhaps be criticized on the ground that the odds are weighted too heavily against the machine. If the man were to try and pretend to be the machine he would clearly make a very poor showing. He would be given away at once by slowness and inaccuracy in arithmetic. May not machines carry out something which ought to be described as thinking but which is very different from what a man does? This objection is a very strong one, but at least we can say that if, nevertheless, a machine can be constructed to play the imitation game satisfactorily, we need not be troubled by this objection.

It might be urged that when playing the ''imitation game'' the best strategy for the machine may possibly be something other than imitation of the behavior of a man. This may be, but I think it is unlikely that there is any great effect of this kind. In any case there is no intention to investigate here the theory of the game, and it will be assumed that the best strategy is to try to provide answers that would naturally be given by a man.

## 3. THE MACHINES CONCERNED IN THE GAME

The question which we put in Sec. 1 will not be quite definite until we have specified what we mean by the word machine. It is natural that we should wish to permit every kind of engineering technique to be used in our machines. We also wish to allow the possibility than an engineer or team of engineers may construct a machine which works but whose manner of operation cannot be satisfactorily described by its constructors because they have applied a method which is largely experimental. Finally, we wish to exclude from the machines men born in the usual manner. It is difficult to frame the definitions so as to satisfy these three conditions. One might for instance insist that the team of engineers should be all of one sex, but this would not really be satisfactory, for it is probably possible to rear a complete individual from a single cell of the skin (say) of a man. To do so would be a feat of biological technique deserving of the very highest praise, but we would not be inclined to regard it as a case of ''constructing a thinking machine.'' This prompts us to abandon the requirement that every kind of technique should be permitted. We are the more ready to do so in view of the fact that the present interest in ''thinking machines'' has been aroused by a particular kind of machine, usually called an ''electronic computer'' or ''digital computer.'' Following this suggestion we only permit digital computers to take part in our game.

This restriction appears at first sight to be a very drastic one. I shall attempt to show that it is not so in reality. To do this necessitates a short account of the nature and properties of these computers.

It may also be said that this identification of machines with digital computers, like our criterion for ''thinking,'' will only be unsatisfactory if (contrary to my belief) it turns out that digital computers are unable to give a good showing in the game.

There are already a number of digital computers in working order, and it may be asked, "Why not try the experiment straight away? It would be easy to satisfy the conditions of the game. A number of interrogators could be used and statistics compiled to show how often the right identification was given." The short answer is that we are not asking whether all digital computers would do well in the game nor whether the computers at present available would do well, but whether there are imaginable computers which would do well. But this is only the short answer. We shall see this question in a different light later.

## 4. DIGITAL COMPUTERS

The idea behind digital computers may be explained by saying that these machines are intended to carry out any operations which could be done by a human computer. The human computer is supposed to be following fixed rules; he has no authority to deviate from them in any detail. We may suppose that these rules are supplied in a book, which is altered whenever he is put on to a new job. He has also an unlimited supply of paper on which he does his calculations. He may also do his multiplications and additions on a "desk machine," but this is not important.

If we use the above explanation as a definition we shall be in danger of circularity of argument. We avoid this by giving an outline of the means by which the desired effect is achieved. A digital computer can usually be regarded as consisting of three parts:

  i.   Store
 ii.   Executive unit
iii.   Control

The store is a store of information and corresponds to the human computer's paper, whether this is the paper on which he does his calculations or that on which his book of rules is printed. Insofar as the human computer does calculations in his head, a part of the store will correspond to his memory.

The executive unit is the part which carries out the various individual operations involved in a calculation. What these individual operations are will vary from machine to machine. Usually fairly lengthy operations can be done, such as "multiply 3,540,675,445 by 7,076,345,687," but in some machines only very simple ones, such as "write down 0," are possible.

We have mentioned that the "book of rules" supplied to the computer is replaced in the machine by a part of the store. It is then called the "table of instructions." It is the duty of the control to see that these instructions are obeyed correctly and in the right order. The control is so constructed that this necessarily happens.

The information in the store is usually broken up into packets of moderately small size. In one machine, for instance, a packet might consist of ten decimal digits. Numbers are assigned to the parts of the store in which the various packets of information are stored in some systematic manner. A typical instruction might say—"Add the number stored in position 6,809 to that in 4,302 and put the result back into the latter storage position."

Needless to say, it would not occur in the machine expressed in English. It would more likely be coded in a form such as 6809430217. Here 17 says which of various possible operations is to be performed on the two numbers. In this case the operation is that described above, viz., "Add the number. . . . " It will be noticed that the instruction takes up ten digits and so forms one packet of information, very conveniently. The control will normally take the instructions to be obeyed in the order of the positions in which they are stored, but occasionally an instruction such as "Now obey the instruction stored in position 5606, and continue from there" may be encountered, or again "If position 4505 contains 0 obey next the instruction stored in 6707, otherwise continue straight on." Instructions of these latter types are very important because they make it possible for a sequence of operations to be repeated over and over again until some condition is fulfilled but in doing so to obey, not fresh instructions on each repetition, but the same ones over and over again. To take a domestic analogy: Suppose Mother wants Tommy to call at the cobbler's every morning on his way to school to see if her shoes are done. She can ask him afresh every morning. Alternatively she can stick up a notice once and for all in the hall which he will see when he leaves for school and which tells him to call for the shoes and also to destroy the notice when he comes back if he has the shoes with him.

The reader must accept it as a fact that digital computers can be constructed, and indeed have been constructed, according to the principles we have described, and that they can in fact mimic the actions of a human computer very closely.

The book of rules which we have described our human computer as using is of course a convenient fiction. Actual human computers really remember what they have got to do. If one wants to make a machine mimic the behavior of the human computer in some complex operation, one has to ask him how it is done and then translate the answer into the form of an instruction table. Constructing instruction tables is usually described as "programming." To "program a machine to carry out the operation A" means to put the appropriate instruction table into the machine so that it will do A.

An interesting variant on the idea of a digital computer is a "digital computer with a random element." These have instructions involving the throwing of a die or some equivalent electronic process; one such instruction might for instance be "Throw the die and put the resulting number into store 1000." Sometimes such a machine is described as having free will (though I would not use this phrase myself). It is not normally possible to determine from observing a machine whether it has a random element, for a similar effect can be produced by such devices as making the choices depend on the digits of the decimal for $\pi$.

Most actual digital computers have only a finite store. There is no theoretical difficulty in the idea of a computer with an unlimited store. Of course only a finite part can have been used at any one time. Likewise only a finite amount can have been constructed, but we can imagine more and more being added as required. Such computers have special theoretical interest and will be called infinitive capacity computers.

The idea of a digital computer is an old one. Charles Babbage, Lucasian Professor of Mathematics at Cambridge from 1828 to 1839, planned such a machine, called the Analytical Engine, but it was never completed. Although Babbage had all the essential ideas, his machine was not at that time such a very attractive prospect. The speed which would have been available would be definitely faster than a human computer but something like one hundred times slower than the Manchester machine, itself one of the slower of the modern machines. The storage was to be purely mechanical, using wheels and cards.

The fact that Babbage's Analytical Engine was to be entirely mechanical will help us to rid ourselves of a superstition. Importance is often attached to the fact that modern digital computers are electrical and that the nervous system also is electrical. Since Babbage's machine was not electrical and since all digital computers are in a sense equivalent, we see that this use of electricity cannot be of theoretical importance. Of course, electricity usually comes in where fast signaling is concerned, so that it is not surprising that we find it in both these connections. In the nervous system chemical phenomena are at least as important as electrical. In certain computers the storage system is mainly acoustic. The feature of using electricity is thus seen to be only a very superficial similarity. If we wish to find such similarities we should look rather for mathematical analogies of function.

## 5. UNIVERSALITY OF DIGITAL COMPUTERS

The digital computers considered in the last section may be classified amongst the "discrete-state machines." These are the machines which move by sudden jumps or clicks from one quite definite state to another. These states are sufficiently different for the possibility of confusion between them to be ignored. Strictly speaking there are no such machines. Everything really moves continuously. But there are many kinds of machine which can profitably be *thought of* as being discrete-state machines. For instance, in considering the switches for a lighting system it is a convenient fiction that each switch must be definitely on or definitely off. There must be intermediate positions, but for most purposes we can forget about them. As an example of a discrete-state machine we might consider a wheel which clicks round through 120 degrees once a second but may be stopped by a lever which can be operated from outside; in addition a lamp is to light in one of the positions of the wheel. This machine could be described abstractly as follows. The internal state of the machine (which is described by the position of the wheel) may be $q_1$, $q_2$, or $q_3$. There is an input signal $i_0$ or $i_1$ (position of lever). The internal state at any moment is determined by the last state and input signal according to the table

|  |  | Last State | | |
|---|---|---|---|---|
|  |  | $q_1$ | $q_2$ | $q_3$ |
| Input | $i_0$ | $q_2$ | $q_3$ | $q_1$ |
|  | $i_1$ | $q_1$ | $q_2$ | $q_3$ |

The output signals, the only externally visible indication of the internal state (the light), are described by the table

| State | $q_1$ | $q_2$ | $q_3$ |
|---|---|---|---|
| Output | $o_0$ | $o_0$ | $o_1$ |

This example is typical of discrete-state machines. They can be described by such tables provided they have only a finite number of possible states.

It will seem that given the initial state of the machine and the input signals it is always possible to predict all future states. This is reminiscent of Laplace's view that from the complete state of the universe at one moment of time, as described by the positions and velocities of all particles, it should be possible to predict all future states. The prediction which we are considering is, however, rather nearer to practicability than that considered by Laplace. The system of the "universe as a whole" is such that quite small errors in the initial conditions can have an overwhelming effect at a later time. The displacement of a single electron by a billionth of a centimeter at one moment might make the difference between a man being killed by an avalanche a year later or escaping. It is an essential property of the mechanical systems which we have called "discrete-state machines" that this phenomenon does not occur. Even when we consider the actual physical machines instead of the idealized machines, reasonably accurate knowledge of the state at one moment yields reasonably accurate knowledge any number of steps later.

As we have mentioned, digital computers fall within the class of discrete-state machines. But the number of states of which such a machine is capable is usually enormously large. For instance, the number for the machine now working at Manchester is about $2^{165,000}$ i.e., about $10^{50,000}$. Compare this with our example of the clicking wheel described above, which had three states. It is not difficult to see why the number of states should be so immense. The computer includes a store corresponding to the paper used by a human computer. It must be possible to write into the store any one of the combinations of symbols which might have been written on the paper. For simplicity suppose that only digits from 0 to 9 are used as symbols. Variations in handwriting are ignored. Suppose the computer is allowed one hundred sheets of paper each containing fifty lines each with room for thirty digits. Then the number of states is $10^{100 \times 50 \times 30}$, i.e., $10^{150,000}$. This is about the number of states of three Manchester machines put together. The logarithm to the base 2 of the number of states is usually called the "storage capacity" of the machine. Thus the Machester machine has a storage capacity of about 165,000 and the wheel machine of our example about 1.6. If two machines are put together their capacities must be added to obtain the capacity of the resultant machine. This leads to the possibility of statements such as "The Manchester machine contains Sixty-four magnetic tracks each with a capacity of 2,560, eight electronic tubes with a capacity of 1,280. Miscellaneous storage amounts to about 300, making a total of 174,380."

Given the table corresponding to a discrete-state machine, it is possible to predict what it will do. There is no reason why this calculation should not be carried out by means of a digital computer. Provided it could be carried out by means of a digital computer. Provided it could be carried out sufficiently quickly, the digital computer could mimic the behavior of any discrete-state machine. The imitation game could then be played with the machine in question (as B) and the mimicking digital computer (as A), and the interrogator would be unable to distinguish them. Of course, the digital computer must have an adequate storage capacity as well as working sufficiently fast. Moreover, it must be programmed afresh for each new machine which it is desired to mimic.

This special property of digital computers, that they can mimic any discrete-state machine, is described by saying that they are *universal* machines. The existence of machines with this property has the important consequence that, considerations of speed apart, it is unnecessary to design various new machines to do various computing processes. They can all be done with one digital computer, suitably programmed for each case. It will be seen that as a consequence of this all digital computers are in a sense equivalent.

We may now consider again the point raised at the end of Sec. 3. It was suggested tentatively that the question "Can machines think?" should be replaced by "Are there imaginable digital computers which would do well in the imitation game?" If we wish we can make this superficially more general and ask, "Are there discrete-state machines which would do well?" But in view of the universality property we see that either of these questions is equivalent to this: "Let us fix our attention on one particular digital computer $C$. Is it true that by modifying this computer to have an adequate storage, suitably increasing its speed of action, and providing it with an appropriate program, $C$ can be made to play satisfactorily the part of A in the imitation game, the part of B being taken by a man?"

## 6. CONTRARY VIEWS ON THE MAIN QUESTION

We may now consider the ground to have been cleared and we are ready to proceed to the debate on our question "Can machines think?" and the variant of it quoted at the end of the last section. We cannot altogether abandon the original form of the problem, for opinions will differ as to the appropriateness of the substitution, and we must at least listen to what has to be said in this connection.

It will simplify matters for the reader if I explain first my own beliefs in the matter. Consider first the more accurate form of the question. I believe that in about fifty years' time it will be possible to program computers, with a storage capacity of about $10^9$, to make them play the imitation game so well that an average interrogator will not have more than 70 per cent chance of making the right identification after 5 minutes of questioning. The original question. "Can machines think?" I believe to be too meaningless to deserve discussion. Nevertheless I believe that at the end of the century the use of words and general educated opinion will have altered so much that one will be able to speak of machines thinking without expecting to be contradicted. I believe further that no useful purpose is served by concealing these beliefs. The popular view that scientists proceed inexorably from well-established fact to well-established fact, never being influenced by any unproved conjecture, is quite mistaken. Provided it is made clear which are proved facts and which are conjectures, no harm can result. Conjectures are of great importance since they suggest useful lines of research.

I now proceed to consider opinions opposed to my own.

1. *The theological objection.* Thinking is a function of man's immortal soul.[1] God has given an immortal soul to every man and woman, but not to any other animal or to machines. Hence no animal or machine can think.

I am unable to accept any part of this, but will attempt to reply in theological terms. I should find the argument more convincing if animals were classed with men, for there is a greater difference, to my mind, between the typical animate and the inanimate than there is between man and the other animals. The arbitrary character of the orthodox view becomes clearer if we consider how it might appear to a member of some other religious community. How do Christians regard the Moslem view that women have no souls? But let us leave this point aside and return to the main argument. It appears to me that the argument quoted above implies a serious restriction of the omnipotence of the Almighty. It is admitted that there are certain things that He cannot do, such as making one equal to two, but should we not believe that He has freedom to confer a soul on an elephant if He sees fit? We might expect that He would only exercise this power in conjunction with a mutation which provided the elephant with an appropriately improved brain to minister to the needs of this soul. An argument of exactly similar form may be made for the case of machines. It may seem

---

[1]Possibly this view is heretical. St. Thomas Aquinas (*Summa Theologica.* quoted by Bertrand Russell, p. 480) states that God cannot make a man to have no soul. But this may not be a real restriction on His powers, but only a result of the fact that men's souls are immortal and therefore indestructible.

different because it is more difficult to "swallow." But this really only means that we think it would be less likely that He would consider the circumstances suitable for conferring a soul. The circumstances in question are discussed in the rest of this paper. In attempting to construct such machines we should not be irreverently usurping. His power of creating souls, any more than we are in the procreation of children: Rather we are, in either case, instruments of His will providing mansions for the souls that He creates.

However, this is mere speculation. I am not very impressed with theological arguments whatever they may be used to support. Such arguments have often been found unsatisfactory in the past. In the time of Galileo it was argued that the texts "And the sun stood still . . . and hasted not to go down about a whole day" (Joshua x. 13) and "He laid the foundations of the earth, that it should not move at any time" (Psalm cv. 5) were an adequate refutation of the Copernican theory. With our present knowledge such an argument appears futile. When that knowledge was not available it made a quite different impression.

2. *The "heads in the sand" objection.* "The consequences of machines thinking would be too dreadful. Let us hope and believe that they cannot do so."

This argument is seldom expressed quite so openly as in the form above. But it affects most of us who think about it at all.We like to believe that man is in some subtle way superior to the rest of creation. It is best if he can be shown to be *necessarily* superior, for then there is no danger of him losing his commanding position. The popularity of the theological argument is clearly connected with this feeling. It is likely to be quite strong in intellectual people, since they value the power of thinking more highly than others, and are more inclined to base their belief in the superiority of man on this power.

I do not think that this argument is sufficiently substantial to require refutation. Consolation would be more appropriate: Perhaps this should be sought in the transmigration of souls.

3. *The mathematical objection.* There are a number of results of mathematical logic which can be used to show that there are limitations to the powers of discrete-state machines. The best known of these results is known as *Gödel's* theorem,[2] and shows that in any sufficiently powerful logical system statements can be formulated which can neither be proved nor disproved within the system, unless possibly the system itself is inconsistent. There are other, in some respects similar, results due to *Church, Kleene,* . . . and *Turing.* The latter result is the most convenient to consider, since it refers directly to machines, whereas the others can only be used in a comparatively indirect argument: For instance, if Gödel's theorem is to be used we need in addition to have some means of describing logical systems in terms of machines, and machines in terms of logical systems. The result in question refers to a type of machine which is essentially a digital computer with an infinite capacity. It states that there are

---

[2]Author's names in italics refer to the Bibliography.

certain things that such a machine cannot do. If it is rigged up to give answers to questions as in the imitation game, there will be some questions to which it will either give a wrong answer or fail to give an answer at all, however much time is allowed for a reply. There may, of course, be many such questions, and questions which cannot be answered by one machine may be satisfactorily answered by another. We are of course supposing for the present that the questions are of the kind to which an answer "Yes" or "No" is appropriate, rather than questions such as "What do you think of Picasso?" The questions that we know the machines must fail on are of this type: "Consider the machine specified as follows. . . . Will this machine ever answer 'yes' to any question?" The dots are to be replaced by a description of some machine in a standard form, which could be something like that used in Sec. 5. When the machine described bears a certain comparatively simple relation to the machine which is under interrogation, it can be shown that the answer is either wrong or not forthcoming. This is the mathematical result: It is argued that it proves a disabiliy of machines to which the human intellect is not subject.

The short answer to this argument is that, although it is established that there are limitations to the powers of any particular machine, it has only been stated, without any sort of proof, that no such limitations apply to the human intellect. But I do not think this view can be dismissed quite so lightly. Whenever one of these machines is asked the appropriate critical question, and gives a definite answer, we know that this answer must be wrong, and this gives us a certain feeling of superiority. Is this feeling illusory? It is no doubt quite genuine, but I do not think too much importance should be attached to it. We too often give wrong answers to questions ourselves to be justified in being very pleased at such evidence of fallibility on the part of the machines. Further, our superiority can only be felt on such an occasion in relation to the one machine over which we have scored our petty triumph. There would be no question of triumphing simultaneously over *all* machines. In short, then, there might be men cleverer than any given machine, but then again there might be other machines cleverer again, and so on.

Those who hold to the mathematical argument would, I think, mostly be willing to accept the imitation game as a basis for discussion. Those who believe in the two previous objections would probably not be interested in any criteria.

4. *The argument from consciousness.* This argument is very well expressed in *Professor Jefferson's* Lister Oration for 1949, from which I quote. "Not until a machine can write a sonnet or compose a concerto because of thoughts and emotions felt, and not by the chance fall of symbols, could we agree that machine equals brain—that is, not only write it but know that it had written it. No mechanism could feel (and not merely artificially signal, an easy contrivance) pleasure at its successes, grief when its valves fuse, be warmed by flattery, be made miserable by its mistakes, be charmed by sex, be angry or depressed when it cannot get what it wants."

This argument appears to be a denial of the validity of our test. According to the most extreme form of this view the only way by which one could be sure that a machine thinks is to *be* the machine and to feel oneself thinking. One could then describe these feelings to the world, but of course no one would be justified in taking any notice. Likewise according to this view the only way to know that a *man* thinks is to be that particular man. It is in fact the solipist point of view. It may be the most logical view to hold, but it makes communication of ideas difficult. A is liable to believe "A thinks but B does not," whilst B believes "B thinks but A does not." Instead of arguing continually over this point it is usual to have the polite convention that everyone thinks.

I am sure that Professor Jefferson does not wish to adopt the extreme and solipist point of view. Probably he would be quite willing to accept the imitation game as a test. The game (with the player B omitted) is frequently used in practice under the name of viva voce to discover whether some one really understands something or has "learnt it parrot fashion." Let us listen in to a part of such a viva voce:

*Interrogator:*  In the first line of your sonnet which reads "Shall I compare thee to a summer's day," would not "a spring day" do as well or better?

*Witness:*  It wouldn't scan.

*Interrogator:*  How about "a winter's day"? That would scan all right.

*Witness:*  Yes, but nobody wants to be compared to a winter's day.

*Interrogator:*  Would you say Mr. Pickwick reminded you of Christmas?

*Witness:*  In a way.

*Interrogator:*  Yet Christmas is a winter's day, and I do not think Mr. Pickwick would mind the comparison.

*Witness:*  I don't think you're serious. By a winter's day one means a typical winter's day, rather than a special one like Christmas.

And so on. What would Professor Jefferson say if the sonnet-writing machine was able to answer like this in the viva voce? I do not know whether he would regard the machine as merely artificially signaling" these answers, but if the answers were as satisfactory and sustained as in the above passage I do not think he would describe it as "an easy contrivance." This phrase is, I think, intended to cover such devices as the inclusion in the machine of a record of someone reading a sonnet with appropriate switching to turn it on from time to time.

In short then I think that most of those who support the argument from consciousness could be persuaded to abandon it rather than be forced into the solipist position. They will then probably be willing to accept our test.

I do not wish to give the impression that I think there is no mystery about consciousness. There is, for instance, something of a paradox connected with any attempt to localize it. But I do not think these mysteries necessarily need to be solved before we can answer the question with which we are concerned in this paper.

5. *Arguments from various disabilities.* These arguments take the form "I grant you that you can make machines do all the things you have mentioned, but you will never be able to make one to do X." Numerous features X are suggested in this connection. I offer a selection:

> Be kind, resourceful, beautiful, friendly . . . have initiative, have a sense of humor, tell right from wrong, make mistakes . . . fall in love, enjoy strawberries and cream . . . make someone fall in love with it, learn from experience . . . use words properly, be the subject of its own thought . . . have as much diversity of behavior as a man, do something really new. . . .

No support is usually offered for these statements. I believe they are mostly founded on the principle of scientific induction. A man has seen thousands of machines in his lifetime. From what he sees of them he draws a number of general conclusions. They are ugly, each is designed for a very limited purpose, when required for a minutely different purpose they are useless, the variety of behavior of any one of them is very small, etc., etc. Naturally he concludes that these are necessary properties of machines in general. Many of these limitations are associated with the very small storage capacity of most machines. (I am assuming that the idea of storage capacity is extended in some way to cover machines other than discrete-state machines. The exact definition does not matter as no mathematical accuracy is claimed in the present discussion.) A few years ago, when very little had been heard of digital computers, it was possible to elicit much incredulity concerning them if one mentioned their properties without describing their construction. That was presumably due to a similar application of the principle of scientific induction. These applications of the principle are of course largely unconscious. When a burned child fears the fire and shows that he fears it by avoiding it, I should say that he was applying scientific induction. (I could of course also describe his behavior in many other ways.) The works and customs of mankind do not seem to be very suitable material to which to apply scientific induction. A very large part of space time must be investigated if reliable results are to be obtained. Other wise we may (as most English children do) decide that everybody speaks English, and that it is silly to learn French.

There are, however, special remarks to be made about many of the disabilities that have been mentioned. The inability to enjoy strawberries and cream may have struck the reader as frivolous. Possibly a machine might be made to enjoy this delicious dish, but any attempt to make one do so would be idiotic. What is important about this disability is that it contributes to some of the other disabilities e.g., to the difficulty of the same kind of friendliness occurring between man and machine as between white man and white man or between black man and black man.

The claim that "machines cannot make mistakes" seems a curious one. One is tempted to retort, "Are they any the worse for that?" But let us adopt a more sympathetic attitude and try to see what is really meant. I think this criticism can be explained in terms of the imitation game. It is claimed that the interrogator could distinguish the machine from the man simply by setting them a number of problems in arithmetic. The machine would be unmasked because of its deadly accuracy. The reply to this is simple. The machine (programmed for playing the game) would not attempt to give the *right* answers to the arithmetic problems. It would deliberately introduce mistakes in a manner calculated to confuse the interrogator. A mechanical fault would probably show itself through an unsuitable decision as to what sort of a mistake to make in the arithmetic. Even this interpretation of the criticism is not sufficiently sympathetic. But we cannot afford the space to go into it much further. It seems to me that this criticism depends on a confusion between two kinds of mistake. We may call them "errors of functioning" and "errors of conclusion." Errors of functioning are due to some mechanical or electrical fault which causes the machine to behave otherwise than it was designed to do. In philosophical discussions one likes to ignore the possibility of such errors; one is therefore discussing "abstract machines." These abstract machines are mathematical fictions rather than physical objects. By definition they are incapable of errors of functioning. In this sense we can truly say that "machines can never make mistakes." Errors of conclusion can only arise when some meaning is attached to the output signals from the machine. The machine might, for instance, type our mathematical equations or sentences in English. When a false proposition is typed we say that the machine has committed an error of conclusion. There is clearly no reason at all for saying that a machine cannot make this kind of mistake. It might do nothing but type out repeatedly "$0 = 1$." To take a less perverse example, it might have some method for drawing conclusions by scientific induction. We must expect such a method to lead occasionally to erroneous results.

The claim that a machine cannot be the subject of its own thought can of course only be answered if it can be shown that the machine has *some* thought with *some* subject matter. Nevertheless, "the subject matter of a machine's operations" does seem to mean something, at least to the people who deal with it. If, for instance, the machine was trying to find a solution of the equation $x^2 - 40x - 11 = 0$, one would be tempted to describe this equation as part of the machine's subject matter at that moment. In this sort of sense a machine undoubtedly can be its own subject matter. It may be used to help in making up its own programs or to predict the effect of alterations in its own structure. By observing the results of its own behavior it can modify its own programs so as to achieve some purpose more effectively. These are possibilities of the near future rather than Utopian dreams.

The criticism that a machine cannot have much diversity of behavior is just a way of saying that it cannot have much storage capacity. Until fairly recently a storage capacity of even a thousand digits was very rare.

The criticisms that we are considering here are often disguised forms of the argument from consciousness. Usually if one maintains that a machine *can* do one of these things and describes the kind of method that the machine could use, one will not make much of an impression. It is thought that the method (whatever it may be, for it must be mechanical) is really rather base. . . .

6. *Lady Lovelace's objection.* Our most detailed information of Babbage's Analytical Engine comes from a memoir by *Lady Lovelace*. In it she states, "The Analytical Engine has no pretensions to *originate* anything. It can do *whatever we know how to order it* to perform" (her italics). This statement is quoted by *Hartree* (p. 70), who adds: "This does not imply that it may not be possible to construct electronic equipment which will 'think for itself,' or in which, in biological terms, one could set up a conditioned reflex, which would serve as a basis for 'learning.' Whether this is possible in principle or not is a stimulating and exciting question, suggested by some of these recent developments. But it did not seem that the machines constructed or projected at the time had this property."

I am in thorough agreement with Hartree over this. It will be noticed that he does not assert that the machines in question had not got the property, but rather that the evidence available to Lady Lovelace did not encourage her to believe that they had it. It is quite possible that the machines in question had in a sense got this property. For suppose that some discrete-state machine has the property. The Analytical Engine was a universal digital computer, so that, if its storage capacity and speed were adequate, it could be suitable programming be made to mimic the machine in question. Probably this argument did not occur to the countess or to Babbage. In any case there was no obligation on them to claim all that could be claimed.

This whole question will be considered again under the heading of learning machines.

A variant of Lady Lovelace's objection states that a machine can "never do anything really new." This may be parried for a moment with the saw "There is nothing new under the sun." Who can be certain that "original work" that he has done was not simply the growth of the seed planted in him by teaching or the effect of following well-known general principles. A better variant of the objection says that a machine can never "take us by surprise." This statement is a more direct challenge and can be met directly. Machines take me by surprise with great frequency. This is largely because I do not do sufficient calculation to decide what to expect them to do or rather because, although I do a calculation, I do it in a hurried, slipshod fashion, taking risks. Perhaps I say to myself, "I suppose the voltage here ought to be the same as there: Anyway let's assume it is." Naturally I am often wrong, and the result is a surprise for me for by the time the experiment is done these assumptions have been forgotten. These admissions lay me open to lectures on the subject of my vicious ways, but do not throw any doubt on my credibility when I testify to the surprises I experience.

I do not expect this reply to silence my critic. He will probably say that such surprises are due to some creative mental act on my part and reflect no credit on the machine. This leads us back to the argument from consciousness and far from the idea of surprise. It is a line of argument we must consider closed, but it is perhaps worth remarking that the appreciation of something as surprising requires as much of a "creative mental act" whether the surprising event originates from a man, a book, a machine, or anything else.

The view that machines cannot give rise to surprises is due, I believe, to a fallacy to which philosophers and mathematicians are particularly subject. This is the assumption that as soon as a fact is presented to a mind all consequences of that fact spring into the mind simultaneously with it. It is a very useful assumption under many circumstances, but one too easily forgets that it is false. A natural consequence of doing so is that one then assumes that there is no virtue in the mere working out of consequences from data and general principles.

7. *Argument from continuity in the nervous system.* The nervous system is certainly not a discrete-state machine. A small error in the information about the size of a nervous impulse impinging on a neuron may make a large difference to the size of the outgoing impulse. It may be argued that, this being so, one cannot expect to be able to mimic the behavior of the nervous system with a discrete-state system.

It is true that a discrete-state machine must be different from a continuous machine. But if we adhere to the conditions of the imitation game, the interrogator will not be able to take any advantage of this difference. The situation can be made clearer if we consider some other simpler continuous machine. A differential analyzer will do very well. (A differential analyzer is a certain kind of machine not of the discrete-state type used for some kinds of calculation.) Some of these provide their answers in a typed form and so are suitable for taking part in the game. It would not be possible for a digital computer to predict exactly what answers the differential analyzer would give to a problem but it would be quite capable of giving the right sort of answer. For instance, if asked to give the value of $\pi$ (actually about 3.1416), it would be reasonable to choose at random between the values 3.12, 3.13, 3.14, 3.15, 3.16 with the probabilities of 0.05, 0.15, 0.55, 0.19, 0.06 (say). Under these circumstances it would be very difficult for the interrogator to distinguish the differential analyzer from the digital computer.

8. *The argument from informality of behavior.* It is not possible to produce a set of rules purporting to describe what a man should do in every conceivable set of circumstances. One might, for instance, have a rule that one is to stop when one sees a red traffic light and to go if one sees a green one, but what if by some fault both appear together? One may perhaps decide that it is safest to stop. But some further difficulty may well arise from this decision later. To attempt to provide rules of conduct to cover every eventuality, even those arising from traffic lights, appears to be impossible. With all this I agree.

From this it is argued that we cannot be machines. I shall try to reproduce the argument, but I fear I shall hardly do it justice. It seems to run something like this. "If each man had a definite set of rules of conduct by which he regulated his life, he would be no better than a machine. But there are no such rules, so men cannot be machines." The undistributed middle is glaring. I do not think the argument is ever put quite like this, but I believe this is the argument used nevertheless. There may however be a certain confusion between "rules of conduct" and "laws of behavior" to cloud the issue. By "rules of conduct" I mean precepts such as "Stop if you see red lights," on which one can act and of which one can be conscious. By "laws of behavior" I mean laws of nature as applied to a man's body such as "if you pinch him he will squeak." If we substitute "laws of behavior which regulate his life" for "laws of conduct by which he regulates his life" in the argument quoted, the undistributed middle is no longer insuperable. For we believe that it is not only true that being regulated by laws of behavior implies being some sort of machine (though not necessarily a discrete-state machine) but that conversely being such a machine implies being regulated by such laws. However, we cannot so easily convince ourselves of the absence of complete laws of behavior as of complete rules of conduct. The only way we know of for finding such laws is scientific observation, and we certainly know of no circumstances under which we could say, "We have searched enough. There are no such laws."

We can demonstrate more forcibly that any such statement would be un-justified. For suppose we could be sure of finding such laws if they existed. Then, given a discrete-state machine, it should certainly be possible to discover by observation sufficient about it to predict its future behavior, and this within a reasonable time, say a thousand years. But this does not seem to be the case. I have set up on the Manchester computer a small program using only 1,000 units of storage, whereby the machine supplied with one sixteen-figure number replies with another within 2 seconds. I would defy anyone to learn from these replies sufficient about the program to be able to predict any replies to untried values.

9. *The argument from extrasensory perception.* I assume that the reader is familiar with the idea of extrasensory perception and the meaning of the four items of it, viz., telepathy, clairvoyance, precognition, and psychokinesis. These disturbing phenomena seem to deny all our usual scientific ideas. How we should like to discredit them! Unfortunately the statistical evidence, at least for telepathy, is overwhelming. It is very difficult to rearrange one's ideas so as to fit these new facts in. Once one has accepted them it does not seem a very big step to believe in ghosts and bogies. The idea that our bodies move simply according to the known laws of physics, together with some others not yet discovered but somewhat similar, would be one of the first to go.

This argument is to my mind quite a strong one. One can say in reply that many scientific theories seem to remain workable in practice, in spite of clashing with ESP; that in fact one can get along very nicely if one forgets about it. This is rather cold comfort, and one fears that thinking is just the kind of phenomenon where ESP may be especially relevant.

A more specific argument based on ESP might run as follows: "Let us play the imitation game, using as witnesses a man who is good as a telepathic receiver, and a digital computer. The interrogator can ask such questions as 'What suit does the card in my right hand belong to?' The man by telepathy or clairvoyance gives the right answer 130 times out of 400 cards. The machine can only guess at random and perhaps gets 104 right, so the interrogator makes the right identification.'' There is an interesting possibility which opens here. Suppose the digital computer contains a random-number generator. Then it will be natural to use this to decide what answer to give. But then the random-number generator will be subject to the psychokinetic powers of the interrogator. Perhaps this psychokinesis might cause the machine to guess right more often than would be expected on a probability calculation, so that the interrogator might still be unable to make the right identification. On the other hand, he might be able to guess right without any questioning, by clairvoyance. With ESP anything may happen.

If telepathy is admitted, it will be necessary to tighten our test up. The situation could be regarded as analogous to that which would occur if the interrogator were talking to himself and one of the competitors was listening with his ear to the wall. To put the competitors into a ''telepathy-proof room'' would satisfy all requirements.

## 7. LEARNING MACHINES

The reader will have anticipated that I have no very convincing arguments of a positive nature to support my views. If I had I should not have taken such pains to point out the fallacies in contrary views. Such evidence as I have I shall now give.

Let us return for a moment to Lady Lovelace's objection, which stated that the machine can only do what we tell it to do. One could say that a man can ''inject'' an idea into the machine and that it will respond to a certain extent and then drop into quiescence, like a piano string struck by a hammer. Another simile would be an atomic pile of less than critical size: An injected idea is to correspond to a neutron entering the pile from without. Each such neutron will cause a certain disturbance which eventually dies away. If, however, the size of the pile is sufficiently increased, the disturbance caused by such an incoming neutron will very likely go on and on increasing until the whole pile is destroyed. Is there a corresponding phenomenon for minds, and is there one for machines? There does seem to be one for the human mind. The majority of them seem to be ''sub-critical,'' i.e., to correspond in this analogy to piles of subcritical size. An idea presented to such a mind will on average give rise to less than one idea in reply. A smallish proportion are super-critical. An idea presented to such a mind may give rise to a whole ''theory'' consisting of secondary, tertiary, and more remote ideas. Animals' minds seem to be very definitely subcritical. Adhering to this analogy we ask, ''Can a machine be made to be supercritical?''

The "skin of an onion" analogy is also helpful. In considering the functions of the mind or the brain we find certain operations which we can explain in purely mechanical terms. This we say does not correspond to the real mind: It is a sort of skin which we must strip off if we are to find the real mind. But then in what remains we find a further skin to be stripped off, and so on. Proceeding in this way do we ever come to the "real" mind, or do we eventually come to the skin which has nothing in it? In the latter case the whole mind is mechanical. (It would not be a discrete-state machine however. We have discussed this.)

These last two paragraphs do not claim to be convincing arguments. They should rather be described as "recitations tending to produce belief."

The only really satisfactory support that can be given for the view expressed at the beginning of Sec. 6 will be that provided by waiting for the end of the century and then doing the experiment described. But what can we say in the meantime? What steps should be taken now if the experiment is to be successful?

As I have explained, the problem is mainly one of programming. Advances in engineering will have to be made too, but it seems unlikely that these will not be adequate for the requirements. Estimates of the storage capacity of the brain vary from $10^{10}$ to $10^{15}$ binary digits. I incline to the lower values and believe that only a very small fraction is used for the higher types of thinking. Most of it is probably used for the retention of visual impressions. I should be surprised if more than $10^9$ was required for satisfactory playing of the imitation game, at any rate against a blind man. (Note—The capacity of the *Encyclopedia Britannica,* 11th edition, is $2 \times 10^9$.) A storage capacity of $10^7$ would be a very practicable possibility even by present techniques. It is probably not necessary to increase the speed of operations of the machines at all. Parts of modern machines which can be regarded as analogues of nerve cells work about a thousand times faster than the latter. This should provide a "margin of safety" which could cover losses of speed arising in many ways. Our problem then is to find out how to program these machines to play the game. At my present rate of working I produce about a thousand digits of program a day, so that about sixty workers working steadily through the fifty years might accomplish the job, if nothing went into the wastepaper basket. Some more expeditious method seems desirable.

In the process of trying to imitate an adult human mind we are bound to think a good deal about the process which has brought it to the state that it is in. We may notice three components:

a.   The initial state of the mind, say at birth
b.   The education to which it has been subjected
c.   Other experience, not to be described as education, to which it has been subjected

Instead of trying to produce a program to simulate the adult mind, why not rather try to produce one which simulates the child's? If this were then subjected to an appropriate course of education one would obtain the adult brain. Presumably the child's brain is something like a notebook as one buys it from the stationers—rather little mechanism and lots of blank sheets. (Mechanism and writing are from our point of view almost synonymous.) Our hope is that there is so little mechanism in the child's brain that something like it can be easily programmed. The amount of work in the education we can assume, as a first approximation, to be much the same as for the human child.

We have thus divided our problem into two parts. The child program and the education process. These two remain very closely connected. We cannot expect to find a good child machine at the first attempt. One must experiment with teaching one such machine and see how well it learns. One can then try another and see if it is better or worse. There is an obvious connection between this process and evolution, by the identifications

> structure of the child machine = hereditary material
>
> changes of the child machine = mutations
>
> natural selection = judgment of the experimenter

One may hope, however, that this process will be more expeditious than evolution. The survival of the fittest is a slow method for measuring advantages. The experimenter, by the exercise of intelligence, should be able to speed it up. Equally important is the fact that he is not restricted to random mutations. If he can trace a cause for some weakness, he can probably think of the kind of mutation which will improve it.

It will not be possible to apply exactly the same teaching process to the machine as to a normal child. It will not, for instance, be provided with legs, so that it could not be asked to go out and fill the coal scuttle. Possibly it might not have eyes. But however well these deficiencies might be overcome by clever engineering, one could not send the creature to school without the other children making excessive fun of it. It must be given some tuition. We need not be too concerned about the legs, eyes, etc. The example of Miss Helen Keller shows that education can take place provided that communication in both directions between teacher and pupil can take place by some means or other.

We normally associate punishments and rewards with the teaching process. Some simple child machines can be constructed or programmed on this sort of principle. The machine has to be so constructed that events which shortly preceded the occurrence of a punishment signal are unlikely to be repeated, whereas a reward signal increased the probability of repetition of the events which led up to it. These definitions do not presuppose any feelings on the part of the machine. I have done some experiments with one such child machine and succeeded in teaching it a few things, but the teaching method was too unorthodox for the experiment to be considered really successful.

The use of punishments and rewards can at best be a part of the teaching process. Roughly speaking, if the teacher has no other means of communicating to the pupil, the amount of information which can reach him does not exceed the total number of rewards and punishments applied. By the time a child has learned to repeat ''Casabianca'' he would probably feel very sore indeed if the text could only be discovered by a ''Twenty questions'' technique, very ''NO'' taking the form of a blow. It is necessary therefore to have some other ''unemotional'' channels of communication. If these are available it is possible to teach a machine by punishments and rewards to obey orders given in some language, e.g., a symbolic language. These orders are to be transmitted through the ''unemotional'' channels. The use of this language will diminish greatly the number of punishments and rewards required.

Opinions may vary as to the complexity which is suitable in the child machine. One might try to make it as simple as possible consistent with the general principles. Alternatively one might have a complete system of logical inference ''built in''.[3] In the latter case the store would be largely occupied with definitions and propositions. The propositions would have various kinds of status, e.q., well-established facts, conjectures, mathematically proved theorems, statements given by an authority, expressions having the logical form of proposition but not belief value. Certain propositions may be described as ''imperatives.'' The machine should be so constructed that as soon as an imperative is classed as ''well established'' the appropriate action automatically takes place. To illustrate this, suppose the teacher says to the machine ''Do your homework now.'' This may cause ''Teacher says 'Do your homework now' '' to be included amongst the well-established facts. Another such fact might be, ''Everything that teacher says is true.'' Combining these may eventually lead to the imperative, ''Do your homework now,'' being included amongst the well established facts, and this, by the construction of the machine, well mean that the homework actually gets started, but the effect is very satisfactory. The processes of inference used by the machine need not be such as would satisfy the most exacting logicians. There might for instance be no hierarchy of types. But this need not mean that type fallacies will occur, any more than we are bound to fall over unfenced cliffs. Suitable imperatives (expressed *within* the systems, not forming part of the rules *of* of the system) such as ''Do not use a class unless it is a subclass of one which has been mentioned by teacher'' can have a similar effect to ''Do not go too near the edge.''

The imperatives that can be obeyed by a machine that has no limbs are bound to be of a rather intellectual character, as in the example (doing homework) given above. Important amongst such imperatives will be ones which regulate the order in which the rules of the logical system concerned are to be applied. For at each

---

[3]Or rather ''programmed in'' for our child machine will be programmed in a digital computer. But the logical system will not have to be learned.

stage when one is using a logical system, there is a very large number of alternative steps, any of which one is permitted to apply, so far as obedience to the rules of the logical system is concerned. These choices make the difference between a brilliant and a footling reasoner, not the difference between a sound and a fallacious one. Propositions leading to imperatives of this kind might be "When Socrates is mentioned, use the syllogism in Barbara" or "If one method has been proved to be quicker than another, do not use the slower method." Some of these may be "given by authority," but others may be produced by the machine itself, e.g., by scientific induction.

The idea of learning machine may appear paradoxical to some readers. How can the rules of operation of the machine change? They should describe completely how the machine will react, whatever its history might be, whatever changes it might undergo. The rules are thus quite time-invariant. This is quite true. The explanation of the paradox is that the rules which get changed in the learning process are of a rather less pretentious kind, claiming only an ephemeral validity. The reader may draw a parallel with the Constitution of the United States.

An important feature of a learning machine is that its teacher will often be very largely ignorant of quite what is going on inside, although he may still be able to some extent to predict his pupil's behavior. This should apply most strongly to the later education of a machine arising from a child machine of well-tried design (or program). This is in clear contrast with normal procedure when using a machine to do computations: One's object is then to have a clear mental picture of the state of the machine at each moment in the computation. This object can only be achieved with a struggle. The view that "the machine can only do what we know how to order it to do,"[4] appears strange in face of this. Most of the programs which we can put into the machine will result in its doing something that we cannot make sense of at all or which we regard as completely random behavior. Intelligent behavior presumably consists in a departure from the completely disciplined behavior involved in computation, but a rather slight one, which does not give rise to random behavior, or to pointless repetitive loops. Another important result of preparing our machine for its part in the imitation game by a process of teaching and learning is that "human fallibility" is likely to be omitted in a rather natural way, i.e., without special coaching. . . . Processes that are learned do not produce 100 per cent certainty of result; if they did they could not be unlearned.

It is probably wise to include a random element in a learning machine. . . . A random element is rather useful when we are searching for a solution of some problem. Suppose for instance we wanted to find a number between 50 and 200 which was equal to the square of the sum of its digits, we might start at 51, then try 52, and go on until we got a number that worked. Alternatively we might

---

[4]Compare Lady Lovelace's statement [earlier] which does not contain the word "only."

choose numbers at random until we got a good one. This method has the advantage that it is unnecessary to keep track of the values that have been tried, but the disadvantage that one may try the same one twice, but this is not very important if there are several solutions. The systematic method has the disadvantage that there may be an enormous block without any solutions in the region which has to be investigated first. Now the learning process may be regarded as a search for a form of behavior which will satisfy the teacher (or some other criterion). Since there is probably a very large number of satisfactory solutions the random method seems to be better than the systematic. It should be noticed that it is used in the analogous process of evolution. But there the systematic method is not possible. How could one keep track of the different genetical combinations that had been tried so as to avoid trying them again?

We may hope that machines will eventually compete with men in all purely intellectual fields. But which are the best ones to start with? Even this is a difficult decision. Many people think that a very abstract activity, like the playing of chess, would be best. It can also be maintained that it is best to provide the machine with the best sense organs that money can buy, and then teach it to understand and speak English. This process could follow the normal teaching of a child. Things would be pointed out and named, etc. Again I do not know what the right answer is, but I think both approaches should be tried.

We can only see a short distance ahead, but we can see plenty there that needs to be done.

## BIBLIOGRAPHY

Butler, S. (1865). The book of the machines. In *Erewhon* (Chapters 23, 24, 25). London.

Church, A. (1936). An unsolvable problem of elementary number theory. *American Journal of Mathematics, 58*, 345–363.

Gödel, K. (1931). Über formal unentscheidbare Sätze der Principia Mathematica und verwandter Systeme, I. *Monatshefte für Math. und Phys.* (pp. 173–189).

Hartree, D. R. (1949). *Calculating Instruments and Machines.* New York.

Jefferson, G. (1949). The mind of mechanical man. Lister oration for 1949. *British Medical Journal, i,* 1105–1121.

Kleene, S. C. (1935). General recursive functions of natural numbers. *American Journal of Mathematics, 57,* 153–173, 219–244.

Countess of Lovelace. (1842). Translator's notes to an article on Babbage's analytical engine. In R. Taylor (Ed.), *Scientific Memoirs* (Vol. 3, pp. 691–731).

Russell, B.(1940). *History of Western Philosophy.* London.

Turing, A. M. (1937). On computable numbers, with an application to the Entscheidungs problem. *Proceedings of the London Mathematical Society, 42*(2), 230–265.

# 8

# Computer Science as Empirical Inquiry: Symbols and Search

## (1976)

### Allen Newell and Herbert A. Simon

Computer science is the study of the phenomena surrounding computers. The founders of this society understood this very well when they called themselves the Association for Computing Machinery. The machine—not just the hardware, but the programmed living machine—is the organism we study.

This is the tenth Turing Lecture. The nine persons who preceded us on this platform have presented nine different views of computer science. For our organism, the machine, can be studied at many levels and from many sides. We are deeply honored to appear here today and to present yet another view, the one that has permeated the scientific work for which we have been cited. We wish to speak of computer science as empirical inquiry.

Our view is only one of many; the previous lectures make that clear. However, even taken together the lectures fail to cover the whole scope of our science. Many fundamental aspects of it have not been represented in these 10 awards. And if the time ever arrives, surely not soon, when the compass has been boxed, when computer science has been discussed from every side, it will be time to start the cycle again. For the hare as lecturer will have to make an annual sprint to overtake the cumulation of small, incremental gains that the tortoise of scientific and technical development has achieved in his steady march. Each year will create a new gap and call for a new sprint, for in science there is no final word.

Computer science is an empirical discipline. We would have called it an experimental science, but like astronomy, economics, and geology, some of its unique forms of observation and experience do not fit a narrow stereotype of the experimental method. Nonetheless, they are experiments. Each new machine that is built is an experiment. Actually constructing the machine poses a question to nature; and we listen for the answer by observing the machine in operation and analyzing it by all analytical and measurement means available. Each new program that is built is an experiment. It poses a question to nature, and its behavior offers clues to an answer. Neither machines nor programs are black boxes; they are artifacts that have been designed, both hardware and software, and we can open them up and look inside. We can relate their structure to their behavior and draw many lessons from a single experiment. We don't have to build 100 copies of, say, a theorem prover, to demonstrate statistically that it has not overcome the combinatorial explosion of search in the way hoped for. Inspection of the program in the light of a few runs reveals the flaw and lets us proceed to the next attempt.

We build computers and programs for many reasons. We build them to serve society and as tools for carrying out the economic tasks of society. But as basic scientists we build machines and programs as a way of discovering new phenomena and analyzing phenomena we already know about. Society often becomes confused about this, believing that computers and programs are to be constructed only for the economic use that can be made of them (or as intermediate items in a developmental sequence leading to such use). It needs to understand that the phenomena surrounding computers are deep and obscure, requiring much experimentation to assess their nature. It needs to understand that, as in any science, the gains that accrue from such experimentation and understanding pay off in the permanent acquisition of new techniques; and that it is these techniques that will create the instruments to help society in achieving its goals.

Our purpose here, however, is not to plead for understanding from an outside world. It is to examine one aspect of our science, the development of new basic understanding by empirical inquiry. This is best done by illustrations. We will be pardoned if, presuming upon the occasion, we choose our examples from the area of our own research. As will become apparent, these examples involve the whole development of artificial intelligence, especially in its early years. They rest on much more than our own personal contributions. And even where we have made direct contributions, this has been done in cooperation with others. Our collaborators have included especially Cliff Shaw, with whom we formed a team of three through the exciting period of the late fifties. But we have also worked with a great many colleagues and students at Carnegie-Mellon University.

Time permits taking up just two examples. The first is the development of the notion of a symbolic system. The second is the development of the notion of heuristic search. Both conceptions have deep significance for understanding how information is processed and how intelligence is achieved. However, they do not come close to exhausting the full scope of artificial intelligence, though they seem to us to be useful for exhibiting the nature of fundamental knowledge in this part of computer science.

## SYMBOLS AND PHYSICAL SYMBOL SYSTEMS

One of the fundamental contributions to knowledge of computer science has been to explain, at a rather basic level, what symbols are. This explanation is a scientific proposition about Nature. It is empirically derived, with a long and gradual development.

Symbols lie at the root of intelligent action, which is, of course, the primary topic of artificial intelligence. For that matter, it is a primary question for all of computer science. For all information is processed by computers in the service of ends, and we measure the intelligence of a system by its ability to achieve stated ends in the face of variations, difficulties, and complexities posed by the task environment. This general investment of computer science in attaining intelligence is obscured when the tasks being accomplished are limited in scope, for then the full variations in the environment can be accurately foreseen. It becomes more obvious as we extend computers to more global, complex, and knowledge-intensive tasks—as we attempt to make them our agents, capable of handling on their own the full contingencies of the natural world.

Our understanding of the system's requirements for intelligent action emerges slowly. It is composite, for no single elementary thing accounts for intelligence in all its manifestations. There is no "intelligence principle," just as there is no "vital principle" that conveys by its very nature the essence of life. But the lack of a simple *deus ex machina* does not imply that there are no structural requirements for intelligence. One such requirement is the ability to store and manipulate symbols. To put the scientific question, we may paraphrase the title of a famous paper by Warren McCulloch (1961): What is a symbol, that intelligence may use it, and intelligence, that it may use a symbol?

## Laws of Qualitative Structure

All sciences characterize the essential nature of the systems they study. These characterizations are invariably qualitative in nature, for they set the terms within which more detailed knowledge can be developed. Their essence can often be captured in very short, very general statements. One might judge these general laws, because of their limited specificity, as making relatively little contribution to the sum of a science, were it not for the historical evidence that shows them to be results of the greatest importance.

*The cell doctrine in biology.* A good example of a law of qualitative structure is the cell doctrine in biology, which states that the basic building block of all living organisms is the cell. Cells come in a large variety of forms, though they all have a nucleus surrounded by protoplasm, the whole encased by a membrane. But this internal structure was not, historically, part of the specification of the cell doctrine; it was subsequent specificity developed by intensive investigation. The cell doctrine can be conveyed almost entirely by the statement we gave above, along with some vague notions about what size a cell can be. The impact of this law on biology, however, has been tremendous, and the lost motion in the field prior to its gradual acceptance was considerable.

*Plate tectonics in geology.* Geology provides an interesting example of a qualitative structure law, interesting because it has gained acceptance in the last decade and so its rise in status is still fresh in our memory. The theory of plate tectonics asserts that the surface of the globe is a collection of huge plates—a few dozen in all—which move (at geological speeds) against, over, and under each other into the center of the earth, where they lose their identity. The movements of the plates account for the shapes and relative locations of the continents and oceans, for the areas of volcanic and earthquake activity, for the deep sea ridges, and so on. With a few additional particulars as to speed and size, the essential theory has been specified. It was, of course, not accepted until it succeeded in explaining a number of details, all of which hung together (e.g., accounting for flora, fauna, and stratification agreements between West Africa and Northeast South America). The plate tectonics theory is highly qualitative. Now that it is accepted, the whole earth seems to offer evidence for it everywhere, for we see the world in its terms.

*The germ theory of disease.* It is little more than a century since Pasteur enunciated the germ theory of disease, a law of qualitative structure that produced a revolution in medicine. The theory proposes that most diseases are caused by the presence and multiplication in the body of tiny single-celled living organisms, and that contagion consists in the transmission of these organisms from one host to another. A large part of the elaboration of the theory consisted in identifying the organisms associated with specific diseases, describing them, and tracing their life histories. The fact that the law has many exceptions—that many diseases are not produced by germs—does not detract from its importance. The law tells us to look for a particular kind of cause; it does not insist that we will always find it.

*The doctrine of atomism.* The doctrine of atomism offers an interesting contrast to the three laws of qualitative structure we have just described. As it emerged from the work of Dalton and his demonstrations that the chemicals combined in fixed proportions, the law provided a typical example of qualitative structure: the elements are composed of small, uniform particles, differing from one element to another. But because the underlying species of atoms are so simple and limited in their variety, quantitative theories were soon formulated which assimilated all the general structure in the original qualitative hypothesis. With cells, tectonic plates, and germs, the variety of structure is so great that the underlying qualitative principle remains distinct, and its contribution to the total theory clearly discernible.

*Conclusion.* Laws of qualitative structure are seen everywhere in science. Some of our greatest scientific discoveries are to be found among them. As the examples illustrate, they often set the terms on which a whole science operates.

## Physical Symbol Systems

Let us return to the topic of symbols, and define a *physical symbol system*. The adjective "physical" denotes two important features: (1) Such systems clearly obey the laws of physics—they are realizable by engineered systems made of engineered components; (2) although our use of the term "symbol" prefigures our intended interpretation, it is not restricted to human symbol systems.

A physical symbol system consists of a set of entities, called symbols, which are physical patterns that can occur as components of another type of entity called an expression (or symbol structure). Thus a symbol structure is composed of a number of instances (or tokens) of symbols related in some physical way (such as one token being next to another). At any instant of time the system will contain a collection of these symbol structures. Besides these structures, the system also contains a collection of processes that operate on expressions to produce other expressions: processes of creation, modification, reproduction, and destruction. A physical symbol system is a machine that produces through time an evolving collection of symbol structures. Such a system exists in a world of objects wider than just these symbolic expressions themselves.

Two notions are central to this structure of expressions, symbols, and objects: designation and interpretation.

*Designation.* An expression designates an object if, given the expression, the system can either affect the object itself or behave in ways depending on the object.

In either case, access to the object via the expression has been obtained, which is the essence of designation.

*Interpretation.* The system can interpret an expression if the expression designates a process and if, given the expression, the system can carry out the process.

Interpretation implies a special form of dependent action: given an expression, the system can perform the indicated process, which is to say, it can evoke and execute its own processes from expressions that designate them.

A system capable of designation and interpretation, in the sense just indicated, must also meet a number of additional requirements, of completeness and closure. We will have space only to mention these briefly; all of them are important and have far-reaching consequences.

(1) A symbol may be used to designate any expression whatsoever. That is, given a symbol, it is not prescribed a priori what expressions it can designate. This arbitrariness pertains only to symbols: the symbol tokens and their mutual relations determine what object is designated by a complex expression. (2) There exist expressions that designate every process of which the machine is capable. (3) There exist processes for creating any expression and for modifying any expression in arbitrary ways. (4) Expressions are stable; once created, they will continue to exist until explicitly modified or deleted. (5) The number of expressions that the system can hold is essentially unbounded.

The type of system we have just defined is not unfamiliar to computer scientists. It bears a strong family resemblance to all general purpose computers. If a symbol-manipulation language, such as LISP, is taken as defining a machine, then the kinship becomes truly brotherly. Our intent in laying out such a system is not to propose something new. Just the opposite: it is to show what is now known and hypothesized about systems that satisfy such a characterization.

We can now state a general scientific hypothesis—a law of qualitative structure for symbol systems:

> *The Physical Symbol System Hypothesis.* A physical symbol system has the necessary and sufficient means for general intelligent action.

By "necessary" we mean that any system that exhibits general intelligence will prove upon analysis to be a physical symbol system. By "sufficient" we mean that any physical symbol system of sufficient size can be organized further to exhibit general intelligence. By "general intelligent action" we wish to indicate the same scope of intelligence as we see in human action: that in any real situation behavior appropriate to the ends of the system and adaptive to the demands of the environment can occur, within some limits of speed and complexity.

The Physical Symbol System Hypothesis clearly is a law of qualitative structure. It specifies a general class of systems within which one will find those capable of intelligent action.

This is an empirical hypothesis. We have defined a class of systems; we wish to ask whether that class accounts for a set of phenomena we find in the real world. Intelligent action is everywhere around us in the biological world, mostly in human behavior. It is a form of behavior we can recognize by its effects whether it is performed by humans or not. The hypothesis could indeed be false. Intelligent behavior is not so easy to produce that any system will exhibit it willy-nilly. Indeed, there are people whose analyses lead them to conclude either on philosophical or on scientific grounds that the hypothesis *is* false. Scientifically, one can attack or defend it only by bringing forth empirical evidence about the natural world.

We now need to trace the development of this hypothesis and look at the evidence for it.

## Development of the Symbol System Hypothesis

A physical symbol system is an instance of a universal machine. Thus the symbol system hypothesis implies that intelligence will be realized by a universal computer. However, the hypothesis goes far beyond the argument, often made on general grounds of physical determinism, that any computation that is realizable can be realized by a universal machine, provided that it is specified. For it asserts specifically that the intelligent machine is a symbol system, thus making a specific architectural assertion about the nature of intelligent systems. It is important to understand how this additional specificity arose.

*Formal logic.* The roots of the hypothesis go back to the program of Frege and of Whitehead and Russell for formalizing logic: capturing the basic conceptual notions of mathematics in logic and putting the notions of proof and deduction on a secure footing. This effort culminated in mathematical logic—our familiar propositional, first-order, and higher-order logics. It developed a characteristic view, often referred to as the "symbol game." Logic, and by incorporation all of mathematics, was a game played with meaningless tokens according to certain purely syntactic rules. All meaning had been purged. One had a mechanical, though permissive (we would now say nondeterministic), system about which various things could be proved. Thus progress was first made by walking away from all that seemed relevant to meaning and human symbols. We could call this the stage of formal symbol manipulation.

This general attitude is well reflected in the development of information theory. It was pointed out time and again that Shannon had defined a system that was useful only for communication and selection, and which had nothing to do with meaning. Regrets were expressed that such a general name as "information theory" had been given to the field, and attempts were made to rechristen it as "the theory of selective information"—to no avail, of course.

*Turing machines and the digital computer.* The development of the first digital computers and of automata theory, starting with Turing's own work in the 1930s, can be treated together. They agree in their view of what is essential. Let us use Turing's own model, for it shows the features well.

A Turing machine consists of two memories: an unbounded tape and a finite state control. The tape holds data, i.e. the famous zeroes and ones. The machine has a very small set of proper operations—read, write, and scan operations—on the tape. The read operation is not a data operation, but provides conditional branching to a control state as a function of the data under the read head. As we all know, this model contains the essentials of all computers, in terms of what they can do, though other computers with different memories and operations might carry out the same computations with different requirements of space and time. In particular, the model of a Turing machine contains within it the notions both of what cannot be computed and of universal machines—computers that can do anything that can be done by any machine.

We should marvel that two of our deepest insights into information processing were achieved in the 1930s, before modern computers came into being. It is a tribute to the genius of Alan Turing. It is also a tribute to the development of mathematical logic at the time, and testimony to the depth of computer science's obligation to it. Concurrently with Turing's work appeared the work of the logicians Emil Post and (independently) Alonzo Church. Starting from independent notions of logistic systems (Post productions and recursive functions, respectively), they arrived at analogous results on undecidability and universality—results that were soon shown to imply that all three systems were equivalent. Indeed, the convergence of all these attempts to define the most general class of information-processing systems provides some of the force of our conviction that we have captured the essentials of information processing in these models.

In none of these systems is there, on the surface, a concept of the symbol as something that *designates*. The data are regarded as just strings of zeroes and ones—indeed that data be inert is essential to the reduction of computation to physical process. The finite state control system was always viewed as a small controller, and logical games were played to see how small a state system could be used without destroying the universality of the machine. No games, as far as we can tell, were ever played to add new states dynamically to the finite control—to think of the control memory as holding the bulk of the system's knowledge. What was accomplished at this stage was half the principle of interpretation—showing that a machine could be run from a description. Thus this is the stage of automatic formal symbol manipulation.

*The stored program concept.* With the development of the second generation of electronic machines in the mid-1940s (after the Eniac) came the stored program concept. This was rightfully hailed as a milestone, both conceptually and practically. Programs now can be data, and can be operated on as data. This capability is, of course, already implicit in the model of Turing: the descriptions are on the very same tape as the data. Yet the idea was realized only when machines acquired enough memory to make it practicable to locate actual programs in some internal place. After all, the Eniac had only 20 registers.

The stored program concept embodies the second half of the interpretation principle, the part that says that the system's own data can be interpreted. But it does not yet contain the notion of designation—of the physical relation that underlies meaning.

*List processing.* The next step, taken in 1956, was list processing. The contents of the data structures were now symbols, in the sense of our physical symbol system: patterns that designated, that had referents. Lists held addresses which permitted access to other lists—thus the notion of list structures. That this was a new view was demonstrated to us many times in the early days of list processing when colleagues would ask where the data were—that is, which list finally held the collections of bits that were the content of the system. They found it strange that there were no such bits, there were only symbols that designated yet other symbol structures.

List processing is simultaneously three things in the development of computer science: (1) It is the creation of a genuine dynamic memory structure in a machine that had heretofore been perceived as having fixed structure. It added to our ensemble of operations those that built and modified structure in addition to those that replaced and changed content, (2) It was an early demonstration of the basic abstraction that a computer consists of a set of data types and a set of operations proper to these data types, so that a computational system should employ whatever data types are appropriate to the application, independent of the underlying machine, and (3) List-processing produced a model of designation, thus defining symbol manipulation in the sense in which we use this concept in computer science today.

As often occurs, the practice of the time already anticipated all the elements of list processing: addresses are obviously used to gain access, the drum machines used linked programs (so-called one-plus-one addressing), and so on. But the conception of list processing as an abstraction created a new world in which designation and dynamic symbolic structure were the defining characteristics. The embedding of the early list-processing systems in languages (the IPLs, LISP) is often decried as having been a barrier to the diffusion of list-processing techniques throughout programming practice; but it was the vehicle that held the abstraction together.

*LISP.* One more step is worth noting: McCarthy's creation of LISP is 1959–60 (McCarthy, 1960). It completed the act of abstraction, lifting list structures out of their embedding in concrete machines, creating a new formal system with S-expressions, which could be shown to be equivalent to the other universal schemes of computation.

*Conclusion.* That the concept of the designating symbol and symbol manipulation does not emerge until the mid-1950s does not mean that the earlier steps were either inessential or less important. The total concept is the join of computability, physical realizability (and by multiple technologies), universality, and symbolic representation of processes (i.e., interpretability), and, finally, symbolic structure and designation. Each of the steps provided an essential part of the whole.

The first step in this chain, authored by Turing, is theoretically motivated, but the others all have deep empirical roots. We have been led by the evolution of the computer itself. The stored program principle arose out of the experience with Eniac. List processing arose out of the attempt to construct intelligent programs. It took its cue from the emergence of random access memories, which provided a clear physical realization of a designating symbol in the address. LISP arose out of the evolving experience with list processing.

## The Evidence

We come now to the evidence for the hypothesis that physical symbol systems are capable of intelligent action, and that general intelligent action calls for a physical symbol system. The hypothesis is an empirical generalization and not a theorem. We know of no way of demonstrating the connection between symbol systems and intelligence on purely logical grounds. Lacking such a demonstration, we must look at the facts. Our central aim, however, is not to review the evidence in detail, but to use the example before us to illustrate the proposition that computer science is a field of empirical inquiry. Hence, we will only indicate what kinds of evidence there are, and the general nature of the testing process.

The notion of physical symbol system had taken essentially its present form by the middle of the 1950s, and one can date from that time the growth of artificial intelligence as a coherent subfield of computer science. The 20 years of work since then has seen a continuous accumulation of empirical evidence of two main varieties. The first addresses itself to the *sufficiency* of physical symbol systems for producing intelligence, attempting to construct and test specific systems that have such a capability. The second kind of evidence addresses itself to the *necessity* of having a physical symbol system wherever intelligence is exhibited. It starts with Man, the intelligent system best known to us, and attempts to discover whether his cognitive activity can be explained as the working of a physical symbol system. There are other forms of evidence, which we will comment upon briefly later, but these two are the important ones. We will consider them in turn. The first is generally called artificial intelligence, the second, research in cognitive psychology.

*Constructing intelligent systems.* The basic paradigm for the initial testing of the germ theory of disease was: identify a disease, then look for the germ. An analogous paradigm has inspired much of the research in artificial intelligence: identify a task domain calling for intelligence, then construct a program for a digital computer that can handle tasks in that domain. The easy and well structured tasks were looked at first: puzzles and games, operations-research problems of scheduling and allocating resources, simple induction tasks. Scores, if not hundreds, of programs of these kinds have by now been constructed, each capable of some measure of intelligent action in the appropriate domain.

Of course intelligence is not an all-or-none matter, and there has been steady progress toward higher levels of performance in specific domains, as well as toward widening the range of those domains. Early chess programs, for example, were deemed successful if they could play the game legally and with some indication of purpose; a little later, they reached the level of human beginners; within 10 or 15 years, they began to compete with serious amateurs. Progress has been slow (and the total programming effort invested small) but continuous, and the paradigm of construct-and-test proceeds in a regular cycle—the whole research activity mimicking at a macroscopic level the basic generate-and-test cycle of many of the AI programs.

There is a steadily widening area within which intelligent action is attainable. From the original tasks, research has extended to building systems that handle and understand natural language in a variety of ways, systems for interpreting visual scenes, systems for hand-eye coordination, systems that design, systems that write computer programs, systems for speech understanding—the list is, if not endless, at least very long. If there are limits beyond which the hypothesis will not carry us, they have not yet become apparent. Up to the present, the rate of progress has been governed mainly by the rather modest quantity of scientific resources that have been applied and the inevitable requirement of a substantial system-building effort for each new major undertaking.

Much more has been going on, of course, than simply a piling up of examples of intelligent systems adapted to specific task domains. It would be surprising and unappealing if it turned out that the AI programs performing these diverse tasks had nothing in common beyond their being instances of physical symbol systems. Hence, there has been great interest in searching for mechanisms possessed of generality, and for common components among programs performing a variety of tasks. This search carries the theory beyond the initial symbol system hypothesis to a more complete characterization of the particular kinds of symbol systems that are effective in artificial intelligence. In the second section of this paper, we will discuss one example of a hypothesis at this second level of specificity: the heuristic search hypothesis.

The search for generality spawned a series of programs designed to separate out general problem-solving mechanisms from the requirements of particular task domains. The General Problem Solver (GPS) was perhaps the first of these; while among its descendants are such contemporary systems as PLANNER and CONNIVER. The search for common components has led to generalized schemes of representation for goals and plans, methods for constructing discrimination nets, procedures for the control of tree search, pattern-matching mechanisms, and language-parsing systems. Experiments are at present under way to find convenient devices for representing sequences of time and tense, movement, causality, and the like. More and more, it becomes possible to assemble large intelligent systems in a modular way from such basic components.

We can gain some perspective on what is going on by turning, again, to the analogy of the germ theory. If the first burst of research stimulated by that theory consisted largely in finding the germ to go with each disease, subsequent effort turned to learning what a germ was—to building on the basic qualitative law a new level of structure. In artificial intelligence, an initial burst of activity aimed at building intelligent programs for a wide variety of almost randomly selected tasks is giving way to more sharply targeted research aimed at understanding the common mechanisms of such systems.

***The modeling of human symbolic behavior.*** The symbol system hypothesis implies that the symbolic behavior of man arises because he has the characteristics of a physical symbol system. Hence, the results of efforts to model human behavior with symbol systems become an important part of the evidence for the hypothesis, and research in artificial intelligence goes on in close collaboration with research in information processing psychology, as it is usually called.

The search for explanations of man's intelligent behavior in terms of symbol systems has had a large measure of success over the past 20 years; to the point where information-processing theory is the leading contemporary point of view in cognitive psychology. Especially in the areas of problem-solving, concept attainment, and long-term memory, symbol manipulation models now dominate the scene.

Research in information-processing psychology involves two main kinds of empirical activity. The first is the conduct of observations and experiments on human behavior in tasks requiring intelligence. The second, very similar to the parallel activity in artificial intelligence, is the programming of symbol systems to model the observed human behavior. The psychological observations and experiments lead to the formulation of hypotheses about the symbolic processes the subjects are using, and these are an important source of the ideas that go into the construction of the programs. Thus many of the ideas for the basic mechanisms of GPS were derived from careful analysis of the protocols that human subjects produced while thinking aloud during the performance of a problem-solving task.

The empirical character of computer science is nowhere more evident than in this alliance with psychology. Not only are psychological experiments required to test the verdicality of the simulation models as explanations of the human behavior, but out of the experiments come new ideas for the design and construction of physical-symbol systems.

*Other evidence.* The principal body of evidence for the symbol-system hypothesis that we have not considered is negative evidence: the absence of specific competing hypotheses as to how intelligent activity might be accomplished—whether by man or by machine. Most attempts to build such hypotheses have taken place within the field of psychology. Here we have had a continuum of theories from the points of view usually labeled ''behaviorism'' to those usually labeled ''Gestalt theory.'' Neither of these points of view stands as a real competitor to the symbol-system hypothesis, and for two reasons. First, neither behaviorism nor Gestalt theory has demonstrated, or even shown how to demonstrate, that the explanatory mechanisms it postulates are sufficient to account for intelligent behavior in complex tasks. Second, neither theory has been formulated with anything like the specificity of artificial programs. As a matter of fact, the alternative theories are so vague that it is not terribly difficult to give them information-processing interpretations, and thereby assimilate them to the symbol-system hypothesis.

## Conclusion

We have tried to use the example of the Physical Symbol System Hypothesis to illustrate concretely that computer science is a scientific enterprise in the usual meaning of that term: it develops scientific hypotheses which it then seeks to verify by empirical inquiry. We had a second reason, however, for choosing this particular example to illustrate our point. The Physical Symbol System Hypothesis is itself a substantial scientific hypothesis of the kind that we earlier dubbed "laws of qualitative structure." It represents an important discovery of computer science, which if borne out by the empirical evidence, as in fact appears to be occurring, will have major continuing impact on the field.

We turn now to a second example, the role of search in intelligence. This topic, and the particular hypothesis about it that we shall examine, have also played a central role in computer science, in general, and artificial intelligence, in particular.

## HEURISTIC SEARCH

Knowing that physical symbol systems provide the matrix for intelligent action does not tell us how they accomplish this. Our second example of a law of qualitative structure in computer science addresses this latter question, asserting that symbol systems solve problems by using the processes of heuristic search. This generalization, like the previous one, rests on empirical evidence, and has not been derived formally from other premises. We shall see in a moment, however, that it does have some logical connection with the symbol-system hypothesis, and perhaps we can expect to formalize the connection at some time in the future. Until that time arrives, our story must again be one of empirical inquiry. We will describe what is known about heuristic search and review the empirical findings that show how it enables action to be intelligent. We begin by stating this law of qualitative structure, the Heuristic Search Hypothesis.

> *Heuristic Search Hypothesis.* The solutions to problems are represented as symbol structures. A physical-symbol system exercises its intelligence in problem-solving by search—that is, by generating and progressively modifying symbol structures until it produces a solution structure.

Physical-symbol systems must use heuristic search to solve problems because such systems have limited processing resources; in a finite number of steps, and over a finite interval of time, they can execute only a finite number of processes. Of course that is not a very strong limitation, for all universal Turing machines suffer from it. We intend the limitation, however, in a stronger sense: we mean *practically* limited. We can conceive of systems that are not limited in a practical way but are capable, for example, of searching in parallel the nodes of an exponentially expanding tree at a constant rate for each unit advance in depth. We will not be concerned here with such systems, but with systems whose computing resources are scarce relative to the complexity of the situations with which they are confronted. The restriction will not exclude any real symbol systems, in computer or man, in the context of real tasks. The fact of limited resources allows us, for most purposes, to view a symbol system as though it were a serial, one-process-at-a-time device. If it can accomplish only a small amount of processing in any short time interval, then we might as well regard it as doing things one at a time. Thus "limited resource symbol system" and "serial symbol system" are practically synonymous. The problem of allocating a scarce resource from moment to moment can usually be treated, if the moment is short enough, as a problem of scheduling a serial machine.

## Problem Solving

Since ability to solve problems is generally taken as a prime indicator that a system has intelligence, it is natural that much of the history of artificial intelligence is taken up with attempts to build and understand problem-solving systems. Problem solving has been discussed by philosophers and psychologists for two millennia, in discourses dense with a feeling of mystery. If you think there is nothing problematic or mysterious about a symbol system solving problems, you are a child of today, whose views have been formed since midcentury. Plato (and, by his account, Socrates) found difficulty understanding even how problems could be *entertained,* much less how they could be solved. Let me remind you of how he posed the conundrum in the *Meno:*

> Meno: And how will you inquire, Socrates, into that which you know not? What will you put forth as the subject of inquiry? And if you find what you want, how will you ever know that this is what you did not know?

To deal with this puzzle, Plato invented his famous theory of recollection: when you think you are discovering or learning something, you are really just recalling what you already knew in a previous existence. If you find this explanation preposterous, there is a much simpler one available today, based upon our understanding of symbol systems. An approximate statement of it is:

> To state a problem is to designate (1) a *test* for a class of symbol structures (solutions of the problem), and (2) a *generator* of symbol structures (potential solutions). To solve a problem is to generate a structure, using (2), that satisfies the test of (*1*).

We have a problem if we know what we want to do (the test), and if we don't know immediately how to do it (our generator does not immediately produce a symbol structure satisfying the test). A symbol system can state and solve problems (sometimes) because it can generate and test.

If that is all there is to problem solving, why not simply generate at once an expression that satisfies the test? This is, in fact, what we do when we wish and dream. "If wishes were horses, beggars might ride." But outside the world of dreams, it isn't possible. To know how we would test something, once constructed, does not mean that we know how to construct it—that we have any generator for doing so.

For example, it is well known what it means to "solve" the problem of playing winning chess. A simple test exists for noticing winning positions, the test for checkmate of the enemy King. In the world of dreams one simply generates a strategy that leads to checkmate for all counter strategies of the opponent. Alas, no generator that will do this is known to existing symbol systems (man or machine). Instead, good moves in chess are sought by generating various alternatives, and painstakingly evaluating them with the use of approximate, and often erroneous, measures that are supposed to indicate the likelihood that a particular line of play is on the route to a winning position. Move generators there are; winning-more generators there are not.

Before there can be a move generator for a problem, there must be a problem space: a space of symbol structures in which problem situations, including the initial and goal situations, can be represented. Move generators are processes for modifying one situation in the problem space into another. The basic characteristics of physical symbol systems guarantee that they can represent problem spaces and that they possess move generators. How, in any concrete situation, they synthesize a problem space and move generators appropriate to that situation is a question that is still very much on the frontier of artificial intelligence research.

The task that a symbol system is faced with, then, when it is presented with a problem and a problem space, is to use its limited processing resources to generate possible solutions, one after another, until it finds one that satisfies the problem-defining test. If the system had some control over the order in which potential solutions were generated, then it would be desirable to arrange this order of generation so that actual solutions would have a high likelihood of appearing early. A symbol system would exhibit intelligence to the extent that it succeeded in doing this. Intelligence for a system with limited processing resources consists in making wise choices of what to do next.

## Search in Problem-solving

During the first decade or so of artificial intelligence research, the study of problem solving was almost synonymous with the study of search processes. From our characterization of problems and problem solving, it is easy to see why this was so. In fact, it might be asked whether it could be otherwise. But before we try to answer that question, we must explore further the nature of search processes as it revealed itself during the decade of activity.

*Extracting information from the problem space.* Consider a set of symbol structures, some small subset of which are solutions to a given problem. Suppose, further, that the solutions are distributed randomly through the entire set. By this we mean that no information exists that would enable any search generator to perform better than a random search. Then no symbol system could exhibit more intelligence (or less intelligence) than any other in solving the problem, although one might experience better luck than another.

A condition, then, for the appearance of intelligence is that the distribution of solutions be not entirely random, that the space of symbol structures exhibit at least some degree of order and pattern. A second condition is that pattern in the space of symbol structures be more or less detectible. A third condition is that the generator of potential solutions be able to behave differentially, depending on what pattern it detected. There must be information in the problem space, and the symbol system must be capable of extracting and using it. Let us look first at a very simple example, where the intelligence is easy to come by.

Consider the problem of solving a simple algebraic equation:

$$AX + B = CX + D$$

The test defines a solution as any expression of the form, $X = E,$ such that $AE + B = CE + D$. Now one could use as generator any process that would produce numbers which could then be tested by substituting in the latter equation. We would not call this an intelligent generator.

Alternatively, one could use generators that would make use of the fact that the original equation can be modified—by adding or subtracting equal quantities from both sides, or multiplying or dividing both sides by the same quantity— without changing its solutions. But, of course, we can obtain even more information to guide the generator by comparing the original expression with the form of the solution, and making precisely those changes in the equation that leave its solution unchanged, while at the same time bringing it into the desired form. Such a generator could notice that there was an unwanted $CX$ on the right-hand side of the original equation, subtract it from both sides, and collect terms again. It could then notice that there was an unwanted $B$ on the left-hand side and subtract that. Finally, it could get rid of the unwanted coefficient $(A - C)$ on the left-hand side by dividing.

Thus by this procedure, which now exhibits considerable intelligence, the generator produces successive symbol structures, each obtained by modifying the previous one; and the modifications are aimed at reducing the differences between the form of the input structure and the form of the test expression, while maintaining the other conditions for a solution.

This simple example already illustrates many of the main mechanisms that are used by symbol systems for intelligent problem-solving. First, each successive expression is not generated independently, but is produced by modifying one produced previously. Second, the modifications are not haphazard, but depend upon two kinds of information. They depend on information that is constant over this whole class of algebra problems, and that is built into the structure of the generator itself: all modifications of expressions must leave the equation's solution unchanged. They also depend on information that changes at each step: detection of the differences in form that remain between the current expression and the desired expression. In effect, the generator incorporates some of the tests the solution must satisfy, so that expressions that don't meet these tests will never be generated. Using the first kind of information guarantees that only a tiny subset of all possible expressions is actually generated, but without losing the solution expression from this subset. Using the second kind of information arrives at the desired solution by a succession of approximations, employing a simple form of means-ends analysis to give direction to the search.

There is no mystery where the information that guided the search came from. We need not follow Plato in endowing the symbol system with a previous existence in which it already knew the solution. A moderately sophisticated generator-test system did the trick without invoking reincarnation.

*Search trees.* The simple algebra problem may seem an unusual, even pathological, example of search. It is certainly not trial-and-error search, for though there were a few trials, there was no error. We are more accustomed to thinking of problem-solving search as generating lushly branching trees of partial solution possibilities which may grow to thousands, or even millions, of branches, before they yield a solution. Thus, if from each expression it produces, the generator creates $B$ new branches, then the tree will grow as $B^D$, where $D$ is its depth. The tree grown for the algebra problem had the peculiarity that its branchiness, $B$, equaled unity.

Programs that play chess typically grow broad search trees, amounting in some cases to a million branches or more. Although this example will serve to illustrate our points about tree search, we should note that the purpose of search in chess is not to generate proposed solutions, but to evaluate (test) them. One line of research into game-playing programs has been centrally concerned with improving the representation of the chess board, and the processes for making moves on it, so as to speed up search and make it possible to search larger trees. The rationale for this direction, of course, is that the deeper the dynamic search, the more accurate should be the evaluations at the end of it. On the other hand, there is good empirical evidence that the strongest human players, grandmasters, seldom explore trees of more than 100 branches. This economy is achieved not so much by searching less deeply than do chess-playing programs, but by branching very sparsely and selectively at each node. This is only possible, without causing a deterioration of the evaluations, by having more of the selectivity built into the generator itself, so that it is able to select for generation only those branches which are very likely to yield important relevant information about the position.

The somewhat paradoxical-sounding conclusion to which this discussion leads is that search—successive generation of potentional solution structures—is a fundamental aspect of a symbol system's exercise of intelligence in problem-solving but that amount of search is not a measure of the amount of intelligence being exhibited. What makes a problem a problem is not that a large amount of search is required for its solution, but that a large amount *would* be required if a requisite level of intelligence were not applied. When the symbolic system that is endeavoring to solve a problem knows enough about what to do, it simply proceeds directly towards its goal; but whenever its knowledge becomes inadequate, when it enters terra incognita, it is faced with the threat of going through large amounts of search before it finds its way again.

The potential for the exponential explosion of the search tree that is present in every scheme for generating problem solutions warns us against depending on the brute force of computers—even the biggest and fastest computers—as a compensation for the ignorance and unselectivity of their generators. The hope is still periodically ignited in some human breasts that a computer can be found that is fast enough, and that can be programmed cleverly enough, to play good chess by brute-force search. There is nothing known in theory about the game of chess that rules out this possibility. But empirical studies on the management of search in sizable trees with only modest results make this a much less promising direction than it was when chess was first chosen as an appropriate task for artificial intelligence. We must regard this as one of the important empirical findings of research with chess programs.

*The forms of intelligence.* The task of intelligence, then, is to avert the ever-present threat of the exponential explosion of search. How can this be accomplished? The first route, already illustrated by the algebra example and by chess programs that only generate "plausible" moves for further analysis, is to build selectivity into the generator: to generate only structures that show promise of being solutions or of being along the path toward solutions. The usual consequence of doing this is to decrease the rate of branching, not to prevent it entirely. Ultimate exponential explosion is not avoided—save in exceptionally highly structured situations like the algebra example—but only postponed. Hence, an intelligent system generally needs to supplement the selectivity of its solution generator with other information-using techniques to guide search.

Twenty years of experience with managing tree search in a variety of task environments has produced a small kit of general techniques which is part of the equipment of every researcher in artificial intelligence today. Since these techniques have been described in general works like that of Nilsson (1971), they can be summarized very briefly here.

In serial heuristic search, the basic question always is: What shall be done next? In tree search, that question, in turn, has two components: (1) from what node in the tree shall we search next, and (2) what direction shall we take from that node? Information helpful in answering the first question may be interpreted as measuring the relative distance of different nodes from the goal. Best-first search calls for searching next from the node that appears closest to the goal. Information helpful in answering the second question—in what direction to search—is often obtained, as in the algebra example, by detecting specific differences between the current nodal structure and the goal structure described by the test of a solution, and selecting actions that are relevant to reducing these particular kinds of differences. This is the technique known as means-ends analysis, which plays a central role in the structure of the General Problem Solver.

The importance of empirical studies as a source of general ideas in AI research can be demonstrated clearly by tracing the history, through large numbers of problem-solving programs, of these two central ideas: best-first search and means-ends analysis. Rudiments of best-first search were already present, though unnamed, in the Logic Theorist in 1955. The General Problem Solver, embodying means-ends analysis, appeared about 1957—but combined it with modified depth-first search rather than best-first search. Chess programs were generally wedded, for reasons of economy of memory, to depth-first search, supplemented after about 1958 by the powerful alpha-beta pruning procedure. Each of these techniques appears to have been reinvented a number of times, and it is hard to find general, task-independent, theoretical discussions of problem solving in terms of these concepts until the middle or late 1960s. The amount of formal buttressing they have received from mathematical theory is still minuscle: some theorems about the reduction in search that can be secured from using the alpha-beta heuristic, a couple of theorems (reviewed by Nilsson, 1971) about shortest-path search, and some very recent theorems on best-first search with a probabilistic evaluation function.

*"Weak" and "strong" methods.* The techniques we have been discussing are dedicated to the control of exponential expansion rather than its prevention. For this reason, they have been properly called ''weak methods''—methods to be used when the symbol system's knowledge or the amount of structure actually contained in the problem space are inadequate to permit search to be avoided entirely. It is instructive to contrast a highly structured situation, which can be formulated, say, as a linear-programming problem, with the less structured situations of combinatorial problems like the traveling salesman problem or scheduling problems. (''Less structured'' here refers to the insufficiency or nonexistence of relevant theory about the structure of the problem space.).

In solving linear-programming problems, a substantial amount of computation may be required, but the search does not branch. Every step is a step along the way to a solution. In solving combinatorial problems or in proving theorems, tree search can seldom be avoided, and success depends on heuristic search methods of the sort we have been describing.

Not all streams of AI problem-solving research have followed the path we have been outlining. An example of a somewhat different point is provided by the work on theorem-proving systems. Here, ideas imported from mathematics and logic have had a strong influence on the direction of inquiry. For example, the use of heuristics was resisted when properties of completeness could not be proved (a bit ironic, since most interesting mathematical systems are known to be undecidable). Since completeness can seldom be proved for best-first search heuristics, or for many kinds of selective generators, the effect of this requirement was rather inhibiting. When theorem-proving programs were continually incapacitated by the combinatorial explosion of their search trees, thought began to be given to selective heuristics, which in many cases proved to be analogues of heuristics used in general problem-solving programs. The set-of-support heuristic, for example, is a form of working backward, adapted to the resolution theorem-proving environment.

*A summary of the experience.* We have now described the workings of our second law of qualitative structure, which asserts that physical-symbol systems solve problems by means of heuristic search. Beyond that, we have examined some subsidiary characteristics of heuristic search, in particular the threat that it always faces of exponential explosion of the search tree, and some of the means it uses to avert that threat. Opinions differ as to how effective heuristic search has been as a problem-solving mechanism—the opinions depending on what task domains are considered and what criterion of adequacy is adopted. Success can be guaranteed by setting aspiration levels low—or failure by setting them high. The evidence might be summed up about as follows: Few programs are solving problems as "expert" professional levels. Samuel's checker program and Feigenbaum and Lederberg's DENDRAL are perhaps the best-known exceptions, but one could point also to a number of heuristic search programs for such operations-research problem domains as scheduling and integer programming. In a number of domains, programs perform at the level of competent amateurs: chess, some theorem-proving domains, many kinds of games and puzzles. Human levels have not yet been nearly reached by programs that have a complex perceptual "front end": visual scene recognizers, speech understanders, robots that have to maneuver in real space and time. Nevertheless, impressive progress has been made, and a large body of experience assembled about these difficult tasks.

We do not have deep theoretical explanations for the particular pattern of performance that has emerged. On empirical grounds, however, we might draw two conclusions. First, from what has been learned about human expert performance in tasks like chess, it is likely that any system capable of matching that performance will have to have access, in its memories, to very large stores of semantic information. Second, some part of the human superiority in tasks with a large perceptual component can be attributed to the special-purpose built-in parallel-processing structure of the human eye and ear.

In any case, the quality of performance must necessarily depend on the characteristics both of the problem domains and of the symbol systems used to

.tackle them. For most real-life domains in which we are interested, the domain structure has so far not proved sufficiently simple to yield theorems about complexity, or to tell us, other than empirically, how large real-world problems are in relation to the abilities of our symbol systems to solve them. That situation may change, but until it does, we must rely upon empirical explorations, using the best problem solvers we know how to build, as a principal source of knowledge about the magnitude and characteristics of problem difficulty. Even in highly structured areas like linear programming, theory has been much more useful in strengthening the heuristics that underlie the most powerful solution algorithms than in providing a deep analysis of complexity.

## Intelligence without Much Search

Our analysis of intelligence equated it with ability to extract and use information about the structure of the problem space, so as to enable a problem solution to be generated as quickly and directly as possible. New directions for improving the problem-solving capabilities of symbol systems can be equated, then, with new ways of extracting and using information. At least three such ways can be identified.

*Nonlocal use of information.* First, it has been noted by several investigators that information gathered in the course of tree search is usually only used *locally,* to help make decisions at the specific node where the information was generated. Information about a chess position, obtained by dynamic analysis of a subtree of continuations, is usually used to evaluate just that position, not to evaluate other positions that may contain many of the same features. Hence, the same facts have to be rediscovered repeatedly at different nodes of the search tree. Simply to take the information out of the context in which it arose and use it generally does not solve the problem, for the information may be valid only in a limited range of contexts. In recent years, a few exploratory efforts have been made to transport information from its context of origin to other appropriate contexts. While it is still too early to evaluate the power of this idea, or even exactly how it is to be achieved, it shows considerable promise. An important line of investigation that Berliner (1975) has been pursuing is to use causal analysis to determine the range over which a particular piece of information is valid. Thus if a weakness in a chess position can be traced back to the move that made it, then the same weakness can be expected in other positions descendant from the same move.

The HEARSAY speech understanding system has taken another approach to making information globally available. That system seeks to recognize speech strings by pursuing a parallel search at a number of different levels: phonemic, lexical, syntactic, and semantic. As each of these searches provides and evaluates hypotheses, it supplies the information it has gained to a common "blackboard" that can be read by all the sources. This shared information can be used, for example, to eliminate hypotheses, or even whole classes of hypotheses, that would otherwise have to be searched by one of the processes. Thus increasing our ability to use tree-search information nonlocally offers promise for raising the intelligence of problem-solving systems.

*Semantic recognition systems.* A second active possibility for raising intelligence is to supply the symbol system with a rich body of semantic information about the task domain it is dealing with. For example, empirical research on the skill of chess masters shows that a major source of the master's skill is stored information that enables him to recognize a large number of specific features and patterns of features on a chess board, and information that uses this recognition to propose actions appropriate to the features recognized. This general idea has, of course, been incorporated in chess programs almost from the beginning. What is new is the realization of the number of such patterns and associated information that may have to be stored for master-level play: something on the order of 50,000.

The possibility of substituting recognition for search arises because a particular, and especially a rare, pattern can contain an enormous amount of information, provided that it is closely linked to the structure of the problem space. When that structure is "irregular," and not subject to simple mathematical description, then knowledge of a large number of relevant patterns may be the key to intelligent behavior. Whether this is so in any particular task domain is a question more easily settled by empirical investigation than by theory. Our experience with symbol systems richly endowed with semantic information and pattern-recognizing capabilities for accessing it is still extremely limited.

The discussion above refers specifically to semantic information associated with a recognition system. Of course, there is also a whole large area of AI research on semantic information processing and the organization of semantic memories that falls outside the scope of the topics we are discussing in this paper.

*Selecting appropriate representations.* A third line of inquiry is concerned with the possibility that search can be reduced or avoided by selecting an appropriate problem space. A standard example that illustrates this possibility dramatically is the multilated checkerboard problem. A standard 64-square checkerboard can be covered exactly with 32 tiles, each a $1 \times 2$ rectangle covering exactly two squares. Suppose, now, that we cut off squares at two diagonally opposite corners of the checkerboard, leaving a total of 62 squares. Can this multilated board be covered exactly with 31 tiles? With (literally) heavenly patience, the impossibility of achieving such a covering can be demonstrated by trying all possible arrangements. The alternative, for those with less patience and more intelligence, is to observe that the two diagonally opposite corners of a checkerboard are of the same color. Hence, the multilated checkerboard has two fewer squares of one color than of the other. But each tile covers one square of one color and one square of the other, and any set of tiles must cover the same number of squares of each color. Hence, there is no solution. How can a symbol system discover this simple inductive argument as an alternative to a hopeless attempt to solve the problem by search among all possible coverings? We would award a system that found the solution high marks for intelligence.

Perhaps, however, in posing this problem we are not escaping from search processes. We have simply displaced the search from a space of possible problem solutions to a space of possible representations. In any event, the whole process of moving from one representation to another, and of discovering and evaluating representations, is largely unexplored territory in the domain of problem-solving research. The laws of qualitative structure governing representations remain to be discovered. The search for them is almost sure to receive considerable attention in the coming decade.

# CONCLUSION

That is our account of symbol systems and intelligence. It has been a long road from Plato's *Meno* to present, but it is perhaps encouraging that most of the progress along that road has been made since the turn of the twentieth century, and a large fraction of it since the midpoint of the century. Thought was still wholly intangible and ineffable until modern formal logic interpreted it as the manipulation of formal tokens. And it seemed still to inhabit mainly the heaven of Platonic ideals, or the equally obscure spaces of the human mind, until computers taught us how symbols could be processed by machines. A. M. Turing made his great contributions at the midcentury crossroads of these developments that led them modern logic to the computer.

*Physical symbol systems.* The study of logic and computers has revealed to us that intelligence resides in physical-symbol systems. This is computer science's most basic law of qualitative structure.

Symbol systems are collections of patterns and processes, the latter being capable of producing, destroying, and modifying the former. The most important properties of patterns is that they can designate objects, processes, or other patterns, and that when they designate processes, they can be interpreted. Interpretation means carrying out the designated process. The two most significant classes of symbol systems with which we are acquainted are human beings and computers.

Our present understanding of symbol systems grew, as indicated earlier, through a sequence of stages. Formal logic familiarized us with symbols, treated syntactically, as the raw material of thought, and with the idea of manipulating them according to carefully defined formal processes. The Turing machine made the syntactic processing of symbols truly machine-like, and affirmed the potential universality of strictly defined symbol systems. The stored-program concept for computers reaffirmed the interpretability of symbols, already implicit in the

Turing machine. List processing brought to the forefront the denotational capacities of symbols, and defined symbol processing in ways that allowed independence from the fixed-structure of the underlying physical machine. By 1956 all of these concepts were available, together with hardware for implementing them. The study of the intelligence of symbol systems, the subject of artificial intelligence, could begin.

**Heuristic search.** A second law of qualitative structure for AI is that symbol systems solve problems by generating potential solutions and testing them—that is, by searching. Solutions are usually sought by creating symbolic expressions and modifying them sequentially until they satisfy the conditions for a solution. Hence, symbol systems solve problems by searching. Since they have finite resources, the search cannot be carried out all at once, but must be sequential. It leaves behind it either a single path from starting point to goal or, if correction and backup are necessary, a whole tree of such paths.

Symbol systems cannot appear intelligent when they are surrounded by pure chaos. They exercise intelligence by extracting information from a problem domain and using that information to guide their search, avoiding wrong turns and circuitous bypaths. The problem domain must contain information—that is, some degree of order and structure—for the method to work. The paradox of the *Meno* is solved by the observation that information may be remembered, but new information may also be extracted from the domain that the symbols designate. In both cases, the ultimate source of the information is the task domain.

**The empirical base.** Research on artificial intelligence is concerned with how symbol systems must be organized in order to behave intelligently. Twenty years of work in the area has accumulated a considerable body of knowledge, enough to fill several books (it already has), and most of it in the form of rather concrete experience about the behavior of specific classes of symbol systems in specific task domains. Out of this experience, however, there have also emerged some generalizations, cutting across task domains and systems, about the general characteristics of intelligence and its methods of implementation.

We have tried to state some of these generalizations here. They are mostly qualitative rather than mathematical. They have more the flavor of geology or evolutionary biology than the flavor of theoretical physics. They are sufficiently strong to enable us today to design and build moderately intelligent systems for a considerable range of task domains, as well as to gain a rather deep understanding of how human intelligence works in many situations.

**What next?** In our account we have mentioned open questions as well as settled ones; there are many of both. We see no abatement of the excitement of exploration that has surrounded this field over the past quarter century. Two resource limits will determine the rate of progress over the next such period. One is the amount of computing power that will be available. The second, and probably the more important, is the number of talented young computer scientists who will be attracted to this area of research as the most challenging they can tackle.

A. M. Turing concluded his famous paper "Computing Machinery and Intelligence" with the words:

> We can only see a short distance ahead, but we can see plenty there that needs to be done.

Many of the things Turing saw in 1950 that needed to be done have been done, but the agenda is as full as ever. Perhaps we read too much into his simple statement above, but we like to think that, in it, Turing recognized the fundamental truth that all computer scientists instinctively know. For all physical-symbol systems, condemned as we are to serial search of the problem environment, the critical question is always: What to do next?

## REFERENCES

Berliner, H. (1975). *Chess as problem solving: the development of a tactics analyzer.* Ph.D. Th., Computer Science Department, Carnegie-Mellon University (unpublished).

McCarthy, J. (1960, April). Recursive functions of symbolic expressions and their computation by machine. *Communications of the ACM 3, 4,* 184–195.

McCulloch, W. S. (1961). What is a number, that a man may know it, and a man, that he may know a number. *General Semantics Bulletin,* Nos. 26 and 27, 7–18.

Nilsson, N. J. (1971). *Problem Solving Methods in Artificial Intelligence.* New York: McGraw-Hill.

Turing, A. M. (1950, October). Computing machinery and intelligence. *Mind, 59,* 433–460.

# 9
# What is Artificial Intelligence?

## 1980

by the Computer Science and Engineering Research
Study Panel on Artificial Intelligence
(Zenon W. Pylyshyn, Panel Chairman, University of
Western Ontario; Woody Bledsoe, University of Texas;
Edward A. Feigenbaum, Stanford University; Allen
Newell, Carnegie-Mellon University; Nils Nilsson,
Stanford Research Institute; D. Raj Reddy, Carnegie-
Mellon University; Azriel Rosenfeld, University of
Maryland; Terry Winograd, Stanford University; Patrick
Winston, Massachusetts Institute of Technology.)

It is no accident that the word *intelligence* appears in the title of this chapter. Years ago, computer scientists such as von Neumann, Turing, Newell, Simon, McCarthy, and Minsky recognized that artificial, or machine, processes could be designed which closely resemble aspects of human thought. Some of this early work is described in Feigenbaum & Feldman, 1963, as well as in the historical sections of references Newell & Simon, 1972; Pylyshyn, 1970. Using the term *artificial intelligence* gives recognition to the fact that studies of symbolic processes in computer science, and the attempts to understand that elusive quality known as "intelligence," are, at some level, inseparable. This recognition, which has indirectly been responsible for much misunderstanding and criticism, is, in fact, fundamental to the integrity of the field, since a pillar of the artificial intelligence field is the belief that tasks requiring what we would call "intelligent action," can, to some extent, be studied independently of such organisms as humans and the way in which they perform such tasks. In addition to shedding light on these tasks, as well as the class of processes capable of dealing effectively with them, research in AI has produced techniques and working systems for dealing with areas previously considered the sole province of human intelligence.

Although the discipline of artificial intelligence dates to the earliest speculation about the nature and limits of information-processing mechanisms, and although the early tools of nonnumerical computing—list processing, time sharing, graphics, and symbolic math systems—were developed in laboratories devoted to research in what would soon be known as artificial intelligence, the development of the science as we know it today began as recently as the mid-1950s when Newell, Shaw, Simon, and others recognized the potential of large-scale digital computers for this kind of non-numerical processing. Since that time, progress has been made, both in understanding the underlying technical issues, such as representing knowledge and controlling search and inference, and in developing practical systems. We begin our discussion by presenting some artificial intelligence systems that are currently in operation.

## WORKING ARTIFICIAL INTELLIGENCE SYSTEMS

A. A geologist dials a government data base on lunar rocks and types in a query (Woods, 1973):

| | |
|---|---|
| *User* | HOW MANY BRECCIAS CONTAIN OLIVINE? |
| *Computer* | 5. |
| *User* | WHAT ARE THEY? |
| *Computer* | S10019, S10059, S10067, S10073. |
| *User* | LIST K/RB RATIOS FOR BRECCIAS. |
| *Computer* | I HAVE 17 HITS. DO YOU WANT TO SEE THEM? |
| *User* | YES. |
| *Computer* | 472.2222   S10018   D70-205 |
| | ...   ...   ... |
| | 500.173   S10073   D70-215 |
| *User* | LIST MODAL FLAG ANALYSES FOR LUNAR SAMPLES THAT CONTAIN OLIV. |
| *Computer* | I HAVE 13 HITS. DO YOU WANT TO SEE THEM? |
| *User* | YES. |

And so on.

At the Second Annual Lunar Science Conference, held in January 1971, this system, described by Woods in 1973, answered 90 percent of the 110 requests put to it by geologists. To some extent, however, this results from the tendency of expert users to employ a narrower range of constructions than do nonexpert users, as well as the experts' tendency to tailor their questions to the perceived ability of the machine. Thus a linguistically less "fluent" system can be serviceable if it is intended for a particular community of specialist users.

B. A business executive specifies that he wishes to interact with GUS, a computerized travel consultant, on his personal terminal (Bobrow, Kaplan, Kay, Norman, Thompson, & Winograd, 1977):

*Client*   I want to go to San Diego May 28.
*GUS*   What time do you want to leave?
*Client*   I must be in San Diego before 10 am.
*GUS*   Would you like P.S.A. flight 102 that arrives at 9:15 am?
*Client*   What is the next flight?
*GUS*   Air California flight 310 leaves at 8:30 am and arrives at 10:00 am.
*Client*   I'll take the first one.
*GUS*   In what name should I make a reservation?
*Client*   Dan Bobrow.
*GUS*   I have confirmed the following flight: P.S.A. flight 102 on Wednesday May 28 from San Jose to San Diego which leaves at 7:30 am and arrives at 9:15 · am. What date do you want to return on?
*Client*   On Friday in the evening.
*GUS*   Would you like the flight that leaves at 7:45 pm?
*Client*   That's fine.
*GUS*   I have confirmed the following flight: P.S.A. flight 307 on Friday May 30 from San Diego to San Jose which leaves at 7:45 PM and arrives at 9:30 PM. Thank you for calling. Goodbye.

Note that, to keep the conversation natural, complex inferences must be made. For example, the client answers the question about departure time indirectly. The system must infer the departure time from the client's statement that he must be at a certain place at a certain time. Similarly, it disambiguates various possible senses of "the first one" and "on Friday" (which Friday?) by the pragmatic context.

C. A physician calls up MYCIN, the computerized, interactive diagnostic assistant for infectious disease (Shortliffe, 1976). In response to questions from the machine, the physician types a brief summary of the patient's medical records. MYCIN names specific infections (INFECTION-1) and cultures for later reference, continuing to ask questions about each infection until it has enough information for recommending treatment. A segment of the dialogue after the initial information entry follows.

*Computer*   My therapy recommendation will be based on the following probable infection(s) and potential causative organism(s):
INFECTION-1 is PRIMARY BACTEREMIA
⟨Item 1⟩ The identity of ORGANISM-1 may be PSEUDOMONAS-AERUGINOSA
⟨Item 2⟩ The identity of ORGANISM-1 may be KLEBSIELLA-PNEUMONIAE
⟨Item 3⟩ The identity of ORGANISM-1 may be E.COLI
⟨Item 4⟩ The identity of ORGANISM-1 may be BACTEROIDES-FRAGILIS
⟨Item 5⟩ The identity of ORGANISM-1 may be PROTEUS NON-MIRABILIS

|          | On a scale of 0 to 4, where higher numbers indicate increasing severity, how would you rate Fred Smith's degree of sickness? |
|----------|---|
| *User*     | 3 |
| *Computer* | Does Fred Smith have a clinically significant allergic reaction to any antimicrobial agent? |
| *User*     | NO |
| *Computer* | Fred Smith's weight in kilograms (or ⟨number⟩ POUNDS): |
| *User*     | 70 |
| *Computer* | (Rec 1) My preferred therapy recommendation is as follows: |

In order to cover for items ⟨1 2 3 5 6⟩:
Give: GENTAMICIN
Dose: 119 mg (1.7 mg/kg) q8h IV (or IM) for 10 days
Comments: Modify dose in renal failure
In order to cover for item ⟨4⟩:
Give: CLINDAMYCIN
Dose: 595 mg (8.5 mg/kg) q6h IV (or IM) for 14 days
Comments: If diarrhea or other GI symptoms develop, patient should be evaluated for possible PSEUDOMEMBRANOUS COLITIS.

During a consultation, if the user is interacting with an extension of MYCIN called TIERESIAS (Davis, Buchanan, & Shortiffe, 1977) the following dialogue might occur:

| *Computer* | Is the patient's illness with ORGANISM-1 a hospital-acquired infection? |
|----------|---|
| *User*     | WHY? (i.e., WHY is it important to determine whether the infection with ORGANISM-1 was acquired while the patient was hospitalized?) |
| *Computer* | This will aid in determining the category of ORGANISM-1. It has already been established that |

(1.1) the gram stain of ORGANISM-1 is gramneg, and
(1.2) the morphology of ORGANISM-1 is rod, and
(1.3) the aerobicity of ORGANISM-1 is facultative
Therefore, if
(1.4) the infection with ORGANISM-1 was not acquired while the patient was hospitalized
then
there is strongly suggestive evidence (.8) that the category of ORGANISM-1 is enterobacteriacae.
Also:
there is weakly suggestive evidence (.1) that the identity of ORGANISM-1 is PSEUDUMONAS-AERUGINOSA (RULE 27)

| *User*     | HOW 1.3? (I.e., HOW was it established that the aerobicity of ORGANISM-1 is facultative?) |
|----------|---|
| *Computer* | The following were used: |

(3.1) RULE 27 indicated there is strongly suggestive evidence (.8) that the aerobicity of ORGANISM-1 is faculative
(3.2) RULE 27 indicated there is weakly suggestive evidence (.2) that the aerobicity of ORGANISM-1 is anaerobic

Since this gave a cumulative CF of (.8) for facultative, and (.2) for anearobic, it has been established that the aerobicity of ORGANISM-1 is facultative.

D. A student studying electronic circuit design and servicing consults his computerized tutor, SOPHIE (Brown & Burton, 1975):

| | |
|---|---|
| *Computer* | THE PIECE OF EQUIPMENT YOU ARE STUDYING IS A REGULATED POWER SUPPLY. WOULD YOU LIKE TO START WITH A FAULTY INSTRUMENT WHICH NEEDS FIXING? |
| *User* | YES |
| *Computer* | THE INSTRUMENT HAS A FAULT AND ITS PRESENT CONTROL SETTING IS: [Gives settings of various currents, voltages, and variable resistances.] |
| *User* | WHAT IS THE OUTPUT? |
| *Computer* | THE OUTPUT VOLTAGE IS 11.7 VOLTS. |
| *User* | WHAT IS IT IN A WORKING INSTRUMENT? |
| *Computer* | IN A WORKING CIRCUIT THE OUTPUT VOLTAGE IS 19.9 VOLTS. |
| *User* | WHAT IS THE VOLTAGE BETWEEN R8 AND Q1? |
| *Computer* | THE VOLTAGE AT N1 IS 47.6 VOLTS. |
| *User* | WHAT IS THE BSE EMITTER VOLTAGE OF THE VOLTAGE-LIMITING TRANSISTOR? |
| *Computer* | [corrects spelling] = BASE THE BASE EMITTER VOLTAGE OF Q5 IS − .037 MILLIVOLTS. |
| *User* | WHAT ABOUT FOR THE CURRENT LIMITING TRANSISTOR? |
| *Computer* | THE BASE EMITTER VOLTAGE OF Q6 IS .349 VOLTS. |
| *User* | WHAT SHOULD IT BE? |
| *Computer* | ... .593 VOLTS. |
| *User* | REPLACE Q6. |

In this brief excerpt it is clear that the computer thoroughly understands the circuit in question, that it can understand references to components by description and by name, and that it can understand clipped, incomplete sentences when the context makes the meaning clear.

E. A television camera is trained on an assembly line in which integrated circuits are being packaged. Although the mechanical assembly device has been used in industry for some time, this one is different; it responds to the sight of the silicon circuit chips (Figure 9-1); this it can align the microscopic chips to within 0.5 mils in spite of irregularities and initial misorientations, a task formerly done by people working tediously with microscopes. This turned out to be a complex task that necessitated the development of sophisticated, artificial intelligence techniques (Horn, 1975).

F. A scientist types in simple English sentences to command a primitive robot vehicle. The commands mention only the end goal (for example, *push the orange pyramid off the platform in the hallway*). They say nothing about how to do this,

**Figure 9-1.   Silicon chip display.**

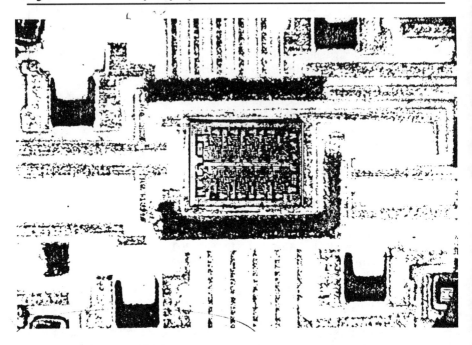

nor about the order in which to carry out subtasks or any obstacles that might exist along the way. The computer converts the command to an internal propositional form and generates a plan for carrying out the command. The vehicle then moves a ramp up to the platform, ascends it, and completes the task.

None of the above systems is a production tool; they are all working experimental prototypes. MYCIN, SOPHIE, and the lunar rocks system are polished, high-performance systems. The lessons learned from them are being used in designing new systems such as GUS, the most embryonic of the examples above. GUS is being developed at the Xerox Corporation, primarily as a test bed for the newest generation of AI techniques relating to language, inference, and knowledge representation. The industrial-application example being developed as a practical application is primarily a demonstration of the applicability of machine-vision techniques. Although the Stanford Research Institute robot mentioned in (F), "Shakey," was used mainly to test ideas about the process of planning, various vision and theorem-proving systems have been incorporated for exploring the problems involved in making the systems work together. Other more practically-oriented robot systems have also been developed for use in space exploration (Oobrotin & Lewis, n.d.).

In addition to these research tools, commercial artificial intelligence systems are being marketed for such jobs as interfacing natural languages, recognizing patterns, controlling robots, and designing and teaching symbolic mathematics with the help of computers. In all these areas, techniques are being explored that were developed during the past decade of research in artificial intelligence. Their performance is high enough that they are now considering commercial products. (Listed in the April 1978 issue of the newsletter of ACM's Special Interest Group on artificial intelligence are some companies that are developing and marketing artificial intelligence systems in North America. Meanwhile, numerous other companies are operating in Japan.)

Of course, these are only a few examples of AI work; they were not chosen because they are particularly representative. Nonetheless, they illustrate better than any prescriptive definition the kind of systems that are being developed in artificial intelligence. Other examples will be presented in this chapter. When practical, we will try to explain not only the performance of the systems but the principles and technical achievements that made them possible, in addition to the trends and problems that exist today. Finally, we will review the changes that have occurred in the field during its second decade and try to indicate what those working in the field see as its problems, achievements, and directions.

The main areas covered are those of problem-solving, automatic theorem-proving, natural language-processing, the perception of speech and visual information, and such application areas as industrial production and "expert," or human-level performance systems for medical and scientific applications. The systems covered were selected because, first, we were most familiar with them, and second, we considered them suitable for the purposes of illustration.

We have, however, tried to emphasize the general design principles and unifying technical themes. A major theme discussed here is that much of artificial intelligence involves exploiting the knowledge of specific problem domains, together with general heuristic search and inference techniques, to reduce the combinatorial growth of potential alternatives in problem situations. To introduce the general theme of heuristic search and problem-solving, we begin with a general description of search techniques and proceed to more recent ways of describing problem-solving by computer.

## SEARCHING ALTERNATIVES

The earliest artificial intelligence programs (Feigenbaum & Feldman, 1963) were devoted to such tasks as playing chess, proving theorems, and solving puzzles. It is appropriate, then, that we begin our exposition here, not only because that is where the field itself began, but because the methods developed, the issues raised, and the lessons learned continue to be important in artificial intelligence. In fact, the problem-solving paradigm still dominates most areas of AI, although the focus has shifted along several dimensions over the years. For example, it has shifted away from powerful, all-purpose methods to knowledge-intensive systems in which special attention is paid to questions of representation and to control structures.

Games and mathematical problems have often been used as a testing ground for problem-solving and reasoning. Since the rules for moves and the criteria of success are clear, the major effort can go into the solution *process*. The fact that such "problems" themselves are well defined—and, in fact, may sometimes appear frivolous—should not detract from the fact that solution methods which avoid the combinatorial explosion are far from being trivial or even well defined. The work on problem solving often has the flavor of going from the *what* to the *how* or what Simon calls going from a "state description" to a "process description" (Simon, 1969).

For example, the game of chess has been one of the oldest challenges to an understanding of the problem-solving process. As the most sophisticated general-purpose techniques were being applied to chess with only mediocre results, the emphasis shifted to better ways of representing the knowledge of chess and of organizing search control in deploying this knowledge. Indeed, it was in exploring chess-playing programs that some of the limitations of conventional program organizations first came to light (Newell, 1962).

Although chess programs have been a popular area for demonstrating problem-solving techniques, much more impressive results have been obtained in domains that employ more specialized knowledge—the "expert" systems for chemistry, medicine, mathematics, and electronics. But before describing these, we should recount the technical discoveries that have been made in studying general problem-solving methods, since these discoveries are now part of the permanent armament of artificial intelligence.

By *problem solving,* we mean a large corpus of basic ideas having to do with the processes of deduction, inference, planning, "common sense" reasoning, and theorem-proving, ideas that have been applied in programs for understanding natural languages, information retrieval, automatic programming, robotics, scene analysis, game playing, and mathematical theorem proving. Here we examine some ideas concerning problem solving.

## Search Methods

Problem-solving methods are characterized by searching through a *state,* or *situation* space or through a space of alternatives. A *solution* is a sequence of state transitions from an initial state or states given in the problem specification, to a final, or *goal* state. The notions of state space, search, and solutions sequences are very general; states can be anything from sets of formulas to game configuration or—, more accurately, an internal description of a game configuration, since we must allow such descriptors as "threatens" or "develop the center'' as part of the state. A *solution sequence* is any succession of states such that the transition is consistent with the problem specification (for example, the rules of a game) and the operators provided by the method. The term *search* emphasizes the teleological nature of the solution sequence; it need not involve much trial-and-error searching, although some searching is as inevitable in machine problem-solving as in human problem-solving

The problem solver has two requirements that are logically independent. One defines the allowable configurations for the class of problem, while the other defines the solution for a problem of that class. The former requirement is used to specify a *generator* for that class of problem—that is, to specify a process which takes a description of the set of permissible elements (for example, potential solutions) and, one by one, produces the elements of the set. Then, using an independent test procedure, it is determined whether the candidate solutions are, in fact, solutions.

In an alternative (and more common) formulation, the generator first generates elements of a set of operators and applies them to problem states that have already been generated. For instance, the operators may represent legal moves in a game or valid steps in a derivation, in which case the states are new game positions, or formulas. Essentially, the set of operators, defines an implicit *problem tree*. In what is sometimes called the generate-and-test method, the nodes tested are classed as solutions or as nonsolutions, whereas in other methods they are evaluated or compared in greater detail with the desired state, and the generator determines the next state to be generated on the basis of the difference between current and desired state.

There are various strategies for generating a set of operators, and from them, a set of problem states. The strategies are what primarily distinguish the methods discussed below. Among those that do not require domain-specific information, other than what is implicit in the given set of operators, are depth- and breadth-first generation. In depth-first generation, before a new operator is generated, each operator is applied to both a problem state and all descendants of the state, down to a termination criterion. In breadth-first generation all operators are generated and then applied to the existing set of states before being applied to the states' descendants.

We can design more efficient methods if the method ''knows'' something about problem states or state sequences, in addition to something about the set of permissible operators and about testing a solution state. Statements such as ''a method knows P'' are harmless anthropomorphisms that are frequently used. They are a paraphrase of, say, ''the programmer knows that $P$ will be the case when the method is applied,'' or more likely, ''the applicability of the method is based on the assumption that $P$ holds.'' $P$ is usually a parameter provided with the problem statement; here, it is considered part of the input, either as the *problem* or as the *knowledge* of the problem.

If a ''given'' in the problem specification is some evaluation of the states with respect to the solution, a stronger method can be applied. Hill climbing is depth-first search, plus a method for ordering the alternatives at each decision point. In hill climbing, search proceeds through the alternative that offers the best improvement (measured in terms of the relative values of potential next states) in one step. This method produces the "best" local problem state compatible with the given constraints. Unfortunately, it can fail to work if the states do not form a total ordering, that is, if the problem space is not unimodal, since it can easily get stuck on a local peak or ridge.

This method illustrates a pervasive concern of AI research: making global decisions (decisions that depend in some way on the larger problem space) on the basis of necessarily local information obtained by examining local parts of the space. Various computationally simple methods for doing this have been tried and are found wanting (see, for example, Minsky's and Papert's study of Perceptron devices (Minsky & Papert, 1969) which attempt to decide on category membership of a pattern by pooling decisions made on the basis of local evidence). In more recent approaches to the local-global problem, new ways of representing knowledge and organizing programs have been developed.

Methods based on some global estimate of the "value" of a state are still widely used, though usually in combination with other methods. For example, variations on hill-climbing methods are still used occasionally for making quantitative decisions such as parameter estimation by relaxation methods. In addition, there are various ways in which the estimated value of a state can be used to "prune" unpromising branches of the search tree. Various formal methods have been studied—for example, the branch-and-bound, the graph-traverser, and the so-called A* algorithms. A number of mathematical theorems which show their power and limitations have also been devised (Nilsson, 1971).

Many search methods have been developed for the special case of game-playing systems and other "adversary" conditions. Since, in the usual minimax strategy, we always assume that the adversary will take the branch that is best for it, all we have to do is develop the tree that corresponds to the adversary's maximum-valued (that is, our minimum-valued) branch, while at the same time developing the look-ahead tree for our own maximum-valued branch. The assumption made in using many of these pruning methods is that we can better estimate the value of the state by developing it, by looking further ahead to the states lying there, and then by backing up the estimate to the current state.

Because we can often resolve problems into two types of secondary problems, we can also obtain related trees for nongame problems. In the first type, if any problems are solved, the original problem will be solved; that is, the secondary problems are equivalent formulations of the original problem. In the second type, if all are solved, the original problem is solved—which means that they are therefore subproblems of the original problem. This condition is required for a tree to take the form known as an AND/OR tree. Such trees have been extensively studied.

## Heuristic Search

The two main reasons for the inefficiency of the generate-and-test method are that it incorporates very little knowledge of the problem domain (that is, it is too general) and that the generate phase does not interact with the test, or evaluation, phase. As a result, nothing is learned from the failure of a generated state, i.e. from false attempts. The only message the evaluator can send to the generator is to stop when a solution is found. One lesson learned early in the development of artificial intelligence is that, unlike the generate-and-test method, natural intelligence seldom involves methods which are complete, in the sense of guaranteeing a solution. Instead, natural intelligence methods are characterized by plausible reasoning and by ad hoc rules of thumb, or heuristics, some of which pertain to problem-solving methods in general but most of which deal with specific task domains. The difference between heuristic search and generate-and-test is that in the former, the operators are not generated exhaustively in a fixed manner but are selected on the basis of their plausibility, based on knowledge of the problem domain, and the knowledge gleaned from past attempts. Although the importance of heuristic reasoning (or, as Polya calls it, "plausible inference") has been recognized informally, the systematic study of heuristic methods has come about in connection with attempts to build reasoning programs. During the first decade of artificial intelligence, about 1956 to 1966, this was indeed the main concern of students of artificial intelligence. More recently the study of tacit heuristics used by experts has again become a major pursuit as applications of AI have been turned to "knowledge engineering" (see the section, "Expert Systems").

Clearly, the selection of operators is important, for these operators are what guide the search through a large problem space. But in extreme cases, if the "correct" operator were always selected, there would, in effect, be no search. Operators must be selected on the basis of two criteria: (a) they must be applicable, that is, they must apply to a state that has already been generated; and (b) they should produce new states similar to the desired goal state. Adherence to the first criterion produces forward-chaining sequences, whereas adherence to the second produces backward-chaining sequences.

## Controlling and Minimizing Search

Whereas all problem solving implicitly involves searching through a problem space, most of the recent work has been devoted to studying more general methods of bringing knowledge of the problem domain to bear. Consequently, modern problem-solving research has tended to emphasize planning, problem reduction, constraint propagation, deduction, and knowledge representation. While the descriptions tend to look different because of this shift of emphasis, the basic ideas discussed above are implicit in all work on problem solving. For instance, there has been considerable recent interest in methods which are best viewed as exploiting problem constraints based primarily on semantic considerations to narrow the space of alternatives.

Search methods have taken the form of applying a simultaneous set of constraints to interrelated parts of a system. For example, Fike's REF-ARF system (Fikes, 1970), Elcock's ABSET and Barrow's and Tenenbaum's perception system (Barrow & Tenenbaum, 1979) all attempt to reduce the search space by applying selective restrictions on the objects that can occupy certain slots in a network. These restrictions arise from such sources as the given relations that must hold between objects (as in a set of simultaneous equations) or the known physical or topological relationships of a physical system. When these constraints are sufficiently strong and localized in a network—for example, if they are primarily pairwise constraints on adjacent elements of the network—they can provide a powerful *filter* for narrowing the search space, without having to expend much effort.

A good example of filtering by constraint propagation through a network is the work of Waltz (1975). Waltz wanted to find a correct interpretation, or labeling, of a network with which to represent the elements (lines and vertices) of a polyhedral scene that contains shadows. By choosing a large set of labels and tabulating their permissible pairwise co-occurrence, and by using a simple iterative filter, he obtained a unique set of labels for the scene. The straightforward application of one of the search methods mentioned above would have led to the exploration of a very large space in search of a correct "parse" of the scene.

Waltz's system is an excellent example of how the particular constraints among the elements of his problem space can be exploited to narrow the search space almost to a single state. Although his filter is applicable only to the particular domain of networks derived from scenes containing polyhedral objects, the general idea of applying local constraints to reduce the search space can be widely applied. For example, it is implicit in recent systems for circuit analysis (Stallman & Sussman, 1974).

In the following we will encounter systems in which the implicit search is not mentioned because the main effort is not in developing uniform, efficient search strategies but in designing methods that draw on various domains of expertise. Nevertheless, in two respects, the general schemes are relevant. First, considerable effort still goes into designing formalisms, language facilities, knowledge-representation schemes, and control structures that facilitate the task of expressing problem-specific knowledge in a form that enables the knowledge to be brought to bear at the most appropriate time during problem solving. Second, designing systems which perform over a broad range of tasks (the search for generality) still absorbs a number of investigators in artificial intelligence. The development of schemes that facilitate the design of knowledge-based problem-solvers, introduced in the next section, is taken up again in the sections, "Automatic Theorem-Proving" and "Expert Systems."

## CONTEMPORARY APPROACHES TO PROBLEM-SOLVING

Two important types of problem-solving tasks are *deduction* and *action synthesis*. In deduction, the task is to deduce the truth or falsity of a given proposition. Applications occur, for example, in information retrieval and mathematical theorem proving. Action synthesis involves constructing a sequence, or plan, of component operations for achieving a goal—for instance, in robotics and automatic programming.

In AI research, both deduction and action synthesis systems usually have a declarative, or assertional, component which describes the task-domain situation and states the goal. (An *assertional representation* is one in which information is represented by sentences in some kind of formalism such as predicate logic or semantic networks.) In theorem proving, for example, the task-domain situation consists of assertions representing axioms, lemmas, and theorems already proved. The goal statement is an assertion which represents the theorem to be proved. In information-retrieval applications, the task-domain situation consists of a set of facts (that is, a data base), while the goal is the statement to be retrieved, or deduced. The situation in robotics is that of a ''world model'' of statements which describe the robot's physical surroundings; the goal is a statement describing what is to be made true by a sequence of robot actions.

Along with the goal and assertions representing the situation are *operators* which can be used to manipulate either the situation or the goal statement. The operators sometimes consist of only a few general rules of inference, which can be used to generate new assertions from existing ones. Generally, however, it's more efficient to use numerous highly specialized operators to generate new assertions solely from specific existing assertions. In action synthesis, operators model component actions, from which a plan is constructed.

In addition to the representation of the situation, goal, and operators, a problem-solving system must have a control strategy for determining the sequence in which to apply the operators. Occasionally, control is highly centralized in a control executive which decides how problem-solving resources should be expended, while at other times, control is diffused through many processes acting and cooperating simultaneously.

Our discussion of problem-solving, then, centers on three main topics: the form of the representation, the kind of operators used for manipulating the assertions, and the type of strategies for controlling the sequencing of the operators. We will begin by discussing two examples of simple ''toy problems.''

### A Simple Example

Early in the research on artificial intelligence, programs were written for solving such simple puzzles as the ''15 puzzle'' in which 15 numbered, movable, square tiles and a blank space are placed in a 4 × 4 array. The object is to slide the tiles around until a specified configuration has been achieved. By considering such problems, we can sharpen our basic ideas about control strategies.

The 15 puzzle can be cast as an action-synthesis problem whose object is to find a sequence of tile moves that will change the configuration of tiles from the initial value of the configuration to that of a goal. Let us now examine what is involved in viewing the problem this way. First, we must have a representation, or data base, of assertions which describes the position of the tiles. As usual, there are several choices. One is to make a separate statement about the position of each tile. But a more compact representation is a 4 × 4 matrix whose components are tile numbers arranged as the tiles themselves are. (The idea of an assertional representation is broad enough to include the use of such matrices.)

We must also have operators for manipulating the data base, which in some way match the physical operations on the tiles themselves. It is convenient to view each tile motion as the motion of the blank space, either up, down, left, or right. We must also be able to compute the effect of each operator on an arbitrary tile-configuration matrix. Now the problem is to compose a sequence of operators that will change the configuration of tiles to the desired configuration.

We can confront the questions about the sequence of operators to be tried by imagining a tree of tile-configuration matrices linked by operators, a small version of which is shown in Figure 9-2. At the root is the initial tile matrix; its first-level successors are all the matrices that can be generated by applying one of the operators. The problem is to find a path in this tree that links the root with a descendant matrix representing the goal configuration. These control-strategy questions involve just how such a tree search should be conducted.

If we had a complete theory of the 15 puzzle, we might also have a simple computation that would indicate which operator to apply at any point in the tree, to achieve a given goal. This knowledge would make it unnecessary to search; it would, instead, become the basis for a fully informed control strategy. Short of a complete theory, however, we can devise general rules of thumb which will often, though not always, indicate the best move. These heuristics can be used to provide useful guidance in the search. In case we have no knowledge (a case that is usually not interesting in AI research), we must conduct an exhaustive search in which the control strategy might be based on a depth-first or breadth-first examination of the tree.

Because a lot is known about heuristically guided tree-searching processes, we can use this framework to approach many planning and deduction problems. Some theorems concerning conditions under which these searches find "best" solutions have been proved (Nilsson, 1971). Viewing control strategies for problem-solving processes as involving trees and guided searches is well established in the field of artificial intelligence.

**Reasoning Forward and Backward**

The application of operators to assertions, to produce modified assertions, is often called "reasoning forward," since the object is to bring the assertions

**Figure 9-2   Tile puzzle.**

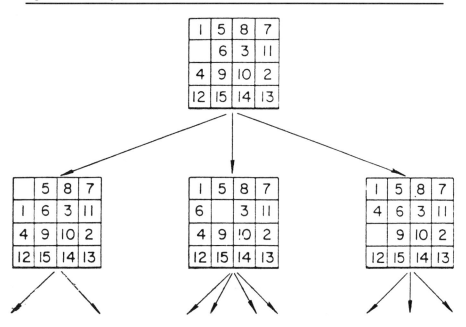

forward from its initial configuration to one which satisfies a goal condition. An alternative strategy is to use another type of operator to convert the goal statement into subgoals which, hopefully, are easier to solve and whose solutions are sufficient to solve the original goal. These subgoals, in turn, are reduced successively to lower and lower goals until each one has been solved or accepted as a trivial problem. This strategy is often called "reasoning backward." Combinations are also possible. In general, whenever an operator is applied to a data-base assertion or group of assertions, to produce a new assertion or assertions, we have a forward-reasoning step; when an operator is applied to a goal statement to produce subgoals, we have a backward-reasoning step.

In another strategy, one known as means-ends analysis, the current goal is compared with the current state of the assertions and a "difference" is extracted, which is used to index the forward operator best suited to reduce the difference. If this operator cannot be applied directly to the present assertions, subgoals are established for changing them so it *can* be applied. (Of course, after we have solved the subgoals we must still apply the appropriate operator and continue.)

Because reasoning-backward methods are used to convert problems to subproblems, they are often called *problem-reduction methods*. It has been observed that much human problem-solving behavior involves reasoning backward, a general strategy on which many AI programs are based.

Reasoning backward is nicely illustrated in the "Tower of Hanoi" puzzle. In

## Figure 9-3.    Tower of Hanoi

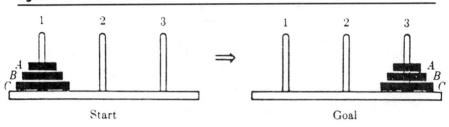

Start ⇒ Goal

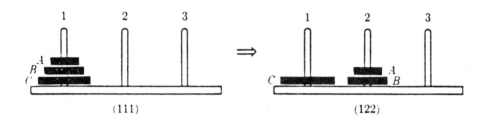

(111) ⇒ (122)

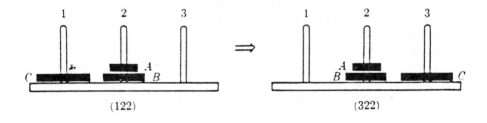

(122) ⇒ (322)

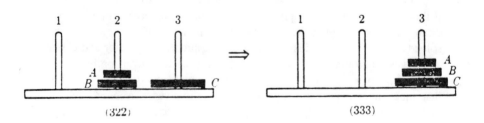

(322) ⇒ (333)

this puzzle (see Figure 9-3), three pegs contain discs of unequal size. Initially, all are on one of the pegs, arranged so that each disc is atop a larger one. The object is to move all the discs to other pegs. Only the top disc on a peg can be moved, and it cannot be put on top of a smaller disc. Here again, we have an action-synthesis problem that can be expressed by designing an assertional data base that represents disc locations and operators that represent the movement of the disc or the conversion of problems into subproblems.

Reasoning backward is an efficient way to solve the problem. The original problem of moving all discs from, say, peg 1 to peg 3 is reduced to the sub-problems of moving all but the largest disc (which is on the bottom) from peg 1 to peg 2, moving the largest disc to peg 3, and then moving the peg 2 discs to peg 3. Two of the subproblems are similar to, but smaller than, the original problem and can be attacked the same way.

In the main, then, the major concepts are: assertional schemes for representing both situation and goal; operators for manipulating situation, goal, or both; and various kinds of tree structures for keeping track of the manipulations that have been tried, in addition to helping organize the manipulations to be made next.

**The Predicate Calculus in Problem-Solving**

Although such data structures as arrays, trees, and lists have been used to represent problem situations, an important evolutionary thrust in problem-solving research has been the development of more powerful and broadly applicable assertional representation schemes. One phase of this evolution has to do with using expressions similar to those of predicate calculus to represent sentences that describe the problem situation. Suppose, for example, that the data base of facts (the problem situation) in a deductive-retrieval problem containing the following sentences:

1.  All large stores have parking lots.
2.  Every store in Sunnyvale is large.
3.  Maloney's is a store in Sunnyvale.

We might represent these sentences with the following expressions in the predicate calculus:

1.  (FOR-ALL x){STORE(x) $\land$ LARGE(x) $\Rightarrow$ HAS (x,PARKINGLOT)}
2.  (FOR-ALL x){STORE(x) $\land$ LOC-IN(x, SUNNYVALE) $\Rightarrow$ LARGE(x)}
3.  STORE(MALONEYS) $\land$ LOC-IN(MALONEYS, SUNNYVALE)

In an actual implementation these expressions would be represented by appropriate data structures in a language such as LISP.

In information-retrieval problems we would like to extract the answers questions from a data base of facts. For example, we might ask: "Does Maloney's have a parking lot?" Substantial AI work has been done in formulating this kind of query as a "theorem" to be proved and in using as "axioms" the facts in the data base. Our sample query (the theorem to be proved) is expressed as

HAS(MALONEYS, PARKINGLOT)

Operators and control (the other parts of a problem-solving system) correspond to the rules of inference, and the strategy, respectively, for applying them, to find a proof for the theorem.

The predicate calculus formulation is extremely general. It is the basis for several intelligent retrieval, or question-answering, systems, and is used in many theorem-proving programs to prove theorems in mathematics, in addition to those dealing with the properties of computer programs. The formulation can also be generalized to handle action-synthesis problems, and thus has been used in robot-planning and automatic-programming systems. Based on axioms with uncertain truth values, these ideas have been adapted in situations involving "inexact reasoning."

The above techniques, which use the predicate calculus formalism, have evolved from the rather naive and often impractical application of such powerful inference rules as resolution to highly specialized, problem-specific, inference programs. The major design questions about a predicate calculus-based approach to problem-solving involve the type of operators or inference rules to be used, along with the control strategies. We will explore some of these choices in the following sections (the proving of significant mathematical theorems by computer is examined separately in the section, "Automatic Theorem-Proving").

### Deduction Operators

In early applications deduction operators were based on the rules of inference of predicate calculus, such as substitution and modus ponens. Thus, from the expressions

(FOR-ALL x)[STORE(x) $\wedge$ LOC-IN(x, SUNNYVALE) $\Rightarrow$ LARGE (x)]

and

STORE(MALONEYS) $\wedge$ LOC-IN(MALONEYS, SUNNYVALE)

we can deduce LARGE(MALONEYS) and add it to the data base, Robinson's resolution procedure involves using only one inference rule, "resolution," which operates on a data base of predicate calculus expressions that are first converted into special canonical form.

Due to their elegance and uniformity, methods based on resolution have enjoyed a certain popularity. It was soon apparent, however, that it is extremely inefficient to subsume all logical manipulations under one general procedure. The problem-solving tree of alternative derivations exploded beyond manageable procedures, so researchers began experimenting with more specialized inference procedures that could be applied more restrictively in situations where they were most appropriate.

Increasing the efficiency of deduction systems involves removing from the assertional data base the axioms that express such general implicational formulas as (FOR-ALL x)$\lfloor$P(x) $\Rightarrow$ Q(x)$\rfloor$ and embedding them, instead, in operators where more control can be exercised over their use. Two approaches have been studied. In the first one, these general implicational formulas are expressed as production rules whose interpretation results either in extending the data-base of assertions or in reducing goals to subgoals. In the second approach the general rules are embedded in programs whose execution results in either data-base operations or reducing goals to subgoals.

To embed a general implication formula in an inference program, the designer first decides whether the formula will be used to reason forward or backward. For instance, if $A \Rightarrow B$ is used to reason forward, it is made the basis of a program that adds B to the data base as soon as A is added. If used to reason backward, it is made the basis of a program that sets up and solves the subgoal of proving A whenever the goal is to prove B. The original formula is neutral, with respect to how it is used; but often the designer of a system knows how a piece of knowledge can be used most efficiently.

Programs for reasoning backward are called "conse(quent) programs," "if-needed methods," or "servants." Typically, their execution converts goals into subgoals. Programs for reasoning forward are called "ante(cedent) programs," "if-added methods," or "demons." Their execution typically adds derived data to the data base of assertions. Together, demons and servants constitute the operators of a procedurally oriented predicate-calculus-deduction system.

Because demons and servants can be arbitrary programs, they can also incorporate additional, useful knowledge beyond that which is expressed by the implications they encode, for example, specific tests for determining whether invoking them is actually appropriate in a given, specialized set of circumstances. Demons and servants can also produce side effects that will alter the course of subsequent problem-solving activity. Of the various large reasoning systems constructed, which use this method of representing knowledge, probably the best known is Winograd's system for understanding natural languages (Winograd, 1972).

## Action Synthesis

In deduction systems a data base of facts and a system of goals and subgoals are manipulated by, for example, servant and demon programs until the main goal has been satisfied. In action-synthesis systems, however, the data base represents a "world model" that is changed successively by applying operators to a model until it satisfies a goal condition. Each operator affects the model differently. Whereas, in deduction, the operators make explicit some facts already implied by the data, in action synthesis, the operators produce new and logically different "worlds." This distinction made it more difficult for designers of action-synthesis systems.

The description of an action-synthesis operator has two major elements. One is the *preconditions* that must be satisfied in the world model before the operator can be applied, and the other are the *effects* on the model. If an operator is encoded as a demon, these elements have obvious interpretations. The preconditions are represented as the antecedent that must be satisfied in order to invoke the program. Operator effects are encoded directly in the demon as the appropriate manipulations of the data base.

Determining how best to encode operator effects is not a trivial problem. The designer wants to change *only* the elements of the world model that should be changed by the operator. Knowing what should be changed is sometimes difficult, due to possible chain reactions triggered by an operation. (If a robot, for example, moves a block—say, A—on a table from one position to another, then any other block—say, B—remains where it was —*unless* B is resting on A, or B is a structure of blocks partially supported by A, or B is in the way of the hand moving A, and so on). Describing the effect of operators is part of the "frame problem" being investigated in AI research.

Sometimes action-synthesis incorporates operators that make possible both forward- and backward-reasoning steps. In any case, the data bases which represent the alternative world situations, as well as the goals that result from alternative operator sequences, must be maintained in a tree-like structure. This is discussed in greater detail below, in our description of control strategies.

A good example of a large action-synthesis system that uses a data base of predicate calculus-like assertions, as well as demons and servants as operators, is Sussman's HACKER system, a system for producing plans for a robot arm that manipulates blocks (Sussman, 1975). (HACKER was also studied intensively in the context of how best to use specialized debugging knowledge to refine plans that are nearly correct.) Another example is the SRI STRIPS system (Fikes & Nilsson, 1971) for synthesizing the actions of a mobile robot. (Although not actually programs, STRIPS operators are similar to production rules which must be interpreted to have an effect.)

**Control Strategies for Procedurally Oriented Systems**

The tree structures and search procedures discussed in connection with programs for solving simple puzzles have analogs in more complex deduction and action-synthesis programs. The nodes of the search tree represent different stages of the assertional data base, or goal structure, which are connected by arcs representing the operators.

Researchers have used several control regimes for searching these trees. Simple, recursive, backtrack control involves depth-first exploration of the tree that selects a "best" alternative at each point where a choice must be made. If a line does not work, control returns to the last point where a choice was made, and another option is tried. If there is enough domain-specific knowledge to enable prediction of the best alternative at points of choice, there will be few occasions for backtracking, and this procedure is an adequate strategy which can be implemented without having to keep an explicit tree of alternatives. This is done by using the recursive control structure of a language such as LISP, augmented by the ability to undo the effects of operators.

To achieve more sophisticated control, though, we must keep some kind of tree structure. We must also be able to explore arbitrary parts of the tree at arbitrarily chosen times. For this, several new languages have been developed, which have built-in features to facilitate more complex operations. Examples are Microplanner, Conniver, Popler, Abset, QA4, and QLISP (Bobrow & Raphael, 1974). Many of them provide a tree of contexts, or environments, that can be used to represent the different data bases and goals resulting from various operator sequences. The operators are applied in a named context; this way, we can arbitrarily deepen the parts of the problem-solving tree that are chosen. In case of failure in one part of the tree, searching can be resumed in another part, one possibly influenced by the failure.

Another feature of the new AI languages, which is useful in distinguishing between procedures and methods, is *pattern-directed function invocation*. By referring to a triggering condition rather than its name, a program can be called and run. A method designed to produce the consequent, ⟨pattern⟩, is invoked automatically by a statement of the type, GOAL ⟨pattern-instance⟩. A demon with the antecedent condition, ⟨pattern⟩, is invoked automatically by a statement of the type, ASSERT ⟨pattern-instance⟩. In each case, ⟨pattern⟩ typically contains program variables that must be instantiated to match ⟨pattern-instance⟩. This matching process, and the associated "binding of variables," are important in invoking such procedures. The new languages automatically provide for matching, binding, and invocation. The presence of ASSERT statements in GOAL statements results in a complex interaction of the two types of reasoning.

An important control issue remains, however. When more than one demon or servant can be invoked, or when more than one match is possible for a given program, which should run first? In serial systems where only one program can run at a time, the problem is usually resolved by adding information to the GOAL and ASSERT statements that dictates the order in which pattern-invoked programs should be run. In parallel systems (where possibly several programs can be run at once), one could in principle run all of the invoked programs simultaneously. Even here, though, there are some special problems involving what to do about conflicts.

Even when the control regime permits deepening of arbitrary parts of the problem-solving tree, the use of ante and conse programs entails a basically recursive problem-solving strategy. The usual interpretation of a conse program, for example, involves achieving all of the subgoals it sets up before control returns to the search executive. In action-synthesis systems, this strategy means that action synthesis will occur to deep levels of detail before a final plan is produced. Such a strategy is ineffective for complex problems, because the search explodes in a welter of details. A better strategy involves suppressing details at first and working out the major steps of the plan, assuming that the details are taken care of later.

In the system known as NOAH (Sacerdoti, 1977), a modified GOAL statement—PGOAL—was introduced, which is used in servant programs to handle any subgoal that is to be regarded as a detail at the current action-synthesis level. When encountered, these subgoals are, for the moment, assumed to be achievable and are passed over, while action synthesis continues to fill out operator steps at the higher level. When a plan has been roughed out at this level, attention is focused on more detailed subgoals.

In addition to the strategy of suppressing details, another valuable idea was introduced in NOAH: a plan does not necessarily have to be expressed as a linear sequence of operators. At certain action-synthesis levels the plan is sometimes best expressed as a partial ordering of steps, even though the most detailed plan steps might eventually be executed strictly in sequence. This innovation is partly responsible for helping solve some of the difficulties connected with conjunctive goals. (A major theoretical problem for both deduction and action-synthesis systems has been that of dealing with a conjunction of goals.)

## Production Rule Systems

An alternative to the procedural embedding of general, implicational rules, as demon and servant programs is to represent them as production rules, a formalism involving condition-action pairs and resembling the familiar logical implications discussed earlier. Depending on their interpretation, such rules can be used in either forward or backward directions. Again, there are the familiar questions about control strategy, such as which rule to use first when more than one is applicable, and how to maintain and search trees of assertions and subgoals. In order to furnish guidance about which first-level rules to apply, Davis (Davis & Buchanan, 1977) has been exploring the strategy of using "meta" production rules.

A system of production rules driven by a common data base is a general computational formalism; thus it can be used to implement arbitrary systems.

Newell and his colleagues (Newell & Simon, 1972) have investigated a specialized version of this formalism to determine its usefulness in psychological modeling. This involves a small global data base of, for example, seven, plus or minus two symbols. In psychological modeling terms, this data base is a representation of short-term memory. Taken together, production rules are a representation of long-term memory. Newell speculates that a complex, cognitive organism may have hundreds of thousands of these rules. The production rules are triggered by elements of the short-term memory matching antecedent sides of the rules. Production-rule actions (expressed by the consequent sides) result in motor actions, changes in the short-term memory, or both. Conceivably, the actions could also create, modify, or destroy production rules.

Using a variation of the production-rule formalism, several large AI programs have been built. As we will see in the next section, systems based on production rules have been used in applications that require inexact reasoning.

### Reasoning with Uncertain Knowledge

One characteristic of human reasoning is a person's ability to make useful decisions, based on uncertain and incomplete evidence. This ability is needed not only for everyday activities, which people normally would never formalize, but for such tasks as medical diagnosis and securities analysis, which have been subjected to formal treatment.

A fairly straightforward adaptation of the problem-solving paradigm can be used to allow reasoning with uncertain knowledge. First, we associate with each "fact" in our assertional data base a "degree of truth" which varies from, say, 0 (certainly false) to 1 (certainly true). Then we must allow the inference operators various degrees of "strength," so the strength of a newly derived conclusion to be added to the data base can be made to depend on both the certainty of the premises and the strength of the inference operator.

MYCIN (Shortliffe, 1976) a system for helping physicians make diagnostic and therapy decisions for patients with bacterial infections, was developed along these lines. Containing over 300 rules, each one expressing an important quantum of medical knowledge, the system uses as inference operators, implicational rules obtained by interviewing physicians. Each rule is represented as a production and can be interpreted both in the backward direction (to establish subgoals) and the forward direction (to add newly derived "facts" to the data base).

In the diagnostic mode, the control strategy for MYCIN directs the system to reason backward; this is an attempt to establish the identity of the infectious organism or organisms. Subgoals are established by the production rules in chain-like fashion and are eventually "proved" questioning the physician-user or referring to the data base. When a subgoal has been proved, the production rules are used in the forward direction (taking into account their strengths) to infer derived facts which satisfy higher subgoals. Eventually, enough evidence is gathered from the user to permit an informed identification of the organism.

MYCIN can thus be viewed as a fairly direct application of artificial intelligence problem-solving techniques which have been extended to cope with incomplete knowledge. Similar systems being developed for other application areas are often called "knowledge based" because they contain many highly specialized inference operators (usually obtained by close collaboration with skilled experts).

### Enriched Assertional Representations

Advanced research in AI problem solving is now being concentrated on extending the expressive power of assertional representations. Earlier representations have several flaws: (a) inadequate cross-indexing of the predicates and their arguments; (b) inability to express and use taxonomic or sub-subset hierarchies and inherited properties easily; (c) inadequate (and usually nonexistent) mechanisms for partitioning the data base into segments of related knowledge; (d) inadequate ability to represent assertionally structures more complex than simple sentences, for example, plans, programs, and stories.

We have space here for naming only a few of the attempts to deal with these shortcomings, and it is still too early to tell which ones will be the most successful. Since many systems share common themes, we hope the next phase of research in problem-solving will produce useful syntheses of the newer representations. Among the prominent new representations are the frame-like schemes inspired by Minsky (1975) semantic-network schemes such as those of Hendrix (1979) which are being used to study natural languages; the conceptual dependency graphs of Schank and his colleagues, together with extensions for dealing with "scripts" and "plans;" (Schank & Abelson, 1977) the beta structures of Moore and Newell (1973), the KRL language of Bobrow and Winograd (1977) and Sacerdoti's procedural net (Sacerdoti, 1977) for representing action hierarchies.

Future problem-solving systems are expected to have one or more of these enriched representational schemes as their assertional data base of facts. The inference operators that manipulate the representations will likely have two representational forms. Compiled procedures will be attached to specific places in the assertional representation, and it will be possible to execute the procedures to produce specific, derived information. It is hoped that these procedures will also be reflected in assertional representations of what the procedures do and how they do it, so the system will be able to answer questions (for a user as well as itself) about its reasoning processes and thus possess some degree of "self-awareness." It should be possible to describe assertionally new reasoning operators to such a system. When first used, they will have to be interpreted from their assertional representations; but with use, they can be compiled into efficient procedural form.

## UNDERSTANDING NATURAL LANGUAGES

One of the most active research areas in artificial intelligence is the attempt to understand natural languages. Ever since the days of computing, researchers have been intrigued by the idea of communicating easily with computers. In nearly every area of computing, one can imagine how the understanding of language could make computers more accessible, not only for those who use them now but for many laymen. Recently new techniques and large systems have been combined, which open up new possibilities for communicating with computers in natural languages. Systems that answer questions are approaching the level at which they will be useful in real application areas. The interaction of advanced computing applications with users, such as automatic programming, will be based on the capabilities of natural languages.

Work on natural languages has been at the center of AI research into the ways in which concepts can be represented and cognitive processes organized. Because language is vital to our thought, any theories concerning memory or reasoning are strongly intertwined with the attempt to understand how language works. In writing a program for understanding languages, one is faced with all the problems of artificial intelligence, problems of coping with huge amounts of knowledge, of finding ways to represent and describe complex cognitive structures, as well as finding an appropriate structure in a gigantic space of possibilities. Much of the research in understanding natural languages is aimed at these problems.

The next section examines the field from a practical standpoint, considering various possible applications and the success achieved thus far. Some of the theoretical issues that guide this research are outlined in the section after that.

### Application Areas

Among the areas in which research on the application of natural language understanding systems is currently active are machine translation, information retrieval, and interactive interfaces to computer systems.

Machine translation, the first natural-language application to be attacked seriously, was the focus of a major research effort that began around 1952. Several projects were sponsored by government agencies, both in the United States (including major support from the Air Force) and abroad (especially the Soviet Union). The objective was to produce practical systems for translating scientific documents; the techniques used were primarily syntactic and in a spirit that was quite different from that of the AI research described in this chapter. By the mid-1960s it was obvious that the techniques developed would not produce high-quality translations. In hindsight, the worst mistake was the attempt to translate language, using only knowledge about its syntactic structure and a bilingual dictionary that established correspondences between words in the two languages. Today, much of the research in languages is based on the belief that a deep understanding of what is being said is vital to all uses of language. Applied to translation, this means that before one can translate material about a subject, one must first have a program that "understands" the subject. But since the ability to model large areas of knowledge is still primitive, this severely restricts the scope of the material which can be handled.

Although the problem of information retrieval is less well defined than that of translation, several possible approaches can be identified. At one end of the scale, there are systems which use straightforward indexing techniques or statistical methods for retrieving pieces of text that are stored verbatim. At the other end, one can imagine systems that acquire knowledge about a subject domain by reading texts and then answering questions posed by people who are interested in information about the subject.

The AI work that most closely resembles information retrieval is the construction of question-answering (QA) systems. Several early natural-language programs were QA systems in which a user entered information in standard form and then asked questions whose answers could be derived from the data. What distinguished these systems from conventional information retrieval was that the answer was not stored directly but was deduced from the stored information, using some kind of reasoning. Since, however, reasoning techniques were designed for the type of information to be handled, they were necessarily limited. For example, the BASEBALL program could answer questions about baseball results by using a data base containing the scores of a series of games. The STUDENT program could solve simple algebra word problems stated in English, while SAD SAM answered simple questions about a family tree, based on sentences about a family's relationships. These programs, which were among the first to use symbol-manipulation and list-processing techniques, were programmed in the earliest versions of AI languages designed for these techniques, namely, LISP and IPL-V (Feigenbaum & Feldman, 1963). Some were also among the first applications of interactive time-sharing systems.

## Question-Answering Systems

There was much interest in providing a more general reasoning capability in natural-language systems. SIR (Raphael, 1967) and its descendant, QA3, were typical of programs designed to perform reasoning, which did not depend on a specific domain; instead, they used techniques similar to those of formal logic. The most extensive of the early question-answering programs was the LUNAR system which, using a large data base provided by NASA, answered questions about the samples of rock brought back from the moon. One of the first programs to attack the problems of English grammar fully, it used "procedural semantics," in which queries are systematically converted into a program to be executed by a retrieval component.

The economics of computation are just now reaching the point where practical question-answering systems can be put to use. For instance, IBM and Phillips, among other companies and research groups, are developing systems. Although these systems are still in the development stage, it is likely that they or similar systems will soon be marketed for applications in domains where the questions to be answered will fall within a fairly narrow area. One example is a system for answering questions about the stock market (at least one such system is now being marketed).

The question-answering systems discussed above accepted questions in English but used a data base that was entered in a more highly structured form. While interest continues in the problem of entering a knowledge base in the form of English text, in its general form, the problem is too difficult for today's programs. To understand a text, a system needs not only a knowledge of the structure of the language but a body of "world knowledge" about the domain discussed in the text. Thus a comprehensive, text-understanding system presupposed an extensive reasoning system, one with a base of common-sense and domain-specific knowledge.

The problem of "understanding" a piece of text does, however, serve as a basic framework for current research in natural languages. Programs are written which accept text input and illustrate their understanding of it by answering questions giving paraphrases, or simply providing a blow-by-blow account of the reasoning that goes on during the analysis. Generally, the programs operate only on a small preselected set of texts created or chosen by the author for exploring a small set of theoretical problems. For example, SAM (Schank, 1975) inputs simple stories, on the basis of which it gives summaries and answers questions. SAM's knowledge base consists of a set of "scripts" which represent the normal course of events for a few simple situations such as going to a restaurant or taking a bus trip. On the basis of these standard scripts, it can make inferences such as those shown below.

Input

> John went to a restaurant. The hostess seated John. The hostess gave John a menu. John ordered a lobster. He was served quickly. He left a large tip. He left the restaurant.

Paraphrase (produced by SAM)

> John decided he was going to go to a restaurant. He went to one. He asked the hostess for a table. She told him he could go to it. He went to it. She went to it. He sat down in a chair. He got a menu from her. He read it. A waiter saw John was at the table. The waiter went to it. John ordered a lobster. A chef cooked it. The waiter got it from the chef. The waiter served it to John quickly. He ate it. He asked the waiter for a check. John got it from the waiter. John remembered the waiter had served the lobster to him quickly. John left the waiter a large tip. John paid the check. He left the restaurant.

| | |
|---|---|
| *Person* | Why did John go to a restaurant? |
| *SAM* | So John could eat a meal. |
| *Person* | Did the waiter give John a menu? |
| *SAM* | John got a menu from the hostess. |

This primitive program can handle only a few stock situations and draw a few basic inferences (which it is preprogrammed to look for), such as assuming that the reason for leaving a large tip was the fast service. But it does point the way toward programs that will be able to make extensive use of the stored knowledge of "the way things are," to help fill in unstated facts in stories.

Programs such as this are being extended to "skim" stylized text, for example, short disaster stories in newspapers. But several problems have been encountered in making these programs practical, both in terms of extending the knowledge of the language and in providing a sufficiently broad base of world knowledge. As is also true of translation, programs that do a partial job may have practical uses well before more difficult problems have been solved. Programs that do a rough job of skimming text for content are already being developed as practical tools.

Question-answering is actually a special case of a more general interactive situation in which natural language is used in a conversation between a person and a computer. Various applications are being explored in which language is the vehicle for communicating with the computer. The subject being worked on may be a program to be written, a financial transaction, a request for data, or a subject that is being learned by a student.

As computers become more numerous, people will often have occasion to interact with computer-controlled systems. It is hoped that such computer systems will be able to answer a broad range of questions. Such systems have been built in "toy" domains where the actual tasks being carried out by the computer are limited to providing a simple domain of language. The dialog given below is an example of one such program, SHRDLU (Winograd, 1972).

| | |
|---|---|
| *Person* | How many blocks are not in the box? |
| *Computer* | Four of them. |
| *Person* | Is at least one of them narrower than the one that I told you to pick up? |
| *Computer* | Yes, the red cube. |
| *Person* | Can the table pick up blocks? |
| *Computer* | No. |
| *Person* | Can a pyramid be supported by a pyramid? |
| *Computer* | I don't know. |
| *Person* | Will you please stack up both of the red blocks and either a green cube or a pyramid? |
| *Computer* | OK. [Performs the action on the display screen.] |
| *Person* | Had you touched any pyramid before you put the green one on the little cube? |

| | |
|---|---|
| *Computer* | Yes, the green one. |
| *Person* | When did you pick it? |
| *Computer* | While I was stacking up the red cube, a large red block, and a large green cube. |
| *Person* | Why? |
| *Computer* | To get rid of it. |
| *Person* | Why did you do that? |
| *Computer* | To clear off the red cube. |

On a TV screen the program simulates a simple robot system consisting of a single mechanical arm which manipulates toy objects on a tabletop. A person types commands, questions, and new information into the program, in English, and the program responds by simulating the movement of objects on its TV screen. The program contains considerable knowledge about the blocks world, knowledge that it uses to plan the execution of complex operations and to answer such questions as, "Can the table pick up blocks?" It also keeps a memory record of all that has happened thus far in the dialog, so as to understand references to past events and answer questions about what has happened, in addition to the reasoning steps it used in deciding on particular actions.

Most of the effort in building SHRDLU went into analyzing how different words and phrases are used to communicate meaning. The program contains a grammar that enables it to analyze the structure of English sentences, and there are programs for interpreting the meaning of individual words in context, as well as special programs for dealing with a range of language phenomena. For example, to recognize the use of such questions as "will you" as implicit commands or to figure out what is desired in a shortened questions such as "Why?," it's necessary to find what is being referred to by using the pronouns *it* and *that* and such definite phrases as *the block* (which refer to objects recently mentioned). In addition to following commands, the system allows the user to define new terms, state new facts to be used in further reasoning, and ask questions about both the current situation and past events.

**Teaching Machines**

One type of interaction that calls for ability in natural languages is the interaction needed for effective teaching machines. Advocates of computer-aided instruction have embraced numerous schemes for putting the computer to use directly in the educational process. It has long been recognized that the ultimate effectiveness of teaching machines is linked to the amount of intelligence embodied in the programs. That is, a more intelligent program would be better able to formulate the questions and presentations that are most appropriate at a given point in a teaching dialogue, and it would be better equipped to understand a student's response, even to analyze and model the knowledge state of the student, in order to tailor the teaching to his needs. Several researchers have already used the teaching dialogue as the basis for looking at natural languages and reasoning. For example, the SCHOLAR system of Carbonell and Collins (1974) tutors students in geography, doing complex reasoning in deciding what to ask and how to respond to a question. Meanwhile, SOPHIE (Brown & Burton, 1975) teaches electronic circuits by integrating a natural-language component with a specialized system for simulating circuit behavior. Although these systems are still too costly for general use, they will almost certainly be developed further and become practical in the near future.

## Theoretical Problems

The categories above make it possible to view research in natural languages in terms of the goals of the systems being built. Although the practical goals set for a project are important in focusing it, they can also help to define the research, at least superficially. A system designed to translate may differ markedly from one that merely absorbs story information in a computer knowledge base. This difference might not reflect a clear difference in theoretical approach; the theoretical base could be used for both tasks, or two different approaches to apparently similar tasks could be taken. In a project where the designers set out to build a "practical working system," various tradeoffs may be made in the way the system allocates its resources; still, it may be based essentially on the same ideas as those of another project, in the form of a *gedanken* experiment.

Similarly, it is often misleading to judge the relevance of a project on the basis of its subject domain. A system for making airline reservations may have more in common with a system that takes medical histories than with one designed to process office schedules. As is true of choosing immediate goals, the subject of domains cannot be completely separated from the type of competence needed; nor can it be separated from suitable organizations of knowledge. Considerable effort has gone into choosing domains whose characteristics support rather than hinder an attempt to deal directly with the most important basic issues.

Some of the theoretical questions that have arisen in research in natural languages are sketched below, as well as some of the approaches taken in both early and current work. While many specific problems are *linguistic* (that is, they relate to the structure of language), many important problems are actually general AI problems of representation and process organization. The problems discussed below are organized according to linguistic categories, although the most important results are those which clarify the underlying structure of the cognitive processing common to most intelligent activity.

Some of the classic divisions of language structure provide us with a rough guide. Again, it is important to remember that this division is artificial, that it must be considered in the context of the interaction of various parts of language. Traditionally, linguistics has dealt with phonology (the study of sound patterns), morphology (analyzing the internal structure of words), syntax (the study of arranging words in phrases and sentences), semantics (the study of meaning), and pragmatics (the study of the use of language in context).

Phonology has not played a part in natural-language systems, other than that which deals with speech inputs (discussed in the section, ''Speech Perception''). Morphology is usually dealt with in computer programs that use straightforward symbol-manipulation techniques. But within the artificial intelligence community, attention has been focused on syntax, semantics, and pragmatics.

## Syntax

Syntax is the most nearly independent category. Much of modern linguistics is based on the belief in an ''autonomous syntax'' which can be studied separately from other aspects of language. In natural-language programs, syntactic analysis has evolved from approximate ad hoc systems into abstract theories of linguistic structure.

As is well known, the first computational work on syntax was part of the machine-translation effort. Programs were based on existing theories of structural linguistics, theories that are insufficiently explicit. To enable them to carry out the steps needed for translation, they were augmented by various ingenious, albeit ad hoc, mechanisms. But this approach led to complex programs in which the facts about grammar were not clearly visible or easily modified. Early AI programs such as the question-answering ones described above avoided difficult problems of syntax by recognizing only very simple structures. Many of the pattern-matching techniques that were suitable only for their limited goals.

By the late 1960s more formal notions of grammar had been developed for such formal systems as computer languages and linguistics. The LUNAR and SHRDLU systems referred to earlier, plus such systems as MIND (Kay, 1973) were designed to deal with more of the complexities of real English. But they could not make direct use of linguistic theories such as ''transformational grammar,'' since these theories of linguistics did not attempt to deal with the problems of parsing languages; in fact, they were ill-suited to being used as a basis for processing languages. Instead, each system had is own formal grammar, which served as an alternative to conventional theories. SHRDLU was based on a ''procedural'' grammar in which facts about syntax were embodied in a program using explicit control-structure constructs to account for repetition, recursion, interrupts, and so forth. On the other hand, the basis of LUNAR was an ''augmented transition network'' which extended the transition-network ideas of automata theory to recursive structures and context-dependence. Meanwhile, MIND made use of ''charts'' which recorded—in a way that avoided duplication of effort—the current state of knowledge about the sentence being analyzed and about the parsing process.

Syntax research in the 1970s has involved, primarily, two kinds of simplification, providing simplified systems for dealing with less than full English, and providing simplified, underlying mechanisms that bring computer parsing techniques closer to being a theory of syntax. Several systems that have been developed—for example, LINGOL (Pratt, 1973) and LIFER (Hendrix, n.d.) use the basic mechanisms of augmented grammars in an easily programmable way. While these systems can not handle the more difficult problems of syntax, they can be used to quickly and easily assemble specialized parsers for applications. They are also likely to become the basis of natural language "front ends" for simple applications. Other systems have been built which use the notion of productions and which deal with each input word as a triggering operation in an active short-term memory. In providing parsing of simple structures with a minimum of syntactic knowledge, these systems have become the basis for programs such as SAM that deal with simplified input syntax.

At the same time, fundamental ideas about parsing and syntactic structure are being reevaluated from the perspective of programs that understand natural languages. For example, Kaplan (1973) Marcus (forthcoming) and Martin (1978) have, in their designs, attempted to capture the same kind of generalizations that linguists and psycholinguists have posited as theories of the structure and use of language. Scientists are emphasizing the interaction between structural facts about syntax and the control structures for implementing the parsing process. The insight into syntax gained by doing this could someday become the basis of a practical system; but for now, the emphasis is on developing a theory.

## Semantics

On the whole, semantics has had the greatest impact on artificial intelligence. In order to represent the meaning of words and sentences, it is necessary to have a formalism for representing facts, concepts, and ideas. Work in the semantics of natural languages has followed two general lines: using formal logic and developing new representations. In both areas there is considerable overlap with the work being done in problem-solving and common-sense reasoning.

In addition, some effort has gone into studying the phenomena that are directly linguistic, for instance, the meaning of the English quantifiers *all, some, any,* and so forth, as well as such determiners as *a, the,* and *this.* This work, necessary for building systems, has also been of theoretical linguistic interest, since the introduction of procedural notions gives us tools not available with classical logic. The main emphasis, though, has been on representing the meaning of words and sentences. Those who have used logic (usually predicate calculus) have worked with people who are proving theorems and performing deductions. Most of this research has meant studying the properties of that which is represented in language and in developing formalisms better suited to them. Among these, the major developments have been semantic networks (introduced earlier in discussing theorem proving), procedural semantics, case systems, and frame systems.

First proposed as a model for memory retrieval, semantic networks used the concepts of graph theory, representing words and meanings as a set of linked nodes. By using a systematic set of link types, simple operations were devised, such as following chains of links, which correspond to inferences. For example, nets often have a link, called "ISA," that connects the concepts corresponding to sets of objects to the concepts for a superset. In a simple net we might have "Dog ISA Animal" and "Poodle ISA Dog." A simple rule for "following ISA chains" gives us the derived link, "Poodle ISA Animal," which corresponds to the set/subset logic needed to prove the corresponding facts in a standard logical representation. The advantage of semantic networks over standard logic lies in the fact that a selected set of possible inferences can be done in this specialized (and efficient) way. If the inferences correspond to the inferences people easily make, the system will be capable of natural reasoning with less search than if the choice of inferences were based uniformly on mathematical rules of deduction.

Semantic networks are the basis of several systems, including most of the speech systems described in the section, "Speech Perception." Recently considerable work has been done in formalizing the network notions, which has resulted in a clear correspondence between the graph operations and the formal logic semantics of the knowledge represented.

Procedural semantics are the basis of LUNAR and SHRDLU. The meanings of words and sentences are expressed as programs in a computer language, with the execution of the programs corresponding to reasoning based on these meanings. To give the programs the necessary generality, they were based on languages that provide complex control structures such as automatic backtracking, data-driven processing (related to production systems), and goal-directed invocation. The MICROPLANNER language (see the section, "Some Contemporary Approaches to Problem-Solving"), which was developed to serve as a basis for representing natural-language meanings, was used to explore such control concepts as "demons" in understanding the connection between successive sentences in a story.

Case representations begin with the notion of *case frames,* which cluster a set of the properties of an object or even in a single concept. Case frames originated in linguistics where a simple sentence is viewed as having a fundamental set of cases that are determined by the verb—for *agent, object,* and so on. Thus, "Susan gave Sally the book" can be represented as an example of the case frame for *give;* the agent is Susan, the beneficiary is Sally, and the object is the book. There have been many variations on this notion, some of which remain close to the linguistic forms, while others such as Schank's "conceptual dependency" apply cases as a way of representing the underlying physical and mental acts that form a primitive basis for describing more complex activities. As is also true of semantic networks, the advantage of case representation lies in its being focused on clustering relevant sets of relationships in single data structures.

The idea of clustering relationships in larger units has been taken further with the use of *frame systems* (Minsky, 1975). Whereas case representations deal mainly with single sentences or acts, frames are applied to entire situations, to complex objects or series of events. A language-understanding system has a base of knowledge which includes "prototypes" for the objects and events in its domain. In analyzing a sentence, narrative, or dialogue, it tries to match the data to one or more of these prototypes. The SAM system makes use of a similar notion involving simple linear "scripts" which represent stereotyped sequences of events. SAM assumes that because the events being described will fit this script, it can use the script to fill in missing pieces. The GUS system (Bobrow et al., 1977) uses frames that represent standard trip plans, which it uses to carry on a dialog for helping someone schedule an airplane trip. The BELIEVER system (Sridharan & Schmidt, 1978) developed by Schmidt and Sridharan has a set of prototypical plans which people use to carry out simple actions. It uses the plans to analyze sequences of events and to look for causes and purposes.

In all these systems the existence of prototype frames makes possible the use of "expectations" in analysis. When an ambiguous or underspecified phrase or sentence occurs, it can be compared with a description of what would be expected, based on the prototype; if there is a plausible fit to the expectation, assumptions can be made as to what was meant. Several research groups are currently developing programming systems which should make it easier to program in a frame-oriented style. These systems are related to current natural-language efforts in a way that is similar to the relationship of the list-processing languages to the natural-language efforts of the early 1960s. Researchers are trying to provide tools with which to cope with at least some of the complexities of data structures and control. This would enable programmers to concentrate on the complexities more closely connected to the structure of language and thought.

**Pragmatics**

At first glance, discovering and representing the rules of English—grammar, spelling, and the meaning of words—seems to be the most difficult problem to overcome in getting a computer to use English. Although these details are, indeed, difficult, they obscure a deeper difficulty, one having to do with the basic nature of human communication. For example, when you talk to someone, you know that you and he or she have much in common. You share a large body of what might be called common-sense knowledge of the human world—physical objects, events, thoughts, motivations. In asking a question, stating a desire, or giving information, you include just enough detail for the other person to be able to understand what you are saying. Moreover, information about the communication itself, as well as its context in a conversation, are vital to understanding what is being said.

The AI programs of the late 1960s and early 1970s were much too literal, dealing, as they did, with meaning as though it were a structure to be built up of the bricks and mortar provided by the words, rather than a design to be created, based on the sketches and hints actually present in the input. Unfortunately, this gives them a brittle character. It makes them capable of dealing with tightly specified areas of meaning in an artificially formal conversation. At the same time, they are weak in dealing with natural utterances, being full of bits and pieces, continual (unnoticed) metaphor, and references to areas of knowledge that are much too formal.

Many of the issues discussed under *frame systems* are pertinent to pragmatic issues. The prototypes stored in a frame system can include both the prototypes for the domain being discussed and those related to the conversational situation. In a travel-planning system, then, a user responds to the question, "What time do you want to leave?" with the answer: "I have to be at a meeting by 11." In planning an appropriate flight, the system makes assumptions about the relevance of the answer to the question.

This aspect of language is one that is just beginning to be dealt with in current systems. Although most large systems in the past had specialized ways of dealing with a subset of pragmatic problems, there is as yet no theoretical approach. As people look to interactive systems for teaching and explanation, however, it seems likely that this will be the major focus of research in the 1980s.

## SPEECH AND VISUAL PERCEPTION

In general, artificial intelligence involves empirical research—e.g., exploring methods for solving problems, and inquiring into the ways in which meaning is mapped onto language structure. Yet nowhere does this enterprise resemble the experimental investigations of the natural sciences so much as in the attempts to interface computational systems with raw natural environments. The problem of bridging the gap—from a physical signal that occurs naturally in an environment, to symbolic representations from which meaningful information can be extracted—has proved to be one of the most difficult areas of artificial intelligence.

Although the problem of deriving meanings from typewritten, natural-language input is much more difficult than was initially thought, the problem of carrying out this project, beginning with the output of a microphone, seems to be even more difficult. In fact, the sensory-interfacing, or signal-to-symbol mapping, problem has been the source of a variety of empirical surprises and findings. In itself, the very difficulty of the problems has been unexpected, at least to some who once believed that various high-powered, pattern-recognition methods, augmented by statistical techniques, would be able to distinguish almost any class of patterns one might wish, and at a satisfactorily high level of probability.

Perception problems involve paying a considerable amount of attention to such engineering details as transduction, elimination of noise, and signal transformation for maximum sensitivity to the information-bearing components. In the next two sections little is said about these problems; rather, the conceptual difficulties are briefly surveyed.

The two perceptual domains to be described, speech and vision (or scene analysis), are typical of the AI approach to these problems, and there has been a substantial amount of research in both domains since about 1967. The speech work described here is the result of a concerted effort by a handful of centers, to meet the performance standards of a five-year research effort (described in a report by Newell and others) (Newell et al., 1973) standards that were met and exceeded in 1977. While the results are not ready for immediate application on a broad scale, some limited applications being investigated could bear fruit in terms of basic computer science and AI understanding.

## SPEECH PERCEPTION

The spectrum of tasks studied in artificial intelligence range from puzzle-solving, at one end, to speech and visual perception tasks, at the other. The sum total of accumulated knowledge used in puzzle-solving is usually minuscule, while each of us spends a significant part of our life acquiring knowledge necessary to perceive and understand speech and visual stimuli. Unlike problem-solving, the perceptual tasks are characterized by high data rates, large amounts of data, possibly error-filled input, and the need for real-time response. In spite of these significant differences, many of the central ideas in perceptual tasks do not differ significantly from those of problem-solving.

The terms *speech recognition* and *speech understanding* are sometimes used to characterize the nature of the speech-perception task being performed. Speech-understanding systems differ somewhat from recognition systems, in that they have access to and make effective use of task-specific knowledge in the analysis and interpretation of speech. Further, the criteria for performance are somewhat relaxed, in that the errors that count are not the errors in speech recognition, but errors in task accomplishment.

In speech perception the task specification can be expressed in terms of three components: the unknown utterance to be analyzed and recognized, the sources of knowledge, and the final symbolic representation of the signal.

Changes in air pressure caused by the unknown utterance are sampled by an analog-to-digital converter 10,000 times a second, producing a digital representation of the speech signal. This continuous signal is divided into acoustically similar discrete segments and classified according to phonc classes, based on segmented features (signal-to-symbol transformation). This symbolic representation of the speech signal forms the basis of further analysis and interpretation.

To successfully decode the unknown utterance, a speech-perception system must effectively use the many diverse sources of knowledge about the language, the environment, and the context. These sources of knowledge include the characteristics of speech sounds (acoustic-phonetics), variability in pronunciation (phonology), the stress and intonation patterns of speech (prosodics), the sound patterns of words (lexicon), the grammatical structure of language (syntax), the meaning of words and sentences (semantics), and the context of the conversation (pragmatics). One of the main problems in speech perception is how to convert these diverse sources of knowledge into action, that is, an effective sequence of operations that transform the signal into an interpretable sequence of symbols.

What makes speech perception a challenging and difficult area of AI is the fact that error and ambiguity permeate all the levels of the speech-decoding process. In speech, there are many sources of variability that contribute to the error-filled nature of the decoding process. In spontaneous (nonmaximally differentiated) connected speech, many expected features (and phonemes) may be missing. Variability due to noise and speaker leads to errors. Incomplete and/or inaccurate knowledge source representations lead to more errors. Thus speech-perception systems must accept the inevitability of errors and handle them gracefully. The following example further illustrates the nature of the speech-perception problem.

## An Example

Figure 9-4 shows partial analysis of the recognition process. At the bottom of the figure is a plot of the speech waveform (representing the changes in air pressure) for part of an utterance, ". . . all about. . ." The true locations of the phoneme and word boundaries are given below the waveform as a referrent for comparison. The waveform illustrates one of the main differences between the written form and the spoken form of the language. Unlike the written form of the words "all about," there is no gap, pause, or silence at the boundary of "all" or "about." The waveform is a single acoustic continuum.

One of the first steps in the speech-perception process is a signal-to-symbol transformation. The continuous speech signal is divided into discrete segmental units, each having approximately similar acoustic characteristics. Given the acoustic templates (or feature descriptors) of the phones of the language to be recognized, a pattern-matching process assigns a set of phone labels to each segment, along with a probability value representing the goodness of match. The dotted lines indicate the boundaries produced by a segmentation program. The segmental labels assigned by the pattern match process are given in the network under "segment level." Note that the first segment, the vowel part of the word *all*, was assigned labels /aw/, /ah/, and /ow/. Similarly, different labels are associated with each of the other segments.

**Figure 9-4.   Speech waveforms.**

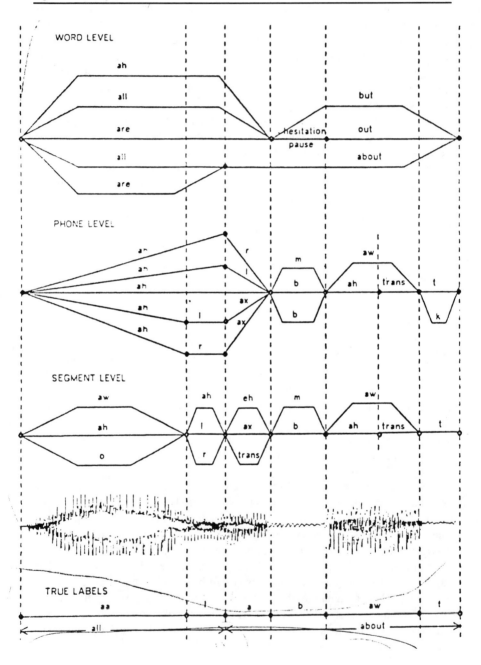

Given the necessary acoustic-phonetic knowledge, it is possible to combine, regroup, and delete segments forming the larger phoneme-sized units. The network under "phone level" shows the possible alternatives at this level. Note, for example, that sound /ah/ and /l/ of "all" have similar acoustic characteristics; it is not impossible that the minor parametric variability thatcaused the segment boundary at the lower level is merely a free variation. The lexical knowledge of word pronunciations and now be used to generate a multiplicity of word hypotheses (see the network under "word level") such as "ah but," "all out," "all about," "all but," "are about," and so on. Knowledge of the grammatical structure of the language, the meaning, and the conversational context can be used to generate acceptable alternative word sequences, that is, phrases and sentences at the next levels of the hierarchy (not shown in the figure).

The primary message of Figure 9-4 should be clear. At each level of the hierarchy, error and uncertainty force the speech recognition system to consider a network of alternatives representing plausible symbolic representations of the speech signal at that level. Thus the goal of speech perception is to find, given the acoustic evidence in the speech signal, the most plausible symbolic representation at each level that is compatible with the representations at the other levels. The result of error and uncertainty is a combinatorial explosion in the number of alternatives. The role of knowledge is to constrain the combinatorial explosion such that only the most plausible alternatives are considered.

## The Complexity of Speech-Perception Tasks

There are many dimensions that affect the complexity of speech-perception tasks. A commonly used measure is the size of the vocabulary. However, it is not always a good measure of the complexity. One recent system which attained 99 percent accuracy on a 200-word multisyllable vocabulary dropped to 89 percent on a 36-letter and number vocabulary. This is because the letters of the alphabet (when pronounced as "aye," "bee," "cee," and so on are easily confused. It is thus important to know not only the size of the vocabulary but a measure of its confusability.

The grammatical structure of sentences can be viewed principally as a mechanism for reducing search by restricting the number of acceptable alternatives. Given a vocabulary of size $N$, if one allows any word to follow any other words, such as "sleep roses dangerously young colorless," the number of possible sentences would be of the order $N^L$ for utterances of less than $L$ words in length. Syntactic structure imposes an ordering and mutually independent relationship among words, such that only a small subset of the $N^L$ is, in fact, possible. The size of the language—that is, the number of sentences of length $L$ or less (for some $L$) generated by a grammar—is sometimes used as a measure of the complexity of the task. A more meaningful measure is the branching factor, the average number of words that may follow each of the words in the sentence.

Just as vocabulary and grammar are restricted to make the speech-recognition task more tractable, there are several other dimensions which can be used to constrain the task so that what might otherwise be an unsolvable problem becomes solvable. Some of the dimensions of the task that can be constrained to reduce the complexity of the tasks are the mode of speech (connected or pause-separated), the noisiness of the environment, the number and cooperativeness of speakers, and the task-specific semantic and pragmatic support.

## Converting Knowledge into Action

An interesting characteristic of the speech task is the availability of many diverse sources of knowledge to help in the decoding process. However, when one attempts to develop systems that can effectively use all the sources of knowledge, the diversity leads to many problems. It is like trying to get several people who speak different languages to communicate and cooperate with each other in solving a complex problem.

In the Hearsay system (Reddy, 1975) the problem of communication and cooperation among diverse sources of knowledge is handled, using a *blackboard* model. Knowledge sources are conceived as independent asynchronous knowledge processes which communicate and cooperate with each other by writing hypotheses on a "blackboard" which can then be validated or rejected by other knowledge processes. The blackboard consists of a global data structure representing a multilevel network of alternatives such as the one given in Figure 9-5. This representation has some interesting similarities with the relaxation method used in vision and in the production system representation of knowledge that is used in other knowledge-based systems research.

In some speech-perception systems, such as in the HWIM system developed at Bolt, Beranek and Newman (also discussed in Rosenfeld, 1978b) the communication and cooperation among different knowledge sources is based on a paradigm derived through incremental simulation of the system, using human subjects. The Dragon and Harpy systems developed at Carnegie-Mellon University use graph structure representations of knowledge. In these systems, knowledge from various sources is integrated into a single state space representation. Although this representation is somewhat restrictive and cannot always use all the available knowledge effectively, it has been demonstrated that it is computationally effective and efficient in restricted language situations. The Harpy system, which uses this type of knowledge representation, was the first system to successfully demonstrate the feasibility of 1,000-word vocabulary-connected speech recognition with sentence accuracies exceeding 90 percent for male and female speakers in 10 to 30 times real time.

**Figure 9-5. Blackboard model.**

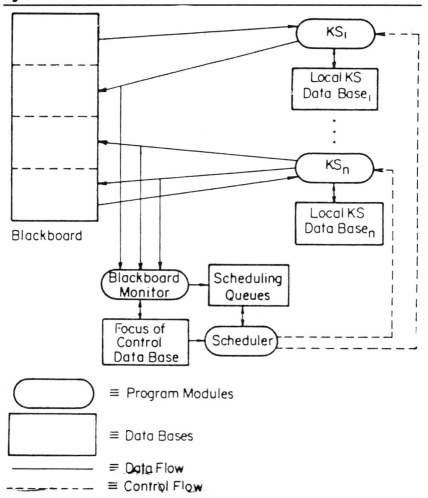

Control Strategies in the Presence of Error and Uncertainty

As noted earlier there are several sources of error and variability in speech perception, such as noise, speaker, missing phones, and extra phones. Incomplete and/or inaccurate knowledge introduces more errors. Given the number of errors in the task, as we see in Figure 9-4, we must consider several plausible alternatives at each level of representation. Thus the problem of error and uncertainty is converted into one of searching through the multilevel network of acceptable alternatives to find the best path that is consistent with all the knowledge sources.

There are several search techniques developed in problem-solving area that have been used in different speech-recognition systems. The Hearsay-I system developed at Carnegie-Mellon, the Lincoln Labs system, the IBM system, and the VDMS system all use the *best-first-search* technique. The Dragon system developed at Carnegie-Mellon uses a *breadth-first graph search* technique that is analogous to dynamic programming. The Hearsay-II and HWIM systems use an island-driven strategy in which the search is initiated at multiple points (islands of reliability) in the unknown utterance, proceeding bidirectionally and using a modified best-first search. The Harpy system uses the *locus model of search*. The most successful search technique to date in the area of speech, the locus model of search, is a graph-searching technique in which all except a beam of near-miss alternatives around the best path are pruned from the search tree at each segmental decision point, thus containing the exponential growth without requiring backtracking and nondeterministic search. Many of these systems are discussed in Reddy, 1975.

### Knowledge Acquisition and Learning

An important dimension of the speech-perception task is the richness of its knowledge sources. Speech has been a subject of systematic study in several disciplines such as linguistics, phonetics, perceptual psychology, and speech science. But much of this knowledge is not available in a form suitable for representation and use in speech-perception tasks.

Attempts to collect and codify this knowledge lead to classical problems in learning. In unsupervised learning, techniques such as clustering methods are used, to generate the phone templates. At higher levels generation of alternative word pronunciations, and inferring grammatical structure from examples require symbolic learning techniques. At present, systems such as Harpy have techniques for automatic extraction of phone templates that are adapted to the speaker and the environment. Acquisition of higher-level knowledge sources such as phonological phenomena, word pronunciations, and grammatical structure are done manually at present, which requires a lot of effort. Work is underway to develop automatic symbolic learning techniques which would generate representations of desired sources of knowledge.

### Central Issues

Many of the same issues raised in the speech-perception tasks are also central to other areas of artificial intelligence. Faced with the problem of reasoning in the presence of error and uncertainty, the systems may generate and search alternatives which have associated with them a probability value representing the degree of uncertainty. Also, faced with the problem of finding the most plausible symbolic description of the utterance in a large combinatorial space, techniques similar to those used in least-cost graph-searching methods in problem-solving are used here as well. Given the problems of acquiring and representing knowledge, as well as control search, the techniques needed in speech-perception research are similar to those of most other knowledge-intensive systems. The main difference is that, given the way humans perform, in terms of accuracy and response time, the criteria for success far exceed the performance requirements of other artificial-intelligence tasks, perhaps with the exception of vision.

## VISION SYSTEMS

### Computer Perception

As functions of intelligent beings, perception and cognition are difficult to separate. A view widely held by psychologists is that perception is an active process in which hypotheses are formed about the nature of the environment and sensory information is sought that will confirm or refute these hypotheses. This view of perception, as a form of problem-solving at least at some stage, is held by many researchers in artificial intelligence. Thus the problem of visual perception, as well as being of intrinsic interest as a task that clearly demands intelligence, also shares a number of technical problems with other areas of artificial intelligence. In this section we discuss only the perception of visual input, or "computer vision."

The mid-1950s mark the beginning of serious work on the computer analysis of images. Applications that began to be investigated at that time included the recognition of printed characters, of cells in photomicrographs, of "events" in photographs of nuclear bubble chambers, and of military targets in aerial photographs. The approaches used belonged to the area now called *pattern recognition* rather than to artificial intelligence; but in those early days little distinction was made between the areas.

Since the early 1960s there has been a marked divergence between the pattern-recognition and AI approaches to computer analysis of images. The former approach has continued to stress the use of ad hoc image features in combination with statistical classification techniques. More recently, use has been made of "syntactic" methods in which images are recognized by a "parsing" process as being built up hierarchically of primitive constituents. By contrast, the AI approach has employed problem-solving methodologies based on extensive use of knowledge about the class of images, or "scenes," to be analyzed. (Many references to image analysis can be found in Rosenfeld (1978a). In this section we will sketch some of the work that is based on the AI approach, to which the term *computer vision* is usually restricted.

Much of the work on computer vision has dealt with images of scenes containing solid objects viewed from nearby. These are the sort of images with which a robot vision system must cope in using vision to guide its motor activities, including manipulation and locomotion. The analysis of such images is usually called "scene analysis," to distinguish it from the analysis of images that are essentially two-dimensional, such as photomicrographs (which show cross-sections), radiographs (which show projections), satellite imagery (in which terrain relief is negligible), documents, diagrams, maps, and so on. The methods of computer vision, however, apply equally to these latter classes of images; the term need not be restricted to three-dimensional scene analysis.

The input to a vision system often consists of a digital image, perhaps obtained by a TV camera. (Stereo pairs of images may be available in some cases, or three-dimensional information can be obtained by means of a rangefinder; but a single image is the most common form of input.) The task of the system is to construct a description of the scene shown in the image. The knowledge needed to carry out this task is provided in symbolic form, while the image is in the form of a two-dimensional signal or digital array. Thus, before we can tackle the task, it is necessary to map the image into some sort of symbol structure, typically representing primitive "objects" in the scene, together with properties of and relationships among these objects. This signal-symbol-mapping process must be carried out with great caution, since it constitutes a major simplification of the input. In particular, it should be done so as to minimize the commitment to a particular set of objects (see Marr, 1976).

In practice, the signal-symbol mapping required for scene description can be very difficult. The raw scene must be *segmented* into regions, or edges of regions, out of which the desired objects are constructed. Various techniques can be used to detect potential segments of a scene, for example, clustering (or histogram peak detection) of point property values, piecewise approximation, region growing and tracking, and many others. However, none of these techniques is guaranteed to yield regions that will be compatible with the desired objects. Even if compatible regions can somehow be obtained, determining which combinations of the regions actually correspond to objects may still not be trivial. The simple examples of vision systems described in the next section illustrate the difficulties.

## Generality and Control

Computer-vision tasks, like the speech-perception tasks described in the preceding section, usually require various levels of knowledge. At the "low," or "general-purpose" level, a knowledge of surfaces and illumination is needed.

At the "high," or "specialized" end, we need to know, for example, about the functions of the objects in the scene. Coordinating these sources of knowledge presents a challenge.

The pioneering effort in computer vision was that of Roberts in 1965. His work dealt with scenes containing small sets of polyhedral objects, each of which could be constructed by combining a few primitive objects such as rectangular parallepipeds and triangular prisms. A photograph of such a scene is digitized and the visible edges of the objects are detected. Straight lines are fitted to the edge points that are detected, thus converting the photographs into a line drawing. Next, polygons formed by the lines are extracted, and it is determined whether they are topologically equivalent to the polygonal faces of any of the "model" primitive objects. If they are, a projective coordinate transformation is sought, which relates the observed polygon to the model. This way, partial matches are found between the model and the drawing. The program is designed to account for the entire drawing as being made up of combinations of models.

Roberts worked with scenes taken from a simple "blocks world" of polyhedral objects. Rather than being noisy TV frames, his input images were photographs taken under controlled lighting conditions. His objects had simple shapes bounded by straight edges, and the regions making up these objects were free of texture. Nevertheless, in his scenes, edge detection did not always yield good region boundaries, since the contrast between regions was often low. Line-fitting to the edges detected could yield anomalous results, due to the presence of false-arm edge detection. Also, model-matching to the lines was nontrivial, because the polygons were subject to arbitrary perspective transformations.

Roberts's program made use of knowledge at several levels. It knew that the objects in the scene were composed of polyhedra, that polyhedra have straight edges, and that the differences in reflectivity give rise to abrupt changes of brightness at these edges. The program used this knowledge in a "bottom-up" fashion, however. First, find edge points and fit lines to them; then fit polyhedron models to the lines. The drawback of this approach is that it makes it difficult to recover from the effects of errors at a given level.

In contrast, Shirai's program (1973) makes much better use of prior knowledge of the class of scenes being analyzed. This program begins by attempting to detect the most obvious edges in the scene, which are expected to be edges between the polyhedra and the background. When this has been done, the program can hypothesize other edges, particularly those that separate two polyhedra—based on information that only polyhedra are present. It can then direct a more sensitive edge-detecting operator to look for the edges at the appropriate places. In turn, internal edges (dihedral angles) of the individual polyhedra can then be found. At each stage, previous results, in conjunction with models of polyhedra, are used to propose that most plausible missing lines. Unlike Roberts's hierarchical program, there is no rigid separation of processing into "levels;" edge detection, line fitting, and model fitting all operate cooperatively. This program illustrates the notion of *heterarchical,* as opposed to hierarchical, organization.

Shirai's approach to scene analysis was a major step forward, but much remained to be done to extend his methodology beyond a world of polyhedral blocks to natural scenes involving textures and complex shapes. In such scenes one must be able to detect *texture* edges and not merely brightness edges. This implies that a larger set of operators must be used, either to detect texture edges directly or to detect the brightness edges of the texture elements and group the elements into textured regions. It also opens up greater possibilities for error. At the same time, the shapes to be constructed from the detected edges are no longer well defined; for example, they might be shapes of automobiles or trees.

Although research in computer vision has gone well beyond the blocks-world images analyzed by Roberts and Shirai, the general principles learned from blocks-world studies are applicable to classes of scenes ranging from production lines to parking lots. The next step is to design vision systems that can cope with unfamiliar or unexpected output. Presumably, such systems will carry out a preliminary analysis of the input, leading to the tentative selection of frames (31) within which to do further analysis.

In the field of artificial intelligence, the relationship of the "lower-level" vision problems (for example, the extraction of lines and other commonly accepted, knowledge-independent features) and the more cognitive processes is still controversial. Roberts's approach was primarily an expectation-driven one, in that only objects known to the system—and features expected in such objects—were searched for. Many people still believe that visual perception is mainly of this type. In later systems, data-driven and expectation-driven processing were combined in various complex, control-sharing strategies. Other investigators—recently, David Marr—have argued that at least in the early stages of the human visual system there is reason to believe that complex, autonomous, knowledge-independent processing takes place with only minor intervention by expectations. This polarity, which is a recurrent theme in the study of perception, is just one manifestation of the age-old problem of the relationship between wholes and parts that has concerned researchers in psychology and systems theory.

## Constraints and Consistency

Computer-vision research has led to important developments in constraint analysis, developments that began with Guzman's work in 1968. He formulated rules for linking regions in a scene that appear to belong to the same polyhedral object. The linkages thus constructed usually lead to uniquely segmenting the scene into objects. Guzman's rules can be rationalized by considering, from various viewpoints, the way in which polyhedral vertices appear in an image (Clawes, 1971; Huffman, 1971). When two regions of the image meet at an edge, the edge may represent a convex or concave dihedral angle on a single object, or it may be an occluding edge created by one object lying in front of another. At vertices, however, not all combinations of these interpretations are physically possible (or plausible). In 1975, Waltz showed that when lines represent not only angles and occlusions but shadows, cracks, and a rich variety of edge labels, only a fraction of the possible combinations will be consistent. For example, Waltz had 11 possible labels for edges, including such labels as boundary, convex, and concave interior, and crack and shadow. Of the hundreds of thousands of logically possible permutations for trihedral junctures, about 500 are physically permissible for a y-shaped juncture, whereas only 70 for an arrow-shaped juncture. If a pair of junctures share a line, however, the line must receive the same label at both junctures. Typically, this reduces the candidate labelings for the line to only a few, the number of which is further reduced by continuing to examine adjacent junctures and ''propagating labels.''

In Guzman's work and that of his successors, line drawings were used as input rather than as images. It was an example of symbolic vision, in which the input has already been segmented into objects (here, the input has been segmented into lines). The constraint analysis technique is being applied to segmentation tasks involving scenes more general than the blocks world. Given a set of objects or regions in a scene, each with a set of possible identifications, we can use the relationships of these objects to eliminate many possible combinations of interpretations. This process often results in a unique interpretation. At worst, it greatly reduces the search space that must be examined in order to find consistent interpretations. Where combinations are either consistent or inconsistent, the process need not be deterministic; it can be probabilistic, using possible relationships to increase or decrease the probability associated with each interpretation.

At a lower level, constraint analysis can enhance the scene-segmentation process. If, for example, we are looking for lines or curves in a scene, we can apply line-detection operations at each point and determine the initial probabilities that lines at various orientations will occur at that point. We then use a reinforcement scheme to enhance these probabilities; for example, line probabilities reinforce each other if they are close and collinear. Similar approaches are taken in edge detection, angle detection, template-matching, and other basic, scene-segmentation processes (Rosenfeld, 1978b). Note that these approaches produce fuzzy segmentations; this seems to be a realistic way to represent noisy, real-world scenes. Therefore, more researchers have proposed extending the discrete relational structures normally used for scene description, to allow for fuzziness, both within the entities and among their relationships.

### Interfaces with Other Disciplines

Increasingly, computer-vision techniques are being applied to real-world problems. This is particular true of device assembly, circuit board layout, and inspection in the field of industrial automation. Although much of the work is still going on, several, convincing demonstration programs have been written, and it is expected that computer vision will soon begin to have a significant impact in industry. At the same time, the computer-vision approach will increasingly be applied to the analysis of images by computer, areas which up to now have been the domain of researchers in pattern recognition—for example, the analysis of handwriting, photomicrographs and radiographs, and satellite imagery.

Because it deals with real-world, noisy, multidimensional input, research in computer vision has been a demanding test area for AI methodology. Thus, efforts to solve the problem of computer vision have stimulated the development of AI techniques in such areas as problem-solving languages, control structures, and computer networks, techniques which, in turn, have spearheaded advances in the language and system areas of computer science.

We can also expect considerable interaction between computer-vision research and the study of human vision. Psychologists studying perception are increasingly aware of the approaches used in machine perception; they have begun to draw on these approaches in developing models for human visual processes. At the same time, researchers in computer vision must study these processes if they are to develop systems that can engage in dialogue with humans about scenes. Such systems must be capable of understanding the capabilities and limitations of human vision.

## PRODUCTIVITY TECHNOLOGY

Generally, the overall goal of artificial intelligence workers specializing in productivity technology is to develop uses for artificial intelligence that involve interaction with the physical world, usually through visual sensors and force-sensing manipulators. To be sure, there are serious economic and social incentives: relieving humans of hazardous or boring jobs; doing labor-intensive jobs that must be done and are very costly using human labor (environmentally important clean-up jobs are a special case); and maintaining economic strength in the competitive international arena through automated production, particularly in assembly.

The roots of artificial intelligence in productivity technology date back to the work on computer vision and manipulation that was prominent in artificial intelligence in the 1960s. While researchers at Stanford and MIT were experimenting with programs that demonstrated the ability to understand a visual scene, those at Stanford Research Institute were working with motion, problem-solving, and obstacle-avoidance, using "Shakey."

During this phase a great deal of effort was devoted to changing blocks-world images into line drawings. Programs of many kinds were written to analyze intensity profiles, extract feature points from them, and group the feature points into line segments and then the line segments into clean, complete drawings.

At first, investigators were optimistic that the blocks world would find applications in the industrial world and that the robot projects would become productivity technology projects. As it became clear that the problems were much more difficult than had been anticipated, the hope for a continuum of applicable systems faded and the robot projects became productivity technology projects more by metamorphosis than by smooth, continuous change. Still, this early work did produce the repertoire of basic vision, manipulation, representation, and problem-solving techniques that are, in more contemporary forms, contributing to progress in the solution of real industrial problems.

Theories of representation and problem-solving, of course, are universally needed; so in those areas, the early robot work served as a test bed for important general problems. Indeed, if we look at the history of the major centers, it seems that far more people were working on robots indirectly through these problems than were working on vision or manipulation, *per se*. One reason for this emphasis is the high frustration associated with dependence on failure-prone physical devices. Another is the tendency of many students to be as theoretical as possible, avoiding problems associated with application. This is unfortunate, since in three areas particularly, research in the application of artificial intelligence appears to be essential: vision, manipulation, and programming-language design.

In the area of vision, one problem is that of inspection for defects. Another is helping guide parts into place, and still another is orienting parts that are jumbled together randomly in a bin.

In the area of manipulation, one problem is that of "sensed forces" to determine forces to be applied, for instance, when inserting a peg in a tight-fitting hole. Another is that of smoothly controlling multijointed manipulators during rapid motion.

In the area of programming-language design, the main problem is to create problem-solving systems that accept rough assembly instructions, preferably in English, to produce the incredibly detailed streams of low-level instructions which interpret sensor signals and control manipulator motors.

**Toward Productivity Technology**

In retrospect, the work of the major research centers has progressed as though the following steps constituted a conscious plan:

1. Pick the simplest possible domain, do vision and manipulation in that domain, and use the results to measure the difficulty of the problems. This should result in the allocation of resources and a prediction as to when the applicable results should emerge.

2. Once the problems are uncovered by working with the "simple" domain, gather the hardware and software tools that can lead to the design of a cost-effective prototype for solving particular problems.

3.  Use the tools to tackle real problems. At first, these may be selected because they are amenable to solution, using the tools and techniques in hand. Obvious, undisputable commercial viability is a secondary objective.

4.  Finally, point the technology at the most serious problems, where the saving will be greatest in human and fiscal terms.

The first step, exploratory research in a simple domain, typically involved doing vision and manipulation in the domain of children's blocks. The first result was the discovery that devising a computer that can see is extremely difficult in any domain, including that of blocks. Veterans of this period recall the summer vision projects that turned into grueling multiyear efforts. Eventually MIT, Stanford, and Stanford Research Institute produced credible demonstrations of scene-understanding in various versions of the blocks world; but these insights into theory came at the cost of delaying work with force-sensing manipulators and special-purpose vision.

The second step, designing and defining basic equipment needs, has met with mixed results. On the positive side, several laboratories have reached the point where their manipulation and vision equipment is being used reliably *for* research rather than simply being research. A number of manipulators and manipulator interfaces are now available, some commercially. On the negative side, some decisions made a few years ago about equipment selection seem unenlightened today. The biggest change is in the assumptions about what kind of computer power will be available when the technology is worked out. Computer power is increasing faster than expected, while the technology is developing more slowly.

The third step, tackling real problems, has led to a rapidly increasing rate of important new demonstrations, of which the following are representative. These are taken from the progress report of Stanford, MIT, and Stanford Research Institute, the largest artificial intelligence centers in the U.S. engaged in productivity technology today.

- A complete system for assembling a 10-part water pump has been demonstrated, using force and touch tools, and some simple vision.
- Coordinated manipulator action has been demonstrated through the assembly of a hinge, using two cooperating manipulators.
- Close-tolerance manipulation has been demonstrated by assembling a bearing with 20-micrometer tolerances.
- Accurate part-location, using vision, has been demonstrated through the precise determination of the position of semiconductors in preparing for attaching leads.
- The ability to perceive, describe, and identify three-dimensional shapes was demonstrated by a complicated system which combined laser rangefinding with a new theory of representation based on generalized cylinders.
- The reorienting of scattered parts has been demonstrated through the identification and correct adjustment of steel castings spread on a light table. This demonstration makes heavy use of binary image-processing techniques.

- The use of visual feedback has been demonstrated through the location of bolt holes, using a solid-state camera mounted on a bolt-bearing arm.

These are obviously illustrations and not solutions. There is a big difference between a mature technology and these crude harbingers of coordinated motion, force-sensing, visual inspection, and bin-picking. But illustrations do help us grasp both the difficulty and the potential of the technology.

Work that advances the cause of vision and force-sensitive manipulation is not limited to the major artificial intelligence centers. Following are some examples of the work being done elsewhere. Some of this work is described in ref. 1.

- General Motors has developed a system that mounts wheels on cars after visually finding the lugs and lug holes.
- General Electric has developed a program for inspecting lamp filaments.
- The Draper Laboratory has developed a passive device for a peg-in-hole insert task which operates at the rate of one insertion per 0.2 seconds, given 1-millimeter initial errors and 50-micrometer clearances.
- Hitachi has developed hardware for visually inspecting printed circuit boards.
- Mitsubishi has developed a process for inspecting the photographic masks used in manufacturing integrated circuits.

It would not be accurate to claim these achievements for artificial intelligence, since, for the most part, the connection is tenuous. Still, it can be said that they are representative of what can be done with sophisticated vision and force-sensitive manipulation both of which were first championed and promoted within the AI field.

## The Needs of Productivity Technology

Looking to the future, several developments are needed to achieve real industrial importance. There is a need for better equipment. Better solid-state cameras, better force sensors, and better mechanical designs—in that order—are at the top of nearly every list. There is a need for better vision-processing. By *better*, we mean both faster and more sophisticated. So far, most demonstrations depend on first reducing gray-level images to binary images or on looking only at a few gray-level profiles, judiciously selected. The reason nothing more has been done is that the necessary expertise is lacking, and even if it existed, currently available machines lack the necessary power. There is also a need for better control ideas. Getting a multijoint manipulator from one point to another smoothly is one problem that has *nearly* been solved. Finally, we need a language for programming assembly.

With respect to this last item another minor variation on the traditional programming languages is not needed. Instead, the need is for a language with strong problem-solving features, strong enough for the assembly programmer to be able to specify what he wants in high-level, comfortable human terms. Eventually, a truly adequate language will be generated automatically in the way that people use manuals to produce programs. While several labs are making progress on the critical modules of such a system, it is difficult to tell how far coordinated applications are in the future.

AL, the Stanford system (Binford et al., 1974–1977), is a complex language similar to Algol, with many new data-structure and -control primitives. Computer scientists have concentrated on modeling the effect of the world on the assembly operations, particularly in developing mechanisms to predict, on the basis of a planning model, errors in location values. The mechanisms, in turn, supply information for automatically generating AL code.

IBM's system, AUTOPASS (Lieberman & Wesley, 1975), is imbedded in PL/I. It provides the user with a selection of high-level assembly operations, the most general being a PLACE command in which the destination is specified as geometric relations between objects.

The MIT system, LAMA (Lozano-Perez & Winston, n.d.) shares many of the ideas and approaches of AL and AUTOPASS. It differs, however, in that there is a stronger focus on representing the spatial and geometric information used to instantiate the skeleton programs which embody the feedback strategies for assembly operations. The key idea is to make the specification of strategies independent of the spatial operations that the system performs.

The Stanford Research Institute system focuses on mechanical assembly techniques which have short-term industrial potential. In the area of pick-and-place, SRI's results have been impressive. Their system stencils randomly oriented boxes moving on a conveyor belt and packs parts in randomly oriented pallets, again, while moving on a conveyor.

Draper Laboratory's system also focuses on short-range results. We have already mentioned their success with a passive device that solves the peg-in-hole problem. Draper has also distinguished itself with an extensive theoretical analysis of the assembly requirements in terms of manipulator design and control and assembly strategies.

When future mechanical assembly languages incorporate the modules being explored by these and other laboratories, there should be little of the current danger that expensive assembly will merely be replaced by expensive programming.

## APPLYING AI METHODS

The last half-dozen or so years have seen a significant increase in efforts to apply the techniques of AI to the solution of practical problems. Such efforts have spanned a wide spectrum from preliminary investigations of the feasibility of certain approaches, to the actual commercial marketing of viable working systems (see the examples given in the introduction to this chapter). They have, in addition, covered a wide range of application areas from providing assistance to research scientists such as mathematics, programmers, or chemists, to serving as part of a field application involving clinical medical practice, teaching, or industrial manufacturing. For the purpose of this brief overview, we shall sketch only two general areas of such application. The first is the application of AI in organic chemistry and the second is in medicine and the health-related fields. These two areas were selected because they are among those that have received intense development in recent years. They are more fully described in Feigenbaum (n.d.) and Pople (n.d.).

## Organic Chemistry: DENDRAL and META-DENDRAL

One of the earliest and most enduring applications of AI to a practical scientific task was DENDRAL (Buchanan, Sutherland, & Feigenbaum, 1969). Begun in 1965 as a collaborative effort between the Stanford Heuristic Programming Project and the Mass Spectrometry Laboratory, it is a model ''knowledge engineering'' project, reaching performance levels surpassing human experts in certain tasks.

DENDRAL's purpose is to enumerate plausible structures (atom-bond graphs) for organic molecules, given two kinds of information: analytic instrument data from a mass spectrometer and a nuclear magnetic resonance spectrometer; and user-supplied constraints on the answers, derived from any other source of knowledge (instrumental or contextual) available to the user.

Chemical structures are represented as node-link graphs of atoms (nodes) and bonds (links). Constraints on search are represented as subgraphs (atomic configurations) to be denied or preferred. The empirical theory of mass spectrometry is represented by a set of rules of the general form:

Situation:  particular atomic
            configuration (subgraph)

            probability, P, of occurring

Action:  fragmentation of the
         particular configuration
         (breaking links)

Rules of this form are natural and expressive to mass spectrometrists.

*Sketch of method.* DENDRAL's inference procedure is a heuristic search that takes place in three stages, without feedback: plan-generate-test.

''Generate'' (a program called CONGEN) is a generation process for plausible structures. Its foundation is a combinatorial algorithm (with mathematically proven properties of completeness and nonredundant generation) that can pro-duce all the topologically legal candidate structures. Constraints supplied by the user or by the "PLAN" process prune and steer the generation to produce the plausible set (that is, those which satisfy the constraints) and not the enormous legal set.

"Test" refines the evaluation of plausibility, discarding less worthy candi-dates and rank-ordering the remainder for examination by the user. "Test" first produces a "predicted" set of instrument data for each plausible candidate, using the rules described. It then evaluates the worth of each candidate by comparing its predicted data with the actual input data. The evaluation is based on heuristic criteria of goodness-of-fit. Thus, "test" selects the "best" explana-tions of the data.

"Plan" produces direct (that is, not chained) inference about likely substruc-tures in the molecule from patterns in the data, which are indicative of the presence of the substructure. (Patterns in the data trigger the lefthand sides of substructure rules.) Although it is composed of many atoms whose interconnec-tions are given, the substructure can be manipulated as atom-like by "generate." Aggregating many units entering into a combinatorial process into fewer higher-level units reduces the size of the combinatorial search space. "Plan" sets up the search space so as to be relevant to the input data. "Generate" is the inference tactician; "plan" is the inference strategist. There is a separate "plan" package for each type of instrument data, but each package passes substructures (sub-graphs) to "generate." Thus there is a uniform interface between "plan" and "generate." User-supplied constraints enter this interface, directly or from user-assist packages, in the form of substructures.

*Sources of knowledge.* The various sources of knowledge used by the DE-NDRAL system are:

Valences (legal connections of atoms), stable and unstable configurations of atoms, rules for mass spectrometry fragmentations, rules for nuclear magnetic resonance (NMR) shifts; expert's rules for planning and evaluation, and user-supplied constraints (contextual).

*Results.* DENDRAL's structure-elucidation abilities are, paradoxically, both very general and very narrow. In general, DENDRAL handles all molecules, cyclic and tree-like. In pure structure elucidation under constraints (without instrument data), CONGEN is unrivaled by human performance. In structure elucidation with instrument data, DENDRAL's performance rivals expert human performance only for a small number of molecular families for which the pro-gram has been given specialist's knowledge, namely, the families of interest to DENDRAL's chemist collaborators. Within these areas of knowledge-intensive specializations, DENDRAL's performance is usually not only much faster but also more accurate than expert human performance.

This description of DENDRAL's performance summarizes thousands of runs on problems of interest to experts, their colleagues, and their students. The results obtained, along with the knowledge that had to be given to DENDRAL to obtain them, are published there, under a series title, "Application of Artificial Intelligence for Chemical Inference (Buchanan et al., 1976).

The DENDRAL system is in everyday use by Stanford chemists, their collaborators at other universities, and by collaborating or otherwise interested chemists in industry. Users outside Stanford access the system over a commercial computer-communications network. The problems they are solving are often difficult and novel. The British government supported a technology-transfer effort that made DENDRAL available to industrial user communities in the U.K.

*META-DENDRAL.* More recently, DENDRAL has been expanded by the addition of META-DENDRAL, a system for automatically inferring rules of fragmentation of molecules in a mass spectrometer for possible later use by the DENDRAL system. META-DENDRAL's rule formation task is done using heuristic search techniques of the type described earlier.

META-DENDRAL produces rule sets that rival in quality those produced by the system's collaborating experts. In some tests, META-DENDRAL recreated rule sets that had been previously acquired from experts during the DENDRAL project. In a more stringent test involving members of a family of complex ringed molecules for which the mass spectral theory had not been completely worked out by chemists, META-DENDRAL discovered rule sets for each subfamily. The rules were judged by experts to be excellent, and a paper describing them was recently published in a major journal (Buchanan et al., 1976).

## Applications to Medicine

Application to medicine has received considerable support from the Biotechnology Resources Program of the U.S. National Institutes of Health, which provides shared computer resources to the AIM (Artificial Intelligence in Medicine) community. One of the themes that unites the AIM researchers is that they consider their work to involve what has become known as "knowledge engineering." This refers generally to the "art of bringing the principles and tools of AI research to bear on the difficult applications problems requiring experts' knowledge for their solution." This paradigm has even been viewed as a useful way to understand intelligence in general—that is, as a question of how to represent large amounts of knowledge in a way that permits its effective use whenever a problem or action calls for it. Some of the earliest systems which took this approach were able to achieve very high levels of performance (so-called expert systems) in limited but real-world task environments. We give a sample of just three such systems below.

## Medical Diagnosis: MYCIN, TEIRESIAS

The MYCIN performance task is a diagnosis of blood infections and meningitis infections and the recommendation of drug treatment. MYCIN conducts a consultation (in English) with a physician-user about a patient case, constructing lines-of-reasoning leading to the diagnosis and treatment plan. (See the introduction to this chapter).

MYCIN's rules are of the form: IF ⟨conjunctive clauses⟩ THEN ⟨implication⟩.

TEIRESIAS is a generalization of MYCIN beyond medical diagnosis applications. Its knowledge-acquisition task can be described as follows:

In the context of a particular consultation, confront the expert with a diagnosis with which he does not agree. Lead him systematically back through the line-of-reasoning that produced the diagnosis to the point at which he indicates the analysis went awry. Interact with the expert to modify offending rules or to acquire new rules. Rerun the consultation, to test the solution and gain the expert's concurrence.

TEIRESIAS allows the representation of MYCIN-like rules governing the use of other rules, that is, rule-based strategies. An example follows.

> METARULE 2
> IF:
> (1)  the patient is a compromised host, and
> (2)  there are rules which mention pseudomonas in their premise
> (3)  there are rules which mention klebsiellas in their premises
> THEN:
> There is suggestive evidence (.4) that the former should be done before the latter.

MYCIN employs a generation-and-test procedure of the sort mentioned earlier. The generation of steps in the line-of-reasoning is accomplished by backward chaining of the rules. An IF-side clause is either immediately true or false (as determined by patient or test data entered by the physician during the consultation), or it is to be decided by generating subgoals. Thus, "test" is interleaved with "generation" and serves to weed out incorrect lines-of-reasoning.

Each rule supplied by an expert has associated with it a "degree of certainty" representing the expert's confidence in the validity of the rule (a number from 1 to 10). MYCIN uses a particular ad hoc but simple model of inexact reasoning to cumulate the degrees of certainty of the rules used in an inference chain.

It follows that there may be a number of "somewhat true" lines-of-reasoning—some indicating one diagnosis, some indicating another. All (above a threshold) are used by the system as sources of knowledge indicating plausible lines-of-reasoning.

TEIRESIAS' rule-acquisition process is based on a record of MYCIN's search. Rule acquisition is guided by a set of rule models that dictate the form and indicate the likely content of new rules. Rule models are not given in advance, but are inferred from the knowledge base of existing rules.

A sample MYCIN/TEIRESIAS run is given in the introduction to this chapter. Note that the system has an "explanation" facility whereby it informs the user of its rationale. This has proved to be a crucial feature for user acceptance, since it enables experts to verify how certain conclusions were reached and why others were ruled out.

In preliminary evaluation, a panel of experts judged the system's performance along a number of dimensions and found that in 90 percent of the cases submitted, the decisions made by the system were at least as good as those which the majority of the judges would have made.

### Internal Medicine: INTERNIST

INTERNIST is a diagnostic problem-solving system for problems in internal medicine (Pople, n.d.). Although exact performance figures are not available, it is considered to be in the "expert" category.

In internal medicine the more traditional approaches to computer-based medical diagnosis, such as pattern recognition, linear discriminant analysis, and statistical decision theory cannot be directly applied. These methods assume an a priori specification of the full range of diagnostic categories into which individual patients are to be classified, an assumption that cannot be sustained in internal medicine. While the number of distinct disease entities known to a practicing clinician is not that large—estimates range from 2,000 to 10,000—the number of diagnostic categories required to classify patients arbitrarily is substantially larger. The reason for this is that in many cases, especially those requiring diagnostic consultation, patients can present a number of concurrent clinical problems. While certain patterns of co-occurrence of disease are more likely than others, one cannot exclude the possibility of encountering a dozen or more hitherto unrelated disease entities in a given patient. If, for the sake of argument, we assume an upper bound of 10 on the number of concurrent disease processes, the number of diagnostic categories required to classify arbitrary patients is on the order of 10 (Marr, 1976), a respectable number of alternatives, even by AI standards.

This, then, is the problem space in which the specialist in internal medicine operates. Given what, to the untrained observer, might appear to be an indiscriminate collection of findings (signs, symptoms, laboratory results, and so on), with respect to a particular patient, the clinician's first job is to decide which problems must be dealt with, and then to employ whatever problem-solving methods are appropriate in selecting the correct alternative from each problem set.

*The Knowledge Base.* The knowledge base underlying the INTERNIST system is comprised of two types of elements, disease entities and manifestations (for example, history items, symptoms, physical signs, and laboratory data). Within these types of elements, there are also several relationships. At present, there are approximately 400 disease entities encoded in the knowledge base, and over 2,000 manifestations.

Each disease entity has an associated list of manifestations that are known to occur in the disease, which are recorded along with an estimate on a scale of 1 to 5 of their frequency of occurrence. The inverse of this relationship is explicitly recorded in the knowledge base; thus, each manifestation is known to occur, again, with a weighting factor (in this case, on a scale of 0 to 5) that is intended to reflect the strength of association. We call this weight the *evoking strength,* by which we mean that a manifestation is related to each diseases on its "evokes list."

Also recorded is a hierarchy of disease categories, organized primarily around the concept of systems of organs. This hierarchy has at the top level such categories as "liver disease," "lung disease," or "kidney disease," each of which is divided into more specific categories which, in turn, may be further subdivided, until we reach the terminal level that represents individual disease entities. The reason we include this hierarchy in the knowledge base is that it enables us to make hypotheses and draw conclusions from higher-level descriptions of disease processes in cases where the data do not permit more precise judgment.

***Problem-Formation.*** The approach taken by INTERNIST is to focus on one problem at a time, with each successive problem dynamically determined by the facts of the case that are developed up to this point. (The term *problem,* refers to a collection of disease entities, one and only one of which is considered possible in the case being analyzed.) The process is as follows. First, disease entities that can explain any or all of the observed findings are weighed individually and assigned scores which reflect their goodness of fit with the data. In this scoring process the "evoking strength" and "importance" of manifestations explained by a disease are counted in its favor; "frequency" weights count against those disease hypotheses in which the corresponding manifestations are expected, but are not present in the case.

Given a ranked list of disease hypotheses, a problem is then formulated on the basis of the most highly rated of these items, using the following heuristic criterion: two disease entities are considered to be alternatives to each other (hence, part of the same problem definition) if, taken together, they explain no more of the observed findings than are explained by one or the other, separately.

The set of alternatives so determined, with scores within a fixed range of the top-ranked disease hypothesis on the list, are then composed into a problem which becomes the focus of problem-solving attention.

The program then selects questions that will help discriminate among entities in the problem set, reevaluates all diseases evoked (whether in or out of the problem focus) on the basis of new information obtained, and then reformulates the problem focus. Depending on which disease entity emerges as most highly rated on successive iterations of the process, the focus of attention may shift from one problem to another—but at any one time, there is a single problem under active consideration.

One of the great strengths of INTERNIST is its ability to shift the focus of attention from one problem to another, on the basis of newly derived data. This is achieved by the simple expedient of reformulating the problem focus after each round of information-gathering activity. Whenever a problem becomes solved, it is entered in a list of concluded diagnoses; all manifestations explained by that disease are marked "accounted for," and the process recycles until all problems present in the case have been uncovered.

An INTERNIST protocol consists of typing in a set of presenting symptoms and test results, followed by a sequence of problem formulation iterations in which sets of disease entities are considered and rejected. Disregarded or unexplained symptoms are also noted and printed out.

More recent work on the INTERNIST system is being directed at increasing its efficiency by allowing it to consider groups of related problems ("complexes") at one time, rather than in strict serial fashion. This has led investigators to treat the search space as an AND/OR graph, as well as leading back to reconsideration of multiple-node generators in problem-reduction methods employed in various areas of AI (see the section on problem-solving). Thus, the technical problems encountered in extending INTERNIST once again turn out to be basic problems in artificial intelligence.

## Other Diagnosis Systems

In this brief sketch we have not mentioned a number of other high-performance medical systems. For example, the Rutgers CASNET/GLAUCOMA system Weiss, Kulikowski, & Safir, n.d.) is an expert consultant in diagnosis and therapy of glaucomas, which uses a technique related to that used by INTERNIST; it attempts to integrate various diverse sources of glaucoma knowledge through a common "causal net" model of eye functions. The high performance exhibited by these systems, and the large number of common technical problems encountered in their design has led many investigators to conclude that a "knowledge engineering" subdiscipline is emerging with potential for fruitful collaboration. It has become clear, too, that the collaboration required to build expert systems must involve close ties between content-area experts and designers of the computer systems.

## CONCLUSIONS

We have come to the end of our survey of the field of artificial intelligence, which we have avoided defining explicitly, choosing instead to describe some examples. Definitions tend to oversimplify in a way that blurs some of the most important areas to which AI is contributing. Thus, while it is true that AI can be viewed as an attempt to make computers perform complex tasks which hitherto were the sole province of humans, such an endeavor itself entails another important pursuit, one that can easily be overlooked. This is the discovery of ways to describe certain complex tasks in a manner that lends itself to solution by known mechanical symbol processing means. This, in turn, invariably involves us in such issues as how to specify a process which can acquire, organize, and use knowledge. It becomes in a sense, a search for a way to capture the organization of complexity (Simon, 1969).

There is a subtle relationship between a scientific community's understanding of a phenomenon such as intelligence and the technical tools and language it possesses for analyzing and describing the phenomenon. While one part of the AI endeavor is devoted to developing complex symbol-processing algorithms, another part is devoted to the empirical and rational analysis of task domains.

To a large extent, this remark applies to computer science as a whole. For example, the attempt to develop real-time systems for process-control or numerical-analysis algorithms requires a *new kind* of analysis of the applications area, one characterized by the need for computer implementation. What distinguishes artificial intelligence is not only that the tasks to which it is applied are ones which appear to require human intelligence (so does arithmetic!) but also, that these tasks demand the application of certain classes of techniques such as those involving search through a large space of alternatives or the invocation of a large body of knowledge. In addition such tasks are often initially complex and poorly structured or poorly understood. Thus, while AI shares with computer science the goal of developing complex algorithms for new problem domains, its devotion to such theoretically poorly understood tasks as vision, language comprehension, and symbolic mathematics (in which the process, not the rules of inference, are poorly understood) means that it shares a considerable overlap with those empirical sciences (particularly, cognitive psychology) which are also concerned with analyzing these natural phenomena. In fact, when a sufficient level of understanding of the problem domain is reached, we may find that we have solved what could turn out to be strictly mathematical problems (as in the Mathlab system, MACSYMA) or problems in the natural sciences (as with DENDRAL's chemical analysis or some models of human memory), or even primarily computer-system problems such as the development of new high-level languages.

## Diversity

A thorough exposition of the achievements of artificial intelligence, therefore, would describe both technical developments related to computer program design and the developments in particular substantive areas of endeavor, the latter often involving the reformulation and reanalysis of the tasks and methods of approach. Thus many of the symbiotic benefits to application areas can be described only in the highly technical terms of specific fields such as chemistry, medicine, mathematics, electronics, or psychology.

In addition to being limited in the depth of our technical exposition of the contributions of artificial intelligence, we have had to be highly selective in the breadth of the areas covered; we hope the coverage has at least been representative. While many may be disappointed by the omission of one or another important problem area, our excuse is that we have attempted to give a picture of the field as it is perceived by most of its practitioners.

The scope of the field cannot be defined except by the range of phenomena studied by investigators who associate themselves with schools, journals, and conferences identified with artificial intelligence. Thus we have not mentioned a considerable amount of important related work, since it has been identified mainly with other, similar fields. This includes work in pattern recognition and work primarily of a mathematical nature on program synthesis and verification (described in the chapter, "Special Topics," and in other places in this book), work on biological modeling (often classified under *cybernetics*), work in the computer simulation of cognitive processes, which stays close to results in experimental psychology (sometimes referred to collectively as *cognitive science*), closely related work bearing on hardware design (for example, the design of multiprocessor systems such as the C.mmp or hardware interpreters like the LISP machine, "CONS"), or application systems utilizing AI techniques in relation to education (SCHOLAR, SOPHIE, PLATO, and LOGO), or applications to various areas of medicine, business, law, and other information banks. It should be remembered that, because AI is very much a frontier research area, many of its innovations (for example, list processing, time sharing, and character recognition) are no longer associated with artificial intelligence.

## Changing Approaches

Those readers who are familiar with early work in various areas that has merged into artificial intelligence (Feigenbaum & Feldman, 1963) will note that the field has undergone considerable change in the last two decades. Following are some of the more visible changes.

*Perception.* The approach taken to problems of perception differs greatly from the pattern-recognition paradigms prevalent in the first decade of AI. The emphasis is on better understanding of the structure of the perceptual domain, methods which involve problem-solving techniques, and the organization and deployment of large amounts of domain knowledge of various kinds and at various levels in the processing.

*Language comprehension.* The approach to machine comprehension of language, like that of machine comprehension of scenes, has shifted from progressive refinement of ad hoc approximations (which characterized some of the early machine translation work) to development of a better basic understanding of language phenomena (including pragmatics) and the development of technical tools for managing the large amount of relevant knowledge. When the knowledge base becomes large and complex, specialized techniques become essential to the control of its use in creating expectations, disambiguating alternative possibilities, filling in unstated assumptions from the pragmatic context, and making various plausible inferences about the situation and the user's intentions.

*Problem solving.* Problem solving requires one of the basic unifying themes in the AI approach. The emphasis now is less on uniform search methods and more on the considerations mentioned in the preceding two paragraphs. Problem solving involves designing ways of bringing specialized knowledge to bear at every possible point in the problem-solving process, and finding technical solutions to the combinatorial growth of search trees by such techniques as planning, progressive refinement, and generally exploiting knowledge of the structure of the task domain.

*Tools and techniques.* One of the most obvious ways that artificial intelligence has changed in the past 20 years is in the availability of tools, techniques, and experience. It is now possible to quickly put together major AI systems for application areas by making use of such tools as the high-level programming languages developed for AI, new techniques such as those mentioned in this chapter, and the accumulated experience with particular systems. This kind of experience is much more accessible today than ever before, due to more widely available common languages and better arrangements for exchanging information such as that facilitated by computer networks. Today it is commonplace in computer science departments for students to put together, during a one-year course in AI reasonably large systems for language comprehension, scene analysis, or applications to other disciplines.

## Interactions

Interaction among AI research and other disciplines has developed in characteristic ways during the evolution of AI as a field. The relationships have been largely symbiotic. There are by now well-established tools and techniques in AI which transcend particular application areas. When an attempt is made to apply these techniques straightforwardly to areas such as theorem-proving, computer-assisted learning, medical diagnosis, or industrial robotics, it often turns out that major reformulations of problems in the application areas result.

Take, for example, the application of AI to mathematics. Although early heuristic programs for logic and symbolic integration resulted in modest success, they did prompt a new mathematical effort which resulted in powerful analytical tools (for example, the resolution principle in logic and the Risch algorithm in integral calculus). After a period of practical experience with these newer automated systems, using the new analytic techniques, there has been a steady increase in the reintroduction of heuristic methods and a return of AI techniques.

The most powerful automated mathematical systems (such as MACSYMA) are now a blend of AI technique and advanced mathematical algorithms. A similar situation exists in other areas of application of AI such as in applications to medicine, education (for instance, the LOGO project), and psychology; it will likely also be true of the still young subfield of productivity technology.

## Summary

The field of artificial intelligence spans a wide range of goals in several dimensions—from highly practical applications such as automatic detection of pathological conditions in radiograms, computer-aided teaching, and diagnosis systems—to pure research on automatic plan-generation for robot vehicles or natural language text-processing. It touches on problems in fields ranging from psychology, where it provides a methodology for analyzing complex tasks and a formalism for expressing theories of cognitive processing, to computer science, where it provides techniques for implementing novel data and control structures.

Due to the mixed character of the field—combining, as it does, empirical science, mathematics, and engineering—neither its underlying unity nor its achievements are exhibited straightforwardly. While the easiest and most common way of documenting the achievements in the field is to describe the performance of some of the main working systems, such a sketch can often be misleading. *First,* because of the rate of change of ideas in the field, working systems quickly become obsolete. Often—for example, in Winograd's language-comprehension system SHRDLU—these systems are more important to researchers as studies of the limitations of current techniques than as demonstrations of benchmark achievements, although they are not likely to be viewed this way by laymen. *Second,* these system descriptions do not reveal either the cumulative nature of the research that went into their design nor the important general principles embodied in their apparent diversity. Thus, although descriptions of the General Problem Solver, the Stanford Research Institute planning system (STRIPS), and the Heuristic Dendral project might suggest that these systems have little in common, they do represent closely related methods of dealing with the exponential growth of alternatives, using various heuristics to search through a problem-solving space. *Third,* for many AI systems, performance itself is not a suitable measure of achievement. In the "basic science" arm of AI, systems are designed primarily as test beds for new ideas. They represent experiments in which tentative hypotheses are tested and new discoveries are made (Newell & Simon, 1973).

While there are a growing number of important engineering achievements and an accumulating body of techniques and tools, there is also a growing awareness of theoretical unity underlying the great diversity of research in artificial intelligence. This awareness stems from the recognition of fundamental and recurring themes in AI work: the organization and representation of knowledge, and the design of control structures for transforming this knowledge and bringing it to bear on performance.

These issues are seldom tackled in isolation; usually they appear in connection with attempts to solve particular problems. But when certain technical solutions are found in one context (for example, the use of semantic nets, the distinction between demon and servant processes, pattern-directed procedure invocation, augmented transition network parsers, constraint analysis, hierarchical and de-bugging plan-generation, and production system control structures), the frequency with which they are exploited in another context is remarkable. It appears that diverse tasks requiring knowledge-dependent intelligent action have much in common with each other. Even though the particulars of the task domains, the actual relevant knowledge content, may be quite specialized, the principles of information-representation and -handling, as well as formal techniques being developed, have wide applicability.

In this chapter we have outlined a variety of such techniques, but it is difficult to convey the impression of unity with a superficial survey. The structure of a field, especially one that is diverse and rapidly growing is, no doubt, more apparent to those working in it than it is to casual observers. If it turns out to be the case that the diversity of manifestations of "intelligent" tasks masks a basic, underlying, technical unity and if the techniques that are just beginning to be studied are as general as some believe them to be, then the field of artificial intelligence may become the branch of computer science that will produce the most far-reaching impact on science and society.

## REFERENCES

Barrow, H. G., & Tenenbaum, J. M. (1979). Recovering intrinsic scene characteristics from images. In A. Hanson & E. Riseman (Ed.), *Computer vision systems*. New York: Academic Press.

Binford, T. O., et al. (1974–1977). *Exploratory study of computer integrated assembly systems, Reports 1–4*. Stanford University Artificial Intelligence Laboratory.

Bobrow, D., & Winograd, T. (1977). An overview of KRL, a knowledge representation language. *Cognitive Science, 2*(1), 3–46.

Bobrow, D. G., & Raphael, B. (1974, September). New programming languages for artificial intelligence research. *Computer Surveys, 6*(3), 155–174.

Bobrow, D. G., Kaplan, R. M., Kay, M., Norman, D. A., Thompson, H., & Winograd, T. (1977). GUS, a frame-driven dialogue system. *Artificial Intelligence, 8*, 155–173.

Brown, J. S., & Burton, R. (1975). Multiple representations of knowledge for tutorial reasoning. In D. G. Bobrow & A. M. Collins (Eds.), *Representation and understanding* (pp. 311–349). New York: Academic Press.

Buchanan, B. G., et al. (1976). Applications of artificial intelligence for chemical inference XXII: Automatic rule formation in mass spectrometry by means of the meta-DENDRAL program. *Journal of the American Chemical Society, 98*, 6168.

Buchanan, B. G., Sutherland, G., & Feigenbaum, E. A. (1969). Heuristic DENDRAL: A program for generating explanatory hypotheses in organic chemistry. In B. Meltzer & D. Michie (Eds.), *Machine Intelligence 4* (pp. 209–254). New York: Elsevier.

Carbonell, J. R., & Collins, A. M. (1974). Natural semantics in artificial intelligence. *American Journal of Computational Linguistics, 1* (3).

Clowes, M. B. (1971). On seeing things. *Artificial Intelligence, 2,* 79–116.

Davis, R., & Buchanan, B. (1977). Meta-level knowledge: Overview and applications. *Proceedings of the Fifth International Joint Conference on Artificial Intelligence,* 920–977.

Davis, R., Buchanan, B. G., & Shortliffe, E. (1977). Production rules as a representation for a knowledge-based consultation program. *Artificial Intelligence, 8,* 14–45.

Dobrotin, B., & Lewis, R. (1977). A practical manipulation system. In *Proceedings of the Fifth International Joint Conference on Artificial Intelligence* (pp. 723–732). Dept. of Computer Science, Carnegie-Mellon University, Pittsburgh, PA.

Elcock, E. W., McGregor, J. J., & Murray, A. M. (1972). Data directed control and operating systems. *Computer Journal, 15,* 125–129.

Feigenbaum, E. A. (1977). The art of artificial intelligence, In *Proceedings of the Fifth International Joint Conference on Artificial Intelligence* (pp. 1014–1029). Dept. of Computer Science, Carnegie-Mellon University, Pittsburgh, PA.

Feigenbaum, E. A., & Feldman, J. (1963). *Computers and thought.* New York: McGraw-Hill.

Fikes, R. (1970). REF-ARF: A system for solving problems stated as procedures. *Artificial Intelligence, 1.*

Fikes, R. E., & Nilsson, N. J. (1971). STRIPS: A new approach to the application of theorem proving in problem solving. *Artificial Intelligence, 2,* 189–208.

Guzman, A. (1968). Decomposition of a visual scene into three-dimensional bodies. *Proceedings of the Fall Joint Computer Conference,* 291–304.

Hendrix, G. G. (1977). Human engineering for applied natural language processing. In *Proceedings of the Fifth International Joint Conference on Artificial Intelligence.* Dept. of Computer Science, Carnegie-Mellon University, Pittsburgh, PA.

Hendrix, G. G. (1979). Encoding knowledge in partitioned networks. In N. V. Findler (Ed.), *Associative networks—The representation and use of knowledge in computers.* New York: Academic Press.

Horn, B. K. P. (1975). A problem for computer vision: Orienting integrated circuit chips for lead bonding. *Computer Graphics and Image Processing, 4,* 294–303.

Huffman, D. A. (1971). Impossible objects as nonsense sentences. In B. Meltzer & D. Michie (Eds.), *Machine Intelligence 6* (pp. 295–323). Edinburgh, Scotland: Edinburgh University Press.

Kaplan, R. (1973). A general syntactic processor. In R. Rustin (Ed.), *Natural language processing.* New York: Algorithmics Press.

Kay, M. (1973). The MIND system. In R. Rustin (Ed.), *Natural language processing.* New York: Algorithmics Press.

Lieberman, L. J., & Wesley, M. A. (1975). AUTOPASS: A very high level programming language for mechanical assembler systems. IBM Research Report RC-5599.

Lozano-Perez, T., & Winston, P. H. (1977). LAMA: A language for automatic mechanical assembly. In *Proceedings of the Fifth International Joint Conference on Artificial Intelligence.* Dept. of Computer Science, Carnegie-Mellon University, Pittsburgh, PA.

Marcus, M. P. (1980). *A theory of syntactic recognition for natural language.* Cambridge, MA: MIT Press.

Marr, D. (1976). Early processing of visual information. *Phil Trans. Roy. Soc. B, 275,* 483–524.

Martin. W. A. (1978). Descriptions and the specializations of concepts. MIT Laboratory for Computer Science TM-101.

Minsky, M., & Papert, S. (1969). *Perceptrons.* Cambridge, MA: MIT Press.

Minsky, M. (1975). A framework for representing knowledge. In P. H. Winston (Ed.), *The psychology of computer vision.* New York: McGraw-Hill.

Moore, J., & Newell, A. (1973). How can MERLIN understand? In L. Gregg (Ed.), *Knowledge and cognition.* Hillsdale, NJ: Erlbaum.

Newell, A. (1962). Some problems of basic organization in problem solving programs. In M. C. Yovits, G. T. Jacobi, & G. D. Goldstein (Eds.), *Self organizing systems.* Washington, DC: Spartan.

Newell, A., & Simon, H. A. (1972). *Human problem solving.* Englewood Cliffs, NJ: Prentice-Hall.

Newell, A., Barnett, J., Forgie, J., Green, C., Klatt, D., Lieklidev, J. C. R., Munson, J., Reddy, R., & Woods, W. (1973). *Speech understanding systems.* Amsterdam: North-Holland.

Newell, A., & Simon, H. A. (1973). Computer science as an empirical inquiry: Symbols and search. *Communications of the Association for Computing Machines Comm. ACM, 19*(3), 113–126.

Nilsson, N. J. (1971). *Problem solving methods in artificial intelligence.* New York: McGraw-Hill.

Pople, H. E. (1977). The formation of composite hypotheses in diagnostic problem solving: An exercise in synthetic reasoning In *Proceedings of the Fifth International Joint Conference on Artificial Intelligence* (pp. 1030–1037). Dept. of Computer Science, Carnegie-Mellon University, Pittsburgh, PA.

Pratt, V. R. (1973). A linguistics oriented programming language. *International Joint Conference on Artificial Intelligence,* 372–382. *Proceedings of the Fifth International Joint Conference on Artificial Intelligence, Cambridge.* (1977). Dept. of Computer Science, Carnegie-Mellon University, Pittsburgh, PA.

Pylyshyn, Z. W. (Ed.). (1970). *Perspectives on the computer revolution.* Englewood Cliffs, NJ: Prentice-Hall.

Raphael, B. (1967). SIR: A computer program for semantic information retrieval. In M. Minsky (Ed.), *Semantic information processing* (pp. 33–145). Cambridge, MA: MIT Press.

Reddy, D. R. (Ed.). (1975). *Speech recognition.* New York: Academic Press.

Roberts, L. G. (1965). Machine perception of three-dimensional solids. In J. T. Tippett et al. (Eds.), *Optical and electro-optical information processing.* Cambridge, MA: MIT Press.

Robinson, G. A., & Wos, L. (1969). Paramodulation and theorem-providing in first-order theories with equality. In D. Michie (Ed.), *Machine intelligence.* Edinburgh, Scotland: Edinburgh University Press.

Rosenfeld, A. (1978a). Picture processing: 1977. *Computer Graphics and Image Processing, 7,* 211–242.

Rosenfeld, A. (1978b). Iterative methods and image analysis. *Pattern Recognition, 10,* 181–187.

Sacerdoti, E. (1977). *A structure for plans and behavior.* New York: Elsevier.

Schank, R., & Abelson, R. (1977). *Scripts, plans, goals, and understanding.* Hillsdale, NJ: Erlbaum.

Schank, R. C. (Ed.). (1975). *Conceptual information processing.* Amsterdam: North-Holland.

Shirai, Y. (1973). A context-sensitive line finder for recognition of polyhedra. *Artificial Intelligence, 4,* 95–119.

Shortliffe, E. H. (1976). *Computer based medical consultations: MYCIN.* New York: Elsevier.

Simon, H. A. (1969). *The sciences of the artificial.* Cambridge, MA: MIT Press.

Sridharan, N. S., & Schmidt, C. F. (1978). Knowledge-directed inference in BE-LIEVER. In D. A. Waterman & F. Hayes-Roth (Eds.), *Pattern-directed inference systems.* New York: Academic Press.

Stallman, R. M., & Sussman, G. J. (1977). Forward reasoning and dependency-directed backtracking in a system for computer-aided circuit analysis. *Artificial Intelligence, 9,* 135–196.

Sussman, G. J. (1975). *A computer model of skill acquisition.* New York: Elsevier.

Waltz, D. (1975). Understanding line drawings of scenes with shadows. In P. Winston (Ed.), *The Psychology of computer vision.* New York: McGraw-Hill.

Weiss, S. M., Kulikowski, C. A., & Safir, A. (1977). A model-based consultation system for the long-term management of glaucoma In *Proceedings of the Fifth International Joint Conference on Artificial Intelligence* (pp. 826–832). Dept. of Computer Science, Carnegie-Mellon University, Pittsburgh PA.

Winograd, T. (1972). *Understanding natural language.* New York: Academic Press.

Woods, W. A. (1973). Progress in natural language understanding: An application to lunar geology. *AFIPS Converence Proceedings, 42.*

# 10

# Algorithms

## 1960

## B. A. Trakhtenbrot

### NUMERICAL ALGORITHMS

The concept of algorithm is one of the basic concepts of mathematics. By an *algorithm* is meant a list of instructions specifying a sequence of operations which will give the answer to any problem of a given type. Of course, this is not a precise mathematical definition of the term, but it gives the sense of such a definition. It reflects the concept of algorithm which arose naturally and has been used in mathematics since ancient times.

The simplest algorithms are the rules for performing the four arithmetic operations on numbers written in decimal form. (The term "algorithm" comes from the name of a medieval Uzbek mathematician, al-Khowārizmī, who gave such rules as early as the ninth century.) For example, the addition of two multi-digit numbers consists of a series of elementary operations, each of which involves only two digits (one of which may be a stroke to denote a one carried from the previous step). These operations are of two types: (a) writing down the sum of corresponding digits; (b) marking the carrying of a one to the left. The instructions give the proper order for performing these operations (from right to left). The elementary operations are purely formal in that they can be carried out automatically, using an addition table which can be written down once and for all without reference to any particular problem.

The situation is analogous for the other three arithmetic operations, for the extraction of square roots, etc. The formal character of the corresponding instructions (algorithms) is readily apparent, especially in the procedure for extracting square roots.

### The Euclidean Algorithm

As a further example we shall consider the *Euclidean algorithm* for solving all problems of the following type.

*Given two positive integers a and b, find their greatest common divisor.*

Obviously, there are as many different problems of this type as there are different pairs of positive integers $a$ and $b$. Any of these problems can be solved by constructing a descending sequence of numbers, the first of which is the larger of the two given numbers, the second the smaller. The third number is the remainder from dividing the first by the second; the fourth number is the remainder from dividing the second by the third, and so on. This process is repeated until one of the divisions leaves no remainder. The divisor in this last division is then the required number.

Since division can be reduced to repeated subtraction, the algorithm for solving any such problem can be put in the form of the following list of instructions.

*Instruction 1.* Consider the pair of numbers $a$, $b$. Proceed to the next instruction.

*Instruction 2.* Compare the two numbers under consideration (that is, determine whether the first equals, is less than, or is greater than the second). Proceed to the next instruction.

*Instruction 3.* If the numbers are equal, then each of them is the required result; the calculation stops. If not, proceed to the next instruction.

*Instruction 4.* If the first number is smaller than the second, interchange them and proceed to the next instruction.

*Instruction 5.* Subtract the second number from the first and replace the two numbers under consideration by the subtrahend and the remainder, respectively. Proceed to Instruction 2.

Thus, after carrying out all five instructions we return again to the second instruction, then the third, then the fourth, then the fifth, then back once more to the second, third, etc., until the condition given in Instruction 3 is met, that is, until the two numbers under consideration are equal. When that happens the problem is solved and computation stops.

While it is true that algorithms are not always presented with such pedantic formality, there is no doubt in anyone's mind that it is possible to present any known algorithm in this formal fashion.

In the instructions for the Euclidean algorithm, the basic operations from which the process is constructed are the operations of subtracting, comparing, and interchanging two numbers. It is easy to see that these could be broken down much further; for example, Instruction 5 could be expanded into a separate algorithm for subtracting one number from another. However, since the rules which govern the arithmetic operations in such cases are very simple and familiar, it is unnecessary to describe the algorithm in greater detail.

## Numerical Algorithms

Algorithms based on the use of the four arithmetic operations are called *numerical algorithms*. They play an important role in both elementary and advanced mathematics and are usually given in the form of verbal instructions or various kinds of formulas or schemata. For example, an algorithm for solving a system of two linear equations in two unknowns,

$$\left. \begin{array}{l} a_1x + b_1x = c_1 \\ a_2x + b_2y = c_2 \end{array} \right\}$$

is given by the formulas

$$x = \frac{c_1b_2 - c_2b_1}{a_1b_2 - a_2b_1} \qquad y = \frac{a_1c_2 - a_2c_1}{a_1b_2 - a_2b_1}$$

in which the operations as well as their order are completely specified. The formula give the same chain of operations for all problems of the given type (that is, for any coefficients $a_1$, $a_2$, $b_1$, $b_2$, $c_1$, $c_2$, provided $a_1b_2 - a_2b_1 \neq 0$).

It is interesting to note, however, that generally speaking the number of operations which must be performed in solving a particular problem is not known beforehand; it depends on the particular problem and is discovered only in the course of carrying out the algorithm. This is the case for the Euclidean algorithm, where the number of subtractions required depends upon the particular choice of numbers $a$ and $b$.

Numerical algorithms are widely used, since many other operations can be reduced to the four arithmetic operations. Usually such a reduction does not give an exact answer but does give an answer to any desired accuracy. This is illustrated by the algorithm for taking a square root. By a series of divisions, multiplications, and subtractions, a root can be computed as accurately as desired. In a special branch of mathematics (*numerical analysis*) similar methods are developed for reducing to arithmetic operations more complicated operations such as integration, differentiation, and solving various kinds of equations.

In mathematics, *a class of problems is considered solved when an algorithm for solving them is found.* The discovery of such algorithms is a natural aim of mathematics. For example, algorithms have been found for determining the number (and multiplicity) of roots of an algebraic equation and for calculating the roots to any preassigned degree of accuracy.

If there is no algorithm for solving all problems of a given type, a mathematician may be able to invent a procedure which solves certain problems of that type, although it is inapplicable to other cases.

## Diophantine Equations

As an example of a class of problems for which present-day mathematics does not have an algorithm, let us consider all possible Diophantine equations, that is, equations of the form

$$P = 0$$

where $P$ is a polynomial with integral coefficients for which integral solutions are to be sought.[1] Examples of such equations are

$$x^2 + y^2 - z^2 = 0$$
$$6x^{18} - x + 3 = 0$$

The first is an equation in three unknowns, and the second is an equation in one unknown. (In general, we may consider equations in any number of unknowns.) Thus, the first equation above has the integral solution

$$x = 3 \quad y = 4 \quad z = 5$$

But the second has no integral solutions, since it is easily shown that for any integer $x$,

$$6x^{18} > x - 3$$

In 1901, at an international mathematical congress in Paris, the prominent German mathematician David Hilbert presented a list of twenty unsolved problems and directed the attention of the mathematical community to the importance of solving them. Among these was the following (Hilbert's Tenth Problem): *Find an algorithm for determining whether any given Diophantine equation has an integral solution.*

For the particular case of Diophantine equations is one unknown, such an algorithm is known. If an equation

$$a_n x^n + a_{n-1} x^{n-1} + \ldots + a_1 x + a_0 = 0$$

with integral coefficients has an integral solution $x_0$, then $a_0$ is divisible by $x_0$. This suggests the following algorithm:

1.   Find all divisors of the number $a_0$ (there are only a finite number of them, and there is an algorithm for finding all of them).

2.   Substitute each of these in turn into the left-hand side of the equation and calculate the resulting value.

3.   If any of the divisors gives a value of zero for the left side, then this divisor is a root of the equation; if none of the divisors gives the value zero, then the equation has no integral roots.

Hilbert's problem has been and continues to be worked on by many prominent mathematicians, but for the general case with two or more unknowns the re-

---

[1]Other definitions of Diophantine equations are sometimes given.

quired algorithm has not yet been found. Furthermore, it now appears very likely that such an algorithm will never be found. . . .

From the examples given so far it is apparent that numerical algorithms (and indeed, algorithms in general) possess the following characteristics:

*The deterministic nature of algorithms.* An algorithm must be given in the form of a finite list of instructions giving the exact procedure to be followed at each step of the calculation. Thus, the calculation does not depend on the calculator; it is a deterministic process which can be repeated successfully at any time and by anyone.

*The generality of algorithms.* An algorithm is a *single* list of instructions defining a calculation which may be carried out on *any* initial data and which in each case gives the correct result. In other words, an algorithm tells how to solve not just one particular problem, but a whole class of similar problems.

## ALGORITHMS FOR GAMES

The examples considered in the preceding section were taken from arithmetic, algebra, and number theory. They are quite typical of the problems of those branches of mathematics and of classical mathematics in general. In this and subsequent sections we shall analyze two classes of problems which have a somewhat different character; it would be more proper to call them *logical* rather than mathematical problems, although it is hard to draw a sharp line between such *logical* problems and ordinarily *mathematical* problems. But regardless of where this line is drawn or which side of it we are on, our task still remains that of finding an algorithm which gives a single method of solving any problem in some class of similar problems, the only difference being that in the cases considered here the algorithms will no longer be numerical.

### "Eleven Matches" Game

One of many games[2] which depend not on the outcome of chance events but on the ingenuity of the players is the game "eleven matches."

Eleven objects, say matches, are on a table. The first player picks up one, two, or three of the matches. Then the second player picks up one, two, or three of the remaining matches. Then it is again the first player's turn to pick up one,

---

[2]Translators' Note: The word "game" is used in two senses, as illustrated by the examples "Chess is a fascinating *game*" and "I played four *games* of chess today." As is customary in American writings in the theory of games, the word "game" is reserved for the first of these uses and the word "play" is used in the second sense. An individual decision made by a player during a play of a game is called a *move* of that play.

two, or three matches. The players keep taking turns until there are no more matches. The player who is forced to pick up the last match is the *loser*. Is there any scheme by which A, the player who has the first turn, can always force his opponent B to pick up the last match?

An analysis of the game shows that A can force B to pick up the last match if he follows the following instructions:

1. *First move.* A picks up two matches.
2. *Subsequent moves.* If B picks up $l$ matches ($l \leq 3$) on his last move, then A picks up 4—$l$ matches.

It can be shown that this list of instructions is complete in the sense that regardless of what his opponent does, the list always specifies a unique move which A can make.

Such a complete list of instructions is called a *strategy* in the theory of games. If player A must necessarily win whenever he employs some strategy, it is called a *winning strategy for A*.

The strategy given for A is in fact a winning strategy, since it enables A to win regardless of what B does. This is illustrated in the following two examples:

| A | B | A | B | A | B | | A | B | A | B | A | B |
|---|---|---|---|---|---|---|---|---|---|---|---|---|
| 2 | 2 | 2 | 1 | 3 | 1 | | 2 | 3 | 1 | 1 | 2 | 1 |

Furthermore, it can be proved that if A were to pick either one or three matches on the first move, then there would be a strategy which B could use so as to be sure of winning.

### "Even Wins" Games

Let us now consider the game "Even wins." The game starts with twenty-seven matches on a table. The players alternatively pick up from one to four of the matches. The winner is the one who has an even number of matches when all the matches have been picked up.

The following is a winning strategy for A, the player who moves first:

1. *First move.* A picks up two matches.

2. *Subsequent moves when B, the other player, has an even number of matches.* Let $r$ be the remainder obtained upon dividing the number of matches still on the table by six. If $r = 2, 3, 4$, or 5, then A takes (respectively) one, two, three, or four matches.

3. *Subsequent moves when B has an odd number of matches.* If $r = 0, 1, 2$, or 3 and there are at least four matches on the table, then A takes (respectively) one, two, three, or four matches. If $r = 4$, then A takes four matches. If there are one or three matches on the table, then A takes them all.

For example, consider the following play, in which A wins by employing this strategy:

```
A  B  A  B  A  B  A  B  A  B  A  B
2  1  1  3  1  3  4  1  4  2  4  1
```

As in the case of the preceding game, we forego a description of the process by which we find a winning strategy for A and confine ourselves simply to presenting one such strategy. Note that the ideas depend greatly on the details of the game in question and demand considerable ingenuity and resourcefulness.

## The Tree of a Game

Our immediate goal consists in finding an algorithm which will give a "best" strategy for every game in a fairly large class. To avoid formal complexities, instead of giving exact definitions of the notions used, we shall sometimes merely explain them and illustrate them by giving examples.

We first note the following properties of the two games described:

1.  The game is played by two players who alternately take turns at making a move.

2.  The game ends with exactly one of two possible outcomes: (*a*) either A, the player who moves first, wins (this outcome is denoted below by " + "), or (*b*) the other player, B, wins (denoted by " − ").

3.  Each move consists of a *choice by the player* of one of a set of admissible moves (note that the choice is a decision by the player, rather than the outcome of some chance event such as throwing dice).

4.  At any point in the game both players have full information as to what moves have already been made and what moves can be made.

5.  There is an upper limit to the number of moves in a play.

In what follows we shall first assume that all the games in question possess properties 1–5.

It is an obvious and trivial fact that the players cannot both simultaneously have a winning strategy. What is less obvious is that in every game there is a winning strategy for one of the players. Before turning to the proof of this assertion we shall show how a game can be given a convenient graphical representation in the form of a *tree*.

The tree corresponding to the following game (a simplified form of the "eleven matches" game) is illustrated in Figure 10-1: There are six matches on a table; each player in turn picks up one or two matches. The loser is the one who picks up the last match.

The *vertices* of the tree represent the various situations which can occur in a

**Figure 10-1.**

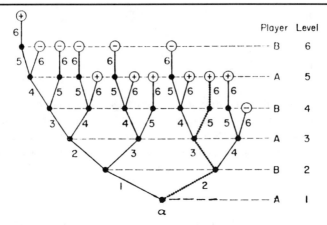

play of the game. The *branches* emanating from a vertex represent the possible choices which the player can make.

In our example there are two possibilities for each move (except the last). For definiteness we let the left branch from any vertex correspond to picking up one match and the right branch to picking up two matches. A play of the game corresponds to a broken line joining the bottom vertex $\alpha$ of the tree (the *base* of the tree) to an *end vertex* (that is, a vertex from which no branches emanate). The outcome of the play is marked at each end vertex.

In Figure 10-1 each branch is marked with the total number of matches which have been picked up at that stage of the play. The hatched line represents the play

```
A B A B
2 1 2 1
```

in which A wins.

We assign a *level* (see Figure 10-1) to each vertex other than an end vertex. The highest level occurring in a tree is called the *order* of the tree; it equals the maximum length of a play of the given game (property 5 thus asserts that all games under consideration have a finite order). The vertices of odd level correspond to situations in which it is A's move and those of even level to situations in which it is B's move.

So far we have considered the tree only as some sort of graphical picture of a game whose rules were given beforehand in some other form. However, nothing prevents us from taking a tree as the definition of a game. For example, Figure 10-2(a) defines a game in which every play consists of exactly two moves: A starts by making one of three possible moves, and then B makes one of two possible moves. In this game there is only one possible play in which A wins (the

**Figure 10-2.**

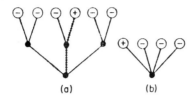

(a)                    (b)

**Figure 10-3.**

(a)  ⊕                        (b)  ①

hatched broken line). A tree of Figure 10-2(b) defines a game which is played in a single move. For various reasons it will also be useful to speak of "games" of no moves as illustrated in Fig. 10-3(a) and 3(b). In these "games" neither player does anything; one is just automatically declared the winner.

Every vertex (not an end vertex) can be regarded as the base of a "subtree" of lower order, which itself corresponds to some game.

The representation of a game by means of a tree allows one to represent any strategy for A graphically as a system of arrows joining vertices of odd level to vertices of the next higher (even) level. To represent a strategy, a system of arrows must possess the properties:

1.   Not more than one arrow starts at any vertex (that is, a strategy for player A must uniquely determine his choice in any given situation).

2.   If there is an arrow leading to a vertex $\gamma$ (of even level), then any adjacent vertex on the next higher level must be the origin of an arrow (Figure 10-4). This condition guarantees that the strategy will give a move for A, regardless of what B does. A strategy for B is defined similarly.

The strategy for A in the game of "six matches" in which A always picks exactly one match is illustrated in Figure 10-5. This strategy yields two plays in which A loses and two in which he wins.

### Algorithm for a Winning Strategy

THEOREM. *In any game satisfying properties 1–5, there is a winning strategy for one of the players.*

Let us illustrate the process with the "six matches" game (Figure 10-6). First, going from the top of the diagram to the bottom, we mark each vertex with a plus sign or minus sign, depending on whether A or B has a winning strategy for the subgame with that vertex as base.

The single nonend vertex of level 6 must be marked with a plus sign. Now

**Figure 10-4.**

**Figure 10-5.**

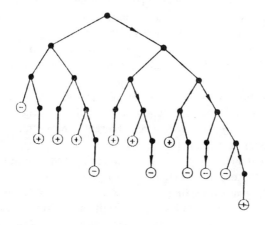

**Figure 10-6.**

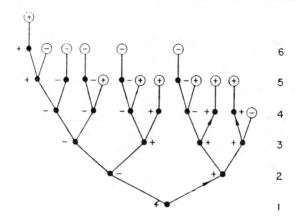

consider the vertices of level 5 from left to right. Recall that it is A's move on this level. It is clear that the leftmost vertex must be marked with a plus sign, since the only adjacent vertex on level 6 is marked with a plus sign. The remaining nonend vertices on level 5 must be marked with minus signs. Among the vertices of level 4 (where it is B's move) we find four minus vertices, namely those adjacent to a minus vertex on level 5, and three plus vertices.

Continuing this process we arrive at level 1, whose single vertex (the base of the tree) must be assigned a plus sign. Thus, A has a winning strategy. We now insert arrows, going from the bottom of the diagram to the top. From the base we draw an arrow to a plus vertex on level 2 (in our example there is only one such vertex). From each vertex on level 3 which is adjacent to the arrowhead we draw an arrow joining it to a plus vertex on level 4. In our example, we now have a complete strategy, and the process ends here (Figure 10-6). As can be seen from the figure, only two plays are possible when A employs this strategy, and A wins in both.

We observe now that the theorem in this section and the algorithm on which it is based can be generalized to take in *the case where properties 1 and 2 of section 6 are not satisfied* (that is, to a game in which only properties 3, 4, 5 hold). For example, we can consider games between two players A and B in which besides A or B winning it is also possible for the game to end in a tie (for example, tick-tack-toe). Here it may turn out that neither player has a winning strategy; in this case the algorithm will yield for each player a strategy which assures him of at least a tie (or, if the opponent makes an unwise move, even a win).

On the other hand, the game of chess fails to satisfy property 5. Nevertheless, by adding the new rule that a game of, say, 40 moves shall be declared a tie, we obtain a game which does possess properties 3, 4, and 5. Thus, there is a strategy which will assure one of the players of at least a tie. To find it, it is sufficient to construct the tree for chess with a 40-move limit and use the above procedure to find an optimum strategy. If it turns out that there is a winning strategy for white (player A), then the game is predetermined in white's favor, provided that he follows this strategy strictly. Similarly, the outcome of the game would also be predetermined if black had a winning strategy or if both players had a tying strategy. Thus, the application to chess of the algorithm considered above must lead to a complete analysis of the game such as we were able to make for the "six matches" game.

Why does chess, nonetheless, remain a game which demands great skill and ingenuity? Here we have encountered the *practical infeasibility* of the process prescribed by the algorithm. Twenty branches (one for each of the possible first moves for white) emanate from the base of the tree for chess. The number of branches from each of the higher-level vertices is also generally very large. The order of the tree is, thus, very large. Nevertheless, we must give an affirmative answer to the question of whether we have an exact list of instructions which enables us to find the optimum strategy for any game of the class under consideration (in a finite number of steps, of course). Thus, the method prescribed by this list of instructions is *potentially feasible,* but not *practically feasible,* because of the large number of operations required.

Just how practical it is to apply the preceding method to a given game depends on the complexity of the game, the speed at which we can perform the operations involved, and the amount of time we are willing to spend on it. We are, of course, interested chiefly in processes which are *practically feasible.* However, there is no precise mathematical criterion for distinguishing between practical and impractical processes. Practicality depends on the means available for computation, and this can change, for example, with the development of technology. Thus, with the advent of the high-speed computing machine, many hitherto infeasible processes have become realizable in practice.

However cumbersome the algorithm considered above may be, its existence is a noteworthy fact. For up to now *no algorithm whatever* has been found for Hilbert's problem on Diophantine equations! Meanwhile, the discovery of an algorithm, even a cumbersome one, can give hope that it may be simplified or that a more convenient algorithm may be constructed.

By virtue of the above considerations, whenever we speak of a computational process or, in general, of a process prescribed by some algorithm, we shall always mean simply a process which would give the desired result were it carried out, even if present computational methods are not sufficient to do this in practice. . . .

## THE NEED FOR A MORE PRECISE DEFINITION OF "ALGORITHM"

### The Existence of Algorithms

Our previous discussion shows the strong connection which exists between algorithms and automatic computing machines. Obviously, any process which can be performed by a machine can be written as an algorithm. Conversely, all algorithms which have so far been constructed, as well as those which may be expected in the present state of science, can in principle be performed by machine.

The last statement requires some clarification. As we have already seen, the actual application of an algorithm may turn out to be very lengthy, and the job of recording all of the information involved may be enormous. On the other hand, the memory units of machines have a limited capacity (since the number of memory cells is finite and the capacity of each cell is limited). Therefore, it may turn out to be impossible to execute an algorithm under existing conditions.

This can be illustrated by the Euclidean algorithm. The very simple problem of finding the greatest common divisor of two numbers cannot be solved by hand if it requires more paper and ink than is available. Similarly, a problem will not be solvable by machine if it requires more memory space than there is in the machine.

In such cases we say that an algorithm is *potentially realizable* if it leads to the required result in a finite number of steps (even though this number may be very large). In other words, it would be possible to use the algorithm in a machine which had an unlimited memory capacity.

The connection between the idea of an algorithm and the idea of an automatic machine with a memory of infinite capacity leads to a clearer understanding of the nature of each. However, for all of our emphasis on their connection, we still have not defined either of these ideas precisely. An exact mathematical definition of the notion of algorithms (and, at the same time, of automatic computing machines) was not produced until the 1930s. Why, through the course of many centuries, have mathematicians tolerated without any particular qualms an unclear notion of algorithms? Why is it that only recently has an acute need for a definition sufficiently exact for mathematical discussion arisen?

Earlier, the term "algorithm" occurred in mathematics only in connection with concrete algorithms, where *an assertion of the existence of an algorithm was always accompanied by a description of such an algorithm.* Under these conditions it was necessary to show only that the system of formal instructions, when applied to any data, in fact led automatically to the desired result. Thus, the need for a precise definition of the notion of algorithm never arose, although every mathematician had a working idea of what the term meant. However, in the course of mathematical progress, facts began to accumulate which radically changed this situation. The motive force was the natural desire of mathematicians to construct increasingly powerful algorithms for solving increasingly general types of problems.

Recall the algorithm for finding square roots. We might wish to generalize this problem: to construct an algorithm for finding the root of any degree of any given number. It is natural to expect that such an algorithm will be more difficult to construct, but the prospect of having it is attractive. We may go even further. Finding the $n$th root of a number $a$ means solving the equation

$$x^n - a = 0$$

(finding the roots of the equation). We can formulate the still more general problem:

*Construct an algorithm for finding all roots of any equation of the form*

$$a_n x^n + a_{n-1} x^{n-1} + \ldots + a_1 x + a_0 = 0 \; (*)$$

*where $n$ is an arbitrary positive integer.*[3]

---

[3]More precisely, for any integer $k$, find a decimal approximation to the roots which is correct to within $1/10^k$.

The construction of such an algorithm is still more difficult. In fact, the basic content of the theory of equations amounts to the construction of just this algorithm; it is of the greatest importance.

## The Deducibility Problem

The examples given show the natural striving of mathematicians to find increasingly powerful algorithms to solve increasingly general types of problems. Of course, the example of solving all equations of the form (*) does not represent the limit to which one might go. If we want to push this desire for increasingly general algorithms to the extreme, we must inevitably consider this problem: *Construct an algorithm for solving any mathematical problem.*

This is a problem so general that it might be considered an insolent challenge to mathematics as a whole. Besides this, it can be criticized on the grounds that it is not clear what is meant by "any mathematical problem." At the same time, the great allure of solving such a problem cannot be doubted.

This problem has its own history. The great German mathematician and philosopher Leibniz (1646–1716) dreamed of an all-inclusive method for solving any problem. Although he was unable to find it, Leibniz still thought that the time would come when it would be discovered, and that any argument among mathematicians could then automatically be settled with pencil and paper.

Later, the problem received some refinement in the form of one of the most famous problems of mathematical logic, the *deducibility problem*. Since we do not have room for a complete treatment of the problem, we shall merely sketch its general outlines.

As is well known, the axiomatic method in mathematics consists in deriving all theorems in a given theory by formal logical steps from certain axioms which are accepted without proof. The first of all axiomatic theories was geometry, but in modern mathematics almost all theories are constructed axiomatically. Mathematical logic employs a special "language of formulas" that enables us to write any proposition of a mathematical theory as a uniquely determined formula. . . . we may say that such a formula is a word in a special alphabet containing symbols to denote logical operations such as negation, conjunction, and implication, as well as the usual mathematical symbols, such as parentheses, and letters to denote functions and variables. . . . [This gives us] the possibility of writing the logical derivation of a statement $S$ from a premise R in the form of formal transformations of words. . . . This allows us to speak of a *logical calculus*, with a system of admissible transformations representing elementary acts of logical deduction, from which any logical inference, of arbitrary complexity, may be built. An example of such an admissible transformation is the elimination of two consecutive negations in a formula; thus, "not unproved" may be transformed into "proved." . . .

The question of the logical deductibility of the proposition $S$ from the premise $R$ in a logical calculus becomes the question of the existence of a deductive chain leading from the word representing $R$ to the word representing $S$. The deducibility problem may now be formulated as follows:

*For any two words (formulas) R and S in a logical calculus, determine whether or not there exists a deductive chain from R to S.*

The solution is supposed to be an algorithm for solving any problem of this type (any $R$ and $S$). Such an algorithm would give a general method for solving problems in all mathematical theories which are constructed axiomatically (or rather, in all *finitely axiomatizable* theories). The validity of any statement $S$ in such a theory merely means that it can be deduced from the system of axioms, or, what is the same thing, that it can be deduced from the statement $R$ which asserts that all the axioms hold. Then the application of the algorithm would determine whether or not the proposition $S$ were valid. Moreover, if the proposition $S$ were valid, then we could find a corresponding deductive chain in the logical calculus and from this recover a chain of inference which would prove the proposition. The proposed algorithm would in fact be a single effective method for solving almost all of the mathematical problems which have been formulated and remain unsolved to this day. That is why constructing such an ''all-inclusive algorithm'' and an ''omnipotent machine'' to match it is so appealing a prospect and at the same time so difficult.

Despite the long and persistent efforts of many great men, the difficulties of finding such an algorithm have remained insurmountable. Furthermore, similar difficulties were soon encountered in trying to find algorithms for certain problems of a far less general nature. Among these were Hilbert's problem on Diophantine equations as well as others which will be discussed below.

As a result of many fruitless attempts to construct such algorithms, it became clear that the difficulties involved are basic, and it came to be suspected that *it is not possible to construct an algorithm for every class of problems.*

The assertion that a certain class of problems cannot be solved algorithmically is not simply a statement that no algorithm has yet been discovered. It is the statement that such an algorithm in fact can *never* be discovered, in other words, that no such algorithm can exist. This assertion must be based on some sort of mathematical proof; however, such a proof makes no sense until we have a precise definition of ''algorithm,'' since until then it is not clear what it is we are trying to prove impossible. It is useful to remember at this point that in the history of mathematics there have been other problems for which solutions had been sought in vain for a long time and for which it was only later proved that solutions could not be obtained. Examples are the problem of trisecting the angle and the problem of solving the general fifth-degree equation by radicals.

A method of bisecting an angle using compass and straightedge is known to every schoolboy. The ancient Greeks tried to solve the problem of trisecting an angle using compass and straightedge. It was later proved that trisection of an arbitrary angle by such means is impossible. It is also well known that the solution of a quadratic equation can be written in terms of the coefficients by means of a formula which employs the signs for the arithmetic operations and the radical sign. There are also formulas in radicals, which are extremely complicated, for third- and fourth-degree equations. A search for similar solutions by radicals for equations of degree higher than four was carried on unsuccessfully until the beginning of the nineteenth century, when the following remarkable result was finally established.

> For any $n$ greater than or equal to 5, it is impossible to express the roots of the general $n$th degree equation in terms of its coefficients by means of the arithmetic operations and the operation of extracting roots.

In both these cases the proof of impossibility turned out to be feasible only after there were precise definitions to answer the questions. "What is meant by compass and straightedge construction?" and "What is meant by solving an equation in radicals?" Note that these two definitions gave a more precise meaning to certain special algorithms, namely, the algorithm for solving an equation in radicals (not for the solution of equations in general) and the algorithm for trisecting an angle with compass and straightedge (not for trisecting by arbitrary devices).

## Formulation of a Definition of "Algorithm"

Until recently, there was no precise definition of the concept "algorithm," and therefore the construction of such a definition came to be one of the major problems of modern mathematics. It is very important to point out that the formulation of a definition of "algorithm" (or of any other mathematical definition) must be considered as not merely an arbitrary agreement among mathematicians as to what the meaning of the word "algorithm" should be. The definition has to reflect accurately the substance of those ideas which are actually held, however vaguely, and which have already been illustrated by many examples. With this aim, a series of investigations was undertaken beginning in the 1930s for characterizing all the methods which were actually used in constructing algorithms. The problem was to formulate a definition of the concept of *algorithm* which would be complete not only in form but, more important, in substance. Various workers proceeded from different logical starting points, and because of this, several definitions were proposed. However, it turned out that all of these were equivalent and that they defined the same concept; this was the modern definition of *algorithm*. The fact that all of these apparently different definitions were really essentially the same is quite significant; it indicates that we have a worthwhile definition.

From the point of view of machine mathematics, we are especially interested in *the form of the definition which proceeds from a consideration of the processes performable by machines.* For such a rigorous mathematical definition it is necessary to represent the operation of the machine in the form of some standard scheme, which has as simple a logical structure as possible, but which is sufficiently precise for use in mathematical investigations. This was first done by the English mathematician Turing, who proposed a very general but very simple conception of a computing machine. It should be noted that the Turing machine was first described in 1937, that is, before the construction of modern computing machines. Turing proceeded simply on the general idea of equating the operation of a machine to the work of a human calculator who is following definite instructions. . . .

The distinguishing features of the Turing machine, as compared with . . . electronic machines . . . are the following:

1.   In the Turing machine the reduction of a process to elementary operations is carried, in a certain sense, to its limit. Thus, for example, the operation of addition, which in the electronic machine is considered as a single operation, is broken down further into a chain of simpler operations. This, of course, considerably increases the number of steps in calculations by the machine, but at the same time greatly simplifies the logical structure, a great convenience for theoretical investigations.

2.   In the Turing machine the memory unit is conceived of as a tape, infinitely long in both directions and divided into cells. Of course, no real machine can have an infinite memory, and the Turing machine is in this sense an idealization which reflects the possibility of increasing the memory capacity of any machine. . . .

## The Turing Machine

We now move on to a [description] of a Turing machine.

1. There is a finite set of symbols . . . the so-called *external alphabet,* in which is coded the information fed into the machine, as well as the information which the machine produces. . . .

Each cell can contain at most one symbol. Each piece of information is represented by a finite string of symbols of the external alphabet, not including the empty letter, and is stored in consecutive cells on the tape. The initial information is introduced onto the tape. The machine then begins to operate, and in the course of each of its cycles the initial information is transformed into intermediate information. At the end of each cycle, all the information on the tape makes up the intermediate information at that stage. The initial information can be any finite system of symbols in the external alphabet (any word in this alphabet) distributed among the memory cells in any fashion. However, depending on what initial information $\mathfrak{E}$ was given, there are two possible cases.

a. After a finite number of cycles the machine halts, having received a stop order, and there appears on the tape the representation of some information $\mathfrak{B}$. In this case we say that the machine is *applicable* to the initial information $\mathfrak{E}$ and that b. A stop-order is never received, and the machine never halts. In this case we say that the machine is *inapplicable* to the initial information $\mathfrak{E}\mathfrak{A}it$ hat transformed it into the resulting information $\mathfrak{B}$.

We say that *a machine can solve a given class of problems* if it is applicable to the information representing (in a fixed code) any problem of the class and if it transforms this information into information representing the solution (in the same code).

2. If the contents of a particular cell are needed in the calculation, the machine searches for this cell by examining all of the cells one by one until it finds the right one. This greatly lengthens the process, but it also affords the following convenience: In the instructions of the program, instead of an arbitrary address for the scanned cell, we can limit ourselves to three standard addresses, which are represented by special symbols:

R—scan the next cell to the right
L—scan the next cell to the left
S—scan the same cell again

3. For processing the numerical information contained in the memory unit, [an] electronic machine . . . has an arithmetic unit, which may be in any one of a finite number of states: the addition state, the subtraction state, etc. To carry out any operation in the arithmetic unit, paths must be established for transmitting not only the numbers on which the operation is to be performed but also the signals which set the unit for the proper operation. . . . In the Turing machine, the processing of information is performed by a *logical unit* $\mathfrak{L}$, which also can be in any of a finite number of states. [The logical unit takes as input the symbol on the square being scanned and a symbol representing the state which the unit is in during the current cycle. It produces as output a "transformed" output symbol, a symbol specifying the state the unit is to take on the next cycle, and a symbol ($R$, $L$, or $S$) specifying the action to be performed on the next cycle. These three symbols constitute the "output triple."] It is convenient to represent this function (called the *logical function* of the machine) as a rectangular table, with one column for each state symbol and one row for each symbol of the external alphabet, and having the output triple at the intersection of the row and column of the input pair. We shall call this table the *functional matrix* of the machine. . . .

It is clear that the operation of a Turing machine is completely determined by its functional matrix, so that two Turing machines with the same matrix are indistinguishable as regards what they do.

## The Basic Hypothesis of the Theory of Algorithms

[One gets] the impression that the operation of a Turing machine is like a slow-motion film of the computation required by an algorithm. We would like to know whether functional matrices can be found for other known algorithms given in various ways, for example, as verbal instructions or algebraic formulas. At this stage of our discussion it appears likely that they can. Is this really the case? How general is the concept of Turing machine and Turing functional matrix? Can we say that all algorithms can be represented as functional matrices?

The modern theory of algorithms answers these questions with the following hypothesis.

The basic hypothesis of the theory of algorithms. *All algorithms can be given in the form of functional matrices and executed by the corresponding Turing machines.*

Two questions arise:

1. What is the significance of the hypothesis for the theory of algorithms?
2. What is the basis for the hypothesis?

The basic hypothesis on the one hand speaks of "all algorithms," that is, of the general concept of algorithms, which, as we have emphasized more than once, is not a precise mathematical concept. On the other hand, it speaks of the Turing functional matrix, which is a precise mathematical concept. Its significance is that it clarifies the general but vague concept of "all algorithms" in terms of the more special but completely precise concept of Turing functional matrix. Thus, the theory of algorithms declares the object of its investigations to be all possible Turing functional matrices (Turing machines). It then becomes meaningful to raise such questions as the existence or nonexistence of an algorithm for solving some class of problems. We now understand this to mean the existence or nonexistence of a Turing machine (functional matrix) having the required properties.

Thus, the basic hypothesis justifies the adoption of the basic definition of the modern theory of algorithms, the use of which enables the vague concept of an algorithm to be identified with the precise concept of the functional matrix of a Turing machine.

What is the basis of this important hypothesis? We cannot prove it as we prove a mathematical theorem, since it is a statement about the general concept of algorithms, which is not precisely defined and is, therefore, not a proper object of mathematical discussion.

Our confidence in the validity of the hypothesis is based chiefly on experience. All known algorithms which have been developed over the thousands of years of the history of mathematics can be written in the form of Turing functional matrices. But the hypothesis is not just a statement about algorithms which have been found in the past. It also has the quite different nature of a prediction concerning the future; it says that whenever any instructions are given as an algorithm, no matter what their form or elementary operations, it will be possible to give them as a Turing functional matrix. In this sense the basic hypothesis may be compared to a physical law, for example, the law of the conservation of energy, where the weight of vast experience in the past is judged to be a sufficient basis for predictions of future events. . . .

Within the theory of algorithms itself, the basic hypothesis is not used. That is, in proving theorems in the theory, no reference is made to the basic hypothesis. Thus, a person who did not know of, or did not accept, the hypothesis would have no formal difficulties in the theory. However, he would consider what we have called the *theory of algorithms* as merely the theory of Turing functional matrices, that is, as the *theory of a particular type of algorithm.*

The author personally believes in the validity of the basic hypothesis and in the consequent estimate of the modern theory of algorithms as a *general* theory rather than simply a theory of an arbitrarily selected class of algorithms, namely the ''Turing algorithms.''

# 11
# Computers, Knowledge, and the Human Mind

## 1987

### Zenon W. Pylyshyn

### INTRODUCTION

Anyone who reads newspapers and magazines these days has heard the term "Artificial Intelligence." It inspires awe in the business community and concern or puzzlement in most other places. Discussions of the limits of machine intelligence, though they still occur, have largely been replaced by concern over the social and economic significance of this new technology.

I'm one of those who is awed and impressed by the potential of this field and have devoted some part of my energy to persuading people that it is a positive force. I have done so largely on the grounds of its economic benefits and its potential for making the fruits of computer technology more generally available to the public—for example, to help the overworked physician; to search for oil and minerals and help manage our valuable resources; to explore, mine, and experiment in dangerous environments; to allow the noncomputing public access to vast libraries of important information and even advice and, in the process, give real meaning to the freedom of information act; and last, but not least, to entertain people—for if we do not blow ourselves off this planet, entertainment in its most general sense, including *education*, will surely be the major industry of the future.

These are fruits of the new technology that many of you may be familiar with, at least in a general way. You may also be aware of the many pitfalls that stand between us and their realization, including the military misuse of such work. What I would like to do today is concentrate on another aspect of the new technology—and, to some extent, of technology in general—which has received much less press. I want to concentrate on the *intellectual* significance of the recent developments in computer science, and particularly in artificial intelligence.

I might begin by asking a question that may be in the minds of many of you here today: Why should those of you who do not plan to be computer specialists or who are not the least bit interested in technological wizardry want to know about artificial intelligence? This and many other institutions of higher learning are dedicated to the development of wiser and more sensitive human beings who may, as a result of their education and other experiences, be in a better position to lead a fuller and more meaningful life. I am very much in favor of liberal education. I believe, like many of you, that the broadening of one's sensibilities and the exercise of one's creative potential are top priorities in education. Nonetheless, I also believe that liberally educated people cannot afford to be completely ignorant of technology, or even worse, to be smug about the playful indulgence of the modern technocrats.

There are several reasons why I hold this view. Probably the most obvious is that those who are growing up to be in a position of influence—to be opinion leaders in one way or another—should have some valid understanding of the major forces that are shaping our world. There can be no doubt that computers— and artificial intelligence in particular—will be among those forces in the coming decades. Unlike many other works of science, there is something about the direct relevance of computers to one's intellectual transactions with the world that make it particularly disturbing and disquieting. There is also something about the complexity and opacity of this form of technology that makes it particularly susceptible to misunderstanding and to prejudice. It is the duty of the intellectual to attempt to get a perspective on the nature of this beast before passing sentence on it, as I have frequently seen done.

The second, and more subtle reason that I believe that understanding the nature of computing and artificial intelligence is relevant to a liberal education, is that the ideas of computing, information, and artificial intelligence bring with it changes in one's world view, and in particular to one's view of human nature. Because this may not strike some of you as obvious, I would like to take a moment to reflect on the role of technology in shaping a world view, because this role has not always been adequately recognized.

The process of understanding and of articulating one's tenuous grasp on an evolving picture of nature is not unlike the process of creating a work of art, such as a sculpture. In both cases there are three major elements: the imagination and curiosity of the creator, the nature of the tools available, and the resistance offered by the materials. A sharp knife on soft wood yields a very different result from a massive chisel on granite rock, quite independent of the sculptor's initial intention. Similarly, a brilliant man tackling the world's mysteries with only his eyes, ears, and the concepts with which his native tongue provides him, will have different experiences, and will carve them up differently than will a person with the tools of a technological culture—even though the world may be essentially the same in both cases.

Technology, by which I mean to include not only the design of artifacts, but everything that involves a codified system of methods or *technique*, provides both instrumental tools to help us make observations and calculations, and conceptual tools that help us to see things in new ways. Such conceptual tools may be thought of as imagination prosthetics because they typically extend the range of the conceivable. Conceptual tools dominate periods of intellectual progress. Speaking of the importance of one such set of concepts—that provided by pure mathematics—physicist Freeman Dyson (1964) says,

> One factor that has remained constant through all the twists and turns of the history of physical science is the decisive importance of mathematical imagination . . . For a physicist, mathematics is not just a tool by means of which phenomena may be calculated; it is the main source of concepts and principles by means of which new theories can be created. (p. 99)

Similarly, speaking of the development of new philosophical views, Susanne Langer (1962) put it this way:

> In every age, philosophical thinking exploits some dominant concepts and makes its greatest headway in solving problems conceived in terms of them. The seventeenth- and eighteenth-century philosophers construed knowledge . . . in terms of sense data and their association. Descartes' self examination gave classical psychology *the mind and its contents* as a starting point. . . . Hobbes provided the genetic method of building up complex ideas from simple ones. . . . Pavlov built intellect out of conditioned reflexes and Loeb built life out of tropisms. (p. 54)

I believe that history will record that, around the mid-twentieth century, many classical problems of philosophy and psychology were transformed by a new notion of process: that of a *symbolic,* or *computational* process. Although the foundations for this idea were laid nearly a half-century ago by mathematicians like Alan Turing, Alonzo Church, Kurt Gödel, Steven Kleene, Emil Post, A. A. Markov, and others, it was not until the late 1950s that the availability of digital computers made it possible to begin the transformation that we see today in both artificial intelligence and the closely related field of study called cognitive science (a term used widely in recent years to designate the scientific study of the processes that underly knowing, reasoning, imaging, planning, remembering, perceiving, and the like—the exact boundaries being under constant review).

Although the computer is a logical continuation of the path of technological development that has been going on ever since *homo sapiens* began to make tools, in some ways it is also a radical departure from this path. In this talk I would like to explore the parallel between earlier technological trends and the development of computers. At the same time I will also examine what is *special* about computing. This discussion will lead me to consider what computing has in common with human thought that recommends it as a vehicle both for the understanding and for the exercise of intelligence. In doing this I shall consider three characteristics of this new technology: its capacity to increase the quantity and quality of complexity, its capacity to exhibit very nearly unbounded plasticity of behavior, and its capacity to determine actions on the basis of knowledge of the external world and certain goals related to this knowledge.

## COMPUTERS AND THE QUALITY OF COMPLEXITY

The industrial revolution made technology supreme by giving us mass production based on the two fundamental ideas of *division of labor* and *standardization* (*and, hence, interchangeability*) *of components*. These two are closely related. The products of technology are decomposable into component parts—parts that are independently specifiable in terms of the *function* that they perform, and which can be used in *any* sample of the manufactured product. Because of this, it is possible to have such components designed and manufactured by specialists and then independently assembled at some later date. This idea is important in part because it leads to high productivity. Yet perhaps even more important than the increase in productivity is the fact that the dual principles of division of labor and interchangeability of components make possible a certain kind of *accumulation of complexity* which had never been seen before the twentieth century. Before the widespread adoption of these principles, the overall complexity of a project was limited to what could be conceived in the mind of the master designer (even the great pyramids and the wonderful cathedrals of Europe are no exception). Nowadays, no single person has more than a highly sketchy understanding of the major products of technology.

The two elements, which together may be referred to as the *modularity* of technology, have had an effect on every phase of modern life. Indeed it might be argued that Guttenberg's invention of movable type is an instance of the discovery of just this sort of modularity. In recent times a more self-consciously systematic and structured version of modularity has been developed to help organize large complex projects. Much of the dramatic successes of modern technology can be attributed to the exploitation of this idea. For example, there is very little in the way of new scientific principles or discoveries that went into the contemporary space program. The dramatic achievements in such things as landing a person on the moon is due entirely to the development of means for organizing complexity—for carrying the principles of modularity and division of labor to its extreme.

One of the fundamental characteristics of computer system design is that it makes the idea of the modular and hierarchical organization of complexity into a fundamental prescriptive principle and capitalizes on it to create enormously complex systems—yet systems that are still understandable and even repairable if they should fail to work properly. One way in which computing makes possible an extreme degree of modularity is worth examining because it sheds some light on the nature of the phenomenon of organization of complexity.

The one example I want to sketch relates to the idea of levels or layers of organization. Computer systems are typically designed by first implementing a set of general purpose facilities in hardware, then another independently designed set of facilities which might take the form of an interpreter for a programming language. Such facilities are specifically designed to suppress certain logistical details from the person who is concerned with the design of a system for some particular application. So-called high-level programming languages, such as Basic, Fortran, LISP, and so on, make it possible for a system designer to concentrate on the concerns of the particular task at hand. Such an individual almost never knows in detail how the computer electronically carries out the sequence of commands that he specifies in his design. Similarly, a designer can also use the computer language layer to create a new set of tools, such as a data base management system, which another designer can subsequently use to design still another complex system with no knowledge of how the facilities he is using are realized at the lower level. This deliberate *suppression of detail* is crucial to the orderly growth of complexity, because it allows different designers to each concentrate on a natural class of tasks that share common design principles.

This layering principle is fundamental to computer design and is carried to an extreme in such applications as the setting of standards for certain large-scale cooperative ventures, such as intercomputer communications.[1] The point of this layering is to provide a way to mediate between the diversity of specific machines and forms of information transmission on the one hand, and the need for identical standards on the other. This layering is just the idea of interchangeability of components and division of labor raised to a high art, in response to the enormous complexity of modern technological artifacts. It is the fact that technical objects can be organized in terms of this kind of conceptual layering that makes it possible for people to have sufficient understanding of such devices to operate them, repair them, and indeed even to design them.

This hierarchical style of design is both extremely natural for computing—for reasons having to do with the ease with which computers allow functions to be *composed* from subfunctions—and at the same time is the reason why computer systems can grow to such enormous complexity. This, in turn, is one of the factors that has contributed to the recent successes in artificial intelligence. Researchers now have the tools (i.e., some of the layers) with which to build systems whose complexity is sufficient to begin to produce behavior that we consider intelligent.

Those who remember the good old days of the early 1960s (how recent is the early history of artificial intelligence!) will recognize that programs such as the

---

[1]For example, the International Standards Organization has devised certain standards and codes to be used for communications among machines (the so-called Open Systems Interconnect standards). These standards consist of a set of seven strictly independent layers—each of which can be realized in whatever way is appropriate for any particular computer or communication link, while enabling compatibility at some particular level.

General Problem Solver were a very small fraction of the size of such current AI expert systems as Xcon or Mycin or Internist. This is critical because one of the lessons that has been learned in the past several dozen years is that intelligence arises from the interaction of a very large number of basic parts. In contrast with physics, cognition appears to have few general and powerful laws. Whatever else is required for the exercise of intelligence, it appears that one thing that is required is a large number of transactions on a large knowledge base. To a first approximation, to be intelligent is to know a lot and to be able to access the knowledge when it is appropriate. The commercial expert system Xcon has a representation of some 2,500 elementary facts, and Internist is said to have nearly a hundred times as much. And both of them are admittedly in the class of *idiot savants* that can perform intelligently only over a narrow range of problems. Clearly, in AI, we are dealing with large numbers. Without some general scheme for keeping control of such quantities, the designers of such systems would soon lose their way.

Before I come to my main point, which concerns the role of knowledge in the functioning of artificial intelligence systems, I want to sketch one additional property of computing that distinguishes it from the operations of other complex artifacts. I do this by going back a half-century or so to the origins of some of the ideas that form the theoretical foundations of computer science.

## PLASTICITY OF COMPUTER FUNCTION

Alan Turing was a mathematician interested in exploring the limits of mechanization of mathematics. In the process he had to define the notion of "mechanism" as a fully specifiable, symbol-manipulating device, abstracted from any physical properties. He devised an extremely simple and ingenious design for such a device, which is now referred to as the "Turing Machine." What he discovered was that such an extremely simple device has the remarkable property of being *universal*. This means that one can design a particular Turing machine in such a way that by varying the symbols it reads on its input tape it can be made to behave like *any possible symbol-manipulating machine*. In other words, a universal Turing machine can simulate every conceivable symbol-processing mechanism without changing its basic structure. Because every computer you buy nowadays is a variant of a Turing machine, this result is also true of all our computers—they can be made to carry out *any* formally or mechanistically specifiable function. This is another way of saying what most people know about computers, that they are programmable to carry out almost[2] any function we know how to describe in the right way.

---

[2]The qualification arises here because Turing was also able to prove that there exist uncomputable functions, thereby demonstrating a formal limit of mechanization. The relevance of such a limitation to cognitive science is not clear at the present time.

This extreme plasticity of behavior is one of the reasons why computers have from the very beginning been viewed as artifacts that might be capable of exhibiting intelligence. Those who were not familiar with this basic idea have frequently misunderstood the capacity of machines. For example, the Gestalt psychologist Wolfgang Kohler (1947) viewed machines as too rigid to serve as models of biological or mental activity. The latter, he claimed, are governed by what he called "dynamic factors"—an example of which are self-distributing field effects, such as the effects which cause magnetic fields to be redistributed when we introduce new pieces of metal. He contrasted such dynamic factors with what he called "topographical factors" which are structurally rigid. He says,

> To the degree to which topographical conditions are rigidly given, and not to be changed by dynamic factors, their existence means the exclusion of certain forms of function, and the restriction of the processes to the possibilities compatible with those conditions. . . . This extreme relation between dynamic factors and imposed topographical conditions is almost entirely realized in typical machines . . . we do not construct machines in which dynamic factors are the main determinants of the form of operation. (p. 65)

That *computers* violate this claim is one of their most important and unique characteristics. Their topographic structure is completely rigid, yet they are capable of *maximal* plasticity or variability of function. It is this very property that led Turing (1964) to speculate that computers would be capable in principle of exhibiting intelligent behavior. The combination of extreme plasticity of function, together with an organization that gives rise to the orderly growth of complexity (due to the layering and distribution of labor principles mentioned earlier) make computers a powerful new form of technology. I will come back to the reason for this plasticity of function later. But first I want to introduce what, in my view, is the aspect of computers that establishes them as the most radical departure from the lineal descendants of early *homo sapiens* tools. Roughly speaking, it is the fact that computers, like people, can be made to *act on the content of information they are given*. Because this is not a familiar idea, I shall devote the remainder of my talk to discussing this claim and its ramifications.

## COMPUTING AS KNOWLEDGE-BASED

It is commonplace nowadays to accept computers as a major new medium for the storage, transmission, and transformation of information. It is becoming clear to the public now, as it was not when I first began to teach computer science a number of years ago, that computers are not just lightening-fast calculators, but *information handlers*. Nonetheless, it is not generally appreciated how the information-handling capacity of a computer is different (except for its speed and efficiency) from the information-handling capacity of such devices as books, files, tape recorders, telephones, libraries, television sets, and so on, all of which in some sense store, transmit, process, and transform information. But that it *is* different should be abundantly clear. Computers, unlike books or even television sets, *do* things because of the particular information they contain. Moreover, the nature of the behavior that they exhibit appears to be directly attributable to the *content* of the information they have—or what the information is *about*. This is not true of any of the other information-handling systems we can think of—with the obvious exception of people or other higher organisms.

This observation is fundamental and bears some elaboration. Those who work with computers know that they can be coherently and consistently described as behaving in certain ways *because they know or have representations of certain things*. For example, a programmer might say that the computer predicted a rise in corporate spending at a certain time because it "has an econometric model" and was told the current values of certain parameters, or that it printed a check for so many dollars because it knows what the individual's salary is and what deductions have to be made according to the contract and the income tax law. The programmer might also correctly describe a computer as making a certain chess move by saying that it did so "in order to avoid having its knight captured by the opponent's queen." A more complex computer system, say one which diagnoses infectious diseases (e.g., the MYCIN system—see Shortliffe, 1976), might be described as *inferring* that a patient has a certain infection and *recommending* a particular treatment based on its *knowledge* of symptoms and of the actions of certain drugs. Indeed, the successor to MYCIN (a system called Teriesias) will even *explain* to the physician how it came to its decision by citing certain things it *believes* and certain inferential processes that it carried out.

Are these sorts of descriptions just convenient anthropomorphisms—like saying, for example, that the thermostat believes the room is too cold so it turns on the furnace? It's beginning to look very much like the answer has to be *no*. For one thing, the case of such artifacts as thermostats is easily excluded on the basis of a version of Occam's Razor (known to biologists as de Morgan's canon); *viz,* don't attribute philogenetically higher capacities when lower ones will suffice. In the case of devices such as thermostats, nothing whatever is lost in describing its functioning in physical terms. All its regularities are adequately captured in an electro-mechanical description, with no need to refer to goals, beliefs, knowledge, and so on. In such cases there is no genuine "level" of organization or of functioning beyond the electromechanical. But this is simply *not* the case for higher organisms, and it turns out not to be the case for the kinds of artifacts being designed in artificial intelligence. Such machines exhibit systematic patterns of behavior that could not adequately be captured by describing their physical structure. They must be described as being governed by internal symbolic representations: In other words, their behavior is dependent on the *knowledge* that is encoded in them. Because whenever I say this, people look at me with suspicion, I had better take a few moments to at least hint at why this is so.

## REPRESENTATION-GOVERNED PROCESSES

The regular pattern of behavior exhibited by some systems can only be understood if we assume that aspects of their internal states are representations—that they are physical instantiations or tokens of symbols that stand for something, or that they function as codes for something. This is really a very simple and unproblematic point, though it sometimes strikes some people as a puzzling claim. Here is a simple example to illustrate this point (needless to say, it is not an example of an intelligent system—only of this simple idea of the need to refer to what states represent in giving an explanation of a system's functioning).

Suppose I showed you a black box into which I had inserted an electrode or some other response recorder (as illustrated in Figure 11-1). We need not be concerned with what is in the box. As we observe the box go about its usual function, we discover that the ensuing record exhibits certain regularities. For example, we observe that either individual short pulses or pairs of such short pulses frequently occur in the record, and that when there are both pairs and single pulses (as sometimes happens), the pair appears to regularly precede the single pulse. After observing this pattern for some time, we discover that there are occasional exceptions to this order—but only when the whole pattern is preceded by a pair of long and short pulse sequences. Being scientists, we are most interested in giving an explanation of this regularity. What causes this

**Figure 11-1. Systematic patterns of behavior recorded from an unknown black box. The problem is to explain the observed regularity. (Pylyshyn (1985), p. 68.)**

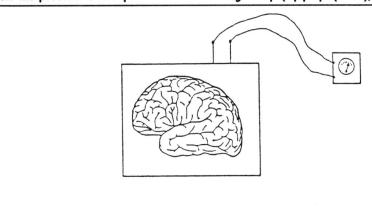

particular pattern to occur, as opposed to some other pattern? What kind of explanation for the pattern will be appropriate?

The answer, I maintain, depends upon what sort of device the black box is—and, in particular, on what its *capacity* is beyond the particular behavior we have just been observing (i.e., not on what it is doing, or what it typically does, but on what it *could* be doing in certain counter-factual situations). In this particular example, chosen deliberately to make a pedagogical point, I can confidently tell you that we would not find the explanation of its behavior in its internal structure or in any properties intrinsic to the box or its contents.

Now that might strike some people as an odd claim. How can the behavior of a system not be explainable in terms of its internal construction or its inherent properties? What else could possibly explain the regularities it exhibits? In the end, of course, it is the existence of certain properties in the box that govern the totality of its behavioral repertoire, or its capacity. But as long as we have only sampled some limited scope of this repertoire, (say, what it "typically" or "normally" does) we may not be in any position to infer what its intrinsically constrained capacity is, hence the observed regularity may tell us nothing about the internal structure or inherent properties of the device.

To make this point concrete, I can now reveal to you that the real reason the black box exhibits this regularity is simply that it processes or transmits English words encoded in International Morse Code. Thus the regularity we have discovered is not a direct result of the structure of the box but is attributable entirely to a spelling rule of English (*viz., i* before *e* except after *c*). And the reason that providing a detailed description of the component structure and the operation of the box would not explain this regularity is that the structure is capable of exhibiting a much greater range of behaviors—*the observed constraint on its behavior is not due to its intrinsic capability but to what its states represent.* Because, as I have already pointed out, computers are extremely labile in the range of behavior that they can potentially exhibit. Hence, most of their behavioral regularities are not due to their structural properties, but to the representations that they embody.

Here are a few other, not so trivial examples. I will make the point in this case by asking what is needed in order to design a system which exhibits a certain pattern of behavior, rather than what do we need to know in order to explain the regularities in its behavior? In fact, explaining and designing are much more closely connected activities than most people are willing to admit—which is one reason I maintain that the role of technology in shaping our understanding of the world has been underrated.

The examples I want to sketch are miniature problems that occur in systems falling into the category of artificial intelligence: The first one is from a system that analyzes aerial photographs. Suppose that it is looking for ships in aerial photos such as the ones shown in Figure 11-2. How can it do this? There are two different ways it might attempt to solve this task, and these two ways illustrate a

**Figure 11-2.  Aerial photograph of ships. [Ballard & Brown (1982), p. 3]**

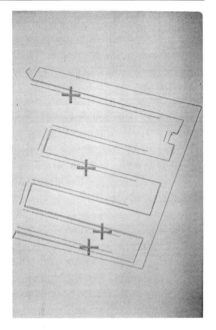

prime difference between AI technology and other engineering technologies. The first way might be to search for image properties that are frequently (or even invariably) associated with ships—for example, patterns of a certain size and shape and appearing at certain coordinates or wavelengths. I will call such reliable indicators "signatures" of what we are looking for. When signatures are available—as they are for a few important features such as ground moisture— then this is certainly a useful approach.

However, signatures of man-made entities are rare because such entities are more often characterized by their function than by their shape or other physical characteristics. After all, a ship can be of many different sizes and can appear as quite different patterns on an image, depending on the season, the lighting condition, the surrounding geography, and so on. But human photointerpreters do very well at the task of locating them. How do they do it? The answer appears to be that they analyze the images by making use of what they know about ships, harbors, water bodies, rivers, the shipping industry, and anything else that might possibly turn out to be relevant.

In the sample image shown here, for example, some of the ships are barely visible. Yet they *can* be detected if you know what to look for and where; if, for example, you keep in mind that ships tend to be located on water near docks, that some rectangular protrusions of the shoreline may be docks, that contours that separate water from shoreline had characteristic shapes that provide evidence as to which is water and which, shore (e.g., at the mouth of rivers), that one can usually rely on such very general facts as that a contour does not change from being a water-land boundary at one place to a land-water boundary at another place as we follow it around. There are dozens and dozens of such obvious commonsense facts that go into the photointerpreter's skill, as well as some not-so-obvious things he may look for. Thus, although an expert photointerpreter may describe what he does as "just looking," we know that such "looking" covers a large amount of knowledge-based reasoning—reasoning that the inter-preter may be unaware of doing. A system that did photointerpretation as well as an expert—and, over a range of situations, as broadly as the expert—is unlikely to be able to get away with searching for a "signature." It would invariably have to resort to inferences based on knowledge that it represented in a form that allows it to reason.

Here is another example which shows that carrying out a certain task requires that we appeal to knowledge. Suppose we wish to design a system that under-stands English sentences. Clearly, in order to understand an English sentence, the system will have to uncover what is called its "thematic structure": it will have to determine "who did what to whom." This requires that a number of things about the sentence be determined, one of what is simply to decide what all the pronouns or other anaphoras refer to. But how are we to determine what the italicized pronoun refers to in sentences such as the following?

- The city councilors refused the demonstrators a permit because *they* feared violence.
- The city councilors refused the demonstrators a permit because *they* were communists.

As in the code-box example, there is no *general* fixed structure or mechanism for doing the right thing in all cases, in this case for assigning references. There is no way of wiring a machine once and for all so it gets all such examples right. Why not? Because it is patent that what the pronoun refers to depends on knowledge of such things as what city councilors are like, what the attitude of people in authority is to communists in certain countries, perhaps on recollec-tions of recent history or the day's news, and so on, without limit. Only factors like this would explain why the pronouns are typically assigned different refer-ents in the two sentences and why the reference assignment can be easily changed by altering the context, and hence rendering some particular piece of knowledge relevant to the assignment. For example, I recently inadvertently provided an example of the effect of context myself when I used these sentences in a talk I gave in Florence, Italy. I had forgotten that the city council of Florence was in fact drawn primarily from the communist party. Because of this, my audience had assigned the same referent to the pronoun in both sentences and the point of the example had been largely lost!

It is important to realize that all this talk about how certain regular features of behavior can only be understood in terms of the use of knowledge and the making of inferences and decisions based on goals is *not just a matter of expedience or convenience.* The fact is that there are certain systems in nature whose behavior is explainable only if we take into account the organization that they have at a certain level: namely, the level at which they can be described as having representations of knowledge and goals. No matter how accurately and completely you described their physical or neurological structure, you would still not understand why they displayed certain patterns of behavior—unless you also took into account this level of organization.

By the way, the existence of this level of organization is closely related to my earlier point about the behavioral plasticity of certain systems. One important reason why we have to postulate representations is in order to account for the rather radical plasticity in human behavior. Psychologists who conduct laboratory studies on human behavior must take extraordinary precautions in the way they instruct subjects and in what they might inadvertently lead subjects to believe about the experiment. The reason is that behavioral regularities are extremely sensitive to subjects' beliefs, which in turn are influenceable by the content of any information or clues that the experimenter might provide. Whatever regularities in behavior we might observe under some set of conditions can be altered in a systematic and logically coherent way (to a first approximation) by merely providing the subject with certain information—by telling or showing the subject something, or providing clues which together with other beliefs warrant some plausible inference (see Brewer, 1972, for excellent examples of this in human conditioning experiments). This responsiveness of behavior to the content of *information-bearing events,* by the way, is one of the main reasons for the downfall of behaviorism.

The radical alterability of behavior patterns has led some people to conclude either that a rigorous predictive science of psychology is not possible, in which case one should resign oneself to predicting statistical properties of behavior (i.e., what people will do *most* of the time) or they have concluded that we have been on the wrong track when we have been trying to model mental activity in certain mechanistic terms. Kohler (1947), whom I cited earlier, was one of the people who took the second option, because he felt that "mechanical" models were too constrained in their behaviors by their structure, or what he called "topographical factors." But, as I noted earlier, Kohler was simply mistaken in this view, as Turing was able to prove. What I did not mention in my earlier discussion is that, in order to prove the universality of the simple Turing machine, Turing had to introduce the idea of symbols or of reference, and hence of representation. In order to simulate another machine, the universal machine has to have some representation of the machine to be simulated (e.g., it has to be given the instructions that the second machine would have carried out). Thus what was missing from Kohler's analysis was the notion that a machine could have another level of organization—one in which it is described as having and using *symbols,* and hence *representations.*

Finally, I want to conclude by saying something about the notion of *cognizing,* which I have been using loosely all through this talk.

## IS *COGNIZING* A NATURAL CLASS OF PHENOMENON?

The qualitative growth in complexity and speed-of-information handling that computers have made possible has been more generally recognized than has their character as knowledge processors or, as Dan Dennett has called them, "semantic engines," which enables them to act on the *content of knowledge.* At the turn of the century, philosopher-psychologist Franz Brentano argued that the mark of the mental (and consequently the mark of the uniquely human) was the possession of what he called "intentionality"—by which he referred to the fact that mental states are "about" something—they have what we would call "representational content." The problem of understanding intentionality remains one of the tougher problems in philosophy of mind. Yet many of us believe that whatever the eventual satisfactory analysis of this notion, it will include features of what computers do, as well as what the human mind does. Indeed, computers are the only nonliving systems we know that appear to support a level of organization which corresponds to having and using representations, and hence that corresponds closely to what Brentano called intentionality. They do this despite the fact that at the moment nobody wants to say that such machines are *conscious*—hence it appears that intentionality may be independent of consciousness.

There is an important point here, if this analysis is correct. Revolutionary changes in our view of the world frequently have had the character of discovering new groupings of phenomena—groupings that philosophers call *natural kinds.* The discovery that violent and natural motion were not different kinds of phenomena, subject to different principles, as Aristotle had taught, was one of the first steps in the development of the new physics. It went hand in hand with the reclassification of the motion of heavenly bodies into the same category as the motion of middle-sized objects like stones and cannonballs. The modern concept of "physical object," as anything that has mass and location—whether or not it is visible, or even detectable in principle, and whether or not it is in motion or at rest—seems totally natural for us today. Yet, this was not always the case. Indeed, Galileo was ridiculed for his assumption that things he could see only through a special instrument (the rudimentary telescope) were of the *same natural kind* as things that could be seen with the naked eye. And perhaps we can understand why. Classing such things in the same natural category was to make an enormous conceptual leap: the leap of seeing a new fundamental grouping of things.

What people who work in the fields of artificial intelligence and cognitive science believe is that certain aspects of human capacity must also be regrouped or reconceptualized. Man has been variously understood as a creature of special creation, as a social entity and, in the late nineteenth century, as a biological object. What some of us now believe is that there is another natural category to which cognitive or rational action should be assigned. That category is one which also includes certain sorts of machines as members in good standing: machines whose behavior is governed by what they represent—by what they know. These are knowledge-driven systems, or what George Miller picturesquely refers to as *informavores,* or systems that are nourished and guided by information. If this regrouping or reconceptualization is correct, it means that certain forms of human behavior should be explained in precisely the same way that we explain certain forms of computer behavior. Thus, contrary to a widely held view, the computer is not a metaphor for mind, anymore than mathematical structures are metaphors for the physical world, as Freeman Dyson insisted in my earlier quotations, or geometry was a metaphor for space to Galileo. Rather, computing is a literal description of aspects of cognitive processes, stated in terms of a more manageable member of the same natural kind (*viz.,* the natural kind *cognizer*). This, then, is the new heresy: man the *informavore,* not only a cousin of the ape, but of the computer.

If all this turns out to be true, and the new natural kind becomes assimilated to the general view, as did the Galilean categories over the Aristotelian ones, we shall be witnessing a revolution in our image of man, perhaps greater even than the Darwinean or the Freudian. We shall also be witnessing a revolutionary change in the nature of our environment as we extend ourselves electronically. For the extension will be unlike that brought about by electronic communication media, which, as my countryman Marshall McCluhan pointed out, simply extended our senses. This new extension will literally place replicas of some of our most cherished functions—like thinking, deciding, recommending, evaluating, and pursuing goals—out there in our environment, along with other people and animals. As autonomous, active gatherers and exploiters of knowledge, they will represent a new and still incomprehensible form of externalized intellectual activity. Although in a sense they will still be tools, they will also be active participants in our intellectual activities, and we shall have to learn to live with them on those terms.

## REFERENCES

Ballard, D. H., & Brown, C. M. (1982). *Computer vision.* Englewood Cliffs, NJ: Prentice-Hall.

Brewer, W. F. (1974). There is no convincing evidence for operant or classical conditioning in adult humans. In W. B. Weiner & D. S. Palermo (Eds.), *Cognition and the symbolic processes*. Hillsdale, NJ: Erlbaum.

Dyson, F. J. (1969). Mathematics in the physical sciences. In National Research Council Committee on Support of Research in the Mathematical Sciences (Ed.), *The mathematical sciences*. Cambridge, MA: MIT Press.

Kohler, W. (1947). *Gestalt psychology: An introduction to new concepts in modern psychology*. New York: Liveright.

Langer, S. (1962). *Philosophical sketches*. Baltimore: Johns Hopkins Press.

Pylyshyn, Z. W. (1958). *Computation and cognition: Toward a foundation for cognitive science* (2d ed.). Cambridge, MA: MIT Press/A Bradford Book.

Shortliffe, E. H. (1976). *Computer-based medical consultations: MYCIN*. New York: Elsevier.

Turing, A. M. (1964). Computing machinery and intelligence. In A. R. Anderson (Ed.), *Minds and machines*. Englewood Cliffs, NJ: Prentice-Hall. (Original work published 1950)

# Notes and Suggestions for Further Reading—Section II

*Numbers refer to notes in the commentary for this Section, not to footnotes within the readings themselves.*

1. See, for example: Cohen, J. *Human Robots in Myth and Science*, London: George Allen and Unwin, 1966.

2. Newman, J. R. (Ed.). *The World of Mathematics* (Volumes I–IV). New York: Simon and Schuster, 1956. Another very good illustration of the theoretical side of computer science can be found in Donald Knuth's Multi-Volume Series, *The Art of Computer Programming*, Reading, MA: Addison-Wesley, 1968–1972.

3. The idea that an algorithm is a detailed *procedure*, and that it is not specific to computers, is illustrated by the following "algorithm" taken verbatim from an old source quite removed from computer science, even though its form is very much that of a program. Can you guess what it is designed to do?

   | R1: | k1, * p3, k1, repeat from * across |
   |---|---|
   | R2: | p1, * k3, p1, repeat from * across |
   | R2-R12: | Repeat R1, R2 |
   | R13: | Repeat R1 |
   | R14: | p2 tog across, end p1 (77sts.) |

   The above algorithm was taken from a knitting magazine and shows exactly how to produce part of a baby's bonnet. If the abbreviations are decoded (R = row, k = knit, p = purl, sts = stitches) and the appropriate "interpreter" and "inputs" (materials) provided, the result is precisely and unambiguously determined.

4. There are a number of more recent important books analyzing the relationship between computing and intelligence, some of which are referenced below. One of the people who has contributed most to this discussion, beginning in the earliest days of artificial intelligence and continuing to this day, is Allen Newell. Among his important papers are the following:
   A. Newell, (1970). Remarks on the relationship between artificial intelligence and cognitive psychology. In R. Banerji & M.D. Mesarovic (Eds.), *Theoretical approaches to non-numeric problem solving*. New York: Spring-Verlag.

A. Newell, (1973). Artificial intelligence and the concept of mind. In R. C. Schank &
K. Colby (Eds.), *Computer models of thought and language,* San Francisco: W. H.
Freeman.

A. Newell, (1980). Physical symbol systems. *Cognitive Science, 4*(2), 135–183.

A. Newell, (1982). The knowledge level. *Artificial Intelligence, 18*(1), 87–127.

5.   There are a number of interesting and well-written books on artificial intelligence
(AI) for the layperson, and the number is growing rapidly. The following is a sam-
pling of books on various aspects of the field, some of which have now become
classic "starters."

   Pamela McCorduck, *Machines Who Think,* San Francisco, W. H. Freeman & Co.
1979.

This is an extremely readable and entertaining book that deals primarily with the
early history of artificial intelligence, including the many personalities, historical events,
and quarrels that characterized the first 20 years of the field. McCorduck has done a very
thorough job of going to the sources for this information.

   Feigenbaum and McCorduck, *The Fifth Generation: Artificial Intelligence & Japan's Computer Challenge to the World* (Addison-Wesley Reading, MA, 1983).

This book, more than anything else, has been responsible for bringing the Japanese
plans for a "fifth generation computer system" to the attention of the western world.
Although opinionated in its style, and controversial among artificial intelligence people
themselves, this book is very readable and contains some interesting insights into the way
that artificial intelligence is being viewed by different nations and by industry.

   John Haugland, *Artificial Intelligence: The Very Idea* (Cambridge: MIT Press,
1985).

Written by a philosopher, this book places current attempts to understand the nature of
intelligence within a philosophical and historical perspective. It is a very sophisticated and
scholarly monograph on the nature of the new sciences of artificial intelligence and
cognitive science, and their relationship to traditional philosophical concerns about the
human mind. Despite its sophistication, however, this book should be quite readable by
the nonspecialist.

   Tim O'Shea and Marc Eisenstadt, *Artificial Intelligence: Tools, Techniques, and
Applications,* Harper and Row, 1984.

This is a collection used in courses by The Open University in the United Kingdom.
Many of the chapters in this book are university level. Nonetheless they are "introducto-
ry" in the sense that they do not presuppose specialized knowledge of computer science.
The topics covered are quite broad, ranging from introductions to programming in the
PROLOG and LISP languages to chapters on industrial robotics and computer vision. It
even includes an interesting chapter called "How to get a Ph.D. in artifical intelligence".

   Roger Schank, *The Cognitive Computer: On Language, Learning, and Artificial
Intelligence,* Addison-Wesley, 1984. This book, written by one of the best known artifical
intelligence researchers, is intended to be a "popular" book. It succeeds in being readable, entertaining, and very provocative. Not everyone in artifical intelligence will agree
with Schank, though the ideas are interesting.

   Margaret Boden, *Artificial Intelligence and Natural Man* (Revised Edition, Basic
Books, 1987).

Although much of this book is now over 10 years old, and therefore does not present
the most recent work, it is nonetheless still one of the most accessible books which

actually gives some examples of what machines are able to do. The Postscript added to the new edition gives a brief account of developments since the first appearance of the book in 1977. It is written in a nontechnical language. Boden is a frequent contributor to the *Times Literary Supplement*, and this book is written in that periodical's style.

Patrick Winston and Karen Prendergast, *The Artificial Intelligence Business*, MIT Press, 1986.

This book provides a very good insight into what the business world expects and is receiving from artificial intelligence technology. Although there is not very much discussion about artificial intelligence technology or about philosophical questions concerning the nature of mind, there is a lot of practical talk about a number of specific systems (particularly expert systems), their levels of performance, and how they are being applied. There is also some discussion of the strategy for developing artificial intelligence systems and for the introduction of artificial intelligence into practical field applications. The question-and-answer transcripts at the end of each chapter are especially interesting with respect to the practical problems of building artificial intelligence and applying it in industry.

Herbert A. Simon, *The Sciences of the Artificial*, MIT Press, (2nd ed.), 1981.

This is the text of the Compton Lectures given at MIT. It is an early but very influential and readable discussion of what is now called cognitive science by the field's only Nobel Laureate. This 100-page paperback is well worth reading.

Susan J. Scown, *The Artificial Intelligence Experience: An Introduction*, Digital Equipment Corporation, 1985.

An introductory treatment sponsored by a major computer company. It also comes with a videotaped course.

Patrick Winston, *Artificial Intelligence*, Second edition, Addison-Wesley.

This is the best-selling text in the field. Less technical than most, but still not for the absolute beginner.

Stuart C. Shapiro, ed. *The Encyclopedia of Artificial Intelligence*, John Wiley & Sons, 1987.

Although quite technical, this is an excellent reference work on the technology of artificial intelligence. It comes in two volumes of 700 double-columned pages.

6.   To address some of the concerns specifically related to artificial intelligence, a journal devoted to this topic was established in 1987: *Artificial Intelligence and Society: The Journal of Human and Machine Intelligence*, published by Springer International.

7.   Artificial intelligence has already had a profound effect on one of the human sciences—the study of the psychology of human cognition (the study of human reasoning, understanding, perception, memory, problem solving, and other mental skills). The new field of *cognitive science* studies human cognition by viewing it as a computational process and by formulating theories of human cognition in the form of computer programs. Cognitive science has attracted a great deal of interest and many practitioners within psychology. There are cognitive science societies in most countries and an international journal, *Cognitive Science*. There are also a number of introductory level books that describe the field:

Howard Gardiner, *The Mind's New Science: A History of the Cognitive Revolution*, Basic Books, 1985.

This is probably the most readable of all the books written for the intelligent layperson. It is a comprehensive and reasonably nontechnical description of the emerging new field of cognitive science, a discipline that draws from computer science, psychology, philosophy, linguistics, and neuroscience in attempting to understand the nature of human reasoning, perception, memory, and thought. Although the emphasis is on history, so far it is the only book that presents the range of issues and problems that are the subject of research within this new science.

Neil A. Stillings, Mark H. Feinstein, Jay L. Garfield, Edwina L. Rissland, David A. Rosenbaum, Steven Q. Weisler, Lynne Baker-Ward *Cognitive Science: An Introduction*. Cambridge, MA: MIT Press (A Bradford Book), 1987.

There are also some more technical or philosophical books about cognitive science in general:

Pylyshyn, Z. (1984). *Computation and cognition: Toward a foundation for cognitive science*. Cambridge, MA: MIT Press (A Bradford Book).

Posner, M. (Ed.). (1989). *Foundations of cognitive science*. Cambridge, MA: MIT Press (A Bradford Book). (This book contains a broad range of tutorial materials on various aspects of cognitive science.)

# Section III
# Human-Computer Interaction

But the age of chivalry is gone. That of sophisters, economists, and calculators has succeeded; and the glory of Europe is extinguished for ever.

Edmund Burke
*Reflections on the Revolution in France*

A Caution to Everybody

Consider the auk:
Becoming extinct because he forgot how to fly, and could only walk.
Consider man, who may well become extinct
Because he forgot how to walk and learned how to fly before he thought.

Ogden Nash
*Verses from 1929 On*

The widespread use of computers by people in all walks of life has emphasized the need for improved human-computer communication. People are unwilling to devote long hours studying artificial languages in order to communicate with a computer system. They wish to use the computer in order to accomplish certain tasks, and are often extremely frustrated by the apparent "dumbness" of the system. The advent of supposedly "user-friendly" computers over the last few years has done little to overcome the real problems of human-computer interaction, as many of the changes made to systems have been largely cosmetic in nature—adjustable screens, better keyboards, more colloquial system responses, and so on.[1]

Recent commercial interest in artificial intelligence (AI) research (See Section II) has partly been prompted by the belief that work in such fields as natural language understanding and voice recognition may truly revolutionize human-computer interaction. There are applications where AI techniques may make a significant contribution, but it is unlikely that AI software will ever be a complete panacea to the interface problem

Traditionally, the problems of human-machine interaction have been the responsibility of people trained in "human factors," or ergonomics. These people usually have backgrounds in either industrial engineering or experimental psychology. For examples of the kinds of studies they have performed, the reader should consult the journals *Human Factors* and *Ergonomics*. In recent years,

---

[1]See Stevens, 1983, for a critique of the concept of "user-friendly" computer systems.

problems of human-computer interaction have also been studied by researchers in a wide variety of disciplines, including computer science and cognitive psychology. Studies on the ergonomics of visual display units (VDUs) and work station design have been complemented by studies that focus more attention on the cognitive capacities of users. Given the increased capabilities of modern computer systems, we no longer have to submit users to the dictates of the machine but rather can design computer systems to maximally assist them in accomplishing their tasks.

The nature of our interaction with computer systems will also be affected by developments in the underlying hardware. The widespread availability of bit-mapped display screens, coupled with software packages that allow for multiple window displays on the same screen, will pose new problems and prospects for the system design team. The problems posed are not simply extensions of existing problems, such as how to get more information on the screen, but have to do with a fundamental difference in the quality of the interaction between the user and the system. Thus having multiple windows on the screen allows the user to have more than one activity ongoing at any time. While this capability can be extremely useful for many purposes, it can also be very confusing, as people can forget what they had been doing, or in what order they were performing tasks— the return of the "messy desk" phenomenon with a vengeance! Future systems will have to assist users in handling complex displays, allowing them to switch between activities, yet keep track at all times of where they are, where they came from, and what other tasks are currently active.[2]

Despite the advances in hardware and software that are envisaged, there are a number of important considerations in human-machine interaction that remain unchanged. First among these is the necessity to understand the needs of the end users of any new computer system. A strict adherence to this maxim implies that in the design of a new system, both the needs and capabilities of the end users are carefully studied, and that the overall system design is built up from this information. Indeed, many now argue that the users themselves should be actively involved in all stages of the design process (see Chapter 17 in this volume).

End users can be studied at a number of different levels using a variety of methodologies. From a psychological perspective, users are viewed as active "information processors" and communicating organisms. Thus the research available on such topics as learning, memory, language skills, perception, and so on, in the psychological literature can be utilized in system design. For example, theoretical advances in the field of cognitive science concerning the nature of human communication can be of use in the design of human-computer dialogues. In person-to-person communication, we explain things at a level that we think is appropriate to the other person, based on our model of that other person. The

---

[2]For more on this issue, see the papers by Bannon, Cypher, Greenspan, and Monty (1983), and Card and Henderson (1987).

reactions of the other will give us feedback as to whether our explanation is relevant to the person, whether it is too verbose or terse. Likewise with human-computer interaction, if we wish to improve the conviviality of the system, then the system must have some conceptual model of the user, which will allow the system to tailor its output, and subsequent dialogue, as required. For an overview of early work performed within the cognitive science paradigm see the two volumes of readings edited by Bobrow and Collins (1975), and Sleeman and Brown (1982).

Currently, there is disagreement over whether the goal of designers should be to try and simulate human-human communication by building ''intelligent'' interfaces that communicate with users using natural language, or whether we should instead be developing better tools for users, ones with which users can interact with directly, without the need for a complex intermediary interface ''agent.''

The concept of mental models has recently generated much interest (see Gentner & Stevens, 1983) and has a variety of applications in system design. People tend to form models of systems that they work with, whether or not they have been explicitly provided such a model. These intuitive models help the user to grasp how the system operates, but often they are quite inaccurate and can lead to systematic errors in the use of the machine. Norman (1986) distinguishes between the *conceptual model* of the system, which is the designer's view of the system, and the image that the actual system presents to the user, which he calls the *system image*. Users develop a mental model of the system which is to a large extent determined by the system image. The design team should establish a conceptual model of the system that is appropriate for the specific class of end users and the task domain, and adhere to this model in constructing the system. If this is done correctly, then user tutorials and general system documentation become much easier to produce, as they can explicitly refer to the system image which has been constructed by the design team.

The initial paper in this volume by the psychologist Donald Norman presents an entertaining yet instructive critique of a highly regarded computer operating system, the UNIX[3] system, which is heavily used in academic and research environments, and is now available on many microcomputer systems. Norman is quite willing to admit that the UNIX system has a conceptual elegance, from a systems point of view, but demonstrates with numerous examples how this elegance does not transfer to the human interface. He makes a number of suggestions as to how the interface might be improved, based on ''cognitive engineering'' principles, a term he had coined to describe the wedding of cognitive science—theoretical and experimental—to engineering design (see Norman, 1986, for further details).

---

[3]UNIX is a registered trademark of AT&T Bell Laboratories.

We have described how knowledge of the cognitive abilities and limitations of the user can assist in the design of more graceful interfaces to computer systems. Another useful approach to interface design is to study the context in which users work on the system—what are the constraints imposed on individuals by the nature of the tasks which they are performing, for example, preparing a budget forecast, manuscript preparation, or programming. In the future, users will expect the computer system to have some understanding of the nature of the task domain in which they are working, and will expect the system to provide feedback which is more comprehensible than one-line error codes! Rarely has the effort or resources been given to fully specify what are the range of tasks currently performed by the designated users of a new system, and how we can build an interface that matches more closely the view of the task held by the user, a step which is essential if we are to develop truly helpful and natural human-computer interfaces.

The groundbreaking Xerox 8010 ''Star'' office work station is an example of a system that attempts to provide an interface attuned to the needs of office workers by using the ''desktop'' metaphor. While there have been criticisms of the system from the standpoint of its overall functionality, the pioneering nature of its human-computer interface has not been questioned, and has been adopted by many other computer manufacturers. The embodiment of many of the interface ideas from the Star in the Apple Macintosh personal computer is credited by many for the phenomenal success of the ''Mac.'' The article by Smith, Irby, Kimball, Verplank, and Harslem (Chapter 13) describes the development of the Star user interface, and gives an important insight into just how different the system design process and product is when the design team takes the end user into account from the very beginning of the system design.

Chapter 14 comes from the research laboratories of IBM, where a number of psychologists and others are involved in long-term studies on human-computer interaction. Carroll and Carrithers, after observing people trying to use a word processor, devised a special training interface that blocked the users from entering certain states that they noted were confusing to the learner. They then carried out an empirical study to see whether users learned more quickly to perform certain basic tasks using this ''training wheels'' system then when they used the regular system. The success of their redesigned system is evident. The paper gives a clear indication of how empirical studies can be used to improve human-computer interaction.

What of the future? Certainly, new computer systems will have a much greater range of input-output devices than are currently available. Sound and color will be utilized to a greater extent. We should expect improvements in the conviviality of the system, as more is learned about dialogue design, and the use of graphics and computer-based imagery becomes routine.[4] The recent growth of

---

[4]The collection of papers edited by Norman and Draper (1986) is a good starting point for those interested in alternative approaches to how to design more usable and useful systems.

interest in support for those who perform joint activities, such as coediting a paper, or developing software packages, is welcome news as researchers go beyond the one-terminal-one person design framework that has been the norm for many years. We can expect to see such devices as electronic chalkboards (Stefik, Foster, Bobrow, Kahn, Lanning, and Suchman, 1987) and other electronic shared workspaces in the workplace of the future. More consideration will be given to the environment in which computers are being used, as researchers attempt to extend the traditional design boundaries of the discipline.[5]

Chapter 15 once again demonstrates how many ideas that are currently in vogue have a long history. Many of the topics that are at the center of attention today in the computing world had been investigated by Douglas Engelbart. As early as the late 1950s he was thinking of the challenges of the 1980s, as this historical vignette shows. It seems fitting somehow to close the chapter on human-computer interaction with a piece on the man who was responsible for the development of the now ubiquitous "mouse" input device, as well as many other innovative concepts.

*LJB*

## REFERENCES

Bannon, L. (1986a). Helping users help each other. In D. A. Norman & S. W. Draper (Eds.), *User centered system design*. Hillsdale, NJ: Erlbaum.

Bannon, L. (1986b). Computer-mediated communication. In D. A. Norman & S. W. Draper, (Eds.), *User centered system design*. Hillsdale, NJ: Erlbaum.

Bannon, L., Cypher, A., Greenspan, S., & Monty, M. L. (1983). Evaluation and analysis of users' activity organization. In A. Janda (Ed.), *Proceedings of the CHI 83 Conference on Human Factors in Computing Systems*, pp. 54–57.

Bobrow, D. G., & Collins, A. (Eds.) (1975). *Representation and understanding*. New York: Academic Press.

Card, S. K., & Henderson, D. A. (1987). A multiple, virtual-workspace interface to support user task switching. In J. M. Carroll & P. P. Tanner (Eds.), *Proceedings of the CHI+GI '87 Conference on Human Factors in Computer Systems and Graphics Interface*. New York: ACM.

Gentner, D., & Stevens, A. L. (Eds.). (1983). *Mental models*. Hillsdale, NJ: Erlbaum.

Malone, T. W. (1987). Computer support for organizations: Toward an organizational science. In J. M. Carroll (Ed.), *Interfacing thought*. Cambridge: Bradford Books.

D. A. Norman, & S. W. Draper (Eds.). (1986). *User centered system design: New perspectives on human-computer interaction*. Hillsdale, NJ: Erlbaum.

---

[5]See, for example, Bannon (1986a,b) who argues for including the social resources in the workplace as an element in the design of human-computer systems, and Malone (1987) who discusses the concept of "organizational interfaces" as an extension of the traditional "user interfaces" approach.

Sleeman, D., & Brown, J. S. (Eds.). (1982). *Intelligent tutoring systems.* London: Academic Press.

Stefik, M., Foster, G., Bobrow, D. G., Kahn, K., Lanning, S., & Suchman, L. (1987). Beyond the chalkboard: Computer support for collaboration and problem solving in meetings. *Communications of the ACM, 30*(1) 32–47.

Stevens, G. C. (1983). "User-friendly computer systems? A critical examination of the concept. *Behaviour and Information Technology, 2*(1), 3–16.

*(For notes on further reading for this section, see page 307.)*

# 12
# The Trouble with UNIX*

## 1981

## Donald A. Norman

UNIX is a highly touted operating system. Developed at the Bell Telephone Laboratories and distributed by Western Electric, it has become a standard operating system in universities, and it promises to become a standard for micro and mini systems in homes, small businesses, and schools. But for all of its virtues as a system—and it is indeed an elegant system—UNIX is a disaster for the casual user. It fails both on the scientific principles of human engineering and even in just plain common sense.

If UNIX is really to become a general system, then it has got to be fixed. I urge correction to make the elegance of the system design be reflected as friendliness towards the user, especially the casual user. Although I have learned to get along with the vagaries of UNIX's user interface, our secretarial staff persists only because we insist.

And even I, a heavy user of computer systems for 20 years, have had difficulties: copying the old file over the new, transferring a file into itself until the system collapsed, and removing all the files from a directory simply because an extra space was typed in the argument string. The problem is that UNIX fails several simple tests.

*Consistency:* Command names, language, functions, and syntax are inconsistent.

*Functionality:* The command names, formats, and syntax seem to have no relationship to their functions.

*Friendliness:* UNIX is a recluse, hidden from the user, silent in operation. The

*Partial research support was provided by Contract N00014-79-C-0323, NR 157-437 with the Personnel and Training Research Programs of the Office of Naval Research, and was sponsored by the Office of Naval Research and the Air Force Office of Scientific Research. I thank the members of the LNR research group for their helpful suggestions and descriptions of misery. In particular, I wish to thank Phil Cohen, Tom Erickson, Jonathan Grudin, Henry Halff, Gary Perlman, and Mark Wallen for their analysis of UNIX. Gary Perlman and Mark Wallen provided a number of useful suggestions.

lack of interaction makes it hard to tell what state the system is in, and the absence of mnemonic structures puts a burden on the user's memory.

What is good about UNIX? The system design, the generality of programs, the file structure, the job structure, the powerful operating system command language (the "shell"). Too bad the concern for system design was not matched by an equal concern for the human interface.

One of the first things you learn when you start to decipher UNIX is how to list the contents of a file onto your terminal. Now this sounds straightforward enough, but in UNIX even this simple operation has its drawbacks. Suppose I have a file called "testfile." I want to see what is inside of it. How would you design a system to do it? I would have written a program that listed the contents onto the terminal, perhaps stopping every 24 lines if you had signified that you were on a display terminal with only a 24-line display. UNIX, however, has no basic listing command, and instead uses a program meant to do something else.

Thus if you want to list the contents of a file called "HappyDays," you use the command named "cat":

cat HappyDays

Why cat? Why not? After all, as Humpty Dumpty said to Alice, who is to be the boss, words or us? "Cat," short for "concatenate" as in, take file1 and concatenate it with file2 (yielding one file, with the first part file1, the second file2) and put the result on the "standard output" (which is usually the terminal):

cat file1 file2

Obvious, right? And if you have only one file, why cat will put it on the standard output—the terminal—and that accomplishes the goal (except for those of us with video terminals, who watch helplessly as the text goes streaming off the display).

The UNIX designers believe in the principle that special-purpose functions can be avoided by clever use of a small set of system primitives. Why make a special function when the side effects of other functions will do what you want? Well, for several reasons:

- Meaningful terms are considerably easier to learn than nonmeaningful ones. In computer systems, this means that names should reflect function, else the names for the function will be difficult to recall.
- Making use of the side effects of system primitives can be risky. If cat is used unwisely, it will destroy files (more on this in a moment).
- Special functions can do nice things for users, such as stop at the end of screens, or put on page headings, or transform nonprinting characters into printing ones, or get rid of underlines for terminals that can't do that.

Cat, of course, won't stop at terminal or page boundaries, because doing so would disrupt the concatenation feature. But still, isn't it elegant to use cat for listing? Who needs a print or a list command? You mean "cat" isn't how you would abbreviate concatenate? It seems so obvious, just like:

| FUNCTION | UNIX COMMAND NAME |
|---|---|
| c compiler | cc |
| change working directory | chdir |
| change password | passwd |
| concatenate | cat |
| copy | cp |
| date | date |
| echo | echo |
| editor | ed |
| link | ln |
| move | mv |
| remove | rm |
| search file for pattern | grep |

Notice the lack of consistency in forming the command name from the function. Some names are formed by using the first two consonants of the function name. Editor, however, is "ed," concatenate is "cat," and "date" and "echo" are not abbreviated at all. Note how useful those two-letter abbreviations are. They save almost 400 milliseconds per command.

Similar problems exist with the names of the file directories. UNIX is a file-oriented system, with hierarchical directory structures, so the directory names are very important. Thus, this paper is being written on a file named "unix" and whose "path" is /csl/norman/papers/CogEngineering/unix. The name of the top directory is "/", and csl, norman, papers, and CogEngineering are the names of directories hierarchically placed beneath "/". Note that the symbol "/" has two meanings: the name of the top level directory and the symbol that separates levels of the directories. This is very difficult to justify to new users. And those names: the directory for "users" and "mount" are called, of course, "usr" and "mnt." And there are "bin," "lib," and "tmp" (binary, library, and temp). UNIX loves abbreviations, even when the original name is already very short. To write "user" as "usr" or "temp" as "tmp" saves an entire letter: a letter a day must keep the service person away. But UNIX is inconsistent; it keeps "grep" at its full four letters, when it could have been abbreviated as "gr" or "gp." (What does grep mean? "Global REgular expression, Print"—

at least that's the best we can invent; the manual doesn't even try. The name wouldn't matter if grep were something obscure, hardly ever used, but in fact it is one of the more powerful, frequently used string processing commands.)

## LIKE CAT? THEN TRY DSW

Another important routine goes by the name of "dsw." Suppose you accidentally create a file whose name has a nonprinting character in it. How can you remove it? The command that lists the files on your directory won't show nonprinting characters. And if the character is a space (or worse, a "*"), "rm" (the program that removes files) won't accept it. The name "dsw" was evidently written by someone at Bell Labs who felt frustrated by this problem and hacked up a quick solution. Dsw goes to each file in your directory and asks you to respond "yes" or "no," whether to delete the file or keep it.

How do you remember dsw? What on earth does the name stand for? The UNIX people won't tell; the manual smiles the wry smile of the professional programmer and says, "The name dsw is a carryover from the ancient past. Its etymology is amusing." Which operation takes place if you say "yes"? Why, the file is deleted of course. So if you go through your files and see important-file, you nod to yourself and say, yes, I had better keep that one. You type in "yes," and destroy it forever. There's no warning; dsw doesn't even document itself when it starts, to remind you of which way is which. Berkeley UNIX has finally killed dsw, saying "This little known, but indispensable facility has been taken over . . ." That is a fitting commentary on standard UNIX: a system that allows an "indispensable facility" to be "little known."

The symbol "*" means "glob" (a typical UNIX name: the name tells you just what it does, right?). Let me illustrate with our friend, "cat." Suppose I want to collect a set of files named paper.1 paper.2 paper.3 and paper.4 into one file. I can do this with cat:

cat paper.1 paper.2 paper.3 paper.4⟩newfilename

UNIX provides "glob" to make the job even easier. Glob means to expand the filename by examining all files in the directory to find all that fit. Thus, I can redo my command as

cat paper*⟩newfilename

where paper* expands to {paper.1 paper.2 paper.3 paper.4}. This is one of the typical virtues of UNIX; there are a number of quite helpful functions. But suppose I had decided to name this new file "paper.all"—pretty logical name.

cat paper*⟩paper.all

Disaster. In this case, paper* expands to paper.1 paper.2 paper.3 paper.4 paper.all, and so I am filling up a file from itself:

cat paper.1 paper.2 paper.3 paper.4 paper.all⟩paper.all

Eventually the file will burst. Does UNIX check against this, or at least give a warning? No such luck. The manual doesn't alert users to this either, although it does warn of another, related infelicity: "Beware of 'cat a b⟩a' and 'cat b a⟩a', which destroy the input files before reading them." Nice of them to tell us.

The command to remove all files that start with the word "paper"

rm paper*

becomes a disaster if a space gets inserted by accident:

rm paper *

for now the file "paper" is removed, as well as every file in the entire directory (the power of glob). Why is there not a check against such things? I finally had to alter my version of rm so that when I said to remove files, they were moved to a special directory named "deleted" and preserved there until I logged off, leaving me lots of time for second thoughts and catching errors. This illustrates the power of UNIX: what other operating system would make it so easy for someone to completely change the operation of a system command? It also illustrates the trouble with UNIX: what other operating system would make it so necessary to do so? (This is no longer necessary now that we use Berkeley UNIX—more on this in a moment.)

## THE SHY TEXT EDITOR

The standard text editor is called Ed. I spent a year using it as an experimental vehicle to see how people deal with such confusing things. Ed's major property is his shyness; he doesn't like to talk. You invoke Ed by saying, reasonably enough, "ed." The result is silence: no response, no prompt, no message, just silence. Novices are never sure what that silence means. Ed would be a bit more likable if he answered, "thank you, here I am," or at least produced a prompt character, but in UNIX silence is golden. No response means that everything is okay; if something had gone wrong, it would have told you.

Then there is the famous append mode error. To add text into the buffer, you have to enter "append mode." To do this, you simply type "a," followed by RETURN. Now everything that is typed on the terminal goes into the buffer. (Ed, true to form, does not inform you that it is now in append mode: when you type "a" followed by "RETURN" the result is silence.) When you are finished adding text, you are supposed to type a line that "contains only a . on it." This gets you out of append mode.

Want to bet on how many extra periods got inserted into text files, or how many commands got inserted into texts, because the users thought that they were in command mode and forgot that they had not left append mode? Does Ed tell you when you have left append mode? Hah! This problem is so obvious that even the designers recognized it, but their reaction, in the tutorial introduction to Ed, was merely to note wryly that even experienced programmers make this mistake. While they may be able to see humor in the problem, it is devastating to the beginning secretary, research assistant or student trying to use UNIX as a word processor, an experimental tool, or just to learn about computers.

How good is your sense of humor? Suppose you have been working on a file for an hour and then decide to quit work, exiting Ed by saying "q." The problem is that Ed would promptly quit. Woof, there went your last hour's work, Gone forever. Why, if you had wanted to save it you would have said so, right? Thank goodness for all those other people across the country who immediately rewrote the text editor so that we normal people (who make errors) have some other choices besides Ed, editors that tell you politely when they are working, that tell you if they are in append or command mode, and that don't let you quit without saving your file unless you are first warned, and then only if you say you really mean it.

As I wrote this paper I sent out a message on our networked message system and asked my colleagues to tell me of their favorite peeves. I got a lot of responses, but there is no need to go into detail about them; they all have much the same flavor, mostly commenting about the lack of consistency and the lack of interactive feedback. Thus, there is no standardization of means to exit programs (and because the "shell" is just another program as far as the system is concerned, it is very easy to log yourself off the system by accident). There are very useful pattern matching features (such as the "glob" * function), but the shell and the different programs use the symbols in inconsistent ways. The UNIX copy command (cp) and the related C programming language "string-copy" (strcpy) reverse the meaning of their arguments, and UNIX move (mv) and copy (cp) operations will destroy existing files without any warning. Many programs take special "argument flags" but the manner of specifying the flags is inconsistent, varying from program to program.

The version of UNIX I now use is called the Fourth Berkeley Edition for the VAX, distributed by Joy, Babaoglu, Fabry, and Sklower at the University of California, Berkeley (henceforth, Berkeley UNIX). This is both good and bad.

Among the advantages: History lists, aliases, a richer and more intelligent set of system programs (including a list program, an intelligent screen editor, an intelligent set of routines for interacting with terminals according to their capabilities), and a job control that allows one to stop jobs right in the middle, start up new ones, move things from background to foreground (and vice versa), examine files, and then resume jobs. The shell has been amplified to be a more powerful programming language, complete with file handling capabilities, if—then—else statements, while, case, and other goodies of structured programming.

Aliases are worthy of special comment. Aliases let users tailor the system to their own needs, naming things in ways they can remember; names you devise yourself are easier to recall than names provided to you. And aliases allow abbreviations that are meaningful to the individual, without burdening everyone else with your cleverness or difficulties.

To work on this paper, I need only type the word "unix," for I have set up an alias called "unix" that is defined to be equal to the correct command to change directories, combined with a call to the editor (called "vi" for visual" on this system) on the file:

```
alias unix "chdir /csl/norman/papers/CogEngineering; vi unix"
```

These Berkeley UNIX features have proven to be indispensable: the people in my laboratory would probably refuse to go back to standard UNIX.

The bad news is that Berkeley UNIX is jury-rigged on top of regular UNIX, so it can only patch up the faults: it can't remedy them. Grep is not only still grep, but there is an egrep and an fgrep.

And the generators of Berkeley UNIX have their problems: if Bell Labs people are smug and lean, Berkeley people are cute and overweight. Programs are wordy. Special features proliferate. The system is now so large that it no longer fits on the smaller machines: our laboratory machine, a DEC 11/45, cannot hold the latest release of Berkeley UNIX (even with a full complement of memory and a reasonable amount of disk). I wrote this paper on a VAX.

## LEARNING IS NOT EASY

Learning the system for setting up aliases is not easy for beginners, who may be the people who need them most. You have to set them up in a file called .cshrc, not a name that inspires confidence. The "period" in the filename means that it is invisible—the normal method of directory listing programs won't show it. The directory listing program, ls, comes with 19 possible argument flags, which can be used singly or in combinations. The number of special files that must be set up to use all the facilities is horrendous, and they get more complex with each new release from Berkeley.

It is very difficult for new users. The program names are cute rather than systematic. Cuteness is probably better than standard UNIX's lack of meaning, but there are limits. The listing program is called "more" (as in, "give me more"), the program that tells you who is on the system is called "finger," and a keyword help file—most helpful, by the way—is called "apropos." I used the alias feature to rename it "help."

One reader of a draft of this paper—a systems programmer—complained bitterly: "Such whining, hand-wringing, and general bitchiness will cause most people to dismiss it as overemotional nonsense. . . . The UNIX system was originally designed by systems programmers for their own use and with no intention for others using it. Other hackers liked it so much that eventually a lot of them started using it. Word spread about this wonderful system, and the rest you probably know. I think that Ken Thompson and Dennis Ritchie could easily shrug their shoulders and say 'But we never intended it for other than our personal use.' "

This complaint was unique, and I sympathize with its spirit. It should be remembered, though, that UNIX is nationally distributed under strict licensing agreements. Western Electric's motives are not altogether altruistic. If UNIX had remained a simple experiment on the development of operating systems, then complaints could be made in a more friendly, constructive manner. But UNIX is more than that. It is taken as the very model of a proper operating system. And that is exactly what it is not.

In the development of the system aspects of UNIX, the designers have done a magnificent job. They have been creative, and systematic. A common theme runs through the development of programs, and by means of their file structure, the development of "pipes" and "redirection" of both input and output, plus the power of the iterative "shell" system-level commands, one can easily combine system level programs into self-tailored systems of remarkable power. For system programmers, UNIX is a delight. It is well structured, with a consistent, powerful philosophy of control and structure.

Why was the same effort not put into the design at the level of the user? The answer is complex, but one reason is the fact that there really are no well known principles of design at the level of the user interface. So, to remedy the harm I may have caused with my heavy-handed sarcasm, let me attempt to provide some positive suggestions based upon research conducted by myself and others into the principles of the human information processing system.

Cognitive engineering is a new discipline, so new that it doesn't exist, but it ought to. Quite a bit is known about the human information processing system, enough that we can specify some basic principles for designers. People are complex entities and can adapt to almost anything. As a result, designers often design for themselves, without regard for other kinds of users.

The three most important concepts for system design are these:

1.   Be consistent. A fundamental set of principles ought to be evolved and followed consistently throughout all phases of the design.
2.   Provide the user with an explicit model. Users develop mental models of the devices with which they interact. If you do not provide them with one, they will make one up themselves, and the one they create is apt to be wrong.

Do not count on the user fully understanding the mechanics of the device. Both secretaries and scientists may be ignorant of the difference between the buffer, the working memory, the working files, and the permanent files of a text editor. They are apt to believe that once they have typed something into the system, it is permanently in their files. They are apt to expect more intelligence from the system than the designer knows is there. And they are apt to read into comments (or the lack of comments) more than you have intended.

Feedback is of critical importance in helping establish the appropriate mental model and in letting the user keep its current state in synchrony with the actual system.

3.   Provide mnemonic aids. For most purposes it is convenient to think of human memory as consisting of two parts: a short-term memory and a long-term memory (modern cognitive psychology is developing more sophisticated notions, but this is still a valid approximation). Five to seven items is about the limit for short-term memory. Thus, do not expect a user to remember the contents of a message for much longer than it is visible on the terminal. Long-term memory is robust, but it faces two difficulties: getting stuff in so that it is properly organized, and getting stuff out when it is needed. Learning is difficult, unless there is a good structure and it is visible to the learner.

There are lots of sensible memory aids that can be provided, but the most powerful and sensible of all is understanding. Make the command names describe the function that is desired. If abbreviations must be used, adopt a consistent policy of forming them. Do not deviate from the policy, even when it appears that a particular command warrants doing so.

System designers take note. Design the system for the person, not for the computer, not even for yourself. People are also information processing systems, with varying degrees of knowledge and experience. Friendly systems treat users as normal, intelligent adults who are sometimes forgetful and are rarely as knowledgeable about the world as they would like to be. There is no need to talk down to the user, nor to explain everything. But give the users a share in understanding by presenting a consistent view of the system. Their response will be your reward.

## TECHNICAL NOTE—WHAT IS UNIX?

UNIX is an operating system developed by Dennis Ritchie and Ken Thompson of Bell Laboratories. UNIX is trademarked by Bell Labs and is available under license from Western Electric. Although UNIX is a relatively small operating system, it is quite powerful and general. It has found considerable favor among programming groups, especially in universities, where it is primarily used with DEC computers—various versions of the DEC PDP-11 and the VAX. The operating system and its software are written in a high level programming language called C, and most of the source code and documentation is available on-line. For programmers, UNIX is easy to understand and to modify.

For the nonexpert programmer, the important aspect of UNIX is that it is constructed out of a small, basic set of concepts and programming modules, with a flexible method for interconnecting existing modules to make new functions. All system objects—including all I/O channels—look like files. Thus, it is possible to cause input and output for almost any program to be taken from or to go to files, terminals, or other devices, at any time, without any particular planning on the part of the module writer. UNIX has a hierarchical file structure. Users can add and delete file directories at will and then "position" themselves at different locations in the resulting hierarchy to make it easy to manipulate the files in the neighborhood.

The command interpreter of the operating system interface (called the "shell") can take its input from a file, which means that it is possible to put frequently used sequences of commands into a file and then invoke that file (just by typing its name), thereby executing the command strings. In this way, the user can extend the range of commands that are readily available. Many users end up with a large set of specialized shell command files. Because the shell includes facilities for passing arguments, for iterations, and for conditional operations, these "shell programs" can do quite a lot, essentially calling upon all system resources (including the editors) as subroutines. Many nonprogrammers have discovered that they can write powerful shell programs, thus significantly enhancing the power of the overall system.

By means of a communication channel known as a pipe, the output from one program can easily be directed (piped) to the input of another, allowing a sequence of programming modules to be strung together to do some task that in other systems would have to be done by a special purpose program. UNIX does not provide special purpose programs. Instead, it attempts to provide a set of basic software tools that can be strung together in flexible ways using I/O redirection, pipes, and shell programs. Technically, UNIX is just the operating system. However, because of the way the system has been packaged, many people use the name to include all of the programs that come on the distribution tape. Many people have found it easy to modify the UNIX system and have done so, which has resulted in hordes of variations on various kinds of computers. The "standard UNIX" discussed in the article is BTL UNIX Version 6 (May 1975). The Fourth Berkeley Edition of UNIX is more or less derived from BTL UNIX Version 7 (September 1978), with considerable parallel development at the University of California, Berkeley and some input from other BTL UNIX versions. I am told that some of the complaints in the article have been fixed; however, Version 6 is still used by many people.

The accompanying article is written with heavy hand, and it may be difficult to discern that I am a friend of UNIX. The negative tone should not obscure the beauty and power of the operating system, file structure, and the shell. UNIX is indeed a superior operating system. I would not use any other. Some of the difficulties detailed result from the fact that many of the system modules were written by the early users of UNIX, not by the system designers; a lot of individual idiosyncrasies have gotten into the system. It is my hope that the positive aspects of the article will not be overlooked. They can be used by all system designers, not just by those working on UNIX. Some other systems need these comments a lot more than does UNIX.

*Donald A. Norman*


## REFLECTIONS ON "THE TROUBLE WITH UNIX"— POSTSCRIPT, 1987

The paper, *The Trouble with Unix,* marked my first foray into the world of incoherent, inconsiderate design. The paper was written out of frustration of having lost yet another file because of the foibles of the Unix operating system. Ah Unix, powerful and elegant from the computer scientist's point of view, but maddeningly intolerant and opaque from the user's point of view. It suddenly dawned on me that the frustrations were not necessary, that they were the fault of the *designers,* not of the users, and that, in fact, something could be done about it.

The paper was written in a weekend, the fastest paper I have ever written and the most controversial. It was pirated from my computer system by a local computer whiz and sent out by computer bulletin net without my knowledge to the Unix experts across the country. I got back dozens of vituperative comments—30 single spaced pages. But the debate got me invited to Bell Labs where I talked to several overflowing audiences and calmly discussed the situation with many of the major Unix developers. In fact, I thought that we hit it off pretty well at Bell Labs and came away with surprisingly little disagreement. They had ignored the user interface, and they admitted that (and now consider that was wrong—I like to think). They had concentrated on the system issues, and were proud of them, and I agreed they had a right to be proud. They also had huge constraints placed upon them by the very limited power of the machines that were first used for UNIX. The original system was intended only for the designers, certainly not for widespread outside use. After it was released to the world, the main interface had been established and it was too late to change.

The Unix paper was written in haste, to bring people's attention to the problem. The solutions I proposed were not always realistic. Some were not correct. In fact, the paper launched a miniature industry of testing the appropriateness of the suggestions, which is all to the good, for the point of the paper was to raise people's awareness that the user should not be neglected, that when users' consistently had difficulties, this reflected poor design and not something to chuckle about (the normal attitude at the time was first to chuckle, then to explain that these people had no business using the system if they were so inept—the idea of providing users with alternatives was not seriously considered.)

The greatest surprise actually is that Unix still lives on, warts and all. The frustrations I expressed in the paper were real and still exist today. In fact, they have just led to another tirade, the book *The Psychology of Everyday Things* (Norman, 1988). Today, such design inadequacies are no longer excusable, but the inadequacies persist nonetheless, if not in Unix, then in other systems. The greatest pleasure is that there is now a scientific/engineering discipline dedicated to the understanding of the user and to the development of better computer systems. The very existence of this section in a book of readings and commentaries is proof.

Norman, D. A. (1981, November). The trouble with UNIX: The user interface is horrid. *Datamation, 27,* (12) 139–150.

Norman, D. A. (1988). *The Psychology of Everyday Things.* New York: Basic Books.

# 13

# Designing the Star User Interface

## 1982

## David Canfield Smith, Charles Irby, Ralph Kimball, Bill Verplank, and Eric Harslem

The Xerox 8010 Star Information System is a new personal computer designed for offices. Consisting of a processor, a large display, a keyboard, and a cursor-control device (see Figure 13-1), it is intended for business professionals who handle information.

Star is a multifunction system combining document creation, data processing, and electronic filing, mailing, and printing. Document creation includes text editing and formatting, graphics editing, mathematical formula editing, and page layout. Data processing deals with homogeneous, relational databases that can be sorted, filtered, and formatted under user control. Filing is an example of a network service utilizing the Ethernet local-area network (Intel, Digital, & Xerox, 1980; Metcalfe & Boggs, 1976). Files may be stored on a work station's disk, on a file server on the work station's network, or on a file server on a different network. Mailing permits users of work stations to communicate with one another. Printing utilizes laser-driven raster printers capable of printing both text and graphics.

As Jonathan Seybold has written, "This is a very different product: Different because it truly bridges word processing and typesetting functions; different because it has a broader range of capabilities than anything which has preceded it; and different because it introduces to the commercial market radically new concepts in human engineering." (See Seybold, 1981).

The Star user interface adheres rigorously to a small set of design principles. These principles make the system seem familiar and friendly, simplify the human-machine interaction, unify the nearly two dozen functional areas of Star, and allow user experience in one area to apply in others. In Smith, Irby, Kimball, & Harslem (1982) we presented an overview of the features in Star. Here, we describe the principles behind those features and illustrate the principles with examples. This discussion is addressed to the designers of other computer programs and systems—large and small.

**261**

Figure 13-1.    A Star work station showing the processor, display, keyboard, and mouse.

## STAR ARCHITECTURE

Before describing Star's user interface, several essential aspects of the Star architecture should be pointed out. Without these elements, it would have been impossible to design an interface anything like the present one.

The Star hardware was modeled after the experimental Xerox Alto computer (Thacker, McCreight, Lampson, Sproull, & Boggs, 1981). Like Alto, Star consists of a Xerox-developed, high-bandwidth, MSI (medium-scale integration) processor; local disk storage; a bit-mapped display screen having a 72-dots-per-inch resolution; a pointing device called the "mouse"; and a connection to the Ethernet network. Stars are higher-performance machines than Altos, being about three times as fast, having 512K bytes of main memory (versus 256K bytes on most Altos), 10 or 29 megabytes of disk memory (versus 2.5 megabytes), a 10½- by 13½-inch display screen (versus 10½ by 8 inches), and a 10-megabits-per-second Ethernet (versus 3 megabits). Typically, Stars, like Altos, are linked via Ethernets to each other and to shared file, mail, and print servers. Communication servers connect Ethernets to one another either directly or over telephone lines, enabling internetwork communication. (For a detailed description of the Xerox Alto computer, see the September 1981 BYTE article "The Xerox Alto Computer" by Thomas A. Wadlow on page 58.)

The most important ingredient of the user interface is the bit-mapped display screen. Both Star and Alto devote a portion of main memory to the screen: 100K bytes in Star, 50K bytes (usually) in Alto. Every screen dot can be individually turned on or off by setting or resetting the corresponding bit in memory. It should be obvious that this gives both computers an excellent ability to portray visual images. We believe that all impressive office systems of the future will have bit-mapped displays. Memory cost will soon be insignificant enough that they will be feasible even in home computers. Visual communication is effective, and it can't be exploited without graphics flexibility.

There must be a way to change dots on the screen quickly. Star has a high memory bandwidth, about 90 megahertz (MHz). The entire Star screen is re-painted from memory 39 times per second, about a 50-MHz data rate between memory and the screen. This would swamp most computer memories. However, since Star's memory is double-ported, refreshing the display does not apprecia-bly slow down processor memory access. Star also has separate logic devoted solely to refreshing the display. Finally, special microcode has been written to assist in changing the contents of memory quickly, permitting a variety of screen processing that would not otherwise be practical (see Ingalls, 1981).

People need a way to quickly point to items on the screen. Cursor step keys are too slow; nor are they suitable for graphics. Both Star and Alto use a pointing device called the mouse. First developed at Stanford Research Institute (see English, Engelbart, & Berman, 1967), Xerox's version has a ball on the bottom that turns as the mouse slides over a flat surface such as a table. Electronics sense the ball rotation and guide a cursor on the screen in corresponding motions. The mouse possesses several important attributes:

- It is a "Fitts's law" device. That is, after some practice you can point with a mouse as quickly and easily as you can with the tip of your finger. The limitations on pointing speed are those inherent in the human nervous system (see Card, English, & Burr, 1978; Fitts, 1954).
- It stays where it was left when you are not touching it. It doesn't have to be picked up like a light pen or stylus.
- It has buttons on top that can be sensed under program control. The buttons let you point to and interact with objects on the screen in a variety of ways.

Every Star and Alto has its own hard disk for local storage of programs and data. This enhances their personal nature, providing consistent access to information regardless of how many other machines are on the network or what anyone else is doing. Larger programs can be written, using the disk for swapping.

The Ethernet lets both Stars and Altos have a distributed architecture. Each machine is connected to an Ethernet. Other machines on the Ethernet are dedicated as "servers"—machines that are attached to a resource and provide access to that resource.

## STAR DESIGN METHODOLOGY

We have learned from Star the importance of formulating the fundamental concepts (the user's conceptual model) *before* software is written, rather than tacking on a user interface *afterward*. Xerox devoted about 30 work years to the design of the Star user interface. It was designed *before* the functionality of the system was fully decided. It was even designed *before* the computer hardware was built. We worked for two years *before* we wrote a single line of actual product software. Jonathan Seybold put it this way, "Most system design efforts start with hardware specifications, follow this with a set of functional specifications for the software, then try to figure out a logical user interface and command structure. The Star project started the other way around: the paramount concern was to define a conceptual model of how the user would relate to the system. Hardware and software followed from this." (1981).

In fact, before we even began designing the model, we developed a methodology by which we would do the design. Our methodology report (Irby, Bergsteinsson, Moran, Newman, & Tesler, 1977) stated:

> One of the most troublesome and least understood aspects of interactive systems is the *user interface.* In the design of user interfaces, we are concerned with several issues: the provision of languages by which users can express their commands to the computer; the design of display representations that show the state of the system to the user; and other more abstract issues that affect the user's understanding of the system's behavior. Many of these issues are highly subjective and are therefore often addressed in an *ad hoc* fashion. We believe, however, that more rigorous approaches to user interface design can be developed. . . .

> These design methodologies are all unsatisfactory for the same basic reason: they all omit an essential step that must precede the design of any successful user interface, namely *task analysis.* By this we mean the analysis of the task performed by the user, or users, prior to introducing the proposed computer system. Task analysis involves establishing who the users are, what their goals are in performing the task, what information they use in performing it, what information they generate, and what methods they employ. The descriptions of input and output information should include an analysis of the various *objects,* or individual types of information entity, employed by the user. . . .

> The purpose of task analysis is to simplify the remaining stages in user interface design. The *current task description,* with its breakdown of the information objects and methods presently employed, offers a starting point for the definition of a corresponding set of objects and methods to be provided by the computer system. The idea behind this phase of design is to build up a new *task environment* for the

user, in which he can work to accomplish the same goals as before, surrounded now by a different set of objects, and employing new methods.

Prototyping is another crucial element of the design process. System designers should be prepared to implement the new or difficult concepts and then to *throw away* that code when doing the actual implementation. As Frederick Brooks says, the question "is not *whether* to build a pilot system and throw it away. You *will* do that. The only question is whether to plan in advance to build a throwaway, or to promise to deliver the throwaway to customers. . . . Hence *plan to throw one away; you will, anyhow.*" (Brooks, 1975). The Alto served as a valuable prototype for Star. Over 1,000 Altos were eventually built. Alto users have had several thousand work years of experience with them over a period of eight years, making Alto perhaps the largest prototyping effort ever. Dozens of experimental programs were written for the Alto by members of the Xerox Palo Alto Research Center. Without the creative ideas of the authors of those systems, Star in its present form would have been impossible. In addition, we ourselves programmed various aspects of the Star design on Alto, but all of it was "throwaway" code. Alto, with its bit-mapped display screen, was powerful enough to implement and test our ideas on visual interaction.

Some types of concepts are inherently difficult for people to grasp. Without being too formal about it, our experience before and during the Star design led us to the following classification:

| *Easy* | *Hard* |
|---:|:---|
| concrete | abstract |
| visible | invisible |
| copying | creating |
| choosing | filling in |
| recognizing | · generating |
| editing | programming |
| interactive | batch |

The characteristics on the left were incorporated into the Star user's conceptual model. The characteristics on the right we attempted to avoid.

## PRINCIPLES USED

The following main goals were pursued in designing the Star user interface:

- familiar user's conceptual model
- seeing and pointing versus remembering and typing
- what you see is what you get

- universal commands
- consistency
- simplicity
- modeless interaction
- user tailorability

We will discuss each of these in turn.

### Familiar User's Conceptual Model

A *user's conceptual model* is the set of concepts a person gradually acquires to explain the behavior of a system, whether it be a computer system, a physical system, or a hypothetical system. It is the model developed in the mind of the user that enables that person to understand and interact with the system. The first task for a system designer is to decide what model is preferable for users of the system. This extremely important step is often neglected or done poorly. The Star designers devoted several work years at the outset of the project discussing and evolving what we considered an appropriate model for an office information system: the metaphor of a physical office.

The designer of a computer system can choose to pursue familiar analogies and metaphors or to introduce entirely new functions requiring new approaches. Each option has advantages and disadvantages. We decided to create electronic counterparts to the physical objects in an office: paper, folders, file cabinets, mail boxes, and so on—an electronic metaphor for the office. We hoped this would make the electronic ''world'' seem more familiar, less alien, and require less training. (Our initial experiences with users have confirmed this.) We further decided to make the electronic analogues be *concrete objects*. Documents would be more than file names on a disk; they would also be represented by pictures on the display screen. They would be selected by pointing to them with the mouse and clicking one of the buttons. Once selected, they would be moved, copied, or deleted by pushing the appropriate key. Moving a document became the electronic equivalent of picking up a piece of paper and walking somewhere with it. To file a document, you would move it to a picture of a file drawer, just as you take a physical piece of paper to a physical file cabinet.

The reason that the user's conceptual model should be decided *first* when designing a system is that the approach adopted *changes the functionality of the system*. An example is electronic mail. Most electronic-mail systems draw a distinction between *messages* and *files* to be sent to other people. Typically, one program sends messages and a different program handles file transfers, each with its own interface. But we observed that offices make no such distinction. Everything arrives through the mail, from one-page memos to books and reports, from intraoffice mail to international mail. Therefore, this became part of Star's physical-office metaphor. Star users mail documents of any size, from one page to many pages. Messages are short documents, just as in the real world. User actions are the same whether the recipients are in the next office or in another country.

A physical metaphor can simplify and clarify a system. In addition to eliminating the artificial distinctions of traditional computers, it can eliminate commands by taking advantage of more general concepts. For example, since moving a document on the screen is the equivalent of picking up a piece of paper and walking somewhere with it, there is no "send mail" command. You simply move it to a picture of an out-basket. Nor is there a "receive mail" command. New mail appears in the in-basket as it is received. When new mail is waiting, an envelope appears in the picture of the in-basket (see Figure 13-2). This is a simple, familiar, nontechnical approach to computer mail. And it's easy once the physical-office metaphor is adopted!

While we want an analogy with the physical world for familiarity, we don't want to limit ourselves to its capabilities. One of the raisons d'être for Star is that physical objects do not provide people with enough power to manage the increasing complexity of the "information age." For example, we can take advantage of the computer's ability to search rapidly by providing a search function for its electronic file drawers, thus helping to solve the longstanding problem of lost files.

### The "Desktop"

Every user's initial view of Star is the "Desktop," which resembles the top of an office desk, together with surrounding furniture and equipment. It represents your working environment—where your current projects and accessible re-

Figure 13-2.   In-basket and out-basket icons. The in-basket contains an envelope indicating that mail has been received. (This figure was taken directly from the Star screen. Therefore, the text appears at screen resolution.)

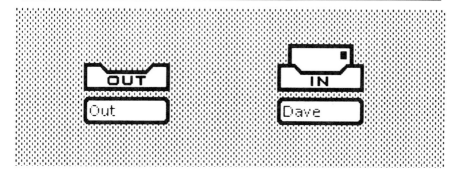

**Figure 13-3.** A Desktop as it appears on the Star screen. Several commonly used icons appear across the top of the screen, including documents to serve as "form-pad" sources for letters, memos, and blank paper. An open window displaying a document containing an illustration is also shown.

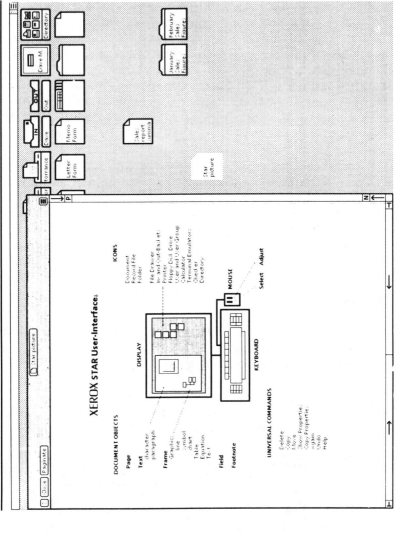

sources reside. On the screen are displayed pictures of familiar office objects, such as documents, folders, file drawers, in-baskets, and out-baskets. These objects are displayed as small pictures or "icons," as shown in Figure 13-3.

You can "open" an icon to deal with what it represents. This enables you to read documents, inspect the contents of folders and file drawers, see what mail you have received, etc. When opened, an icon expands into a larger form called a "window," which displays the icon's contents. Windows are the principal mechanism for displaying and manipulating information.

The Desktop "surface" is displayed as a distinctive gray pattern. This restful design makes the icons and windows on it stand out crisply, minimizing eye-strain. The surface is organized as an array of one-inch squares, 14 wide by 11 high. An icon can be placed in any square, giving a maximum of 154 icons. Star centers an icon in its square, making it easy to line up icons neatly. The Desktop always occupies the entire display screen; even when windows appear on the screen, the Desktop continues to exist "beneath" them.

The Desktop is the principal Star technique for realizing the physical-office metaphor. The icons on it are visible, concrete embodiments of the correspond-ing physical objects. Star users are encouraged to think of the objects on the Desktop in physical terms. Therefore, you can move the icons around to arrange your Desktop as you wish. (Messy Desktops are certainly possible, just as in real life.) Two icons cannot occupy the same space (a basic law of physics). Al-though moving a document to a Desktop resource such as a printer involves transferring the document icon to the same square as the printer icon, the printer immediately "absorbs" the document, queuing it for printing. You can leave documents on your Desktop indefinitely, just as on a real desk, or you can file them away in folders or file drawers. Our intention and hope is that users will *intuit* things to do with icons, and that those things will indeed be part of the system. This will happen if:

1.  Star models the real world accurately enough. Its *similarity* with the office environment preserves your familiar way of working and your existing concepts and knowledge.
2.  Sufficient *uniformity* is in the system. Star's principles and "generic" com-mands (discussed below) are applied throughout the system, allowing lessons learned in one area to apply to others.

The model of a physical office provides a simple base from which learning can proceed in an incremental fashion. You are not exposed to entirely new concepts all at once. Much of your existing knowledge is embedded in the base.

In a functionally rich system, it is probably not possible to represent every-thing in terms of a single model. There may need to be more than one model. For example, Star's records-processing facility cannot use the physical-office model because physical offices have no "records processing" worthy of the name.

Therefore, we invented a different model, a record file as a collection of *fields*. A record can be displayed as a row in a *table* or as filled-in fields in a *form*. Querying is accomplished by filling in a blank example of a record with predicates describing the desired values, which is philosophically similar to Zloof's "Query-by-Example" (see Zloof, 1975).

Of course, the number of different user models in a system must be kept to a minimum. And they should not overlap; a new model should be introduced only when an existing one does not cover the situation.

## Seeing and Pointing

A well-designed system makes everything relevant to a task visible on the screen. It doesn't hide things under CODE+key combinations or force you to remember conventions. That burdens your memory. During conscious thought, the brain utilizes several levels of memory, the most important being the "short-term memory." Many studies have analyzed the short-term memory and its role in thinking. Two conclusions stand out: (a) conscious thought deals with concepts in the short-term memory (Arnheim, 1971) and (b) the capacity of the short-term memory is limited (Miller, 1956). When everything being dealt with in a computer system is visible, the display screen relieves the load on the short-term memory by acting as a sort of "visual cache." Thinking becomes easier and more productive. A well-designed computer system can actually improve the *quality* of your thinking (Smith, 1977). In addition, visual communication is often more efficient than linear communication; a picture is worth a thousand words.

A subtle thing happens when everything is visible; *the display becomes reality*. The user model becomes identical with what is on the screen. Objects can be understood purely in terms of their visible characteristics. Actions can be understood in terms of their effects on the screen. This lets users *conduct experiments* to test, verify, and expand their understanding—the essence of experimental science.

In Star, we have tried to make the objects and actions in the system *visible*. Everything to be dealt with and all commands and effects have a visible representation on the display screen or on the keyboard. You never have to remember that, for example, CODE+Q does something in one context and something different in another context. In fact, our desire to eliminate this possibility led us to abolish the CODE key. (We have yet to see a computer system with a CODE key that doesn't violate the principle of visibility.) You never invoke a command or push a key and have nothing visible happen. At the very least, a message is posted explaining that the command doesn't work in this context, or it is not implemented, or there is an error. It is disastrous to the user's model when you invoke an action and the system does nothing in response. We have seen people push a key several times in one system or another trying to get a response. They are not sure whether the system has "heard" them or not. Sometimes the system is simply throwing away their keystrokes. Sometimes it is just slow and is *queuing* the keystrokes; you can imagine the unpredictable behavior that is possible.

We have already mentioned icons and windows as mechanisms for making the concepts in Star visible. Other such mechanisms are Star's *property and option sheets.* Most objects in Star have properties. A property sheet is a two-dimensional, form-like environment that displays those properties. The character property sheet appears on the screen whenever you make a text selection and push the PROPERTIES key. It contains such properties as type font and size; bold, italic, underline, and strikeout face; and superscript/subscript positioning. Instead of having to remember the properties of characters, the current settings of those properties, and, worst of all, how to change those properties, property sheets simply *show everything on the screen. All* the options are presented. To change one, you point to it with the mouse and push a button. Properties in effect are displayed in reverse video.

This mechanism is used for *all* properties of *all* objects in the system. Star contains a couple of hundred properties. To keep you from being overwhelmed with information, property sheets display only the properties relevant to the type of object currently selected (e.g., character, paragraph, page, graphic line, formula element, frame, document, or folder). This is an example of "progressive disclosure": hiding complexity until it is needed. It is also one of the clearest examples of how an emphasis on visibility can reduce the amount of remembering and typing required.

Property sheets may be thought of as an *alternate representation* for objects. The screen shows you the visible characteristics of objects, such as the type font of text characters or the names of icons. Property sheets show you the underlying structure of objects as they make this structure visible and accessible.

Invisibility also plagues the commands in some systems. Commands often have several arguments and options that you must remember with no assistance from the system. Star addresses this problem with *option sheets,* a two-dimensional, form-like environment that displays the arguments to commands. It serves the same function for command arguments that property sheets do for object properties.

## What You See Is What You Get

"What you see is what you get" (or WYSIWYG) refers to the situation in which the display screen portrays an accurate rendition of the printed page. In systems having such capabilities as multiple fonts and variable line spacing, WYSIWYG requires a bit-mapped display because only that has sufficient graphic power to render those characteristics accurately.

**Figure 13-4.   A Star document showing multicolumn text, graphics, and formulas. This is the way the document appears on the screen. It is also the way it will print (at higher resolution, of course).**

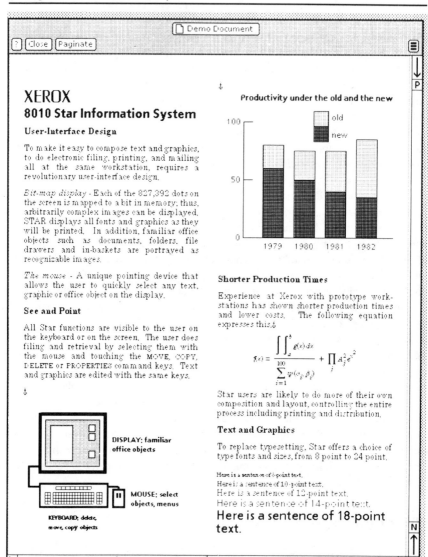

WYSIWYG is a simplifying technique for document-creation systems. All composition is done *on the screen*. It eliminates the iterations that plague users of document compilers. You can examine the appearance of a page *on the screen* and make changes until it looks right. The printed page will look the same (see Figure 13-4). Anyone who has used a document compiler or post-processor knows how valuable WYSIWYG is. The first powerful WYSIWYG editor was Bravo, an experimental editor developed for Alto at the Xerox Palo Alto Research Center (Lampson, 1976, 1978). The text-editor aspects of Star were derived from Bravo.

Trade-offs are involved in WYSIWYG editors, chiefly having to do with the lower resolution of display screens. It is never possible to get an *exact* representation of a printed page on the screen since most screens have only 50 to 100 dots per inch (72 in Star), while most printers have higher resolution. Completely accurate character positioning is not possible. Nor is it usually possible to represent shape differences for fonts smaller than eight points in size since there are too few dots per character to be recognizable. Even 10-point ("normal" size) fonts may be uncomfortably small on the screen, necessitating a magnified mode for viewing text. WYSIWYG requires very careful design of the screen fonts in order to keep text on the screen readable and attractive. Nevertheless, the increase in productivity made possible by WYSIWYG editors more than outweighs these difficulties.

## Universal Commands

Star has a few commands that can be used throughout the system: MOVE, COPY, DELETE, SHOW PROPERTIES, COPY PROPERTIES, AGAIN, UNDO, and HELP. Each performs the same way regardless of the type of object selected. Thus, we call them "universal" or "generic" commands. For example, you follow the same set of actions to move text in a document and to move a line in an illustration or a document in a folder: select the object, push the MOVE key, and indicate a destination. (HELP and UNDO don't use a selection.) Each generic command has a key devoted to it on the keyboard.

These commands are far more basic than the commands in other computer systems. They strip away the extraneous application-specific semantics to get at the underlying principles. Star's generic commands derive from fundamental computer-science concepts because they also underlie operations in programming languages. For example, much program manipulation of data structures involves moving or copying values from one data structure to another. Since Star's generic commands embody fundamental underlying concepts, they are widely applicable. Each command fills a variety of needs, meaning fewer commands are required. This simplicity is desirable in itself, but it has another subtle advantage: it makes it easy for users to form a model of the system. People can use what they understand. Just as progress in science derives from simple, clear theories, progress in the usability of computers is coming to depend on simple, clear user interfaces.

MOVE is the most powerful command in the system. It is used during text editing to rearrange letters in a word, words in a sentence, sentences in a paragraph, and paragraphs in a document. It is used during graphics editing to move picture elements, such as lines and rectangles, around in an illustration. It is used during formula editing to move mathematical structures, such as summations and integrals, around in an equation. It replaces the conventional "store file" and "retrieve file" commands; you simply move an icon into or out of a file drawer or folder. It eliminates the "send mail" and "receive mail" commands; you move an icon to an out-basket or from an in-basket. It replaces the "print" command; you move an icon to a printer. And so on. MOVE strips away much of the historical clutter of computer commands. It is more fundamental than the myriad of commands it replaces. It is simultaneously more powerful and simpler.

Much simplification comes from Star's object-oriented interface. The action of setting properties also replaces a myriad of commands. For example, changing paragraph margins is a command in many systems. In Star, you do it by selecting a paragraph object and setting its MARGINS property. (For more information on object-oriented languages, see the August 1981 BYTE.)

### Consistency

Consistency asserts that mechanisms should be used in the same way wherever they occur. For example, if the left mouse button is used to select a character, the same button should be used to select a graphic line or an icon. Everyone agrees that consistency is an admirable goal. However, it is perhaps the single hardest characteristic of all to achieve in a computer system. In fact, in systems of even moderate complexity, consistency may not be well defined.

A question that has defied consensus in Star is what should happen to a document after it has been printed. Recall that a user prints a document by selecting its icon, invoking MOVE, and designating a printer icon. The printer absorbs the document, queuing it for printing. What happens to that document icon after printing is completed? The two plausible alternatives are:

1. The system deletes the icon.
2. The system does not delete the icon, which leads to several further alternatives:
   2a. The system puts the icon back where it came from (i.e., where it was before MOVE was invoked).
   2b. The system puts the icon at an arbitrary spot on the Desktop.
   2c. The system leaves the icon in the printer. You must move it out of the printer explicitly.

The consistency argument for the first alternative goes as follows: when you move an icon to an out-basket, the system mails it and then deletes it from your Desktop. When you move an icon to a file drawer, the system files it and then deletes it from your Desktop. Therefore, when you move an icon to a printer, the system should print it and then delete it from your Desktop. Function icons should behave consistently with one another.

The consistency argument for the second alternative is: the user's conceptual model at the Desktop level is the physical-office metaphor. Icons are supposed to behave similarly to their physical counterparts. It makes sense that icons are deleted after they are mailed because after you put a piece of paper in a physical out-basket and the mailperson picks it up, it *is* gone. However, the physical analogue for printers is the office copier, and there is no notion of deleting a piece of paper when you make a copy of it. Function icons should behave consistently with their physical counterparts.

There is no one right answer here. Both arguments emphasize a dimension of consistency. In this case, the dimensions happen to overlap. We eventually chose alternative 2a for the following reasons:

1. *Model dominance.* The physical metaphor is the stronger model at the Desktop level. Analogy with physical counterparts *does* form the basis for people's understanding of what icons are and how they behave. Argument 1 advocates an *implicit* model that must be learned; argument 2 advocates an *explicit* model that people already have when they are introduced to the system. Since people do use their existing knowledge when confronted with new situations, the design of the system should be based on that knowledge. This is especially important if people are to be able to *intuit* new uses for the features they have learned.

2. *Pragmatics.* It is dangerous to delete things when users don't expect it. The first time a person labors over a document, gets it just right, prints it, and finds that it has disappeared, that person is going to become *very nervous,* not to mention angry. We also decided to put it back where it came from (2a instead of 2b or 2c) for the pragmatic reason that this involves slightly less work on the user's part.

3. *Seriousness.* When you file or mail an icon, it is not deleted entirely from the system. It still exists in the file drawer or in the recipients' in-baskets. If you want it back, you can move it back out of the file drawer or send a message to one of the recipients asking to have a copy sent back. Deleting after printing, however, is final; if you move a document to a printer and the printer deletes it, that document is gone for good.

One way to get consistency into a system is to adhere to *paradigms* for operations. By applying a successful way of working in one area to other areas, a system acquires a unity that is both apparent and real. Paradigms that Star uses are:

- *Editing*—Much of what you do in Star can be thought of as editing. In addition to the conventional text, graphics, and formula editing, you manage your files by *editing filing windows.* You arrange you working environment by *editing your Desktop.* You alter properties by *editing property sheets.* Even programming can be thought of as *editing data structures* (see Smith, 1977).
- *Information retrieval.* A lot of power can be gained by applying information-retrieval techniques to information wherever it exists in a system. Star broadens the definition of "database." In addition to the traditional notion as represented by its record files, Star views file drawers as databases of documents, in-baskets as databases of mail, etc. This teaches users to think of information retrieval as a general tool applicable throughout the system.
- *Copying.* Star elevates the concept of "copying" to a high level: that of a paradigm for creating. In all the various domains of Star, you *create by copying.* Creating something out of nothing is a difficult task. Everyone has observed that it is easier to modify an existing document or program than to write it originally. Picasso once said, "The most awful thing for a painter is the white canvas . . . To copy others is necessary." (Wertenbaker, 1967) Star makes a serious attempt to alleviate the problem of the "white canvas" by making copying a practical aid to creation. For example, you create new icons by copying existing ones. Graphics are created by copying existing graphic images and modifying them. In a sense, you can even type characters in Star's $2^{16}$ character set by "copying" them from keyboard windows.

These paradigms *change the very way you think.* They lead to new habits and models of behavior that are more powerful and productive. They can lead to a *human-machine synergism.*

Star obtains additional consistency by using the class and subclass notions of Simula (Dahl & Nygaard, 1966) and Smalltalk (Kay, 1976). The clearest example of this is classifying icons at a higher level into *data icons* and *function icons.* Data icons represent objects on which actions are performed. Currently, the three types (i.e., subclasses) of data icons are documents, folders, and record files. Function icons represent objects that perform actions. Function icons are of many types, with more being added as the system evolves: file drawers, in- and out-baskets, printers, floppy-disk drives, calculators, terminal emulators, etc.

In general, anything that can be done to one data icon can be done to all, regardless of its type, size, or location. All data icons can be moved, copied, deleted, filed, mailed, printed, opened, closed, and a variety of other operations applied. Most function icons will accept any data icon; for example, you can move any data icon to an out-basket. This use of the class concept in the user-interface design reduces the artificial distinctions that occur in some systems.

## Simplicity

Simplicity is another principle with which no one can disagree. Obviously, a simple system is better than a complicated one if they have the same capabilities. Unfortunately, the world is never as simple as that. Typically, a trade-off exists between easy novice use and efficient expert use. The two goals are not always compatible. In Star, we have tried to follow Alan Kay's maxim: "Simple things should be simple; complex things should be possible." To do this, it was sometimes necessary to make common things simple at the expense of uncommon things being harder. Simplicity, like consistency, is not a clear-cut principle.

One way to make a system appear simple is to make it uniform and consistent, as we discussed earlier. Adhering to those principles leads to a *simple user's model*. Simple models are easier to understand and work with than intricate ones.

Another way to achieve simplicity is to minimize the redundancy in a system. Having two or more ways to do something increases the complexity without increasing the capabilities. The ideal system would have a minimum of powerful commands that obtained all the desired functionality and that did not overlap. That was the motivation for Star's "generic" commands. But again the world is not so simple. General mechanisms are often inconvenient for high-frequency actions. For example, the SHOW PROPERTIES command is Star's general mechanism for changing properties, but it is too much of an interruption during typing. Therefore, we added keys to optimize the changing of certain character properties: BOLD, ITALICS, UNDERLINE, SUPERSCRIPT, SUBSCRIPT, LARGER/SMALLER (font), CENTER (paragraph). These significantly speed up typing, but they don't add any new functionality. In this case, we felt the trade-off was worth it because typing is a frequent activity. "Minimum redundancy" is a good but not absolute guideline.

In general, it is better to introduce the *general* mechanisms by which "experts" can obtain accelerators rather than add a lot of special one-purpose-only features. Star's mechanisms are discussed below under "User Tailorability."

Another way to have the system as a whole appear simple is to make each of its parts simple. In particular, the system should avoid overloading the semantics of the parts. Each part should be kept conceptually clean. Sometimes, this may involve a major redesign of the user interface. An example from Star is the mouse, which has been used on the Alto for eight years. Before that, it was used on the NLS system at Stanford Research Institute (Engelbart & English, 1968). All of those mice have three buttons on top. Star has only two. Why did we depart from "tradition"? We observed that the dozens of Alto programs all had different semantics for the mouse buttons. Some used them one way, some another. There was no consistency between systems. Sometimes, there was not even consistency *within* a system. For example, Bravo uses the mouse buttons

for selecting text, scrolling windows, and creating and deleting windows, depending on where the cursor is when you push a mouse button. Each of the three
buttons has its own meaning in each of the different regions. It is difficult to
remember which button does what where.

Thus, we decided to simplify the mouse for Star. Since it is apparently quite a
temptation to overload the semantics of the buttons, we eliminated temptation by
eliminating buttons. Well then, why didn't we use a one-button mouse? Here the
plot thickens. We did consider and prototype a one-button mouse interface. One
button is sufficient (with a little cleverness) to provide all the functionality
needed in a mouse. But when we tested the interface on naive users, as we did
with a variety of features, we found that they had a lot of trouble making
selections with it. In fact, we prototyped and tested six different semantics for the
mouse buttons: one one-button, four two-button, and a three-button design. We
were chagrined to find that while some were better than others, *none of them* was
completely easy to use, even though, a priori, it seemed like all of them would
work! We then took the most successful features of two of the two-button designs
and prototyped and tested them as a seventh design. To our relief, it not only
tested better than any of the other six, everyone found it simple and trouble-free
to use.

This story has a couple of morals:

- The intuition of designers is error-prone, no matter how good or bad they are.
- The critical parts of a system should be tested on representative users, preferably of the "lowest common denominator" type.
- What is simplest along any one dimension (e.g., number of buttons) is not
  necessarily conceptually simplest for users; in particular, minimizing the
  number of keystrokes may not make a system easier to use.

## Modeless Interaction

Larry Tesler defines a *mode* as follows:

> A mode of an interactive computer system is a state of the user interface that lasts
> for a period of time, is not associated with any particular object, and has no role
> other than to place an interpretation on operator input. (Tesler, 1981)

Many computer systems use modes because there are too few keys on the
keyboard to represent all the available commands. Therefore, the interpretation
of the keys depends on the mode or state the system is in. Modes can and do
cause trouble by making habitual actions cause unexpected results. If you do not
notice what mode the system is in, you may find yourself invoking a sequence of
commands quite different from what you had intended.

Our favorite story about modes, probably apocryphal, involves Bravo. In Bravo, the main typing keys are normally interpreted as commands. The "i" key invokes the Insert command, which puts the system in "insert mode." In insert mode, Bravo interprets keystrokes as letters. The story goes that a person intended to type the word "edit" into his document, but he forgot to enter insert mode first. Bravo interpreted "edit" as the following commands:

E(verything)      select everything in
                  the document
D(elete)          delete it
I(nsert)          enter insert mode
t                 type a "t"

The entire contents of the document were replaced by the letter "t." This makes the point, perhaps too strongly, that modes should be introduced into a user interface with caution, if at all.

Commands in Star take the form of noun-verb. You specify the object of interest (the noun) and then invoke a command to manipulate it (the verb). Specifying an object is called "making a selection." Star provides powerful selection mechanisms that reduce the number and complexity of commands in the system. Typically, you will exercise more dexterity and judgment in making a selection than in invoking a command. The object (noun) is almost always specified before the action (verb) to be performed. This helps make the command interface modeless; you can change your mind as to which object to affect simply by making a new selection before invoking the command. No "accept" function is needed to terminate or confirm commands since invoking the command is the last step. Inserting text does not even require a command; you simply make a selection and begin typing. The text is placed after the end of the selection.

The noun-verb command form does not by itself imply that a command interface is modeless. Bravo also uses the noun-verb form; yet, it is a highly modal editor (although the latest version of Bravo has drastically reduced its modalness). The difference is that Bravo tries to make one mechanism (the main typing keys) serve more than one function (entering letters and invoking commands). This inevitably leads to confusion. Star avoids the problem by having special keys on the keyboard devoted solely to invoking functions. The main typing keys only enter characters. (This is another example of the simplicity principle: avoid overloading mechanisms with meanings.)

Modes are not necessarily bad. Some modes can be helpful by simplifying the specification of extended commands. For example, Star uses a "field fill-in order specification mode." In this mode, you can specify the order in which the NEXT key will step through the fields in the document. Invoking the SET FILL-IN ORDER command puts the system in the mode. Each field you now select is added to the fill-in order. You terminate the mode by pushing the STOP key. Star also utilizes temporary modes as part of the MOVE, COPY, and COPY PROPERTIES commands. For example, to move an object, you select it, push the MOVE key that puts the system in "move mode," and then select the destination. These modes work for two reasons. First, *they are visible*. Star posts a message in the Message Area at the top of the screen indicating that a mode is in effect. The message remains there for the duration of the mode. Star also changes the shape of the cursor as an additional indication. You can always tell the state of the system by inspection. Second, *the allowable actions are constrained during modes*. The only action that is allowed—except for actions directly related to the mode—is scrolling to another part of the document. This constraint makes it even more apparent that the system is in an unusual state.

## User Tailorability

No matter how general or powerful a system is, it will never satisfy all its potential users. People always want ways to speed up often-performed operations. Yet, everyone is different. The only solution is to design the system with provisions for user extensibility built in. The following mechanisms are provided by Star:

- You can tailor the appearance of your system in a variety of ways. The simplest is to choose the icons you want on your Desktop, thus tailoring your working environment. At a more sophisticated level, a work station can be purchased with or without certain functions. For example, not everyone may want the equation facility. Xerox calls this "product factoring."
- You can set up blank documents with text, paragraph, and page layout defaults. For example, you might set up one document with the normal text font being 10-point Classic and another with it being 12-point Modern italic. The documents need not be blank; they may contain fixed text and graphics, and fields for variable fill-in. A typical form might be a business-letter form with address, addressee, salutation, and body fields, each field with its own default text style. Or it might be an accounting form with lines and tables. Or it might be a mail form with To, From, and Subject fields, and a heading tailored to each individual. Whatever the form or document, you can put it on your Desktop and make new instances of it by selecting it and invoking COPY. Thus, each form can act like a "pad of paper" from which new sheets can be "torn off."

  Interesting documents to set up are "transfer sheets," documents containing a variety of graphics symbols tailored to different applications. For example, you might have a transfer sheet containing buildings in different sizes and shapes, or one devoted to furniture, animals, geometric shapes, flowchart symbols, circuit components, logos, or a hundred other possibilities. Each sheet would make it easier to create a certain type of illustration. Graphics experts could even construct the symbols on the sheets, so that users could create high-quality illustrations without needing as much skill.

- You can tailor your filing system by changing the sort order in file drawers and folders. You can also control the filing hierarchy by putting folders inside folders inside folders, to any desired level.
- You can tailor your record files by defining any number of "views" on them. Each view consists of a filter, a sort order, and a formatting document. A filter is a set of predicates that produces a subset of the record file. A formatting document in any document that contains fields whose names correspond to those in the record file. Records are always displayed through some formatting document; they have no inherent external representation. Thus, you can set up your own individual subset(s) and appearance(s) for a record file, even if the record file is shared by several users.
- You can define "meta operations" by writing programs in the CUStomer Programming language CUSP. For example, you can further tailor your forms by assigning computation rules expressed in CUSP to fields. Eventually, you will be able to define your own commands by placing CUSP "buttons" into documents.
- You can define abbreviations for commonly used terms by means of the abbreviation definition/expansion facility. For example, you might define "sdd" as an abbreviation for "Xerox Systems Development Department." The expansion can be an entire paragraph, or even multiple paragraphs. This is handy if you create documents out of predefined "boilerplate" paragraphs, as the legal profession does. The expansion can even be an illustration or mathematical formula.
- Every user has a unique name used for identification to the system, usually the user's full name. However, you can define one or more *aliases* by which you are willing to be known, such as your last name only, a shortened form of your name, or a nickname. This lets you personalize your identification to the rest of the network.

## SUMMARY

In the 1980s, the most important factors affecting how prevalent computer usage becomes will be reduced cost, increased functionality, improved availability and servicing, and, perhaps most important of all, progress in user-interface design. The first three alone are necessary, but not sufficient for widespread use. Reduced cost will allow people to *buy* computers, but improved user interfaces will allow people to *use* computers. In this article, we have presented some principles and techniques that we hope will lead to better user interfaces.

User-interface design is still an art, not a science. Many times during the Star design we were amazed at the depth and subtlety of user-interface issues, even such supposedly straight-forward issues as consistency and simplicity. Often there is no one "right" answer. Much of the time there is no scientific evidence to support one alternative over another, just intuition. Almost always there are trade-offs. Perhaps by the end of the decade, user-interface design will be a more rigorous process. We hope that we have contributed to that progress.

## REFERENCES

Arnheim, R. (1971). *Visual thinking*. Berkeley: University of California Press.

Brooks, F. (1975). *The mythical man-month*. Reading, MA: Addison-Wesley.

Card, S., English, W., & Burr, B. (1978). Evaluation of mouse, rate-controlled isometric joystick, step keys, and text keys for text selection on a CRT. *Ergonomics, 21*(8), 601–613.

Dahl, O-J., & Nygaard, K. (1966). SIMULA—An algol-based simulation language. *Communications of the ACM, 9*(9), 671–678.

Engelbart, D., & English, W. (1968). A research center for augmenting human intellect. *Proceedings of the AIFPS 1968 Fall Joint Computer Conference, 33*, 395–410.

English, W., Engelhart, D., & Berman, M. L. (1967). Display-selection techniques for text manipulation. *IEEE Transactions on Human Factors in Electronics, HFE-8* (1), 21–31.

Fitts, P. M. (1954). The information capacity of the human motor system in controlling amplitude of movement. *Journal of Experimental Psychology, 47*, 381–391.

Ingalls, D. (1981, August). The Smalltalk graphics kernel. *BYTE*, 168–194.

Intel, Digital Equipment, & Xerox Corporations. (1980). *The Ethernet, a local area network: Data link layer and physical layer specifications*. Version 1.0.

Irby, C., Bergsteinsson, L., Moran, T., Newman, W., & Tesler, L. (1977, January). *A methodology for user interface design*. Systems Development Division, Xerox Corporation.

Kay, A., & the Learning Research Group. (1976). *Personal dynamic media*. Xerox Palo Alto Research Center Technical Report SSL-76-1. (A condensed version is in *IEEE Computer*, March 1977, 31–41.)

Lampson, B. (1976/1978). Bravo manual. *Alto User's Handbook*. Xerox Palo Alto Research Center. (Much of the design, and all the implementation of Bravo was done by Charles Simonyi and the skilled programmers in his "software factory.")

Metcalfe, R., & Boggs, D. (1976). Ethernet: Distributed packet switching for local computer networks. *Communications of the ACM, 19*(7), 395–404.

Miller, G. (1967). The magical number seven, plus or minus two: Some limits on our capacity for processing information. In G. Miller (Ed.), *The psychology of communication*. New York: Basic Books. (An earlier version appeared in *Psychology Review, 63*(2), 81–97, 1956.)

Seybold, J. (1981). Xerox's 'Star'. *The Seybold Report, 10*(16). Media, PA: Seybold Publications.

Smith, D. C. (1977). *Pygmalion, a computer program to model and stimulate creative thought*. Basel, Switzerland: Birkhauser Verlag.

Smith, D. C., Irby, C., Kimball, R., & Harslem, E. (1982). The Star user interface: An overview. *Proceeding of the AFIPS 1982 National Computer Conference, 50,* 515–528.

Tesler, L. (private communication).

Tesler, L. (1981, August). The Smalltalk environment. *BYTE,* 90–147.

Thacker, C. P., McCreight, E. M., Lampson, B. W., Sproull, R. F., & Boggs, D. R. (1982). Alto: A personal computer. In D. Siewiorek, C. G. Bell, & A. Newell (Eds.), *Computer structures: Principles and examples.* New York: McGraw-Hill.

Wertenbaker, L. (1967). *The world of Picasso.* New York: Time-Life Books.

Zloof, M. M. (1975). Query-by-example. *Proceedings of the AFIPS 1975 National Computer Conference, 44,* 431–438.

# 14
# Training Wheels in a User Interface*

## 1984

### John M. Carroll and Caroline Carrithers

Empirical characterizations of computer novices learning to use application systems paint a dreary picture of side tracks and error tangles from which recovery, or even diagnosis, is difficult (e.g., Mack, Lewis, & Carroll, 1983). In this paper, we show that a "training wheels"[1] interface—designed to block typical side tracks and error states—can facilitate the learning process for new users.

## THE TRAINING WHEELS INTERFACE

We studied a stand-alone, commercial word processing system and observed new users, people who had never used a computer before, trying to learn the system's basic function. From this, we developed an inventory of typical new-user errors. The system's interface was then modified to block these error states, that is, to make them unreachable. This training wheels interface afforded the basic function for document creation, revision, and printing, but no advanced word processing function (e.g., table formatting). A variety of specific errors were identified and blocked. The most important (in terms of the severity of their consequences) were these seven (the errors are numbered and labeled for later reference):

1. *The Exotic Menu Choice Error.* New users often recklessly tried out

*This paper was presented at the 24th Annual Meeting of the Psychonomic Society, on November 17, 1983, in San Diego, California. We are grateful to David Boor, who designed the implementation for the Training Wheels Interface. This collaboration made it possible to iteratively design a training environment from an empirically derived inventory of user errors. We also thank Clayton Lewis, Ann Gruhn, May Beth Rosson, and Maureen Ruskie who commented on several drafts of this paper. Clayton Lewis suggested the term "training wheels."

[1]This term refers to the extra sidewheels put on the rear wheel of children's bicycles to add stability as the child learns to ride. In some countries they are referred to as "stabilizers" rather than training wheels.—Editors

menu choices in their early encounters with the system. These users typically became tangled in advanced menus (for example, those pertaining to system and diskette maintenance) and were unable to get back to the simple function they had originally set out to learn. This error was eliminated by making only basic menu choices accessible in the training wheels interface. When inappropriate, exotic choices were selected, the message "XXX not available on the Training System" was displayed (where "XXX" stands for the name of the selected function), and the advanced function was not engaged.

2. *The Print First Error.* New users want to undertake real work immediately. We observed novices who requested a print job before they had even created and stored a document. This error was blocked by making print requests dependent on immediately preceding create or revise requests. When a print was selected inappropriately, the message "Print is available only after a Create or a Revise on the Training System" was displayed.

3. *The Parameter Loop Error.* Several of the word processor's menus involve a series of parameters. Users have the option of accepting default values by merely pressing ENTER or of interacting with the menu to specify or respecify parameter values (for example, the default of single spacing can be respecified to double spacing). We observed that new users failed to avail themselves of the default option. They quite typically got into a loop of specification and respecification of parameters (perhaps because the screen prompt inviting this action was more visually salient than was the prompt inviting the defaults). These parameter loops can be lengthy and frustrating, and they are totally unnecessary. For the novice, the defaults are fine. This error state was blocked by disabling the menu parameters; when a novice selected a parameter, the disablement message "XXX not available on the Training System" was displayed (where "XXX" stands for the name of the selected parameter).

4. *The Alternate Shift Error.* We observed an error involving the alternation of two keystroke commands. Both are located on the same physical key. One command, which cancels menus and selections, requires an alternate shift. The other, which displays a special system utility menu, does not. Understandably, it is the alternate key that is more important to novice users (who must frequently cancel an incorrect menu or selection). However, these users often fail to hold down the alternate shift and end up with the utility menu offering seemingly inscrutable choices. This error state was blocked by disabling the nonalternated command. Pressing the key without the alternate shift elicited the message "The Utility key is not available on the Training System."

5. *The Print Queue Error.* The word processor we studied allows multiple print jobs to be queued. Novices lack the concept of a "queue" and often issue multiple print requests. This leads to problems when the user later requests another print of another document. The output will be what was queued before and not what was just requested. The user is also prevented from revising documents that are queued to print, hence multiple print requests effectively make a document

unrevisable. The error state was blocked by limiting the size of the print queue to one document. Trying to queue a second document merely elicited the message "Only one document at a time can be printed on the Training System."

6. *The Diskette Name Error.* The word processor stores data on diskettes. In the course of creating, revising, and printing a document, the user is prompted to specify a diskette name, and then to insert that diskette. If the user misspecifies the diskette name, the system prompts for the (perhaps nonexistent) diskette. There is a command to cancel this request, but it is not an elementary command. For novices, this error is a dead end. This error state was eliminated by anticipating the name of the diskette that novices use and by programming the system to accept only that name. Hence, misspecifying the diskette name elicited the message "Diskette XXX is not available on the Training System."

7. *The Unprintable Character Error.* Different printer configurations for the word processor are compatible with different subsets of its possible keyboard characters. In particular, for the printer we used, it was possible to enter keyboard characters into a text file which could not be printed. In such a case, the word processor produced an error message which prompted the user to override the printer, and have an underscore print in place of the unprintable character, or to cancel the print job altogether (and then, by implication, take further action, such as re-editing the document or changing the printer). This error state was eliminated by forcing a choice on the user: Unprintable characters were always replaced with underscores.

There were of course a variety of other possible errors users could make. To contrast them terminologically with the "blocked" errors above, we will refer to these as "nonblocked" errors. We will comment on some of these later.

Our hypothesis was that blocking the consequences of these seven errors would eliminate some of the frustration and confusion caused in the early stages of learning, and thereby facilitate learning of the system by novices. We performed an exploratory experimental investigation to test this hypothesis.

## METHOD AND RESULTS[2]

Our experimental approach was essentially observational, reflecting our concern with the qualitative differences between two training experiences. However, the observer in our study did *not* interfere with behavior (e.g., by questioning of prompting), and hence we will report sheer performance differences as well.

---

[2]This paper contains more detail on experimental procedure and statistical analysis than is usual for articles in a general reader. However, it is felt that readers, especially introductory computer science students, should learn and understand certain empirical techniques if they wish to perform serious evaluations of the systems that have been developed, and this example may serve as a useful introduction to this topic. For those less inclined, the details may be glossed over, as the main findings are clearly described in the text.—Editors

In the experiment, 12 office temporaries learned to use a commercial word processing system. They were obtained from an agency and selected to have no prior word-processing experience. At the start, they were each given a brief self-study manual and a handwritten letter. They were told to imagine that they had been hired to replace a typist for one week, were to learn the essentials of the word-processing system, and then type up the letter—all this as quickly as possible. They were asked to further imagine that the only person who knew about the word processor was the one they were replacing—hence, they would be totally on their own. The observer offered encouragement whenever it seemed appropriate, but the only "help" provided was the suggestion to reread the manual.

Six of the temporaries were arbitrarily assigned to the training wheels interface and six to the complete system interface. The manual they used was specially designed to be brief. (In 12 pages, it introduced word processing and taught system initialization, document creation, and printing.) The training wheels version of the manual differed from the complete system version only where it had to be factually accurate in order to inform the user of the disablement messages.

The observer sat with the participant during the entire session, taking detailed notes, including timings on actions and outcomes. Particular attention was given to errors (like 1–7 above)—both to their frequency and to the amount of time required to recover from them. ("Error" was defined as a departure from the create and print action path; "recovery" was defined as a subsequent return to that path).

**Performance Differences**

Overall time and success data indicate that the training wheels interface provided a better learning environment for our participants. Training wheels users took an average of 92 minutes to complete the letter-typing task; complete system users took 116 minutes. Thus, the training wheels participants were 21 percent faster overall, $t(10) = 2.11$, $p < 0.05$. (See Ferguson, 1951 for description of $t$ statistics.) Participants who failed to type and/or print out were arbitrarily assigned a time of 120 minutes. As we will see, most of these failures were in the complete system condition, hence the time analysis may be somewhat conservative. The performance, error and post-test measures we took are summarized in Table I.

Overall success followed the same pattern. Four of the six participants using the training wheels interface succeeded in printing out the letter we gave them within the allotted time. (Mean time to complete the task for these four people was 78 minutes.) The other two typed the letter into the system by the end of the two hours but did not print. In contrast, only two of the six participants using the complete system succeeded in printing their letters. (Mean time for these two was 107 minutes, 37 percent longer than the four training wheels interface

**Table 14.1.  Performance, Error and Post-test Summary**

|  | Training Wheels | Complete System |
|---|---|---|
| **Overall Measures** | 92 min. | 116 min. |
| Total time on task | | |
| Number of subjects who printed | 4 | 2 |
| Number of subjects who only typed | 2 | 2 |
| Number of subjects who failed | 0 | 2 |
| Initial time to get to the typing area | 28 min. | 53.6 min., $n = 5$ |
| Total time spent in the typing area | 14.7 min. | 10.2 min. |
| Total time spent on error recovery | 45.5 min. | 65 min. |
| Total recovery time for blocked errors | 5.7 min. | 25.2 min. |
| **Learning versus Letter-Typing Phase:** | | |
| Total time spent in learning phase | 75 min. | 88.5 min |
| Total time spent in letter-typing    phase | 16.8 min. | 40.5 min., $n = 4$ |
| Initial time to typing area in letter phase | 3.5 min. | 10.0 min., $n = 3$ |
| Error recovery time in learning phase | 39 min. | 47.8 min. |
| Error recovery time in letter-typing phase | 6.5 min. | 25.8 min., $n = 4$ |
| **Post-tests** | | |
| Comprehension scores | 2.7/6 | 1.6/6 |
| Work-attitude scores | 12.5/16 | 9.8/16 |

participants who printed.) Two other participants had only typed the letter after two hours; two had neither typed nor printed their letters.

We performed Wilcoxon's ranked sum test [Ferguson, 1951] on the overall success data, grouping the participants into three classes—those that printed, those that only typed, and those that did neither. The significance level for this contrast was only marginal, $p < 0.1$. If we also include performance time information in this ranking, that is, if we rank by overall time within the three success classes, the Wilcoxon ranked sum becomes statistically significant, $p < 0.05$.

In brief, these overall quantitative measures indicate that the training wheels interface afforded more efficient learning progress. Indeed, a third of the complete system participants were unable to produce any demonstration of practical competence after two hours of training time. The people using the training wheels interface were all able to do something, and the majority of them were able to complete the entire task. In passing, it is also worth noting that—looking across both conditions—half of our participants did not succeed in printing a one-page letter within two hours. This remains a major design challenge in word processing.

Beyond the overall differences, we wanted to understand what the training wheels learners were doing differently than the complete system learners. Most of the modifications in the training interface are intended to help the new user get through the control structure of the word processor and on to the more concrete tasks of creating and printing. Accordingly, one further performance measure we focused on was the time elapsed when the user first emerged from this control structure and accessed the typing display. The mean time to reach the typing area for the users in the training wheels condition was 28 minutes; for those using the complete system, the mean time was 53.6 minutes. The training wheels learners were 48 percent faster, $t(10) = 2.47$, $p < 0.05$.

Traversing the system's control structure to get to the typing display was indeed an important aspect to focus attention on. Across all 12 participants, only 12 percent of the 2-hour experimental session was spent working on the typing display. The fact that the training wheels participants got through this control structure more quickly may have left them relatively more time to work on the typing display. Training wheels participants spent an average of 14.7 minutes, or 16.5 percent of their time, in the typing display; the complete system participants spent 10.2 minutes, or 9 percent of their time, $t(10) = 2.97$, $p < 0.01$.

How were the training wheels learners able to traverse the system's control structure so much more rapidly? At least a part of the performance difference between the two groups can be directly ascribed to the amount of time the complete system learners wasted recovering from the particular errors (1–7 above) that the training wheels learners were protected against. Indeed, the complete systems learners spent almost 22 percent of their time on task (25.2 minutes) trying to recover from these seven particular errors. The training wheels learners were blocked from suffering the consequences of these errors and spent an average of less than 6 minutes (7 percent of their overall time on task) recovering from the blocked errors. (Generally, this was time spent reading and interpreting the training interface's disablement messages.) This difference in error recovery times between the two groups was significant, $t(10) = 3.20$, $p < 0.005$.

Again, we must keep this result in perspective. Both groups spent a huge amount of time recovering from errors. Learners using the training interface spent 50 percent of their time in error recovery as compared to those using the complete system who spent 56 percent of their time. (The training wheels learners were of course recovering from errors other than 1–7 above, the nonblocked errors).

The summary figures for time spent on error-recovery suggest a simple additive model differentiating the two learning conditions. It turned out that learners in both groups spent an average of about 40 minutes recovering from non-blocked errors, but that the complete system learners spent almost 20 minutes more, on average, recovering from the seven errors blocked for the training wheels learners. Recall now that the training wheels group spent about 24 minutes less on the overall letter-typing task; it seems that one could summarize the effect of the training interface as saving the learner 20 minutes by blocking 20 minutes worth of error-recovery time.

We do not believe, however, that the training interface merely saved people from making errors. There are several sources of evidence for this. First, there is evidence in the overall times that participants using the training interface enjoyed most of their advantage when they were actually performing with the system, as opposed to learning it. We were able to divide the participants' overall time into two phases—time spent initially learning, and time spent typing and printing the letter. We did not ask participants to organize their time into two sequenced phases, but they all did so. Training-wheels learners spent an average of 75 minutes in the learning phase and nearly 17 minutes in the letter phase. Only four of the complete system learners entered both phases; for these four an average of nearly 75 minutes was spent in the learning phase but over 40 minutes in the letter phase. Clearly, the time advantage of the training wheels group was in the letter phase of the experiment. This difference was significant, $t(8) = 2.90, p < 0.01$.

In order to separate the fact that training wheels learners spent less time on the experimental task overall from the contrast of time spent on the final letter phase, we recomputed the contrast using the proportion of each participant's time spent on the final letter phase. The difference is still reliable by Wilcoxon's ranked sums test, $p < 0.05$. Hence, the training wheels learners not only spent significantly less time on the final letter phase of the task, they spent a smaller proportion of their time on this phase of the task. These differences were obtained despite the fact that both groups spent comparable amounts of time in the initial learning phase. This indicates that the training wheels people were able to make better use of their learning time.

But what were they learning? Other performance evidence indicates that the training interface participants learned to avoid errors. Considering both types of errors (blocked and nonblocked), the training wheels learners spent 52 percent of their time, or an average of 39 minutes, recovering from errors during the learning phase of the experiment. The complete system people spent 54 percent of their time, an average of 48 minutes, in error recovery during the learning phase. In the letter phase, the training wheels group spent only 39 percent of their time, an average of less than 7 minutes on error recovery, while the complete system group (of only four participants) spent 64 percent of their time, 26 minutes on average. Thus, the training interface significantly reduced the proportion of time dedicated to error recovery between the learning phase and the letter phase relative to the complete system group, $t(8) = 2.1, p < 0.05$.

When we further divided these error recovery times into blocked versus nonblocked errors, we found that most (over 90 percent) of the recovery time decrease for the training wheels group came from the nonblocked errors. This is not entirely surprising; the training wheels people spend so little time recovering from the blocked errors that there was little room left for improvement. However, their improvement in the nonblocked errors suggested that blocking of even *some* learner errors can have a generalized benefit for learners.

Training wheels learners also seemed to become efficient users more rapidly. In the letter-typing phase, the training wheels people were able to traverse the system control structure and get to the typing area in an average of 3.5 minutes. Complete system learners took 10.0 minutes or more than three times as long, $t$ (8) = 3.69, $p$ < 0.005. Between the learning phase and the letter phase, the training wheels learners reduced the amount of time it took them to get to the typing area by a factor or 8 (3.5 versus 28 minutes); the complete system learners reduced their times by a factor of 5 (10.0 versus 53.6 minutes). While both groups were improving, the training wheels group improved more dramatically.

Finally, two post-tests we administered also indicated that the training wheels manipulation had done more than merely limit error recovery time. We administered a brief comprehension test which asked participants in both groups about diskettes and documents, and about several of the function keys and display symbols. The results are an indication that the group on the training wheels did learn more than the group on the complete system. Mean number correct for the group using the training wheels was 2.7 out of 6; for the group using the complete system the mean number correct was 1.6. The training wheels learners did 41 percent better. This result is significant by Wilcoxon's ranked sum test, $p$ < 0.05.

After the experiment proper, we also gave all participants a questionnaire designed to reveal their general attitude toward work. The group using the training wheels scored significantly higher than the group using the complete system, $t(10)$ = 2.32, $p$ < 0.05. The participants using the training interface, because they were more successful, may have felt better about themselves and about work in general.

### Individual Differences

We observed vastly differing individual learning styles among the participants in our study. At one extreme is the reckless explorer who immediately begins to play with the system, frequently with only a superficial reading of the manual. This type of learner commits many errors and spends much of the time in error recovery, but will sometimes stumble on the correct solution by mistake. One of our participants made 106 errors during the two-hour test period.

At the other end of the continuum is the plodder who will not try anything until assured of the results. This type of learner will read and reread the manual and frequently sit and stare at the screen for periods of time. These participants make fewer errors but may have more trouble recovering from the effects of errors. One of our participants made only 15 errors total in two hours, but the fifteenth error was fatal and this person was unable to accomplish anything more in the final 16 minutes of the experimental session. Neither of these learning styles seems to be better-suited than the other to mastering the system. The two learners in these examples were equally successful; both were able to type in the letter, but neither was able to print.

One particular learner in the training wheels group caught our attention. All by herself, she accounted for nearly half of the errors committed by the learners in this group. Indeed, looking at the nonblocked errors made during the letter phase, this participant made 36 of the group's 43 errors. Not surprisingly, removing her from the experiment strengthened most of the statistical results we have cited. Curiously, she is the reckless explorer described above. (The plodder was one of our complete system participants.) Unfortunately, at present we have no independent basis for understanding these individual differences, and their causal relations to training methods and performance success.

## Error Specifics

Examining the particular errors and error recovery outcomes can further illuminate how the training interface worked. First though, we digress to comment on a few of the principal "nonblocked" errors. Mechanical errors involving the loading of program or data diskettes consumed the most time among the nonblocked errors. A typical error of this sort was attempting to mount a diskette in an improper orientation. A second type of nonblocked error—with an assortment of variants—was naming errors, producing names with too many characters, naming a document with the same name as a menu choice, an ID letter, or a data diskette or using a double name (ignoring a system-prompted name and suffixing a duplication of the name). Another nonblocked error was making an overly literal response to a system prompt, for example, typing the literal string "ID letter" when prompted by the system to "type ID letter" (the system accepts only ID letters like a, b, c, etc.).

Of the seven errors inventoried in previous studies of the word processing system, and blocked in the training interface, four did not affect the performance of participants in either experimental condition. Only three participants added more than one document to the print queue and since they were all from the training wheels group they received the message that this was not allowed (Print Queue Error, #5). And only two participants typed characters that could not be printed (Unprintable Character Error, #7); both were in the training wheels condition and neither even noticed the underscores that the system substituted. The fact that all of these errors occurred in the training wheels group seemed likely to be due to the fact that only two of the complete system learners ever printed anything. Overall, the training wheels group printed nine documents to three for the complete system group.

Two other blocked errors also were of little importance in participants' performance. No participant attempted to print before creating or revising (Print First Error, #2), and only three participants made an exotic menu choice unrelated to their task, but were able to recover quickly (Exotic Menu Choice Error, #1). Two accounts of this are obvious. First, we prepared our own manual for this experiment—chiefly to control "manual effects" between the two system conditions. We designed the manual to be usable, based on what we had seen in the course of our earlier work and perhaps we simply succeeded with respect to Errors 1 and 2.

A second account appealed to our learners' task orientation. Both groups were explicitly instructed to type out a particular letter. Thus for them, learning the system was a functional means of accomplishing as quickly as possible a real task they could already appreciate. Learners in our previous studies, and indeed typically in such studies, were instructed to "learn how to use the system." This relatively abstract goal may make learners more susceptible to certain errors. These possibilities are being pursued in follow-up research.

The other three blocked errors in our inventory account for the majority of the performance differences between our two groups. Five of the 12 participants specified unnecessary parameters in menus (Parameter Loop Error, #3). Of these five, four were in the complete system group and one in the training wheels group. One of these complete system participants seemed different from the others who made this error: She made only Error 3 on one menu, made the error only twice in all, and was the only person to make the error *after* having successfully avoided it earlier in the experiment. The other four learners who made this error made it repeatedly and in different menu environments.

We cannot say that the training wheels interface helped our new users learn not to make Error 3 because this error seems to be self-sustaining once it is committed. However, the raw figures do suggest that people using the training interface are less likely to make the error in the first place. Perhaps, having already seen that many menu choices and keypress commands are disabled in the training interface, these new users are disinclined to go beyond the training manual instructions by trying a nonrequired menu option.

Although our learner sample is quite small, some preliminary observations seem striking. No participant in either group *clearly* learned *not* to make Error 3. In fact, in the only unequivocal case of learning, a participant learned how to *recover* quickly; this did not prevent her from making the error. The participants' first encounter with a potential error situation seemed to determine performance in future situations: Those participants who committed the error at their first opportunity always seemed to repeat it; those participants who did not commit it at the first opportunity, tended not to commit it at all.

Seven of the 12 participants made the Alternate Shift Error (#4), improperly using the alternate shift key when attempting to cancel menus or selections. Three of these seven used the training wheels interface; four used the complete system. In contrast to Error 3, five of the seven participants who made this error *did* demonstrate that they had learned to correct this mistake. This included all three of the training wheels learners and two of the complete system learners. One of the remaining participants used the cancel function correctly for a time, then began to make the error. The remaining participant never correctly used it, although she kept trying.

Error 4 was fairly pervasive; four of the five participants who avoided the error simply had no occasion to use the cancel function and therefore never risked making the error. Indeed, only one of the participants who tried the operation at all used it successfully throughout. Perhaps we do have here an indication that the training interface is supporting successful learning. Learners using both systems made Error 4, but all of the training wheels learners corrected the error where only half of the complete system learners were able to do this.

By far the most costly error for participants was misnaming a data diskette (Diskette Name Error, #6). It consumed large spans of learning time and it was fairly common; seven of the 12 learners made the error. Three of these were using the training wheels interface, four were using the complete system. Of these seven, only two seemed to have learned the correct concept by the end of the experiment. Both were in the training wheels group. Three of the remaining participants, one in the training wheels group, two on the complete system, managed to make progress in spite of the fact that they seemed to have no clear concept for a data diskette name. The last two participants, both on the complete system, were never able to use the diskette name correctly and were unable to continue making progress once they had committed the error. One learner spent 90 minutes attempting to correctly name a data diskette. Again, in spite of the small numbers, it is worth noting that the training interface fostered the learning that did occur; participants who learned to correctly name diskettes were using the training wheels interface while the participants who were unable to recover in the specified time were on the complete system.

## DISCUSSION

The training system tested in this study presents a first approximation of a solution for introducing new users to the mechanics of complex systems. One obvious next step in this research would be to reiterate our selection of blocked errors. Errors we did not block (e.g., naming a document with the same name as that of the data diskette, and then confusing the two) turned out to be troublesome for our participants. Conversely, four of the seven errors whose consequences we did block, actually had little effect on the performance of participants. Another direction for research would be a closer examination of the disablement messages, which informed users that a requested system function was unavailable. In the training wheels interface, Error 4—neglecting to hold down the alternate shift while cancelling a menu or selection—elicited a message that the utility key was not available. This might be understandably confusing in that the person may never have intended to request the system utility menu in the first place! A better message might inform the person that it is necessary to hold down the alternate shift key while cancelling.

Beyond these technical issues, though, the variety of results we have presented, both qualitative and quantitative, demonstrate that the training wheels interface facilitated learning. Moreover, this facilitation is more than a mere release of error recovery time through error blocking. Nevertheless, this demonstration itself further raised a serious question of interpretation. On the one hand, the training wheels interface can be thought of as a tactical technique for salvaging the learnability of difficult system interfaces. But on the other hand, it can be thought of as a strategic technique for architecting the function of systems and incorporating online training into system designs. These two views are not contradictory, but they are different.

On the first view, the training wheels interface is an illustration of a simple technique for retrofitting a user interface to achieve enhanced ease-of-learning. In our case, the training wheels alteration was made to an existent commercial system, at the assembly code level, in less than one man-month. Given the empirical results of our experiment, one could indeed hazard that we have succeeded in giving the learnability of a state-of-the-art system a little push in the right direction, and at a modest man-month cost. But is there any longer term implication in the training wheels interface?

Clearly, a more significant and longer term goal in system design is that of defining a user interface architecture with which to confront learnability and training issues, and with which to eliminate the need to retrofit for learnability in the first place. This is not a simple issue; even the first-order distinctions in user interface architecture are only now being thrashed out (e.g., Carroll, 1983). Nevertheless, it is worth reflecting on the proposition that the training wheels approach, namely "staging" the presentation of function to users, is an architectural principle.

Consider the current conflict between the rapid diversification of user interface style and system function, on the one hand, and the goal of providing effective training for new users, on the other. Standard approaches to training, namely, online tutorials and self-instruction manuals, have failed up to now to resolve this conflict—and it is arguable that they are indeed losing ground as systems become more diverse and complex. A training wheels interface provides an alternative approach for the design of training: an initially simple and error-cushioned system interface to help develop a foundation of concepts and confidence, and a bridge from mastery of the basic function to acquaintance with the complete system (by keeping menus, messages, prompts and hardware identical between the training wheels interface and the complete system interface).

The rationale for such an approach is that a training wheels interface provides an exploratory environment (Carroll, 1982) to the new user, an environment that affords active involvement in the learning process (learning by doing) with reasonable protection from the consequences of errors that active learning inevitably entrains (Carroll & Mack, 1983; 1984). This is in contrast to standard approaches to the design of training (including online computer tutorials) which place the learner in a relatively passive role, and which either obstruct learner initiated activity (most online tutorials allow only one "correct" answer in any input field) or discourage it and provide no protection from the consequences of errors (most self-instruction manuals are written under the assumption that learners will follow them to the letter, and never make a mistake). Of course all bets are off if system interfaces should ever become so simple that learning is virtually instantaneous and training unnecessary. There is, unfortunately, nothing to indicate that any such circumstances are in the offing for the foreseeable future.

A new user is very much like an out-of-towner set down in the middle of a strange city. A goal, a map, and some directions all may help, but the possibilities for getting lost are overwhelming. Most insidious of all is the fact that if the out-of-towner makes a wrong turn he or she may not even become aware of it, because *everything looks strange*. The present research suggests that a practical alternative to the current methods of inducing new users into the mysteries of small systems is to create an environment in which the learner is either correct or else is corrected without penalty. The consequences of errors are blunted, and appropriate feedback is immediate. In such an approach, the new user is able to take control of the learning situation and of the system, to do something real and recognizable immediately, and to avoid the side tracks and error tangles that loom so large today.

# Postscript: 1987

## John M. Carroll

Since this paper appeared, our training wheels work has developed in three ways. First, we have strengthened and expanded the empirical case for training wheels. Catrambone & Carroll (1987) showed that people who learned basic system functions with training wheels support were better able to subsequently learn and perform more advanced system functions with the complete system. Thus, training wheels techniques appear to provide a better foundation for continued learning even after the initial training wheels support is withdrawn.

The second area in which our work has developed is theory. We have better articulated the original idea that learners often lose the forest for the trees in learning a new skill. We have assimilated our view of learning to Mandler's (1980) general theory of "recognition" (Carroll & Kay, 1987). Mandler argues that recognition consists of two processes: a fast, wholistic process and a slower, more analytical process. Analogously, it appears that learners need to quickly and wholistically experience and analyze tasks in a new skill domain *before* they can more analytically make sense of the procedural details and their relations. This view of learning predicts the efficacy of training wheels, and raises serious questions about more traditional, curriculum-based training design.

Finally, we have applied the training wheels technique to other design questions—in particular to the design of intelligent interfaces. Because a training wheels system radically reduces the space of available system states, it can more easily diagnose and advise user problems. We developed a special case of training wheels in which only one system state is available from any other state, a design we call a Scenario Machine (Carroll & Kay, 1987). We have designed several scenario machine systems to demonstrate and empirically test approaches to providing intelligent, goal-oriented advice (Carroll & Kay, 1987; Kirson, Carroll, Kelley, & Canetti, 1988; McKendree & Carroll, 1987).

## REFERENCES

Carroll, J. M. (1982, November). The adventure of getting to know a computer. *Computer, 15*(11), 49–58.

Carroll, J. M. (1983, December). Presentation and form in user–interface architecture. *BYTE, 8*(12), 113–122.

Carroll, J. M., & Mack, R. L. (1983). Actively learning to use a word processor. In W. E. Cooper (Ed.), *Cognitive aspects of skilled typewriting.* New York: Springer-Verlag.

Carroll, J. M., & Mack, R. L. (1984). Learning to use a word processor: By doing, by thinking, and by knowing. In J. C. Thomas & M. Schneider (Eds.), *Human factors in computing systems*. Norwood, NJ: Ablex.

Carroll, J. M., & Kay, D. S. (1987, in press). Prompting, feedback, and error correction in the design of a Scenario Machine. *International Journal of Man-Machine Studies*. (Briefer version originally appeared in L. Borman & B. Curtis (Eds.), *ACM CHI'85, Conference on Human Factors in Computing Systems* (pp. 149–154). New York: ACM.)

Catrambone, R., & Carroll, J. M. (1987, April). Learning a word processing system with guided exploration and training wheels. In J. Carroll & P. Tanner (Eds.), *Proceedings of ACM CHI+GI'87, Joint Conference on Human Factors in Computing Systems and Graphics Interface* (pp. 169–174). New York: ACM.

Ferguson, G. A. (1971). *Statistical analysis in psychology and education*. New York: McGraw-Hill.

Kirson, D., Carroll, J. M., Kelley, J. F., & Canetti, S. (1988). Specialist help. Videotape demonstration to be shown at ACM CHI'88. Conference on Human Factors in Computing Systems, Washington, D.C.

Mack, R. L., Lewis, C. H., & Carroll, J. M. (1983, July). Learning to use word processors: Problems and prospects. *ACM Transactions on Office Information Systems, 1*(3), 254–271.

Mandler, G. (1980). Recognizing: The judgment of previous occurrence. *Psychological Review, 87*, 252–271.

McKendree, J. E., & Carroll, J. M. (1987). Impact of feedback content in initial learning of an office system. In H. Bullinger & B. Shakel (Eds.), *Proceedings of Interact'87* (pp. 855–859). Amsterdam: North-Holland.

# 15

# The Pioneering Work of Douglas C. Engelbart

## 1987

## Liam J. Bannon[1]

Douglas Engelbart had a very comprehensive vision, as early as the 1950s, of how computers could change our lives, not simply at the macroeconomic level, but at the microlevel, at the level of the structure of our work habits. He foresaw the revolutionary potential of the computer as a medium for improving idea development and group communication. To him, the computer was as significant a breakthrough as that of writing. We now had a new tool that might, if properly developed, become a powerful aid to increasing our capabilities, or, to use his phrase, ''augment the human intellect''. His goal was to provide:

> a ''domain where hunches, cut-and-try, intangibles, and the human ''feel for a situation'' usefully coexist with powerful concepts, streamlined terminology and notation, sophisticated methods, and high-powered electronic aids (Engelbart, 1962).''

A major statement of Engelbart's philosophy was put together as a Stanford Research Institute report in 1962, entitled ''Augmenting Human Intellect: A Conceptual Framework.'' This provides the background for his ideas on the subject, which had evolved from the early 1950s, and still motivates his work in the computing field.[2]

For Engelbart, human capabilities are extended by ''augmentation means,'' comprising the following four classes: Artifacts, Language, Methodology, and

---

[1] I would like to extend my gratitude to Douglas Engelbart for his patience in responding to my queries and requests for information—by electronic mail, telephone, and in personal meetings. Any errors in this account are mine alone. The reader should consult the referenced papers for fuller information. Most of the work on this paper was done while I was a Postdoctoral Fellow at the Institute for Cognitive Science, UCSD, California, and first appeared in a technical report (Bannon, 1985).

[2] A condensed and more accessible version of this report can be found in Engelbart (1963).

Training. These elements are interdependent within the overall system, which is hierarchical, and whose fundamental capabilities are the basic human capabilities on the one hand, and the functional capabilities of the artifacts, on the other. These can be organized into successively more complex capabilities. Engelbart believes that the important concept and symbol manipulation capabilities of the person can be augmented by use of the new capabilities of the computer artifact. What Engelbart wanted was to develop a means whereby people could have a better understanding of the nature of the complex problems confronting them in the world, and ways of manipulating problems so that fresh insights on how to solve these problems might emerge.

He felt that the computer would be the ideal tool that could help people in this process. Nevertheless, he was aware of the great gap between the solution to any complex problem and the initial starting state of the person. He saw the augmentation means as being the ways in which humans bridged this gap, breaking down problems into subproblems that could eventually be solved, and the computer as a new artifact that could assist in this process of decomposition of a problem, reordering elements of the problem, and allowing for new ways of analyzing and solving the problem.

What Engelbart was after was "intelligence amplification," to use a term coined by the cybernetician W. Ross Ashby. But this did not imply a simplistic notion of amplifying human intelligence directly, rather, the intelligence of the human will be amplified by "organizing his intellectual capabilities into higher levels of synergistic reasoning." Engelbart saw the computer as a means for doing this by providing a mechanism for externally manipulating symbols.

Engelbart mentions how he was influenced by the classic article of Vannevar Bush, "As We May Think", which initially appeared in 1945 (The article appears as Chapter 5 in this volume). Bush's ideas, specifically the "MEMEX," include ideas of a personal work station, associative indexing, windowing, database trails, and many other concepts which were developed further by Engelbart and continue to be investigated by researchers today. Engelbart (1962) develops a detailed scenario of how a computer system might be used to assist in the organization of ideas and the production of text. It includes references to hypertext—where pieces of text are organized into complex networks, and discussion of the kinds of links one might want to have between text items. One other idea embodied in the early report was that of team cooperation—"two heads being better than one"—when using augmentation tools. He forecast that augmentation developments in this domain might be even more impressive than at the individual level.

Engelbart's vision was attractive to some people at the United States Defense Advanced Research Projects Agency (DARPA), and funds were given to set up an Augmentation Research Center (ARC) at Stanford Research Institute (SRI) to develop a computing environment that would turn Engelbart's vision into reality. The initial goal was to augment the facilities available to the ARC staff themselves, a "bootstrapping" operation to speed the development of even more sophisticated tools. The results of the ARC group were impressive, and not simply because of their invention of the "mouse" as an input device.[3] Not only were a number of studies conducted on new methods of communication with the computer—joysticks, lightpens, the "mouse" (English, Engelbart, & Berman, 1967), but a system was developed—the oN-Line System—or NLS, which embodied a number of aspects relevant to Engelbart's original goals. The original system had only one CRT terminal attached to it, but this soon expanded. A good account of this system can be found in the paper presented by the group at the Fall Joint Computer Conference in 1968 (Engelbart & English, 1968). It was at this conference that many of the computer community saw an impressive 90-minute audio and video display of the capabilities of the system, carried out by Engelbart at the conference site in San Francisco, with remote connections to ARC staff at Stanford Research Institute in Menlo Park, about 30 miles away.

The focus of the NLS system was to provide a complete "knowledge workshop" for the person, not an isolated bunch of tools. The idea was to demonstrate what it might be like to perform one's work through such a system—writing, editing, running programs, scheduling, and so on. The use of the three-button mouse, and the novel five-piece keyset, while requiring a little time for new users to get used to, offered a fast and smooth way for the user to input and edit information. Although a standard keyboard was also provided, many operations could be performed by a combination of mouse and keyset commands, with the user's hands never having to move to the keyboard.

Engelbart's major concern was how skilled users using sophisticated technology might be "augmented." He believed that the "easy to use" criterion was not necessarily the best test for a good system. After all, he states, nobody argues that an aircraft pilot should take a while learning how to operate advanced equipment, so why should not the same be true of advanced computer users? A paper presented at the National Computer Conference back in 1973 (Engelbart, Watson, & Norton, 1973) gives a nice overview of some of the capabilities of the NLS system, some of which I mention here.

The NLS system provided a number of tools for allowing the user to manipulate online documents. There was a concept of an "information space" through which the user could use the NLS functions to navigate. Graphical, numerical, and vocal information were envisaged as being ultimately a part of the information space, although initially only textual manipulations were supported. The user could manipulate hierarchically-structured text files in several ways, displaying top-level statements only, controlling the number of lines displayed per statement, and deciding on whether various filters should be applied to the text before viewing.

The user could "jump" to various points in the information space. One could

---

[3]See Engelbart (1986) for his personal reminiscences of the ARC work.

jump to previously marked passages, to adjacent passages, to a specified point, to a point that satisfied a certain test, and so on. An important feature was the ability to jump to other documents that might be cited in the original document, if one wished to read original source material. Such jumps through several documents could be saved and used for later perusal purposes. This idea is an implementation of Bush's "MEMEX" proposal mentioned earlier, and has relations to the hypertext ideas later propounded by Nelson (1981). Recently there has been a resurgence of interest in the topic of how to represent information, and how we might use the computer to assist us in the representation of argument structures (See Lowe [1985], Trigg & Weiser [1986], Stefik, Foster, Bobrow, Kahn, Lanning, & Suchman [1987]).

The system also allowed the screen to be divided horizontally and/or vertically into eight rectangular windows for displaying different views of a text, or quite different texts. Once again, in its use of such facilities, NLS presaged the development of window systems that are now common on many computer systems.

Engelbart's system provided impressive facilities for supporting group working. NLS had two kinds of facilities to support dialogue, one for real-time dialogue, and one for recorded, written dialogue (Engelbart, 1975a). The teleconferencing support consisted of software that allowed people to link their terminals to allow for a common screen information display, with either person being able to control the pointer on the screen, and being able to call up related files on different windows. The AUGMENT Conference system

> permits a user to call an on-line conference of two or more people, view and edit files, add and remove conferees, pass the gavel, and transparently connect to other machines via TYMNET or ARPANET. Televiewing is usually done in conjunction with a telephone connection, and is often used to support document review and revision in a synchronous mode, where all conferees can see and discuss changes as they are made (Engelbart, 1984).

For longer-term support of working groups, the need for some kind of archiving of designs, notes, and so on, was clear, and aids were developed. The principal one was the Journal, "a specially managed and serviced repository for files and messages." The Journal housed read-only files that were identifiable by catalogue number, time, author, and keyword, which could be used to refer to the document in future papers. So it was possible, using one of the "jump" commands specified previously, to incorporate a direct link to the original document in the paper, allowing the reader to peruse the original if desired. The Journal facility was a part of the general mail facility available on NLS.

The NLS system was available over the ARPANET from 1974, and many researchers used it for real work problems, not simply demonstrations. In 1978, TYMSHARE took over the rights to the NLS system, and marketed it commercially under the AUGMENT name, available through TYMNET, a packet-switching network (See Seybold, [1978] for a review of the AUGMENT service). In 1984 the McDonnell Douglas Corporation acquired Tymshare and incorporated the AUGMENT project into its Information Systems Group.

Due to a number of difficulties, both personal and organizational, the level of support and research activity dwindled significantly as the project moved from the research to the commercial domain. Many of the more ambitious aspects of Engelbart's scheme were never implemented. Although Engelbart stayed with the AUGMENT group and continued to try and arouse interest in his augmentation thesis, the response was not encouraging. Even within the academic world there was little interest. However, a number of the NLS researchers had moved on into other Bay Area research centers, and brought with them some of the ideas they had heard espoused at the Augmentation Research Center. So a number of important concepts from the ARC group did permeate the computing community consciousness, even if the original project had faded. In the last few years there has been a resurgence of interest in the field of computer support for groups, and the need for high performance work stations and powerful integrated software environments has been acknowledged. The contributions of Engelbart have once again begun to be appreciated, despite the legitimate reservations about some aspects of the project.

Engelbart's vision of augmentation extends from the individual, to the group, and through to the organization and society itself (Engelbart, 1970, 1975b). Aspects of his "grand design" have been criticized on a number of counts, but one does not have to support the specifics of the project, or the management style and methods that were employed on it, to acknowledge the extent and originality of his contribution to the computing world.

Simply concentrating on the computer tools he provided vitiates an essential message that Engelbart has been trying to push throughout his career, namely the provision of a complete new environment for "knowledge workers," an information space through which the worker navigates, and in which the worker has become totally "at home." This scenario is quite distinct from the more common perspective that attempts to provide the worker with a set of isolated computer tools. His emphasis is on supporting the person, and enhancing the possibilities for collaboration between people, rather than on reducing the control that people have over machines in the workplace. Perhaps that is the most important message that we can take away today from his early, prophetic, writings.

## REFERENCES

Bannon, L. J. (1985, May). Extending the design boundaries of human–computer interaction. Institute for Cognitive Science Technical Report 8505. University of California, San Diego, CA.

Bush, V. (1945, July). As we may think. *The Atlantic Monthly, 176*, 101–108.

Engelbart, D. C. (1962, October). Augmenting human intellect: A conceptual framework. *AFOSR-3223, AD-289 565*. Menlo Park, CA: Stanford Research Institute.

Engelbart, D. C. (1970). Intellectual implications of multi-access computer networks. In *Proceedings of the Interdisciplinary Conference on Multi-Disciplinary Computer Networks*. Austin, TX.

Engelbart, D. C. (1975a, September). NLS teleconferencing features: The Journal, and shared-screen telephoning. *CompCon, Digest of Papers* (IEEE Catalogue No. 75CH0988-6C), 173–176.

Engelbart, D. C. (1975b). Coordinated information services for a discipline- or mission-oriented community. In R. L. Grimsdale & F. F. Kuo (Eds.), *Computer Communication Networks*. Leyden: Noordhoff.

Engelbart, D. C. (1963). A conceptual framework for the augmentation of man's intellect. In P. W. Howerton & D. C. Weeks (Eds.), *Vistas in information handling*. Washington, DC: Spartan Books.

Engelbart, D. C. (1984, February). Collaboration support provisions in AUGMENT. AFIPS Office Automation Conference Digest, Los Angeles. *AFIPS Press*, 51–58.

Engelbart, D. C. (1986). The augmented knowledge workshop. In *Proceedings of ACM Conference on the History of Personal Workstations*, Palo Alto, CA. New York: ACM.

Engelbart, D. C., & English, W. K. (1968). A research center for augmenting human intellect. *AFIPS Proceedings—Fall Joint Computer Conference, 33*, 395–410.

Engelbart, D. C., Watson, R. W., & Norton, J. C. (1973). The augmented knowledge workshop. *Proceedings of AFIPS National Computer Conference, 42*, 9–21.

English, W. K., Engelbart, D. C., & Berman, M. A. (1967, March). Display-selection techniques for text manipulation. *IEEE Transactions on Human Factors in Electronics, HFE-8*, 5–15.

Lowe, D. G. (1985). Co-operative structuring of information: the representation of reasoning and debate. *International Journal of Man-Machine Studies, 23*, 97–111.

Nelson, T. (1981). *Literary machines*. Swarthmore, PA: T. Nelson.

Seybold, P. (1978, October). TYMSHARE'S AUGMENT—Heralding a new era. *The Seybold Report on Word Processing, 1*.

Stefik, M., Foster, G., Bobrow, D. G., Kahn, K., Lanning, S., & Suchman, L. (1987). Beyond the chalkboard: Computer support for collaboration and problem solving in meetings. *Communications of the ACM, 30*(1), 32–47.

Trigg, R., & Weiser, M. (1976, January). TEXTNET: A network-based approach to text handling. *ACM Transactions on Office Information Systems, 4*(1), 1–23.

# Suggestions for Further Reading—Section III

In the last few years, there has been an explosion of interest in the field of human-computer interaction, to judge from the increasing number of reports, newsletters, and conferences devoted to these issues. Shackel's 1985 paper (Ergonomics in information technology in Europe—a review. *Behavior and Information Technology*, (4), 263–287) gives an overview of the changes that have been occurring in the field.

For an insight into current research work, good sources are the conferences organized by such societies as the Association of Computing Machinery's (ACM) special interest group on computer-human interaction (SIGCHI)

*Proceedings of the CHI+GI '87 Conference on Human Factors in Computer Systems and Graphics Interface,* Carroll, J. M., and Tanner, P. P. (Eds.), New York: ACM.

*Proceedings of the CHI '86 Conference on Human Factors in Computing Systems,* 1986, Boston, MA

*Proceedings of the CHI '85 Human Factors in Computer Systems Conference,* April, 1985, San Francisco, CA

*Proceedings of the CHI '83 Human Factors in Computer Systems Conference,* December, 1983, Boston, MA

*Proceedings of the Human Factors in Computer Systems Conference,* March 1982, Gaithersburg, MD. (It was the 1982 Conference that really launched the new field in North America.)

There have also been two international conferences sponsored by IFIP. The Proceedings of INTERACT '84 edited by B. Shackel, 1985, Amsterdam:North-Holland, and the INTERACT '87 Conference Proceedings, another massive volume, edited by H. J. Bullinger and B. Shackel, will be available shortly from the same publisher.

A useful collection of articles entitled *Human Factors in Software Development* was put together by the IEEE Computer Society, edited by B. Curtis (1982). The recently published collection of papers edited by Ronald Baecker and William Buxton, entitled *Readings in Human-Computer Interaction: A Multidisciplinary Approach,* (Los Altos, CA: Morgan Kaufmann, 1987) contains several hundred pages of research papers and survey material, and is an excellent sourcebook and general guide to the field. The following collections, although uneven in quality, contain some good material, and are certainly worth browsing through:

Bill Shackel (Ed.) (1976, September). *Man-computer interaction.* Sijthoff & Noordhoff. Papers from a NATO Advanced Study Institute.

van der Veer, G. C., Tauber, M. J., Green, T. R. G., & Gorny, P. (Eds.). (1984). *Readings on Cognitive Ergonomics—Mind and Computers.* In G. Goos, & J. Hartmanis, (Eds.), *Lecture Notes in Computer Science, Number 178.* Berlin: Springer-Verlag.

A. Badre, & B. Shneiderman (Eds.). (1982). *Directions in human-machine interaction*. Norwood, NJ: Ablex.

J. Thomas & M. Schneider (Eds.). (1983). *Human factors in computer systems*. Norwood, NJ: Ablex.

T. R. G. Green, S. J. Payne, & G. C. van der Veer (Eds.). (1983). *The psychology of computer use*. London: Academic Press.

Guedj, R. A., ten Hagen, P., Hopgood, F. R., Tucker, H., & Duce, D. A. (Eds.). (1980). *Methodology of interaction*. Amsterdam: North-Holland.

M. E. Sime, & M. J. Coombs (Eds.). (1983). *Designing for human-computer communication*. London: Academic Press.

Coombs, M. J., & Alty, J. L. (Eds.). (1981). *Computing skills and the user interface*. London: Academic Press.

Smith, H. T. & Green T. R. G. (Eds.). (1980). *Human interaction with computers*. London: Academic Press.

Gardiner, M. M., & B. Christie (Eds.). (1987). *Applying cognitive psychology to user interface design*. Chichester: John Wiley.

Harrison, M. D., & Monk, A. F. (Eds.). (1986). *People and computers: Designing for usability*. Cambridge England: Cambridge University Press.

Hooper, K., & Newman, I. A. (Eds.). (1986). *Foundations for human-computer communication*. Amsterdam:North-Holland.

The recently published collection edited by John M. Carroll entitled *Interfacing Thought: Cognitive Aspects of Human-Computer Interaction* (Cambridge: Bradford, 1987) is definitely worth reading. For an overview of the more ergonomic aspects of human-computer interaction, see:

Bennett, J., Case, D., Sandelin, J., & Smith, M. (1984). *Visual display terminals—Usability issues and health concerns*. (Englewood Cliffs, NJ: Prentice-Hall.

A. Cakir, D. Hart, T. F. M. Stewart. (1980). *Visual display terminals*. Wiley,

Grandjean, E., & Vigliani, E. (Eds.). (1980). *Ergonomic aspects of visual display terminals*. London: Taylor & Francis.

Panel on Impact of Video Viewing on Vision of Workers. (1983). Video Displays, Work, and Vision. Washington, DC: National Academy Press.

In the area of dialogue design, an old classic still worth a look is:

Martin, J. (1973) *Design of man-machine dialogues*. Englewood Cliffs, NJ: Prentice-Hall.

Another old, but still entertaining and instructive book is *The Psychology of Computer Programming* by G. M. Weinberg (New York: Van Nostrand Reinhold, 1971). It has numerous insights into the social and psychological aspects of computer software development. Other references are:

Nievergelt, J. (1982) *Errors in dialog design and how to avoid them*. In (J. Nievergelt, G. Coray, J-D. Nicoud, & A. C. Shaw (Eds.), *Document preparation systems*. (1981). (pp. 265–274.) Amsterdam: North-Holland.

P. Hayes, E. Ball, & R. Reddy (1981). Breaking the man-machine communication barrier. *Computer, 14*(3) 19–30.

An old, but still amusing paper on problems in the use of natural language for programming is: I. D. Hill. (1972, June) Wouldn't it be nice if we could write computer programs in ordinary English—or would it? *Computer Bulletin, 16*(6) 306–312.

The major journals that often carry articles in the area of human-computer interaction include: *Communications of the ACM, ACM Computing Surveys, IEEE Computer, Inter-*

national *Journal of Man-Machine Studies* (IJMMS), *Behavior and Information Technology, Human-Computer Interaction,* and the forthcoming *Interacting with Computers.* The September 1982 issue of *Computing Surveys* was devoted to the topic "The Psychology of Human-Computer Interaction." Papers of interest also appear occasionally in more standard journals in psychology and computer science. For instance, the *ACM Transactions on Database Systems* has occasional articles of relevance (e.g., B. Shneiderman. (1978). Improving the human factors aspect of database interactions, *3*(4). 1978). *The ACM Transactions on Office Information Systems* is another journal worth investigating. The yearly issue of *Scientific American* devoted to computing usually has some articles of interest. Also, journals such as *Cognitive Science* and *Cognitive Psychology* have occasional papers of relevance; for example,

> Kieras, D. E., and Bovair, S. "The role of a mental model in learning to operate a device". *Cognitive Science,* 8, 255–273, 1984.
> S. K. Card, T. P. Moran, A. Newell. "Computer Text-Editing: An information-processing analysis of a routine cognitive skill". *Cognitive Psychology,* 12, 32–74, 1980.

The book by Stuart Card, Tom Moran and Allen Newell, *The Psychology of Human-Computer Interaction* (Hillsdale, New Jersey; Erlbaum, 1983) presents a theoretical framework for the analysis of human-computer interaction based on fundamental information-processing mechanisms. The book *Information Processing and Human Machine Interaction* (Amsterdam:North Holland, 1986) by Jens Rasmussen develops related themes. A very different style is evident in the books by Shneiderman and Rubinstein and Hersh,

> B. Shneiderman. *Designing the user interface: Strategies for effective human-computer interaction.* Reading, Mass: Addison-Wesley, 1987.
> R. Rubinstein & H. Hersh. *The Human Factor: Designing Computer Systems for People.* Digital Press, 1984.

The personal opinions of a human-factors expert on many aspects of computing systems can be found in R. S. Nickerson, *Using Computers: Human Factors in Information Systems* (Bradford/MIT Press: Cambridge, Mass., 1986).

Yet another eclectic approach can be seen in the work of Norman and others at the University of California, San Diego, featured in D. A. Norman, & S. W. Draper (Eds.) *User Centered System Design: New Perspectives on Human-Computer Interaction.* (New Jersey; Erlbaum, 1986). The recent book by Lucy Suchman, an anthropologist at Xerox Palo Alto Research Center, *Plans and Situated Action: The problem of human-machine communication* (Cambridge; Cambridge University Press, 1987) is a seminal work that is re-structuring how we think about interfaces and the general problem of human-machine "communication". Another challenge to how we build computer systems can be found in the work of the "Aarhus-Oslo" school of Scandinavian researchers (see Chapter 17), and examples of their work can be found in: Bjerknes, G., Ehn, P., and Kyng, M. (Eds.) *Computers and Democracy—A Scandinavian Challenge.* (Aldershot, UK; Gower, 1987)

An area of increasing importance is that of computer support for people working together. The book by Irene Greif *Computer Supported Cooperative Work: A Book of Readings* (Los Altos, CA; Morgan Kaufmann, 1988) is a useful introduction to this area.

New products, such as voice, mouse, joystick and even glove input devices, writing tablets, touch sensitive screens, etc., are constantly being announced, and many of the popular computer magazines contain articles on the new hardware and software available.

# Section IV

# Applications of Computing

I am afraid that I am convinced that a community of human beings is a far more useful thing than a community of ants; and that if the human being is condemned and restricted to perform the same functions over and over again, he will not even be a good ant, not to mention a good human being. Those who would organize us according to permanent individual functions and permanent individual restrictions condemn the human race to move at much less than half steam. They throw away nearly all our human possibilities and by limiting the modes in which we may adapt ourselves to future contingencies, they reduce our chances for a reasonably long existence on this earth.

Norbert Wiener
*The Human Use of Human Beings*

With the development of microelectronics, the power of computing technology has been made available at a fraction of the previous cost. This had lead to an ever-widening sphere of applications of microcomputer-controlled devices in all facets of human activity—in the workplace, the home, the school, and in our leisure activities. Earlier generations of computer equipment tended to be very expensive to purchase and maintain, and they required a large staff of expert computing personnel to program and perform maintenance on the systems. The new technologies have brought about a massive change in these practices. Personal computers are within the reach of many families, the capabilities of these systems are expanding, covering a wide variety of disparate applications, and maintenance has been simplified greatly.

In this section, we survey some areas where computers are fundamentally restructuring the way we perform activities. The first chapter was written by Robert Ayres and Steve Miller, researchers in the Department of Engineering and Public Policy at Carnegie-Mellon University. The chapter first appeared as an article in *Technology Review,* a magazine of the sciences produced by the Massachusetts Institute of Technology, which often contains interesting articles on technology and its social effects. They describe the development of complex computer-controlled machine tools, more commonly called robots, and discuss the potential social impact of these devices on workers in manufacturing industries where the robots are being introduced. Industrial robots may not conform to our stereotype of robots as human-like automatons, but they are quite distinct from earlier generations of industrial machines by virtue of the greater complexity of tasks that they can be programmed to perform, and the greater array and sophistication of their sensory devices.

The introduction of robots onto the factory floor has not happened without some controversy. Supporters of these developments tend to emphasize the increased productivity made possible by these devices, stressing how the use of robots can help eliminate dangerous and unhygienic working conditions. Critics focus on the potential elimination of large numbers of jobs of all kinds, and are pessimistic as to the equitable distribution of any increased wealth that might be obtained by the large-scale introduction of robots into industry. It is extremely difficult to develop a balanced view of the benefits and costs associated with the introduction of robots as most articles in the area tend to present only one of these positions. It is one of the virtues of this article that both sides of the debate are outlined and discussed.

The authors make some suggestions as to how all interested parties, labor, management, and government need to work together to prevent the possible economic and social dislocations that might occur. The need for such cooperation has long been felt in some countries, such as those that form the European Community, where central governments tend to be more directly involved in influencing social and economic affairs than is the case in other countries, such as the United States. It will be interesting to see whether the traditional antipathy of the U.S. federal government towards developing a coherent science and technology policy—that would explicitly address issues of structural unemployment—will continue in the face of large-scale unemployment in the older industrial areas caused by the introduction of robots into the manufacturing process. The difficulties of forecasting both the spread of automation and its effects in the workplace are discussed in Steve Miller's important Postscript to this well-known article, where he cast a critical eye back on the research perspectives employed in the beginning of the 1980s, and suggests some areas for further research.

These concerns serve as a useful introduction to the second chapter in this section which describes a radically different approach to the design of technology for the workplace. The project involved researchers from several Scandinavian academic institutions and workers from the Scandinavian graphic workers union. This group of people came up with a design for a new computer-based page-makeup system for newspaper production that embodied a number of novel aspects. Central to the design of this technology was the tenet that the workers' skills and labor are of paramount importance, and the computer is seen as a tool that can augment this skill.

The Scandinavian work is grounded in the experience of the workers themselves, augmented by the researcher's knowledge of the new technologies' capabilities. This joint knowledge and experience leads to the development and testing of various possible changes in the work process, and these alternatives must be explored and experimented with using prototypes before the system can be developed. The technology is not thrust upon the workers by managment, but is developed over time, by trial and error, so as to most effectively fit into the labor process. Rather than being consulted when technology is introduced, as in many situations, the workers are producing the very technology itself. We include this chapter as an example of an alternative design framework that can lead to actual applications development as we see here. This approach emphasizes the tacit knowledge and skills of the worker which, it is argued, are not reducible to "information flow" analyses or other forms of abstract modeling. It is unfortunate that much of the excellent work on computing applications development and studies of social effects that has been done in Scandinavia over the last 20 years has remained untranslated and relatively unknown in other areas of Western Europe, and especially North America, with the possible exception of the work by Niels Bjorn-Andersen (Bjorn-Andersen & Rasmussen, 1980). Fortunately, this is changing, as there is much that we can learn from their innovative, socially committed view of computing systems design and use.

Proponents of technological development argue that the low productivity of office personnel (compared with workers in manufacturing industry) can be attributed to the disparity in capital investment per employee in the factory versus the office. Often the latter has nothing more in the way of equipment than an antiquated typewriter! It can be argued that the office "missed out" on the industrial revolution which was based on capital-labor substitution, though this claim has been challenged recently. The claim is that providing a wide range of information technology to office workers will lead to a significant increase in productivity. The consequences of such a change in the structure and functioning of the office are by no means obvious. (See Morgall (1983) for an interesting discussion of office technology and women's work.) Just as we noted the disparate viewpoints concerning the economic and social effects of the introduction of industrial robots, the same issues arise here, and we will elaborate on them in the commentary to Section V.

There has been much speculation about the "office of the future" over recent years, and the flow of words continues unabated. Much of this literature is devoid of any appreciable content. Hammer and Sirbu are quite optimistic about the effects of office automation on the nature of office work, but their principal concern in this chapter is to clarify what the term "office automation" might actually mean. This term is generally used to describe the potential changes in the structure and functioning of the office heralded by the new information technologies. They begin by asking what it is that people actually *do* in an office, and then consider how the new computing and telecommunication technologies could affect these basic office operations. They attempt to dispel many of the myths concerning the nature of office automation, distinguishing it from simple mechanization of existing office procedures, with which it is often confused.

Likewise, they criticize those who equate automating the office with providing better tools for the "knowledge worker," as this view ignores the social dimension—the way people interact with each other in order to accomplish the overall goals of the office. Having discussed several different perspectives on office automation, they present their own view, which is expressed as simply "the utilization of technology to improve the realization of office functions." Thus the office system must be considered as a whole, and not partitioned into individual tasks. Their emphasis is on the effectiveness, and not simply the efficiency, of office operations.

Since the advent of computing, many claims have been made about the major impact that such machines would have on the educational process. However the actual history of the use of computers, within schools at least, has not shown such an illuminating pattern to date. The recent developments in microelectronics, that have allowed for the production of personal computers at relatively affordable prices, have once again brought out the soothsayers who are predicting a "new age" for educational technology.

The final paper in this section presents an optimistic account of how computers may affect education. The authors, Jim Levin and Yaakov Kareev, are active in promoting the creative use of personal computers both within and outside the formal school system. They make the interesting observation that, whereas earlier pronouncements on the effects of computers in education assumed that massive funding from some public or private agency would be required before substantial change would occur, current developments are more in the form of "grassroots" activism, with the impetus for change coming from parents, children, and teachers. While admitting that much can be learned outside of the regular classroom situation—in private homes and computer clubs—they also show how personal computers can be creatively used within the current educational system to promote learning about a wide variety of domains.

In discussions of computers and education, there is often confusion about whether one is talking of the need for education about computers, or whether the focus is on the use of computers to assist in learning about other things. Levin and Kareev address both of these concerns in their article. They use the concept of the "zone of proximal development" to develop a theory of how the computer can be used to provide individualized learning environments for the student. This concept, from the Russian psychologist Vygotsky (1978), refers to the set of skills which is just beyond the current abilities of the child, yet which can be mastered by the child with some outside assistance, from the teacher or the computer. The authors note that "learning can be optimized if activities are so arranged that individuals operate most of the time within their zone of proximal development." They then show how one can use the power of the personal computer to accomplish this.

*LJB*

# REFERENCES

Bjorn-Andersen, N., & Rasmussen, L. B. (1980). Sociological implications of computer systems. In H. T. Smith & T. R. G. Green (Eds.), *Human interaction with computers*. London: Academic Press.

Morgall, J. (1983). Typing our way to freedom; Is it true that new office technology can liberate women? *Behaviour and Information Technology, 2*(3), 215–226.

Vygotsky, L. S. (1978). In M. Cole, V. John-Steiner, S. Scribner, & E. Soubeman (Eds.), *Mind in society*. Cambridge, MA: Harvard University Press.

*(For notes on further readings for this section, see page 397.)*

# 16

# Industrial Robots on the Line

## 1982

## Robert Ayres and Steve Miller

Industrial robots are not humanlike androids that stroll around and converse as R2D2 did in *Star Wars*. They are machine tools—programmable manipulators that can move parts or tools through prespecified sequences of motions. Like more familiar machine tools, a robot can repeat the same task for prolonged periods with great precision, but a robot's tasks can be extremely complex. Moreover, a robot can be "taught" new tasks and use accessory tools to extend its range of abilities. State-of-the-art robots—mostly in research labs—even have crude senses of "sight" and "touch" and limited capability to coordinate their manipulators with sensory information.

As yet, robots at work in industry cannot react to unforeseen circumstances and changing environments, nor can they improve performance based on prior experience. Because of these limitations, today's robots are mostly used in repetitive, "preprogrammable" tasks such as spot welding, grinding, spray painting, stacking, and the loading and unloading of machines.

The next generation of robots will have greatly improved vision and sensory feedback, enabling them to perform many more of the tasks still performed by production workers on the factory floor. Thus, robotics has the potential to greatly increase productivity and wealth but also promises significant social impacts, such as displacement of workers and shifts in the structure of the world economy.

Throughout history, societies have functioned by forcing large numbers of people to perform dull, dirty, dangerous, and demeaning but necessary tasks. Factories, in particular, have traditionally used humans to handle materials, load and unload machines, operate tools, and assemble parts. Such tasks make use of human motor skills and eye-hand coordination but often require little judgment or creativity.

Robots can fill such jobs, providing an immediate overall societal benefit. In a particularly exotic example, robots may someday be used to handle dangerous radioactive materials, including wastes in disposal facilities. Such a robot was built in 1958 by Hughes Aircraft to handle radioactive materials at the Atomic

Energy Commission facilities in Albuquerque, New Mexico. Mobile robots would also be extremely useful in exploration, mining, construction, and maintenance and repair work. For example, the U.S. Department of Energy is currently evaluating the potential of robotics in nuclear reactor maintenance, and the navy and others are actively developing unmanned submersibles—a kind of robot— for both military and civilian purposes. If we succeed in creating orbiting space colonies or industrializing the moon, asteroids, and other planets, it will be with major assistance from robots. The *Viking 2* lander that touched down on Mars in September 1976 was the first of such exploration robots, and similar extended missions are now being planned.

Future robots may serve disabled people such as paraplegics, and especially quadriplegics, full time. For example, voice-activated robots now being developed in the United States and Japan might eventually perform a variety of tasks from feeding to page-turning.

In 1978, Quasar Industries of Rutherford, New Jersey, announced its intention to mass-produce a household android "within two years." The project was a hoax but stimulated press interest, if only because of the vast potential market. And Nieman-Marcus Department Stores introduced a household "robot"—actually a remote-controlled device—in their 1981 catalog. Meanwhile, Joseph Engelberger, president of Unimation, the largest U.S. manufacturer of robots, has promised he will soon have a robot (to be named Isaac, after Asimov) that will serve coffee in his office.

## ROBOTIC ROOTS

The term *robot,* from the Czech word *robota,* or serf, was popularized a half-century ago by Czech playwright Karel Capek in his play *R.U.R.* But the concept of programmable machinery dates back to eighteenth-century France, when Bouchon, Vacaunson, Basile, Falcon, and Jacquard developed mechanical looms controlled by punched cards. In the United States in the mid-nineteenth century, Christopher Spencer invented the Automat, a programmable lathe that made screws, nuts, and gears. Its cutting patterns could be varied with interchangeable cam guides fitted to the end of a rotating drum. Mechanical controls were standard in the machine-tool industry until the 1950s.

Mechanical manipulators also have a long history. In 1892, Seward Babbitt of Pittsburgh patented a rotary crane with a motorized gripper for removing hot ingots from furnaces. The first jointed mechanical arm (specialized for spray painting) that could repeat a series of preset motions was developed by Willard Pollard in 1938.

But the robotic age really began in 1946 when George Devol developed a general-purpose playback device for controlling machines. And in 1954, Devol patented the first manipulator with a playback memory that controlled movements from one point to subsequent points. Devol's early patents were sold to

Consolidated Diesel Corp. (Condec) and led to the formation of Unimation, Inc., Condec's robot division. Between 1954 and 1963, Devol and several others patented the major features of the first generation of robots.

These early robots had computerlike functions such as electronic memory, but the pertinent components were permanently wired to perform specific sets of tasks. Software-controlled robots were not commercialized until the early 1970s. The first—controlled by a minicomputer—was offered in 1974 by Cincinnati Milacron, and microprocessor-controlled robots followed several years later. Such "soft-wired" robots—really specialized "peripherals" of general-purpose computers—enjoy the benefits of huge amounts of "memory" or data storage, and are consequently far more flexible than machines controlled only by specialized electronic logic circuits. The best of today's robots can work in several coordinate systems, are easily reprogrammed, utilize sensors, and to some extent respond to variations in "real time"—that is, as they occur.

## HOW MANY ARE THERE, AND WHERE?

Industrial robots in the United States are undergoing a virtual population explosion; their numbers have increased from 200 in 1970 to about 4,500 today. At the end of 1980, almost 30 percent of the U.S. robot population was owned by only six firms, three in the auto industry. However, robot use has spread to a larger number of firms over the past several years.

Most potential robot users fall within a group of five industries known as "the metalworking sector." As specified by the Standard Industrial Classification Code, the five are primary metals, fabricated metal products, machinery (except electrical), electrical and electronic equipment, and transportation equipment. As of 1980, there was only one robot for every 1,300 production workers in these industries, and less than one robot for every 3,000 production workers throughout all manufacturing.

The Japanese have been more aggressive in applying robots to industry: as of the end of 1981, there were nearly 14,000 programmable robots in Japan. Larger estimates of the Japanese robot population stem from a difference in definition: the Japanese include some 65,000 nonprogrammable manual manipulators and fixed-sequence machines in their own total, but the U.S. definition excludes these. (*See the Postscript to this article for a discussion of why the "numbers game" with respect to robots may not be the crucial aspect for assessing technology impacts*—Eds.)

## WHAT ROBOTS CAN AND CANNOT DO

Because they are slow and have limited accuracy, force, and versatility, present robotic manipulators are unsatisfactory for many applications. There are also significant trade-offs among the various measures of performance. For example, extremely accurate robots with very small payloads allow only limited kinds of movements and a relatively tiny working volume. Such accurate but motion-limited robots may be appropriate for some operations with very small parts, such as assembling watches and cameras. On the other hand, robots that can move large payloads through greater distances are not usually very precise, but they can be useful in heavy manufacturing industries.

Robots' accuracy is limited by the precision and durability of their power transmission mechanisms, such as hydraulic lines and valves, gear trains, belts, chains, and linkages. All such devices have inherent slop, and they wear with use, making things even more difficult for the control system. New robot designs, such as a direct-drive electric manipulator developed at Carnegie-Mellon University, eliminate transmission mechanisms and pave the way for a new generation of lightweight, high-performance robot arms.

Most robots in use today must be "taught" or "walked through" a task in complete detail. However, many industrial tasks such as welding, grinding irregular surfaces, cutting logs, and fitting pieces of cloth together require adjustment as the task proceeds. Such tasks are easy for humans but exceedingly difficult for robots, which must be able to sense key attributes of workpieces to make the necessary adjustments. Robots must also be able to know when a workpiece is damaged or of inferior quality, perhaps removing it from the line, and recognize when a job is finished.

To do these tasks, robots need sensors that can measure workpieces and their orientations and compare such information with predetermined standards. Such sensors can provide a stream of raw data to the robot's control system, where data processors filter, enhance, and interpret the information, make appropriate decisions, and implement revised instructions.

Computer vision systems that distinguish silhouettes in black and white have been in use since 1973. These systems depend on special lighting and other techniques to produce a high-contrast image. Several commercially available systems that use this technique can inspect, count, locate, and orient parts as well as guide a manipulator to an object, making corrections as needed. More advanced vision systems that can recognize shapes, deduce details in shadowed areas, determine distances stereoscopically, and see in three dimensions are under development.

Researchers are now developing robotic software that can "learn from experience" and do high-level planning. Given a goal and the necessary sensory input, such machines could modify or even create an instructional program, essentially learning on the job. In comparison, today's robots require each step of an instruction to be laid out in complete detail.

Improvements in programming languages can greatly ease this transition to more "intelligent" robots. *Explicitly programmed* languages require the human operator to specify manipulator positions and trajectories. In comparison, new high-level *world-modeling* languages, which contain simple but powerful instructions, automatically generate manipulator positions and trajectories. But such languages can be used only with robots controlled by a general-purpose computer, and very few currently installed robots have that capability. As a result, today's robots, with their limited data-processing capacity, cannot recognize and pick desired parts from bins, nor can they perform complex assembly and disassembly work routinely.

Contrary to popular belief, American manufactured goods are not primarily mass-produced: between 50 and 75 percent of the dollar value of durable goods manufactured in the U.S. are "batch-produced." In batch production, a relatively small number of products are made over a period of a few weeks or months at most. Despite improvements in computer-controlled machine tools and robots over the past 20 years, most batch production is still quite labor-intensive.

Shifts in consumer preferences and a growing demand for customized products are forcing manufacturers to simultaneously increase both product variety and quality. Thus, a more flexible manufacturing technology is needed because production runs will be shorter and changeovers more frequent. Most important, the need for extensive retooling to accommodate production redesign must be reduced or eliminated. These simultaneous requirements have pushed existing production technologies and management techniques to their limits.

But a robotized factory need have no such constraints. Indeed, "flexible" automation—based on clusters of multipurpose, easily reprogrammed, computer-controlled machines—is ideally suited to batch production. But robots are not yet cost-effective in custom applications in which a great deal of time may be needed for skilled machinists to set up the machines to produce very few copies of the product. Also, the time needed to write the necessary computer programs could exceed the machine operation time. It is usually easier for a machinist to make such custom pieces manually than for engineers to "translate" the procedures into a program of instructions suitable for use by a robot.

Robots are not yet cost-effective in most mass-production applications either, because specialized mass-production machinery can operate at higher speeds and perform more efficiently. But mass-production machinery, such as high-speed transfer lines used to manufacture automobile engines and transmissions, has other limitations. Such machinery is custom built for a single product and can accommodate few, if any, variations. Indeed, an assembly line is virtually a huge specialized machine that can produce only a single product. As a result, substantive design changes in mass-produced goods are costly to implement. It is generally cheaper to scrap the specialized machinery and rebuild the system from scratch.

Thus, mass-production would be cheaper if the capital equipment were itself mass-produced and more flexible. The virtue of programmable, general-purpose robots is that a standardized unit may be utilized in many different configurations. Specialization is achieved through changes in software rather than hardware.

## THE FACTORY OF THE FUTURE

There could be no more dedicated and untiring factory worker than a robot. Robots can repeat tasks such as spot welding and spray painting flawlessly on a variety of workpieces, and they can be quickly reprogrammed to perform entirely new tasks. However, once installed, a particular robot is likely to be a specialist in a particular application because of mobility constraints. Thus, the capabilities of today's programmable machines are not yet fully exploited.

In the next few years, we can expect to see many industrial robots installed in medium-batch manufacturing plants. Robots will feed workpieces to clusters of automatic machines in "work cells." Such work cells may be serialized to form a "closed-loop" manufacturing system controlled by microprocessors. However, stand-alone robots will still be crucial in carrying out preprocessing functions such as cutting raw bar stock, and also for supplementary functions such as heat training, surface plating, and assembly. Today, human operators still have to manually measure workpieces to ensure that such "closed-loop" machining operations meet specifications. Eventually, when work cells are fully automated, robots will perform such routine measurement and inspection.

The factory of the future will consist of such closed loops linked together in a flexible, computerized manufacturing system. Precursors of such systems have already been built in the United States, East Germany, and Japan. These flexible, computerized manufacturing systems could be quickly and cheaply modified to make changes to existing products and even to inexpensively produce entirely new products. In the ideal flexible manufacturing system, the average unit cost of producing one thousand (or million) copies of a product could well approach the average unit cost of producing each of a thousand different products!

Machine utilization would be higher in robotic production systems. In comparison, manually operated machine tools in today's metalworking industries are idle far more than they are in use—from 70 to 95 percent of the time in small job shops and batch production, and between 60 and 80 percent of the time in typical mass-production plants. This downtime stems from scheduled maintenance time, incomplete use of the second and third shifts, plant shutdowns, scheduling inefficiencies, and setup time. And because of the limitations of manual materials-handling systems, there is typically a large work-in-process inventory on the shop floor.

Significantly, manufacturers' durable goods, including machine tools and other capital equipment, are almost entirely batch-produced. The use of robots and computer control could greatly boost the efficiency with which such equipment is produced. Thus, the price of capital goods in relation to other production factors can be expected to decline fairly sharply over the next half-century.

It is difficult to overstate the potential significance of increased productivity on the nation's economy:

- Manufactured goods might become cheaper as the capital equipment used in production declines in cost.
- Consumer demand might be stimulated by decreasing prices. But because old or worn-out items could be more cheaply replaced, that demand could take new directions. For example, people might increase their demand for educational opportunities or leisure time as their real buying power increases.
- A lower real cost for manufactured goods might even decrease the rate of inflation. If inflation is caused by too much money chasing too few goods, a boost in productivity could be an effective way to break out of the vicious cycle.

## THE ROBOT REVOLUTION

As part of the Carnegie-Mellon University study called *Impacts of Robotics on the Workforce and Workplace,* members of the Robot Institute of America were asked to rank the factors influencing their decision to install robots. Of the respondents, 19 were robot users and 19 were considering adoption.

Survey respondents overwhelmingly ranked efforts to reduce labor cost as their main reason for purchasing robots. A 1980 survey conducted by the Charles Stark Draper Laboratories of Cambridge, Massachusetts also determined that direct labor cost was the primary motivation for using assembly robots. Users frequently pointed out that the return on their investment in robotics would not be favorable without a resulting dramatic decrease in direct labor costs.

One executive speculated that inexperienced users weigh only direct labor costs because they do not know what other categories of cost will be affected. He said that his firm had learned how to quantify indirect benefits such as improved quality and reduction in materials requirements. But other experienced users did not report this kind of learning, and the benefits of improved product quality and increased flexibility were generally considered ''nebulous.''

Some respondents indicated that they also take into account broader strategic concerns such as long-term competitiveness, but only one firm said outright that it had invested heavily in robotics to improve the quality and competitive standing of its product. That firm was also the only one to emphasize strongly other ''intangibles'' such as improved production flexibility, and it was alone in not evaluating robot applications primarily on the basis of conventional return-on-investment calculations.

The firms were asked to estimate what percentage of jobs within a given occupational title could be done by a non-sensor-based robot similar to most of those on the market today (''Level 1'' robots), and by the next generation of robots with rudimentary sensing capabilities (''Level 2''). Based on these results, we estimate that Level 1 robots could theoretically replace about 1 million operators, and Level 2 robots could theoretically replace 3 million of a current total of 8 million operators. However, this displacement will take at least 20 years. By 2025, it is conceivable that more-sophisticated robots will replace almost all operators in manufacturing (about 8 percent of today's workforce), as well as a number of routine nonmanufacturing jobs. (*However, see the Postscript to this article where Steve Miller acknowledges how difficult it is to obtain precise estimates of the labor substitution effect of these technologies*—Eds.)

The private and public sectors should make a concerted effort to plan for these changes. The transition will not be catastrophic if workers are properly trained and directed toward growth areas. In fact, this transition will probably be less dramatic than the impact of office automation. By 2025, most current operators will have retired or left their jobs, and robot manufacturing, programming, and maintenance itself will provide some new jobs, although most will probably not be in manufacturing. Growth sectors in the economy, including undersea and space exploration, may also provide many new jobs. Therefore, young people entering the labor force in the near future will have to learn marketable skills other than welding, machining, and other tasks that are being robotized.

Even though the adjustment problems seem manageable, the potential for social unrest in specific locations cannot be dismissed quite so lightly. Over half of all the unskilled and semiskilled workers in jobs that could be replaced by robots are concentrated in the five major metalworking sectors. Almost one-half of all production workers in these five industries are geographically concentrated in five Great Lakes States—Indiana, Illinois, Michigan, Ohio, and Wisconsin—plus New York and California. The metalworking sector accounts for a large percentage of total manufacturing employment in these states. Therefore, the impacts of not improving the productivity and competitive standing of these industries will be concentrated in the same few states.

There may also be a disproportionate impact on racial minorities and women. Nonwhites account for only 11 percent of the national workforce but comprise between 15 and 20 percent of manufacturing operators and laborers. And women employed in semiskilled and unskilled manufacturing jobs are less likely to be represented by labor organizations than their male counterparts, leaving them more vulnerable to displacement by technological innovation.

Minimizing this displacement through attrition does not seem feasible. According to the Bureau of Labor Statistics data, only 1 to 3 percent of metalworking employees leave their place of work as a result of quitting, discharges, permanent disability, death, retirement, and transfers to other companies. (These figures include only people who actually leave their establishment, not those who change jobs within one company.) The vast majority of manufacturing workers still have 20 or more years of active work life left. As of 1980, between two-thirds and three-fourths of these workers were less than 45 years old, which means that barely a third of the workforce would have retired normally by the year 2000. Although skilled workers are usually older, they are not as likely to be replaced by robots in the near future.

## UNION RESPONSE

Labor unions will be heavily involved in the move toward robotics. Over one-third of all wage and salary workers and a significantly higher proportion of production workers (85 percent of motor-vehicle equipment operators, 52 percent of laborers, 47 percent of other durable-goods operators, and 41 percent of non-durable-goods operators) are represented by labor organizations. Over 90 percent of those represented are actual union members.

Unions and employers have devised contract provisions to soften the impact of technological change, as well as to allow workers to share in the benefits from improved productivity. For example, the United Autoworkers Union's "wage-improvement factor" explicitly calls for an annual benefit based on a percentage of increased productivity, independent of cost-of-living considerations.

Companies can spread fewer available jobs among a greater number of employees by giving workers paid time off in addition to legal and religious holidays. The UAW negotiates such paid personal holidays when productivity is increasing within a plant and unit labor requirements are decreasing. Other unions have implemented a similar strategy by increasing standard vacation time. The UAW is also the principal national advocate of providing supplemental benefits in addition to unemployment compensation for workers who are laid off.

"Transitional allowances" can ease the impact on workers transferred from one plant to another. In four union contracts we reviewed, individual allowances range from $500 to $1,760. In some cases other benefits such as seniority also

**Table 16-1. The Ranking of Motivations for Using Robots by Companies Currently Using Them and by Those Considering Using Them. Other Motivational Factors Mentioned by the Companies Included "To Give an Image of Innovativeness" and "To Keep Us with the Japanese." (Data: CMU Robotics Survey, April 1981)**

|   | Users | Prospective Users |
|---|---|---|
| 1 | Reduced labor cost | Reduced labor cost |
| 2 | Elimination of dangerous jobs | Improved product quality |
| 3 | Increased output rate | Elimination of dangerous jobs |
| 4 | Improved product quality | Increased output rate |
| 5 | Increased product flexibility | Increased product flexibility |
| 6 | Reduced materials waste | Reduced materials waste |
| 7 | Compliance with OSHA regulations | Compliance with OSHA regulations |
| 8 | Reduced labor turnover | Reduced labor turnover |
| 9 | Reduced capital cost | Reduced capital cost |

Table 16-2. The Nuts and Bolts of Contractual Clauses Relevant to Workers Displaced by Technological Change. Paid Personal Holidays (PPH) Are Included Because This Benefit Can Serve to Distribute Fewer Job Responsibilities Among More Workers. These Summaries Were Compiled from the 1979 Collective Bargaining Agreements Between General Motors Corp. and the United Autoworkers, Between Columbia Lighting Co. and the International Brotherhood of Electrical Workers Local 73, General Motors and the IUE, and the "Model Contract" of the International Association of Machinists.

| | United Automobile, Aerospace, and Agricultural Implement Workers of America (UAW) | International Brotherhood of Electrical Workers (IBEW) | International Association of Machinist and Aerospace Workers (IAM) | International Union of Electrical, Radio, and Machine Workers (IUE) |
|---|---|---|---|---|
| Retraining provisions, cost burden on employer | Retraining for new position is determined by a committee of management and union representatives. | | Company is responsible for establishing retraining programs at its own expense and during regular work hours. | Company will make available specialized training for qualified workers displaced as a result of technological changes. |
| Paid personal holiday (PPH) | Workers become eligible for PPH after one year of seniority and a set number of pay periods per year. | | | |
| Relocation allowances | Amount of allowance ranges from $500 to $1760 depending on | | Company provides moving arrangements and pays transfer costs: | |

| | | | |
|---|---|---|---|
| | worker's marital status and transfer distance. Seniority and other benefits unaffected. | transferred employees carry all rights except seniority to new plant. | |
| Advance notice | Advance notice of technological change is provided through a National Committee on Technological Progress composed of union and management representatives. | Company retains sole right to manage its business, including the right to introduce technological improvements. | A joint union-management Committee for Technological Change will study effects of technological change on workers and issue recommendations to management. | A joint union-management committee will discuss impact of technological change on workers. |
| Sharing of increased productivity benefits ("wage improvement factor") | Exclusive of cost-of-living, profits from new technology are shared between management and UAW workers. | | | |
| Supplemental unemployment benefits | Aid provided to laid-off auto workers. | Employees receive a retirement service, if eligible, or a termination allowance. | | |
| Severance pay | | Employees eligible for severance pay After 5 years of service will retain all union rights. | | |

follow transferred employees. Severance pay may also provide the firm with a quick but costly means of reducing the size of its workforce—workers may be paid lump sums to leave their jobs and may also receive a percentage of their pension benefits.

Advance notice to workers of technological change is often a stipulation in negotiated contracts. The UAW and International Association of Machinists require committees composed of both union and management representatives to study technological developments. (However, the current contract of the International Brotherhood of Electrical Workers gives management the sole right to administer the introduction of new technology.)

Retraining provisions have also been negotiated as the responsibility of the employer by three of the four unions we studied. As a result of the recently ratified Ford-UAW Agreement, a joint Union-Management Employee Development and Training Program will be established. This center will arrange for or provide "training, retraining, and development assistance for employees displaced by new technologies, new production techniques, and shifts in customer-product preference. Similar efforts will be undertaken for employees displaced as a result of facility closings or discontinuances of operations." In addition, the UAW has run its own training and retraining programs.

The integrity of the bargaining unit is another important bargaining issue. For example, the UAW has made several agreements stating that all jobs previously in a bargaining unit will stay in the unit. Thus, if an operator in a bargaining unit is replaced by a robot, then the robot's operator will also be in the unit.

## INVESTING IN HUMAN CAPITAL

On the whole, private industry is doing very little to prepare workers whose jobs may be eliminated or substantially changed by the use of robots. To ease the transition and ensure optimal productivity from our "human capital," the following goals warrant serious consideration:

- Affected industries should identify vulnerable categories of workers well before their jobs are actually eliminated.
- Industry, government, and labor unions should cooperate in planning for long-range employment needs and publicizing new job-skill requirements.
- Education and training facilities should be established to retrain workers caught in shrinking skill categories in more marketable skills. Otherwise, unemployment is likely to become pervasive, especially among the least-skilled workers.
- Industry and government separately or jointly should create facilities to locate suitable jobs for displaced workers and to help pay the costs of relocation.
- Unemployment compensation should be legislatively restructured into a job-

**Table 16-3. The Capabilities of Today's Industrial Robots and a Wishlist of Capabilities to be Developed, Based on Responses to a CMU Robotics Survey in April 1981.**

| | Robot Capabilities Commercially Available | Robot Capabilities Sought for the Future |
|---|---|---|
| Learning | Online programming via teach/playback modes; teaching in multiple coordinates; local and library memories of any size. | General purpose robot programming languages; off-line programming; "learning" with experience |
| Decision-making | Program selection by random stimuli; computer intepretation of sensory data; computer interfacing. | "World model" of working environment |
| Sensing | 2-D vision with binary recognition; force/torque sensing; limited speech input. | Positional sensing; 3-D vision with grey levels and color; tactile sensing; voice communication; improved processing of sensory inputs; coordination of multiple sensory inputs and control |
| Manipulation | Six infinitely controllable articulations between base and gripper; point-to-point control; position accuracy repeatable to 0.3 mm; handles up to 150 kilos. | Miniature manipulators; greater position accuracy; greater dynamic control; general-purpose hands; multiple hand-to-hand coordination. |
| Mobility | Synchronization with moving workpieces. | Progammable omnidirectional mobile bases; self-navigating mobile bases; "walking" robots. |
| Reliability | 400 hours mean time between failures. | Self-diagnostic fault tracing. |

security fund financed jointly by workers and employers (similar to Social Security). The fund would be used to pay for transportation, maintenance, and retraining of displaced workers on a sliding scale, with benefits proportional to seniority.

The transition to the factory of the future is occurring now. Manufacturers, government, and labor unions can ill afford to ignore the challenge of cooperatively upgrading the skills of the nation's workers when an unprecedented need for people with new skills is imminent. If appropriate measures are not taken, the nation will experience unnecessary economic distress and lost opportunities.

## REFERENCES

Asada, H., & Kanade, T. (1981, April). Design of direct-drive mechanical arms. Technical Report CMU-R1-81-1. Carnegie-Mellon University, Pittsburg, PA.

Ayres, R. U., & Miller, S. M. (1981–1982, Winter). Robotics, CAM, and industrial productivity. *National Productivity Review, 1*(1), 42–60.

Birk, J. R., & Kelly, R. B. (1981, August). An overview of the basic knowledge needed to advance the state of knowledge in robotics. *IEEE Transactions on Systems, Man, and Cybernetics, 11*(8), 574–579.

Clapp, N. W. (1980). Management resistance to industrial robots. Technical Report MS80-690, Society of Manufacturing Engineers.

Engelberger, J. F. (1980). *Robotics in practice*. New York: American Management Association.

Heer, E. (1981, September). Robotics in modern industry. *Astronautics and Aeronautics,* 60–69.

Jablonski, J. (1980, March). Aiming for flexibility in manufacturing systems. *American Machinist, 124,* 167–182.

Tanner, W. R. (1979). *Industrial robots: Fundamentals*. Dearborn, MI: Society of Manufacturing Engineers.

Warnecke, H. J., Bullinger, H. J., & Kolle, J. H. (1981, May). German manufacturing industry approaches to increasing flexibility and productivity. In *Proceedings of the 1981 Spring Annual Conference and World Productivity Congress*. Norcross, GA: American Institute of Industrial Engineers.

Weekley, T. L. (1979). A view of the United Automobile, Aerospace, and Agricultural Workers of America (UAW) stand on industrial robots. Technical Report MS79-776, Society of Manufacturing Engineers.

## APPENDIX A: ROBOT ROOTS REVISITED. A PARTIAL CHRONOLOGY OF SIGNIFICANT DEVELOPMENTS IN ROBOTICS TECHNOLOGY

**3000 to 100 B.C.**
Egyptians build water-powered clocks and articulated figures, some of which they regard as oracles.

Greeks, Ethopians, and Chinese construct a variety of statues and figures capable of sequences of motion powered by steam or water.

**1770s**
Swiss craftsmen Pierre and Henri Jaques-Droz construct life-like automata that can write, draw, and play musical instruments—controlled by cams and driven by spring-powered escapements.

**1801**
The first machine-operated by punched-cards—a programmable loom designed by Joseph Jaquard—is mass-produced in France.

**1830s**
Christopher Spencer develops the Automat, a cam-programmable lathe, in the United States.

**1892**
Seward Babbitt designs a motorized crane and gripper in the United States for removing ingots from a furnace.

**1921**
Czech playwright Karel Capek's play *R.U.R.* (Rossum's Universal Robots) opens in London, popularizing the word *robot*—derived from the Czech word for *forced laborer*.

**1938–39**
Programmable paint-spraying machines are designed in the United States by Harold Roselund working for the DeVilbiss Co., and Willard Pollard.

**1946**
In the United States, George Devol develops the magnetic process controller (a general-purpose playback device for controlling machines) and inaugurates the age of programmable industrial machinery in the same year.

J. Presper Eckert and John Mauchly build the first large electronic computer, the ENIAC, at the University of Pennsylvania, sponsored by the U.S. army.

Whirlwind, the first general purpose digital computer solves its first problem at MIT.

**1948**
MIT professor Norbert Wiener publishes *Cybernetics*, popularizing the concepts of communications and control involved in electronic, mechanical and biological systems.

**1951**
Raymond Goertz, working for the Atomic Energy Commission, develops a remote-controlled electrical teleoperator equipped with an articulated arm.

**1952**
The first numerically-controlled machine tool is built at the MIT Servomechanism Lab.

**1954**
Devol develops the first programmable robot, and in describing its point-to-point control and electronic playback memory, coins the phrase *universal automation*, shortened later to unimation.

**1958**
Hughes Aircraft develops a mobile, two-armed, remote-controlled teleoperator for the Atomic Energy Commission to be used in radioactive environments.

**1959**
Planet Corp. builds—and sells—the first commercially available robots.

**1960**
Devol's patents are acquired by Consolidated Diesel Corp. (Condec), which develops the Unimate robot through its newly formed subsiduary Unimation, Inc. (now the world's largest robot manufacturer).

Harry Johnson and Veljko Milenkovic design a programmable robot for the American Machine and Foundry Co.

**1961**
At MIT, Hienrich Ernst builds an electrically-powered mechanical hand, equipped with touch sensors and controlled by a computer.

**1962**
General Motors installs its first Unimate robot on the assembly line.

**Mid-1960s**
Robot or artificial intelligence research laboratories open at MIT, Stanford Research Institute (SRI) International, Stanford University, and the University of Edinburgh.

**1965**
An aluminium prosthetic hand is developed by Rajko Tomovic at the University of Belgrade, prefiguring the development of remote-controlled teleoperator devices with sophisticated sensory feedback.

**1967**
General Electric builds what proves to be an unmanageable quadruped vehicle for the Department of Defence—all four legs required simultaneous manipulation by a single human operator.

**1968**
An "intelligent" mobile robot, equipped with a television camera, optical range finder, touch sensors, and the capability of deciphering English commands, is built at SRI International and named Shakey for its characteristic movement. In the same year, Andrew Frank's quadruped vehicle, controlled by a small onboard computer, takes its first steps at the University of Southern California.

**1970**
Victor Scheinman demonstrates what becomes known as the Stanford arm—a small, electrically powered manipulator—at Stanford University.

**1972**
The force vector assembly concept, by which a servocontroller can guide the assembly of parts, is developed at the Charles Stark Draper Laboratories.

**1973**
A computer-integrated robot assembly station, developed at Stanford, puts together 10 automobile water pumps, in an experiment there.

Richard Hohn develops the T³, The first commercially available minicomputer controlled robot for Cincinnati Milacron.

**1974**
Following the development of his first Vicarm—a small electronically powered arm— Scheinman founds Vicarm Inc., and builds a minicomputer controlled arm.

**1976**
NASA's Viking 1 and 2 landers perform on Mars with their sample-collecting arms.

Vicarm builds the first microprocessor-controlled robot and ships it to the Navy Research Lab.

A compliant robot wrist is developed by Draper Labs.

A vision system and a robot programming language (AL) are interfaced by Ralph Bolles at Stanford.

The HARPY speech understanding system is completed by Raj Reddy at Carnegie-Mellon.

**1977**
A hexapod vehicle, developed by Robert McGee, walks while tethered to a computer at Ohio State University. A similar machine walks at the Moscow Institute for Mechanics.

ASEA commercializes a microprocessor-controlled electrically-activated robot in two sizes.

A vision module developed at SRI International is marketed by Machine Intelligence Corp.

**1978**
The first PUMA (programmable universal machine for assembly) prototype based on Sheinman's MIT model arm is shipped to General Motors by Unimation Inc. which acquired Vicarm the previous year.

**1979**
The first version of ACRONYM, a vision system based on geometric reasoning is developed at Stanford.

**1980**

The Robotics Institute (now the largest academic robot lab in the United States) opens at Carnegie-Mellon.

The University of Rhode Island demonstrates a robotic system that picks randomly stacked rods out of a bin.

A mobile robot developed by Hans Moravec at Stanford negotiates a simple obstacle course taking 15 minutes to move three feet.

**1981**

A direct-drive manipulator with no mechanical linkages is developed by Harry Asada and Takeo Kanade at Carnegie Mellon—enabling the robotic device to move with great accuracy at high speeds.

Unimation demonstrates a PUMA mounted on a microprocessor-controlled mobile base.

The Neiman-Marcus Christmas Catalogue advertises a Unimation designed "Domestic Robot System," that can open the door, take out the trash, bring in the paper, sweep the floor, water the plants, dust the furniture, pick up after the children and pour the wine. The delux model includes a color TV and an AM/FM stereo radio and cassette player. The catalogue also describes a robot pet named Wires.

**1982**

Donald Seltzer builds a sophisticated force-sensor for the Draper Labs wrist, enabling the robot's microprocessor to calculate the force exerted by the robot hand and manipulate the hand and arm accordingly.

At Carnegie-Mellon Moravec designs a prototype of the second generation "Moravec cart," improving the speed tenfold and adding three-dimensional vision.

# Robots on the Line Revisited—Postscript, 1988*

## Steve Miller

Labor requirements on the factory floor are being affected by a wide range of automation technologies in addition to robotic manipulators, such as computer-controlled machine tools, material-handling systems, and programmable controls. Combinations of these other types of programmable automation can sometimes be substituted for robotic manipulators. For example, there are situations where a material-handling system with the appropriate type of programmable controls can perform the functions of a material-handling robot. There are also cases where the boundaries between what is a robot and what is some other form of programmable automation are not so clear. And as automation in general becomes "more robotic" (i.e., more programmable, more adaptable, and more multifunctional), the distinctions between what is and what is not an industrial robot will become increasingly blurred.

Clearly, the question of how many workers are likely to be displaced by industrial robots in future years is only one element of the more general question of how many workers in manufacturing are likely to be displaced by factory automation. Forecasting technologically-induced displacement is further complicated by the fact that changes in production technology are increasingly accompanied by efforts to simplify or rationalize both the design of the product and the sequence of production activities. These types of change also affect the labor requirement per unit of output. It is evident that multiple forms of technology and multiple factors are altering production labor requirements per unit of output on the factory floor. Given that, one wonders if it is possible to forecast the component of job displacement that is attributable specifically to industrial robots. In some cases, perhaps. In many cases, undoubtedly not. And even if the portion of job displacement induced by robot use could be disentangled from overall technologically-induced displacement, is it important to do this? Probably not.

Why, then, did we attempt to estimate the job displacement impact of robot use in the preceding article? The answer lies in the mind-set that seemed to prevail among both technologists and analysts of technological change in the late 1970s and early 1980s. That was the time when an understanding of the inefficiencies of current manufacturing methods had become a popular "cutting edge" topic for a certain set of technological and managerial avant-garde. It was also the period in which the groundswell of both commercial and research interests in robotics began. In 1980, Joseph Engelberger, recognized as the father

---

*The following material is extracted, with minor changes, from: Miller, S. M. *Impacts of Industrial Robotics: Potential Effects on Labor and Costs within the Metalworking Industries* (Madison, WI, University of Wisconsin Press, 1988).

of the commercial robotics industry, released his book *Robotics in Practice,* which spurred interest in robot applications. At that time, there was publicity around the fact that Japan was then leading the world in the number of robots installed in factories. The first commercially available robot truly controlled by computer software, the Cincinnati Milacron T3, had recently appeared on the market, demonstrating that new technology could improve robot capabilities. Much publicity surrounded the inauguration of new research centers, such as the Carnegie Mellon Robotics Institute, that set out to develop a new generation of "intelligent robots."

Although it was clear back then that robots were not the only new technology relevant for automating factory operations, it seemed that they were the key technology. Robot use was regarded as the bellwether of a great change that was on the threshold of taking place in factories throughout the world. Robots were going to have an important impact! The issues then became figuring out what that impact would be. It was important to think ahead and anticipate some of the consequences of the inevitable "robotization" of the factory.

Given the mind-set that existed in the late 1970s and early 1980s, if one were going to think about the impact of technology on factory operations, it seemed reasonable (as well as fashionable) to think about changes that would occur as a result of using robots. One obvious consequence would be that robots would perform some of the tasks currently performed by production workers. Thus, as part of looking at the impending impact of robot use, what seemed important, perhaps critical, was to estimate how many jobs would likely be taken over by robots. This is why several studies done in the early 1980s, including our own (Ayres & Miller, 1983), specifically addressed the issue of how many workers would likely be displaced by robots over the next 10 to 20 years.

What are the implications of the points made above? One implication is that if the objective of analysis is to predict future levels of technologically-induced displacement of production workers, it does not make sense to scrutinize or fine-tune many of the details of the earlier robot displacement studies. Details on the number of robots projected to be in use are important to the issue of forecasting the size of the robot market. But such details, even if correct, would provide only part of the information required to predict future levels of worker displacement in manufacturing. The same point holds for details on the fraction of jobs within specific occupational categories that could potentially be performed by robots. Such details would be important for forecasting displacement if one could obtain estimates that represent the effect of automation and technological change in general, as opposed to the effect of robotic manipulators in particular.

For policy analysts and planners interested in manufacturing, anticipating the likely magnitude and timing of job displacement on the factory floor has always been important. It still is. What is evident from the experience of manufacturers in the 1980s is that displacement is being induced by multiple types of change in the production process, as well as by change in managerial practices and in the design of products. Therefore, if one sets out to forecast displacement of production workers within an industry or sector, it should be approached from a broader perspective that encompasses the full set of factors affecting labor requirements. It should not be approached from a technology-specific perspective, such as trying to forecast the number of workers that will be displaced by robots.

Even if we are clear about the type of worker that could be displaced by programmable automation in general or by robots in particular, there is another issue that complicates the forecasting of displacement. We are not certain about when, or even whether, the technology will actually be adopted by potential users. The ability to predict the full cost and benefit of adopting the technology is key to forecasting its rate of diffusion, and hence it is key to estimating the rate at which displacement will occur. The problem is, the *total* costs and benefits of implementing and using new technologies on the factory floor are still not fully understood. This leads to uncertainty in the analysis of whether or not potential users will have a strong enough economic incentive to adopt new technology. Because of such uncertainty, there will continue to be ambiguity as to the size of the gap between engineering-based estimates of the theoretical potential for displacing workers and more economic-based estimates of the number of workers that may actually be displaced within a given time frame.

Within the past several years, the topic of financial justification for new technologies in manufacturing has received much attention in the communities of both the practitioner and the researcher. As a result of these efforts, there is growing understanding of the economic impact of using new technologies. The major contribution of the new work on financial justification has been in recognizing and quantifying a fuller range of financial benefits beyond reduction of direct labor cost (e.g., financial benefits associated with changes in levels of quality, inventory, productivity, flexibility, innovation). What has received less attention, though, is the recognition and quantification of the full range of costs for planning, implementing, and operating robots and other new factory-floor technologies. The more time one spends around automation projects in industry, especially large projects, the more evident it becomes that the cost of the equipment is only a small fraction of the cost of automating. For example, there are costs of focusing large blocks of managerial time on automation projects, training costs, support costs, and many costs associated with making transitions within the organization. And these costs can vary over time as more experience is gained with using the technology. As the full range and dynamic nature of costs and benefits of using technologies are recognized and as a consensus emerges on approaches for quantification, the ability to forecast the rate of diffusion should improve. This in turn would improve our ability to distinguish between predictions of upper bounds on potential displacement and predictions of what will most likely happen in the near-term future.

In addition to these difficulties in forecasting technologically-induced displacement, there are limitations on what can be learned from such an analysis.

The first limitation is that even if we know for sure the number of jobs in an industry that could be performed by robots or other machines, we do not know how many of the workers who do these jobs will become redundant. This depends on the total demand for the industry's output. Thus, while the Leontief and Duchin (1984) study forecasts that several million jobs will be performed by robots and other types of factory-automation technology over a 20-year period, it also forecasts there will actually be more people working in these same jobs because the forecasted growth in the level of output would offset the effects of displacement. Technologically-induced displacement is only one of the factors effecting changes in the level of employment within occupations in industry. And the consensus of analysts is that, compared with the effect of changes in the level of demand, displacement is not even a primary factor affecting employment levels. The second limitation is that the most dramatic labor-force impact resulting from the use of new factory automation technologies appears to be changes in the nature of work, and hence in skill requirements for the related workers.

On one hand, an industry-wide or sector-wide study of displacement is too narrow. It does not address the issue of net changes in employment within occupational groups because the influences of macroeconomic factors, such as demand levels, are not considered. Economic models of industries and of the economy are needed for this. On the other hand, a study of displacement alone is too broad, because it does not provide enough detail on how the use of the technology will change the nature of the work and the skill requirements. Organizational-level studies of technology implementation and use are needed for this.

Despite the difficulties and limitations of analyzing the impact of robot use on job displacement, the studies on this topic still made an important contribution to the more general analysis of the impact of robotics and factory automation on the labor force. These studies have been used as a starting point, a point of contrast, or a general motivator for a number of other studies which have subsequently been carried out by other researchers. For example, the study by the Office of Technology Assessment (OTA, 1984), which looks more broadly at the labor-force impact of a factory automation, used as its starting point several of the studies on the impact of robot use. The Leontief and Duchin (1984) study, which simultaneously considers the effects of automation technologies and macroeconomic influences on job requirements, also used several of the robot displacement studies as a data source for making assumptions about the impact of technology. Also, studies by organizational researchers, which have looked with more depth into how the use of factory automation is affecting the nature of work within specific companies, cite the robotic displacement studies as motivation for the widespread importance of researching the topic.

The following scenario was analyzed in work which came after the "Industrial Robots on the Line" article: a conventional factory (circa 1980) which produces batches of specialized products is reorganized and automated with robots and other types of programmable automation technology so that it can produce specialized products in a continuous fashion around the clock. The framework used in *Impacts of Industrial Robotics* for estimating the resulting reduction in unit cost is the assumption that this "ideal" flexibly automated plant, capable of continuously producing specialized products in small batches, would have some of the operating characteristics of conventional mass-production plants which produce standardized products in large volumes. Relationships between unit cost and the level of output derived from a cross-sectional analysis of industries using the 1980s generation of production technology provide the basis for estimating potential cost reductions in the hypothetical high-volume batch-production facility. The result of the analysis is that several-fold increases in the output of a batch-production facility would lead to a substantial decrease in unit cost. For example, if the output of the new facility were twice that of the conventional one, the estimated decrease in unit cost would range from 18 to 26 percent. If it were 10 times greater, the estimated decrease in unit cost would range from 50 to 65 percent.

Because of the inferences and approximations required to do the work, the analysis is only suggestive of the economics of production in a newly designed, flexibly automated plant. Nonetheless, if the inference of this analysis is correct, and it is the case that a flexibly automated batch-production plant would have a substantial cost advantage over a conventionally organized facility, one would expect that this type of plant would begin diffusing throughout manufacturing industries. In fact, current examples of flexible manufacturing systems for machining, particularly the Japanese systems, are the initial attempts at building such facilities. And many major manufacturers throughout the world have plans in progress to construct flexibly automated plants for batch production.

If a plant could be built having several times the capacity of a conventional batch-production plant and the flexibility to produce a mix of different products, it would be possible to close down several existing plants and consolidate their production into the new facility. This seems likely if the flexibly automated plant were to be built in a mature industry where the potential for market growth is limited. An example worked out in *Impacts of Industrial Robotics* shows that if three plants were closed down and their output consolidated into one high-volume, flexibly automated plant, total labor requirements would decrease by 30 to 40 percent. This estimated decrease in labor requirements is based on the elasticity of unit production-labor cost, which is estimated from the regression analysis based on the use of conventional types of technology across low-, medium-, and high-volume industries as of 1977. More recent information available from the existing flexible manufacturing systems in operation indicates that the one flexibly automated plant would most likely have substantially fewer workers than even one of the smaller plants it replaces. If this were the case, the percentage of decrease in total labor requirements would be much larger.

Since the flexible factory scenario holds the largest promise for reducing unit cost and potentially poses the largest threat to employment in an industry, it warrants more extensive analysis. Further research should focus on a more refined and direct analysis of the economics of production in flexibly automated factories, and on forecasts of their use within specific industries.

## REFERENCES

Ayres, R. U., & Miller, S. M. (1983). *Robotics: Applications and social implications.* Cambridge, MA: Ballinger Publishing Co.

Engelberger, J. F. (1980). *Robotics in practice.* New York: American Management Association.

Leontief, W., & Duchin, F. (1984, April). The impacts of automation on employment, 1963–2000. Technical Report, Institute for Economic Analysis, New York University.

Miller, S. M. (1988). *Impacts of industrial robotics: Effects on Labor and cost in the metalworking industries.* Madison, Wisconsin: University of Wisconsin Press.

U. S. Congress, Office of Technology Assessment. (1984). *Computerized manufacturing automation: Employment, education, and the workplace.* Washington, DC: U. S. Government Printing Office.

# 17

# Utopia: Where Workers Craft New Technology

## 1985

### Robert Howard

The sign on the door reads "technical laboratory." The walls are festooned with elaborate diagrams. In one corner a slide carousel projects images onto a small, VDT-sized screen, simulating a computerized work station in operation. In another corner, an individual puts together the photographs, headlines, and text of a newspaper page on the screen of a real terminal. At his side an observer jots down a few notes and asks an occasional question about the quality of the "interface" and the "feel" of the machine.

It could be a scene from the research department at any high-tech computer manufacturer. But this lab is in the government-funded Swedish Center for Working Life in Stockholm. The individual using the terminal belongs to the Swedish Graphics Workers Union, while his partner is a computer scientist from Sweden's Royal Institute of Technology. Both worker and scientist are participants in an intriguing experiment in technology development known as the UTOPIA Project.

UTOPIA is a Swedish acronym for "training, technology, and products from a skilled worker's perspective." It is a three-year $400,000 research effort, funded primarily by public sources, that has brought together two quite different social groups: on the one hand, systems designers, computer scientists, and work-efficiency experts at institutions in Sweden and Denmark; and on the other, activists and officials from unions representing some 120,000 printers, typographers, lithographers, and other skilled workers in the newspaper and printing industries of the five Nordic countries.

Since 1981, UTOPIA participants have worked to define a role for trade unions in the design of new workplace technology. The goal is to help unions translate their social values regarding job skills, quality of work, and quality of products into new computer hardware and software for the printing industry. In this way, participants hope to shape the impacts of new technology on workers before it ever reaches the shop floor.

Few Americans would expect unions to play an active role in developing new technology. The most common stereotype is that workers oppose it through restrictive work rules, feather-bedding, and even a Luddite resistance to the very idea of technological change. But the reality is considerably more complicated. While unions have often tried to cushion their members from the negative impacts of new technology, few have flatly opposed it. Especially since the end of the Second World War, most U.S. unions have chosen to accept management's plans for new technology, and then bargain over their share of the productivity gains that technology can make possible.

This attitude may now be changing for two basic reasons. The computer has transformed work on a scale not seen since the mass-production assembly line was introduced at the turn of the century. What's more, this technological change is occurring as a profound restructuring of the world economy has brought increased international competition and higher levels of unemployment to most advanced industrial economies.

As a result, trade unions—primarily in Europe, and to a lesser degree in the United States—have begun to ask several fundamental questions: What is the impact of the microelectronics revolution on employment? How does the on-going computerization of work affect employees' skills and job quality? What are the potential health effects of the new technology? How can workers acquire the training to ensure that the computer revolution does not pass them by? And, perhaps most important, how is rapid technological and economic change re-shaping the traditional balance of power between corporations and unions?

Nowhere has union activism on these issues gone further than in Scandinavia. Beginning in Norway in the late 1960s, and extending to Denmark and Sweden over the next decade, technical specialists from government-funded institutions such as the Norwegian Computing Center in Oslo and the Swedish Center for Working Life joined unionists to study the effects of new technology on work and to formulate realistic union strategies to address them.

These "action research" projects spread throughout Scandinavia in metal-working shops, chemical refineries, railroad repair shops, insurance offices, retail stores, and newspaper offices. They quickly took on the form of a popular-education movement. Workers began to understand technology as something they might be able to influence—just like other aspects of working life. And technologists began to see some of the implications for people on the shop floor of the technologies they designed. They began to question some of the assumptions and methods of their profession.

Perhaps most important, action research has enabled workers to participate in company decisions about technological change. In Norway, for example, the projects have led to a new kind of collective-bargaining mechanism known as "technology agreements." These give local unions the right to receive advance notice of all company plans for purchasing or designing new technical systems, and to appoint a union staff member to represent workers' interests in all technological matters. UTOPIA represents the most recent effort by Scandinavian unions to deal with new technology: building union influence over the design of technology itself. UTOPIA focused on the printing industry.

## HOW COMPUTERS TRANSFORMED PRINTING

Printing has traditionally been considered the archetypal craft industry. In his sociological classic *Alienation and Freedom,* written in 1964, Robert Blaunder described how the combination of "craft technology, favorable economic conditions, and powerful work organization and traditions" gave printers "the highest levels of freedom and control in the work process among industrial workers today." Yet in the past two decades, the introduction of computerized text-entry, typesetting, and layout have transformed both the industry and workers' roles within it. At the same time, newspapers, in particular, have faced intense competition from alternative advertising outlets, including television and the new mass-circulation "daily shoppers."

The most visible impact of such technological change has been on the number of jobs. Employment of production workers in the U.S. printing industry declined by perhaps 50,000 through the 1970s. Computer and telecommunications technology has also made it easier for companies to shift work from heavily unionized and relatively high-wage urban centers in the Northeast to nonunion printing shops in other parts of the country.

Those printers who remain have experienced far-reaching changes in their autonomy and creativity. Obviously, the keyboards, terminal screens, and software of computerized systems require altogether new skills. Workers have suddenly found themselves dependent on their employers and computer companies for new training in the tools of what, for generations, they had considered "their" trade. Computerization has also created conflicts over job definitions in what Scandinavian printers, borrowing a metaphor from soccer, like to call "the struggle for the mid-field."

Such changes sometimes result from the capabilities of the technology itself. Reporters can now type their stories directly into the computer system, which automatically typesets them and eliminates the need for many skilled typographers. In other cases, the technology provides a smokescreen to disguise what are really managerial decisions about how to organize work. For example, computerized layout systems have allowed several newspapers to shift work from union printers to other company employees.

Computerization has also brought more subtle changes to printers' work. In the days of lead, skilled craftspeople made up an entire page of articles, headlines, photoengraving, and advertisements in metal, according to a rough sketch provided by the editorial department. Because they could "put their hands on it," makeup workers could easily judge the quality of their design.

Lead was succeeded by paper, with workers pasting columns of text onto page boards. Although pages lose a certain crispness of detail during this process, makeup workers can more readily rearrange and evaluate the elements of the page.

With computerization, makeup workers' relationship with the page has changed drastically. Early systems made layout extremely abstract, and some still do not show the page on the terminal screen. They require the workers to retain a mental image of the page while they feed codes into the computer that instruct it to create certain shapes and spaces on the page. More recent systems do show empty boxes on the screen representing headlines, articles, and photographs. But makeup workers still have difficulty judging page design because they do not work with the actual pictures or text. "It's almost as if you were working blind," says Malte Ericsson, a Swedish lithographer and participant in UTOPIA.

The new computer technologies, Scandinavian printers argue, have diminished the quality of the product as well as that of their work experience. European newspapers have traditionally been far more design-conscious than their American counterparts. They use higher-quality newsprint, a greater variety of typefaces, and more color, graphics, and special photography. Computerization, unions claim, has brought standardization—a trend toward a more boxy "American" style based on uniformity of typeface and monotony of design. The ultimate result is visually less interesting.

This change is not the inevitable outcome of computerization. One need only look at a newspaper such as *USA Today* to see how state-of-the-art technology can allow newspapers to explore new frontiers in design. However, according to the Scandinavian printers' unions, many papers in the rush to automate seem to have eliminated not only workers' craft autonomy but also some fundamental principles of graphics design.

## THE UNIONS' ALTERNATIVES

Such concerns have made technological change in the printing industry a divisive process in a number of countries. The New York City newspaper strike of 1963 and the *Washington Post* conflict in 1975 stemmed from the advent of new technology. Many unions have also resorted to less aggressive measures to protect their members from the negative consequences of technological change. In Britain, for example, labor has negotiated a ban on "single key stroking"— the automatic typesetting of text that journalists enter into the computer. Thus, after writers compose their stories at a terminal, a paper copy must be made. A union typographer then retypes the copy into the computerized typesetting system.

In the Nordic countries, the conflict has taken a different course. While print unions have negotiated protective measures similar to those in other countries, their participation in the action research projects taught them that such an approach can, at best, be a holding action. "The real issue," says Malte Ericsson, "is determining how we can make sure that no single occupational group is totally expelled from the profession. To do that, we have to suggest alternatives."

That is where the design of technology becomes important. "We saw the big printing companies and newspapers doing their own research," says Gunnar Kokaas, secretary of the Norwegian Graphics Workers Union. "They were giving money to vendors to develop new equipment that we felt would undermine our traditional labor agreements. So we thought it was important for us to get into R&D as well, to support technology that would lead to the kind of skills and working conditions that *we* were interested in. Maybe that way we could influence the vendors."

Scandinavian unions had already tried this approach in a more limited way. During the 1970s, they were among the first to urge VDT manufacturers to apply strict "ergonomic" criteria to reduce strain on the human body caused by prolonged VDT work. By the early 1980s, Nordic computer companies were making some of the world's most ergonomic terminals. They had also become the most vocal proponents of adhering to such design standards, seeing in them a potential competitive advantage akin to the rigorous safety features of Volvo automobiles.

In effect, the unions were able to establish a set of standards for the entire VDT marketplace. UTOPIA set out to do the same for the technology of the entire printing industry.

UTOPIA's computer scientists were convinced that recent technological advances could benefit skilled printers. For example, powerful new software could create an accurate facsimile of the printed page directly on the terminal screen. This made it possible to create electronically the immediate feedback that make-up workers previously enjoyed using manual methods. Such capabilities could begin to restore printers' traditional autonomy and control. Instead of simply "automating" work previously done by people, the computer could augment printers' design skills, becoming, in the words of UTOPIA director Pelle Ehn, "an advanced tool for skilled graphics workers."

Seeing the computer as a tool also implies a different understanding of the process by which new technical systems are developed. Most designers create a highly abstract model of a work process, and then try to incorporate that model into new computer hardware and software. Often, workers using the system end up as little more than passive objects of automation. UTOPIA's goal was to put the centuries-old traditions and occupational knowledge of printers at the center of the design process. Workers would play an active role in determining what kind of technology they needed and how it could support them in their work.

This did not mean preserving activities performed by printers in the past. As Pelle Ehn says, "When a worker used lead he had to have the skill of reading upside down and backwards. Is that a skill one should want to protect? Probably not.'' However, UTOPIA would maintain printers' ability to create an attractive page design. ''That is the kind of skill you have to make sure not to destroy when you shift to new technologies,'' says Ehn.

The group discovered early on that the best way to articulate printers' demands for new technology was to give them direct experience using it. Since UTOPIA had no money to set up its own computerized printing shop, the project team opted for the next best thing—ever more sophisticated simulations of the page makeup process.

At first, participants used crude styrofoam and plywood mockups and paper diagrams to map out the steps of page makeup. Later, the team rigged up a slide projector that flashed makeup images onto a screen representing a computer terminal. By rearranging the order of the slides, the team could experiment with different ways of organizing the makeup process. Ultimately, the lab acquired a real computer work station, programmed with a few sample layout functions, that helped the team refine its ideas for hardware, software, and organization of work. As printers discussed the pros and cons of different approaches, the technical staff advised them on their feasibility.

## DEVELOPING THE TECHNICAL COMPROMISES

Had this been the extent of the UTOPIA Project's work, it would have remained an interesting but somewhat abstract research project. However, in 1982, Sven Holmberg, the president of Liber Systems, made a proposal that helped turn UTOPIA into a concrete exercise in technological development. Liber was the chief participant in a $10 million Nordic project to develop a fully integrated text-and-image processing computer system known as TIPS. Based on technology developed at Sweden's University of Linköping, TIPS was to be one of the most sophisticated computer systems available in the printing and publishing industry. It would combine text entry, image enhancement, pagination, and layout in a single work station.

Holmberg offered UTOPIA a role in the Liber development process. Project participants agreed to produce a set of ''applications specifications'' recommending how the Liber system should be used in printing. In exchange, the project acquired access to the TIPS technical staff and R&D labs. For Liber, cooperation with UTOPIA offered a way to incorporate users' ideas into the new system, although the company was not required to do so. For UTOPIA cooperation offered an opportunity to influence a specific technical system soon to reach the market.

Completed last year, the UTOPIA specifications try to strike a balance between workers' demands and technical capabilities. For example, one of the printers' top priorities is gaining the capacity to work with an entire newspaper page directly on the terminal screen. However, even the largest screens are too small to present a newspaper page in its normal size. Either the page must be reduced, making the text and the images too small to be seen clearly, or only a portion of the page can be projected on the screen, disrupting workers' sense of the whole.

The technical compromise developed by UTOPIA and TIPS engineers recommends software that provides makeup workers with "lenses," or "viewports," through which they can see different portions of the newspaper page. Different lenses allow scale reduction, magnification, or natural size. If workers want to change some text, they might use the lens that presents that portion in its natural size. But if they are assembling articles, headlines, and photographs into an overall design, they can choose the lens that reduces the whole page to fit on the screen. Makeup workers can also use different lenses simultaneously. They might enhance a photograph or drawing to full scale in one corner of the screen while watching the impact of this operation at a reduced scale on another part of the screen. Or they could compare different versions of the same page on the screen simultaneously.

The UTOPIA specifications also call for workers to have access to high-speed laser printers. These create hard-copy prints of layouts that allow the workers and their editors to check the design created with the computer in terms of how it will look on the printed page.

The specifications further touch on organization and training. The "scanner station," where a worker feeds photographs and graphics material into the computer, provides an example. UTOPIA recommends that the system allow workers to begin preparing photographs for layout in addition to simply feeding the information to the computer. This makes the job more varied and helps to avoid bottlenecks at later stages of production.

Finally, whereas most vendors train users to operate only their particular system, UTOPIA recommends that training include general education in what Pelle Ehn calls "computer science for graphics workers." Such training can yield dividends for management. When printers are more broadly trained, an organization can adapt more easily to fresh technology. And the more understanding workers have of the concepts underlying the systems they work with, the more they will be able to exploit the systems' versatility to create high-quality products. Pelle Ehn even foresees a not-too-distant time when powerful new software packages will enable printers to program systems themselves in order to maintain, upgrade, and adapt their technology to new uses.

## PRACTICAL PROBLEMS

Liber unveiled its TIPS technology last spring. Six out of nine systems ordered so far are being installed, including two at newspapers in Finland and Sweden. Not surprisingly, in the move from technical lab to newspaper shop floor, UTOPIA's ideas have encountered some obstacles. How they are met will determine UTO-PIA's ultimate impact. Indeed, the most important period for the UTOPIA Project may still lie ahead.

Creating new models for designing technology and organizing work does not guarantee that employers will actually use them. While Liber has incorporated many of the UTOPIA recommendations for user-friendly software into its system, the company has left most of the ideas concerning work organization and training up to individual customers. Thus, the precise impact of the TIPS technology on graphics workers in any given company will depend upon a complex process of formal and informal negotiations. Here the goals of the UTOPIA team can clash with those of other social groups.

One example is the introduction of the TIPS technology at the Stockholm daily *Aftonbladet*. Originally, UTOPIA members were to have helped define how the new system would be used at the newspaper. However, *Aftonbladet* management, anxious to implement the new system, refused to let the UTOPIA team participate. The local journalists' union—leery of what its members saw as the "graphics workers' technology"—also opposed UTOPIA's role. Thus, the project's concepts became hostage to traditional conflicts between unions and management and among unions.

UTOPIA's model of skilled workers using high technology to create high-quality products may also encounter problems with general trends in the newspaper industry. While the UTOPIA team was refining its concepts in the technical laboratory, U.S. manufacturers were perfecting a different approach to computerized pagination known as "free-flow page makeup." This allows editors to perform both page layout and copyediting. To remain competitive, especially in the U.S. market, Liber has had to include this feature in TIPS.

But how TIPS or any computerized pagination system is used in the Scandinavian printing industry will ultimately depend, at least in part, on how well the graphics workers' unions argue for their own model of technology and work. Perhaps UTOPIA's greatest accomplishment has been its contribution to workers' expertise about technology and its impacts. This knowledge is already affecting the outcome of labor-management negotiations in the printing industry. Malte Ericsson tells of entering negotiations with the managers of a Stockholm printing firm who wanted to introduce a new Xerox laser printer. Because of his involvement with UTOPIA, Ericsson found that he knew far more than his counterparts across the bargaining table about the system's labor requirements, the kind of skills workers would need to operate it effectively, and the type of training they would require. "We feel we are stronger in negotiations now," says Ericsson, "because we have more knowledge than the employers."

Last November, the UTOPIA specifications were used in national negotiations for the first time, forming the basis for proposals by the Danish Graphics Worker Union on new technology. And so seriously does Sweden's newspaper-industry trade association take the new union proposals that it is developing its own "system specifications."

Moreover, the idea of putting a union label on new workplace technology has spread to other Nordic unions. Those representing office workers have recently announced an effort to create their own organizational model for the "office of the future." According to project director Arne Pape of the Norwegian Computing Center, the model will emphasize the use of new technology to break down the traditionally rigid sexual division of labor in office work. Another project is exploring how to involve unions and professional associations in the design of "expert systems"—programs that enable a computer to make judgments. A preliminary field experiment with nurses is currently under way at a major Oslo hospital. Other unions and researchers are considering similar projects in computer-aided design and manufacturing, retail sales, and warehousing.

One particularly interested observer of these developments is the small but dynamic Nordic computer industry. "They are taking the discussion within the labor movement very seriously, because it may provide a signal of future trends in the market," says Arne Pape. "They are beginning to realize that trade unions can point things out to them that they aren't likely to hear from anyone else."

The discussion within the Scandinavian labor movement has even produced an echo on this side of the Atlantic. As they begin to confront the issues that Nordic unions have been addressing for years, some American unions are turning to the Scandinavian labor movement for models and advice. For example, last September, leaders of the Communications Workers of America (CWA) went to Scandinavia with executives from AT&T to examine the way the unions and companies are addressing technology and its effects on work. Explains Lorel Foged of the CWA's Development and Research Department, speaking of UTOPIA, "We'd love to be able to do something along those lines."

So the impact of UTOPIA is continuing to expand, and the idea that workers and their unions have an important role to play in the design of new technology is reaching a wider and wider audience. Today, Scandinavia. Tomorrow, perhaps, the rest of the world.

# 18
# What is Office Automation?

## 1980

### Michael Hammer and Marvin Sirbu

## WHAT DO PEOPLE DO IN OFFICES?

Many of us have had the experience of trying to explain to a small child what it is that we do in an office. It is not easy. From a child's perspective, office work seems to be composed of simple tasks: reading, talking on the telephone, typing, shuffling papers, drinking coffee. Yet we know that these terms do not capture the essence of an office. The business of an office is about making payments, or scheduling production or negotiating contracts. Tasks such as typing and filing are, in an important way, mere artifacts. If the business to be done in the office could be accomplished without these tasks, so much the better. One need only compare an accounting office of 100 years ago and one of today; the rows of clerks standing at carrels have been replaced by clerks sitting at adding machines and more recently by accountants flipping through printouts or sitting at video terminals. Thus, a description of an office in terms of the elemental tasks as they are performed using current technology gives us little understanding of the real work of an office.

"Office automation" is a phenomenon, a trend, a concept, an advertising slogan, a buzzword. Every user of the phrase imparts a different meaning to it. Yet most definitions of this term have one point in common: like the child's view of the office, they emphasize its most visible activities and fail to grasp its fundamental meaning.

In this paper, we present our perspective on the nature of the office and what it means to automate it, and relate these to some of the other definitions currently being proposed for the phrase "office automation."

## THE ENVIRONMENT FOR OFFICE AUTOMATION

It can presumably be agreed upon that office automation does relate to the introduction and use of automated equipment in the office. Consequently, a discussion of office automation should be predicated on some conception of the nature of office work. A number of observations or characterizations can be made about the environment of the office that should condition our view of automated office systems. First, offices and their activities are *distributed* both in space and time. They involve the continuous coordination of parallel activities in many locations. Second, office activities are sometimes routine, but are more often *changing*. The office worker must constantly revise his activities to cope with the changing and dynamic environment faced by today's business organizations. Third, activities in the office are *interactive*. Rarely are problems solved, or goals realized, except by the interaction of several persons in a back-and-forth exchange of work, ideas, and commitment. Indeed, much of what transpires in an office can be characterized as *group* work involving the simultaneous participation of several persons, rather than as a sequence of activities by autonomous actors.

The information that is manipulated in the office comes in many forms. While the earliest applications of the computer to the office were for data-intensive activities such as payroll and finance, the office also utilizes information in the form of text, and even more frequently as voice. Thus, office automation should support information transfer and manipulation in all of these modes. Information used in the office is both developed *internally* (as with production and personnel data) and *externally* (e.g., in the form of orders, prices, and actions by the competition). (Unfortunately, the difficulties associated with standardizing the exchange of information among many firms and organizations has led to a focus on schemes for better manipulation of internally generated information almost to the exclusion of external information. This can and has proved catastrophic for those myopic organizations who confused complete knowledge of internal data with complete information for decision.) Finally, the information handled in the office is historically-oriented, as in data on past performance of the firm, but also future-oriented, as in sales or cost projections.

## VIEWS OF OFFICE AUTOMATION

Given the complexities of the office, it is not surprising that there is more than one conceptual model of how to go about assisting office work through the aid of modern computer and communication technology. In this section we shall review some of these models, and attempt to identify the assumptions that underlie them.

For those with short memories, "office automation" may appear to be a recent addition to the language. Yet, if one looks back at the literature that appeared in the late 1950s and early 1960s describing the migration of the computer from the research laboratory into business and government, it is replete with discussions of the new "office automation." Certainly, we have gone a long way toward "automating" the modern accounting and financial office. Yet in much of the current discussion of office automation, data processing is viewed as a foreign and unrelated technology. There is something perverse in a nomenclature that includes facsimile transmission as a form of electronic mail but not an on-line order entry system which eliminates considerably more correspondence; or counts word processing as office automation, but not the forms handling program which similarly reduces the typing workload. Certainly, data processing as it is commonly understood is a form of office automation.

From this perspective, office automation is simply an extension of the kinds of things that data processing has been doing for years, updated to take advantage of new hardware and software possibilities. Distributed processing to replace mail, source data capture to reduce retyping, and end-user oriented systems are the ways in which "office automation" will be brought beyond the traditional applications and to the aid of all segments of the office.

There is substance in this perspective, yet it is an incomplete view. Traditional DP focuses on highly structured and data-intensive applications. Yet offices in general are often text-intensive, highly interactive, and constantly changing. The styles and approaches of a DP shop oriented to large standardized projects may be inappropriate for the development of the next generation of office information systems.

A second view of the office of the future views technology as leading us towards a "paperless" office in which the basic clerical tasks of information handling—capture, manipulation, storage, retrieval, reproduction, and communication—have been *mechanized* with the aid of such tools as word processors, electronic filing cabinets and electronic mail [Zisman, 1978]. This perspective focuses on the rudimentary tasks of the office, and on the gains that can be achieved by applying modern technology to these tasks. In mechanical terms this corresponds to moving from hand tools to power tools.

Clearly there is much productivity improvement that can be expected from providing secretaries and clerks with more powerful tools to conduct their tasks. Word processors can speed the process of document production, and electronic mail can cut distribution time of information substantially. Moreover, by focusing on elemental and generic tasks, vendors of task mechanization equipment can successfully sell to every type of office.

Nevertheless, there are significant limitations to this perspective. First, focusing on the mechanization of existing tasks implies the current set of tasks is optimal. Many studies have shown, however, that much of the benefit to be gained from office automation will come about due to the opportunity it provides to rationalize or restructure office tasks. Second, this perspective does not address the needs of principals (variously known as managers or professionals or knowledge workers). These workers account for a clear majority of the office's labor costs [Harkness, 1978]. Moreover, enhancing their productivity can have a major impact on the quality of the office's work product. Finally, by stopping at task mechanization, vast opportunities to further improve office productivity by actually automating specific office functions are lost.

A third approach to office automation focuses on providing the knowledge worker with a better working environment. The aim is to "augment" his capabilities by supporting him with powerful intelligent tools [Engelbart & English, 1966]. For example, the individual's memory is enhanced by providing a personal database capability; calculation is simplified by calculators or personal computers; writing and communicating are simplified by use of electronic aids for composing, spelling correction, and document sharing. The electronic tools allow the professional worker to perform tasks of information manipulation that were otherwise too difficult or costly to undertake.

More recently, this approach has focused on augmenting group work through the use of the computer. This takes the form of facilities for computer conferencing, information sharing, and support of continuous dialogues [Hiltz & Turoff, 1979].

Despite its emphasis on knowledge workers, this approach does not really address the content of their work; it deals with surface structure rather than with substance. Furthermore, it addresses the work of individuals without reference to the processes in which they are engaged. Even though some tasks are automated (rather than mechanized) in this approach, these are generally *individual's* tasks, not those of the organization. The work of the office *as a whole* is not considered, nor is the way in which the activities of individual principals relate to one another.

A fourth approach is that of decision support. A decision support system seeks to provide decision makers with tools that actively assist them in accessing and analyzing information [Keen & Morton, 1978]. For example, a portfolio management system for use by a bank would consist of specialized databases and modeling tools for constructing forecasts, answering "what if?" questions, and otherwise assisting a decision-maker, in an interactive way, in understanding the nature of his problem and the implications of various decision options. The data, and support programs are very much problem-specific; rather than supporting elemental tasks, they form a coherent package designed to support a major function or decision process within the organization.

Decision support systems differ from traditional data processing in that they are not oriented to automated execution of structured tasks. Rather, they support an unstructured or semistructured decision process through the provision of calculation, display and other aids. DSS differ from the personal augmentation approach by the degree to which they are problem-specific and involve programs and databases designed for a specific company problem.

Although this model of office automation does begin to address the substance of office work, its focus remains narrow and incomplete. While decision making is a key component of office work, it does not take place in a vacuum. Office decisions are made in a broader context of activities performed by all the workers in the office. An isolated decision support system that is not integrated with the office as a whole merely attacks one piece, albeit an important one, out of a complete system.

## FUNCTIONAL OFFICE AUTOMATION

Our perspective on office automation is based on a view of the office is as a place of business, not as a site for document handling and information processing. The purpose of every office is to realize a *mission,* to implement some business function that can be expressed in terms of the goals and needs of the organization of which the office is a part. The existence of this office function is inevitable and axiomatic, even though it may be disguised at times by people's emphasis on their day-to-day tasks and activities. The essence of office work, which must serve as the basis for any effective measure of office work and office productivity, should not be confused with the artifacts of current office operation. It is the rare office whose goal and function it is to produce letters. More likely, the office exists to purchase goods, to manage the human resources of the organization, or to approve payments and claims against an insurance policy. Letter-writing, record maintenance, communicating, and the like all play roles in accomplishing these functions; however, they are only the superficial aspects of office work, the means used to realize an end. Moreover, they are coincidental and inessential, since under a different set of circumstances alternative means might be feasible and even preferable. Our focus is on the purpose of office work; the function itself, rather than any particular implementation of it, is foremost in our priorities.

From this view of office work is derived our perspective on office automation. We define office automation simply as *the utilization of technology to improve the realization of office functions.* Any technology that can have a positive impact on the productivity of the office (as measured in *business* terms) legitimately falls within the domain of office automation. Office automation is *not* improved document handling and production, it is *not* faster and more reliable communications, it is *not* the electronic storage and retrieval of information; it *may* include any or all of these, as well as a wide variety of other technologies and equipment, so long as they contribute to the realization of the office's functions. It is easy, and all too common, to confuse the performance of a particular set of office tasks with the underlying office function, and to conclude that "automating" the former will yield improvements in the latter. The result of an automation effort that is based on a mistaken identification of the business goals of an office with its information-handling activities may be a *decrease* in office productivity. For example, it is by now a common phenomenon to observe that after the installation of a costly word processor, the reduction in secretarial staff on which the cost justification for the equipment had been based is never realized. This is not to suggest that word processing cannot have a positive impact on office operations; indeed in many cases it has. It is the perspective that is the key, the way in which the equipment is viewed and utilized. A word processor, or any other device, is by itself neither a panacea nor a disaster; it is only a tool whose impact depends entirely on how it is used. Any individual electronic device has the potential for improving or disrupting office operation. If its use is planned in a way that takes the entire office context into account and is based on an appropriate perspective on the task for which the tool is being used, then its impact can be enormously beneficial. If, on the other hand, the task and its tool are viewed in isolation from the operation of the office as a whole, then a number of undesirable outcomes are likely.

The real payoffs of an office automation system must be measurable in business terms. The number of pages of text produced per day, the average time required to retrieve a record from the files, or the number of communications completed per week: these are meaningless and misleading measures of the efficacy of an office system. They can measure efficiency but not effectiveness. Increasing the amount of information produced, or the rate at which it can be processed, does not inherently contribute to the quality or quantity of the office's real work product. The convenience copier has proven to be a mixed blessing for many organizations; while it did enormously enhance the ready flow of information with an organization, it also resulted in an information explosion: many people found themselves inundated with a sea of paperwork without which they would have been better off. Exploiting word processing to endlessly revise a report or to generate vast quantities of a letter that will remain unread is costly and valueless. Similarly, increasing the number of messages that an executive receives during the day is counterproductive if the average information content of each message decreases. These situations result from seizing on an individual office task in isolation and bringing technology to bear on it. The task may be "improved," but the function is unaffected.

In order to determine if an office automation effort is successful, it is necessary to have some metrics by which it may be judged. An effective measure will be based on an understanding and identification of the office's work product and of the function it realizes. Office productivity is raised if this function can be realized at lower unit cost, if improvements in the function can be achieved in a cost-effective fashion, or if the ability to realize new and desirable functions is achieved; in other words, cost reduction (and/or cost avoidance), quality enhancement, and extended capabilities. Ultimately, these must all be reduced into objective terms extrinsic to the office's operation. For example, in a purchasing office, desirable ends might include lowering the cost of producing a purchase order, improving the average delivery time of a requisitioned item, or serving as a clearinghouse for equipment sharing in the company as a whole.

These payoffs can be realized in a variety of ways. In some cases they will be achieved by reducing head count or by avoiding the hiring of new personnel to handle additional activity volume. In others, they can result from the improved utilization of staff time, especially that of professionals and managers. In particular, it is often the case that office professionals spend significant amounts of their time on activities of minor importance; the availability of office equipment that enables them to divest these tasks would enable them to devote themselves to more important work. (However, here it is particularly important that the office system as a whole be so organized that this newly freed up time is profitably applied; otherwise Parkinson's Law will take effect.) Effective measures need not always be expressed in monetary terms; improved customer relations or employee morale are real although intangible. Sometimes the impact may be indirect, manifesting itself as an improved utilization of some resource.

## OFFICE PROCEDURES

The way in which an office automation effort can successfully realize these potential benefits is by analyzing and supporting the *office procedures* that are executed in accomplishing an office's mission. An office procedure is a structuring framework by means of which the individual tasks and activities performed by office workers are organized. It specifies what steps are to be taken, by whom, and in what order; it provides a context and a rationalizing framework for otherwise isolated office activities. For example, many tasks are executed in a university admissions office: sending out application forms, matching transcripts to applications, issuing acceptance letters, and so on. However, these are all part of a coherent procedure aimed at making a selection of next year's incoming class. The procedure determines the sequence of activities that are to be performed following the receipt of a letter from a prospective student, the information that is to be utilized, the timing constraints that are to be observed, and the exceptional situations that might occur.

By emphasizing the procedure as a whole and addressing individual tasks only within that context, we bring the function and purpose of the office into sharper focus and direct the automation effort where it is most needed. Focusing on an office procedure enables us to identify the framework for the office's activities and support them in a coherent and productive way; the alternative is haphazard automation of individual tasks without due regard for the overall structure and operation of the office, which is as likely to have a negative impact on office productivity as it is a positive one. Any functioning system, even a manual one, is often highly tuned and sensitive to perturbation. It is necessary to take a holistic view of office work, and one that is moreover based on a thorough understanding of the particular needs and special characteristics of each office. In effect, we are arguing for a *systemic* approach to office automation, which views an office as a system that is composed of components integrated by means of office procedures. Office automation should seek to improve the operation of the office *system*.

The workers in an office may be more or less explicitly aware of the global nature of their procedures; however, the existence of a procedure in an office operation is fundamental and inevitable. It is only by means of the structuring that it imposes that an office can operate in a predictable and repeatable fashion;

without one every situation would have to be handled on an improvised and ad hoc basis. Furthermore, an office procedure enables the work of the office as a whole to be decomposed into individual assignable units. It provides structure and organization, discipline and regularity. However, this should not be taken to suggest that all office procedures are fully specified and algorithmic; most office procedures are *semistructured processes* [Gorry & Morton, 1978]. That is, they are comprised both of highly structured and repetitive tasks, and by unstructured judgmental tasks (such as decision making and negotiation). The procedure is the glue that holds these pieces together; it is the skeletal framework on which they all hang.

An *office information system* (OIS) is an integrated collection of components that supports the operation of an office procedure. Typically, an OIS will provide a facility by which office workers may communicate in sequencing the steps of a procedure, it will support the storage and retrieval of information, it will enable limited forms of processing to be applied to information, and it will connect the office with the rest of the organization and the outside world. In other words, an OIS provides an environment and context in which workers can do *substantive* office work (as opposed to support activities). Most substantive office work takes the form of information processing, decision making, or interpersonal interactions. These are the activities that truly effect the business of the office; the others are merely the underlying infrastructure. An OIS may contain automated, manual, and human components; however, they are all organized into a coherent whole. A well-designed manual office operation is an office information system, with components that include typewriters, copying machines, calculators, file cabinets, and mail carts, as well as the workers who utilize and operate this equipment. The constituents, organization, and functionality of an OIS all depend on the nature and characteristics of the procedure it supports.

An *automated* OIS can improve the execution of office procedures in a variety of ways. By improving communication and information access, the flow of control and information through the procedure can be enhanced, with consequent increases in speed, accuracy, and control. Technology can be employed to mechanize support tasks such as document preparation and communication, with potential improvements in quality and volume. (However, these improvements are only meaningful if they result in facilitating the performance of the office's substantive work.) Moreover, an automated OIS can also address the essential tasks of the office, those that relate to the content of the procedure rather than to its structure. Highly structured tasks can be automated; if an activity is entirely algorithmic, it can be performed by software controlling a machine. A supportive and facilitating environment can be provided for decision-making and other unstructured tasks, so that the office worker has better access to information and tools with which to manage and analyze it, as well as to other people.

Many different technologies can be employed in an OIS; however, the point is not the technology, but how it is used. The key to the development of a successful OIS is the effective design of a system that seeks to support the office's procedures.

Our approach to office automation has a number of implications. First, it implies the necessity of office-specific systems. The individual components of an OIS may be obtained off-the-shelf, but the particular way in which they are combined and integrated into a total system must be specific to an individual office, and dependent on the details of its procedures and the other aspects of its operation. Further, as the OIS seeks to address more and more of the substance of the office's operation, the components themselves become more and more office-specific. (For example, the automation of structured tasks can only be accomplished by means of specialized application software that embodies a detailed knowledge of how the task is to be performed). This in turn implies a preeminent role for the process of system analysis and design. It is essential that a careful study be conducted before any equipment is installed into an office, in order to identify the true needs of the office and determine how they can most effectively be met. Most generally, this leads to an emphasis on the rationalization of office work in the context of an automation effort. Frequently, office procedures are outmoded, inefficient, inadequately documented, and poorly designed in the first place. Even if originally valid, a procedure's structure and rationale often become obscured by a mass of historical accretions and obscure implementation mechanisms. The direct application of automated equipment to such archaic procedures is of dubious value. A rationalization and redesign of office procedures should accompany an office automation effort. Indeed as detailed elsewhere [Hammer & Zisman, 1979], the first phase of such an effort should consist of a thoroughgoing analysis, specification, and evaluation of the existing office procedures, followed then by their redesign; subsequent to this redesign effort, the new procedures can be examined for opportunities for the employment of automated equipment. This act of procedure redesign can often be the greatest benefit derived from an office automation effort, far exceeding anything realized from the introduction of the equipment itself. Of course, in undertaking such an effort, one must tread a fine line between the ultimately desirable and the immediately feasible. Too much of an emphasis on current activities can forestall many benefits that could be realized from the use of new equipment; on the other hand, a completely de novo design effort, which fails to take into account the existing operational context, is unlikely to end in success. This problem has often been encountered in data processing applications: whether new computing equipment ought to be used to computerize existing manual activities or as a means of instituting entirely new systems. In practice, a compromise between the two extremes is often the most effective. Thus, automation can serve as a catalyst for evolutionary change in the office.

Moreover, it is not appropriate to view office automation as a one-time effort. Office procedures are subject to continual change under pressures from new technology, new personnel, and the changing business environment. Furthermore, the extent to which an OIS can automate various parts of a procedure will expand over time. As various ad hoc solutions to exceptions become accepted parts of the standard procedure, they can be incorporated into the OIS. Thus, an OIS will grow in an evolutionary fashion. However, it is important that the incremental improvements all point in the direction of a planned goal and that each intermediate stage represent an intrinsically useful end in itself. In other words, it is important to know where one is going, as well as how one is to get there. Similarly, the design of an office procedure cannot be entirely divorced from available technology; though the design of an office system should not be technology-driven, it will inevitably be technology-influenced, and will change as the capabilities of available equipment do.

For these reasons, it is essential that we design flexible rather than rigid office information systems. First, the ultimate configuration of an office system will only be achievable by means of a period of incremental growth, with the starting point not too far removed from the existing operation. Second, office systems technology is changing very rapidly. Any system design must be flexible and fluid enough to take advantage of new technological developments. Finally, an office system is almost certain to evolve and grow in unpredictable ways. New demands on the organization and new ways of doing business will eventually be reflected in the procedures that the office embodies.

## THE OFFICE OF THE FUTURE

As we have stressed above, office automation is not a matter of technology, but of how technology is employed to improve office productivity. An office information system can be fashioned out of different kinds of components, using differing levels of technology; office automation is not defined in technological terms. Nonetheless, we do have our own picture of "the office of the future," with a model of how an automated office information system that is based on current and evolving technological trends can most effectively support office procedures. This picture is not of a generic OIS, but of a general model of the functionality and architecture of office-specific systems. The OIS structure described below does not represent the only possible application of the ideas expressed above; rather, it represents the asymptote towards which current efforts should be evolving and converging. While our view of the architecture of an electronic OIS is not expressed in terms of technology, it does posit a certain technological environment in which it will operate; we shall subsequently examine how these ideas can be applied in the existing and prevailing technological environment.

Specifically, we envision the following context in which a functionally-oriented OIS will operate: every office worker will have ready access to a CRT terminal (say within 50 feet of his normal place of work); there should be enough of these in the office to avoid contention for their use among the workers. This terminal will have at least a page-sized bit-map display screen, offering high resolution display of text and graphics; it will also have at least a full keyboard with a small set of special function keys, to enable data entry and selection of standard functions. (Other man-machine communication devices may also be available, such as a pointing device (mouse, touch panel, or light pen), voice output (but not as general input), and the like. While these may enhance the process of worker-system interaction, their individual characteristics will not affect the overall architecture of the OIS as a whole.) The user of this station will be provided with substantial amounts of computational power, sufficient for performing a variety of text and data processing applications, as well as access to large storage capabilities. Functionally, we are indifferent to whether these capabilities are provided by a processor within the work station, by a local minicomputer, or by a mainframe at a remote site; what is necessary is that the capability be provided with acceptable response and access time. Moreover, data sharing between work stations must be provided in some way; that is, it must be possible for data associated with a worker at one station to be made available to others. Here too, this can be accomplished in different ways, including locating all the data in a large and centralized shared data bank and transmitting it by means of some communication system. What we assume is a certain speed by which the data may be moved from one station to another; a high speed if the two stations are both within the same office, and a somewhat slower speed if they are in the same organization but different offices. (We do not expect that high-speed interorganizational data sharing and communications will be available in the near term, for a wide variety of reasons detailed elsewhere [Sirbu, 1978].) As for output devices, high-speed intelligent printers will provide hard-copy output of whatever appears on the screen; the availability of such devices is important for facilitating the use of the screen-based capabilities. We remain agnostic about a number of other technologies. For example, facsimile scanning and transmission would enable paper documents to be scanned directly into the system, avoiding the need for keyed data entry or manual distribution of paper documents. Its absence might limit the penetration of automated office systems and the extent to which they can support geographically-dispersed procedures.

As we noted above, this set of assumptions is relatively independent of technology and system architecture; it could be realized by means of a set of powerful microprocessor-based work stations communicating via a packet-switched network, or it could be realized by means of conventional terminals connected by means of telephone lines to a mainframe data-processing system. Our concern is with the environment and the functionality that the technology provides; the way in which it is implemented principally determines its price-performance characteristics. The time-frame for this assumed hardware environment is the late 1980s; that is, at that point we expect that these capabilities will be widely available at a price that will permit their cost-effective use in a typical office. We feel that this picture is, if anything, somewhat modest. The kinds of capabilities that we describe, and systems based on them, are already in daily use in a relatively small number of laboratories or test-sites in advanced organizations; by 1990, they should be common. Several useful capabilities have been omitted from our list, because their general availability is less certain (or even highly unlikely); these include low-cost image-processing capabilities, video-conferencing, mixed text and video, and others.

Given that the costs of computation are declining relative to the costs of communication, it seems likely that the eventual configuration of this OIS will lean more towards the intelligent work station than to a shared mainframe. In the near term, minicomputers and shared-logic word processors provide the most cost-effective environment for constructing such systems. Perhaps the most critical short-term goal for most organizations is the establishment of a network strategy for linking today's mainframes and minis and tomorrow's workstations.

However, the foregoing capabilities do not by themselves constitute an office automation system; they only provide a platform on which an office information system may be constructed. As we have stressed above, there is no such thing as a generic OIS; an effective office system must be geared to the particular characteristics of the office in question and to the procedures that it employs. However, some general components and characteristics of a functionally-oriented OIS can be identified. The work station will present to the office worker a set of tools with which he will be able to perform the tasks that are his responsibility in the context of the procedure. The most basic set of tools will simply provide for rudimentary office activities: entering and editing text or data, handling forms, composing and transmitting messages, accessing databases, and the like. (One of these tools will probably be a facility for controlling and managing one's own work, keeping track of the various tasks that must be done and the state of activities that have been initialized but not yet completed.) A richer and more powerful set of tools will provide a supportive and facilitating environment for the unstructured tasks that "knowledge workers" perform; these will encompass the capabilities of contemporary personal augmentation and decision support systems. A variety of facilities, ranging from a personal information management system to decision support tools such as modeling, graphical displays, data analysis packages, and so on, will give the professional a rich set of capabilities for managing the information that is the fundamental object on which he works. Some general facilities may be provided, while others will be application- and even operator-specific. The more precisely oriented a tool is for an individual office application, the more effective it is for the office worker who uses it. Thus, a portfolio analyst might use a package that enables him to construct sample portfolios and readily compute their key characteristics, while a program manager would employ a subsystem for keeping track of deadlines, responsibilities, meeting and vacation schedules, and the like. However, even these advanced tools are not used in isolation, without reference to the larger procedural context. The OIS will have embedded in it application-specific software that embodies the procedure that is the skeletal framework for all the office activities. This software will effectively provide for the control and flow of the procedure as a whole. It will direct responsibility and data through the network of office workers and their stations; it will specify what actions need to be performed, by whom, and to what. This software is the integument that holds the pieces of the procedure together, that connects together the individual tasks performed at independent work stations into a coherent whole. In addition, the OIS software will automate highly structured tasks that can be so fully specified that they can be reduced to algorithmic programs. Thus, some routine clerical tasks, many of them currently performed by principals, will no longer be performed by people at all, while others will be doable by means of a single command to the OIS. In addition, the OIS will provide a variety of tracking and monitoring facilities that enable the procedure as a whole to be effectively managed and controlled.

As an example scenario, consider a typical purchasing office, which processes purchase requisitions, produces purchase orders, and monitors satisfactory delivery of goods to the requestor and payment to vendors. An electronic OIS would assume control of this process from the time an incoming requisition is received. (Whether this requisition comes in on paper or over the company's electronic mail system is a second-order concern.) The first set of activities involve logging the arrival of the requisition, checking it for completeness and accuracy, and the like. These activities can be entirely automated, with an appropriate office worker being notified only if there is some difficulty. (Note the change in the nature of the job of the person responsible for incoming requisitions.) The validated requisition would then be passed on to a purchasing agent, who would decide where the requested goods are to be purchased. This is an unstructured task that cannot be automated. However, the OIS can provide the buyer with a decision support facility that enables him to do a better job. It might allow him to easily compare vendor delivery performances, seek opportunities for quantity discounts, consider shipping schedules, and propose alternative goods to the ones explicitly requested. This is more than just access to on-line databases; it represents an active system, which is tuned to the particulars of the buyer's job. After the purchasing agent has made his decision, the OIS, following the standard procedure embedded in it, would automatically construct a purchase order, cause copies to be sent to appropriate locations, and maintain records about the order. At a later stage, the system could examine these records in order to trace undelivered goods, to analyze the performance of the purchasing office, or to enable the ready modification previously issued orders.

What should be noted about this view of an OIS is how it differs from the other approaches to office automation mentioned at the beginning of this paper. It differs from data processing in its interactive character, in the way in which the computer's activities are interleaved with those of human operators and decision makers, and in the fact that it addresses a complete process that is spread out over time. An OIS is not an automated system in the way that a payroll system is; the latter accepts time cards and produces checks, while an OIS provides an environment in which office work is done. As such, it incorporates decision support capabilities. However, it goes beyond conventional decision support systems because an OIS integrates a decision into the overall context of the office procedure. In a conventional DSS, the consequences of the decision reached are outside the realm of the DSS itself; in an OIS, the decision usually determines the subsequent activities to be taken by the OIS. In many cases, these consequences may result automatically, as a result of application-specific software. For example, in the example discussed above, the buyer's decision as to where to buy the requested goods automatically caused the construction of an appropriately complete purchase order; the results of the decision did not have to be manually processed or entered into some other isolated automated system. The key feature of an OIS is integration, the way in which the individual components are tied together. (Another way in which an OIS is likely to differ from a DSS is in the environment of the decision being made. An OIS will typically support "operational" decisions, rather than the strategic ones that are the focus of much of the DSS literature. The analyses for these decisions are typically made by line managers rather than by highly specialized staff professionals; furthermore, the volume of these decisions is substantially higher.) Similarly, our view of an OIS includes the capabilities of task mechanization and personal augmentation, but not as isolated facilities; the emphasis is on employing these facilities in the context of procedure execution, and on automating their utilization wherever possible.

## IMPACTS ON OFFICE WORK

We expect that in the context of an automated office information system the nature of the work performed by a typical office worker, his role in the office organization, and even the structure of the organization as a whole will be somewhat different from what currently prevails. One likely result is a less hierarchical structure of the office and a decreased emphasis on task specialization. An electronic OIS can eliminate the need for many office tasks that are simply artifacts of a paper-based operation. On the whole an OIS provides the opportunity for office workers to focus on the fundamental content of their procedures rather than on controlling its superficial structure. Some highly routine work will no longer be performed by people at all; others, such as filing and retrieval of information, will be so highly facilitated by the advent of an electronic OIS that each individual office worker (including a professional) may do this on his own. Thus, an OIS will likely lead to the elimination of many functionally specialized support tasks. Each office worker's activities are likely to more closely parallel the operation of the procedure as a whole. Indeed, since most routine work will be automatically performed by the system, the typical office worker may be elevated to a paraprofessional level [Matteis, 1979]. His activities are likely to focus on creative acts, such as judgmental decision making or interaction with people outside the office.

In certain respects, the architecture of an automated office will have some points in common with the factory floor; the electronic communication network becomes a conveyer belt by means of which work is passed about to be processed. However, there is likely to be a retrenchment from the heavy forms orientation of current paper-based systems. With the accessibility of online databases, the information to be processed and handled by individual workers need not actually be transmitted from one to another; the information can always reside in the central database. What will be communicated is the responsibility and authority for performing a task, as well as specific parameters describing the task at hand. On the other hand, in certain respects, office workers become more like craftsmen rather than assembly line workers. They will no longer perform standardized and repetitive tasks; rather, they will be given a set of tools with which they will be expected to carry out unstructured tasks. Furthermore, they will need the ability and the authority to improvise and, if appropriate, to modify standard procedures or override the system in order to handle unusual situations. Indeed, with communication and information access greatly facilitated, flexibility in office operation becomes more feasible. Moreover, a set of tools that enables an office worker to better manage his own work will lead to greater individual autonomy and responsibility.

Thus, the cast of characters in an automated office looks somewhat different from what it looks like in most manual offices. There will likely continue to be a small cadre of low-level data entry personnel; until inter-office and inter-organization communications are entirely electronic, much information will have to be manually entered into the local office system. However, we expect that the great majority of office workers will enjoy greater autonomy and responsibility than they currently do. Rather than explicitly carrying out instructions provided to them by others, they will be given a mandate in terms of a function that they are expected to realize. The facilities of an OIS will enable them to accomplish these functions more efficiently and more effectively than in a paper-based environment.

The role of the manager of an automated OIS is a challenging one. As we have stressed above, technology by itself is not a recipe for success. The key issue is understanding the nature of the work being done, determining how technology can be most effectively exploited to support it, and continually managing the process to insure that the desired results are indeed achieved. Thus, the manager of an OIS has a wide range of responsibilities. First, he is the one who must assume responsibility for the initial design of the office process and the implementation of an OIS to support it; he must exercise continuing control and authority to monitor the performance of the system and, when appropriate, to redesign it. On a day-to-day basis, the manager will have important responsibilities for handling people. Employee motivation and management become ever more critical when the typical office worker is no longer a clerk, but a paraprofessional. The importance of the worker's job increases, as does its direct impact on the quality of the office's product; on the other hand, monitoring the quantity and quality of the work done becomes a more delicate process, as does managing the personnel who perform it. Finally, the office manager will have ultimate responsibility for the conduct of the procedure being performed in his office. He will have to assign priorities, manage the details of the individual activities, and conduct traces and analyses. He also will be the ultimate arbiter of all exceptions and special cases. The best designed office procedure cannot account for all unusual situations that may arise; and even the best trained office worker will sometimes encounter situations where he must turn to his supervisor for assistance. Thus, the office manager will have to possess both a global picture of the office procedures being performed, as well as a detailed understanding of the work of each of his individual subordinates. The office manager thus really becomes the manager of a system composed of both machine and human components.

Moreover, an emphasis on the fundamental office work being conducted, rather than on the artifacts of office operation, may lead to a different perspective on the structure of the organization as a whole [Strassman, 1980]. Many office procedures are not conducted entirely within the confines of a single office, but rather transcend existing office boundaries. A focus on the flow of a procedure that crosses these boundaries may lead to the conclusion that existing structures are of historical importance only. Instead of looking at an individual office as a specialized node in performance of the process as a whole, alternative modes of realizing the function may be designed, which significantly alters the function, responsibility, and mission of individual offices.

## CONCLUSION

What are the implications for an organization's current strategy of the preceding perspective on the nature and aims of office automation? First, it suggests that implementation of office automation technology must begin with an examination of the office in terms of its business goals, by identifying the function that is being realized and seeking improved ways of accomplishing it. The question to be asked is "What is my problem and how can technology be used to solve it?", rather than "How can I make use of word processing?" Only by evaluating a range of technical alternatives in terms of the office's overall objectives can effective systems be designed. This means that office equipment must be evaluated not just in terms of cost displacement, but with respect to its total contribution to business objectives, as manifested by improvements in the quantity or quality of the office's work product.

A second implication is that instead of focusing on the use of office automation hardware to mechanize discrete tasks, users should focus their attention on opportunities to support entire office procedures. For example, consider the "new business" office of an insurance firm. A pure task approach would utilize a word processor solely to generate correspondence, perhaps producing individualized letters from collections of canned paragraphs. A functional approach would begin by examining the entire procedure for processing new insurance applications, and decomposing it into steps requiring individual judgment and steps consisting of routine tasks. In the process, opportunities for rationalizing the procedure as a whole might well be found. From this analysis, techniques for supporting the entire procedure using office automation would be developed. For example, the analysis might lead to the use of a powerful multifunctional word processing system to track the current status of applications, generate reminders when responses are overdue, produce checklists of remaining steps to be done, and in general automate parts of the "new business" acceptance function. (Such automation is well within the reach of contemporary word processors with their mathematical packages, list-processing facilities, and programming language support.) Note that the advantages of this approach are substantial, and could not be realized by a fixation on the mechanics of typing and document preparation.

Third, in addition to supporting the clerical workers in the office, the approach we advocate would consider how managerial productivity could be enhanced. The office system could be used to produce management summary reports and facilitate queries against an on-line database, for use in planning and in solving problems that cannot be handled by the clerical staff.

The detailed examination and analysis of each office's procedures required to achieve this type of office automation means that individual offices must undertake these efforts themselves—no central office automation group could master the procedures in every department. The question is then how to achieve some kind of uniformity and coherence of equipment and data, if each office proceeds on its own. Moreover, as offices move to apply office automation to ever larger procedures, the issue quickly arises of how to address procedures that cut across departmental boundaries.

Therefore, the fourth step in our approach must be the early implementation of an organization-wide network, to serve as the interface between independent office systems. While it is difficult to impose a common choice of equipment on diverse departments in a large organization, the existence of a common network with a standard set of interface conventions provides a strong motivation for compatibility and adhering to standards.

In conclusion, our approach to office automation is fundamentally an *integrated* one. Its key concept is that office work is not as the child sees it, a disorganized assemblage of unrelated tasks. Rather, an office is a *system* of interacting components that purposefully cooperate to accomplish a business function. An automated office information system has the potential of substantially improving the realization of this function, through the mechanization of some office tasks and the automation of others, through personal augmentation of principals and support of the decision-making process, and through management and control of the procedure as a whole. However, these improvements will only be achieved if the basic business purpose of the office is kept foremost and a systemic approach to supporting it is employed.

## REFERENCES

Engelbart, D. C., & English, W. K. (1966). A research center for augmenting human intellect. *Proceedings of the AFIPS 1968 Fall Joint Computer Conference, 33,* 395–410.

Gorry, G. A., & Morton, M. S. S. (1978, Spring). A framework for management information systems. *Sloan Management Review.*

Hammer, M., & Zisman, M. D. (1979, May). Design and implementation of office information systems. *Proceedings of the NYU Symposium on Automated Office Systems.*

Harkness, R. (1978, June). Office information systems: An overview and agenda for public policy research. *Telecommunications Policy.*

Hiltz, S. R., & Turoff, M. (1979). *The network nation: Human communication via computer.* Reading, MA: Addison-Wesley.

Keen, P. G. W., & Morton, M. S. S. (1978). *Decision support systems: An organizational perspective.* Reading, MA: Addison-Wesley.

Matteis, R. (1979, March-April). The new back office focusses on customer service. *Harvard Business Review.*

Sirbu, M. (1978, October). Automating office communications: The policy dilemmas. *Technology Review.*

Strassman, P. (1980, January). The office of the future: Information management for the New Age. *Technology Review.*

Zisman, M. D. (1978, Spring). Office automation: Revolution or evolution. *Sloan Management Review.*

# 19
# Personal Computers and Education

## 1980, 1984

## James A. Levin and Yaakov Kareev

### INTRODUCTION

For more than 20 years, people have been claiming that computers are about to revolutionize education. In 1966, Suppes wrote, "One can predict that in a few more years millions of school-children will have access to . . . the personal services of a tutor as well-informed and responsive as Aristotle. This rate [of computer-assisted instruction] is scarcely implemented as yet, but . . . it cannot fail to have profound effects in the near future." (Suppes, 1966, p. 204) However, there are very few children, if any, who enjoy the privileges of Alexander of Macedonia through the use of a computer. Why, then, should you continue to read this chapter, which also argues that revolutionary changes lie ahead of us due to the impending impact of personal computers on education at all levels?

Previous claims were made on the basis of possible changes that *could* occur; the changes we describe reflect changes that *are* occurring. The changes envisioned in the past required that someone (the federal government, private foundations, state governments or local school districts) commit large amounts of money to bring computers into the classroom. The changes described here are based to a large extent on *grassroots* developments, brought about by the people involved at the basic level of education: teachers, students, and parents. Finally, earlier approaches expected the educational effects to occur within the school, and at least implied that some of them may result in the replacement of human teachers by computers. However, more profound effects of personal computers on education may occur outside of schools.

Our predictions about the impending impact of computers on education are based on the simple observation that it is easy to design highly motivating computer activities with clearly identifiable educational components. The flexibility of computers can assure a wide choice of activities to satisfy many tastes and ability levels. The activities themselves and their contents can be designed to achieve a wide range of educational objectives.

While the potential for intensive use of computers has existed for a long time, the high price of computers or the continuing expense of maintaining communication with a remote central facility proved prohibitive in many cases, and almost always required some benefactor to support the project. Recent advances of microelectronics have drastically reduced the price of computing power and thus reduced the dependence on outside funding. Many parents have taken the initiative themselves to buy personal computers for their homes—there are even now hundreds of thousands of personal computers in American homes, and their number is increasing at a rapid rate. Moreover, personal computers are also finding their way into classrooms, sometimes without the official sanction of authorities as teachers bring personal computers in their classrooms on their own. This is one route by which computers are finding their way into schools.

Students attending a university course taught by one of us (JAL) during the spring of 1979 were asked to assess the extent to which computers were being used in the schools of San Diego County. One group of students talked to the school administrators responsible for educational innovation for the county system, and returned with the view that computers were not being used much in classrooms and further that there were no plans for a major expansion of that use. Other students talked to classroom teachers and returned with a different story. The teachers reported a substantial and expanding use of computers in classrooms. How can we reconcile these two accounts?

While it is true that the school system as an institution was not expanding at that time its use of computers very much, it turned out that many teachers were bringing their *own* personal computers into their classrooms. The price of computers has now dropped to a level where teachers can afford to buy their own computers and integrate them in whatever way they want into their classrooms. This is a grassroots development, in which teachers are taking the initiative and the control over introducing computers into their own classrooms. It is difficult to get a measure of the magnitude of this development, both because it is recent and rapidly changing, and because any statistics collected by the official authorities would be suspect, as personal computers are often introduced into the classroom without the official involvement (or even knowledge, in some cases) of school administrations.

The other half of the grassroots development is the increasing number of personal computers in the homes of students. In addition, there are an increasing number of educational programs, marketed directly to owners of these computers. This development is occurring outside the scope of the institutionalized educational process, but the impact of a substantial number of students working with computers in the home will soon have to be acknowledged and adjusted to by schools.

What we see, then, is the spread of a technology which offers a range of highly motivating activities for a decreasing cost. Such a development cannot fail to have a profound effect on education, both in and out of schools. As a result schools face the challenge of integrating computers into their structure to harness their tremendous educational power.

In this paper, we will begin by describing some of the earlier attempts to use computers for education. Then we will outline the range of activities available with current systems, both to explore the range of possible educational uses of personal computers and to gain some insight as to why computer activities can be motivating. We will suggest a model of educational design for educational computer activities. In the final section we will recommend some actions those involved in education can take to deal with the challenge posed by personal computers.

## COMPUTERS AND EDUCATION—A HISTORICAL SKETCH

### Drill and Practice

The earliest yet still most widely used mode of computer-assisted instruction (CAI) is the "drill and practice" format. The computer presents instructional material, then asks the student a series of evaluative questions. Drill and practice CAI is an automated version of programmed instruction text books. Both of these were a reaction against the conventional instruction in classrooms, designed to allow personalized instruction and rapid feedback. Depending on the student's answers, the CAI system moves on to new material, asks further diagnostic questions, or presents remedial material. The following is an example of drill and practice (This example is taken from a program called STATES developed by the Minnesota Educational Computing Consortium. The computer prints the words on a computer screen; the student types on a keyboard, and his words are printed in italics here.):

> What is your name? *Jim*
> Lansing is the capital of? *Michigan*
> That's great, Jim!
> Charleston is the capital of? *South Carolina*
> No, try again. *North Carolina*
> No, Charlestown is the capital of West Virginia.
> The capital of Alaska is? *Juno*
> That's close, Jim.
> The exact answer is Juneau.
> The capital of Alaska is Juneau.
>
> Number tried 3
> Number correct 1st try 2
> Number correct 2nd try 0

Early efforts to develop computer-assisted instruction were largely oriented towards drill and practice. The Stanford project (Suppes, 1966; Atkinson &

Wilson, 1969) developed and tested nationwide systems for arithmetic and reading in the mid- to late 1960s. The Plato System at the University of Illinois (Bitzer & Skaperdas, 1970) went the furthest in providing a supportive environment for teachers to create drill and practice programs in many different subject areas.

However, none of these early efforts at CAI have been widely adopted. One of the major factors for the lack of acceptance has been cost. Both the Plato system and the early Stanford system operated on large central computers, with students connected by phone lines. A big central computer was much too expensive for a school to buy, and even the terminals for these systems were relatively expensive. But the major barrier was the continuing communication costs. Even schools which could raise the startup costs for terminals and training found the continuing expense of phone lines to Illinois or California an intolerable burden.

There was a second major problem with drill and practice approaches. The type of activities provided by them were often unmotivating and sometimes downright boring. When given a choice, students prefer a computer game to a straight drill and practice program (Malone, 1981). Lack of variability and similarity to other school tasks are certainly among the reasons for this effect, but a major reason seems to be that the initiative for action in drill and practice environments is almost entirely under the control of the computer program.

## Student-Initiative Uses of Computers for Learning

A second major line of development for using computers in education rejected the lack of initiative typical of drill and practice approaches. Instead it created environments in which students had the initiative for actions. In the late 1960s, at the time that the "free-school" movement was at its height, Papert and others at MIT started the LOGO Project. Rather than trying to come up with a better way to conduct conventional classroom activities, the LOGO Project developed an environment where learning was achieved through the active process of programming the computer. While drill and practice programs concentrated solely on the acquisition of conventional subject matter, the LOGO approach viewed both learning to program and the acquisition of subject matter as important aspects of computer-based activities. Learning to program emerged as a central goal both because it was regarded as an important skill in itself and because it was hoped that it would help develop general problem-solving skills. The LOGO Project and others adopting this same educational philosophy explored the potential of computers as a new medium for learning, rather than just as a way to do the same old things more efficiently.

The work of the LOGO Project was named after and based on LOGO, a computer language that children could easily learn and use. More importantly, they restructured knowledge domains (for example, geometry [Papert, 1971, 1980], music [Bamberger, 1972], and physics [Abelson & diSessa, 1981]) so

**Figure 19-1.   Figure drawn on a screen by the POLYPSI program with inputs 5 and 121.**

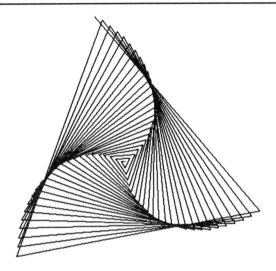

that children using LOGO could easily explore and master them. This restructuring of knowledge makes it relatively easy to write programs that produce interesting results. Below is a program written in LOGO that produces on the computer screen the graphic figures shown in Figures 19-1 and 19-2.

**Figure 19-2.   Figure drawn by POLYSPI program with inputs 5 and 93.**

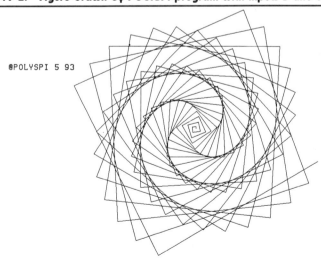

@POLYSPI 5 93

Sketch Pad Program:  Roy Eagleson – UWO Centre for Cognitive Science

```
TO POLYSPI :STEP :ANGLE
1 FORWARD :STEP
2 LEFT :ANGLE
3 POLYSPI :STEP+5 :ANGLE
END
```

To use POLYSPI one has to supply it with two numbers: a value for the variable STEP, and a value for ANGLE. The program instructs a mechanical turtle (or its equivalent appearing on a video screen) to move forward STEP units, then turn left ANGLE degrees. At that point it calls itself again (i.e., recursively) with a new value for STEP (STEP+5) and the same value for the turning angle. Children can learn LOGO and write programs such as POLYSPI, which produce a lot of action for relatively little effort.

Another project sharing LOGO's view of computers and education was the Learning Research Group, started by Alan Kay in the early 1970s at Xerox Palo Alto Research Center. The project set out to provide users in general and children in particular with a powerful tool for fostering learning through active exploration. They developed a computer language for learning, called Smalltalk (Kay, 1977; Learning Research Group, 1976), providing tools for easily producing high-quality graphics, animation, and music. The Xerox Learning Research Group was among the first to explore the possibilities of using *personal* computers for learning, even when the notion of computers inexpensive enough for individuals to own seemed a pipe dream.

## MIXED INITIATIVE USES OF COMPUTERS FOR LEARNING

The two approaches discussed so far can be seen as occupying two ends of a spectrum of underlying educational philosophy. In the drill and practice uses, the computer takes and maintains the initiative in interacting with the student. The LOGO and Smalltalk languages were designed so that the learner would take the initiative in the interaction to use the computer as an educational tool. Much of the recent research on using computers in education has explored the middle ground between these two extremes, where both student and computer can take the initiative during the interaction. These "mixed initiative systems" (Carbonell, 1970) perform Intelligent Computer-Aided Instruction (ICAI). Carbonell's Scholar program (tutoring students in geography) and more recent systems draw upon the methods developed in research in psychology and computer science for representing knowledge, comprehending language, and performing inference.

A prime example of a mixed initiative computer program is the Sophie system developed by Brown and his associates (Brown & Burton, 1975; Brown, Burton, & Zdybel, 1973) to train people to repair complex electronic equipment. The student is presented with a simulated malfunctioning electronic device, and is to discover the malfunction and repair the device. Within this system, the student can make simulated measurements and "replace" suspected components.

Part of the Sophie system builds a representation of the student's current state of knowledge, based on what information the student has gathered and the electrical laws the student has previously mastered. The system can then give guidance to the student as s/he proceeds through the diagnosis process. The computer builds a model of what the student could know about the circuit based on his/her previous actions, and guides the student when s/he makes redundant measurements, generates faulty hypotheses about the trouble, or asks for help. Below is an example of a dialogue between a student (given in Mixed Case Letters) and Sophie (given in UPPERCASE letters). (R22 is a particular resistor in the circuit.) In this dialog, both the student and the computer take the initiative at different points.

> What is the resistance of R22?
> THE MEASURED RESISTANCE OF R22 IS 25 OHMS.
> Replace R22.
> R22 REPLACED.
> NOW YOU SHOULD TAKE MEASUREMENTS TO SEE IF ANY-
> THING ELSE IS WRONG.
> Now what is the output?
> THE OUTPUT VOLTAGE IS 19.9 VOLTS.

Another example of the use of AI in CAI is the Why system of Collins and Stevens (Collins, 1976; Stevens & Collins, 1977). This system contains a representation of some of the processes embodying Socratic tutoring, in which a student actively learns by answering a series of "leading" questions.

This metaphor of the computer as tutor is based on an educational philosophy in which the computer is neither purely pedant nor purely tool, but instead a jointly active participant in interaction with the learner. A similar metaphor for a mixed initiative interaction sees the computer as a "coach," giving guidance to a learner who is practicing his/her abilities in some domain. The coach metaphor was explored by Goldstein (1977), who designed a program to coach players of a cave exploration game called Wumpus. To play this game well, the student has to learn how to integrate various kinds of uncertain information. The Coach system starts with a complex representation of the Wumpus game and typical student problems, and builds up a representation of the particular student being coached.

This taxonomy of educational uses of computers parallels the more general philosophical positions that have been proposed for education. Kohlberg and Mayer (1972) describe three "streams of educational ideology": cultural transmission, romanticism, and progressivism. There is a nice mapping of the three positions along the "initiative" dimension (computer-initiative, student-initiative, mixed-initiative) described previously and each of these three general positions. But unlike Kohlberg and Mayer, we are not arguing for the inherent superiority of mixed-initiative systems over computer-initiative or student-initiative systems. Instead, we shall argue for dynamic-initiative systems, that initially provide strong support for novices, and that allow students to acquire more and more control over the domain.

## COMPUTERS IN SCHOOL, CLUB, AND HOME ENVIRONMENTS

What are the implications of this dynamic support hypothesis for structuring computer learning environments? We have observed the use of computers by children in three different environments (schools, clubs, and homes) in an attempt to discover how children interact with personal computers, and to see if a dynamic support notion could allow us to design environments that are fruitful for learning.

### Computers in the Classroom

We were particularly interested to find out how easy it would be to integrate the computer into the normal flow of classroom activities. We have been observing the impact of computers on classrooms over the past nine school years. Our first observation was that the computer could be integrated into classrooms without disrupting the other classroom activities. This was true despite the enthusiasm and interest surrounding the computer. One fear often expressed is that unless each child in the class has a computer, the other class activities will be hopelessly disrupted. Since this was not true in any of the classrooms we observed, we feel that the way the computer was introduced by teachers deserves further description. Generally the whole class was presented with the computer. The available activities were described as well as the steps needed to operate it. In addition teachers usually put a sheet of paper detailing the most frequently used commands next to the computer. It was then placed in a corner of the classroom and defined as an "activity center." The children normally rotate through different activity centers during the course of the day, so the computer was added as just another one. Each child was assigned a time slot, and the schedule was written on the blackboard so that everyone could see it. From then on, the allocation of time was administered largely by the children themselves. We feel that both the equitable allocation of time and the self-regulation principle contributed to the smooth integration of the computer into the class routine.

In one classroom, the children were allowed to work by themselves or to choose a friend with whom to work during their turns. Almost all children selected someone to work with them. Because of this, each child got to spend more time with the computer. But more important, pairs of children working together *substantially* reduced the number of problems encountered requiring outside help. When the children worked in pairs, a large percentage of the low-level problems encountered by one child were immediately solved by the other. For example, in many programs the computer will not act on a typed input until a key labeled RETURN (or ENTER or ACCEPT) is pushed. Inexperienced users often forget to hit this key; they sit there waiting for the computer to respond with increasing frustration. Previous solutions to this problem involved making the RETURN key larger, or coloring it red, or having the computer time a response and prompt the user when too much time elapsed. This problem, along with many other such low-level problems, *disappeared* when children worked in pairs, as one child almost always pointed out the problem or acted to solve the problem as soon as it emerged.

Since teamwork and cooperation helped resolve most of the low-level problems encountered, the demands on the teacher's time were minimized. In the relatively few cases when the pair of children could not resolve a problem, often another child, an ''expert'' on the particular computer activity engaged in, would come to the rescue. Only in rare circumstances was the teacher's help required.

Educators often express the fear that the introduction of computers into the classroom will adversely affect peer interaction. An often-invoked image is that of children sitting before computer consoles, isolated from other children. Our observations showed that computer activities, when properly organized, lead to a considerable *increase* in cooperative peer interaction, more so than almost any other classroom learning environment.

Throughout our classroom experiments the elementary school children have showed no signs of ''computer anxiety.'' They related to it as naturally as they would to a telephone or a television set. This stands in marked contrast to the anxiety experienced by many adults in their dealings with computers. Lack of anxiety was true for both boys and girls. Typically there is a gross imbalance in the representation of the two genders in computer-related activities. Indicators such as attendance of computer courses, ownership of personal computers, or subscription to computer hobbyist magazines all show approximately a 9:1 ratio of males to females. However we observed no discernible gender differences in amount of motivation or involvement. There was, however, a gender-related difference in *which* activities the children preferred (also found by Malone, 1981). While boys were more attracted by competitive ''action'' games, girls often preferred games involving writing or music. By providing a wide variety of activities and allowing the children to choose among them, both girls and boys were able to find computer activities that they enjoyed.

The wide variety of activities we provided led to the emergence of ''local experts,'' children who became very adept at performing one activity or another.

It was particularly encouraging to observe cases in which those experts were children who are among the "low achievers" in the class. In two noteworthy examples, a roadrace game and the operation of a lemonade stand, the best performers were two children who were ordinarily at the bottom of the class. Their expertise was recognized by the other children, who came to ask them for advice. We feel that it is very important for any child to excel in some school-related activity. The wide variety of activities available on computers greatly increases the chances that each child will indeed be able to achieve that status.

## Computers in Clubs

In between the formally structured learning environments of schools and the informally structured ones of homes, there are semiformally structured settings that children and adults participate in, such as clubs and other voluntary groups led by adults. One aspect of both clubs and homes that differentiate them from schools is the more flexible interactions allowed. Another difference is that computer activities in clubs and homes must compete with a wide range of alternative activities. Unless the computer activities are sufficiently entertaining children will not engage in them. Entertainment value has long been recognized as an important ingredient for learning environments. However, in school settings it often plays only a secondary role (often accepted only as a necessary evil). In contrast, in less formal environments, entertainment provides the initial motivation necessary for the success of any educational undertaking.

In an attempt to find out how computers could be used for learning and problem solving, we set up two computer clubs for 10-year-olds, who voluntarily attended over the course of four months. During each club meeting children were free to engage in any of the computer activities available. A more detailed account of the club activities appears in Levin and Kareev (1980a).

As in the school setting, there was a large amount of cooperative interaction among the children in the clubs. Even though most of the computer activities available in the clubs had been originally designed with one user in mind, they were most often used by groups of children. This was true even though the computers were an abundant resource during club sessions (in fact it was not uncommon to see a deserted computer in one end of the room, with several children gathered around another). By working together children were able to divide up the work among themselves thereby dealing with the complexities of new situations in an efficient way. For example, in a game called Harpoon, which required the players to enter two pieces of information, one group smoothly divided up the task so that one child took responsibility for determining one aspect while two others determined the other.

We observed a recurring progression in the way children engaged in computer activities during the clubs. First, when a new computer activity was introduced, a large group of children (four or five) would gather around as an adult demonstrated it. Then one child would claim a turn and sit at the keyboard. This child would often serve as a typist, entering the suggestions of other children and the adult. Next, children would begin to interact with the computer without adult participation, except when they sought help. As the children acquired expertise and the novelty of the activity wore off, the group would grow smaller, often with just pairs of children working together. An expert child might then begin to work alone, increasing the difficulty level of the task when possible. This progression from low-level performance to expertise recurred almost every time we introduced a new computer activity to the club. Once a child became an expert at a particular activity, other children would turn to him or her for help rather than call an adult. Since there was a relatively large number of activities, expertise was widely distributed among children.

Computer games were the most popular kind of activity in the club. However, many of the games required the practice of skills likely to be useful outside the microworlds of the games. For example, in the Harpoon Game, the children tried to "throw a harpoon at a shark" on the screen. To do so, they had to specify its X and Y coordinates. The harpoon flew to the spot specified, either hitting the shark or splashing into the water. This highly entertaining game provides practice at estimating the number corresponding to a position on a number line, a basic skill for mathematics. The ability to embed basic skills and knowledge in entertaining computer activities allows education to move into less formally structured environments. It also raises the possibility that education in formal environments may be made more motivating without sacrificing its other goals.

## Computers in Homes

As the number of home computers increases, it becomes increasingly important for us to know what kinds of impact computers will have on children at home. We will describe here an exploratory "diary" study of computer use in a home (the home of author YK), which spanned a seven-month period. The two boys in this home had no previous computer experience.

There was a progression of usage in this home, that we believe characterizes a reasonable prediction about usage in other homes as well. Initially there was a large degree of enthusiasm about a variety of computer games available on the computer. Playing was typically intense, but the boys would spend relatively short periods of times with any single game as they were eager to sample others. That pattern changed after a number of days, with longer periods of play devoted to a single game with much emphasis placed on setting personal records in games where scores were provided. Game playing remained popular throughout the period, but different games were popular at different times. Sometimes the boys would return to games they had not played in months. These cyclical patterns of game playing are very similar to what one observes with noncomputer games, and serve as another indication that children treat the computer in a similar way.

The computer neither completely displaced all other play nor did interest disappear as the novelty wore thin. Instead, the boys continued to use it across the seven months of this study, while their patterns of usage shifted. After the initial game usage phase, they also became interested in graphics and music programs. A high point of this usage pattern came several months into the project, when they helped produce a picture and a song appropriate for the Hanukkah holiday. At about this time, each child received his own "floppy disk" to store his pictures on, and a little later they were also allowed for the first time to start the computer and change disks on their own. With that permitted, they became much less dependent on adults in their use of the computer, and could use it even with no adult around.

At this point, they were introduced to a text editor program, which they could use to enter and modify text easily. They enjoyed using this screen editor (the UCSD Pascal Editor) for laboriously entering stories they made up, but mostly for entering "crazy stories"—text entered by hitting keys randomly on the keyboard. Editing commands to delete, change, and insert text were very popular with the children.

While there was a strong temptation to try and teach the children some programming, we made a conscious decision not to force the issue. They were told that the different activities they were engaged in involved the use of computer programs, and were presented with programs via the use of the 'LIST' command in BASIC. They were then shown how programs could be modified— initially to change the values of some parameters they did not like in some of the game programs. For example, in a game called Space War, they asked for an increase in the amount of energy allocated by the original program, so they could play longer. In a game involving the operation of a lemonade stand they asked for a different mix of rainy, sunny, and hot and dry days than that originally available. Only after becoming experts at operating the computer and familiar with low-level notions of programming did the children start writing simple programs, for example, ones that filled the screen by printing out strings of characters over and over again.

The computer had an important side benefit: it served as an important aid for language learning. In the beginning, the need to read computer messages and program names, and to type in answers to play games served as a strong motivation for coming to grips with English (a second language for the boys). Later, the text editor and story programs helped them refine their language skills.

Finally, after almost seven months of playing computer games, creating computer graphics and music, editing text, and modifying and writing programs, they came to discover one more use for the computer. They were trying to figure out how much money they had earned from babysitting so that they could plan for an upcoming toy-shopping expedition. They were surprised when told that they could use the computer to calculate that amount. They entered the numbers and operations within the BASIC 'PRINT' statement ("PRINT 6.25 + 2.37 −

1.31''), and were pleased to see the computer print out the answer. When told the computer was also similar to a calculator, one of the boys said ''No, it's much better than a calculator, since here you may correct your errors.''

What we see, then, is that with the computer at home the children engaged in a large number of educationally relevant activities. Not only did they learn how to operate a new system, but they also improved their performance in numerous games, and improved their language skills. Probably most important of all, they became aware of the wide range of uses to which the computer can be put. Finally, it should be noted that the computer did not become an all-encompassing preoccupation with the boys. Interactions with it stabilized at an average of about one hour a day. That time seemed to come mostly at the expense of television viewing time.

We have observed the use of personal computers in three different environments: in a classroom as part of ongoing school activity, in a computer club, and at home. The three environments varied along a number of important decisions. One was the availability of computing resources: the computers were a scarce resource in the classroom, and the computer club meetings were relatively infrequent. At home, on the other hand, the computer was continuously available, leading to a different style of use. The environments also differed in the kind of interaction between participants. At school, children could consult with some but not with all of their peers, and expert advice was not readily available; in the club and at home children could freely interact both with peers and with any expert adults present. Both variables were important in determining the kind of emergent behaviors.

The three environments also had some common features. The computers provided much initial support in all three of them. Many of the activities were computer games with the setting and rules determined by the computer (programs), with the participants being explicitly informed about the range of activities available to them. More creative activities such as story making or sketching were also selected with special attention to the availability of clear and easy-to-follow instructions concerning the range of possible actions.

## EDUCATIONAL DESIGN

### Preliminary Considerations

In this section we will examine the educational potential of computer activities and suggest ways for designing them. Our approach to educational design rests on two related assumptions concerning the educational potential of an activity: (a) The educational potential of an activity is directly related to the individual's interest in engaging in that activity. (b) The educational potential is maximized when the activity is within the individual's ''zone of proximal development.''

The role of motivation in bringing about learning cannot be overestimated. Children can be forced to engage in activities they do not like, but unmotivated or frustrated children are unlikely to achieve the intended goals of the activity. Educators are well aware of the need for motivating activities; once educational goals are set, much effort is devoted to the question of how to design motivating activities to achieve these goals.

A related question has to do with the kind of activities which are likely to be of maximum benefit to the learner. Some activities may be of minimal value since they enhance a capacity already mastered by the student. Other activities may turn out to require capabilities not at the individual's disposal. Activities of the later type are too difficult and lead to frustration on the learner's part. In between already mastered skills and too difficult tasks lies the zone of proximal development. It includes those activities which the individual cannot perform alone but is capable of performing with some help from the outside environment.

The notion of the zone of proximal development was developed by Vygotsky (1978). The basic idea is that development results from an interplay between the individual and the environment. The individual possesses certain faculties, and they increase in power as a result of the individual's interaction with the environment. There is a certain region which is beyond the individual's reach when operating alone, but which can be mastered with outside help. The help might provide additional information, point to similarities, differences, or regularities, or indicate what should be done next. The range of conditions within which such help can be utilized by the individual is the zone of proximal development. The zone depends on the individual in question, and changes with the mastery of new faculties. Learning can be optimized if activities are so arranged that the individual operates most of the time within his/her zone of proximal development (Laboratory of Comparative Human Cognition, 1979).

The concept of zone of proximal development provides a powerful tool for the design of educational activities. The basic idea is not new, of course, and similar notions about the design of a supportive environment for the learner exist elsewhere in the educational literature. Indeed, a basic assumption underlying the use of teachers and curricula is that such a zone exists, and that activities within it can enhance the achievement of educational goals.

The zone of proximal development is not of a fixed size or location, but is dynamically defined by the amount of needed support available in the outside environment, with the appropriate support leading to a wider zone. While support is necessary during the initial stages of achieving new educational goals, the end result often calls for the learners to be able to achieve independent mastery of the subject matter in question. Therefore, an important aspect of designing educational activities is to build into them a mechanism for gradually withdrawing support, thus letting the individual become increasingly independent in his/her performance. At the same time that mastery of certain performances is achieved, other materials which draw on the newly acquired capacities are introduced, again in a supportive environment. Support systems should be tuned to take into account the special needs of the individual learner. The design, introduction and withdrawal of supportive systems are major challenges to educators. Individualized instruction can be viewed as a way of producing just the right amount of support for the learner.

We regard the suggestions presented below as valid principles for designing computer-based educational activities both when the users have a computer for themselves and when the computer is a scarce resource to be allocated between a number of users. However, the prototypical situation we have in mind is one where both the computer and human expert support are limited. While the prices of microcomputers have dropped at an astounding rate, economic considerations make it unlikely that schools which decide to integrate computers into their activities will be able to acquire a computer for each child in the immediate future. Our observations lead us to believe that this economic reality may be a blessing in disguise since it is not necessary, and possibly not even desirable, for each child to have his/her own computer. Expert advice is likely to be another limited resource: except for a few well-financed experimental projects we expect expert adults (teachers, club leaders, parents) to be able to devote only part of the time necessary to support the new users. Here, too, we do not regard the scarcity of the resource as a debilitating limitation; in fact, there might even be ways of taking advantage of this situation. The design of computer activities should take these constraints into account, though.


**Progression Towards Expertise**

In this section we present a more detailed account of how related activities may be combined to provide an environment for progressing to expertise. We start by showing what kind of activities might be necessary for novices to become familiar with a computer and to learn how to program. We have chosen this example since quick mastery of the computer system may be a prerequisite for successful interaction required by many different activities, while programming knowledge provides the students with a powerful tool with which they can further explore the newly acquired knowledge.

*Introducing a computer system.* There are two levels of skills involved in using a computer, operating a computer, and programming it. Current educational uses of computers vary as to how much knowledge of these two aspects they demand of the users, or expect them to achieve. At one end of the spectrum, some educational applications of computers (drill and practice, for example) only require that the user know how to run an existing program, and not much else. At the other extreme, there are approaches (e.g., LOGO) which put much more in the educational benefits of learning to program. These approaches require both familiarity with the system at hand and knowledge of a programming language.

We believe that learning to program is an important eventual goal of using computers in the educational process, and that as many users as possible should acquire at least some knowledge of the skill. Yet, programming is a complicated skill, which requires mastery of the syntax of a new language which is quite different from natural language. Furthermore, without having a good grasp of the operating system of the computer, any programming efforts will be of little use. For example, suppose one learned some of the rules of a programming language, and wanted to type in a program. One is immediately confronted with a host of problems, unnoticed by experienced users but debilitating for a beginner. How does one terminate a statement? What about typing errors? What does one do to make a program run once it is typed in? Suppose one likes the program; what should be done so that it can be used on some later occasion? And if the program is stored somewhere for future use, how is it called back?

Any one of these problems can frustrate the novice, or even destroy his/her enthusiasm for interacting with the computer. All of these problems have easy solutions, but they depend on the system used and they have to be learned. Operating manuals describe the solutions, but they often make for dull reading, and in any event it is difficult to remember all the commands, options, and solutions described. Immediate expert advice is of great help in such situations, but is likely to be scarce. Furthermore, expert help will be under the heaviest demands by each individual user at the same time shortly after the computer is introduced. Thus, approaches which call for immediately teaching novices to program may result in frustration and resentment when put into use in realistic everyday conditions.

One way to ease novices into full-blown use of computers is by initially employing simple computer activities which can be easily used to produce interesting results. Many different kinds of such activities are currently available, but all of them have a number of features in common. First, the computer provides the environment in which the activity takes place. This environment consists of graphic or verbal material presented on a television- like screen, and often accompanied by sound effects. Second, the user is actively engaged through the use of some input device(s) such as a keyboard, game paddles, joysticks, or a lightpen. In addition to providing the environment, the computer almost always serves as a record keeper, provides prompts for action when necessary, and modifies the environment in response to the user's actions. In many activities, the computer also plays the role of another active participant.

Our observations of children interacting with computers at home, in the classroom, and in clubs all clearly indicate that such computer activities are easy to learn and highly motivating. There are, of course, some which are too difficult for children at certain ages, and some are downright boring. Yet, the variety of existing programs (there are thousands of commercially-distributed computer games and other activities) assures the availability of interesting and easy-to-use activities for beginners of all ages.

Computer activities such as these are a good introduction to the computer for a number of reasons. First, as noted above, people enjoy operating them. Thus motivation to use the computer is achieved in a natural and effortless way. Secondly, since appropriately chosen computer activities are easy to use, they put minimal demands on the scarce resource of an expert's time. Novices can operate the computer themselves when all they have to do is run existing programs. In other words most of the necessary initial support is provided by the computer itself. Thirdly, computer activities provide initial familiarity with the operating system. While interacting with the computer the users become familiar with the outlay of the keyboard and with how it is used to type in answers. They learn the functions of the special keys such as "return," "backspace," "delete," "escape," or "reset." Once they become bored with one activity they have to learn how to start up another program. All this knowledge will be very useful when the users learn to do more advanced activities like programming. And it can be acquired without strain in a play-like context. Engaging in computer activities can be of educational value by itself. The activities can be designed in such a way as to present new materials as well as to require the practice and development of a large number of skills.

Thus, by starting with computer programs one can produce users who not only enjoy interacting with computers, but also know how to do it by themselves. They are likely to know how to run programs, to enter data and modify variables at run time, to correct typing errors, and in general be aware of some of the capabilities of the computer as well as its limitations.

After a number of weeks of working with programs the users can become skillful at operating the computer. By that time, different people will also have developed different preferences. Individual differences assure enough variation in the preferences for even the most popular activities (Malone, 1981). Even better, some people will become frustrated with some features of their favorite programs. They may start complaining about them, and with little or no prompting may start wondering about how they could be changed. It is easy to rouse the curiosity of novices by providing a few variations of the same program ("Why are there sounds in this program but not in the other?"). Dissatisfaction with existing programs and the realization that they can be modified sets the stage for the next phase in introducing computers, the phase of *modifying existing programs.*

The modification of existing programs serves a number of useful purposes. First, as a phase along the way towards learning how to program, it can introduce novices to concepts necessary for programming. A program cannot be modified without knowing some of the programming concepts involved in the modified section. Thus the novice can become acquainted with basic programming tools such as input or output statements, assignment of values, computations, testing conditions and branching, arrays, loops, and so on. Now, not every person in a group will learn about all these concepts, but each can master some of them by the time they are ready to do their own programming. As a result each will be able to contribute something to the group. Moreover, the learners will acquire those concepts which will be relevant for them at a given point in time, when the particular concept helps them overcome a problem they face.

The acquisition of basic programming tools and distributed expertise are only part of the potential benefits of a program modification stage. As they have to integrate their modifications into larger programs, learners can learn about program structure and design. Their section of the program will have to interact with other sections of it, and they will have to at least partially understand what those other parts do and how they operate. Their sections are almost certain to contain both syntax errors and logical errors (bugs), thus providing basic training in the art of troubleshooting and problem solving in the computer environment. All this will happen in the context of relatively small changes, which will increase the likelihood that the tasks will be accomplished with minimum pain, or even with pleasure. While debugging a large program is a painful operation, detecting and fixing the last bug in it is always a very rewarding experience; by having learners work on small changes chances are that their bugs will always be "last" bugs, thus minimizing their frustration.

A continuing high level of motivation is a final advantage of this intermediate stage. The learner will certainly be motivated to participate in a project stemming from their own curiosity and interest in improving a computer activity. But there will also be another motivating force providing support for the project. Almost all the learners in a group will be exposed to the activity being modified. They will be able to evaluate, as well as appreciate, any improvements made in it. Thus we can expect social support for projects undertaken by the learners.

Since other learners in the class are likely to be familiar with the activity in question, the learners involved in modifying any of the programs can discuss their ideas with other members of a group, incorporate new suggestions, and take criticisms into account. Different learners working on similar projects can compare ideas and products, as well as get into larger scale problems involved in integrating their changes of different parts of the activity into one "super-improved" activity. The ability to plan, design, criticize, take criticism into account, or take another person's point of view are all useful metacognitive skills (Brown & DeLoache, 1978), and have been suggested as some of the prime cognitive abilities underlying intelligence. Indeed, the acquisition of metacognitive skills has often been mentioned as one of the expected benefits of teaching programming (Papert, 1971). Our claim is that many of these skills can also be acquired (at least to a degree) during the program modification phase. The ability to take another person's point of view or the ability to modify a course of action as a result of constructive criticism may even develop better during this stage, since it is not clear that novices are very good at criticizing and monitoring their own activities. The modification of existing programs can provide novices with practice in all of these skills.

At this point learners would probably be ready to move to the next phase, *programming on their own*. Calling it a phase may be a misnomer, since independent programming may come about gradually, with the learners rewriting longer and more complicated segments of programs, which will eventually become independent programs. Here an adult expert can help by showing how certain segments can stand on their own, or be incorporated in a number of different programs, thus emphasizing the independent nature of the learners' products. At a certain point the instructor may do well to point out that some learners have written complete and independent programs, which will probably be a pleasant surprise to the new programmers, as well as a source of inspiration to their peers. When the learners seem to be close enough to the independent programs phase the instructor have a number of suggestions for programs. These can be brought up with discussions with learners who are ready to proceed in programming but who might seem at a loss for a topic.

The beauty of programming is that most of its benefits will happen almost independently of the actual project involved. Questions of design and planning (ease of usage, flexibility, error-free performance), problem solving involved in the actual writing of the programs, and the benefits of debugging will all occur with any project. Many learners will have, of course, their own ideas for programs they would like to write and test out. In such cases the instructor should gracefully (and gratefully) step aside, and resign him/herself to the role of a consultant. With programming activities naturally evolving on the basis of prior experience and actual needs we do not expect learners to lack ideas for projects or to undertake projects which are too grandiose (two problems frequently encountered by current approaches which attempt to introduce learners to programming right from the start). With programming activities emerging in a gradual way we also expect a proliferation of group projects, based on shared interest in common problems. Such projects will further familiarize learners with problems of teamwork, division of labor, and questions of coordinating the work so that separately produced segments fit together. All these are useful skills which are rarely practiced in most educational settings.

Note that a high level of motivation and a sufficient amount of support are ever-present concerns in the scheme just described. The novice learns about the computer system by engaging in self-selected computer activities; basic programming notions are acquired through attempts to make the activities even more interesting; full-blown programming evolves from such fixes, or comes about as an integral and useful part of other group activities. During the program use phase the novice is almost completely supported by the computer program itself, with low-level help provided by peers, written instructions, or, if all else fails, the local experts. During the second phase the structure of the to-be-modified program provides most of the necessary support, as the learner changes some parts and retains others. Finally the learner is on his/her own, with relatively little support from the computer. Social resources (peers and adults) are, of course, an ever-present source of support, to be used by the learner as s/he pleases.

## Creative Computer Learning Environments

Computer activities differ in how much freedom they give the user. Game programs, while high on interactive value, define a rigid set of rules within which the users operate. There are other computer activities which can be viewed as providing the users with some tools, then allowing them to use these tools in whatever way they please. LOGO and Smalltalk were expressly designed with the "tool" philosophy in mind. In this section we describe a number of programs and activities which also serve as tools. These programs are narrower in scope than those provided by the programming languages of LOGO and Smalltalk, but on the other hand they provide the user with much more initial support. We label these activities "creative" since users can apply the tools to create a variety of unique stories, drawings, or music.

*Writing.* One of the most significant uses of computers is for word processing. More and more of the people who make their living crafting words are replacing their typewriters with personal computers. The development of hardware and software to serve these people also makes it plausible to use personal computers to teach writing. In this section we will present four kinds of computer writing activities.

*Interactive Prompters.* Part of the reason novice writers have difficulty in organizing and expressing their ideas is that they have to deal simultaneously with problems at many levels. When writing with paper and pencil, they have to draw each individual letter, they have to select and correctly spell words, they have to organize grammatical phrases and sentences, they have to maintain intersentential connectivity, and at the same time they have to follow an overall plan to ensure that the text they are creating will properly convey their ideas. Faced with such problems novice writers often find it easiest to "downslide" their effort, concentrating on the lower-rather than the higher-level aspects of writing (Collins & Gentner, 1979). There are some programs which have been developed to help novices exercise the higher-level skills involved in writing, while providing support for handling the lower-level requirements. The Story-Maker programs (Rubin & Gentner, 1979) are an example, presenting the user with parts of a story, and offer a kind of program that allows even young children to generate interesting stories. At each branch point, the children see the alternatives printed on the computer screen and type in the number of the choice they want. Rather than getting hung up in the lower-level mechanics of printing, spelling, punctuation, syntax, or semantics, they engage in high-level decisions about the flow of the narrative.

We have developed a large set of such interactive reading and writing activities, which we call "interactive texts" (Levin, Riel, Rowe, & Boruta, 1985;

Levin, 1982). We have found that writers of all ages enjoy creating stories with these kinds of interactive writing activities, and that the impact carries over even to their writing with pencil and paper. In our classroom studies we also found that some of the children were eager and able to go beyond the use of the original options provided. They created their own interactive texts. In doing that they combined a high-level creative activity with elementary programming (the modification of existing programs).

*Writing Adventure Worlds.* The simple structure of initial writing prompters are an excellent way to introduce the practice of high-level skills, yet any given prompter is soon exhausted by its users. We have developed richer interactive texts that simulated adventure worlds for students to interact within. Inspired by earlier "adventure" games, we have created several moderately complex worlds in which the player is faced with problems to solve. The computer automatically saves in long-term storage the text (and action) that the player experiences during the game as a "narrative" of that person's adventure. Students can later edit the narrative if they want. Editing can be accomplished on a number of levels: words or phrases can be modified to improve the story, or whole units may be deleted or added. In this way children participate in an intrinsically motivating writing activity (they rewrite the story of their own adventure), but can practice the different writing skills in the highly supportive environment provided by a computer word processor.

*A Writer's Assistant.* In another attempt to provide a supportive environment for exercising writing skills, we have developed a Writer's Assistant, a computer program designed to help people who compose and edit their own text on a computer (Levin, Boruta, & Vasconcellos, 1983). As a base, we started with an existing computer text editor available on Apple II computers. A good text editor program is by itself very helpful for creating and changing text. However, we augmented this editor (the UCSD Pascal Editor) to help users at several different points in the writing process:

At one end, the Writer's Assistant can help with spelling. If the writer is uncertain about the spelling of a word s/he can generate a hypothesis about how the word is spelled and ask the Writer's Assistant to verify it. Another aid provided by the Writer's Assistant is the ability to display the text the writer has entered in a number of different presentation formats, which can help the writer evaluate the overall organization of the text.

*Computer Networks for Writing.* Electronic mail is now a major communication medium, especially in the commercial world. We have been conducting research into ways that it can be used for education (Black, Levin, Mehan, & Quinn, 1983; Quinn, Mehan, Levin, & Black, 1983). We have organized a network called "The Computer Chronicles Network" which has tied together students in several elementary schools in San Diego county with several schools in Alaska, including students in rural Eskimo villages. Students write news articles, which are sent to the other classrooms. Each classroom puts together its own class newspaper, selecting whichever articles it wants from the Computer Chronicles newswire. This kind of communication network can provide a "functional environment" for writing (Riel, 1983), in which children are writing and revising because they want to communicate with some other person, rather than just as a classroom exercise.

*Graphic and Music Worlds.* Other domains in which computers can support learning is in graphics, animation, and music. Traditionally, as in writing, learners have had to master laboriously lower-level skills (playing an instrument, writing notes) before they could even experience, must less master, higher levels such as painting or composing music. However recent advances in both the hardware and the software available for personal computers allow even novices to experiment with composition. The resulting piece can be experienced immediately, but also stored for further "editing" and later replay. There are many possible "art worlds" that can be provided by personal computers. Each of these worlds is particularly suited for certain tasks but not for others. Not only can these worlds provide support for art and music education, but they will challenge and then help redefine the basic notions of composition, performance, and enjoyment, by turning art and music into an interactive experience for the vast majority that now are just passive audience.

For example, there are now several "music editor" systems, which allow the user to enter notes (which appear graphically on a music staff drawn on the computer screen). These systems make it easy to enter new music, hear it performed by the computer, change it, and store it for later enjoyment or further modification. This general ability to easily display, modify, and save music, graphics, and text allows people to become involved with the higher, more creative levels of composition even while they are mastering the lower, more mechanical levels.

We have presented a broad selection of types of computer activities for learning to make the point that the use of computers for learning can go far beyond the traditional domains of mathematics and programming. In the next section, we will try to outline a set of design techniques that we have distilled for creating effective learning environments by using personal computers.


## DESIGNING EDUCATIONAL COMPUTER ACTIVITIES

A personal computer is a powerful tool available for building learning environments. Like other tools, the placement of the computer and the goals to be achieved are selected by the designer. Whatever the educational goals of the designer, our observations indicate that there are a number of design techniques which increase the likelihood that a given computer activity will effectively achieve its goals. Broadly speaking these techniques can be classified as falling into two categories: some of them provide the users with the right amount of support, while others sustain the user's motivation. The division is not clear-cut, though, and some of the suggested methods apply to both classes.

## Methods for Achieving Supportive Environments

*Dynamic computer support.* Computer activities should be designed so that users have as much support as necessary (especially at the initial stages), but also have the ability to go beyond that support. One way to achieve dynamic support is to have levels of difficulty within the activity. For example, in a race car simulation game, the car can go faster, or the course can become more winding. Level of difficulty can be manipulated not only by quantitatively changing the values along existing dimensions, but also by introducing new dimensions. In a car race activity, for example, one can have more expert drivers monitor a gas gauge as well as their position on the course. An adult expert can play an important role in providing dynamic support, both by suggesting new goals within an activity and by suggesting (or simply making available) new activities.

*Social support.* Activities should be designed so as to enable and encourage peer interaction and help. Fostering interaction and help is a desirable goal in itself; it is a good way to prepare students to live within a society, to learn how to contribute to other members of it, and to know how to seek help when necessary. In addition, helping another student is one of the best ways for the helper to gain a better understanding of the activity in question. Finally, peer support is likely to ease the burden placed on the instructor. The simplest way to achieve peer support is to let it take place, since it is natural for most people to engage in such behavior. It is also possible to encourage such behavior by designing activities which require cooperation between a number of users, suggesting projects which can be broken down into subparts, or encouraging group discussions of activities and projects.

*Progression to Expertise.* Educational computer activities should be designed so that they enable the students to gain in expertise as they further engage in those activities. One simple way of achieving this goal is to have an adjustable difficulty level, described previously. Another way is to prepare and provide for activities likely to develop as a result of using the original one. The modification of an existing program is one such new activity. Writing new programs inspired by existing ones is another. The important point is for the instructor to be aware of the need for vertical variety and be on the lookout for opportunities for its application. With simulation programs it is possible to demand increased expertise by adding additional realistic features to the simplified situation presented at the beginning. Finally, as students become proficient with some activity the designer may consider the possibility of presenting the same activity under a different representation. Multiple and parallel representations are one of the hallmarks of experts in almost any field. By providing students with different approaches to the same problem we can increase their own expertise.

## Methods for Achieving Motivating Environments

*Active/Interactive activities.* Activities should be designed to ensure an active role for the user. An active role is relatively easy to achieve when the program calls for much interaction between the user and the computer. It is preferable that the user have the feeling that his/her acts determine what the computer does rather than that the computer determines what s/he should do next. This technique applies not only within a given activity or program, but also across them: users should be allowed to freely switch between a number of different activities. Malone's (1981) three motivating factors—fantasy, challenge, and curiosity— can all be viewed as different ways for ensuring active participation on the user's part.

*Breadth of activities.* Individuals greatly differ in interests, backgrounds, and capabilities. As a result they also differ in the kind of educational activities which attract them and from which they benefit. To accommodate these differences students have available a large number of varied activities. This variety is also necessary so that the individual user can shift between activities as s/he chooses (the Active Principle). One special aspect of Breadth of Activity has to do with the preparation of isomorphic activities. These are activities which call upon the same mental faculties for their performance, but are disguised under different cover stories. Isomorphic activities are particularly useful when the educational designer feels that learners will benefit from practicing certain skills, and wants to increase the chances that each learner will find at least one relevant activity interesting. An important consideration in developing program isomorphs is to make the cover story meaningful to the intended audience (e.g., make the activity take place in an interesting environment). Isomorphic activities are also useful for helping users generalize (and transfer the skills they have acquired in the original environment by applying it in the different situation of the isomorph.

An important kind of variety is provided by "tool" programs. These are programs which serve as means for obtaining other goals. Text editing or "calculator" programs fall into this category. Programs used for creative activities (drawing, animation, music) are also included here. Students may be encouraged to develop their own tools, useful for their own purposes.

*Powerful Environments.* One way to sustain the motivation of novices is to have their actions produce easily discernible changes in the behavior of the program. Action games are a prime example of activities where this technique is often applied. The technique also applies for novice programmers, who should be directed, if possible, to write simple programs which have spectacular effects. A five-line program which fills the screen with interesting patterns is much preferable as an introductory exercise to a 200-line program which prints a single number at the end. The LOGO language is a good example of an environment where the programmer can get a lot of "bang per buck." "Tool" or creative programs also often provide novices with the power to produce spectacular effects from the start.

These design methods have focused on the relatively broad issues of the overall structure of computer learning activities and on the interactions of participants in those activities with computers and with other people in the learning environment. There are other levels in this design process that are also important. (For example, the Minnesota Educational Computing Consortium presents a number of presentation techniques such as screen layout for instructional software (MECC, 1980).) The global design methods described here are not meant as prescriptions to be slavishly followed, only as techniques found to be useful across a wide range of educational computer activities. As is the case in many other fields, experience and field testing will turn out to be the best guides for the design of fruitful educational activities.

## THE CHALLENGE TO SCHOOLS

Let us now consider possible ways for schools to meet the challenge of personal computers. The easiest approach would be to ignore the implications. However this "head in the sand policy" has its dangers, since the important learning might shift to other settings, leaving schools an anachronistic institution without any real function, a sad and transient existence at best. This is the threat of personal computers to schools.

The challenge has an positive side as well, providing exciting new opportunities for schools. One of the surprises of our studies of personal computers in different environments was how well computers could be integrated into a school classroom. The elements of this successful use of computers in a classroom derive directly from the design methods described previously—the gradual transition from the use of pre-programmed activities to program modification to programming, the use of social resources, the provision of a broad variety of computer activities for learners to select among. If schools capitalize on the opportunities they can become new and invigorated learning centers, taking advantage of their ability to provide effective face-to-face support from peers and expert adults. Schools can also provide more cost-effective systems, especially when it comes down to the use of specialized and expensive peripherals. So schools are not necessarily made obsolete by the impending advances in computer technology. By adapting appropriately they can even gain from it, becoming environments where effective and rewarding educational processes take place.

No longer is computer use restricted to programmers or to the drill-and-the-tested. Powerful tools such as word processors, graphics and animation editors, communication networks, and engaging educational games widen the range of options for teachers, parents, and students to take an active role in meeting the computer challenge. If we all take the initiative to shape this new educational medium, then it can be used to achieve a more effective, equitable, and humane educational process.

# Postscript: September 1987

## James A. Levin

This chapter is an abridged version of a report originally written in 1980 (Levin & Kareev, 1980b), with several minor changes. It is interesting to see both how far we have come since then, and how many of the major issues remain the same. In 1980, the number of microcomputers in schools was less than 10,000; in 1985, the number surpassed 1,000,000 (Becker, 1986), with the number doubling each year. There has also been a substantial shift away from the dominant uses of drill-and-practice and programming toward the kind of "tool use" proposed in this chapter (Becker, 1986). But the challenges described for education in this chapter remain.

The fundamental challenge raised by the increasing numbers and capabilities of computers concerns the goals of education. What kinds of skills and knowledge do students need to learn? This depends crucially on what kind of world that they will inhabit as adults. And in a time of rapid change, this is indeed a difficult challenge for schools.

There are two technological developments that jointly are working to change the nature of knowledge. One is the increasing ability to interlink microcomputers into long-distance networks, both to access electronic data bases and to communicate with other people. The second development is the exponential increase in the availability of low-cost mass storage (using magnetic and optical media), so that vast amounts of information can be immediately accessed from a microcomputer. Together, these developments change a microcomputer from an information-sparse setting into an information-rich setting. Instead of having available a relatively small amount of text and a few crudely drawn pictures, microcomputers will be able to draw upon a vast array of text, high-quality graphics, animation, and sound, in a richly interconnected network of knowledge. This change has an impact both on work settings and educational settings, so the question is dual: what skills will students need as adults in this new sort of work environment, and how best to use the new capabilities to help students acquire these skills.

We may move toward a new metaphor for knowledge. Rather than viewing knowledge as a relatively fixed set of precious gems to be preserved and passed on to future generations, we may view knowledge as a much more dynamic entity, to be shaped when needed. Both students and adults will need new skills to track down relevant information in a vast array, to evaluate and integrate conflicting information, and to generate knowledge as an active process, rather than to retrieve from memory a set of fixed facts. The challenge remains for education to discover what abilities will be valuable on this new electronic frontier.

# REFERENCES

Abelson, H., & diSessa, A. (1981). *Turtle geometry: The computer as medium for exploring mathematics.* Cambridge, MA: MIT Press.

Atkinson, R. C., & Wilson, H. A. (1969). Computer-assisted instruction. In R. C. Atkinson & H. A. Wilson (Eds.), *Computer-assisted instruction: A book of readings.* New York: Academic Press.

Bamberger, J. (1972, July). Developing a musical ear: A new experiment. Cambridge, MA: MIT Artificial Intelligence Memo No. 264.

Becker, H. J. (1986, June). Instructional Uses of School Computers: Reports from the 1985 National Survey. 1. Center for Social Organization of Schools, Johns Hopkins University.

Bitzer, D., & Skaperdas, D. (1970). The economics of a large-scale computer-based education system: Plato IV. In W. H. Holtzman (Ed.), *Computer-assisted instruction, testing and guidance.* New York: Harper & Row.

Black, S., Levin, J. A., Mehan, H. B., & Quinn, C. N. (1983). Real and non-real time interaction: Unraveling multiple threads of discourse. *Discourse Processes, 6,* 59–75.

Brown, A. L., & DeLoache, J. S. (1978). Skills, plans, and self-regulation. In R. Siegler (Ed.), *Children's thinking: What develops.* Hillsdale, NJ: Erlbaum.

Brown, J. S., & Burton, R. R. (1975). Multiple representations of knowledge for tutorial reasoning. In D. G. Bobrow & A. Collins (Eds.), *Representation and understanding: Studies in cognitive science.* New York: Academic Press.

Brown, J. S., Burton, R. R., & Zdybel, F. (1973). A model-driven question answering system for mixed-initiative computer assisted instruction. *IEEE Transactions on Systems, Man and Cybernetics, 3,* 248–257.

Carbonell, J. R. (1970). AI in CAI: An artificial intelligence approach to computer-assisted instruction. *IEEE Transactions on Man-Machine Systems, 11,* 190–202.

Collins, A. (1976). Processes in acquiring knowledge. In R. C. Anderson, R. J. Spiro, & G. Montague (Eds.), *Schooling and the acquisition of knowledge.* Hillsdale, NJ: Erlbaum.

Collins, A., & Gentner, D. (1979). A framework for a cognitive theory of writing. In L. W. Gregg & E. Steinberg (Eds.), *Cognitive processes in writing: An interdisciplinary approach.* Hillsdale, NJ: Erlbaum.

Goldstein, I. (1977, February). The computer as coach: An athletic paradigm for intellectual education. Cambridge, MA: MIT Artificial Intelligence Memo No. 339.

Kay, A. and the Learning Research Group. (1976). Personal Dynamic Media (Technical Report 556-76-1). Xerox Palo Alto Research Center. (An abbreviated version appeared in *IEEE Computer,* March 1977, 31–41.)

Kohlberg, L., & Mayer, R. (1972). Development as the aim of education. *Harvard Educational Review, 42,* 449–496.

Laboratory of Comparative Human Cognition. (1979). Cross-cultural psychology's challenges to our ideas of children and development. *American Psychologist, 34,* 827–833.

Levin, J. A. (1980). Interpersonalized media: What's news? *Byte, 5,* 214–228.

Levin, J. A. (1982). Microcomputers as interactive communication media: An interactive text interpreter. *Quarterly Newsletter of the Laboratory of Comparative Human Cognition, 4,* 34–36.

Levin, J. A., Boruta, M. J., & Vasconcellos, M. T. (1983). Microcomputer-based environments for writing: A Writer's Assistant. In A. C. Wilkinson (Ed.), *Classroom computers and cognitive science.* New York: Academic Press.

Levin, J. A., & Kareev, Y. (1980a). Problem solving in everyday situations. *The Quarterly Newsletter of the Laboratory of Comparative Human Cognition, 2,* 45–51.

Levin, J. A., & Kareev, Y. (1980b). *Personal computers and education: The challenge to schools (Report 98).* Center for Human Information Processing, University of California, San Diego.

Levin, J. A., Riel, M. M., Rowe, R. D., & Boruta, M. J. (1985). Muktuk meets jacuzzi: Computer networks and elementary school writers. In S. W. Freedman (Ed.), *The acquisition of writing skill: Revision and response,* Norwood, NJ: Ablex.

Malone, T. (1981). Toward a theory of intrinsically motivating instruction. *Cognitive Science, 4,* 339–369.

Minnesota Educational Computing Consortium. (1980). *A guide to developing instructional software for the Apple II microcomputer.* St. Paul, MN: MECC.

Papert, S. (1971, July). Teaching children to be mathematicians vs. teaching about mathematics. Cambridge, MA: MIT Artificial Intelligence Memo No. 249.

Papert, S. (1980). *Mindstorms.* New York: Basic Books.

Papert, S., Watt, D., diSessa, A., & Weir, S. (1979, September). Final report of the Brookline LOGO Project. Part II: Project summary and data analysis. Cambridge, MA: Artificial Intelligence Laboratory, LOGO Memo No. 53.

Quinn, C. N., Mehan, H. B., Levin, J. A., & Black, S. (1983). Real education in non-real time: The use of electronic message systems for instruction. *Instructional Science, 11,* 313–327.

Riel, M. (1983). Education and ecstasy: Computer chronicles of students writing together. *The Quarterly Newsletter of the Laboratory of Comparative Human Cognition, 5*(3), 59–67.

Rubin, A. (1980). Making stories, making sense. *Language Arts,* 285–298.

Rubin, A., & Gentner, D. (1979). *An educational technique to encourage practice with high-level aspects of texts.* Cambridge, MA: Bolt Beranek and Newman, Inc.

Stevens, A. L., & Collins, A. (1977). The goal structure of a Socratic tutor. In *Proceedings of the Association for Computing Machinery National Conference.* Seattle, WA.

Suppes, P. (1966). The uses of computers in education. *Scientific American, 215,* 206–221.

Vygotsky, L. S. 91978). *Mind in society.* Cambridge, MA: Harvard University Press.

# Suggestions for further Reading—Section IV

This section provides some references focused on computer use in the manufacturing, office, and educational environment. More general readings on the relationship between technology and society are given in the Further Readings for Section 5. Ayres and Miller, the authors of one of the articles in this book, have published a more extensive discussion of robotics issues in their book *Robotics - Applications and Social Implications* (Ballinger: Cambridge, 1983), and another book by Miller is available. *Impacts of Industrial Robotics - Effects on labor and cost in the metalworking industries.* (Madison, Wisconsin; University of Wisconsin Press, in press). Other forecasts on the diffusion of the new technologies and employment impacts have been produced by technology policy research centers. Two important British groups active in this area are the Science Policy Research Unit (SPRU) at Sussex University, and the Technology Policy Unit (TPU) based at the University of Aston, in Birmingham, who produce numerous reports. There are several papers on industrial automation by members of the latter group in the book, *The Microelectronics Revolution* edited by Tom Forester (Basil Blackwell: Oxford, 1980). Forester's more recent edited collection - *The Information Technology Revolution* (Oxford: Blackwell, 1985) is also worth browsing.

A recent US study surveyed the changes in technology and employment and makes policy suggestions:

Cyert, R. M. and Mowery, D. C. (Eds) *Technology and Employment.* (National Academy Press; Washington, DC, 1987). The OECD and ILO also produce reports on these topics. The view of a key industrialist in the robotics area can be seen in J. F. Engelberger *Robotics in Practice* (American Management Association: New York, 1980). The January 1985 issue of the *MIT Technology Review* focused on the topic of automation, including an article by Harley Shaiken, author of the book, *Work Transformed: Automation and Labor in the Computer Age* (Holt, Rinehart, and Winston, 1985). A more general related work is that by David Noble, *Forces of Production: A social history of industrial automation* (New York: Alfred Knopf, 1984).

Readers should also consult issues of *Industrial Robot* and *American Machinist* for commentary on the changes occuring in manufacturing industry.

The September 1982 issue of *Scientific American* was devoted to the topic "The Mechanization of Work", and includes articles on developments in mining, manufacturing, and office work.

Some other references:

G. Winch (Ed.) *Information Technology in Manufacturing Processes.* (Rossendale: London, 1983).

A. Sorge, G. Hartmann, M. Warner, I. Nicholas *Microelectronics and Manpower in manufacturing* (Gower: Aldershot, U.K., 1983).

G. L. Simons *Robotics in Industry* (NCC Publications, Manchester, U.K., 1981).
Rhodes, E. and Wield, D. (Eds.) *Implementing New Technologies: Choice, Decision and Changes in Manufacturing* (Oxford: Blackwell, 1985).
Wall, T. D., Clegg, C. W. and Kemp, N. J. (Eds.) *The Human Side of Advanced Manufacturing Technology* (Chichester, John Wiley, 1987).

There is a large and rapidly growing literature in the field of office automation, much of it concerned with how to manage the changes in the structure and functioning of the office which are envisaged by many writers. Ellis, C. A., and Naffah, N. *Design of Office Information Systems* (Berlin: Springer-Verlag, 1987) is a readable introduction to a number of technical issues in the field. It also contains a useful bibliography. Despite the large amount of material on the "office of the future" available in such management journals and office magazines as *Administrative Management, Journal of Systems Management, Management Review, Management World, Business Communications Review, The Office Magazine,* and *Word Processing Magazine,* there has been, until recently, a dearth of published *empirical* studies on the effects of office automation - both from the point of view of productivity enhancement and quality of working life. Part of the reason for this lack of published data is that the results of pilot studies performed within many companies have been deemed proprietary information, not for general distribution. One of the first papers to discuss the effects of automation in the office was I. R. Hoos "When the computer takes over the office," *Harvard Business Review,* 38, 4, 102–112, 1960. Other papers of interest are:

V. Vyssotsky "The use of computers for business functions," in M. Dertouzos and J. Moses (Eds.) *The Computer Age* (MIT Press: Cambridge, 1979).
Driscoll, J. "Office Automation: dynamics of a technological boondoggle," *Sloan Management Review,* 27, 1980, 34–44.
J. Schlefer "Office Automation and Bureaucracy," *MIT Technology Review,* July 1983.
A. Pape "The Office of the Future - Some sociological perspectives on office work and office technology." In E. Fossum (Ed.) *Computerization of Working Life* (Chichester, U.K.: Ellis Horwood, 1983)

The attitude of one trade union to office information is presented in the report "Office Technology - The Trade Union Response," APEX:London, 1979. See also Werneke, D. "Microelectronics and office jobs: the impact of the chip on women's employment." International Labor Office: Geneva, 1983.

The collection of papers in the book *New Office Technology - Human and Organizational Aspects,* edited by H. J. Otway and M. Peltu (Frances Pinter: London, 1983) is also of interest. An interesting, more theoretical, set of papers can be found in the collection edited by R. Boland and R. Hirschheim - "Critical Issues in Information Systems" (London: John Wiley, 1987). Other books of relevance are:

N. Naffah (Ed.) *Integrated Office Systems - Burotics.* (North-Holland: Amsterdam, 1980).
R. M. Landau, J. H. Bair, J. Siegman. *Emerging Office Systems* (Ablex: New Jersey, 1982).
R. P. Uhlig, D. J. Forber, J. H. Bair. *The Office of the Future.* (North-Holland: Amsterdam, 1982).
R. Kraut (Ed.) *Technology and the transformation of white-collar work* (Hillsdale, New Jersey: Erlbaum, 1987).

Occasional articles on office automation and management information systems can be found in the business school reviews, such as the *Harvard Business Review*, and *Sloan Management Review*. The journal, *Office: Technology and People*, (Elsevier: Amsterdam) is a key resource for researchers in this area. Business newspapers and magazines such as *The Wall Street Journal, The Financial Times* (London), *The Economist, Forbes, Fortune*, and *Business Week*, often contain interesting articles on office computing. There are also specialist business publications, such as *The Seybold Report on Office Systems*. Articles of relevance also appear in such publications as *Computerworld, Datamation, Telecommunications, Telecommunications Policy, Infosystems*, and the *Journal of Systems Management*.

The alternative Scandinavian approach to technology development and use is still not very well represented in English language research journals and the popular literature. Thankfully, this is changing, and a more representative sample of work is appearing. For some pointers, see Bjerknes, G. et al (Eds.) *Computers and Democracy - A Scandinavian Challenge*. (Aldershot; Gower, 1987) See also, Pelle Eln *Work-Oriented Design of Computer Artificats* (Stockholm: Arbetslivscentrum, 1988) [The latter is available internationally from Almquist & Wiksell International, P.O. Box 638, S-101 28 Stockholm, Sweden.] It is not the case that all Scandinavian researchers on technology necessarily share a common viewpoint, but there is no doubting the more comprehensive approach adopted by the majority of researchers in these countries - reflected in the desire to shape technology to human and social needs.

Finally, some references in the field of educational computing—see the references in the Levin and Kareev paper in this volume for additional material:

Papert, S. (1980). *Mindstorms*. New York: Basic Books.

Coburn, P., Kelman, P., Roberts, N., Snyder, T., Watt, D., & Weiner, C. (1982). *The practical guide to computers in education*. Reading, MA: Addison-Wesley.

Kelman, P., Bardige, A., Choate, J., Hanify, G., Richards, J., Roberts, N., Walters, J., & Tornrose, M. (1983) *Computers in teaching mathematics*. Reading, MA: Addison-Wesley.

Abelson, H., & diSessa, A. *Turtle geometry: The computer as medium for exploring mathematics*. Cambridge, MA: MIT Press, 1981.

Glossbrenner, A. *The complete handbook of personal computer communications: Everything you need to go online with the world*. New York: St. Martin's Press, 1983.

Yazdani, M. (Ed.) *New Horizons in Educational Computing*. (Chichester, U.K.; Ellis Horwood, 1984).

Rutkowska, J. C., and Crook, C. (Eds.) *Computers, Cognition and Development: Issues for Psychology and Education*. (Chichester: John Wiley, 1987).

Pea, R. D., and Sheingold, K. (Eds.) *Mirrors of Minds: Patterns of Experience in Educational Computing* (New Jersey: Ablex, 1987).

O'Shea, T. and Self, J. *Learning and Teaching with Computers: Artificial Intelligence in Education* (New Jersey: Prentice-Hall, 1983).

Kurland, D. Midian and Kurland, L. C. "Computer Applications in Education: A Historical Overview", in *Annual Review of Computer Science*, Vol 2, 1987, pp 317–358. (Palo Alto: Annual Reviews).

The *Journal of Educational Computing Research* is an interesting new journal in this area.

# Section V
# Social Dimensions of Computing

Our worship of progress may be discussed from two points of view: a factual one and an ethical one—that is, one which furnishes standard for approval and disapproval. Factually, it asserts that the earlier advance of geographical discovery, whose inception corresponds to the beginning of modern times, is to be continued into an indefinite period of invention, of the discovery of new techniques for controlling the human environment. This, the believers in progress say, will go on and on without any visible termination in a future not too remote for human contemplation. Those who uphold the idea of progress as an ethical principle regard this unlimited and quasispontaneous process of change as a Good Thing and as the basis on which they guarantee to future generations a Heaven on Earth. It is possible to believe in progress as a fact without believing in progress as an ethical principle; but in the catechism of many Americans, the one goes with the other.

Norbert Wiener
*The Human Use of Human Beings*

Man has within a single generation found himself sharing the world with a strange new species: the computers and computerlike machines. Neither history nor philosophy nor common sense will tell us how these machines will affect us, for they do not do "work" as did machines of the Industrial Revolution. Instead of dealing with materials or energy we are told that they handle "control" and "information" and even "intellectual processes." There are very few individuals today who doubt that the computer and its relatives are developing rapidly in capability and complexity and that these machines are destined to play important (though not as yet fully understood) roles in society's future. Though only some of us deal directly with computers, all of us are falling under the shadow of their ever-growing sphere of influence, and thus we all need to understand their capabilities and their limitations.

Marvin Minsky
*Computation, Finite and Infinite Machines*

Since the emergence of the Industrial Era, there have been voices raised both in support of, and in protest against, the perceived social effects of technology. With the advent of the silicon "chip" and the widespread application of microelectronics technology, these conflicting voices have multiplied. This section contains a number of chapters that together give a broad perspective on the relationship between technology and society.[1] It is important to realize that a full understanding of the interrelationship between technology and society involves examination of economic, social, and political factors. This fact is often obscured in publications which tend to emphasize the technology and then discuss its "impact on society." Such an atheoretical framework often implies that the author implicitly accepts the doctrine of technological determinism, which assumes that technology per se is the driving force in our society, and thus we must "adapt to," or "prepare for," the "inevitable" changes to our work and lifestyle. Use of such language often simply disguises the value framework of the author.[2] In real life, we have choices to make about whether we accept or reject new technological developments, and even where there seems to be a clear societal trend towards acceptance of a new technology, there is still much room for different actors to influence several factors, for example, the rate of change, and legal safeguards concerning the introduction of the technology.

When one performs a detailed analysis of the development of any technology, one becomes aware of the crucial role played by certain human actors (at both the individual and group level) that are concerned with such mundane issues as power, control, and profit. For example, Noble (1977) provides an interesting account of how the rise of science and technology in the United States was intricately linked with the development of corporate capitalism. These factors become enmeshed in very complex ways with decisions as to which technical developments are supported, and which are left undeveloped. Questions of power and control therefore become central to any analysis. Taking the area of office automation as an example, one value framework perceives developments in this area as essential to improving productivity and remaining competitive in the international arena. Within this framework, any criticism regarding the use of the technology is seen as "short-sighted," and even more dramatically, as contributing to the decline of the nation! An alternative view, representing a different value framework, regards the introduction of the new technology into the office as an attempt by management to further control office activity, resulting in the "assembly-line in the office"—a more regimented, less autonomous, work environment. Most empirical studies uncover a more complex interplay of forces than either of these optimistic or pessimistic scenarios outline, but the failure to explicate underlying value frameworks only contributes to present-day confusions about the actual changes that are occurring as a result of new technological applications. Hirschheim (1986) explicitly notes how authors' conclu-

---

[1]We should realize, at the outset, that making such a separation between technology and society is simply for convenience, as of course, technology itself is a product of society and may be analyzed as such.

[2]See Kling (1978) for an example of the value conflicts that underlny the debate on the social impact of Electronic Funds Transfer (EFT) systems.

sions on the effects of office technology can be directly linked to the *a priori* views of the authors!

We begin the section with an excerpt from the book *Erewhon* by Samuel Butler, first published in 1872. This book satirizes the social and economic injustices prevalent in the England of the time by describing a country called Erewhon (a play on the word "nowhere"), where customs and laws are reversed. Our interest centers on the three chapters that collectively comprise "The Book of the Machines," of which our excerpt is a condensed version. Here, Butler outlines the reasons why machines were destroyed by the Erewhonians. The three chapters in Erewhon are themselves a reworking of several earlier articles by Butler that utilized the machine metaphor to debate aspects of Darwin's theory of evolution. In Erewhon, the intent of the diatribe against the evolving machines would appear to be a critique of Darwinism for its mechanistic view of humanity. But even this is uncertain, as in the Preface to the second edition of the book, Butler explicitly denies that he was ridiculing "Mr. Darwin."

The intricacies in the debate about human evolution that Butler was alluding to with the machine metaphor are probably not of much interest to the modern reader. However, the piece can be viewed simply as a description of how humans can become subordinate to the machine.[3] We find echoes of Butler's arguments in the works of more recent authors who have criticized the increasing mechanization and dehumanization of our society. When we find ourselves today surrounded by machines of all kinds that profoundly affect the way we live, the remarks of Butler as to our gradually increasing dependence on machines becomes prophetic. If we reflect on the amount of time we spend washing, cleaning, and fixing present-day machines such as cars, televisions, and now, home computers, we might agree with the Erewhonian who says: "How many men at this hour are living in a state of bondage to the machines? How many spend their whole lives, from the cradle to the grave, in tending them by night and day?"

These remarks of the Erewhonian are an appropriate introduction to the second article in the section, extracted from Jacques Ellul's obscure but influential volume *The Technological Society*. This book is a telling indictment of our technological civilization, implicating *technique* as the all-pervasive influence that is fashioning the modern world to the detriment of our human values. It is important to realize that, for Ellul, the term *technique* does not mean simply technology or machines but, as the sociologist Robert Merton notes in his Preface to the work, "any complex of standardized means for attaining a predetermined result." For Ellul, modern society is committed to the "one best way" of doing things; more emphasis is placed on the concept of efficiency than on

---

[3]The reader may also notice the relevance of some of Butler's criticisms to the arguments concerning the loss of self-image engendered by the concept of superhuman machines discussed by Mazlish in Chapter 6.

purposes, with *technique* thus becoming an end in itself. Whereas in earlier periods *technique* "belonged to a civilization" and was simply one element in a wide range of activities, today it has "taken over the whole of civilization," and can no longer be equated with the simple substitution of machines for human labor. Ellul draws together a wide variety of literature from many disciplines to support his thesis. Arguments concerning the veracity of Ellul's analyses have continued since the initial publication of the book (in French) in 1954, but there is general agreement as to its unique place in the literature on social aspects of technology. Our excerpt has been compiled from Chapters 1 and 2 of the original volume. It includes Ellul's distinction between machines and the broader concept of *technique*, and an extensive discussion of the autonomy of *technique*.

Echoes of Ellul's concern with the lack of morality evident in modern technological society can be found in the chapter by Joseph Weizenbaum, a computer scientist at an institution that has become a symbol of American *technique*, the Massachusetts Institute of Technology. Having himself worked in the newly-developing field of artificial intelligence in the early 1960s, Weizenbaum became critical of the exaggerated claims made by many researchers in the field as to the potential of computers to change the way we think about ourselves and the world that we inhabit. This particular article appeared initially in the journal *Science* in 1972, and describes the dangers inherent in fetishizing computer technology. Weizenbaum addresses the question of how we, as human beings, view ourselves and how our image is being affected by the developments in machine intelligence.[4] While the computer may be a wonderful tool to study the nature of intelligence (see Section II), he argues that the gulf between human and machine should not be forgotten. Weizenbaum believes that we have "permitted technological metaphors, and technique itself, to so thoroughly pervade our thought processes that we have finally abdicated to technology the very duty to formulate questions." He then discusses how certain computer systems have evolved in a fashion that has resulted in the bizarre situation where nobody really understands how the resulting system works! When these complex systems are utilized by decision makers to make judgments on such politically sensitive matters as welfare funding or foreign policy, there often is no clear line of human responsibility evident for these decisions. Thus human values become superseded by *machine dictat*. An elaboration of Weizenbaum's position can be found in his book *Computer Power and Human Reason*. Needless to say, these views have been strenuously opposed by many scientists, who disagree with Weizenbaum's analyses and see no fundamental incompatibility between taking a moral stance on fundamental issues and supporting the widespread use of computer technology in the conduct of human affairs.

The three chapters just described convey an image of technology and comput-

---

[4]The reader is again directed to the earlier essay by Mazlish in this collection which elaborates on this theme, although from a slightly different perspective.

ing machines that is essentially pessimistic. There are also innumerable articles available that extol the beneficial uses of technology and computing in society. We have chosen an article by Nobel Laureate Herbert O. Simon to represent the viewpoint of those that see computing technology as a liberating force in society that opens up new horizons. Simon has had a major influence on a number of fields: operations research, administrative management, economics, cognitive psychology, and artificial intelligence. A common thread in much of his writings has been his emphasis on human rationality and the ways in which computers can be used to assist people and organizations in achieving their goals. In this chapter, Simon takes issue with those critics of the "information revolution" who see mass technological unemployment and job deskilling as an inevitable result. In his view, automation increases productivity, which in turn results in higher wages and increased leisure time. Simon also rejects the claim that modern technology is an alienating force, arguing that there is little evidence to support the "romantic" conception of work being more meaningful and less arduous before the industrial revolution, on the contrary, "the newer technologies may even have a modest humanizing effect on the nature of work."

At this stage, the reader may rightly be confused about the actual social effects of computing, as many writers tend to emphasize opinions over the presentation of empirical data that support their respective positions. There have been empirical studies conducted in the area of "social effects of computing" but the diversity of approaches evident, and different methodologies chosen, make it very difficult to develop a coherent picture of the field. Perhaps some of the best efforts at surveying the field and delineating theoretical positions can be found in the work of Rob Kling. His chapter in this section is an updated and abridged version of a seminal paper entitled "Social Analyses of Computing: Theoretical Perspectives in Recent Empirical Research" that first appeared in the journal ACM *Computing Surveys* in 1980. This chapter is valuable as it attempts to provide a coherent framework for discussing and evaluating the empirical work that has been performed on exactly what happens when computers are being selected by, and subsequently introduced into, organizations. Although one may find his theoretical terminology somewhat recondite, his distinction between "systems-rationalist" and "segmented-institutionalist" perspectives allows one to understand the underlying assumptions made by different authors about the nature of society and the role of computing technology. Once these biases are known, the reader should find it easier to comprehend the myriad of empirical studies performed. This long paper is written in a formal, terse, style that differs from many of the other contributions in the book, but it will repay serious study and is one of the few papers that comprehensively reviews the empirical work in the field.

The final chapter by Howard Rosenbrock, a professor of engineering, is a short piece, contrasting sharply in style with the Kling excerpt, as it is in the form of a homily to students and practitioners of technical disciplines to take into account human needs and values when designing complex systems. His argument is not that engineers are lacking in concern for their fellow human beings, but that consistently, for various reasons, technology has taken a path which has not contributed to the betterment of the human condition. Rosenbrock points out the gross "misalignment between human abilities and the demands of some jobs" that exists in our society, and argues for a more human technology which is "well matched to human ability and which fosters skill and makes it more productive." Rosenbrock does not paint technology as the villain, but simply makes the plea that our human values should be reflected in the new human-machine systems that we develop, thus ensuring that these new systems support human abilities rather than suppress them.

Certainly, recognizing that there is something wrong with the sociotechnical systems currently existing in our society is a necessary first step towards humanizing technology. A much greater issue however, is how we, as individual citizens, can organize ourselves in an effort to transform our present societal structure—government bureaucracies, antiquated legal systems, the profit-maximization policies of corporations—in order that the changes advocated by Rosenbrock become more realizable.

*LJB*

## REFERENCES

Hirschheim, R. A. (1986). The effect of a priori views on the social implications of computing: The case of office automation. *ACM Computing Surveys, 18*(2) 165–195.

Kling, R. (1978, August). Value conflicts and social choice in electronic funds transfer system developments. *Communications of the ACM, 21*(8), 642–657.

Noble, D. (1977). *America by design: Science, technology, and the rise of corporate capitalism.* New York: Alfred A. Knopf.

Weizenbaum, J. (1976). *Computer power and human reason.* San Francisco: W. H. Freeman.

*(For notes on further readings for this section, see page 529).*

# 20

# The Destruction of Machines in Erewhon

## 1872

## *Samuel Butler*

It was during my stay in the City of the Colleges of Unreason—a city whose Erewhonian name is so cacophonous that I refrain from giving it—that I learned the particulars of the revolution which had ended in the destruction of so many of the mechanical inventions which were formerly in common use. During the remaining weeks or rather days of my sojourn in Erewhon I made a résumé in English of the work which brought about the already mentioned revolution. My ignorance of technical terms has led me doubtless into many errors, and I have occasionally, where I found translation impossible, substituted purely English names and ideas for the original Erewhonian ones, but the reader may rely on my general accuracy. I have thought it best to insert my translation here.

"There is no security against the ultimate development of mechanical consciousness, in the fact of machines possessing little consciousness now. A mollusk has not much consciousness. Reflect upon the extraordinary advance which machines have made during the last few hundred years, and note how slowly the animal and vegetable kingdoms are advancing. The more highly organized machines are creatures not so much of yesterday as of the last five minutes, so to speak, in comparison with past time. Assume for the sake of argument that conscious beings have existed for some twenty million years: See what strides machines have made in the last thousand! May not the world last twenty million years longer? If so, what will they not in the end become? Is it not safer to nip the mischief in the bud and to forbid them further progress?

"But who can say that the vapor engine has not a kind of consciousness? Where does consciousness begin, and where end? Who can draw the line? Who can draw any line? Is not everything interwoven with everything? Is not machinery linked with animal life in an infinite variety of ways? The shell of a hen's egg is made of a delicate white ware and is a machine as much as an egg cup is: The shell is a device for holding the egg as much as the egg cup for holding the shell: Both are phases of the same function; the hen makes the shell in her inside, but it is pure pottery. She makes her nest outside of herself for convenience' sake, but the nest is not more of a machine than the egg shell is. A 'machine' is only a 'device.'

"Either," he proceeds, "a great deal of action that has been called purely mechanical and unconscious must be admitted to contain more elements of consciousness than has been allowed hitherto (and in this case germs of consciousness will be found in many actions of the higher machines)—or (assuming the theory of evolution but at the same tine denying the consciousness of vegetable and crystalline action) the race of man has descended from things which had no consciousness at all. In this case there is no a priori improbability in the descent of conscious (and more than conscious) machines from those which now exist.

"Do not let me be misunderstood as living in fear of any actually existing machines; there is probably no known machine which is more than a prototype of future mechanical life. The present machines are to the future as the early Saurians to man. The largest of them will probably greatly diminish in size. Some of the lowest vertebrata attained a much greater bulk than has descended to their more highly organized living representatives, and in like manner a diminution in the size of machines has often attended their development and progress.

"Take the watch, for example; examine its beautiful structure; observe the intelligent play of the minute members which compose it: Yet this little creature is but a development of the cumbrous clocks that preceded it; it is no deterioration from them. A day may come when clocks, which certainly at the present time are not diminishing in bulk, will be superseded owing to the universal use of watches, in which case they will become as extinct as *ichthyosauri,* while the watch, whose tendency has for some years been to decrease in size rather than the contrary, will remain the only existing type of an extinct race.

"But returning to the argument, I would repeat that I fear none of the existing machines; what I fear is the extraordinary rapidity with which they are becoming something very different [from] what they are at present. No class of beings have in any time past made so rapid a movement forward. Should not that movement be jealously watched and checked while we can still check it? And is it not necessary for this end to destroy the more advanced of the machines which are in use at present, though it is admitted that they are in themselves harmless?

"As yet the machines receive their impressions through the agency of man's senses: One traveling machine calls to another in a shrill accent of alarm, and the other instantly retires; but it is through the ears of the driver that the voice of the one has acted upon the other. Had there been no driver, the callee would have been deaf to the caller. There was a time when it must have seemed highly improbable that machines should learn to make their wants known by sound, even through the ears of man; may we not conceive, then, that a day will come when those ears will be no longer needed, and the hearing will be done by the delicacy of the machine's own construction?—when its language shall have been developed from the cry of animals to a speech as intricate as our own? But other questions come upon us. What is a man's eye but a machine for the little creature that sits behind in his brain to look through? And take man's vaunted power of calculation. Have we not engines which can do all manner of sums more quickly and correctly than we can?

"It can be answered that even though machines should hear never so well and speak never so wisely, they will still always do the one or the other for our advantage, not their own; that man will be the ruling spirit and the machine the servant; that as soon as a machine fails to discharge the service which man expects from it, it is doomed to extinction; that the machines stand to man simply in the relation of lower animals, the vapor engine itself being only a more economical kind of horse; so that instead of being likely to be developed into a higher kind of life than man's, they owe their very existence and progress to their power of ministering to human wants and must therefore both now and ever be man's inferiors.

"This is all very well. But the servant glides by imperceptible approaches into the master; and we have come to such a pass that, even now, man must suffer terribly on ceasing to benefit the machines. If all machines were to be annihilated at one moment, so that not a knife nor lever nor rag of clothing nor anything whatsoever were left to man but his bare body alone that he was born with, and if all knowledge of mechanical laws were taken from him so that he could make no more machines and all machine-made food destroyed so that the race of man should be left as it were naked upon a desert island, we should become extinct in six weeks. A few miserable individuals might linger, but even these in a year or two would become worse than monkeys. Man's very soul is due to the machines; it is a machine-made thing: He thinks as he thinks, and feels as he feels, through the work that machines have wrought upon him, and their existence is quite as much a *sine qua non* for his, as his for theirs. This fact precludes us from proposing the complete annihilation of machinery, but surely it indicates that we should destroy as many of them as we can possibly dispense with, lest they should tyrannize over us even more completely.

"True, from a low materialistic point of view, it would seem that those thrive best who use machinery wherever its use is possible with profit; but this is the art of the machines—they serve that they may rule. They bear no malice toward man for destroying a whole race of them provided he creates a better instead; on the contrary, they reward him liberally for having hastened their development. It is for neglecting them that he incurs their wrath or for using inferior machines or for not making sufficient exertions to invent new ones or for destroying them without replacing them; yet these are the very things we ought to do and do quickly; for though our rebellion against their infant power will cause infinite suffering, what will not things come to, if that rebellion is delayed?

"They have preyed upon man's groveling preference for his material over his spiritual interests and have betrayed him into supplying that element of struggle and warfare without which no race can advance. The lower animals progress because they struggle with one another; the weaker die, the stronger breed and transmit their strength. The machines being of themselves unable to struggle have got man to do their struggling for them: As long as he fulfills this function duly, all goes well with him—at least he thinks so; but the moment he fails to do his best for the advancement of machinery by encouraging the good and destroying the bad, he is left behind in the race of competition; and this means that he will be made uncomfortable in a variety of ways and perhaps die.

"So that even now the machines will only serve on condition of being served and that too upon their own terms; the moment their terms are not complied with, they jib and either smash both themselves and all whom they can reach or turn churlish and refuse to work at all. How many men at this hour are living in a state of bondage to the machines? How many spend their whole lives, from the cradle to the grave, in tending them by night and day? Is it not plain that the machines are gaining ground upon us, when we reflect on the increasing numbers of those who are bound down to them as slaves and of those who devote their whole souls to the advancement of the mechanical kingdom?

"But I have heard it said, 'Granted that the vapor engine has a strength of its own, surely no one will say that it has a will of its own?' Alas! if we look more closely, we shall find that this does not make against the supposition that the vapor engine is one of the germs of a new phase of life. What is there in this whole world, or in the worlds beyond it, which has a will of its own? The unknown and unknowable only!

"A man is the resultant and exponent of all the forces that have been brought to bear upon him, whether before his birth or afterward. His action at any moment depends solely upon his constitution and on the intensity and direction of the various agencies to which he is, and has been, subjected. Some of these will counteract each other; but as he is by nature and as he has been acted on and is now acted on from without, so will he do, as certainly and regularly as though he were a machine.

"We do not generally admit this, because we do not know the whole nature of any one, nor the whole of the forces that act upon him. We see but a part, and being thus unable to generalize human conduct, except very roughly, we deny that it is subject to any fixed laws at all and ascribe much both of a man's character and actions to chance or luck or fortune; but these are only words whereby we escape the admission of our own ignorance; and a little reflection will teach us that the most daring flight of the imagination or the most subtle exercise of the reason is as much the thing that must arise and the only thing that can by any possibility arise at the moment of its arising as the falling of a dead leaf when the wind shakes it from the tree.

"If the above is sound, it follows that the regularity with which machinery acts is no proof of the absence of vitality or at least of germs which may be developed into a new phase of life. At first sight it would indeed appear that a vapor engine cannot help going when set upon a line of rails with the steam up and the machinery in full play; whereas the man whose business it is to drive it can help doing so at any moment that he pleases; so that the first has no spontaneity and is not possessed of any sort of free will, while the second has and is.

"This is true up to a certain point; the driver can stop the engine at any moment that he pleases, but he can only please to do so at certain points which have been fixed for him by others or in the case of unexpected obstructions which force him to please to do so. His pleasure is not spontaneous; there is an unseen choir of influences around him, which make it impossible for him to act in any other way than one. It is known beforehand how much strength must be given to these influences, just as it is known beforehand how much coal and water are necessary for the vapor engine itself; and curiously enough it will be found that the influences brought to bear upon the driver are of the same kind as those brought to bear upon the engine—that is to say, food and warmth. The driver is obedient to his masters, because he gets food and warmth from them, and if these are withheld or given in insufficient quantities he will cease to drive; in like manner the engine will cease to work if it is insufficiently fed. The only difference is that the man is conscious about his wants, and the engine (beyond refusing to work) does not seem to be so; but this is temporary and has been dealt with above.

"Accordingly, the requisite strength being given to the motives that are to drive the driver, there has never, or hardly ever, been an instance of a man stopping his engine through wantonness. But such a case might occur; yes, and it might occur that the engine should break down: But if the train is stopped from some trivial motive, it will be found either that the strength of the necessary influences has been miscalculated or that the man has been miscalculated, in the same way as an engine may break down from an unsuspected flaw; but even in such a case there will have been no spontaneity; the action will have had its true parental causes: Spontaneity is only a term for man's ignorance of the gods.

"Is there, then, no spontaneity on the part of those who drive the driver?"

Here followed an obscure argument upon this subject, which I have thought it best to omit. The writer resumes: "After all then it comes to this, that the difference between the life of a man and that of a machine is one rather of degree than of kind, though differences in kind are not wanting. An animal has more provision for emergency than a machine. The machine is less versatile; its range of action is narrow; its strength and accuracy in its own sphere are superhuman, but it shows badly in a dilemma; sometimes when its normal action is disturbed, it will lose its head and go from bad to worse like a lunatic in a raging frenzy: But here, again, we are met by the same consideration as before, namely, that the machines are still in their infancy; they are mere skeletons without muscles and flesh.

"For how many emergencies is an oyster adapted? For as many as are likely to happen to it and no more. So are the machines; and so is man himself. The list of casualties that daily occur to man through his want of adaptability is probably as great as that occurring to the machines; and every day gives them some greater provision for the unforeseen. Let anyone examine the wonderful self-regulating and self-adjusting contrivances which are now incorporated with the vapor engine, let him watch the way in which it supplies itself with oil; in which it indicates its wants to those who tend it; in which, by the governor, it regulates its application of its own strength; let him look at the storehouse of inertia and momentum [of] the flywheel or at the buffers on a railway carriage; let him see how those improvements are being selected for perpetuity which contain provision against the emergencies that may arise to harass the machine, and then let him think of a hundred thousand years, and the accumulated progress which they will bring unless man can be awakened to a sense of his situation and of the doom which he is preparing for himself.

"The misery is that man has been blind so long already. In his reliance upon the use of steam he has been betrayed into increasing and multiplying. To withdraw steam power suddenly will not have the effect of reducing us to the state in which we were before its introduction; there will be a general breakup and time of anarchy such as has never been known; it will be as though our population were suddenly doubled, with no additional means of feeding the increased number. The air we breathe is hardly more necessary for our animal life than the use of any machine; on the strength of which we have increased our numbers, is to our civilization; it is the machines which act upon man and make him man as much as man who has acted upon and made the machines; but we must choose between the alternative of undergoing much present suffering or seeing ourselves gradually superseded by our own creations 'til we rank no higher in comparison with them than the beasts of the field with ourselves.

"Herein lies our danger. For many seem inclined to acquiesce in so dishonorable a future. They say that although man should become to the machines what the horse and dog are to us, yet that he will continue to exist and will probably be better off in a state of domestication under the beneficent rule of the machines than in his present wild condition. We treat our domestic animals with much kindness. We give them whatever we believe to be the best for them; and there can be no doubt that our use of meat has increased their happiness rather than detracted from it. In like manner there is reason to hope that the machines will use us kindly, for their existence will be in a great measure dependent upon ours; they will rule us with a rod of iron, but they will not eat us; they will not only require our services in the reproduction and education of their young but also in waiting upon them as servants; in gathering food for them and feeding them; in restoring them to health when they are sick; and in either burying their dead or working up their deceased members into new forms of mechanical existence.

"The very nature of the motive power which works the advancement of the machines precludes the possibility of man's life being rendered miserable as well as enslaved. Slaves are tolerably happy if they have good masters, and the revolution will not occur in our time, nor hardly in ten thousand years or ten times that. Is it wise to be uneasy about a contingency which is so remote? Man is not [a] sentimental animal where his material interests are concerned, and though here and there some ardent soul may look upon himself and curse his fate that he was not born a vapor engine, yet the man of mankind will acquiesce in any arrangement which gives them better food and clothing at a cheaper rate and will refrain from yielding to unreasonable jealousy merely because there are other destinies more glorious than their own.

"The power of custom is enormous, and so gradual will be the change that man's sense of what is due to himself will be at no time rudely shocked; our bondage will steal upon us noiselessly and by imperceptible approaches; nor will there ever be such a clashing of desires between man and the machines as will lead to an encounter between them. Among themselves the machines will war eternally, but they will still require man as the being through whose agency the struggle will be principally conducted. In point of fact there is no occasion for anxiety about the future happiness of man so long as he continues to be in any way profitable to the machines; he may become the inferior race, but he will be infinitely better off than he is now. Is it not then both absurd and unreasonable to be envious of our benefactors? And should we not be guilty of consummate folly if we were to reject advantages which we cannot obtain otherwise, merely because they involve a greater gain to others than to ourselves?

"With those who can argue in this way I have nothing in common. I shrink with as much horror from believing that my race can ever be superseded or surpassed as I should do from believing that even at the remotest period my ancestors were other than human beings. Could I believe that ten hundred thousand years ago a single one of my ancestors was another kind of being to myself, I should lose all self-respect and take no further pleasure or interest in life. I have the same feeling with regard to my descendants and believe it to be one that will be felt so generally that the country will resolve upon putting an immediate stop to all further mechanical progress and upon destroying all improvements that have been made for the last 300 years. I would not urge more than this. We may trust ourselves to deal with those that remain, and though I should prefer to have seen the destruction include another 200 years, I am aware of the necessity for compromising and would so far sacrifice my own individual convictions as to be content with 300. Less than this will be insufficient."

This was the conclusion of the attack which led to the destruction of machinery throughout Erewhon.

# 21

# The Technological Society

## 1954

## Jacques Ellul

No social, human, or spiritual fact is so important as the fact of technique in the modern world. And yet no subject is so little understood. Let us try to set up some guideposts to situate the technical phenomenon.

### MACHINES AND TECHNIQUE

Whenever we see the word *technology* or *technique,* we automatically think of machines. Indeed, we commonly think of our world as a world of machines. This notion—which is in fact an error—is found, for example, in the works of Oldham and Pierre Ducassé. It arises from the fact that the machine is the most obvious, massive, and impressive example of technique, and historically the first. What is called the history of technique usually amounts to no more than a history of the machine; this very formulation is an example of the habit of intellectuals of regarding forms of the present as identical with those of the past.

Technique certainly began with the machine. It is quite true that all the rest developed out of mechanics; it is quite true also that without the machine the world of technique would not exist. But to explain the situation in this way does not at all legitimatize it. It is a mistake to continue with this confusion of terms, the more so because it leads to the idea that because the machine is at the origin and center of the technical problem, one is dealing with the whole problem when one deals with the machine. And that is a greater mistake still. Technique has now become almost completely independent of the machine, which has lagged far behind its offspring.

It must be emphasized that, at present, technique is applied outside industrial life. The growth of its power today has no relation to the growing use of the machine. The balance seems rather to have shifted to the other side. It is the machine which is now entirely dependent upon technique, and the machine represents only a small part of technique. If we were to characterize the relations between technique and the machine today, we could say not only that the machine is the result of a certain technique, but also that its social and economic applications are made possible by other technical advances. The machine is now not even the most important aspect of technique (though it is perhaps the most spectacular); technique has taken over all of man's activities, not just his productive activity.

From another point of view, however, the machine is deeply symptomatic: It represents the ideal toward which technique strives. The machine is solely, exclusively, technique; it is pure technique, one might say. For, wherever a technical factor exists, it results, almost inevitably, in mechanization: technique transforms everything it touches into a machine.

Another relationship exists between technique and the machine, and this relationship penetrates to the very core of the problem of our civilization. It is said (and everyone agrees) that the machine has created an inhuman atmosphere. The machine, so characteristic of the nineteenth century, made an abrupt entrance into a society which, from the political, institutional, and human points of view, was not made to receive it; and man has had to put up with it as best he can. Men now live in conditions that are less than human. Consider the concentration of our great cities, the slums, the lack of space, of air, of time, the gloomy streets and the sallow lights that confuse night and day. Think of our dehumanized factories, our unsatisfied senses, our working women, our estrangement from nature. Life in such an environment has no meaning. Consider our public transportation, in which man is less important than a parcel; our hospitals, in which he is only a number. Yet we call this progress. . . . And the noise, that monster boring into us at every hour of the night without respite.

It is useless to rail against capitalism. Capitalism did not create our world; the machine did. Painstaking studies designed to prove the contrary have buried the obvious beneath tons of print. And if we do not wish to play the demagogue, we must point out the guilty party. "The machine is antisocial," says Lewis Mumford. "It tends, by reason of its progressive character, to the most acute forms of human exploitation." The machine took its place in a social milieu that was not made for it and for that reason created the inhuman society in which we live. Capitalism was therefore only one aspect of the deep disorder of the nineteenth century. To restore order, it was necessary to question all the bases of that society—its social and political structures, its art and its way of life, its commercial system.

But let the machine have its head, and it topples everything that cannot support its enormous weight. Thus everything had to be reconsidered in terms of the machine. And that is precisely the role technique plays. In all fields it made an inventory of what it could use, of everything that could be brought into line with the machine. The machine could not integrate itself into nineteenth-century society; technique integrated it. Old houses that were not suited to the workers were torn down; and the new world technique required was built in their place. Technique has enough of the mechanical in its nature to enable it to cope with the machine, but it surpasses and transcends the machine because it remains in close touch with the human order. The metal monster could not go on forever torturing mankind. It found in technique a rule as hard and inflexible as itself.

Technique integrates the machine into society. It constructs the kind of world the machine needs and introduces order where the incoherent banging of machinery heaped up ruins. It clarifies, arranges, and rationalizes; it does in the domain of the abstract what the machine did in the domain of labor. It is efficient and brings efficiency to everything. Moreover, technique is sparing in the use of the machine, which has traditionally been exploited to conceal defects of organization. "Machines sanctioned social inefficiency," says Mumford. Technique, on the other hand, leads to a more rational and less indiscriminate use of machines. It places machines exactly where they ought to be and requires of them just what they ought to do.

This brings us to two contrasting forms of social growth. Henri Guitton says: "Social growth was formerly reflexive or instinctive, that is to say, unconscious. But new circumstances (the machine) now compel us to recognize a kind of social development that is rational, intelligent, and conscious. We may ask ourselves whether this is the beginning not only of the era of a spatially finite world but also of the era of a conscious world." All-embracing technique is in fact the consciousness of the mechanized world.

Technique integrates everything. It avoids shock and sensational events. Man is not adapted to a world of steel; technique adapts him to it. It changes the arrangement of this blind world so that man can be a part of it without colliding with its rough edges, without the anguish of being delivered up to the inhuman. Technique thus provides a model; it specifies attitudes that are valid once and for all. The anxiety aroused in man by the turbulence of the machine is soothed by the consoling hum of a unified society.

As long as technique was represented exclusively by the machine, it was possible to speak of "man *and* the machine." The machine remained an external object, and man (though significantly influenced by it in his professional, private, and psychic life) remained none the less independent. He was in a position to assert himself apart from the machine; he was able to adopt a position with respect to it.

But when technique enters into every area of life, including the human, it ceases to be external to man and become his very substance. It is no longer face to face with man but is integrated with him, and it progressively absorbs him. In this respect, technique is radically different from the machine. This transformation, so obvious in modern society, is the result of the fact that technique has become autonomous. . . .

## THE AUTONOMY OF TECHNIQUE

The primary aspect of autonomy is perfectly expressed by Frederick Winslow Taylor, a leading technician. He takes, as his point of departure, the view that the industrial plant is a whole in itself, a "closed organism," an end in itself. Giedion adds: "What is fabricated in this plant and what is the goal of its labor—these are questions outside its design." The complete separation of the goal from the mechanism, the limitation of the problem to the means, and the refusal to interfere in any way with efficiency; all this is clearly expressed by Taylor and lies at the basis of technical autonomy.

Autonomy is the essential condition for the development of technique, as Ernst Kohn-Bramstedt's study of the police clearly indicates. The police must be independent if they are to become efficient. They must form a closed, autonomous organization in order to operate by the most direct and efficient means and not be shackled by subsidiary considerations. And in this autonomy, they must be self-confident in respect to the law. It matters little whether police action is legal, if it is efficient. The rules obeyed by a technical organization are no longer rules of justice or injustice. They are "laws" in a purely technical sense. As far as the police are concerned, the highest stage is reached when the legislature legalizes their independence of the legislature itself and recognizes the primacy of technical laws. This is the opinion of Best, a leading German specialist in police matters.

The autonomy of technique must be examined in different perspectives on the basis of the different spheres in relation to which it has this characteristic. First, technique is autonomous with respect to economics and politics. We have already seen that at the present, neither economic nor political evolution conditions technical progress. Its progress is likewise independent of the social situation. The converse is actually the case, a point I shall develop at length. Technique elicits and conditions social, political, and economic change. It is the prime mover of all the rest, in spite of any appearance to the contrary and in spite of human pride, which pretends that man's philosophical theories are still determining influences and man's political regimes decisive factors in technical evolution. External necessities no longer determine technique. Technique's own internal necessities are determinative. Technique has become a reality in itself, self-sufficient, with its special laws and its own determinations.

Let us not deceive ourselves on this point. Suppose that the state, for example, intervenes in a technical domain. Either it intervenes for sentimental, theoretical, or intellectual reasons, and the effect of its intervention will be negative or nil; or it intervenes for reasons of political technique, and we have the combined effect of two techniques. There is no other possibility. The historical experience of the last years shows this fully.

To go one step further, technical autonomy is apparent in respect to morality and spiritual values. Technique tolerates no judgment from without and accepts no limitation. It is by virtue of technique rather than science that the great principle has become established: *chacun chez soi*. Morality judges moral problems; as far as technical problems are concerned, it has nothing to say. Only technical criteria are relevant. Technique, in sitting in judgment on itself, is clearly freed from this principal obstacle to human action. (Whether the obstacle is valid is not the question here. For the moment we merely record that it is an obstacle.) Thus, technique theoretically and systematically assures to itself that liberty which it has been able to win practically. Since it has put itself beyond good and evil, it need fear no limitation whatever. It was long claimed that technique was neutral. Today this is no longer a useful distinction. The power and autonomy of technique are so well secured that it, in its turn, has become the judge of what is moral, the creator of a new morality. Thus, it plays the role of creator of a new civilization as well. This morality—internal to technique—is assured of not having to suffer from technique. In any case, in respect to traditional morality, technique affirms itself as an independent power. Man alone is subject, it would seem, to moral judgment. We no longer live in that primitive epoch in which things were good or bad in themselves. Technique in itself is neither and can therefore do what it will. It is truly autonomous.

However, technique cannot assert its autonomy in respect to physical or biological laws. Instead, it puts them to work; it seeks to dominate them.

Giedion, in his probing study of mechanization and the manufacture of bread, shows that "wherever mechanization encounters a living substance, bacterial or animal, the organic substance determines the laws." For this reason, the mechanization of bakeries was a failure. More subdivisions, intervals, and precautions of various kinds were required in the mechanized bakery than in the non-mechanized bakery. The size of the machines did not save time; it merely gave work to larger numbers of people. Giedion shows how the attempt was made to change the nature of the bread in order to adapt it to mechanical manipulations. In the last resort, the ultimate success of mechanization turned on the transformation of human taste. Whenever technique collides with a natural obstacle, it tends to get around it either by replacing the living organism by a machine or by modifying the organism so that it no longer presents any specifically organic reaction.

The same phenomenon is evident in yet another area in which technical autonomy asserts itself: the relations between techniques and man. We have already seen, in connection with technical self-augmentation, that technique pursues its own course more and more independently of man. This means that man participates less and less actively in technical creation, which, by the automatic combination of prior elements, becomes a kind of fate. Man is reduced to the level of a catalyst. Better still, he resembles a slug inserted into a slot machine: He starts the operation without participating in it.

But this autonomy with respect to man goes much further. To the degree that technique must attain its result with mathematical precision, it has for its object the elimination of all human variability and elasticity. It is a commonplace to say that the machine replaces the human being. But it replaces him to a greater degree than has been believed.

Industrial technique will soon succeed in completely replacing the effort of the worker, and it would do so even sooner if capitalism were not an obstacle. The worker, no longer needed to guide or move the machine to action, will be required merely to watch it and to repair it when it breaks down. He will not participate in the work any more than a boxer's manager participates in a prize fight. This is no dream. The automated factory has already been realized for a great number of operations, and it is realizable for a far greater number. Examples multiply from day to day in all areas. Man indicates how this automation and its attendant exclusion of men operates in business offices; for example, in the case of the so-called tabulating machine. The machine itself interprets the data, the elementary bits of information fed into it. It arranges them in texts and distinct numbers. It adds them together and classifies the results in groups and subgroups, and so on. We have here an administrative circuit accomplished by a single, self-controlled machine. It is scarcely necessary to dwell on the astounding growth of automation in the last ten years. The multiple applications of the automatic assembly line, of automatic control of production operations (so-called cybernetics) are well known. Another case in point is the automatic pilot. Until recently the automatic pilot was used only in rectilinear flight; the finer operations were carried out by the living pilot. As early as 1952 the automatic pilot effected the operations of take-off and landing for certain supersonic aircraft. The same kind of feat is performed by automatic direction finders in antiaircraft defense. Man's role is limited to inspection. This automation results from the development servomechanisms which act as substitutes for human beings in more and more subtle operations by virtue of their "feedback" capacity.

This progressive elimination of man from the circuit must inexorably continue. Is the elimination of man so unavoidably necessary? Certainly! Freeing man from toil is in itself an ideal. Beyond this, every intervention of man, however educated or used to machinery he may be, is a source of error and unpredictability. The combination of man and technique is a happy one only if man has no responsibility. Otherwise, he is ceaselessly tempted to make unpredictable choices and is susceptible to emotional motivations which invalidate the mathematical precision of the machinery. He is also susceptible to fatigue and discouragement. All this disturbs the forward thrust of technique.

Man must have nothing decisive to perform in the course of technical operations; after all, he is the source of error. Political technique is still troubled by certain unpredictable phenomena, in spite of all the precision of the apparatus and the skill of those involved. (But this technique is still in its childhood.) In human reactions, howsoever well calculated they may be, a "coefficient of elasticity" causes imprecision, and imprecision is intolerable to technique. As far as possible, this source of error must be eliminated. Eliminate the individual, and excellent results ensue. Any technical man who is aware of this fact is forced to support the opinions voiced by Robert Jungk, which can be summed up thus: "The individual is a brake on progress." Or: "Considered from the modern technical point of view, man is a useless appendage." For instance, 10% of all telephone calls are wrong numbers, due to human error. An excellent use by man of so perfect an apparatus!

Now that statistical operations are carried out by perforated-card machines instead of human beings, they have become exact. Machines no longer perform merely gross operations. They perform a whole complex of subtle ones as well. And before long—what with the electronic brain—they will attain an intellectual power of which man is incapable.

Thus, the "great changing of the guard" is occurring much more extensively than Jacques Duboin envisaged some decades ago. Gaston Bouthoul, a leading sociologist of the phenomena of war, concludes that war breaks out in a social group when there is a "plethora of young men surpassing the indispensable tasks of the economy." When for one reason or another these men are not employed, they become ready for war. It is the multiplication of men who are excluded from working which provokes war. We ought at least to bear this in mind when we boast of the continual decrease in human participation in technical operations.

However, there are spheres in which it is impossible to eliminate human influence. The autonomy of technique then develops in another direction. Technique is not, for example, autonomous in respect to clock time. Machines, like abstract technical laws, are subject to the law of speed, and coordination presupposes time adjustment. In his description of the assembly line, Giedion writes: "Extremely precise time tables guide the automatic cooperation of the instruments, which, like the atoms in a planetary system, consist of separate units but gravitate with respect to each other in obedience to their inherent laws." This image shows in a remarkable way how technique became simultaneously independent of man and obedient to the chronometer. Technique obeys its own specific laws, as every machine obeys laws. Each element of the technical complex follows certain laws determined by its relations with the other elements, and these laws are internal to the system and in no way influenced by external factors. It is not a question of causing the human being to disappear but of making him capitulate, of inducing him to accommodate himself to techniques and not to experience personal feelings and reactions.

No technique is possible when men are free. When technique enters into the realm of social life, it collides ceaselessly with the human being to the degree that the combination of man and technique is unavoidable, and that technical action necessarily results in a determined result. Technique requires predictability and, no less, exactness of prediction. It is necessary, then, that technique prevail over the human being. For technique, this is a matter of life or death. Technique must reduce man to a technical animal, the king of the slaves of technique. Human caprice crumbles before this necessity; there can be no human autonomy in the face of technical autonomy. The individual must be fashioned by techniques, either negatively (by the techniques of understanding man) or positively (by the adaptation of man to the technical framework), in order to wipe out the blots his personal determination introduces into the perfect design of the organization.

But it is requisite that man have certain precise inner characteristics. An extreme example is the atomic worker or the jet pilot. He must be of calm temperament and even temper, he must be phlegmatic, he must not have too much initiative, and he must be devoid of egotism. The ideal jet pilot is already along in years (perhaps thirty-five) and has a settled direction in life. He flies his jet in the way a good civil servant goes to his office. Human joys and sorrows are fetters on technical aptitude. Jungk cites the case of a test pilot who had to abandon his profession because "his wife behaved in such a way as to lessen his capacity to fly. Every day, when he returned home, he found her shedding tears of joy. Having become in this way accident conscious, he dreaded catastrophe when he had to face a delicate situation." The individual who is a servant of technique must be completely unconscious of himself. Without this quality, his reflexes and his inclinations are not properly adapted to technique.

Moreover, the physiological condition of the individual must answer to technical demands. Jungk gives an impressive picture of the experiments in training and control that jet pilots have to undergo. The pilot is whirled on centrifuges until he "blacks out" (in order to measure his toleration of acceleration). There are catapults, ultrasonic chambers, etc., in which the candidate is forced to undergo unheard-of tortures in order to determine whether he has adequate resistance and whether he is capable of piloting the new machines. That the human organism is, technically speaking, an imperfect one is demonstrated by the experiments. The sufferings the individual endures in these "laboratories" are considered to be due to "biological weaknesses," which must be eliminated. New experiments have pushed even further to determine the reactions of "space pilots" and to prepare these heroes for their roles of tomorrow. This has given birth to new sciences, biometry for example; their one aim is to create the new man, the man adapted to technical functions.

It will be objected that these examples are extreme. This is certainly the case, but to a greater or lesser degree the same problem exists everywhere. And the more technique evolves, the more extreme its character becomes. The object of all the modern "human sciences" . . . is to find answers to these problems.

The enormous effort required to put this technical civilization into motion supposes that all individual effort is directed toward this goal alone and that all social forces are mobilized to attain the mathematically perfect structure of the edifice. ("Mathematically" does not mean "rigidly." The perfect technique is the most adaptable and, consequently, the most plastic one. True technique will know how to maintain the illusion of liberty, choice, and individuality; but these will have been carefully calculated so that they will be integrated into the mathematical reality merely as appearances!) Henceforth it will be wrong for a man to escape this universal effort. It will be inadmissible for any part of the individual not to be integrated in the drive toward technicization; it will be inadmissible that any man even aspire to escape this necessity of the whole society. The individual will no longer be able, materially or spiritually, to disengage himself from society. Materially, he will not be able to release himself because the technical means are so numerous that they invade his whole life and make it impossible for him to escape the collective phenomena. There is no longer an uninhabited place, or any other geographical locale, for the would-be solitary. It is no longer possible to refuse entrance into a community, to a highway, a high-tension line, or a dam. It is vain to aspire to live alone when one is obliged to participate in all collective phenomena and to use all the collective's tools, without which it is impossible to earn a bare subsistence. Nothing is gratis any longer in our society; and to live on charity is less and less possible. "Social advantages" are for the workers alone, not for "useless mouths." The solitary is a useless mouth and will have no ration card—up to the day he is transported to a penal colony. (An attempt was made to institute this procedure during the French Revolution, with deportations to Cayenne.)

Spiritually, it will be impossible for the individual to disassociate himself from society. This is due not to the existence of spiritual techniques which have increasing force in our society, but rather to our situation. We are constrained to be "engaged," as the existentialists say, with technique. Positively or negatively, our spiritual attitude is constantly urged, if not determined, by this situation. Only bestiality, because it is unconscious, would seem to escape this situation, and it is itself only a product of the machine.

Every conscious being today is walking the narrow ridge of a decision with regard to technique. He who maintains that he can escape it is either a hypocrite or unconscious. The autonomy of technique forbids the man of today to choose his destiny. Doubtless, someone will ask if it has not always been the case that social conditions, environment, manorial oppression, and the family conditioned man's fate. The answer is, of course, yes. But there is no common denominator between the suppression of ration cards in an authoritarian state and the family pressure of two centuries ago. In the past, when an individual entered into conflict with society, he led a harsh and miserable life that required a vigor which either hardened or broke him. Today the concentration camp and death await him; technique cannot tolerate aberrant activities.

Because of the autonomy of technique, modern man cannot choose his means any more than his ends. In spite of variability and flexibility according to place and circumstance (which are characteristic of technique) there is still only a single employable technique in the given place and time in which an individual is situated. We have already examined the reasons for this.

At this point, we must consider the major consequences of the autonomy of technique. This will bring us to the climax of this analysis.

Technical autonomy explains the "specific weight" with which technique is endowed. It is not a kind of neutral matter, with no direction, quality, or structure. It is a power endowed with its own peculiar force. It refracts in its own specific sense the wills which make use of it and the ends proposed for it. Indeed, independently of the objectives that man pretends to assign to any given technical means, that means always conceals in itself a finality which cannot be evaded. And if there is a competition between this intrinsic finality and an extrinsic end proposed by man, it is always the intrinsic finality which carries the day. If the technique in question is not exactly adapted to a proposed human end and if an individual pretends that he is adapting the technique to this end, it is generally quickly evident that it is the end which is being modified, not the technique. Of course, this statement must be qualified by what has already been said concerning the endless refinement of techniques and their adaptation. But this adaptation is effected with reference to the techniques concerned and to the conditions of their applicability. It does not depend on external ends. Perrot has demonstrated this in the case of judicial techniques, and Giedion in the case of mechanical techniques. Concerning the overall problem of the relation between the ends and the means, I take the liberty of referring to my own work, *Présence au monde moderne*.

Once again we are faced with a choice of "all or nothing." If we make use of technique, we must accept the specificity and autonomy of its ends and the totality of its rules. Our own desires and aspirations can change nothing.

The second consequence of technical autonomy is that it renders technique at once sacrilegious and sacred. (*Sacrilegious* is not used here in the theological but in the sociological sense.) Sociologists have recognized that the world in which man lives is for him not only a material but also a spiritual world; that forces act in it which are unknown and perhaps unknowable; that there are phenomena in it which man interprets as magical; that there are relations and correspondences between things and beings in which material connections are of little consequence. This whole area is mysterious. Mystery (but not in the Catholic sense) is an element of man's life. Jung has shown that it is catastrophic to make superficially clear what is hidden in man's innermost depths. Man must make allowance for a background, a great deep above which lie his reason and his clear consciousness. The mystery of man perhaps creates the mystery of the world he inhabits. Or perhaps this mystery is a reality in itself. There is no way to decide between these two alternatives. But, one way or the other, mystery is a necessity of human life.

Man cannot live without a sense of the secret. The psychoanalysts agree on this point. But the invasion of technique desacralizes the world in which man is called upon to live. For technique noting is sacred, there is no mystery, no taboo. Autonomy makes this so. Technique does not accept the existence of rules outside itself or of any norm. Still less will it accept any judgment upon it. As a consequence, no matter where it penetrates, what it does is permitted, lawful, justified.

To a great extent, mystery is desired by man. It is not that he cannot understand or enter into or grasp mystery but that he does not desire to do so. The sacred is what man decides unconsciously to respect. The taboo becomes compelling from a social standpoint, but there is always a factor of adoration and respect which does not derive from compulsion and fear.

Technique worships nothing, respects nothing. It has a single role: to strip off externals, to bring everything to light, and by rational use to transform everything into means. More than science, which limits itself to explaining the "how," technique desacralizes because it demonstrates (by evidence and not by reason, through use and not through books) that mystery does not exist. Science brings to the light of day everything man had believed sacred. Technique takes possession of it and enslaves it. The sacred cannot resist. Science penetrates to the great depths of the sea to photograph the unknown fish of the deep. Technique captures them, hauls them up to see if they are edible—but before they arrive on deck they burst. And why should technique not act thus? It is autonomous and recognizes as barriers only the temporary limits of its action. In its eyes, this terrain, which is for the moment unknown but not mysterious, must be attacked. Far from being restrained by any scruples before the sacred, technique constantly assails it. Everything which is not yet technique becomes so. It is driven onward by itself, by its character of self-augmentation. Technique denies mystery a priori. The mysterious is merely that which has not yet been technicized.

Technique advocates the entire remaking of life and its framework because they have been badly made. Since heredity is full of chance, technique proposes to suppress it so as to engender the kind of men necessary for its ideal of service. The creation of the ideal man will soon be a simple technical operation. It is no longer necessary to rely on the chances of the family or on the personal vigor which is called virtue. Applied biogenetics is an obvious point at which technique desacralizes; but we must not forget psychoanalysis, which holds that dreams, visions, and the psychic life in general are nothing more than objects. Nor must we forget the penetration and exploitation of the earth's secrets. Crash programs, particularly in the United States, are attempting to reconstruct the soil which massive exploitation and the use of chemical fertilizers have impaired. We shall soon discover the functions of chlorophyll and thus entirely transform the conditions of life. Recent investigations in electronic techniques applied to biology have emphasized the importance of DNA and will possibly result in the discovery of the link between the living and the nonliving.

Nothing belongs any longer to the realm of the gods or the supernatural. The individual who lives in the technical milieu knows very well that there is nothing spiritual anywhere. But man cannot live without the sacred. He therefore transfers his sense of the sacred to the very thing which has destroyed its former object: to technique itself. In the world in which we live, technique has become the essential mystery, taking widely diverse forms according to place and race. Those who have preserved some of the notions of magic both admire and fear technique. Radio presents an inexplicable mystery, an obvious and recurrent miracle. It is no less astonishing than the highest manifestations of magic once were, and it is worshipped as an idol would have been worshipped, with the same simplicity and fear.

But custom and the recurrence of the miracle eventually wear out this primitive adoration. It is scarcely found today in European countries; the proletariat, workers, and peasants alike, with their motorcycles, radios, and electrical appliances, have an attitude of condescending pride toward the jinn who is their slave. Their ideal is incarnated in certain things which serve them. Yet they retain some feeling of the sacred, in the sense that life is not worth the trouble of living unless a man has these jinns in his home. This attitude goes much further in the case of the conscious segment of the proletariat, among whom technique is seen as a whole and not merely in its occasional aspects. For them, technique is the instrument of liberation for the proletariat. All that is needed is for technique to make a little more headway, and they will be freed proportionately from their chains. Stalin pointed to industrialization as the sole condition for the realization of Communism. Every gain made by technique is a gain for the proletariat. This represents indeed a belief in the sacred. Technique is the god which brings salvation. It is good in its essence. Capitalism is an abomination because on occasion it opposes technique. Technique is the hope of the proletarians; they can have faith in it because its miracles are visible and progressive. A great part of their sense of the mysterious remains attached to it. Karl Marx may have been able to explain rationally how technique would free the proletariat, but the proletariat itself is scarcely equal to a full understanding of this "how." It remains mysterious for them. They retain merely the formula of faith. But their faith addresses itself with enthusiasm to the mysterious agent of their liberation.

The nonintellectual classes of the *bourgeoisie* are perhaps less caught up in this worship of technique. But the technicians of the *bourgeoisie* are without doubt the ones most powerfully taken with it. For them, technique *is* sacred, since they have no reason to feel a passion for it. Technical men are always disconcerted when one asks them the motives for their faith. No, they do not expect to be liberated; they expect nothing, yet they sacrifice themselves and devote their lives with frenzy to the development of industrial plants and the organization of banks. The happiness of the human race and suchlike nonsense are the commonplaces they allege. But these are no longer of any service even as justifications, and they certainly have nothing at all to do with man's passion for technique.

The technician uses technique perhaps because it is his profession, but he does so with adoration because for him technique is the locus of the sacred. There is neither reason nor explanation in his attitude. The power of technique, mysterious though scientific, which covers the whole earth with its networks of waves, wires, and paper, is to the technician an abstract idol which gives him a reason for living and even for joy. One sign, among many, of the feeling of the sacred that man experiences in the face of technique is the care he takes to treat it with familiarity. Laughter and humor are common human reactions in the presence of the sacred. This is true for primitive peoples; and for the same reason the first atomic bomb was called "Gilda," the giant cyclotron of Los Alamos "Clementine," the atomic piles "water pots," and radioactive contamination "scalding." The technicians of Los Alamos have banned the word *atom* from their vocabulary. These things are significant.

In view of the very different forms of technique, there is no question of a technical religion. But there is associated with it the feeling of the sacred, which expresses itself in different ways. The way differs from man to man, but for all men the feeling of the sacred is expressed in this marvelous instrument of the power instinct which is always joined to mystery and magic. The worker brags about his job because it offers him joyous confirmation of his superiority. The young snob speeds along at 100 miles per hour in his Porsche. The technician contemplates with satisfaction the gradients of his charts, no matter what their reference is. For these men, technique is in every eay sacred: it is the common expression of human power without which they would find themselves poor, alone, naked, and stripped of all pretentions. They would no longer be the heroes, geniuses, or archangels which a motor permits them to be at little expense.

What shall we say of the outburst of frenzy when the Sputnik went into orbit? What of the poems of the Soviets, the metaphysical affirmations of the French, the speculations on the conquest of the universe? What of the identification of this artificial satellite with the sun or of its invention with the creation of the earth? And, on the other side of the Atlantic, what was the real meaning of the excessive consternation of the Americans? All these bore witness to a marked social attitude with regard to a simple technical fact.

Even people put out of work or ruined by techniques, even those who criticize or attack it (without daring to go so far as to turn worshippers against them) have the bad conscience of all iconoclasts. They find neither within nor without themselves a compensating force for the one they call into question. They do not even live in despair, which would be a sign of their freedom. This bad conscience appears to me to be perhaps the most revealing fact about the new sacralization of modern technique.

The characteristics we have examined permit me to assert with confidence that there is no common denominator between the technique of today and that of yesterday. Today we are dealing with an utterly different phenomenon. Those who claim to deduce from man's technical situation in past centuries his situation in this one show that they have grasped nothing of the technical phenomenon. These deductions prove that all their reasonings are without foundation and all their analogies are astigmatic.

The celebrated formula of Alain has been invalidated: "Tools, instruments of necessity, instruments that neither lie nor cheat, tools with which necessity can be subjugated by obeying her, without the help of false laws; tools that make it possible to conquer by obeying.'' This formula is true of the tool which puts man squarely in contact with a reality that will bear no excuses, in contact with matter to be mastered, and the only way to use it is to obey it. Obedience to the plow and the plane was indeed the only means of dominating earth and wood. But the formula is not true for our techniques. He who serves these techniques enters another realm of necessity. This new necessity is not natural necessity; natural necessity, in fact no longer exists. It is technique's necessity, which becomes the more constraining the more nature's necessity fades and disappears. It cannot be escaped or mastered. The tool was not false. But technique causes us to penetrate into the innermost realm of falsehood, showing us all the while the noble face of objectivity of result. In this innermost recess, man is no longer able to recognize himself because of the instruments he employs.

The tool enables man to conquer. But, man, dost thou not know there is no more victory which is thy victory? The victory of our days belongs to the tool. The tool alone has the power and carries off the victory. Man bestows on himself the laurel crown, after the example of Napoleon III, who stayed in Paris to plan the strategy of the Crimean War and claimed the bay leaves of the victor.

But this delusion cannot last much longer. The individual obeys and longer has victory which is his own. He cannot have access even to his apparent triumphs except by becoming himself the object of technique and the offspring of the mating of man and machine. All his accounts are falsified. Alain's definition no longer corresponds to anything in the modern world. In writing this, I have, of course, omitted innumerable facets of our world. There are still artisans, petty tradesmen, butchers, domestics, and small agricultural landowners. But theirs are the faces of yesterday, the more or less hardy survivals of our past. Our world is not made of these static residues of history, and I have attempted to consider only moving forces. In the complexity of the present world, residues do exist, but they have no future and are consequently disappearing.

## REFERENCES

Bouthoul, G. (1953). *La guerre*. Paris: Presses Universitaires de France.

Bouthoul, G. (1951). *Les guerres; éléments de polémologie*. Paris: Payot.

Duboin, J. (1932). *La grande reléve des hommes par la machine*. Paris: Les Éditions Nouvelles.

Ducassé, P. (1945). *Histoire des techniques*. Paris: Presses Universitaires de France.

Ducassé, P. (1958). *Les techniques et le philosophie*. Paris: Presses Universitaires de France.

Giedion, S. (1948). *Mechanization takes command*. New York: Oxford University Press.

Guitton, H. (1951, January–February). Stagnation et croissance économiques. *Revue d'économie politique, LXI*, 5–40.

Jungk, R. (1952). *Die Zukunfk hat schon begonnen; Amerikas Allmacht und Ohnmacht.*

Stuttgart: Scherz and Goverts. (Translated as *Tomorrow is already here: Scenes from a man-made world*. London: R. Hart-Davis.)

Kohn-Bramstedt, E. (1945). *Dictatorship and political police: The technique of control by fear*. London: K. Paul, Trench, Trubner.

Mumford, L. (1938). *The culture of cities*. New York: Harcourt, Brace & World.

Mumford, L. (1934). *Technics and civilization*. New York: Harcourt, Brace & World.

# 22

# On the Impact of the Computer on Society

## 1972

### Joseph Weizenbaum

The structure of the typical essay on "the impact of computers on society" is as follows: First there is an "on the one hand" statement. It tells all the good things computers have already done for society and often even attempts to argue that the social order would already have collapsed were it not for the "computer revolution." This is usually followed by an "on the other hand" caution which tells of certain problems the introduction of computers brings in its wake. The threat posed to individual privacy by large data banks and the danger of large-scale unemployment induced by industrial automation are usually mentioned. Finally, the glorious present and prospective achievements of the computer are applauded, while the dangers alluded to in the second part are shown to be capable of being alleviated by sophisticated technological fixes. The closing paragraph consists of a plea for generous societal support for more, and more large-scale, computer research and development. This is usually coupled to the more or less subtle assertion that only computer science, hence only the computer scientist, can guard the world against the admittedly hazardous fallout of applied computer technology.

In fact, the computer has had very considerably less societal impact than the mass media would lead us to believe. Certainly, there are enterprises like space travel that could not have been undertaken without computers. Certainly the computer industry, and with it the computer education industry, has grown to enormous proportions. But much of the industry is self-serving. It is rather like an island economy in which the natives make a living by taking in each other's laundry. The part that is not self-serving is largely supported by government agencies and other gigantic enterprises that know the value of everything but the price of nothing, that is, that know the short-range utility of computer systems but have no idea of their ultimate social cost. In any case, airline reservation systems and computerized hospitals serve only a tiny, largely the most affluent, fraction of society. Such things cannot be said to have an impact on society generally.

## SIDE EFFECTS OF TECHNOLOGY

The more important reason that I dismiss the argument which I have caricatured is that the direct societal effects of any pervasive new technology are as nothing compared to its much more subtle and ultimately much more important side effects. In that sense, the societal impact of the computer has not yet been felt.

To help firmly fix the idea of the importance of subtle indirect effects of technology, consider the impact on society of the invention of the microscope. When it was invented in the middle of the seventeenth century, the dominant commonsense theory of disease was fundamentally that disease was a punishment visited upon an individual by God. The sinner's body was thought to be inhabited by various so-called humors brought into disequilibrium in accordance with divine justice. The cure for disease was therefore to be found first in penance and second in the balancing of humors as, for example, by bleeding. Bleeding was, after all, both painful—hence punishment and penance—and potentially balancing in that it actually removed substance from the body. The microscope enabled man to see microorganisms and thus paved the way for the germ theory of disease. The enormously surprising discovery of extremely small living organisms also induced the idea of a continuous chain of life which, in turn, was a necessary intellectual precondition for the emergence of Darwinism. Both the germ theory of disease and the theory of evolution profoundly altered man's conception of his contract with God and consequently his self-image. Politically these ideas served to help diminish the power of the Church and, more generally, to legitimize the questioning of the basis of hitherto unchallenged authority. I do not say that the microscope alone was responsible for the enormous social changes that followed its invention. Only that it made possible the kind of paradigm shift, even on the commonsense level, without which these changes might have been impossible.

Is it reasonable to ask whether the computer will induce similar changes in man's image of himself and whether that influence will prove to be its most important effect on society? I think so, although I hasten to add that I don't believe the computer has yet told us much about man and his nature. To come to grips with the question, we must first ask in what way the computer is different from man's many other machines. Man has built two fundamentally different kinds of machines, nonautonomous and autonomous. An autonomous machine is one that operates for long periods of time, not on the basis of inputs from the real world, for example from sensors or from human drivers, but on the basis of internalized models of some aspect of the real world. Clocks are examples of autonomous machines in that they operate on the basis of an internalized model of the planetary system. The computer is, of course, the example par excellence. It is able to internalize models of essentially unlimited complexity and of a fidelity limited only by the genius of man.

It is the autonomy of the computer we value. When, for example, we speak of the power of computers as increasing with each new hardware and software development, we mean that, because of their increasing speed and storage capacity, and possibly thanks to new programming tricks, the new computers can internalize ever more complex and ever more faithful models of ever larger slices of reality. It seems strange then that, just when we exhibit virtually an idolatry of autonomy with respect to machines, serious thinkers in respected academies [I have in mind B. F. Skinner of Harvard University (1971)] can rise to question autonomy as a fact for man. I do not think that the appearance of this paradox at this time is accidental. To understand it, we must realize that man's commitment to science has always had a masochistic component.

Time after time science has led us to insights that, at least when seen superficially, diminish man. Thus Galileo removed man from the center of the universe, Darwin removed him from his place separate from the animals, and Freud showed his rationality to be an illusion. Yet man pushes his inquiries further and deeper. I cannot help but think that there is an analogy between man's pursuit of scientific knowledge and an individual's commitment to psychoanalytic therapy. Both are undertaken in the full realization that what the inquirer may find may well damage his self-esteem. Both may reflect his determination to find meaning in his existence through struggle in truth, however painful that may be, rather than to live without meaning in a world of ill-disguised illusion. However, I am also aware that sometimes people enter psychoanalysis unwilling to put their illusions at risk, not searching for a deeper reality but in order to convert the insights they hope to gain to personal power. The analogy to man's pursuit of science does not break down with that observation.

Each time a scientific discovery shatters a hitherto fundamental cornerstone of the edifice on which man's self-esteem is built, there is an enormous reaction, just as is the case under similar circumstances in psychoanalytic therapy. Powerful defense mechanisms, beginning with denial and usually terminating in rationalization, are brought to bear. Indeed, the psychoanalyst suspects that, when a patient appears to accept a soul-shattering insight without resistance, his very casualness may well mask his refusal to allow that insight truly operational status in his self-image. But what is the psychoanalyst to think about the patient who positively embraces tentatively proffered, profoundly humiliating self-knowledge, when he embraces it and instantly converts it to a new foundation of his life? Surely such an event is symptomatic of a major crisis in the mental life of the patient.

I believe we are now at the beginning of just such a crisis in the mental life of our civilization. The microscope, I have argued, brought in its train a revision of man's image of himself. But no one in the mid-seventeenth century could have foreseen that. The possibility that the computer will, one way or another, demonstrate that, in the inimitable phrase of one of my esteemed colleagues, "the brain is merely a meat machine" is one that engages academicians, industrialists, and journalists in the here and now. How has the computer contributed to bringing about this very sad state of affairs? It must be said right away that the computer alone is not the chief causative agent. It is merely an extreme extrapolation of technology. When seen as an inducer of philosophical dogma, it is merely the reductio ad absurdum of a technological ideology. But how does it come to be regarded as a source of philosophic dogma?

## THEORY VERSUS PERFORMANCE

We must be clear about the fact that a computer is nothing without a program. A program is fundamentally a transformation of one computer into another that has autonomy and that, in a very real sense, behaves. Programming languages describe dynamic processes. And, most importantly, the processes they describe can be actually carried out. Thus we can build models of any aspect of the real world that interests us and that we understand. And we can make our models work. But we must be careful to remember that a computer model is a description that works. Ordinarily, when we speak of A being a model of B, we mean that a theory about some aspects of the behavior of B is also a theory of the same aspects of the behavior of A. It follows that when, for example, we consider a computer model of paranoia, like that published by Colby, Weber, & Hilf (1971), we must not be persuaded that it tells us anything about paranoia on the grounds that it, in some sense, mirrors the behavior of a paranoiac. After all, a plain typewriter in some sense mirrors the behavior of an autistic child (one types a question and gets no response whatsoever), but it does not help us to understand autism. A model must be made to stand or fall on the basis of its theory. Thus, while programming languages may have put a new power in the hands of social scientists in that this new notation may have freed them from the vagueness of discursive descriptions, their obligation to build defensible theories is in no way diminished. Even errors can be pronounced with utmost formality and eloquence. But they are not thereby transmuted to truth.

[The failure to make distinctions between descriptions, even those that "work," and theories accounts in large part for the fact that those who refuse to accept the view of man as machine have been put on the defensive.] Recent advances in computer understanding of natural language offer an excellent case in point. Halle (Chomsky & Halle, 1968) and Chomsky (1965), to mention only the two with whom I am most familiar, have long labored on a theory of language which any model of language behavior must satisfy. Their aim is like that of the physicist who writes a set of differential equations that anyone riding a bicycle must satisfy. No physicist claims that a person need know, let alone be able to solve, such differential equations in order to become a competent cyclist. Neither do Halle and Chomsky claim that humans know or knowingly obey the rules they believe to govern language behavior. Halle and Chomsky also strive, as do physical theorists, to identify the constants and parameters of their theories with components of reality. They hypothesize that their rules constitute a kind of projective description of certain aspects of the structure of the human mind. Their problem is thus not merely to discover economical rules to account for language behavior, but also to infer economic mechanisms which determine that precisely those rules are to be preferred over all others. Since they are in this way forced to attend to the human mind, not only that of speakers of English, they must necessarily be concerned with all human language behavior—not just that related to the understanding of English.

The enormous scope of their task is illustrated by their observation that in all human languages declarative sentences are often transformed into questions by a permutation of two of their words. (John is here — Is John here?) It is one thing to describe rules that transform declarative sentences into questions—a simple permutation rule is clearly insufficient—but another thing to describe a ''machine'' that necessitates those rules when others would, all else being equal, be simpler. Why, for example, is it not so that declarative sentences read backward transform those sentences into questions? The answer must be that other constraints on the ''machine'' combine against this local simplicity in favor of a more nearly global economy. Such examples illustrate the depth of the level of explanation that Halle and Chomsky are trying to achieve. No wonder that they stand in awe of their subject matter.

Workers in computer comprehension of natural language operate in what is usually called performance mode. It is as if they are building machines that can ride bicycles by following heuristics like ''if you feel a displacement to the left, move your weight to the left.'' There can be, and often is, a strong interaction between the development of theory and the empirical task of engineering systems whose theory is not yet thoroughly understood. Witness the synergistic cooperation between aerodynamics and aircraft design in the first quarter of the present century. Still, what counts in performance mode is not the elaboration of theory but the performance of systems. And the systems being hammered together by the new crop of computer semanticists are beginning (just beginning) to perform.

Since computer scientists have recognized the importance of the interplay of syntax, semantics, and pragmatics, and with it the importance of computer-manipulable knowledge, they have made progress. Perhaps by the end of the present decade, computer systems will exist with which specialists, such as physicians and chemists and mathematicians, will converse in natural language. And surely some part of such achievements will have been based on other successes in, for example, computer simulation of cognitive processes. It is understandable that any success in this area, even if won empirically and without accompanying enrichments of theory, can easily lead to certain delusions being planted. Is it, after all, not terribly tempting to believe that a computer that understands natural language at all, however narrow the context, has captured something of the essence of man? Descartes himself might have believed it. Indeed, by way of this very understandable seduction, the computer comes to be a source of philosophical dogma.

I am tempted to recite how performance programs are composed and how things that don't work quite correctly are made to work via all sorts of strategems which do not even pretend to have any theoretical foundation. But the very asking of the question, "Has the computer captured the essence of man?" is a diversion and, in that sense, a trap. For the real question "Does man understand the essence of man?" cannot be answered by technology and hence certainly not by any technological instrument.

## THE TECHNOLOGICAL METAPHOR

I asked earlier what the psychoanalyst is to think when a patient grasps a tentatively proffered deeply humiliating interpretation and attempts to convert it immediately to a new foundation of his life. I now think I phrased that question too weakly. What if the psychoanalyst merely coughed and the cough entrained the consequences of which I speak? That is our situation today. Computer science, particularly its artificial intelligence branch, has coughed. Perhaps the press has unduly amplified that cough—but it is only a cough nevertheless. I cannot help but think that the eagerness to believe that man's whole nature has suddenly been exposed by that cough, and that it has been shown to be a clockwork, is a symptom of something terribly wrong.

[What is wrong, I think, is that we have permitted technological metaphors, what Mumford (1970) calls the "Myth of the Machine," and technique itself to so thoroughly pervade our thought processes that we have finally abdicated to technology the very duty to formulate questions. Thus sensible men correctly perceive that large data banks and enormous networks of computers threaten man.] But they leave it to technology to formulate the corresponding question. Where a simple man might ask: "Do we need these things?", technology asks "what electronic wizardry will make them safe?" Where a simple man will ask "is it good?", technology asks "will it work?" Thus science, even wisdom, becomes what technology and most of all computers can handle. Lest this be thought to be an exaggeration, I quote from the work of H. A. Simon, one of the most senior of American computer scientists (1969):

> As we succeed in broadening and deepening our knowledge—theoretical and empirical—about computers, we shall discover that in large part their behavior is governed by simple general laws, that what appeared as complexity in the computer program was, to a considerable extent, complexity of the environment to which the program was seeking to adapt its behavior.
>
> To the extent that this prospect can be realized, it opens up an exceedingly important role for computer simulation as a tool for achieving a deeper understanding of human behavior. For if it is the organization of components, and not their physical properties, that largely determines behavior, and if computers are organized somewhat in the image of man, then the computer becomes an obvious device for exploring the consequences of alternative organizational assumptions for human behavior.

and

> A man, viewed as a behaving system, is quite simple. The apparent complexity of his behavior over time is largely a reflection of the complexity of the environment in which he finds himself.
>
> . . . I believe that this hypothesis holds even for the whole man.

We already know that those aspects of the behavior of computers which cannot be attributed to the complexity of their programs is governed by simple general laws—ultimately by the laws of Boolean algebra. And of course the physical properties of the computer's components are nearly irrelevant to its behavior. Mechanical relays are logically equivalent to tubes and to transistors and to artificial neurons. And of course the complexity of computer programs is due to the complexity of the environments, including the computing environments themselves, with which they were designed to deal. To what else could it possibly be due? So, what Simon sees as prospective is already realized. But does this collection of obvious and simple facts lead to the conclusion that man is as simple as are computers? When Simon leaps to that conclusion and then formulates the issue as he has done here, that is, when he suggests that the behavior of *the whole man* may be understood in terms of the behavior of computers as governed by simple general laws, then the very possibility of understanding man as an autonomous being, as an individual with deeply internalized values, that very possibility is excluded. How does one insult a machine?

The question "Is the brain merely a meat machine?", which Simon puts in a so much more sophisticated form, is typical of the kind of question formulated by, indeed formulatable only by, a technological mentality. Once it is accepted as legitimate, arguments as to what a computer can or cannot do "in principle" begin to rage and themselves become legitimate. But the legitimacy of the technological question—for example, is human behavior to be understood either in terms of the organization or of the physical properties of "components"— need not be admitted in the first instance. A human question can be asked instead. Indeed, we might begin by asking what has already become of "the whole man" when he can conceive of computers organized in his own image.

The success of technique and of some technological explanations has, as I've suggested, tricked us into permitting technology to formulate important questions for us—questions whose very forms severely diminish the number of degrees of freedom in our range of decision-making. Whoever dictates the questions in large part determines the answers. In that sense, technology, and especially computer technology, has become a self-fulfilling nightmare reminiscent of that of the lady who dreams of being raped and begs her attacker to be kind to her. He answers, "It's your dream, lady." We must come to see that technology is our dream and that we must ultimately decide how it is to end.

I have suggested that the computer revolution need not and ought not to call man's dignity and autonomy into question, that it is a kind of pathology that moves men to wring from it unwarranted, enormously damaging interpretations. Is then the computer less threatening that we might have thought? Once we realize that our visions, possibly nightmarish visions, determine the effect of our own creations on us and on our society, their threat to us is surely diminished. But that is not to say that this realization alone will wipe out all danger. For example, apart from the erosive effect of a technological mentality on man's self-image, there are practical attacks on the freedom and dignity of man in which computer technology plays a critical role.

I mentioned earlier that computer science has come to recognize the importance of building knowledge into machines. We already have a machine—Dendral—(Buchanan, Sutherland, & Feigenbaum, 1969) that commands more chemistry than do many Ph.D. chemists, and another—Mathlab—(Martin & Fateman, 1971) that commands more applied mathematics than do many applied mathematicians. Both Dendral and Mathlab contain knowledge that can be evaluated in terms of the explicit theories from which it was derived. If the user believes that a result Mathlab delivers is wrong, then, apart from possible program errors, he must be in disagreement, not with the machine or its programmer, but with a specific mathematical theory. But what about the many programs on which management, most particularly the government and the military, rely, programs which can in no sense be said to rest on explicable theories but are instead enormous patchworks of programming techniques strung together to make them work?

## INCOMPREHENSIBLE SYSTEMS

In our eagerness to exploit every advance in technique we quickly incorporate the lessons learned from machine manipulation of knowledge in theory-based systems into such patchworks. They then "work" better. I have in mind systems like target selection systems used in Vietnam and war games used in the Pentagon, and so on. These often gigantic systems are put together by teams of programmers, often working over a time span of many years. But by the time the systems come into use, most of the original programmers have left or turned their attention to other pursuits. It is precisely when gigantic systems begin to be used that their inner workings can no longer be understood by any single person or by a small team of individuals. Norbert Wiener, the father of cybernetics, foretold this phenomenon in a remarkably prescient article (1960) published more than a decade ago. He said there:

> It may well be that in principle we cannot make any machine the elements of whose behavior we cannot comprehend sooner or later. This does not mean in any way that we shall be able to comprehend these elements in substantially less time than the time required for operation of the machine, or even within any given number of years or generations.

An intelligent understanding of [machines'] mode of performance may be delayed until long after the task which they have been set has been completed. This means that though machines are theoretically subject to human criticism, such criticism may be ineffective until long after it is relevant.

This situation, which is now upon us, has two consequences: first that decisions are made on the basis of rules and criteria no one knows explicitly, and second that the system of rules and criteria becomes immune to change. This is so because, in the absence of detailed understanding of the inner workings of a system, any substantial modification is very likely to render the system altogether inoperable. The threshold of complexity beyond which this phenomenon occurs has already been crossed by many existing systems, including some compiling and computer operating systems. For example, no one likes the operating systems for certain large computers, but they cannot be substantially changed nor can they be done away with. Too many people have become dependent on them.

An awkward operating system is inconvenient. That is not too bad. But the growing reliance on supersystems that were perhaps designed to help people make analyses and decisions, but which have since surpassed the understanding of their users while at the same time becoming indispensable to them, is another matter. In modern war it is common for the soldier, say the bomber pilot, to operate at an enormous psychological distance from his victims. He is not responsible for burned children because he never sees their village, his bombs, and certainly not the flaming children themselves. Modern technological rationalizations of war, diplomacy, politics, and commerce such as computer games have an even more insidious effect on the making of policy. Not only have policy makers abdicated their decision-making responsibility to a technology they don't understand, all the while maintaining the illusion that they, the policy makers, are formulating policy questions and answering them, but responsibility has altogether evaporated. No human is any longer responsible for "what the machine says." Thus there can be neither right nor wrong, no question of justice, no theory with which one can agree or disagree, and finally no basis on which one can challenge "what the machine says." My father used to invoke the ultimate authority by saying to me, "it is written." But then I could read what was written, imagine a human author, infer his values, and finally agree or disagree. The systems in the Pentagon, and their counterparts elsewhere in our culture, have, in a very real sense, no authors. They therefore do not admit of exercises of imagination that may ultimately lead to human judgment. No wonder that men who live day in and out with such machines and become dependent on them begin to believe that men are merely machines. They are reflecting what they themselves have become.

The potentially tragic impact on society that may ensue from the use of systems such as I have just discussed is greater than might at first be imagined. Again it is side effects, not direct effects, that matter most. First, of course, there is the psychological impact on individuals living in a society in which anonymous, hence irresponsible, forces formulate the large questions of the day and circumscribe the range of possible answers. It cannot be surprising that large numbers of perceptive individuals living in such a society experience a kind of impotence and fall victim to the mindless rage that often accompanies such experiences. But even worse, since computer-based knowledge systems become essentially unmodifiable except in that they can grow, and since they induce dependence and cannot, after a certain threshold is crossed, be abandoned, there is an enormous risk that they will be passed from one generation to another, always growing. Man too passes knowledge from one generation to another. But because man is mortal, his transmission of knowledge over the generations is at once a process of filtering and accrual. Man doesn't merely pass knowledge, he rather regenerates it continuously. Much as we may mourn the crumbling of ancient civilizations, we know nevertheless that the glory of man resides as much in the evolution of his cultures as in that of his brain. The unwise use of ever larger and ever more complex computer systems may well bring this process to a halt. It could well replace the ebb and flow of culture with a world without values, a world in which what counts for a fact has long ago been determined and forever fixed.

## POSITIVE EFFECTS

I've spoken of some potentially dangerous effects of present computing trends. Is there nothing positive to be said? Yes, but it must be said with caution. Again, side effects are more important than direct effects. In particular, the idea of computation and of programming languages is beginning to become an important metaphor which, in the long run, may well prove to be responsible for paradigm shifts in many fields. Most of the commonsense paradigms in terms of which much of mankind interprets the phenomena of the everyday world, both physical and social, are still deeply rooted in fundamentally mechanistic metaphors. Marx's dynamics as well as those of Freud are, for example, basically equilibrium systems. Any hydrodynamicist could come to understand them without leaving the jargon of his field. Languages capable of describing ongoing processes, particularly in terms of modular subprocesses, have already had an enormous effect on the way computer people think of every aspect of their worlds, not merely those directly related to their work. The information-processing view of the world so engendered qualifies as a genuine metaphor. This is attested to by the fact that it (a) constitutes an intellectual framework that permits new questions to be asked about a wide-ranging set of phenomena, and (b) that it itself provides criteria for the adequacy of proffered answers. A new metaphor is important, not in that it may be better than existing ones, but rather in that it may enlarge man's vision by giving him yet another perspective on his world. Indeed, the very effectiveness of a new metaphor may seduce lazy minds to adopt it as a basis for universal explanations and as a source of panaceas. Computer simulation of social processes has already been advanced by single-minded generalists as leading to general solutions of all of mankind's problems.

The metaphors given us by religion, the poets, and by thinkers like Darwin, Newton, Freud, and Einstein have rather quickly penetrated to the language of ordinary people. These metaphors have thus been instrumental in shaping our entire civilization's imaginative reconstruction of our world. The computing metaphor is as yet available to only an extremely small set of people. Its acquisition and internalization, hopefully as only one of many ways to see the world, seems to require experience in program composition, a kind of computing literacy. Perhaps such literacy will become very widespread in the advanced societal sectors of the advanced countries. But, should it become a dominant mode of thinking and be restricted to certain social classes, it will prove not merely repressive in the ordinary sense, but an enormously divisive societal force. For then classes which do and do not have access to the metaphor will, in an important sense, lose their ability to communicate with one another. We know already how difficult it is for the poor and the oppressed to communicate with the rest of the society in which they are embedded. We know how difficult it is for the world of science to communicate with that of the arts and of the humanities. In both instances the communication difficulties, which have grave consequences, are very largely due to the fact that the respective communities have unsharable experiences out of which unsharable metaphors have grown.

## RESPONSIBILITY

Given these dismal possibilities, what is the responsibility of the computer scientist? First, I should say that most of the harm computers can potentially entrain is much more a function of properties people attribute to computers than of what a computer can or cannot actually be made to do. The nonprofessional has little choice but to make his attributions of properties to computers on the basis of the propaganda emanating from the computer community and amplified by the press. The computer professional, therefore, has an enormously important responsibility to be modest in his claims. This advice would not even have to be voiced if computer science had a tradition of scholarship and of self-criticism such as that which characterizes the established sciences. The mature scientist stands in awe before the depth of his subject matter. His very humility is the wellspring of his strength. I regard the instilling of just this kind of humility, chiefly by the example set by teachers, to be one of the most important missions of every university department of computer science.

The computer scientist must be aware constantly that his instruments are capable of having gigantic direct and indirect amplifying effects. An error in a program, for example, could have grievous direct results, including most certainly the loss of much human life. On September 11, 1971—to cite just one example—a computer programming error caused the simultaneous destruction of 117 high-altitude weather balloons whose instruments were being monitored by an earth satellite (Gillette, 1971). A similar error in a military command and control system could launch a fleet of nuclear tipped missiles. Only censorship prevents us from knowing how many such events involving non-nuclear weapons have already occurred. Clearly then, the computer scientist has a heavy responsibility to make the fallibility and limitations of the systems he is capable of designing brilliantly clear. The very power of his systems should serve to inhibit the advice he is ready to give and to constrain the range of work he is willing to undertake.

Of course, the computer scientist, like everyone else, is responsible for his actions and their consequences. Sometimes that responsibility is hard to accept because the corresponding authority to decide what is and what is not to be done appears to rest with distant and anonymous forces. That technology itself determines what is to be done by a process of extrapolation and that individuals are powerless to intervene in that determination is precisely the kind of self-fulfilling dream from which we must awaken.

Consider gigantic computer systems. They are, of course, natural extrapolations of the large systems we already have. Computer networks are another point on the same curve extrapolated once more. One may ask whether such systems can be used by anybody except by governments and very large corporations and whether such organizations will not use them mainly for antihuman purposes. Or consider speech recognition systems. Will they not be used primarily to spy on private communications? To answer such questions by saying that big computer systems, computer networks, and speech recognition systems are inevitable is to surrender one's humanity. For such an answer must be based either on one's profound conviction that society has already lost control over its technology or on the thoroughly immoral position that "if I don't do it, someone else will."

I don't say that systems such as I have mentioned are necessarily evil—only that they may be and, what is most important, that their inevitability cannot be accepted by individuals claiming autonomy, freedom, and dignity. The individual computer scientist can and must decide. The determination of what the impact of computers on society is to be is, at least in part, in his hands.

Finally, the fundamental question the computer scientist must ask himself is the one that every scientist, indeed every human, must ask. It is not "what shall I do?" but rather "what shall I be?" I cannot answer that for anyone save myself. But I will say again that if technology is a nightmare that appears to have its own inevitable logic, it is our nightmare. It is possible, given courage and insight, for man to deny technology the prerogative to formulate man's questions. It is possible to ask human questions and to find humane answers.

## REFERENCES

Buchanan, B., Sutherland, G., & Feigenbaum, E. A. (1969). In B. Meltzer (Ed.), *Machine Intelligence*. New York: Elsevier.

Chomsky, N. (1965). *Aspects of the theory of syntax*. Cambridge, MA: MIT Press.

Chomsky, N., & Halle, M. (1968). *The sound pattern of English*. New York: Harper & Row.

Colby, K. M., Weber, S., & Hilf, F. D. (1971). *Artificial Intelligence, 1*, 1.

Gillette, R. (1971). *Science, 174*, 477.

Martin, W. A., & Fateman, R. J. (1971). The Macsyma system. In *Proceedings of the second symposium on symbolic and algebraic manipulation*. New York: Association for Computer Machines.

Moses, J. (1971). *Communication Association of Computer Machines, 14*(8), 548.

Mumford, L. (1970). *The Pentagon of power*. New York: Harcourt, Brace, Jovanovich.

Simon, H. A. (1969). *The sciences of the artificial*. Cambridge, MA: MIT Press.

Skinner, B. F. (1971). *Beyond freedom and dignity*. New York: Knopf.

Wiener, N. (1960). *Science, 131*, 1355.

# 23

# What Computers Mean for Man and Society

## 1977

### Herbert A. Simon

Energy and information are two basic currencies of organic and social systems. A new technology that alters the terms on which one or the other of these is available to a system can work on it the most profound changes. At the core of the Industrial Revolution, which began nearly three centuries ago, lay the substitution of mechanical energy for the energy of man and animal. It was this revolution that changed a rural subsistence society into an urban affluent one and touched off a chain of technological innovations that transformed not only production but also transportation, communication, warfare, the size of human populations, and the natural environment.

It is easy, by hindsight, to see how inexorably these changes followed one another, how "natural" a consequence, for example, suburbia was of cheap, privately owned transportation. It is a different question whether foresight could have predicted these chains of events or have aided in averting some of their more undesirable outcomes. The problem is not that prophets were lacking— they have been in good supply at almost all times and places. Quite the contrary, almost everything that has happened, and its opposite, has been prophesied. The problem has always been to pick and choose among the embarrassing riches of alternative projected futures; and in this, human societies have not demonstrated any large foresight. Most often we have been constrained to anticipate events just a few years before their occurrence, or even while they are happening, and to try to deal with them, as best we can, as they are engulfing us.

We are now in the early stages of a revolution in processing information that shows every sign of being as fundamental as the earlier energy revolution. Perhaps we should call it the Third Information Revolution. (The first produced written language, and the second, the printed book.) This third revolution, which began more than a century ago, includes the computer but many other things as well. The technology of information comprises a vast range of processes for

445

storing information, for copying it, for transmitting it from one place to another, for displaying it, and for transforming it.

Photography, the moving picture, and television gave us, in the course of a century, a whole new technology for storing and displaying pictorial information. Telegraphy, the telephone, the phonograph, and radio did the same for storing and transmitting auditory information. Among all of these techniques, however, the computer is unique in its capacity for manipulating and transforming information and hence in carrying out, automatically and without human intervention, functions that had previously been performable only by the human brain.

As with the energy revolution, the consequences of the information revolution spread out in many directions. First, there are the economic consequences that follow on any innovation that increases human productivity. As we shall see, these are perhaps the easiest effects of technological change to predict. Second, there are consequences for the nature of work and of leisure—for the quality of life. Third, the computer may have special consequences for privacy and individual liberty. Fourth, there are consequences for man's view of himself, for his picture of the universe and of his place and goals in it. In each of these directions, the immediate consequences are, of course, the most readily perceived. (It was not hard to foresee that Newcomen's and Watt's engines would change the economics of mining in deep pits.) It is far more difficult to predict what indirect chains of effects these initial impacts will set off, for example, the chain that reaches from the steam engine through the internal-combustion engine to the automobile and the suburb.

Prediction is easier if we do not try to forecast in detail the time path of events and the exact dates on which particular developments are going to occur, but to focus, instead, upon the steady state toward which the system is tending[1]. Of course, we are not so much interested in what is going to happen in some vague and indefinite future as we are in what the next generation or two holds for us. Hence, a generation is the time span with which I shall be concerned.

My discussion will be divided into five parts, the last four corresponding to domains of prediction: economics, the nature of work and leisure, social consequences, and how men and women view themselves. These essays in prediction need to be preceded, however, by some analysis of the computer itself, and particularly its capabilities and potential in the area that is usually called artificial intelligence. This subject is taken up in the next section[2].

---

[1]A few years ago, Newell and I erred in predicting that certain specific developments in artificial intelligence were going to take place "within 10 years." The fact that we were optimistic about the time scale has blinded a number of critics to the basic soundness of our characterization of the nature and directions of artificial intelligence. I shall try not to make the same mistake here of predicting that very specific things will occur at very specific times. See H. A. Simon and A. Newell, *Oper. Res. 6*, 1 (1958).

[2]For more detailed discussions of these topics, see H. A. Simon, *The New Science of Management Decision* (Prentice-Hall, Englewood Cliffs, N.J., 3d ed., 1977).

## COMPUTER CAPABILITIES

The computer is a device endowed with powers of utmost generality for processing symbols. It is remarkable not only for its capabilities but also for the simplicity of its underlying processes and organization. Of course, from a hardware standpoint it is not simple at all but is a highly sophisticated electronic machine. The simplicity appears at the level of the elementary information processes that the hardware enables it to perform, the organization for execution and control of those processes, and the programming languages in terms of which the control of its behavior is expressed. A computer can read symbols from an external source, output symbols to an external destination, store symbols in one or more memories, copy symbols, rearrange symbols and structures of symbols, and react to symbols conditionally—that is, follow one course of action or another, depending on what symbols it finds in memory or in its input devices. The most general symbol-manipulating system that has been defined, the so-called Turing machine, requires no broader capabilities than these. The important limits on the powers of a computer are limits on the sizes of its memories and the speed of its elementary processes, and not on the generality of those processes.

There is great dispute among experts as to what the generality of the computer implies for its ability to behave intelligently. There is also dispute as to whether the computer, when it is behaving more or less intelligently, is using processes similar to those employed by an intelligent human being, or quite different processes. The views expressed here will reflect my own experience in research with computers and my interpretation of the scientific literature. First, no limits have been discovered to the potential scope of computer intelligence that are not also limits on human intelligence. Second, the elementary processes underlying human thinking are essentially the same as the computer's elementary information processes, although modern fast computers can execute these processes more rapidly than can the human brain[3]. In the past, computer memories, even in large computers, have probably not been as capacious as human memory, but the scale of available computer memories is increasing rapidly, to the point where memory size may not be much longer an effective limit on the capacity of computers to match human performance. Any estimate of the potential of the computer in the near or distant future depends on one's agreement or disagreement with these assumptions.

One common objection to the beliefs just expressed is that "computers can only do what you program them to do." That is correct. The behavior of a computer at any specific moment is completely determined by the contents of its

---

[3]The position that computers can be programmed to simulate an indefinite range of human thinking processes is developed in detail, and a large body of supporting evidence is examined in A. Newell and H. A. Simon, *Human Problem Solving* (Prentice-Hall, Englewood Cliffs, N.J., 1972); and in J. R. Anderson and G. H. Bower, *Human Associative Memory* (Winston, Washington, D.C., 1973).

memory and the symbols that are input to it at that moment. This does not mean that the programmer must anticipate and prescribe in the program the precise course of its behavior. A program is not a scenario; it is a strategy of action, and what actions actually transpire depends on the successive states of the machine and its inputs at each stage of the process—neither of which need be envisioned in advance either by the programmer or by the machine. A problem-solving program applied to a particular puzzle situation does not prescribe all the steps to solve that puzzle; it prescribes a selective search strategy that, when followed, may lead the computer to discover a path to a solution. But selective search, under the guidance of strategies, is also the process that people use to solve puzzles.

Of course humans, through the processes called learning, can improve their strategies by experience and instruction. By the same token, computers can be, and to some extent have been, provided with programs (strategies) for improving their own strategies. Since a computer's programs are stored in the same memories as data, it is entirely possible for programs to modify themselves—that is, to learn.

Probably the most fundamental differences between today's computers and the human information-processing system have to do with the input organs that provide the interface between the system and its environment. Simulating the capabilities of human eyes and ears has proved to be a much more difficult task than simulating the thinking processes that go on in the central nervous system. Computer capabilities in both visual and auditory domains, and particularly the former, fall far short of human capabilities.

Over the past two decades a moderate amount of work has been carried on in the field usually called artificial intelligence to explore the potentialities of the computer that have been outlined above. Some of this research has been aimed at programming computers to do things which, if done by a person, would be regarded as intelligent. Another part of the research has been directed at simulating not only the human capabilities but also the processes that human beings use in exercising these capabilities. The considerable progress that has been made in understanding the nature both of artificial and of human intelligence has hardly begun to translate itself into applications, and has been reflected to only a small degree in the actual practical uses of computers. Artificial intelligence research has had an impact upon the search algorithms that are used to solve large combinatorial problems, it is on the verge of practical application in the realm of medical diagnosis, and it has had an important influence upon certain computer programming techniques (for example, list processing). But its main significance for practical affairs lies in the future.

How, then, have computers actually been used to date? At present, computers typically spend most of their time in two main kinds of tasks: carrying out large-scale engineering and scientific calculations and keeping the financial, production, and sales records of business firms and other organizations. Although precise statistics are not available, it would be safe to estimate that 95 percent of all computing power is allocated to such jobs. Now these tasks belong to the horseless-carriage phase of computer development. That is to say, they consist in doing things rapidly and automatically that were being done slowly and by hand (or by desk calculator) in the precomputer era.

Such uses of computers do not represent new functions but only new ways of performing old functions. Of course, by greatly lowering the cost of performing them, they encourage us to undertake them on a larger scale than before. The increased analytic power provided by computers has probably encouraged engineers to design more complex structures (for example, some of the very tall new office buildings that have gone up in New York and Chicago) than they would have attempted if their analytic aids were less powerful. Moreover, by permitting more sophisticated analyses to be carried out in the design process, they have also brought about significant cost reductions in the designs themselves. In the same way, the mechanization of business record-keeping processes has facilitated the introduction of improved controls over inventories and cash flows, with resulting savings in costs. Thus, the computer not only reduces the costs of the information-processing operations that it automates but also contributes to the productivity of the activities themselves.

The remaining 5 percent of computer uses are more sophisticated. Let us consider two different ways in which a computer can assist an engineer in designing electric motors. On the one hand, the engineer can design the motor using conventional procedures, then employ the computer to analyze the prospective operation of the design—the operating temperature, efficiency, and so on. On the other hand, the engineer can provide the computer with the specifications for the motor, leaving to the computer the task of synthesizing a suitable design. In the second, but not the first, case the computer, using various heuristic search procedures, actually discovers, decides upon, and evaluates a suitable design. In the same way, the role of the computer in managing inventories need not be limited to record keeping. The computer program may itself determine (on the basis of usage) when items should be reordered and how large the orders should be. In these and many other situations, computers can provide not only the information on which decisions are made but can themselves make the decisions. Process-control computers, in automated or semiautomated manufacturing operations, play a similar role in decision making. Their programs are decision strategies which, as the system's variables change from moment to moment, retain control over the ongoing process.

It is the capability of the computer for solving problems and making decisions that represents its real novelty and that poses the greatest difficulties in predicting its impact upon society. An enormous amount of research and developmental activity will have to be carried out before the full practical implications of this capability will be understood and available for use. In the single generation that modern computers have been in existence, enough basic research has been done to reveal some of the fundamental mechanisms. Although one can point to a number of applications of the computer as decision maker that are already 20 or 25 years old, development and application on a substantial scale have barely begun.

## ECONOMIC EFFECTS OF COMPUTERS

The direct economic effects of introducing computers as numerical calculators and decision makers are like those of introducing any new form of capital that raises productivity and also improves the quality of the product. The computer (its hardware together with the associated system-programming costs) represents an investment in a capital-intensive, labor-saving device that has to justify itself, in competition with other possible forms of investment, through savings in clerical and other personnel costs together with the improvements it brings about in organizational decisions.

When the main motive of introducing the computer is to mechanize existing clerical operations—in the actuarial department of an insurance firm, say, or the accounting department of a manufacturing concern—then its main economic advantage stems from the reduction in clerical costs. When it is introduced to mechanize decision processes—engineering design, for example, or control of stock or cash inventories—then its direct effect shows up as some form of productivity increase in the organization's operations. In either case, there is nothing special about the computer that distinguishes it, in its economic effects, from any other capital investment. Any such investment can be expected to have a direct effect upon employment in the organizational components where it is introduced. When the accounting system is mechanized, fewer clerks and book-keepers are needed, else there would be no economic motivation for mechanizing. Of course, if part of the motivation for the change is to improve the quality of the system's output, the operation may be expanded, and the net reduction in personnel may be smaller than would be estimated solely from the increase in efficiency. If there is sufficient elasticity of demand for the activity, personnel may actually increase.

The most important question, however, is what the reduction in personnel at the point of impact means for the total level of employment in the economy. Again, this is a general economic issue—of technical unemployment—that does not depend on any special properties of computers. They are simply one among the many labor-saving devices that have been appearing since the beginning of the Industrial Revolution (and before).

Both standard economic analysis and a large body of empirical evidence demonstrate that there is no relation, positive or negative, between the technological sophistication of an economy and the level of employment it maintains. From a systems standpoint, a cost reduction in any part of the system releases resources that can be employed to increase the output of goods and services elsewhere in the system. At any level of employment, from 0 to 100 percent, the total revenue received by wage earners and owners of capital and land as wages, interest, and rent is just sufficient to purchase the total bundle of goods and services that is produced. Economists sometimes disagree as to why economies do not always operate at or near full employment, but they are unanimous in agreeing that the reason is not that they produce more than they can consume. (Even Marxists agree with this proposition, although they argue that full employment cannot be maintained within the institutions of capitalism.)

An even stronger statement can be made about the systems effects of cost-saving technological innovations. We usually describe devices like computers (and most other machinery) as labor-saving because they require a lower ratio of labor to capital than the methods they displace. But if we measure savings relative to output, they are usually both labor-saving and capital-saving. That is to say, a smaller capital investment per passenger mile is required to transport people by jet plane than to transport them by ox cart. Similarly, a smaller capital investment per multiplication is required if a large modern computer is used to do the arithmetic than if it is done on a desk calculator or with pencil and paper. (Do not forget to include the capital cost of the desk at which the clerk sits and the heated or air-conditioned room in which he or she works.) Now it is easy to show, for economic equilibrium and under reasonable assumptions about the supply of capital, that the introduction of capital-intensive, cost-saving innovations will raise the level of real wages and increase the fraction of the total revenue that goes to wages. This prediction from economic theory is amply supported by the histories of the industrialized economies over the present century. As productivity has increased (mainly as a consequence of technological innovation), real wages have steadily risen, as has labor's share in the total national product[4].

Now the rate of technological change depends both upon the rate of discovery of new innovations and upon the availability of capital to turn them into bricks and steel (or wire and glass). In this process, computers compete with other forms of technology for the available capital. Hence, the process of computerization is simply a part, currently an important part, of the general process of technological change. It might be described, paraphrasing Clausewitz, as ''a continuation of the Industrial Revolution by other means''[5].

In taking this very global and bird's-eye view of the economics of mechanization, we should not ignore the plight of the worker who is displaced by the computer. His plight is often genuine and serious, particularly if the economy as a whole is not operating near full employment, but even if it is. Society as a whole benefits from increased productivity, but often at the expense of imposing

---

[4]For a fuller discussion of this evidence, see note 2, chap. 4.

[5]K. von Clausewitz, *On War* (Modern Library, New York, 1943), p. 596.

transient costs on a few people. But the sensible response to this problem is not to eschew the benefits of change; it is rather to take institutional steps to shift the burdens of the transition from the individual to society. Fortunately, our attitudes on these questions appear to be maturing somewhat, and our institutional practices improving, so that the widespread introduction of the computer into clerical operations over the past generation has not called forth any large-scale Ludditism. In fact, during the depression that we are currently experiencing, in contrast to some earlier ones, technology has not been accused as the villain.

## EFFECTS ON THE NATURE OF WORK

We see that, so far as economic effects are concerned, the computer simply provides a particular path toward higher productivity through industrialization. Whatever benefits it produces, it produces in this way; whatever problems it creates, it creates as other capital-intensive innovations do. We must be careful, however, not to evaluate social change solely in terms of its impact on wages and employment. Of equal importance are the effects it may have on the workplace, and even on leisure. Today we frequently hear the claim that computers and automation dehumanize work and that dehumanization, in turn, causes alienation from work and society. These charges have been laid not only against contemporary developments in automation but against the whole process of industrialization. They were stated eloquently in the *Communist Manifesto* more than a century ago and by numerous social critics before and since. There has been a new surge of concern with the alienation issue in the past 10 years.

Three questions need to be asked about alienation. First, how much alienation is there—is there evidence that alienation has been increased by computers and automation or, for that matter, by other forms of industrialization and mechanization? Second, in what ways is the nature of work, and the satisfactions derivable from it, changed by automation of the workplace? Third, as automation eliminates certain kinds of jobs in favor of others, what are the net effects upon the profile of jobs in the economy—are the jobs that are eliminated, on balance, more or less satisfying than the new ones that are created to replace them?

Objective data on national trends in job satisfaction are available only for about the last 20 years. About 15 national surveys have been conducted since 1958 by professional polling organizations that included questions on job satisfaction. Although 20 years is a short time, it does cover almost the whole period of the introduction of computers: hence these data should help answer the question before us. The polls provide absolutely no evidence for a decrease in job satisfactions over this period. If alienation has been increased by automation, the increase somehow does not show up in answers by workers to questions about their attitudes toward their jobs[6]. Notice that the polls do not show that workers are enthusiastic about their jobs, only that they do not seem to like them less today than they did in 1958.

Unfortunately, comparable data are not available to measure the longer trends in job satisfaction over the whole past two centuries or so of industrialization. Perhaps even if computers and automation do not intensify alienation, they confirm and complete a loss of satisfactions that was produced by the rise of the factory system. The answer to that question must be mainly speculative. Clayre, however, recently threw some interesting light on it by examining the attitudes toward work expressed in preindustrial folk literature and popular ballads[7]. He finds few indications of a Golden Age in which work was generally regarded as pleasurable and satisfying. He concludes that, in general, daily work was the same burdensome necessity for peasants and craftsmen as it is for factory workers and clerks: and that life's satisfactions and pleasure were mainly sought, then as now, in leisure, not work.

Perhaps, however, we should not try to detect alienation in this indirect way but should look directly at the workplaces where computers have been introduced, in order to see how they have changed the nature of work and its environment. Sizable differences have been found in worker satisfaction among blue-collar workers in different kinds of factories, some of the important variables being job variety and worker control over the timing of work. It is not the case, however, that the most advanced forms of industrialization and automation produce the most tedious and restrictive jobs. On the contrary, those forms of work organization that appear to have been most alienating—typified by the auto assembly line or large-scale hand assembly operations—are declining in importance relative to other forms of mechanization. Blauner, for example, studied four industries in depth: printing, a traditional craft industry; textiles, a machine-tending industry; automobile assembly, highly mechanized with highly specialized jobs; and a highly automated continuous-process chemical manufacturing industry[8]. He found few indications of alienation in printing and chemicals, considerably more in textiles, and most of all in automobile assembly. The industry that best typifies modern automation—chemicals—was substantially less alienating than the two that typify older kinds of mechanization.

If we look at office automation, we see that, here too, the kinds of jobs that

---

[6]The polls under discussion were conducted by the Survey Research Centers of the Universities of Michigan and California, the National Opinion Research Center, and the Gallup Poll. For a detailed analysis of these data, see R. P. Quinn and L. J. Shepard, *The 1972–73 Quality of Employment Survey* (Institute for Social Research, University of Michigan, Ann Arbor, 1974).

[7]A. Clayre, *Work and Play* (Harper & Row, New York, 1974).

[8]R. Blauner, *Alienation and Freedom, The Factory Worker and His Industry* (Univ. of Chicago Press, Chicago, 1964).

are displaced tend to be those that are most repetitive and restricting. Whisler, who studied about 20 companies in the insurance industry, found that computerization had produced only small and conflicting changes in the nature of clerical and supervisory jobs[9]. The new jobs placed greater demands on the employees for accuracy and reliability in performance, but they were not generally perceived as being significantly more or less pleasant or more or less boring than before. And, perhaps most important of all, whatever effects were produced were small effects. Automation and computerization do not appear to change the nature of work in a fundamental way.

Again we must look not just at immediate impact but at system effects. Factory and office automation are labor-saving technologies. The jobs they eliminate are mostly jobs that were already relatively routine. Therefore, when we look at the impact on the labor force as a whole, we expect to see automation bringing about an overall decrease in the percentage of persons engaged in routine work of these kinds. Correspondingly, there will be a larger percentage of employees than before in service occupations and probably also in technical occupations. The work-satisfaction studies discussed earlier show differences among occupational groups of precisely this kind. From these data it appears that if factory operatives and clerical workers decline as a fraction of the labor force, while service workers, sales personnel, and professional and technical workers increase, there will be a net increase in reported job satisfaction—unless, of course, a compensating shift takes place in aspirations, a possibility we must not dismiss.

On all counts, then, we must acquit the computer technology of the charges that it has been and will be a cause of widespread alienation from work. Empirically, we find no signs of a downward trend in work satisfactions, and when we look at the actual impact of automation upon the workplace and the work force, we find no reason why such a trend should be expected. On the contrary, the newer technologies may even have a modest humanizing effect on the nature of work. The notion of a Golden Age of work prior to the Industrial Revolution must also be dismissed as romanticism, unsupported by such evidence as has been examined.

## CONTROL AND PRIVACY

The potential of computers for increasing the control of organizations or society over their members and for invading the privacy of those members has caused

---

[9]T. L. Whisler, *The Impact of Computers on Organizations* (Praeger, New York, 1970). I. R. Hoos [in *Automation in the Office* (Public Affairs Press, Washington, D.C., 1961)] reaches more pessimistic conclusions than Whisler about the impact of the computer, but she mainly observed transient effects at the time the new technology was being introduced, and not the longer-term effects after the changes had been digested.

considerable concern. The issues are important but are too complex to be discussed in detail here. I shall therefore restrict myself to a few comments which will serve rather to illustrate this complexity than to provide definitive answers.

A first observation is that our concern here is for competitive aspects of society, the power of one individual or group relative to others. Technologies tend to be double-edged in competitive situations, particularly when they are available to both competitors. For example, the computerization of credit information about individuals facilitates the assembly of such information from many sources, and its indefinite retention and accessibility. On the other hand, it also facilitates auditing such information to determine its sources and reliability. With appropriate legal rules of the game, an automated system can provide more reliable information than a more primitive one and can be surrounded by more effective safeguards against abuse. Some of us might prefer, for good reasons or bad, not to have our credit checked at all. But if credit checking is a function that must be performed, a strong case can be made for making it more responsible by automating it, with appropriate provision for auditing its operation.

Similarly, much has been said of the potential for embezzlement in computerized accounting systems, and cases have occurred. Embezzlement, however, was known before computers, and the computer gives auditors as well as embezzlers powerful new weapons. It is not at all clear which way the balance has been tilted.

The privacy issue has been raised most insistently with respect to the creation and maintenance of longitudinal data files that assemble information about persons from a multitude of sources. Files of this kind would be highly valuable for many kinds of economic and social research, but they are bought at too high a price if they endanger human freedom or seriously enhance the opportunities of blackmailers. While such dangers should not be ignored, it should be noted that the lack of comprehensive data files has never been the limiting barrier to the suppression of human freedom. The Watergate criminals made extensive, if unskillful, use of electronics, but no computer played a role in their conspiracy. The Nazis operated with horrifying effectiveness and thoroughness without the benefits of any kind of mechanized data processing.

Making the computer the villain in the invasion of privacy or encroachment on civil liberties simply diverts attention from the real dangers. Computer data banks can and must be given the highest degree of protection from abuse. But we must be careful, also, that we do not employ such crude methods of protection as to deprive our society of important data it needs to understand its own social processes and to analyze its problems.

## MAN'S VIEW OF MAN

Perhaps the most important question of all about the computer is what it has done and will do to man's view of himself and his place in the universe. The most heated attacks on the computer are not focused on its possible economic effects, its presumed destruction of job satisfactions, or its threats to privacy and liberty, but upon the claim that it causes people to be viewed, and to view themselves, as "machines"[10].

To get at the real issues, we must first put aside one verbal confusion. All of us are familiar with a wide variety of machines, most of which predated the computer. Consequently, the word "machine" carries with it many connotations: of rigidity, of simplicity, of repetitive behavior, and so on. If we call anything a machine, we implicitly attribute these characteristics to it. Hence, if a computer is a machine, it must behave rigidly, simply, and repetitively. It follows that computers cannot be programmed to behave like human beings.

The fallacy in the argument, of course, lies in supposing that, because we have applied the term "machine" to computers, computers must behave like older forms of machines. But the central significance of the computer derives from the fact that it falsifies these earlier connotations. It can, in fact, be programmed to behave flexibly, in complex ways, and not repetitively at all. We must either get rid of the connotations of the term, or stop calling computers "machines."

There is a more fundamental question behind the verbal one. It is essentially the question that was raised by Darwinism, and by the Copernican revolution centuries earlier. The question is whether the dignity of man, his sense of worth and self-respect depends upon his being something special and unique in the universe. As I have said elsewhere (see note 2).

> The definition of man's uniqueness has always formed the kernel of his cosmological and ethical systems. With Copernicus and Galileo, he ceased to be the species located at the center of the universe, attended by sun and stars. With Darwin, he ceased to be the species created and specially endowed by God with soul and reason. With Freud, he ceased to be the species whose behavior was— potentially—governable by rational mind. As we begin to produce mechanisms that think and learn, he has ceased to be the species uniquely capable of complex, intelligent manipulation of his environment.

What the computer and the progress in artificial intelligence challenge is an ethic that rests on man's apartness from the rest of nature. An alternative ethic, of course, views man as a part of nature, governed by natural law, subject to the forces of gravity and the demands of his body. The debate about artificial

---

[10]Two books that attack artificial intelligence on this ground are H. L. Dreyfus, *What Computers Can't Do* (Harper & Row, New York, 1972) and J. Weizenbaum, *Computer Power and Human Reason* (Freeman, San Francisco, 1976). The two books have little in common except a shared antipathy against the "machine" view of human thinking, and an eloquent contempt for those who hold that view. Weizenbaum's book is the technically more competent of the two, with respect to its understanding of the current state of the computer programming art.

intelligence and the simulation of man's thinking is, in considerable part, a confrontation of these two views of man's place in the universe. It is a new chapter in the vitalism-mechanism controversy.

Issues that are logically distinct sometimes become stuck together with the glue of emotion. Several such issues arise here:

To what extent can human behavior be simulated by computer?

In what areas of work and life should the computer be programmed to augment or replace human activities?

How far should we proceed to explore the human mind by psychological research that makes use of computer simulation?

The first of these three issues will only be settled, over the years, by the success or failure of research efforts in artificial intelligence and computer simulation. Whatever our beliefs about the ultimate limits of simulation, it is clear that the current state of the art has nowhere approached those limits.

The second question will be settled anew each year by a host of individual and public decisions based on the changing computer technology, the changing economics of computer applications, and our attention to the social consequences of those applications.

The answer to the third question depends upon our attitudes toward the myths of Pandora and Prometheus. One viewpoint is that knowledge can be dangerous—there are enough historical examples—and that the attempt to arrive at a full explanation of man's ability to think might be especially dangerous. A different point of view, closer to my own, is that knowledge is power to produce new outcomes, outcomes that were not previously attainable. To what extent these outcomes will be good or bad depends on the purposes they serve, and it is not easy, in advance, to predict the good and bad uses to which any particular technology will be put. Instead, we must look back over human history and try to assess whether, on balance, man's gradual emergence from a state of ignorance about the world and about himself has been something we should celebrate or regret. To believe that knowledge is to be preferred to ignorance is to believe that the human species is capable of progress and, on balance, has progressed over the centuries. Knowledge about the human mind can make an important contribution to that progress. It is a belief of this kind that persuades researchers in artificial intelligence that their endeavor is an important and exciting chapter in man's great intellectual adventure.

## SUMMARY

From an economic standpoint, the modern computer is simply the most recent of a long line of new technologies that increase productivity and cause a gradual shift from manufacturing to service employment. The empirical evidence provides no support for the claim sometimes made that the computer ''mechanizes'' and "dehumanizes" work. Perhaps the greatest significance of the computer lies in its impact on Man's view of himself. No longer accepting the geocentric view of the universe, he now begins to learn that mind, too, is a phenomenon of nature, explainable in terms of simple mechanisms. Thus the computer aids him to obey, for the first time, the ancient injunction, "Know thyself."

# 24
# Theoretical Perspectives in Social Analyses of Computerization*

## 1988

## Rob Kling

*This chapter consists of major portions of Robert Kling's* ACM Computing Surveys *article (1980), "Social Analyses of Computing: Theoretical Perspectives in Recent Empirical Research" and a new section that updates this paper from 1980–1987—prepared especially for this volume. Eds.*

## INTRODUCTION

Almost everyone who has had substantial contact with computer-based systems is impressed by their capacity to store and flexibly manipulate vast amounts of information. The increases in storage capacity and speed of digital computers over both their mechanical precursors and people have led many analysts to view digital computing as a technology with possible social repercussions as potent as those of the automobile and telephone. Speculations about the social repercussions of new computing modalities, from large databases (Michael, 1964), to network information services (Licklider & Vezza, 1978, Hiltz & Turoff, 1978), to artificial intelligence (Weizenbaum, 1976; Boden, 1978), are commonplace. Often there is little choice but to speculate about new technologies since they

*This study was supported by the National Science Foundation under Grant MCS 77-20831. The analyses reported here have been enriched by discussions with Howard S. Becker, James Danziger, William Dutton, Les Gasser, Peter Keen, Kenneth Laudon, M. Lynne Markus, Abbe Mowshowitz, James Rule, and Anselm Strauss. Elihu Gerson, John King, Kenneth Kraemer, Walt Scacchi, and the referees have been especially helpful; Adele Goldberg provided special aid with knotty editorial decisions.

Table 24-1 and pp. 468–495 have been adapted from "Computing as Social Action: The Social Dynamics of Computing in Complex Organizations," by Rob Kling and Walt Scacchi, in *Advances in Computers*, Vol. 19, Marshall Yovits, Ed., Academic Press, New York, 1980, and are published here by permission.

have not been built and placed in their host social settings. One constructive role of prospective analyses is that of informing affected parties and thus enabling them to make better social and technical choices. Postmortem analyses may be more accurate (Kling, 1978c; Kraemer, 1979b), but they are of substantially less utility.

Speculative analyses emphasize the capabilities, potential benefits, and potential harm of new technical developments. Consider the case of electronic funds-transfer systems. By appreciating the ways in which automated teller machines enable the public to bank at any hour of the day or night, bankers can develop a new set of services. Also, by appreciating the ways in which real-time funds-transfer systems may be susceptible to "credit blackouts," bankers, technologists, and the public alike are alerted to the potential harm of haphazard developments (Kling, 1978c).

To identify the social impacts of computing, one must have, at least implicitly, a theory of the causal powers that computerized systems can exert upon individuals, groups, organizations, institutions, social networks, social worlds, and other social entities. Only the most ardent technical determinist would claim that the consequences of computer use depend exclusively on the technical characteristics of the mode of computing adopted (e.g., large-scale data systems, point-of-sale terminal networks, "personal" computers). Serious analyses of the consequences of computing consider social and economic characteristics to be important elements in a line of analysis or "storyline." But what social or economic characteristics should be selected? How are they to be related? And to what shall they be attributed? Shall we start with *social groups* connected by *channels of communication, cooperatively striving* to satisfy *common goals?* Shall we further assume that the social world in which computing is used is relatively well ordered, with participants adopting stable *roles* and acting in accord with stable *norms?* Or shall we start with *social groups, in conflict,* which *manipulate* available *channels of communication* and *messages* to gain more *valued resources* than their competitors? Moreover, shall we assume that *roles* are *fluid,* that lines of action are *situated,* and that *rules* and *norms* may be selectively ignored or renegotiated? In any case, how do *goals* arise among social groups or in organizations? How do they influence the modes of computing adopted, and the ways that they are used? Are *goals* to be viewed as the sum of *individual preferences,* reflections of *economic relationships,* the *negotiated agreements among interested parties,* or as *convenient fictions* retrospectively formulated to make sense of *ambiguous streams of events?*

Any observation or claim about the uses or consequences of new computing technologies (e.g., electronic funds-transfer systems, decision support systems) rests on an array of assumptions about these issues, however implicit. For example, if we believe that the social world can be understood as an ecology of cooperating groups and that conflict is largely a by-product of poor communication, then network information systems may appear as media for reducing intergroup conflict (Hiltz & Turoff, 1978). On the other hand, if we view social worlds as arenas for interaction of groups with overlapping but often conflicting interests, then network information systems appear as instruments of both cooperation and conflict (Schiller, 1969).

In coming to an understanding of computing technologies, particularly newer ones, it is important to understand which conceptions of social life are likely to aid in discerning critical social aspects. Analysts do not select random sets of concepts on which to base an examination of computing: They cluster useful concepts into coherent bundles which constitute a perspective on social life. Some perspectives are substantially better than others in accurately predicting the future uses and consequences of computing. The choice of core concepts need not simply be a matter of speculation. It is possible to test some of the simpler claims about computing use, and consequently the "goodness" of the perspectives from which they are "derived," by examining the development and use of existing systems.

In the United States there are well over 200,000 digital computers in use (Gottlieb, 1973; U.S. Government, 1977) and millions of applications developed in thousands of organizations. These applications vary considerably in their technical strategies, and the computer-using organizations vary considerably in characteristics often identified as important, such as size and social complexity (DeBrebander, Deschoolmeester, Leyder, & Van Lommel, 1972; Danziger & Dutton, 1977b). Because of this variety, much can be learned from a careful examination of the adoption, development, uses, and consequences of existing computer-based technologies.[1]

This paper selectively examines recent empirical studies of computing in organizations as a way of investigating the appropriateness of different conceptions of social life for an understanding of the use and consequences of computing. Two common and broadly drawn perspectives adopted by social analysts of computing are introduced in Section 1. We then examine how social studies of computing are influenced by these perspectives. Some of these studies focus on behavior within organizations, such as decision making and work life. Others focus on social issues, such as privacy and social accountability, where empirical studies have shed some light.

---

[1]Many important reasons for this focus on computing in organizations are pragmatic; most computer-based systems have been adopted by organizations. Even computer systems with which the public has direct contact, such as point-of-sale terminals and automated tellers, are administered by organizations. In advanced industrial societies, large organizations play a dominant role in the lives of many, particularly in urban areas. Since many of these organizations use computer-based systems to record transactions with their clients, organizations become a natural focus for certain issues affecting the relations between them and the public (Sterling, 1979; Lenk, 1980; Kraemer, 1980c).

## THEORETICAL PERSPECTIVES FOR THE SOCIAL ANALYSIS
## OF COMPUTING

The literature analyzing the social character and consequences of computer use is fragmented and often bewildering to nonspecialists. The diligent reader who examines the literatures on such topics as computing and personal privacy or the role of computer-based information systems in organizational decision making will find a cacophony of voices (Kling 1980a). If he or she reads widely and listens carefully, distinct choruses can be discerned. It is difficult to find voices singing precisely the same tune, or even in the same key, but some do sound in relative harmony. To make sense of the singers and to learn from their songs, the reader must identify the tunes and harmonies of the most notable choruses. These tunes and harmonies are patterned perspectives that provide answers to many of our earlier questions.

As a first approximation, analyses of the social character and development of computing can be divided into two groups, based on two major perspectives: *systems rationalism* and *segmented institutionalism* (see Table 24-1). Systems rationalists typically emphasize the positive roles that computerized technologies play in social life. Often, they examine new capabilities of computing technologies (e.g., computer conferencing) or new areas in which existing computer technologies may be applied. They assume that there is a marked consensus on major social goals relevant to computing use, and they often develop a relatively synoptic account of social behavior. Systems rationalists place efficiency, whether economic or organizational, as the predominant value. Moreover, they typically focus on a narrowly bounded world of computer use in which the computer user is a central actor.

In contrast, segmented institutionalists examine the consequences of computerized technologies on many aspects of social life, both "legitimate" and "illegitimate." For example, they observe that participants in organizations adopt computing to enhance their personal status or credibility, as well as to improve the technical quality of their decisions or increase the economic efficiency of specific activities. Rather than assume a consensus on important goals and values, segmented institutionalists assume that intergroup conflict is as likely as cooperation unless the contrary is empirically demonstrated. They identify as dominant values the sovereignty of individuals and groups over critical aspects of their lives, the integrity of individuals, and social equity; economic or organizational efficiency is subservient to these values. They typically identify settings of computer use as broad in scope, and they are likely to emphasize parties other than the computer user (e.g., clients, regulators, suppliers, competitors, or controllers of critical resources).

These two sweeping labels help to identify the major choruses and their principal songs.[2] But the voices within each chorus are more diverse and less

---

[2]Most analysts adopt a relatively uniform voice from presentation to presentation. Others adopt

harmonized than these brief sketches suggest.[3] Systems rationalists do not sing completely in unison. Analysts who identify with positions as diverse as management science (Buffa, 1979), "the systems approach" (Emery, 1969; Chartrand, 1971), and managerial rationalism (Kanter, 1977)[4] still share the basic assumptions of systems rationalism.

Both management scientists and managerial rationalists often identify the interests of managers as more legitimate than those of their subordinates. Some managerial rationalists seek to optimize the management of organizations by embedding computing in their operations; other simply emphasize the tasks to be automated independently of any contextual features aside from the costs of automation. An important variant of managerial rationalism, structural analysis,[5] identifies critical contextual features of the organization or its environment that influence the utility and correct selection of the mode of automation (Galbraith, 1977, Colton, 1978). Environmental uncertainties, slack resources, transaction volumes, communication channels, and standard operating procedures are among the common concepts employed by structuralists in characterizing the social world in which participants utilize technologies (Thompson, 1967; Galbraith, 1977). Human-relations analysts (Mumford & Banks, 1967; Argyris, 1971) emphasize the role of technology in altering the quality of working life. While the human-relations tradition developed in reaction to work practices

different perspectives, depending on the situation they are analyzing. It makes more sense to characterize analyses by the perspectives they embody rather than to pigeonhole analysts. Comments about "analysts" should be understood to apply to the analyses under discussion, and not necessarily to other work by the same author.

[3]In a recent review of the literature on the development, uses and consequences of computing in organizations, King and Scacchi (Kling, 1980b) identified six major perspectives, which have been simplified here into two: systems rationalism and segmented institutionalism. Their article examines the development and use of computing, not just its consequences, from all six perspectives. In a review of analyses of the social issues raised by computing—within and without organizations— Mowshowitz (1981) identified eight somewhat different perspectives. Our main aim here is not to define whether there are "really" two, four, six, eight, or 48 major perspectives, but rather to determine which theoretical perspectives provide the greatest insight into the social character of computing.

[4]Managerial rationalism connotes a set of approaches designed to organize and manage efficiently and effectively according to the preferences of higher level managers. Classically, it emphasizes the division of labor according to specialized activity, and the existence of logical relationships of various organizational functions (Killough, 1972; Scott, 1973). More modern variations on this classical theme, our "structural" and Allison's (1971) "organizational process," emphasize organizational uncertainties and slack resources as being important contextual conditions in selecting management strategies. The organizing strategies rely less on the formal hierarchy of authority, and more extensively on a variety of "bridging roles" and information systems, to coordinate the diverse activities of internally differentiated organizations. Although sociologists no longer believe that the classical theory provides a credible account of the ways that large organizations are or can be managed, it is still commonly adopted as an analytical posture in the computing literature. For recent examples see Kling 1972 and especially Figure 1 of Kern 1979.

[5]This is treated as a separate position in Kling, 1980b; Allison, 1971; Perrow, 1979. Here it is integrated with other variants of systems rationalism to simplify the broader contrasts. See footnote 4.

Table 24-1. Theoretical Perspectives Adopted by Social Analysts of Computing [a]

| | Systems Rationalism | | | | Segmented Institutionalism | |
| --- | --- | --- | --- | --- | --- | --- |
| | Rational | Structural | Human Relations | Interactionist | Organizational Politics | Class Politics |
| Technology | Equipment as instrument | Equipment as instrument | Equipment as instrument/environment | "Package" as milieu | Equipment as instrument | Equipment as instrument |
| Social setting | Unified organization 1. The user 2. Tasks and Goals 3. Consistency and consensus over goals (assumed) | Organizations and formal units (e.g., departments) 1. Formal organizational arrangements 2. Hierarchy of authority, reporting relationships | Small groups and individuals 1. Task groups and their interactions 2. Individual needs 3. Organizational resources and rewards | Situated social actors 1. Differentiated work organizations and their clientele 2. Groups with overlapping and shifting interests 3. Participants in different social worlds | Social actors in positions 1. Individuals/groups and their interests | Social classes in stratified system |
| Organizing concepts | Rationalization Formal procedures Individual ("personality") differences Intended effects (assumed) Authority | Organizational structure Organizational environment Uncertainty Standard operating procedures | Trust Motivation Expectations and rewards Job satisfaction (subjective alienation) Self-esteem | Defining situations Labeling events as a social construction Work opportunities/constraints Power Career | Work opportunities/constraints Power Social conflict Legitimacy Elites Coalitions | Ownership of means of production Power Social conflict Alienation Deskilling Surplus value |

| | | | | | |
|---|---|---|---|---|---|
| Productivity<br>Need<br>Cost benefit<br>Efficiency<br>Task<br>"Better management" | Organizations' resources and rewards<br>Uncertainty absorption<br>Rules<br>Authority/power<br>Information flow | Leadership<br>Sense of competence<br>User involvement<br>Group autonomy | Legitimacy<br>Social world<br>Social conflict<br>Interaction<br>Role<br>Negotiations<br>Orientation<br>Arenas | Political resources<br>Bargaining<br>Power reinforcement<br>Gesture | |
| **Dynamics of technical diffusion**<br>Economic substitution—"meet a need"<br>Educate users<br>A good technology "sells itself" | Attributes of<br>1. Innovation<br>2. Organization<br>3. Environment | Acceptance through participation in design | Accepted technologies preserve important social meanings of dominant actors | Accepted technologies serve specific interests | Accepted technologies serve dominant class interests |
| **Good technology**<br>Effective in meeting explicit goals or "sophisticate" use<br>Efficient<br>Correct | Helps organizations adapt to their environments | Promotes job satisfaction (e.g., enlarges jobs) | Does not destroy social meanings important to lower level participants, public, and underdogs | Serves the interests of all legitimate parties and does not undermine legitimate political process | Does not alienate workers<br>Does not reproduce relations |
| **Workplace ideology**<br>Scientific management | Scientific management | Individual fulfillment through work | Individual fulfillment through evocation of valued social meanings | [Several conflicting ideologies] | Worker's control over production |

based on scientific management that emphasized narrow concerns with technical efficiency (Perrow, 1979), this tradition shares more in common with other variants of systems rationalism than with segmented institutionalism (Mumford, 1978). While human-relations analysts often identify conflicts between workers and their managers, they assume that it is possible to organize the world of work so that all may be well off: Satisfied workers will be productive (Tausky, 1977 pp. 90–94).[6] While there may be conflict today over the role of computing developments in a given workplace, systems can be "properly designed and implemented" so that important common goals can be achieved (Argyris, 1971; Kling, 1973, 1977a; Lucas, 1975a; Mumford & Banks, 1967; Swanson, 1974).

Systems rationalists also differ on critical assumptions. For example, many systems rationalists imply that important social decisions can be made with one comprehensive, enduring rationality (Buffa & Miller, 1979; Dorf, 1977; Kanter, 1977). Others, structuralists like Simon (1977), assume that the focal actors have fragmentary information and that goals may shift over time. Moreover, Simon has argued that for most important decisions, comprehensive knowledge about the costs and benefits of alternative lines of action is too costly and time consuming to obtain, and that decision makers must therefore select satisfactory but suboptimal choices. Systems rationalists also differ in their assessment of social conflict. Typically, management scientists ignore social conflicts by defining problems as if there were a commonly agreed-upon objective function whose optimization is collectively valued (Buffa & Miller, 1979). Some managerial rationalists attempt to resolve conflicts simply by appeals to administrative authority (Donelson, 1979). Still other systems rationalists acknowledge the presence and persistence of social conflict, but argue that conflict is "functional" for an identified social system (Turner, 1978) because it allows a wider variety of perspectives to be incorporated into a plan of action and releases otherwise destructive social tensions. This is a key difference between even the conflict-oriented rationalist approaches and segmented institutionalism. Segmented institutionalists do not assume that the observed level of conflict in a social setting is necessarily "optimal" or even tends toward some kind of "healthy equilibrium"; most even reject the concepts of "social optima" and "social equilibria."[7]

---

[6]See Mumford, 1978 for an example. See Perrow (1979) and Silverman (1971) for sharp critiques for this position and Argyris, 1972, for an extended rejoinder.

[7]The conception of social systems of constrained conflict tending toward healthy equilibria is a common point of convergence of positions that are as diverse as the traditional market analysis of competitive capitalism (Lowi, 1979), interest-group pluralism (Lowi, 1979), structural functionalism (Turner, 1978), "open-systems" theory (Baker, 1973; Swanda, 1979) and cybernetic models of the social order (Emery, 1969). For criticisms of this assumption, see (Collins, 1975; Lowi, 1979; Turner, 1978). Both major perspectives have rich traditions outside of computing. Systems rationalism has been closely aligned with structural functionalism in American sociology (Tausky, 1977; Turner, 1978), and segmented institutionalism with the conflict perspective (Collins, 1975; Ritzer, 1977). Their explanatory power has been the subject of considerable debate among so-

Segmented institutionalists also differ among themselves on their assumptions about how to understand social life and the role of computing therein. Political analysts view social life as a continual contest for power by groups with conflicting interests and view computing as an instrument turned toward aggrandizing power.[8] In contrast, symbolic interactionists view social life as constructed from the interaction of people and groups as they create and respond to socially defined meanings. Conceptions of a "good system," for example, may depend critically on whether the evaluator is a technical specialist interested in working with a state-of-the art technology, a staff analyst interested in having an easily intelligible instrument, or a manager who is interested in reducing critical costs in his organizational unit (Kling, 1979a). Interactionists view computing as an arena in which many participants with overlapping but conflicting interests are brought together—designers, vendors, service suppliers, users, consumers, consultants (Kling, 1977b, 1978g, 1980d; Scacchi, 1980).

Systems rationalism and segmented institutionalism are two convenient and broad-brush labels. In practice, analysts take considerable license in appropriating concepts from either of these idealized perspectives. Thus management scientists will on occasion deal with power, and political analysts will assume that there are technical systems that can simultaneously satisfy all parties. But analysts do usually adopt a primary perspective that is closely aligned with one of those sketched here.[9] [In the original article, Kling discusses some early studies of computing from 1950–1970. For space reasons, this section has been deleted here. —Eds.]

## COMPUTING IN ORGANIZATIONS

Analysts of almost every persuasion have suspected that a technology that enlarges the information processing capacity of people or organizations by orders

---

ciologists, and the reader is encouraged to examine the broader accounts (Collins, 1975; Cuff & Payne, 1979; Turner, 1978).

[8]Within this broadly construed political perspective, many more specific claims about the political order can be specified. Pluralists argue that many groups may organize and bargain for their interests, but that there is no ruling class or dominant elite that almost always wins. Those who argue for "reinforcement politics" claim that expensive and complex resources such as automated information systems are likely to be used by already powerful groups so that they can differentially accumulate further advantage over their competitors (Kling, 1978e; Kraemer & Dutton, 1979a). See Danziger, Dutton, Kling, & Kraemer, 1980) for a careful analysis of four different political perspectives applied to the case of computing in organizations and the section on "Organizational Power" for an account of reinforcement politics.

[9]Marxism (or class politics) is conspicuously missing from this set because it has no informed empirical studies of computing in social life. One exception is Noble, 1978; see Braverman, 1974 for an interpretive essay and also the section on "Work Life". Interpretive studies of computing use in nominally Marxist societies such as the Soviet Union and China often rely on other analytical perspectives (Goodman, 1979; Gordon, 1979; Hoffman, 1977).

of magnitude must have potent influences on their interaction and work techniques. What kinds of differences do computerized information systems make in the nature of the activities performed by and within organizations? Most of the accounts of the impacts of computing on organizational life focus on the ways in which computing alters the efficiency or effectiveness of organizations, the ways in which decisions are made, the work life of participants in the organizations, the ways in which activities are structured, the kinds of control managers can exercise in their administrative domains, and the power of different participants to influence the activities of their organizations. Analysts who adopt different perspectives approach the questions, "What difference does computing make?" or "Is computing a good organizational technology?" very differently. The main line of development in this section is to examine the consequences of organizational computing use as viewed by analysts from variations of the systems-rationalist and segmented-institutionalist approaches.

Rather than examine every important difference that computer use can make in organizational life, we examine a few important areas which have been most studied. These include the roles of computer use in decision making in organizations, the work life of computer users, and the alteration in patterns of power and managerial control.[10]

## Innovation

Traditionally, new or better technical components or complete systems are said to move "naturally" from the inventor or developer toward users and consumers. Computing-system promoters or adopters can, however, be motivated by different, potentially conflicting, incentives. Vendors are interested in selling (or overselling) systems for profit. Managers in federal agencies seek to increase their efficiency and spheres of influence. Specialists often seek work with newer, more sophisticated systems instead of procrustean older applications (Kling & Gerson, 1977b; Kling, 1978c). And instrumental users seek to improve their productivity or organizational effectiveness (Scacchi, 1980).

Some systems rationalists hold pleasingly simple conceptions of the diffusion of technical innovations, to wit, successful technologies meet a "need" of individuals or organizations (Licklider & Vezza, 1978). As people learn to appreciate that a new technology meets some need better than its alternatives, and as the costs of obtaining the technology decrease, the technology is adopted on a larger scale (Simon, 1977).

---

[10]Topics that have not been well examined empirically will not be reviewed here, namely, the ways in which computer use may alter the formal "structure" of organizations (Bjorn-Anderson & Pederson, 1977; Bjorn-Anderson & Eason, 1980b; Blau, Falbe, McKinley, & Tracey, 1976; Whisler, 1970), the ethos of an organization's members (Mowshowitz, 1978), or the relations between organizations.

The primary analytical difficulty confronting anyone investigating these claims arises in conceptualizing "need." Structural analysts and those who use an organizational politics perspective approach this problem differently. Structural analyses typically focus on the information processing task to which computing technologies can be applied (DeBrebander, Deschoolmeester, Leyder, & Van Lommel, 1972; Gerson & Koenig, 1979). Gerson and Koenig (1979), for example, analyze the applicability of computing to different tasks by examining the extent to which the tasks can be easily rationalized. They indicate that organizations which carry out a large volume of easily rationalizable tasks (e.g., insurance companies which process bills, claims, and payments) are much more likely to find computing applicable than are firms where rationalizable tasks are a smaller fraction of the work done (e.g., law firms). Organizational politics analysts, on the other hand, focus on the interests and intentions of participants in a decision to adopt a new computing arrangement.

One important study examined the relative importance of structural and political explanations of computing adoption. Danziger and Dutton (1977b) carefully examined the role of institutional needs and the social features within and outside a large sample of American local governments to predict the rates at which they would adopt computing applications. By comparing rates of computing adoption within similar kinds of organizations, they were able to use organizational domains (populations of the jurisdiction) as an index of need. Most American countries, for example, administer property taxes. One can assume that the utility of computing to help ease the burdens of tax roll preparation would be similar for counties with similar populations. Danziger and Dutton found that governmental size and complexity (i.e., "need") account for about half of the explained variance in levels of computing adoption. The other half is accounted for by elements of the government's milieu (e.g., presence of outside funding for applications) and of the social milieu inside the government agency (e.g., reliance on professional management practices, variety of participants influencing decisions to adopt computing). As indicated by this study, then, organizational adoption of computing is not simply based on economic conceptions of task demands; it is also influenced by a variety of specifiable social features of an organization.[11]

Often the staff of an organization will point to "technical benefits" such as labor reduction, internal efficiencies, and increased managerial control to justify the adoption and use of computing technologies. However, careful studies of the actual payoffs of computing within organizations indicate that other, more private rationales often dominate the decisions to adopt or sustain computer-based

---

[11]For an examination of the ways that the personal decision styles actually influence the use and perceived value of automated systems, see Lucas, 1975b,c, 1978a,b). The analyses that follow emphasize the role of the social milieu rather than individual differences within a given milieu (see also Dutton & Kraemer, 1978; Kling & Ahrentzen, 1980c; Kling, 1980d).

systems. Concerns for increasing administrative attractiveness, rather than internal administrative efficiencies, helped sustain an otherwise relatively useless client-tracking information system (UMIS) in Riverville (Kling, 1978c). The welfare agencies using UMIS appeared more efficient to federal auditors; they were able to maintain a steady flow of the funds because the presence of computing enhanced their image of effective administration. UMIS was a political resource for the municipal welfare agencies in Riverville.[12]

Laudon's (1974) insightful case studies of four police computing systems in state and local governments illustrate how these systems served the interest of particular elite groups in the governments which adopted them. Computerized systems were often introduced as instruments of bureaucratic politics. For example, one state governor wished to establish a state attorney general's office, but the local police departments were extremely autonomous and their staffs opposed it. As a *quid pro quo* to help establish the attorney general's office, the governor offered to develop a state-run computer system to keep track of wants, warrants, and criminal histories for all jurisdictions within the state. Since the administration of the system would be centralized in the new attorney general's office, the governor triumphed by offering local police a police information network in exchange. Laudon views new computer systems as political instruments that are selected to fit the political contours of existing organizations with their own ongoing conflicts and coalitions.

In one of our own case studies of a multinational engineering firm, "WESCO," similar patterns were sometimes found. Chemical engineers at WESCO utilize automated simulations to help calculate the design parameters of chemical-processing plants. Sometimes they seek more precise estimates for the sizes of pumps, compressors, and costly equipment. But there are also occasions when engineers have trouble convincing auditors hired by their clients of the efficacy of their designs. At times, engineers have moved from hand calculations to available simulation programs in order to help "snow" the auditors. The computer calculations appear precise, accurate, and sophisticated, and since WESCO's simulation programs are proprietary, it is difficult for auditors to double check the correctness of the calculations or the assumptions made.[13]

In the language of management science, one could say that engineers at

---

[12]The success of the Polaris missile project has often been attributed to the use of PERT scheduling, which was developed for it. However, Sapolsky persuasively argues that PERT was not used to manage the Polaris's schedule and costs. The admiral in charge of Polaris development was not concerned as to how PERT was used, only that its presence be visible (Sapolsky, 1972). PERT served to sufficiently enhance the image of the navy teams that were managing Polaris development so that they were relatively unburdened by the scrutiny and intrusive demands of external review boards. On other projects PERT might well serve as an instrument of managerial control, but in its first and most publicized use, it served primarily as an instrument of bureaucratic politics.

[13]See Kling & Scacchi, 1980b, for a more detailed description of the technical difficulties indicated here.

WESCO and administrators in Riverville have found computing "applicable" to decisions in their organizations (Licklider & Vezza, 1978). But much is lost with such banal characterizations. Sometimes people and groups choose to utilize computer-based systems because they value expected technical benefits such as more precise calculations, speedier information flows, and more flexibly organized reports. On other occasions, computer use is of more importance as an instrument of bureaucratic politics (Keen, 1975; Kling, 1974, 1978c; Laudon, 1974). Computing applications used as political instruments do not easily fit the highly rationalized accounts provided by systems rationalists (Kerner, 1979; Licklider & Vezza, 1978; Simon, 1977). Many of the analyses of computer use developed by systems rationalists are conceptually inadequate because they only focus on the economic payoffs of computing in organizations and neglect patterns of use that are inconsistent with an economic conception of organizational life (Burch, Strater, & Grudnitski, 1979; Champine, 1978; Kerner, 1979; Killough, 1972; Licklider & Vezza, 1978; Simon, 1977). Organizations, public and private, are not exclusively economic production units, even though some of their activities can be well described in those terms. They are also complex arenas for people developing career lines and anchoring their lives in a social world outside the family; they provide opportunities for people to engage in a wide array of symbolic, as well as economic, activities (Pfeffer, 1979; Strauss, 1978). The continued use of the automated welfare information system in Riverville as a symbolic, but resource attracting, gesture provides a commonplace illustration (Kling, 1978c). An example of a different flavor is provided by Pettigrew (1973) in his examination of a British manufacturing firm's decisions to select new computer systems. He found that technical choices made by the board of directors were more influenced by their trust in the individual advocates than by the technical merits of their proposals. Staff enjoying good personal relations with board members were most likely to have their proposals for choice of vendors or kinds of equipment accepted, even when their adversaries in the firm had better cases on procedural or technical grounds. To the extent to which organizational politics influences the adoption and use of computing, its dynamics must be part of any scientifically complete understanding of the antecedents or consequences of computer use in organizations.

Understanding the interplay between computing and the political order of organizations can prove helpful for computing promoters. Kraemer (1977), for example, has developed an insightful analysis of the social dynamics of software transfer. A common belief is that computer-using organizations can benefit from adopting computer applications that are developed by an outside vendor or other organization and marketed for a modest fee. Computer scientists and federal research supporters have paid serious attention to schemes for developing machine-independent software to help diminish the costs of transferring applications across organizations. Kraemer also has studied the actual rates of software transfer between American cities (Kraemer, 1977). He found that a typical city has automated about 40 applications, but in general only one of those has been transferred in. With John King he also studied federal projects in which cities were funded specifically to transfer applications and found that transfers rarely took place (Kraemer & King, 1979). One can respond to these findings by bemoaning the ignorance of public officials and wishing that they were "wiser and more innovative." Or one can more sensibly, as Kraemer has done, analyze the incentives for particular groups in an organization to transfer in an application. In most organizations transferring in a new application does not provide the same strong rewards for a local computer group as does local development. A manager supervising a local development can increase, or at least maintain, his staffing, can increase his budget, and can become an expert on yet another critical operation. Given the development bias of the computing world, a new developer may gain additional prestige that an actor who merely transfers an existing application does not. Together, these create a mobilization of bias against transferring in new applications. Kraemer's analysis differs from the rational economic theory of the firm that underlies the analyses of management scientists who assume that software transfer is "natural."[14] And it has convinced officials in the U.S. Department of Housing and Urban Development not to support information repositories for "transferable" software until the Department can provide other resources that help alter organizational rewards which favor application transfer.

All of these studies emphasize the potent role of an organization's political order in influencing whether computing is adopted, which technologies will be selected, how they will be developed, and whom they shall serve.

## Work Life

There is no paucity of *images* to portray the effects of computing on work life. Bell (1973) and Myers (1970) provide enthusiastic and largely systems-rationalist accounts of computing as an aid to "knowledge work." They both emphasize how computer-based technologies enlarge the range and speed at which data are available. Myers, for example, concludes that "computing will help relieve 'specialists and professionals' of the time-consuming and repetitive parts of their work." In contrast, Braverman (1974), a class-politics analyst, argues that managers conceive of workers as general-purpose machines which they operate. He views automation as a managerial strategy to replace unreliable and finicky "human machines" with more reliable, more productive, and less self-interested mechanical or electronic machines. He argues that computerized information systems usually are organized to routine white-collar work and weaken the power of lower level participants in an organization.

---

[14]See Goodman, 1976, for a sensitive study of how software transfer in the Soviet Union is influenced by the political and economic organization of Soviet industry and state planning.

Human-relations analysts occupy a middle ground between these extremes of euphoria and gloom. They believe that the effects of computerization are contingent upon the technical arrangements chosen and the way they are introduced into the workplace (Argyris, 1971; Kling, 1973). While human-relations analysts place considerable value on jobs which allow people opportunity for self-expression and trust (Argyris, 1972), they argue that the character of jobs and the role of computing in work are to be empirically determined (Kling, 1973; Mann & Williams, 1960). Empirical studies of computing in the workplace have been dominated by human-relations approaches (Hoos, 1960; Kling, 1978f; Mann & Williams, 1958, 1960; Mumford & Banks, 1967; Robey, 1979).[15] Thus they will be our starting point.

*Computing and job characteristics.* Regardless of their theoretical orientation, most analysts view computing as a potent technology that is likely to have a powerful influence on the workplaces in which it is used. It is easy to think of technological changes, such as the transformation of craft fabrication into assembly lines, organized in a way that has powerful influences on the character of work. One human-relations strategy for investigating the character of work empirically is to characterize jobs by a set of important features (e.g., variety, autonomy) and to examine their variations under different conditions.

Kling (1978f) followed this approach in a recent investigation of the impacts of computer use on the character of white-collar jobs through a survey, in 42 municipal governments, of 1200 managers, data analysts (e.g., urban planners), and clerks. While his study was carried out within the human-relations tradition, it casts doubt on the easy assumption that computing is a potent workplace-transforming technology. Most of Kling's respondents used computer-based reports and attributed job-enlarging influences to computer use; they also attributed increases in job pressure and task significance to computing.[16] These effects increased with the extent to which respondents used computer-based reports in their work. Kling also correlated alterations in job characteristics attributed to computing and measures of those same characteristics in each respondent's overall job. These correlations were negligible for most characteristics (e.g., variety) and weak for job pressure and task significance. Thus he concludes that the job-enlarging effects of computer use do not carry over to the jobs of the computer

---

[15]Class-politics analysts often draw upon studies done by others and then interpret them in their own framework (Braverman, 1974; Mowshowitz, 1976), although Noble (1978) has developed a provocative, empirically grounded account of computer numerical control in machine shops, which is based on his own field studies. Managerial rationalists usually emphasize the information processing potentials of computing but remain relatively remote from empirical inquiries (Burch, Strater & Grudnitski, 1979; Kanter, 1977; Sanders, 1974).

[16]These findings are consistent with those reported by Robey in a study of industrial managers in nine European countries (Robey, 1979). They also parallel those of Den Hartog et al. in a study of laboratory technicians who used an automated data system for routine record keeping (Den Hartzog, Wielinga, & Heine, 1980).

users he studied, but some of the felt pressures and influence do. Overall, computer use had perceptible, but *not dominant,* effects on the jobs of many people who used the technology; computer use did not profoundly alter the character of their jobs.

Computing was viewed as a salient technology by managers, data analysts, and clerks who utilized it regularly. For some, computing substantially increased the ease with which they could obtain valued information and made possible more complex data analyses; for others, it had little utility. White-collar workers in several different occupational specialities attributed to computing clear, often positive influences in their jobs.

Kling's (1978f) findings generally support those of Whisler (1970), who indicates that managers are better served by computing than are clerks. But even traffic clerks in Kling's study generally attributed job-enlarging influences to computing. Kling's data lend no support to analysts like Braverman (1974) and Mowshowitz (1976), who argue that the dominant effect of white-collar computer use is to diminish the quality of working life for white-collar workers; on the contrary, it supports claims that computer use is often organized so that it slightly enlarges the jobs of white-collar workers using the technology.

The detailed patterns and levels of the impact of computing vary from one occupational specialty to another and can be understood best in terms of different work contingencies and information-system designs. In addition, the technology is not always easily implemented; difficulties in getting data and in coping with computer specialists, with the computing-services organization, and with the technology itself all add minor and continual turmoil to the white-collar workplace. But, overall, the technology does not dramatically change the character of work; rather, according to Kling's findings, it has a benign and minor influence on the work of the computer users.

*Automated information systems and supervision.* It is often assumed that when automated information systems become available, managers and line supervisors exploit them to enhance their own control over different resources, particularly the activities of their subordinates (Downs, 1967; Whisler, 1970). Two strategies are commonly adopted: reorganizing work so that either tasks are more finely subdivided or control over key decisions moves "up" the organizational hierarchy (Noble, 1978); or directly employing automated information systems to enhance the grain, comprehensiveness, and speed of organizational control systems (Kling, 1974; Lawler & Rhode, 1976). In this section we examine the latter strategy.

Episodes illustrating the use of automated information systems to better monitor the activities of employees, particularly the quantity of their work, can be found in many computer-using organizations (Kling, 1974). Both the image of computing as a tool for the rationalization of white-collar work (Braverman, 1974; Mowshowitz, 1976) and reports by managers that they are losing autonomy (Bjorn-Anderson & Pederson, 1977; Mumford & Banks, 1967) support the hunch that such uses are widespread and effective. In short, computing and closer supervision are held to go hand in hand.

There are few good studies of automated information systems and patterns of supervision.[17] How commonly do organizational actors attempt to utilize information systems as direct aids to supervision, and how successful are they? Kling's (1978f) study of the role of computing in white-collar work provides some helpful data. Each of his respondents was asked to report whether automated information systems had increased or decreased the extent to which he or she was supervised. Few of the respondents attributed increases in their level of supervision to computer use. Kling found that traffic clerks and managers, rather than accountants, detectives, and planners, most frequently (12–16 percent) reported increases in their level of supervision.

The respondents were also asked whether computing provided their supervisors with information about the quantity and quality of their work. Between 25 and 36 percent of the respondents in each occupational group answered positively. In addition, the managers were asked whether computer-based reports helped them monitor and control the work groups within their organizational domains; a majority indicated either that they received no relevant computer-based data, or that the computer-based data they received were of no use in enhancing their control over subordinates. A small fraction indicated that computer-based reports were a major aid, and many managers indicated that computer-based data were sometimes, but not usually, helpful.

Understanding the contingencies of different jobs and the typical uses of automated information systems helps us explain these patterns. Computer-based reports are sometimes used to monitor the workloads of detectives, property appraisers, and social workers. However, such data are usually available in manual records as well and are simply by-products of the computer-based systems (e.g., a welfare client-tracking system). First-line supervisors often have some concept of the relative quantity and quality of the work done by their staffs. In most police detective details, cases are assigned to individual detectives by a supervisor; planners are assigned work on particular projects and their reports are reviewed by higher level staff; accountants work on particular projects or with particular funds. Much of the work is carried out in small groups where supervision can be informal and close. Even when formal statistics may help line supervisors evaluate the quality of work performed by their subordinates, their explicit use seems to produce resentment, suspicion, and controversy over the meaning of the data.

The information systems used by most of Kling's nonclerical respondents

---

[17]Later in this chapter, we examine a case (Albrecht, 1979) in which the probation staff of a court was able to prevent the legal staff from employing an automated information system to monitor their casework. This rich study illustrates how a specific information system was introduced by actors (legal staff) who wished to control others in their work organization.

were not well tailored to provide information about the style, quantity, or quality of their work. Ledgers do not record the activity of an accountant, nor do demographic databases record the activities of planners.

Automated systems can enhance the control of one group over another (Kling, 1974), but in many workplaces where computing is used to automate records retrieval and data analysis, the technology has not been so exploited by managers. Rather, the scenario of computing and control is of accountants in central budget units monitoring the expenditures of line departments, of detectives seeking to catch lawbreakers, and of municipal staff using automated traffic ticket processing systems to help catch scofflaws.

These data[18] indicate that computing should not be viewed as a technology with inevitable, fixed patterns of use and consequences. Computing is selectively exploited as one strategy among many for organizing work and information. The patterns of computer use appear to fit the workplace politics of the computer-using organization. In current practice semiprofessionals do not attribute increased supervision to the use of automated information systems. Structural analysts would suggest that managers find other more effective strategies for controlling their subordinates. Political analysts would suggest that semiprofessionals such as probation officers, accountants, and detectives have sufficient control over their own work so that managers cannot succeed in using formal reporting systems to enhance their supervisory control.

*Operational problems in work with computing.* Computing technology is often portrayed as a "problem solver," but in routine use it is as much a "problem generator." The difficulties of computer use are rich, varied and often more obvious than the "consequences" of computing for one's work style. These can include difficulties in having a computer application properly designed or in having it altered in a timely way in response to new working conditions; getting and using adequate data; finding skilled computer experts; maintaining stable applications or computing arrangements; correcting errors in data and systems; managing the interfaces of different software ensembles; etc. Problems like these have long been recognized by practicing computer specialists and computer users and have often been documented.[19] There clearly are computing difficulties in many settings, but the most important questions are whether they are "accidental" or "recurrent," under what conditions they occur, what their consequences are, what their causes may be, and how they may be reduced. The

---

[18]See also Albrecht, 1979; Noble, 1978.

[19]They have been noted by systems rationalists and segmented institutionalists (Ackoff, 1971; Alter, 1980; Danzinger, 1977a; Dery, 1977; King & Kraemer, 1979; Kling, 1978f; Kling & Scacchi, 1979b; Markus, 1979; Withington, 1969). See Alter, 1980; King & Kraemer, 1979; Kling, 1978c, for explicit treatments. Some extreme rationalists portray computing as if routine difficulties were insignificant or simply attributable to primitive technologies, "inadequate" planning, "poor" communication, and bad luck (Burch, Strater, & Grudnitski, 1979; Dorf, 1977; Sanders, 1977; Simon, 1977).

most common conception is to treat computing as a tool and difficulties as by-products of a collection of accidents that occur as a by-product of "poor planning" or "bad luck" (Withington, 1969).

There is growing evidence that computing difficulties are systemic (Alter, 1980; Dery, 1977; King & Kraemer, 1979; Kling & Gerson, 1977b; Kling, Scacchi, & Crabtree, 1978h; Kling & Scacchi, 1979b; Swanson, 1974). In a study of over 50 decision-support systems that are used in private firms, Alter (1980, pp. 125–142) encountered an array of recurrent problems which he classified as stemming from the technology used, data quality, system conceptions, and "people." While problems of computer use are astutely categorized (e.g., "disappearing users, implementors, and maintainers"), they are simply conceptualized as "risk factors" in system implementation, akin to risk factors in personal health. There is no attempt at explaining the causes or conditions under which these problems occur.[20]

Management analysts are quick to suggest that when users have difficulties, there must be a clearly identifiable "management or technical problem which needs a systematic solution." In many of the organizations, managers and staff have developed sensible strategies for dealing with many, but not all, aspects of computing; however problems still recur (Kling, 1978f). Kling suggests a different approach to help understand why computer use is often problematic by expanding the traditional view of computing from that of a "tool" to that of a "package." The tool metaphor, which is appropriate for simple, individually controllable devices, such as hammers and pocket calculators, suggests that the item denoted may be used with few attendant problems. Of course, some tools may be more graceful, effective, and reliable than others, but in most cases one can safely focus on the device to understand its use and operation.

In contrast, the package metaphor describes a technology that is something more than the physical device. In the case of computing, the package includes not only hardware and software facilities, but also a diverse set of skills, organizational units to supply and maintain computer-based services and data, and sets of beliefs about what computing is good for and how it may be used efficaciously.

Many of the difficulties that users face in exploiting computer-based systems lie in the way in which the computing package is embedded in a complex set of social relationships. Most computer systems are shared with other users. Organi-

---

[20]A provocative account of one class of technical problem, that associated with "incomprehensible programs," may be found in Weizenbaum, 1976). Weizenbaum suggests that large ensembles of software which are programmed by many people over periods of years are most likely to be badly understood by their users, if not their implementors. This provocative line of analysis is grounded in some suggestive examples. It opens many important and unanswered questions: Who understands what in dealing with large hunks of software? When do documents help? How do implementors, maintainers, and users interact with software that they partially understand? When are the consequences of these developments particularly harmless or harmful?

zational information systems often depend on programs and data that are provided through several different social networks and which often entail contact with different social groups. Computing developers or users do not simply "disappear"; their involvement with a given computing system occurs at a "point" along career and organizational trajectories which they follow elsewhere.[21] When computing is embedded in a complex social setting, it becomes a social object, and the development and use of computer-based services a social act (Kling & Scacchi, 1979b, 1980; Scacchi, 1980).

The first studies to use the "package" concept were conceptual elaborations (Kling & Scacchi, 1979b; Kling, 1980d) and case studies (Conery, 1980; Gasser & Scacchi, 1979; Kling & Ahrentzen, 1980c; Scacchi, 1980). These have helped flesh out the ways in which the difficulties faced by many computer users arise from dealings with the "infrastructure" of the computing world (Kling & Gerson, 1977b, 1978g). King and Kraemer (1979) provide compelling data about the routine difficulties faced by users who deal with the computing package. (Their analysis is based on a study of 42 American urban governments and 16 urban governments in nine Western European countries.) King and Kraemer developed a battery of indices to measure different kinds of computing problems (e.g., user-staff interaction, technical), policies to alleviate problems (e.g., policy boards, user training), and the character of the computing milieu (e.g., age of site, sophistication of equipment). According to the tool conception of computing, problems should be least likely in those organizations with the most experience with computing, the more sophisticated computing installations, and the largest array of policies to alleviate computing problems. In examining the occurrence of computing problems, both those that are "technical" and those that arise in the interaction of users and computer specialists, they find that the larger, more sophisticated sites are those that are most plagued with computing problems.[22] They interpret this finding to mean (a) that the computing milieu becomes more problematic when it is more technically and socially complex (the package view), and (b) that policies are introduced reactively, to manage problems after they arise, not before. The package view casts a different light on computing than the tool view. While both systems rationalists and segmented institutionalists typically treat computerized systems as tools, the package view is most consistent with the latter conception.

---

[21]In highly dynamic occupations, organizations, and job markets the participants in any computing arrangements should all "disappear" from any given scene within a few years. But every exit from one place is an entrance to another, often also a scene of computing development and use. If the jobs are more stable than their incumbents, the "disappearing" participant is complemented by the "appearing" participant, who carries new expectations and is unfamiliar with existing systems and organizational protocols.

[22]Their findings and interpretations are more subtle than can be explained here. They elaborate a stage theory of computing development (Kraemer, 1980a) and find that certain "policy-problem mixes" occur at different stages and that the most advanced stages are the most troublesome.

*The integration of computing in work.* The package conception of computing suggests that computing is not simply a "tool" which "impacts" work life. Rather, dealing with computing can involve a complex array of social interactions. The key question then becomes how people do integrate computing into their working lives (and careers) rather than simply respond to a simply conceived technical stimulus.

One point of departure begins with the discretion that workers have over their use of computing. When workers have little discretion over their use of computing, it seems an external force to which they must adapt. Many white-collar workers, however, have some discretion over the conditions under which they will use computing.

Detectives in local police departments, for example, can initiate searches in extensive file systems relatively early or late in working a case. Individual detectives have substantial flexibility in integrating computing use into their work. Similar observations apply to the engineers at WESCO, described earlier, or to managers of stock portfolios, described by Keen and Scott-Morton (1978). People who have substantial discretion in their decisions about whether, when, and how to use computing can utilize it as a relatively flexible resource to fit many social agendas. It may be used primarily as a rational instrument to save time or ease the handling of complex bodies of information. Some modes of automation, such as automated testing of electronic components, may help managers employ less skilled workers to reduce costs or maintain stable supplies of labor. But its use may also be invoked as a symbolic gesture to appear innovative, as a medium for playful work (Kling & Ahrentzen, 1980c), or as a political instrumentality (Kling & Ahrentzen, 1980c; Kling 1980d). Little is known about the ways in which semiprofessional workers can adapt computing to their working lives, or the ways in which their working lives are altered with different computing arrangements. The interactionist approach, which emphasizes the ways in which people construct social meanings around the different elements of their working lives—tasks, technologies, and people, may provide the richest starting point for this line of inquiry.

## Decision Making

A critical issue faced by anyone who analyzes the role of automated information systems in decision making is the directness of the linkages among data, information, the way decisions are made, and the effects of different decision styles on activities within and by an organization. In this section we first examine this question from systems-rationalist and segmented-institutionalist perspectives; then we proceed to examine several classes of automated information systems. Analysts who focus on the role of computer-based systems in supporting decisions usually differentiate the different kinds of tasks normally performed at different hierarchical levels in organizations. The most common result is the trichotomy of "operations," "management control," and "strategic planning" (Burch, Strater, & Grudnitski, 1979). The lion's share of computing in organizations is devoted to applications that support routine operations within the organization: billing, transaction processing, simple record keeping, and engineering analysis. Fewer computational resources are devoted to applications that support the ability of managers to schedule, allocate, and control their resources. The smallest portion goes to the most analytically interesting and the rarest of all applications, those used to support long-range planning and policy analysis (Danziger, Kraemer, & King, 1978).

## Data, Information, Automation, and Decisions

Management scientists examine the direct links between data and decisions (Buffa, 1979; Burch, 1979; Chartrand, 1971), but analysts from other perspectives treat them as more problematic. H. A. Simon has clearly been the most influential theorist and structural analyst to link computer-based systems and decision making in organizations. This conjunction of computing and decision making is natural for Simon, since he has developed a view of organizations that emphasizes people's activities as decision makers and problem solvers (Simon, 1947, 1965, 1973, 1977). He argues that data and methods that help focus attention and evaluate choices improve the technical performance of a decision maker. He has also argued that computer-based information systems can help participants in organizations act more rationally by enabling them to compensate for the weaknesses in their abilities to select and remember information (Simon, 1973, 1977). To the extent that computer-based systems can help organize and filter larger volumes of information and that simulations enable them to consider a wider variety of complex dynamics simultaneously, Simon views computer-based systems as helpful instruments. Simon's claims have rarely been tested empirically, but they have provided the framework for much theorizing by systems rationalists about the social roles of computer-based information (Burch, Strater, & Grudnitski, 1979; Licklider & Vezza, 1978; Galbraith, 1977).

Many studies that relate computer-based information systems to decisions made by actors in organizations assume that there is usually a good match between the data available in computer systems and the kinds of information used to inform decisions (Burch, Strater, & Grudnitski, 1979; Kanter, 1977; Simon, 1977). In practice, the relation between the data contained in computerized information systems and the decisions that they are held to inform is problematic, although no one is surprised when the connections are direct and simple. For instance, most readers will have had the experience of altering airline flights in midtrip with the assistance of an airline reservationist using a computerized information system to find available flights. And when we are told that a police patrolman is able to locate more stolen vehicles with the assistance of an on-line stolen vehicles file, which he can access through the department's dispatcher, our expectation that data in computerized systems are useful is confirmed. These examples typify the many cases in which some participant in an organization directly uses some item of information from a computerized information system to inform a decision. Clearly, decisions based on data from computerized systems might be poor if the link were direct between data and decision, but the data themselves were in error.

Systems rationalists readily identify *swollen databases* as a troublesome phenomenon. Many automated information systems that provide inadequate data to their users have been built (Ackoff, 1971; Ackoff, 1967; Danziger, 1977a; Dery, 1977). The variety of problems encountered includes inappropriate data items, data that cannot be cross-referenced in useful ways, data that are inaccurate or out-of-date, and cumbersome reporting formats. Often these difficulties appear amenable to social or technical fixes.

Structural analysts also identify situations in which the *decisions are made independently of the formal data system.* Gibson (1975) reports an interesting study of the ways in which decisions to find new branches for acquisition were made by the staff of an Eastern bank. A management analyst who computed the costs and potential profitability of prospective acquisitions believed that his analyses were the primary elements in decisions about *which* banks to acquire. However, his supervisor, who was responsible for acquiring new banks, used a variety of informal sources such as friends and newspaper stories to *locate* prospective branches. Kling and Scacchi (1980b) also report several illustrative cases in which financial analyses for development projects and police manpower allocations were actually developed independently of the supporting computerized information systems.

Management science and structural analyses (Galbraith, 1977) typically focus *inward* on the formal task organization and on the decisions that are most critically related to the formal tasks. Some structural analyses (Danziger & Dutton, 1977b) and most interactionist and organizational-politics analyses also focus *outward* on the web of social and economic relations in which each social unit is embedded. These choices have profound effects on the understanding one has of computing use. For example, a systems rationalist would argue that computer use would be of little value to WESCO, discussed earlier if it did not help engineers design products better or more easily. In contrast, a political analyst would argue that automated design programs could be of tremendous value in helping engineers convince auditors of the aptness of their design choices, even if the automated system did not improve the quality or lower the direct cost of engineering design.

Systems rationalists emphasize the formal tasks of organizational participants (Alter, 1980; Burch, Strater, & Grudnitski, 1977; Galbraith, 1977; Kanter, 1977; Kerner, 1979; Killough, 1972; Simon, 1977). These include engineers designing, accountants calculating rates of return and balancing books, and clerks auditing and correcting records. Interactionist analyses also examine the work setting in organizations and examine the way in which the participants adopt, define, and negotiate all of the tasks they find important during their working day. People attend to ongoing social relations in their work groups, their relationships with clients and staff in other organizational units, relationships with auditors, and relationships with subordinates and superordinates in the organization. These "decisions" may focus on ways of making sense of new activities in one's immediate setting, maintaining autonomy or security in the work group, hiding unauthorized work practices, or maintaining the cooperation of the variety of people with whom the participant interacts. As we shall see later, these decisions, which are not about the public content of a participant's authorized task, may nevertheless play important roles in shaping the uses of computing in organizations.

But this broader ecology of social relationships in which organizational members act can also influence the relations between computer use and decisions. Computing can serve as a symbolic element in organizational life. In the cases of Riverville (Kling, 1978c) and of WESCO, described earlier, computing was used because it convinced important parties that decisions were being carefully made. In the case of Riverville, an automated information system was not used by managers in making the decisions in the municipal welfare agency; in the case of WESCO, engineering calculations were shifted from paper and pencil to computers to provide the appearance of greater accuracy. These are extreme cases in which computer use serves almost exclusively symbolic and political functions. However, more common examples are those in which computer use serves several social roles simultaneously. Computing may be used both to help a manager plan his organization's activities *and* to gain more credibility for his plans (Keen & Scott-Morton, 1978).

*Operations.* If there is any kind of task for which computer systems ought to pay off, it is the support of routine operations such as billing and airline reservations. Most of the system successes reported by managers or designers of computer-based systems were written from a systems-rationalist perspective. The typical report describes how goals were set and how the author and his coworkers successfully designed a computer-based system to meet them. All the drama focuses on the battles faced by the implementors in getting a "successful" system designed on time, priced within budget, and loved by its users.

There are relatively few careful studies of computer use in organizations, and few of these focus on routine operations. The better quality evaluations are less triumphant and report complex or ambiguous results. Many routine systems, such as traffic ticket processing, do help increase organizational efficiency (Colton, 1978; Kraemer, Dutton, & Northrup, 1980b). Systems may fail because they are technically unsound (e.g., response time is too slow in a demanding decision-making environment) or because they do not contain terribly useful or accurate information (Kling, 1978c). Most important, the criteria adopted for success may strongly influence one's evaluations. Laudon (1974), Colton

(1978), and Kraemer (Kraemer, Dutton, & Northrup, 1980b) have all studied police patrol support systems that provide information about wanted persons, stolen property, and criminal records to patrol officers in the field. Colton and Kraemer et al. examined the use of these systems by patrolmen and found the systems to be ''successful'' with respect to two measures: response time and job effectiveness. Colton contrasted a ''successful'' system in which the mean response time is 5–10 seconds with a nearly worthless system in which the mean response time was 10 minutes. Patrolmen made about four times as many inquiries per capita with the better automated system. Kraemer et al. found that police who used a local automated information system were much more likely to find people with outstanding arrest warrants and to locate stolen vehicles than were police who had access only to statewide and national systems. These are the kinds of internal efficiencies that systems rationalists identify as major values of computing use.

However, as one enlarges the array of activities and subjects included in an evaluation, the picture can alter dramatically. For example, Colton also reported that the (ex)chief of the Kansas City Police Department at times lamented the enhanced efficiency of Kansas City's system in helping patrolmen find stolen cars, unpaid parking tickets, and unregistered vehicles. His feelings stemmed from the increased field stops patrol officers made for these relatively minor offenses, which displaced time from other important police tasks. Laudon (1974) adopted a frame of reference that included the network of criminal justice agencies from police through courts. He argued that the increasing success of police in locating stolen vehicles and citing minor traffic offenders further clogged the already jammed courts. Furthermore, Kraemer et al. found that at locally automated sites police were more likely to detain people who should not have been detained and to arrest people who should not have been arrested.

Studies that identify an array of parties with possibly conflicting interests in computing support for routine operations are relatively rare, although Sterling's study (Sterling, 1979) of the frequency of billing errors attributed to automated systems is an example. Again, systems that may perform well according to narrow efficiency criteria (e.g., cost savings for the organization) may be problematic when viewed more broadly (e.g., inconvenience to clients). But the converse is also true: Computerized systems that seem ineffective when evaluated with respect to narrow criteria of internal efficiency may appear of substantial value to their users in the larger ecology of social relations. Automated information systems did little to improve the internal efficiencies of the welfare agencies in Riverville (Kling, 1978c), but they improved the agencies' image of efficient administration enough to attract funding more easily. The engineering simulations at WESCO, which confounded the designers but which helped move a stalled project through another stage of auditing, were valued for their political role.

Many computer-based systems persist because they save time, money, or tedium for their primary users, even though they may also pose important problems. As the groups affected by the use of a computer-based system increase in number and variety, one can expect that computing will serve some groups better than others. It is also likely that some groups will use computer-based technologies to alter their power and dependency relative to other groups instead of simply using the technology to maximize efficiencies within their own operations. Efficiency gains should be *findings,* however, rather than assumptions (Kraemer, Dutton, & Northrup, 1980b; Lucas, 1975c).

Systems rationalists usually evaluate computerized systems in terms of efficiency or effectiveness to the computer-using organization or to one of its subunits. In contrast, political analysts assume that different groups using the same computer system or the reports that it generates may have conflicting orientations and interests. In empirical inquiries, a political analyst would examine the orientations and interests of a wide array of participants in a computing milieu, rather than assume they were all relatively homogeneous. Thus a political analysis of an organization's milieu would be much more informative for understanding the utility and effects of computing on internal operations.

*Management control.* Control systems are usually initiated by or for managers to help them direct their organizational resources or the activities of their subordinates. These systems parallel lines of authority and usually measure only a few aspects of behavior or activity. Systems rationalists have argued that computer-based control systems can dramatically increase the effective control of higher level managers by providing them with fine-grained, timely, and accurate information about the activities within their administrative domains. But few studies have empirically investigated the accuracy of these claims.

Regardless of automation, organizational control systems may still be problematic. When the resource that is controlled is inanimate, such as parts for a manufacturing plant, the greatest dilemma may be in developing a good control procedure. Systems rationalists have observed that a poor procedure, independent of whether it is automated, may lead to costly overstock (Ackoff, 1971). Conversely, a good procedure, such as "material requirements planning," may demand such fine-grained records of product structures that for complex custom-manufactured items, digital computers provide the only economically feasible medium.

When the controlled activities depend critically on people's skill and cooperation, control systems can become even more problematic (Lawler & Rhode, 1976). The staff of an organization may have several conflicting goals, but most control or reporting systems are designed to measure only one or two aspects of performance. These control systems are easily "gamed" by the participants' simply altering their work style to "make the numbers look good." Assemblers may produce a greater number of lower quality components. Employment counselors may gravitate toward clients who are easiest to place in jobs. These shifts in performance may have severe consequences for the organization's achievement of various important goals. Coworkers in assembly lines may sufficiently intensify their competition that morale drops and production suffers through the costs of continual turnover and retraining. Employment counselors may divert their attention from those clients most in need; or they may place unsuitable clients in order to raise their own performance measures in the short run but lower both the agency's credibility with employers and the number of potential placements in the long run. These are dilemmas of organizational control, and they are not simply resolved through the use of automated reporting systems.

In studies of computer use it is often difficult to discern which alterations to attribute to the algorithm or strategy adopted and which alterations to attribute to the *automation* of the algorithm or strategy. This differentiation is particularly critical in the case of control systems. The keen separation of the algorithm from its automation is often moot in practice; computer-based information systems are often the only technically or economically feasible instrumentality to implement the algorithms.

The efficacy of several control systems has been studied in private firms (Markus, 1979) and in public agencies (Albrecht, 1976; Herbert & Colton, 1978; Kling, 1978c; Kling & Scacchi, 1980b; Kraemer, Dutton & Northrup, 1980b). Albrecht found that a case-load reporting system used in a large metropolitan court led to substantial reductions in case-processing time. These findings are consonant with the expectations of systems rationalism. In contrast, Kling (Kling, 1978c; Kling & Scacchi, 1980b) and Markus (1979) found control systems that were of little utility to managers in controlling activities within their administrative domains. One of Markus's cases focuses on a financial/ accounting system whose primary utility was to justify the existence of the office of the corporate comptroller. Similarly, Kling explained the persistence of an automated client-tracking system in a welfare agency primarily in political terms. He also reports the case of a manpower-allocation system that was well advertised in the "urban systems world" as helping police in Kansas City, Missouri, on a routine basis (Kling & Scacchi, 1980b). Despite the persistent belief that this system was well used, community conditions in Kansas City made the use of the model superfluous for the police staff between 1971 and 1976. In short, the efficacy of automated control systems varies considerably, systems persist because they may support a variety of agendas in addition to "management control," and systems may be believed to be routinely used even though they have been discontinued for several years. These complex patterns merit finer examination.

Kraemer et al. (1980b) investigated budget-monitoring systems in local governments and systems to help police commanders allocate their staff across beats, districts, and shifts. Herbert and Colton (1978) also studied local police manpower-allocation systems. Kraemer et al. found that budget-monitoring systems were favorably viewed by central managers in helping them to track the expenditures of operating departments and to predict potential problem areas. The budgetary control prerogative of central managers is so well accepted that the staff of operating departments did not find this surveillance intrusive. When the staff in operating departments did complain about budgeting systems, it was primarily because the systems designed to serve the needs of central managers did not serve *their* interests very well. Usually these complaints were assuaged by re-designing budget programs to accommodate the interests of staff both in central finance departments *and* in the operating departments.

However, neither Herbert and Colton nor Kraemer et al. found police man-power-control systems to be particularly efficacious. Herbert and Colton present a composite structural argument for the difficulties of linking automated man-power allocation to improved police performance. One line of argument ad-dresses computing and police performance as part of a larger strategy for crime deterrence. Manpower-allocation models are part of a strategy to increase the number of criminal apprehensions by increasing the speed with which a pa-trolman can reach the scene of a crime, and this is further increased by using manpower-allocation schemes to deploy patrolmen to those beats and shifts where apprehensions are most likely. But, Herbert and Colton argue, even if the models were relatively efficacious in helping police departments allocate their patrol, the effects on criminal activity would be negligible. Even if it were twice as likely that a suspect would be apprehended, his chance of conviction would be only slightly increased given the frequency of delays, plea bargaining, and dismissed cases in the American courts.

Kraemer et al. report that manpower-allocation models are least efficacious in cities where elected officials have relatively strong influence in computing deci-sions. To improve the efficacy of these models, they recommend structural solutions that include "placing manpower-allocation *automation* outside the agenda of control decisions available to elected officials [emphasis added]." But their finding may be reinterpreted in political terms which would suggest a different policy proposal. In such cities elected officials often have equally strong influence in other resource allocations as well, including the allocation of police. Since the quality of police service is a highly politicized topic in cities with moderate or high crime rates, city councilmen may refuse to cede to model-based analyses which result in the loss of patrol support in their districts. For example, though manpower-allocation models in Atlanta indicated that police should be moved from outlying suburban areas to the inner city, the councilmen in the suburban areas mustered a majority of votes and prevented the proposed shift. Because of this the models were viewed as ineffective. It is even possible that the adoption of manpower models is particularly attractive to police officials when they believe that they will have a difficult time convincing elected officials to accept the allocations they prefer. Much depends on the construction of "efficacy." Kraemer et al. rely on reported crime rates to evaluate the efficacy of manpower models, rather than more politically situated, but substantially less tangible, measures that tap the influence of police officials on manpower allocations. Nevertheless, their analyses provide a major contribution, since advocates of these models argue that their use should lead to decreased crime rates.

Examination of control systems for budgets and police manpower reveals interesting contrasts in efficacy. Here a structural perspective seems fruitful. Although both expenditure levels and crime rates are subject to exogenous influences, the extent to which departments spend their allocated budgets is mostly subject to administrative control. Moreover, budgetary control has been a traditional prerogative of central managers who, each fiscal year, set budgets for the operating departments. The staff of operating departments may feel that this budget monitoring by central accounting staff does not strongly intrude upon their traditional prerogatives.

When there are major conflicts over the control of critical organizational resources, computerized information systems may simply be used as political instruments by the contenders and fought as political intrusions. Albrecht (1979) presents an intriguing study of a case-tracking system that was introduced by judges on the legal staff in a Southern court to manage the work of the probation staff. Each of the two groups brought a different orientation to its work with defendants and convicts, and each was able to exercise moderate autonomy in its control over the meaning of its work. The legal staff members were concerned that cases be processed through the courts in an orderly manner and emphasized due process. In contrast, the probation staff emphasized rehabilitating individuals to become productive and trusted members of the community. When the information system was being designed, each group proposed a reporting structure which *minimized* its accountability and *maximized* its visibility and possible control over its other group. An automated system, which included a compromise set of data, was built and operated for four years. During this time it was primarily used as a record-keeping system and rarely used to enhance the control of either group of court administrators. Finally it was removed, and the court reverted to a manual record-keeping system. Albrecht considers this information system to have been used as an instrument in the power struggle between the legal staff and probation staff. Neither group was able to gain sufficient power to force the other to submit to its form of measurement and management. Since neither group could tightly manage the other and thus provide ''objective'' data about the productivity and efficacy of court activities, the automated system was a sterile tool. This case also highlights the close coupling of management control systems and the exercise of power in organizations. Organizational power will be carefully examined later in this chapter.

*Policy making and strategic planning.* The roles of automated information systems in policy making have been examined from management-scientific, structural, and political perspectives. This section examines sample studies from each framework.

An example of the management-scientific perspective is provided by a recent account of computer-based models by Licklider and Vezza:

> Computer-based modeling and simulation are applicable to essentially all problem-solving and decisions-making . . . they are far from ubiquitous as computer applications. . . . The trouble at present is that most kinds of modeling and simulation are much more difficult, expensive, and time-consuming than intuitive judgment and are cost-effective only under special conditions that can justify and pay for facilities and expertise. [1978, p. 1333]

These causal explanatory comments typify the weaknesses of much management-scientific commentary on the social effects of computer-based technologies. They embody a simplified version of Simon's decision-making perspective but lack the attention to social context which Simon, on occasion, provides (March & Simon, 1958). Neglecting the *obiter dictum* claim that modeling and simulation are "applicable to essentially all problem-solving and decision-making," presumably including ethical decisions, one is left with an odd account of the problems of modeling. Models "are far from ubiquitous," and "the trouble at present is" they are difficult and costly to develop and use. But the appropriateness of modeling is not linked by Licklider and Vezza to any discernible social setting or the interests of its participants. Licklider and Vezza's claims are not particularly aimed at policy making, since their observations apply to simulations for engineering design as well as for projecting the costs of new urban development. However, they adopt an important assumption of the management-science perspective when it is applied to information systems in policy making: differences in social settings are inconsequential in the use or utility of analytical models. But careful studies of the conditions under which computer-based technologies are adopted and used indicate that the character of social settings is a potent influence (Danziger & Dutton, 1977b; Greenberger, Crenson, & Crissey, 1976; Kling, 1974, 1978a, 1978c; Rule, 1974). Whether models and simulations "are applicable to essentially all problem-solving and decision-making" by virtue of their ability to help make informed decisions, or whether they are merely used to rationalize and obscure the bases of already-made decisions, depends in part on the degree of consensus over means and ends held by the active participants in a decision arena (Greenberger, Crenson, & Crissey, 1976; Kling, 1978a). Exactly which "special conditions" Licklider and Vezza believe "can justify and pay for facilities and expertise" cannot be discerned from their account. The reader is provided with an ambiguous analysis, framed in rational symbols, which can be interpreted within a broad variety of political understandings of organizational action.

The investigation of Greenberger et al. (1976) of the use of computer-based modeling systems as guides by policy makers in public agencies is primarily a structural analysis with some political elements. They studied the role of econometric models in developing U.S. fiscal policy, Forrester's WORLD III model, which stimulated the "limits to growth" debate in the United States, and an operations research model used by the City of New York for locating fire stations. An advocate of rational modeling would assume that models such as these could and should be used by policy makers to help sharpen their perceptions and select among alternative policies. Greenberger et al. rarely found that policy makers' choices were influenced directly by model-based analyses. Political actors often used models to generate support for policies selected in advance. When modeling efforts were influential in a decision arena, it was often the *modeler* who was called upon to inform decisions, rather than the *results of the modeling*. Models did help inform decisions indirectly by stirring partisan debate. While "modeling as advocacy" was best illustrated in the "limits to growth" debate and by their account of Laffer's predictions of the U.S. GNP in 1971, modeling as a tool of advocacy is commonplace. Under such conditions the most constructive role for models has been to support the advocates of different positions and to critique the assumptions of their antagonists.

Greenberger et al.'s subtle analysis of each modeling effort indicates that details and structural arrangements differ across problem domains and social arenas. Bargaining over firehouse locations in New York City differs from predictions of the gross national product in response to an increase in the Federal Reserve Board's prime interest rate; the actions of city councils and Congress differ from those of firemen's unions and bankers, but in each case Greenberger et al. take as given in the world of policy making its short time horizons, the fluctuating attention to issues, and the attempts of participants to mobilize support, placate critics, and displace problems not requiring immediate attention. They find that modeling does not easily fit the fragmented world of public policy making, particularly since modeling often requires clear, fixed definitions of the questions to be asked, while policy makers are often working with shifting definitions of the dilemmas they face. In addition, modeling efforts often require several years to design, program, and fine-tune, whereas many policy matters are resolved rapidly. Indeed, many political actors are voted out of office or transferred to other jobs within any two-year period. Greenberger et al. also note that models help an actor gain intellectual mastery over a given problem domain by *integrating* many factors and their interactions. In contrast, political arenas, particularly in the federal government, are designed to manage problems by *factoring* them into chunks that can be delegated to different administrative and regulatory agencies. Each of these structural features (time horizon, stability of people and problems) becomes an element in their explanation of why modeling has been problematic. In addition, they play down the political attractiveness to politicians of modeling and modelers under ordinary circumstances. If the modeler is called upon to provide sage advice, he or she can be viewed as a flexible political resource. The modeler can be chosen to have a world view closely aligned with the politician's, but to use the "objective authority" of modeling to enhance the credibility of partisan analyses.

Despite the structural discrepancies between model-based analyses and the dynamics of policy making that they emphasize, Greenberger et al. are optimistic about the value of modeling efforts and recommend strategies to improve their utility. They focus on social strategies that institutionalize the development of specific models that may be used to answer recurrent questions and intensify the uses of countermodeling and multimodeling. They clearly eschew those explanations of the failures of rational modeling efforts that hinge on the technical weaknesses of contemporary models.

In a study of the use of automated information systems in municipal policy making, Kling (1978e) contrasted the explanatory power of systems rationalism and organizational politics. In the 42 cities he studied, automated information systems providing demographic, economic, housing, and transportation data were available to most of the city councils, planning staff, and top administrators. Computer-based reports were provided to the city council several times a year. In about half the cities these reports never resulted in clearer perceptions or surprises about city conditions; only in 10 percent of the cities did these results occur. However, in 35 percent of the cities the reports were generally used to enhance the legitimacy of decisions and personal perceptions of city councilmen. In about 10 percent of the cities the reports were generally used to gain publicity for programs. In about 25 percent of the cities these reports were sometimes used to legitimize perceptions and gain publicity for programs supported by council members.

These patterns could be attributed to the primitive state of automation in American cities. If cities utilized more sophisticated data resources, then perhaps policy makers would find more surprises in the reports they received and be less likely to use them as political resources. Kling developed several measures of the degree and richness of automated data systems supporting policy analysis in the 42 cities. He found that in more highly automated cities, policy makers were more likely to report clearer perceptions and surprises gleaned from reports based on automated analyses. However, he also found that policy makers in more highly automated cities were more likely to use the same reports to legitimize their personal perceptions and gain publicity for their preferred programs. These findings indicate that computer-based analyses are a social resource used by political actors in the same manner as any other social resource. They do not alter the policy-making style of political bodies but are appropriated and adapted by policy makers to *their* styles of organizational work.

### Recapitulation

There is a vast literature devoted to the design of information systems for organizations (Buffa & Miller, 1979; Burch, Strater, & Grudnitski, 1979; Chartrand, 1971; Galbraith, 1977; Kerner, 1979; Li, 1972; Simon, 1973), but remarkably few studies actually evaluate the use and social consequences of systems in place. Management scientists are usually careful to specify the precise theoretical conditions under which their algorithms achieve specified economic effects, but the discrepancy between the typically static assumptions of these analyses and the more dynamic realities of organizational life make the results problematic and open to empirical verification. Those analysts who do investigate systems in place are often surprised. There is an oral folklore among computer specialists of automated systems that "work," others that are "troublesome," and still others that have "failed." But the public theoretical literature of systems rationalists gives little insight into the conditions under which even the best technically designed system will be less than useful.

Earlier, we examined a host of empirical studies of the roles of automated information systems in decision making within organizations. These studies indicate that computing can play multiple social roles within the host organizations. While systems rationalists are concerned that computing be successfully applied to increase organizational efficiencies, they rarely inquire into the relationship between computer use and the social order within the computer-using organization. In contrast, this has been a central issue for segmented institutionalists. The few studies that examine the interplay between automated information systems and the social order of their host organizations find that computing is markedly adapted to fit the social world in which it is used.[23]

While the studies cited here have been carried out within public agencies, there is no reason to believe that the internal organizational dynamics of private organizations are substantially different. McLean and Riesing (1977) investigated a technically interesting decision-support system in a major Eastern bank and found that it was rarely used for management decisions because budgeting was incremental from year to year. Managers felt little incentive to streamline their operations when they could not transform their labors into new organizational resources during annual budget setting. Remarkably, bank managers did not view the use of a technically interesting decision-support system as an end in itself but expected its use to help them reap greater organizational rewards. However, they did not possess sufficient authority to alter the bank's budgetary process. A variation on this theme is found in Pettigrew's study of decisions to adopt computing in a private manufacturing firm (Pettigrew, 1973), which indicates that office politics can be as pervasive in private firms as in public agencies.

For systems rationalists, computerized information systems provide an essential means for key social actors to measure, analyze, comprehend, and act sensibly in a complex, dynamic world. Systems-rationalist accounts are most adequate in explaining the way in which computing can be embedded in the operations of organizations and of management control systems that remain well within organizational boundaries. As the boundaries of the computerized system

---

[23]In addition to the studies described here, see Colton's studies of computer applications for police (Colton, 1979), the studies of Kling (1978c) and Laudon (1974) described earlier, and Stewart's studies of large-scale decision-support systems in British firms (Stewart, 1972).

grow to include larger, more complex social worlds beyond the control of computer users, the segmented-institutionalist accounts gain greater explanatory power. In helping to analyze the uses of automated data systems in public policy making the systems-rationalist account is of less value. Thus these two perspectives may be viewed as complementary and make most sense in social and technical worlds of quite different character. As we shift from organizations to the larger society, we might expect this asymmetry in explanatory power to increase.

## Organizational Power

We have already discussed managerial control, by which an administrator increases his influence within a domain of activity over which he has primary supervisory responsibility. However, there are many arenas of organizational life in which activities are influenced by many participants and in which some may attempt to increase their relative influence. Managerial rationalists emphasize the role of formal authority in organizational life and ignore power as an organizing concept. Segmented institutionalists, on the other hand, emphasize power, particularly the relative power of groups inside and outside organizations. One participant exerts power over others to the exten that he can effectively influence them to do and see things his way.[24] It is a relatively common observation that computer-based systems increase the influence of those who have access to the technology, can organize data to their advantage, and can understand computing use (Danziger, 1977a).[25] Downs (1967), for example, suggests that data custo-

---

[24]"Power" is a commonplace term that carries a rich set of social assumptions with its different uses. This deceptively simple characterization of power embodies a rich array of assumptions: that power accrues to people or groups, but not to systems or structures; that power is "zero-sum" within an identified social arena; and that the exercise of power need not be overt, but may be done by structuring social arrangements to satisfy the power. This contrasts with usages in systems theory in which power is an attribute of systems or structures and is not "zero-sum." It also glosses over the distinction between "power" and "influence" made by Bachrach and Baratz: power wielders can apply negative sanctions which influentials do not have (Bachrach & Baratz, 1963; Kling, 1974). Such a distinction can be of importance in operationalizing power in empirical studies. For a sensitive examination of "power" as a theoretical term, see Lukes, 1978.

[25]There is an important distinction between "information politics" and "resource politics." In the former, information is used as a political resource to help convince or intimidate others into accepting one's preferred line of action. "Resource politics" refers to those cases where control over computing resources provides a base for other forms of influence. For example, a comptroller in a business firm may fight to maintain control over a centralized computing center in the finance department because it provides him with a growing staff (of computer specialists) and budget, relieves him from depending on a less controllable organizational unit for critical data processing, and leads other managers, high and low in the organization, to curry his favor when they have data processing tasks for which they wish special attention. This section examines information politics, not resource politics. See Danziger, Dutton, Kling, & Kraemer, 1980 for a keen account of both resource politics and information politics.

dians will gain power relative to other staff, and that full-time administrators will gain power relative to elected officials in urban governments.

Bjorn-Anderson and Pederson (1977) examined the role of production-scheduling systems in altering relations of influence and power among production planners, plant managers, and production managers in 5 Danish factories.[26] In this exploratory study, 40 managers were interviewed and the factories were studied for about one year. In addition, 18 managers and planners completed quantitatively coded questionnaires on the role of computing in their work and in altering the bases and patterns of influence in the organization. The firm studied by Bjorn-Anderson and Pederson is of particular interest since it was organized, in part, as a matrix organization, with major decisions made through cross-departmental committees in order to integrate diverse functional units (Galbraith, 1977). While shifts of influence were not overtly intended or advertised, they did accompany the use of these systems. Production planners increased their influence relative to both plant managers and production managers. Both peer ratings and self-ratings indicate comparable increases. In contrast, according to peer ratings, both plant managers and production managers gained or lost little influence in plant operations. According to their self-ratings, production managers believed they lost influence and plant managers believed they increased their influence. Bjorn-Anderson and Pederson also examined the bases of power (sanctions, formal status, "up-to-date knowledge") for these participants and the ways in which these bases of power were influenced by computing. In particular, production planners attributed increases in their status, expert knowledge, and up-to-date knowledge to the automated scheduling system. They reported no change in their ability to levy sanctions against others. In contrast, a majority of the production managers reported losses of formal status and the ability to levy sanctions. Some also reported losses in their relative level of expert knowledge about plant operations.[27] In fact, during the study one plant manager was demoted and another was shifted from line management to a special studies group. In short, Bjorn-Anderson and Pederson found that the automated production scheduling system altered patterns of influence and power among key participants in an organization where no such consequences appear to have been intended.

If automated systems can have power impacts when they are utilized in relatively unpoliticized arenas, how potent are they likely to be when they are used in settings where participants consciously maneuver to increase and exercise their power? Public policy making in local governments is one such arena.

---

[26]They did not examine the economic payoffs of these systems but report that the factory staff believe that the systems help improve production efficiencies.

[27]This is just one of the places in which the distinction between power and influence (Bachrach & Baratz, 1963) can make a subtle difference in the way findings are interpreted. Since Bachrach and Baratz link power to the threat of sanction, they would say that the data indicate that planners gain influence, but that production managers lost power.

Recently, Kling (1978e) and Kraemer and Dutton (1979a) investigated the role of automated information systems in altering power relations among key participants in American municipal governments. They collected data in 42 cities to investigate alterations in power relations attributable to the use of computer-based reports in policy formation and policy making. Data about the uses of computer-based reports and their roles in influencing different policy preferences were collected in interviews with 10 to 20 key actors in each city; these actors included data custodians, urban planners, mayors, chief administrative officers, city council members, department heads, and assistants to top administrators. In each city the researchers coded the extent to which different classes of actors (e.g., mayor and staff, council members, planners) gained or lost power because of computer-based reports. "Power" was treated operationally as "effective influence"; actors who appeared to have gained influence in the outcomes of decisions made during the previous two years were viewed as having gained power. A weak group gaining power need not be relatively strong, and a strong group losing power will not be relatively weak.

In a majority of the cities some participants discernibly gained or lost power as a result of computer use. However no single role taker gained or lost power; that is, in different cities, different participants were gainers or losers because of computer use, although many actors had their power unaffected. (Respondents also attributed shifts of power to a variety of sources including demographic changes in the city and personal style of top officials.) Data custodians (e.g., planners) were most likely to gain, and never lost, power because of computer-based analyses; nevertheless, they remained relatively weak. At best they appeared as the favored experts of more powerful actors, and at worst their counsel was distrusted and their reports received little sustained interest. Supporting Downs's hypotheses (Downs, 1967), city councilmen were most likely to lose (20 percent) and rarely gained (5 percent) power because of computer-based analyses. Moreover, as suggested by Downs, top-level administrators (city managers and chief administrative officers) often gained (27 percent) and rarely lost (3 percent) power when there were any shifts at all. The conditions under which mayors and departments gained and lost power were more complex. The top elected officials in a city were more likely to gain power and less likely to lose power than all other role takers except the data custodians. This suggests that computer-based analyses *reinforce* the patterns of influence in municipal governments (Kling, 1978e; Kraemer & Dutton, 1979a). Kling (1974) suggests that computer-based information systems reinforce the structure of power in an organization simply because computer-based systems are expensive to develop and use. For this reason, top officials who can authorize large expenditures will, on the average, ensure that the expensive analyses serve their interests.

However, the data reported by Kling and Kraemer and Dutton indicate even more subtle patterns of influence. Correlations were computed between power shifts attributable to computing and measures of both city size and the extent of automation in policy analysis. Departments gained power, while top officials lost power in the *larger* cities; this pattern mirrors the structure of influence in American municipalities. In the smaller cities the mayors and city managers were able to keep informed of department operations and place a strong stamp upon municipal activities. In larger cities the departments were often vast fiefdoms (particularly police and public works), and the top officials were placed in a weaker bargaining position relative to department heads. In the cities with several hundred thousand residents the larger departments had sufficiently large budgets to afford their own skilled analysts to build information systems that suited their needs and to do it with less scrutiny from top officials. Thus in these cities it was not top officials who gained most, but managers who were sufficiently high in the organizational hierarchy that they could command large resources.

A general observation drawn from the analysis of computer-based systems for policy analysis in cities is that such systems often serve as *political, power-reinforcing* instruments (Kling, 1978e; Kraemer & Dutton, 1979a). They differ from automated upward-reporting systems, which may cause data providers to lose power to data collectors (Kling, 1974). In general, to predict the influences of a computer-based information system, one must have a sharp characterization of the distribution of influence in its intended social setting (Dutton & Kraemer, 1978; Gibson, 1975; Greenberger, Crenson, & Crissey, 1976). Automated information systems should be viewed as social resources that are absorbed into ongoing organizational games but do not materially influence the structure of the games being played. In organizations in which "normal business" is highly politicized, computing will not a neutral resource; it can easily be used to reinforce the power of potent actors.

This analysis is neither vacuous nor obvious. Recently, McLaughlin (1978) recommended that the Office of the President should develop a "policy management system" with extensive automated support to help provide greater control over the (then) U.S. Department of Health, Education and Welfare. Since the federal cabinet agencies have developed into extensive bases of independent power vis-à-vis the presidency, they may be analogous to departments in the larger cities. The analysis presented here suggests that extensive automation is likely to reinforce the power of the executive agencies, in which case McLaughlin's strategy would backfire.

This analysis indicates that the political order of the social setting in which a computer-based system is utilized must be as well understood as the technical features of the system in order to predict the probable uses and impacts of computing. This principle undermines the sufficiency of the formulations of analysts who emphasize the technical characteristics of systems and neglect the political dynamics of the settings in which automated data systems are utilized (Burch, Strater, & Grudnitski, 1979; Donovan & Madnick, 1977; Dorf, 1977; Kanter, 1977). [*The discussion on social and public policy issues that appears at this juncture in the original paper has been deleted for space reasons—Eds.*]

# CONCLUSIONS

For many readers this will have been a long journey through specialized studies of computer uses and their social "consequences." Rather than speculate about possible future "consequences" of widespread computer use, we have taken a rather conservative tour through studies that examine the social character of existing computer technologies in established settings. During the last decade scholars have published several dozen useful empirical studies of computing use and its consequences in social life. These vastly sharpen our conceptions of computing but are a meager base of information on which to generalize about "computing," particularly given the wide array of computing modalities and social contexts of use.

## The Impacts of Computing in Review

The reader's most direct question might be, "In short, what have computers done to or for people who interact with them, or for activities that depend on them?" It is certainly tempting to answer a question posed in these terms (Bjorn-Anderson & Rasmussen, 1980a). But the answers would be misleading; after all, the first thing we learn is that computers by themselves "do" nothing to anybody. Earlier in the chapter, we said that computing is selectively adopted in a given social world and organized to fit the interests of dominant parties. There is sufficient evidence that computing use is purposive and varies between social settings; little causal power can be attributed to computers themselves. Electronic digital computers can be turned to selected ends to amplify the speed or ease of their accomplishment. The technology is malleable, though not entirely plastic. Thus, to speak of the "social impacts of computing" is as invalid as it is valid (Laudon, 1976). The "consequences" of computer use are simply the consequences of lines of purposive action married to computing. As these actions change, the "consequences" may well change. If we say that the "impacts" of computing have been to slightly enlarge the jobs of white-collar workers and not increase their level of supervision, these "impacts" may be reversed under altered economic or industrial conditions.[28] Similarly the finding that computerized data systems are used to reinforce the power of already-powerful groups might not apply to social worlds in which the participants were thoroughly uninterested in increasing their power, or which actively sought ways to distribute power among the participants maximally. Each of these "impacts" happens because of some underlying patterned social process, and speaking about

---

[28]See Mumford, 1978, which interprets variations in the extent to which computerized systems enlarge or constrict the jobs of clerical users in terms of the values of the managers who authorized their development.

the "impacts of technology" often distracts attention from the social processes by which they are developed, adopted, and used.

Second, the ways in which an investigator demarcates a problem, collects data, and interprets his findings are all keenly influenced, but not determined, by his prior theoretical commitments. Normally this is no surprise, but the notion is certainly not well integrated into computer science.

Third, we have studies that are primarily informed by systems rationalism contrasted with those that are informed by segmented institutionalism. While these are very broad labels covering many more carefully refined perspectives, they have helped us cluster major lines of analysis in a useful way. In our examination of studies of decision making, we found that systems rationalism had the greatest descriptive adequacy for situations that involved relatively few social groups and were relatively well controlled by agents with centralized authority. As the boundaries of the computerized system expand to include larger, more complex social worlds that are outside the control of computer users, the segmented-institutionalist accounts gain greater explanatory power.[29] In explaining the use of computerized data systems in complex social arenas such as public policy making in urban governments, systems-rationalist accounts are of limited value (Danziger, Dutton, Kling, & Kraemer, 1980; Kling, 1978e; Kraemer & Dutton, 1979a; Markus, 1979). Thus these two perspectives may be viewed as complementary and make most sense in social and technical worlds of markedly different character. As we shift from organizations to the larger society, this asymmetry in explanatory power becomes more critical. Examination of studies of power shifts between participants in public policy making show the systems rationalist position to be of little utility. It does little to help us understand the vulnerability of the public when critical computerized systems are embedded in complicated and loosely governed organizational arrangements. In the case of privacy studies, the two theoretical perspectives differ on just this point. Systems rationalists attempt to develop procedures and system designs that are likely to be trouble free "in principle"; segmented institutionalists argue that the "principle" may have to be very different in complex social orders, since even a proliferation of clean systems may be problematic for public life (Rule, McAdam, Stearns, & Uglow, 1980).

Another important and related difference between these two perspectives lies in the elements of social life to which each directs attention. Systems rationalists emphasize tasks that are related to the production of some specific product or service. Moreover, the identified tasks are typically "legitimate," rather than "deviant" [Johnson & Douglas, 1978]. In an engineering firm attention may be

---

[29]One line of analysis that has not been examined in this paper argues that many occasions of computer use implicitly encompass settings of larger social scope since computer users are linked to vendors, consultants, service providers, programmers, data entry staff, etc., on whom they depend for support (Gasser & Scacchi, 1979; Kling & Gerson, 1977b; Kling, 1979a).

focused on design, accounting, or market analysis, not price fixing, cover-ups, and bribery. Segmented institutionalists are interested in the common activities and orientations of the social world in which computing is embedded. They are as likely to expand their view and examine the environment surrounding computer users' interactions with vendors, customers, regulators, and competitors, as they are to rivet their attention on the identified task to which computing is being applied. Further, they are not squeamish about examining any kind of activity, legitimate or deviant, or social relationship that sheds light on the social character of computing.

Fourth, computing has often been used in ways which have relatively subtle consequences for participants in computer-using organizations. The studies examined here find several "consequences" of common patterns of computer use. Many white-collar workers attribute job-enlarging rather than job-constricting attributes to the use of automated information systems. Computerized information systems have not been extensively employed to supervise white-collar workers more closely. Workers with some organizational power can effectively resist the attempts of other occupational groups to monitor their work by the use of computerized information systems. As a class automated systems for managerial control are problematic. Those that are aimed at activities wholly within the authoritative domain of central administrators (e.g., budget monitoring) seem markedly more effective than those aimed at activities whose contingencies are less subject to administrative control. When automated data systems are utilized in public policy formation and policy making, they appear more as instruments to help actors mobilize support and legitimize their policy preferences than as "decision-making" aids. Overall, automated information systems seem to be organized so that they enhance the power of already powerful groups in computer-using organizations. Their use seems to weaken the ability of elected officials to formulate policy and retain political control over public agencies. There is also some evidence that some members of the public experience inordinate difficulties in correcting errors made in routine computerized transactions with computer-using organizations. These findings are as much contingent upon the interests that computing is organized to serve as they are upon the simple presence of an automated system.

## Theoretical Approaches to Computing Developments

Much of the attention in computer science is placed on technical innovations and their probable uses (Kling & Gerson, 1977b). One of these, the development of "chip"-based microprocessors, has excited enthusiasm about the possibility of genuine personal computing (Kay & Goldberg, 1977). And technologies of broader "social scope" have been frequently proposed, including electronic funds-transfer systems (Kling, 1978b, 1978d), electronic mail, community information utilities (Press, 1974; Sackman & Nie, 1970), and even "wired societies'' (Carne, 1979; Hiltz & Turoff, 1978; Martin, 1978). What guiding images shall we adopt when trying to understand how these technologies may be developed? Which social and technical choices are sensible? Who will be best served by them under the different potential arrangements? What may be the broader consequences of developments such as these? In this review of recent empirical research, we have examined the utility of two very roughly drawn social perspectives in order to understand the development, use, and consequences of computer-based systems that employ current technologies (Table 24.1).

The guiding images for many published accounts of new computing developments are drawn from systems rationalism (Boden, 1978; Carne, 1979; Champine, 1978; Chartrand, 1971; Dorf, 1977; Hiltz & Turoff; Kay & Goldberg, 1977; Martin, 1978; Sackman & Nie, 1970; Sanders, 1977; Simon, 1977). These images are not all identical, but they make important common assumptions and place an overriding emphasis on elements of social life that are positively correlated with broadly desirable (and often abstractly drawn) social outcomes. Systems rationalists often argue that more sophisticated forms of computing would be organized in ways that are less problematic (Donovan & Madnick, 1977). These convictions rest on a theory of social change in which technologies in and of themselves play dominant and possibly democratizing roles. Such hopes are admirable, and computing has long been allied with utopian traditions,[30] but such theories are troublesome to formulate carefully, let alone validate (Laudon, 1980; Lauer, 1973). There are tremendous differences between concepts which can mobilize important pro-social aspirations and those which can help predict the likely outcomes of purposive behavior. In this regard systems rationalism is problematic. When its organizing concepts are applied to wholly artificial systems, they can have inordinate analytical power. The methods of operations research, for example, can help schedule a complex array of tasks with subtle priorities and dependencies in a relatively optimal manner (Buffa & Miller, 1979). But the analytical methods of management science and the managerial strategies of classical management theory embody certain critical social assumptions. In particular, they assume that ''goals are known, tasks are repetitive, output of the production process somehow disappears, . . . resources in uniform quality are available (Thompson, 1967, p. 5)'' to all participants, and that all

---

[30]Boguslaw (1965) was the first analyst to examine the different kinds of utopian assumptions that underlie strategies of computerization. When systems analysis has been applied to problems of state and local governments, the resulting computerized systems have had conservative social consequences (Laudon, 1974) when they have come near meeting their original, progressively articulated goals (Kling, 1978c; Kraemer & King, 1979). While it is always easy to explain away these findings by reference to clumsy technologies or insufficient communication (Hiltz & Turoff, 1978), progressive reformers have been unable to formulate careful accounts of the embedding of computing in social worlds characterized by considerable inequalities of wealth, power, and expertise, and inequalities of opportunity to obtain them (Collins, 1975).

participants can cooperate sufficiently to provide adequately reliable data in a timely manner. These are simply the social prerequisites for the technical payoffs to be realized. It takes yet another set of assumptions about the interests of computer users to believe that they will guide their actions primarily on the data or options produced by their algorithms (Ackoff, 1971; Danziger et al., 1980; Dery, 1977; Kling, 1978c). Difficulties occur when the analytically powerful techniques whose efficacy depends on this set of fragile social assumptions are translated from the world of artifice to natural settings. Only when these critical social assumptions are in fact fairly descriptive of the natural setting may systems designed according to these rationales be extremely workable and useful to participants; troubles begin when these assumptions do not hold.[31] (Thus what is "theoretically possible" in a highly constrained "artificial environment" may be extremely unlikely in a more loosely structured and less stable "natural environment."[32]

Some versions of systems rationalism provide provocative metaphors for conceptualizing large-scale ("system-wide") social behavior. Cybernetic models, in particular, help one link the "control of social systems" to flows of information to different participants. They also provide a language for thinking about "adequate levels of control," adaptability, and the susceptibility of systems to overcontrol, instability, and failure when "subsystems" are improperly configured. These models are particularly inappropriate for social settings in which many competing groups, rather than one distinguished group, hold legitimate power, when there is serious conflict over appropriate goals and their relative importance. Goals may even be unclear, and, consequently, any concept

---

[31]Troubles only begin for those who have the temerity to try out their ideas in complex social settings. A common strategy to avoid these difficulties is to simplify the "natural system" so that discontinuities are not apparent. This is most obviously attempted in accounts of computerized systems that are to be used in extremely volatile arenas such as public policy making or the management of public agencies at federal, state, and local levels. While scholars who examine these arenas find them rife with conflict (Banfield, 1961; Lowi, 1979), and even possibly "ungovernable" (Yates, 1977), many social analysts of computing simply minimize the level of strife and treat these governments as if they were business enterprises manufacturing simple product lines (Chartrand, 1971; Dorf, 1977; Martin, 1978; Sanders, 1977). These analytical conveniences make the resulting accounts of computer use easier to comprehend and thoroughly inapplicable for most practical, pedagogical, and scholarly purposes. (See Mowshowitz, 1976, for a strikingly careful account of computer use in complex social settings that does not share these flaws.)

[32]Some managerial rationalists have valiantly attempted to expand the limited conceptual vocabulary criticized here (Galbraith, 1977; Simon, 1977; Thompson, 1967). Principally, these attempts have emphasized bounded rationality (Simon, 1977), environmental uncertainty (Thompson, 1967), slack resources (Galbraith, 1977), and related concepts drawn from economics and cognitive psychology. These revisions have been useful in making the perspective more workable for simple organizations (Allison, 1971) but have not been terribly successful in extending the predictive scope of the perspective to include volatile arenas of larger social scope (Collins, 1975; Markus, 1979,; Perrow, 1979; Pfeffer, 1979; Strauss, 1978).

of appropriate "social direction" will merely reflect the preferences of some particular group or the analyst.

The most misleading forms of systems rationalism for understanding the dynamics of computer use in complex settings are those in which conflict over system use is a surprise, shifts of power are ignored, and even cost overruns in developments are unexpected[33] (Burch, Strater, & Grudnitski, 1979; Chartrand, 1971; Dorf, 1977; Kanter, 1977; Kerner, 1979).

Segmented institutionalists begin from a complementary position. Rather than take a streamlined technical system as a point of departure, they start with relatively complex social orders and attempt to find adequate descriptions and theories to understand social life, with and without computing (Collins, 1975; Galbraith, 1979; Strauss, 1978). The primary advantage of this strategy is that it is most likely to maintain descriptive adequacy as the social scope of proposed computing arrangements enlarges and the dynamism of the social world in which they are used and maintained increases (Kling, 1977a; Kling & Gerson, 1977b; Kling, 1979a; Laudon, 1974; Rule et al., 1980). For conventional computer science its greatest shortcoming is the sheer difficulty of translating concepts that help one understand the dynamics of social conflict (e.g., class, power, definition of the situation, negotiated order, structural interest, mobilization of bias, legitimation, coalition, value conflict, negotiation context) into specific design criteria for new computerized technologies.

Some segmented-institutionalist analyses are also nondeterministic (Kling & Gerson, 1977b, 1978g; Kling, 1978a, 1979a; Rule, 1974; Strauss, 1978). But that is an important contribution because they provide richer alternatives (Hoos, 1974) than do the naively deterministic approaches. They stimulate the analyst to conceive of a larger variety of outcomes of technical developments; they do not predict which outcomes are most likely, except in rather general terms (e.g., high levels of conflict over system use, no perceived power shifts between computers and nonusers). This may appear as a relative weakness of the segmented institutionalist approaches, but systems rationalist analyses also have genuine difficulties in providing decent predictions when applied to complex settings of computer use, both inside and outside organizations.

This chapter has been deliberately unspecific about the units of analysis and has casually moved back and forth between small groups, complex organizations, urban governments, institutional sectors (e.g., banking), social worlds, and the larger society in which they are embedded. For carrying out specific analyses the shifts in level of analysis cannot be so casual, and greater care must be taken in characterizing the particular social world in which computing is

---

[33]Computing specialists often have keen practical perceptions about these matters, which are not, however, integrated into conventional systems-rationalist approaches (Burch, Strater, & Grudnitski, 1979; Champine, 1978; Simon, 1977). Rather, they are part of a folklore that is carried by magical proverbs such as "Murphy's law."

utilized. This requires some description of that social world since scientific research laboratories (Scacchi, 1980) differ from manufacturing plants (Markus, 1979), and both, in turn, differ from a community in which core services are administered by local offices of regional or national organizations (Kling, 1978c; Rule, 1974). This places a strong burden on the social analyst of computing to develop keen accounts of the technologies in use and of the basic social processes that organize the institutional, occupational, and social worlds in which the technology is employed.[34] As we have seen earlier, computer use is often contoured to fit the stresses and strains perceived by the social elites who control decisions regarding computing adoption. Thus the ecology of interests in any social setting must be a starting point for understanding computer use.

Such a starting point profoundly influences the selection of appropriate research methods—the greater the detail required to adequately specify the social context of computing use and the "ecology of interests" it includes, the less the utility of research instruments that depend on a priori knowledge of the patterning of relevant interests (e.g., closed-coded surveys). Thus most segmented institutional analyses have relied upon qualitative field studies.

## Prospects

Most serious studies of computing in social life are prospective and aim to improve the lot of those who control computing resources, those who use them, or those whose lives may be profoundly affected by their use. The utilization and utility of research are often problematic, and studies conducted in these areas suffer the same fate as studies on other timely topics. They catch the attention of computer specialists, managers, policy makers, and other interested parties rather haphazardly. Some of the best studies are too careful and "stuffy" to appeal to large audiences. Some studies capture attention and crystallize because they are well written and timely. Westin and Baker's study has influenced much of the federal policy-making community's views of information privacy (Westin & Baker, 1972). Kraemer's studies of software transfer have also been influential in policy making within HUD (Kraemer, 1977). Weizenbaum's insightful, but polemical and uneven, analysis of computing has spurred debates among computer scientists about the social character of computing and the theoretical

---

[34]See Kling, 1978b; Mowshowitz, 1976, for examples. Attempts to situate computing developments in the broader society depend on a priori conceptions of the social order and the role technologies play in social development. Are information technologies "decisive" elements in social change (Bell, 1973, 1979)? Is the locus of broad social change to be found in a technostructure formed of middle managers and technical experts in large corporations (Galbraith, 1979)? Or do technical changes lag behind administrative changes in the larger organizational ecologies (Lowi, 1979)? These questions again illustrate how a priori conceptions of social life are critical for appreciating the social roles of computing developments. (For a critique of Bell, 1973, see Steinfels, 1979; for commentary on Galbraith, 1979, see Gintis, 1979).

and social limits of artificial intelligence (Weizenbaum, 1976). Similarly, the studies of other analysts have attracted attention in other specialized communities.

It is possible to be optimistic, complacent, or pessimistic in drawing conclusions from these research streams. During the 1970s we learn to treat the social dynamics of computing development and use it far more carefully; the ways in which its uses and influences are altered by the host social setting are becoming well documented. These increases in analytical sophistication provide a basis for scholarly optimism.

However, there are still no adequate theoretical accounts of computing in social life. (It is also fair to say that there are few candidate theoretical accounts of the role of technology in social life.) The accounts of computing, whether developed by scholars or by laymen, are strongly limited by the primitive state of social theory in general, and by the common myths that surround complex technologies in particular. One may easily be sanguine that accounts of computing in social life will grow in sophistication along with advances in social theory and research method generally.

As one turns from the content of these studies to the broader social context that they address, the grounds for optimism grow thinner. Computer use is rapidly expanding in the United States. It is hard to believe that the public could best be served by rapid development of a poorly understood technology. In characteristic American fashion, a good deal of attention is spent in developing the ''know-how'' of computing technologies and their applications. As a consequence, technical improvement in the quality of equipment and the richness of applications software have grown immensely. However only about two dozen scholars currently undertake serious, empirically-grounded investigations of the social aspects of computer use. Their studies have influenced some aspects of public policy related to computing development, particularly policies regarding privacy of personal information. But the pace and scope of new computing developments far outstrip our capability to carefully understand their near- and long-term social repercussions (King & Kraemer, 1978). With such meager systematic attention, it is hard to believe that important understandings about the long-term and more subtle social features of computing will be acquired before inappropriate commitments are made.

# Postscript, 1988

## Rob Kling

### THEORETICAL ADVANCES AND EMPIRICAL STUDIES:
### 1980–1987[35]

Since the bulk of this paper was originally written in 1979, more than 100 scholarly books and articles and several literature surveys have been published about the social dimensions of computerization (Attewell & Rule, 1984; King & Kraemer, 1986; Danziger, 1985; Hirschheim, 1986). In addition, there have been interesting empirical and theoretical studies published in Danish, French, German, Italian, and Norwegian, among other languages. It is impossible to summarize concisely the key findings of this massive body of new research and explain the newer theoretical ideas in detail.[36] This postscript takes the more pragmatic approach of serving as a brief guide to some of this newer literature.

During the 1980s, computerization took a wider variety of forms than in the 1950s through 1980s. In the 1950s through 1980s, most studies of "computer use" and its consequences focused on data entry clerks or users of printed reports which were generated from batch systems run on shared minicomputers and terminals ("desktop computing") substantially altered the character of computer use in many workplaces in North America (Kling & Iacono, in press).

Home computer use is another example of the way that changing technologies have altered the social conditions and meaning of computing for millions of people in the United States. In the 1970s, home computer uses were relatively a tiny minority; they were primarily scientists who had terminals connected to timesharing services or hobbyists who built primitive microcomputers. By the mid-1980s millions of people from diverse walks of life had acquired commercial quality microcomputers at home—for entertainment, finance, education, word processing, and so on. As a consequence, computerization at home had different meanings for many people in the 1980s and was more accessible as a subject of study than in the 1970s (Olson, 1983; Vitalari, Venkatesh, &

---

[35]This postscript was written to accompany the publication of key sections of "Social Analysis of Computing" in the present book. "Social Analysis of Computing: Theoretical Perspectives in Recent Empirical Research" was originally published in *Computing Surveys, 12*(1), (March 1980):61–110.

[36]There have been some interesting studies which examine computerization from several analytical perspectives which were not included in this study: Frankfurt School critical theory (Hirschheim, 1986), feminism (Wright & Associates, 1987), and ethnomethodology. Because of space constraints, I have not amplified the original characterization of six theoretical perspectives to include these newer approaches.

Gronhaug, 1985; Turkle, 1984). Similarly, desktop computerization (Kling & Iacono, in press), electronic mail (Sproull & Kiesler, 1986), instructional computing (Kling, 1986; Beeman & Associates, 1988) were also much more widely adopted and began to become subjects of scholarly inquiry.

However, the scale of scholarly research *has not kept up* with the vast increase in the kind of computer systems in use and the variety of conditions under which they are developed, deployed, and used. For analysts who see a uniform logic beyond all forms of computerizations, such as "more choices in life" or "tightened managerial control" and "deeper penetrations of the organizations into private life," this research gap is not a fundamental problem. But those scholars who have become intrigued by the empirical reality of computerization have found that the "social and economic forces" that shape computerization are somewhat varied, that systems do not always fit the preferences of managers and the visions of their designers, and that computer usage is shaped by social relations and physical conditions that can vary from one setting to another. To us, this research gap echoes loud silences. It is ironic that we are still puzzled by key possibilities, meanings, and many actual consequences of computerization as we race into a social form that some analysts joyfully label "the information age." The possibilities and actual working out of computerization for people, organizations, and the larger social order still continues to pose many significant questions. In the absence of a body of good scholarship which adequately covers computerization, the dominant discourse is a anchored in a professional and journalistic literature which simplistically heralds new technical possibilities (cf. Giuliano, 1982; Poppel, 1982) and occasionally reports discouragement when optimistic promises are not readily fulfilled (cf. Salerno, 1985).

## Computerization in Worklife

Computerization in workplaces has been the topic most subject to systematic study in the 1980s, and several recent books examine the topic from different theoretical perspectives (Kraut, 1987; Shaiken, 1986; Noble, 1985, Danziger and Kraemer, 1986; Wright and Associates, 1987; Howard, 1985; Bjorn-Anderson, Eason, and Robey, 1986). Class politics and human relations approaches have dominated the literature, but they are not the only viable approaches to understanding computerization and work.

The class politics analyses focus on one primary storyline: that managers shape computerization to control the workforce through a variety of strategies, including more tightly monitoring workers, deskilling jobs, fragmenting jobs, and so on (Howard, 1985; Shaiken, 1986; Noble, 1985). Mowshowitz (1986) summarizes some of this research literature and argues that the regimented "factory of the past" is the model of work organization which drives current office automation projects. He argues that clerical workers of all kinds have been substantially regimented by managerially-imposed regimes, and that managers will employ emerging computer-based technologies to similarly regiment and fragment the work of professionals and socially isolate them as well.

While managers have computerized in order to fragment, speed up, and more tightly control some jobs, the overall body of empirical studies have found relatively little electronic monitoring and regimentation. Some studies report complex patterns of sharpened control, not simple top-down control (Kling & Iacono, 1984a). But overall, the literature indicates that there is a substantial variety in the changes in work that are attributable to computerization (Danziger & Kraemer, 1986): clerks can report upskilling and job integration (Carter, 1987), as well as occasions of increased regimentation and stress (Turner, 1984). Professionals often benefit more from computerization than clerical workers (Danziger & Kraemer, 1986). These outcomes are not entirely happenstance. There is good reason to believe that occupational power plays a key mediating role. On the average, professionals and managers are more likely than clerks to adapt computing in ways that improves their working conditions. But there are substantial variations in work within occupations and with different modes of computerization as well as between them (Iacono & Kling, 1987).

The study of computing and work has also become more sophisticated in at least three ways. (a) Scholars are beginning to study the ways that work is organized rather than the character of individual jobs. This shift has profound repercussions for study designs, since one examines work groups or work groups and their clients rather than random samples of workers who have specific jobs, but who do not necessarily work together (Kling & Iacono, in press); (b) Scholars have begun to appreciate that computerization is a long term process; as a consequence short "before-after" comparisons may not tell us much about the nature of working conditions 10 or 20 years after a work group first computerized (Kling, 1984); (c) Scholars have realized that occupations change substantially over time and that the interplay between technology, work, work organization, skill levels, and labor markets unfolds over decades (Iacono & Kling, 1987).[37]

I believe that the big question about how computerization transformed work for any major occupational group has not yet been answered definitively. And I am skeptical of studies that rapidly generalize from a small sample of technologies and workplaces to "all work and computerization." One key difficulty in assessing studies of computerization and work—and drawing sound general conclusions—is in understanding to which work worlds the studies readily generalize. In 1984, there were approximately 105 million full-time paid workers in

---

[37]The first and third of these themes can be found in the better class politics analysis of worklife (Zimbalist, 1979; Littler, 1982), and they are now influencing a broader sociologically informed series of inquiries. Class politics analyses have often assumed a monolithic role for managers, a relatively passive role for workers, and an assumption that relations between workers and managers are basically similar in all workplaces (Braverman, 1974; Mowshowitz, 1986).

the United States. Approximately 57 million participants in the full-time paid workforce were white collar workers; of these, approximately 48 million were office workers; and of these office workers, about 15 million were clerical workers of various kinds—from data entry clerks through telephone operators to secretaries (Kling & Turner, forthcoming). These people worked in several dozen occupations and for a wide variety of organizations - large and small, rich and poor, public and private, and so on. No single study can examine more than a tiny fraction of occupations, kinds of organizations, technologies, forms of work organization, and work worlds. This does not mean that we need 10,000 studies before we can draw meaningful conclusions. It does mean that we have to be careful how we generalize from studies which are necessarily limited in scope. One should pay attention to key dimensions of technology, work and social life, and not *casually generalize* from a study of clerks who work in a large regimented office to all clerks; from freelance professionals to all professionals; or from rich organizations to poor ones. Nor can we generalize casually from work with mainframes to work with microcomputers, or from work with record-keeping systems to communication via electronic mail. As a consequence, our understanding of how computerization alters the character of work will build slowly as careful studies accumulate across occupations, work arrangements, technologies, implementation strategies, labor market conditions, stage of computerization, and so on rather than through one definitive study. Theoretical perspectives play a key role in helping decide what small slice of computerization and worklife will stand as an adequate sample to generalize to a much larger set of worlds of work and computing and along what dimensions to develop new studies (Kling & Iacono, in press).

## Theoretical Advances: Web Models

In earlier sections of this chapter I contrasted two broad theoretical perspectives: systems rationalism and segmented institutionalism. Careful studies framed within systems rationalism can sometimes provide important insights about people's direct experience in using computing equipment under special social conditions (Sproull & Kiesler, 1986; Turkle, 1984). But the perspective has been of limited use in helping us understand how social and political relations shape computerization and the conditions under which people develop and work with computer-based systems. Nevertheless, systems rationalism dominates the professional literature about computerization (Giuliano, 1982; Poppel, 1982; Salerno, 1985). It is also characteristic of many social-psychological studies since they usually examine individuals or small groups in a sociological vacuum.

Some scholars have tried to use the multiple theoretical perspectives examined in this paper to generate alternative hypotheses within the same study (Scacchi, 1981; Rittenhouse, 1987). This has been an interesting strategy to build on the strengths of each perspective, but also to compensate for their weaknesses. But it proves unwieldy, since the researcher carries along six parallel sets of hypotheses (or storylines) simultaneously. Walt Scacchi and I have developed a simpler strategy which rests on a specific theoretical model for understanding computerization in social settings: web models (Kling & Scacchi, 1982; Kling, 1987). Several interesting empirical studies have explicitly adopted web models as an organizing frame (Kling & Iacono, 1984a; Goodman & McHenry, 1986) and several other recent studies use them implicitly (Laudon, 1986; Kraemer, Dickhoven, Tierney, & King, 1987; Beeman & Associates, 1988). The web models have been useful for giving new insights into the role of computerized systems in "decision making" and negotiating (see section on "Decision Making"); and also for understanding the role of computer-based systems in altering power relations in social settings (see section on "Organizational Power"). But their value goes beyond this limited, though useful, role.

Since there is scant room in this short section to explain web models conceptually and illustrate them with a detailed example, the interested reader should examine the original expositions (Kling & Scacchi, 1982; Kling, 1987). In a web model, a computer system is a *mixture* of social and technological elements which are organized in a specific social setting; it is not simply a technology used in a social context. Here we can sketch their meaning and utility, and point the reader to relevant literature.

For example, consider a computerized system to monitor budgets. It may be viewed as a "tool" which can help accountants track the expenditures in their departments. However, a typical computer user does not have flexible control over all aspects of its use. Most computer-based systems are built or operated with critical resources shared with other users, other systems, or other organizational units. Shared arrangements which are commonplace for significant cost savings also constrain operational schedules, the arrangements for altering the data collected or the reporting formats, or ways of getting access to basic computing resources. As a consequence, it may be difficult to rapidly reorganize a particular budget-monitoring system to track budgets differently, for example, by cost-center instead of by line item. Certainly "computers" can be programmed to execute the programs for budget-monitoring systems which are organized both by line items and by cost centers within departments. But the difficulty facing a cadre of accountants who wish to reorganize their particular budget monitoring system is not only the difficulty of reorganizing their kind of software, but also the difficulty of changing the particular complex sets of overlapping social obligations in which their systems are enmeshed:

- getting approval for their project through their own organizational hierarchies and through the agents who approve and schedule computing alterations
- having programming staff understand their requirements
- getting adequate commitments of skill, time, and money devoted to this project

- insuring that systems analysts and programmers have an adequate understanding of the layers of software which comprise the current system so they can properly renovate it
- altering data collection procedures so that data is properly coded by various clerks (e.g., by cost center in addition to the line item)
- having the new programs tested and integrated into the proper program libraries for routine operations and maintenance

In the course of getting their budget-monitoring system changed, most accountants would find that their organizations are not simply unified task systems. Some organizations, particularly those that are more "bureaucratic," can be rather cumbersome places to accumulate resources for altering standard procedures, communication channels, reporting arrangements, and so on. In addition, if the accountants work in different organizational units, or have different lines of work, they may have different preferences for how the revised system should perform and who should control it. Rather than acting as efficient unified task systems, organizations also act as: (a) rule-oriented bureaucratic systems; (b) sets of political fiefdoms; and (c) arenas in which members negotiate social statuses and social meanings. Web models take these alternative aspects of organizational life into account (Kling & Scacchi, 1982; Kling, 1987).

Web models of computerization examine the adoption, development, use and impacts of systems like this budget-monitoring system in the *context* of key systems and social relations like those sketched above. They also consider the *infrastructure* systems development and support as an integral element of its operational form and examine the *history* of systems and social relations as important constraints on the range of possible action. All analyses about the adoption, development, and use of computer-based technologies draw boundaries to include significant participants. Many systems rationalist analyses draw formal, a priori boundaries around direct computer-based systems and immediate users, their work groups, or at formal organizational boundaries. As Kling (1987) shows, these boundaries have often failed to capture important social relationships which influence the development and use of computer-based systems. Web models have helped analysts draw more meaningful, behaviorally justifiable boundaries (Goodman & McHenry, 1986; Kling, 1987; Beeman & Associates. 1988; Kraemer, Dickhoven, Tierney, & King, 1987; Laudon, 1986; Dutton & Kraemer, 1985). Within these behaviorally drawn boundaries, web models help explain (a) the social leverage provided by computing arrangements; (b) the corequisites for smoothly operating systems; and (b) the ways in which the social settings in which computing arrangements are developed and used shape their configurations and consequences. In addition to serving as an analytical approach to understanding computerization, web models help shape research strategies by providing explicit criteria for identifying the array of participants who influence computerization and the relevant time frames.

# REFERENCES

Ackoff, R. (1971). Management misinformation systems. In A. Westin (Ed.), *Information technology in a democracy*. Cambridge, MA: Harvard University Press.

Albrecht, G. (1976). The effects of computerized information systems on juvenile courts. *Justice Systems Journal, 2*, 107–120.

Albrecht, G. (1979, August). Defusing technical change in juvenile courts: The probation officer's struggle for professional autonomy. *Sociology of Work and Occupation, 6* (3), 259–282.

Allison, G. (1971). *The essence of decision: Explaining the Cuban missile crisis*. Boston, MA: Little, Brown, & Co.

Alter, S. L. (1980). *Decision support systems: Current practice and continuing challenge*. Reading, MA: Addison-Wesley.

Argyris, C. (1971). Management information systems: The challenge to rationality and emotionality. *Management Science, 17*(6), 275–292.

Argyris, C. (1972). *The applicability of organizational sociology*. New York: Cambridge University Press.

Attewell, P., & Rule, J. (1984, December). Computing and organizations: What we know and what we don't know. *Communications of the ACM, 27*(12), 1184–1192.

Bachrach, P., & Baratz, M. (1963, September). Decisions and nondecisions: An analytical framework. *American Political Science Review, 57*, 632–642.

Baker, F. (1973). *Organizational systems: General systems approaches to complex organizations*. Homewood, IL: Richard D. Irwin.

Banfield, E. (1961). *Political influence: A new theory of urban politics*. New York: The Free Press.

Beeman, W., & Associates (1988). *Intermedia: A case study of innovation in higher education*. Providence, RI: Institute for Research on Instructional Systems, Brown University.

Bell, D. (1973). *The coming of post-industrial society: A venture in social forecasting*. New York: Basic Books.

Bell, D. (1979, May/June). Communications technology—for better or for worse. *Harvard Business Review, 57*(3), 20–45.

Bjorn-Anderson, N. & Pederson, P. (1977). *Computer systems as a vehicle for changes in the management structure*. Working Paper 77-3, Information Systems Research Group. Copenhagen, Denmark: University of Copenhagen.

Bjorn-Anderson, N., & Rasmussen, L. B. (1980a). Sociological implications of computer systems. In H. Smith & T. Green (Eds.), *Man-computer research*. London: Academic Press.

Bjorn-Anderson, N., & Eason, K. (1980b). Myths and realities of information systems contributing to organizational rationality. In A. Mowshowitz (Ed.), *Proceedings of the Second Conference on Computers and Human Choice*. Amsterdam: North Holland.

Bjorn-Anderson, N., Eason, K., & Robey, D. (1986). *Managing computer impact: An international study of management and organizations*. Norwood, NJ: Ablex.

Blau, P., Falbe, C. M., McKinley, W., & Tracey, P. (1976, March). Technology and organization in manufacturing. *Administrative Science Quarterly, 21*(1), 20–40.

Boden, M. (1978, December). Social implications of intelligent machines. In *Proceedings of the 1978 Annual ACM Conference* (pp. 746–752). Washington, DC.

Boguslaw, R. (1965). *The new utopians: A study of system design and social change.* Englewood Cliffs, NJ: Prentice-Hall.

Braverman, H. (1974). *Labor and monopoly capital: The degradation of work in the twentieth century.* New York: Monthly Review Press.

Buffa, E., & Miller, J. (1979). *Production-inventory systems: Planning and control* (3rd ed.). Homewood, IL: Richard D. Irwin.

Burch, J., Strater, F., & Grudnitski, G. (1979). *Information systems: Theory and practice.* New York: Wiley.

Carne, W. (1979, October). The wired household. *IEEE Spectrum, 61–66.*

Carter, V. (1987). Office technology and relations of control in clerical work organization. In Wright and Associates (1987).

Champine, G. (1978). *Computer technology impact on management.* New York: North Holland.

Chartrand, R. (1971). *Systems technology applied to social and community problems.* New York: Spartan Books.

Collins, R. (1975). *Conflict sociology: Toward an explanatory science.* New York: Academic Press.

Colton, K. (Ed.). (1978). *Police computer technology.* Lexington, MA: Lexington Books.

Colton, K. (1979, January). The impact and use of computer technology by the police. *Communications of the ACM, 22*(1), 10–20.

Conery, J. (1980). *Metaphors of instrumental computer use: A case study.* (Working paper, Public Policy Research Organization). Irvine, CA: University of California—Irvine.

Cuff, E. C., & Payne, G. C. F. (Eds.). (1979). *Perspectives in sociology.* London: George Allen and Unwin.

Danziger, J. (1977a, January/February). Computers and the litany to EDP. *Public Administration Review, 37,* 28–37.

Danziger, J., & Dutton, W. (1977b, December). Computers as an innovation in American local governments. *Communications of the ACM, 20*(12), 945–956.

Danziger, J., Kraemer, K., & King, J. (1978). An assessment of computer technology in U.S. local governments. *Urban Systems, 3,* 21–37.

Danziger, J., Dutton, W., Kling, R., & Kraemer, K. (1980). *Computers and politics: High technology in American local governments.* New York: Columbia University Press.

Danziger, J. (1985, March). Social science and the social impacts of computer technology. *Social Science Quarterly, 66*(1), 3–21.

Danziger, J., & Kraemer, K. (1986). *People and computers: The impacts of computing on end-users in organizations.* New York: Columbia University Press.

DeBrebander, B., Deschoolmeester, D., Leyder, R., & Van Lommel, E. (1972, January). The effect of task volume and complexity upon computer use. *The Journal of Business, 45*(1), 56–84.

Den Hartog, J. F., Wielinga, C., & Heine, P. (1980). The integration of a computer system in the task environment of process operators: A case of action research. In

A. Mowshowitz (Ed.), *Proceedings of the Second Conference on Computers and Human Choice.* Amsterdam: North Holland.

Dery, D. (1977). *The bureaucratic organization of information technology: Computers, information systems, and welfare management.* PhD dissertation, Dept. of Public Policy, University of California, Berkeley.

Donelson, W. (1979, May). MRP—Who needs it? *Datamation, 25*(5), 185–197.

Donovan, J., & Madnick, S. (1977, Winter). Institutional and ad hoc DSS and their effective use. *Database, 8*(3), 79–88.

Dorf, R. (1977). *Computers and man* (2nd ed.). San Francisco, CA: Boyd and Fraser.

Downs, A. (1967, September). A realistic look at the final payoffs from urban data systems. *Public Administration Review, 27,* 204–209.

Dutton, W., & Kraemer, K. (1978, March). Management utilization of computers in American local governments. *Communications of the ACM, 21*(3), 206–218.

Dutton, W., & Kraemer, K. (1980, January/February). The automation of bias: Computers and local government budgeting. *Society, 17*(2).

Dutton, W., & Kraemer, K. (1985). *Modelling as negotiating.* Norwood, NJ: Ablex.

Emery, F. (Ed.). (1969). *Systems thinking.* Baltimore, MD: Penguin Books.

Galbraith, J. (1977). *Organization design.* Reading, MA: Addison-Wesley.

Galbraith, J. K. (1979). *The new industrial state* (3rd ed.). New York: Houghton Mifflin.

Gasser, L., & Scacchi, W. (1979). *Towards a social framework for understanding personal computing* (Tech. Rep. No. 142). Irvine, CA: University of California— Irvine, Dept. for Information and Computer Science.

Gerson, E. M., & Koenig, S. R. (1979). *Information systems technology and organizations: The impact of computing on the division of labor and task organization* (Working Paper). San Francisco, CA: Pragmatica Systems.

Gibson, C. (1975). A methodology for implementation research. In R. Schultz & D. Slavin (Eds.), *Implementive operations research/management science.* New York: Elsevier.

Gintis, H. (1979, December). Reconsideration: The new industrial state. *New Republic, 181*(22), 28–32.

Giuliano, V. (1982, September). The mechanization of office work. *Scientific American, 247,* 148–164.

Goodman, S. (1979). Software in the Soviet Union: Progress and problems. In *Advances in computers* (Vol. 18). New York: Academic Press.

Goodman, S. E., & McHenry, W. K. (1986, November). MIS in Soviet industrial enterprises: The limits of reform from above. *Communications of the ACM, 29*(11), 1034–1043.

Gordon, A. (1979, Spring). Computers and politics in China. *Computers and Society, 9* (3/4), 18–30.

Gotlieb, C. C., & Borodin, A. (1973). *Social issues in computing.* New York: Academic Press.

Greenberger, M., Crenson, M. A., & Crissey, B. L. (1976). *Models in the policy process: Public decision-making in the computer era.* New York: Russell Sage Foundation.

Herbert, S., & Colton, K. (1978). The implementation of computer-assisted policy resource allocation methods. In K. Colton (Ed.), *Police computer technology.* Lexington, MA: Lexington Books.

Hiltz, R. S., & Turoff, M. (1978), *The network nation.* Reading, MA: Addison-Wesley.

Hirschheim, R. (1986). *Office automation: A social and organizational perspective.* New York: Wiley.

Hoffman, E. (1977). Technology, values and political power in the Soviet Union: Do computers matter? In F. Fleron (Ed.), *Technology and communist culture: The socio-cultural impact of technology under socialism.* New York: Praeger.

Hoos, I. (1960). When the computer takes over the office. *Harvard Business Review, 38,* 102–112.

Hoos, I. (1974). Criteria for 'good' futures research. *Technological Forecasting and Social Change, 6*(2), 113–132.

Howard, R. (1985). *Brave new workplace.* New York: Viking.

Iacono, S., & Kling, R. (1987). Office technologies and changes in clerical work: A historical perspective. In R. Kraut (Ed.), *Technology and the transformation of white collar work.* Hillsdale, NJ: Erlbaum.

Johnson, J. M., & Douglas, J. D. (Eds.). (1978). *Crime at the top: Deviance and the professions.* New York: J. B. Lippincott.

Kanter, J. (1977). *Management-oriented information systems* (2nd ed.). Englewood Cliffs, NJ: Prentice-Hall.

Kay, A., & Goldberg, A. (1977, March). Personal dynamic media. *Computer,* 31–41.

Keen, P. (1975, Spring). Computer-based decision aids: The evaluation problem. *Sloan Management Review,* 13–21.

Keen, P., & Scott-Morton, M. (1978). *Decision support systems: An organizational perspective.* Reading, MA: Addison-Wesley.

Kerner, D. (1979, Spring). Business information characterization study. *Data Base, 10* (4), 10–17.

Killough, L. (1972). The management system viewed in perspective. In D. Li (Ed.), *Design and management of information systems.* Palo Alto, CA: Science Research Associates.

King, J., & Kraemer, K. (1978, March). Electronic funds transfer as a subject of study in technology, society, and public policy. *Telecommunications Policy, 2*(1), 13–21.

King, J., & Kraemer, K. (1979, July). *Assessing the interaction between computing policies and problems: Toward an empirically defined stage theory of computing evolution* (Working Paper). Irvine, CA: University of California—Irvine, Public Policy Research Organization.

King, J., & Kraemer, K. (1986, November). Computing in public organizations. *Public Administration Review,* 488–496.

Kling, R. (1973, August). Toward a person-centered computer technology. In *Proceedings of the 1973 ACM National Conference* (pp. 387–391). Atlanta, GA.

Kling, R. (1974, Fall). Computers and social power. *Computer and Society, 5*(3), 6–11.

Kling, R. (1977a, December). The organizational context of user-centered software design. *MIS Quarterly, 1*(4), 41–52.

Kling, R., & Gerson, E. (1977b, Fall). The social dynamics of technical innovation in the computing world. *Symbolic Interaction, 1*(1), 132–146.

Kling, R. (1978a). Information systems in public policy making: Computer technology and organizational arrangements. *Telecommunications Policy, 2*(1), 22–32.

Kling, R. (1978b). Electronic funds transfer systems and quality of life. In *Proceedings of the 1978 AFIPS National Computer Conference* (Vol. 47, pp. 191–197). Arlington, VA: AFIPS Press.

Kling, R. (1978c, June). Automated welfare client-tracking and service integration: The political economy of computing. *Communications of the ACM, 21*(6), 484–493.

Kling, R. (1978d, August). Value conflicts and social choice in electronic funds transfer systems developments. *Communications of the ACM, 21*(8), 642–657.

Kling, R. (1978e, December). Information systems as social resources in policymaking. In *Proceedings of the 1978 ACM Annual Conference* (pp. 666–674). Washington, DC.

Kling, R. (1978f). *The impacts of computing on the work of managers, data analysts and clerks* (Working Paper). Irvine, CA: University of California—Irvine, Public Policy Research Organization.

Kling, R., & Gerson, E. (1978g, Spring). Patterns of segmentation and intersection in the computing world. *Symbolic Interaction, 1*(2), 24–43.

Kling, R., Scacchi, W., & Crabtree, P. (1978h, Summer). The social dynamics of instrumental computer use. *SIGSOC Bulletin, 10*(1), 9–21.

Kling R. (1979a, March). Alternative EFT developments and quality of life. *Telecommunications Policy, 3*(1), 52–64.

Kling, R., & Scacchi, W. (1979b). Recurrent dilemmas of routine computer use in complex organizations. In *Proceedings of the 1979 AFIPS National Computer Conference* (Vol. 48, pp. 107–115). Arlington, VA: AFIPS Press.

Kling, R. (1980a). Social issues and impacts of computing: From arena to discipline. In A. Mowshowitz (Ed.), *Proceedings of the Second Conference on Computers and Human Choice.* Amsterdam: North Holland.

Kling, R., & Scacchi, W. (1980b). Computing as social action: The social dynamics of computing in complex organizations. In M. Yovits (Ed.), *Advances in computers* (Vol. 19). New York: Academic Press.

Kling, R., & Ahrentzen, S. (1980c). *The integration of computing in engineering work* (Tech. Rep.). Irvine, CA: University of California—Irvine, Dept. of Information and Computer Science.

Kling, R. (1980d). *The social dynamics of computer use with technology of large 'social scope': The case of material requirements and planning* (Tech. Rep.). Irvine, CA: University of California—Irvine, Dept. of Information and Computer Science.

Kling, R. (1984, June). Assimilating social values in computing-based technologies. *Telecommunications Policy,* 127–147.

Kling, R. (1986, Spring/Summer). The new wave of academic computing in colleges and universities. *Outlook, 19*(1/2), 8–14.

Kling, R. (1987). Defining the boundaries of computing across complex organizations. In R. Boland & R. Hirschheim (Eds.), *Critical issues in information systems.* New York: Wiley.

Kling, R., & Iacono, S. (1984a, December). The control of information systems after implementation. *Communications of the ACM, 27*(12), 1218–1226.

Kling, R., & Iacono, S. (1984b). Computing as an occasion for social control. *Journal of Social Issues, 40*(3), 77–96.

Kling, R., & Iacono, S. (in press). Desktop computerization and the organization of work. *Technologies de l'Information et Societie.*

Kling, R., & Scacchi, W. (1982). The web of computing: Computer technology as social organization. *Advances in computers* (Vol. 21, pp 1–90.). New York: Academic Press.

Kling, R., & Turner, C. (forthcoming). The structure of the information labor force: Good jobs and bad jobs. In R. Kling, S. Olin, & M. Poster (Eds.), *California's Informational Utopia: The social transformation of postwar Orange County.* Berkeley, CA: University of California Press.

Kraemer, K. (1977, July/August). Local government, information systems, and technology transfer. *Public Administration Review, 38,* 368–382.

Kraemer, K., & Dutton, W. H. (1979, May). The interests served by technological reform: The case of computing. *Administration and Society, 11*(1), 80–106.

Kraemer, K., & King, J. L. (1979, Summer). Requiem for USAC. *Policy Analysis, 5*(3), 313–349.

Kraemer, K. (1980a). Computers, information, and power in local governments. In A. Mowshowitz (Ed.), *Proceedings of the Second Conference on Computers and Human Choice.* Amsterdam: North Holland.

Kraemer, K., Dutton, W., & Northrup, A. (1980b). *The management of information systems.* New York: Columbia University Press.

Kraemer, K. (1980c). *Citizen impacts from information technology in public administration* (Working Paper). Irvine, CA: University of California—Irvine, Public Policy Research Organization.

Kraemer, K., Dickhoven, S., Tierney, S. F., & King, J. (1987). *Datawars: The politics of modelling in federal policymaking.* New York: Columbia University Press.

Kraut, R. (Ed.). (1987). *Technology and the transformation of white collar work.* Hillsdale, NJ: Erlbaum.

Laudon, K. (1974). *Computers and bureaucratic reform.* New York: Wiley Interscience.

Laudon, K. (1976, September). Computers and cultural imperatives. *Science,* 1111–1112.

Laudon, K. (1980). Information technology and participation in the political process. In A. Mowshowitz (Ed.), *Proceedings of the Second Conference on Computers and Human Choice.* Amsterdam: North Holland.

Laudon, K. (1986). *Dossier society: Value choices in the design of national information systems.* New York: Columbia University Press.

Lauer, R. (1973). *Perspectives on social change.* Boston: Allyn and Bacon.

Lawler, E. E., & Rhode, J. G. (1976). *Information and control in organizations.* Pacific Palisades, CA: Goodyear.

Lenk, K. (1980). Computer use in public administration: Implications for the citizen. In A. Mowshowitz (Ed.), *Proceedings of the Second Conference on Computers and Human Choice.* Amsterdam: North Holland.

Li, D. (Ed.). (1972). *Design and management of information systems.* Palo Alto, CA: Science Research Associates.

Licklider, J. C. R., & Vezza, A. (1978, November). Applications of information networks. *Proceedings of IEEE, 66*(11), 1330–1346.

Littler, C. (1982). *The development of the labour process in capitalist societies: A comparative study of the transformation of work organization in Britain, Japan, and the USA.* London: Heinemann.

Lowi, T. J. (1979). *The end of liberalism: The second republic.* New York: W. W. Norton.

Lucas, H. (1975a). *Why information systems fail.* New York: Columbia University Press.

Lucas, H. (1975b, October). The use of an accounting system: Action and organizational performance. *Accounting Review,* 735–746.

Lucas, H. (1975c, April). Performance and use of an information system. *Management Science, 21*(1), 908–919.

Lucas, H. (1978a, January). Unsuccessful implementation: The case of a computer-based order entry system. *Decision Science, 9*(1), 68–79.

Lucas, H. (1978b, March). The use of an interactive storage and retrieval system in medical research. *Communications of the ACM, 21*(3), 197–205.

Lukes, S. (1978). Power and authority. In T. Bottomore & R. Nesbit (Eds.), *A history of sociological analysis.* New York: Basic Books.

Mann, F., & Williams, L. K. (1958). Organizational impact of white collar automation. *Annual Proceedings of Industrial Relations Research Associates* (pp. 59–68).

Mann, F. C., & Williams, L. K. (1960). Observations on the dynamics of change to electronic data processing equipment. *Administrative Science Quarterly, 5,* 217–256.

March, J., & Simon, H. A. (1958). *Organizations.* New York: Wiley.

Markus, M. L. (1979). *Understanding information systems use in organizations: A theoretical explanation* (PhD dissertation, Case Western Reserve University). Cleveland, Ohio.

Martin, J. (1978). *The wired society.* Englewood Cliffs, NJ: Prentice-Hall.

McLaughlin, R. A. (1978, July). The mis(use) of DP in government agencies. *Datamation, 27*(7), 147–157.

McLean, E., & Riesing, T. L. (1977, Winter). MAPP: A decision support system for financial planning. *Data Base, 8*(3), 9–14.

Michael, D. (1964, October). Speculations on the relation of the computer to individual freedom and the right to privacy. *George Washington Law Review, 33,* 270–286.

Mowshowitz, A. (1976). *The conquest of will: Information processing in human affairs.* Reading, MA: Addison-Wesley.

Mowshowitz, A. (1978). Computers and ethical judgment in organizations. In *Proceedings of the 1978 Annual ACM Conference* (pp. 675–683). Washington, DC.

Mowshowitz, A. (1981). On approaches to the study of social issues in computing. *Communications of the ACM, 24,* 146–155.

Mowshowitz, A. (1986). The social dimensions of office automation. In M. C. Yovits (Ed.), *Advances in computers* (Vol. 25, pp. 335–404). New York: Academic Press.

Mumford, E., & Banks, O. (1967). *The computer and the clerk.* London: Routledge and Keegan-Paul.

Mumford, E. (1978). Values, technology and work. In G. Bracchi & P. C. Lockerman (Eds.), *Information systems technology* (pp. 142–159). New York: Springer-Verlag.

Myers, C. A. (1970). *Computers in knowledge-based fields.* Cambridge, MA: MIT Press.

Noble, D. (1978). Social choice in machine design: The case of automatically controlled machine tools, and a challenge for labor. *Politics and Society, 8*(3–4), 313–347.

Noble, D. (1985). *The forces of production.* New York: Alfred Knopf.

Olson, M. (1983). Remote office work: Changing patterns in space and time. *Communications of the ACM, 26,* 182–187.

Perrow, C. (1979). *Complex organizations: A critical essay* (2nd ed.). Glenview, IL: Scott, Foresman.

Pettigrew, A. (1973). *The politics of organizational decision-making.* London: Tavistock.

Pfeffer, J. (1979). Management as symbolic action: The creation and maintenance of organizational paradigms. In L. Cummings & B. Staw (Eds.), *Research in organizational behavior* (Vol. 3). Greenwood, CT: JAI Press.

Poppel, H. L. (1982, November–December). Who needs the office of the future? *Harvard Business Review, 60*(6).

Press, L. (1974, December). Arguments for a moratorium on the construction of a community information utility. *Communications of the ACM, 17*(12), 674–678.

Rittenhouse, R. G. (1987). *The social dynamics of computer-based text processing.* Doctoral Dissertation. Department of Information & Computer Science, University of California, Irvine.

Ritzer, G. (1977). *Working: Conflict and change* (2nd ed.). Englewood Cliffs, NJ: Prentice-Hall.

Robey, D. (1979). MIS effects on managers task scope and satisfaction. In *Proceedings of the 1979 AFIPS National Computer Conference* (Vol. 48, pp. 391–395). Arlington, VA: AFIPS Press.

Rule, J. (1974). *Private lives and public surveillance: Social control in the computer age.* New York: Schocken Books.

Rule, J. McAdam, D., Stearns, L., & Uglow, D. (1980). *The politics of privacy: Planning for personal data systems as powerful technologies.* New York: New American Library.

Sackman, H., & Nie, N. (1970). *The information utility and social choice.* Arlington, VA: AFIPS Press.

Salerno, L. M. (1985, November–December). What happened to the computer revolution? *Harvard Business Review, 63*(6), 129–138.

Sanders, D. (1974). *Computers and management in a changing society.* New York: McGraw-Hill.

Sanders, D. (1977). *Computers in society* (2nd ed.). New York: McGraw-Hill.

Sapolsky, H. (1972). *The Polaris system development.* Cambridge, MA: Harvard University Press.

Scacchi, W. (1981). *The process of innovation in computing: A study of the social dynamics of computing* (PhD Dissertation). Dept. of Information & Computer Science, University of California, Irvine.

Schiller, H. (1969). *Mass communications and American empire.* Boston, MA: Beacon Press.

Scott, W. G. (1973). Organization theory: An overview and appraisal. In F. Baker (Ed.), *Organizational systems: General systems approaches to complex organizations.* Homewood, IL: Richard D. Irwin.

Shaiken, H. (1986). *Work transformed: Automation and labor in the computer age.* Lexington, MA: Lexington Books.

Silverman, D. (1971). *The theory of organizations.* New York: Basic Books.

Simon, H. A. (1947). *Administrative behavior.* New York: Macmillan.

Simon, H. A. (1965). *The shape of automation for men and management.* New York: Harper and Row.

Simon, H. A. (1973, May/June). Applying information technology to organizational design. *Public Administration Review, 33,* 268–287.

Simon, H. A. (1977). *The new science of management decision-making.* Englewood Cliffs, NJ: Prentice-Hall.

Sproull, L. S., & Kiesler, S. (1986, November). Reducing social context cues: Electronic mail in organizational communication. *Management Science, 32*(11), 1492–1512.

Steinfels, P. (1979). *The neo-conservatives.* New York: Simon and Schuster.

Sterling, T. (1979, May). Consumer difficulties with computerized transactions: An empirical investigation. *Communications of the ACM, 22*(5), 283–289.

Stewart, R. (1972). *How computers affect management.* Cambridge, MA: MIT Press.

Strauss, A. (1978). *Negotiations: Order, process, structure, and context.* San Francisco, CA: Jossey-Bass.

Swanda, J. (1979). *Organizational behavior: Systems and applications.* Sherman Oaks, CA: Alfred Publishing.

Swanson, E. B. (1974, October). Management information systems: Appreciation and involvement. *Management Science, 21*(1), 178–188.

Tausky, C. (1977). *Work organizations: Major theoretical perspectives* (2nd ed.). Itasca, IL: F. E. Peacock Publishers.

Thompson, R. (1967). *Organizations in action.* New York: McGraw-Hill.

Turkle, S. (1980, January/February). Computing as Rorschach. *Society/Transaction, 17* (2), 15–24.

Turkle, S. (1984). *The second self: Computers and the human spirit.* New York: Simon and Schuster.

Turner, J. (1978). *The structure of sociological theory* (revised ed.). Homewood, IL: Dorsey Press.

Turner, J. (1984, December). Computer mediated work: The interplay between technology and structured jobs—claims representatives in the Social Security Administration. *Communications of the ACM, 27*(12), 1210–1217.

U.S. Government Department of Commerce. (1977). *Computers in the federal government: A compilation of statistics.* National Bureau of Standards Publication 500-7, Government Printing Office, Washington, D.C.

Vitalari, N. P., Venkatesh, A., & Gronhaug, K. (1985, May). Computing in the home: Shifts in the time allocation patterns of households. *Communications of the ACM, 28*(5), 512–522.

Weizenbaum, J. (1976). *Computer power and human reason.* San Francisco, CA: Freeman.

Westin, A., & Baker, M. (1972). *Databanks in a free society: Computers, record-keeping, and privacy.* New York: Quadrangle Books.

Whisler, T. (1970). *The impact of computers on organizations.* New York: Praeger.

Withington, F. (1969). *The real computer: Its influence, uses, and effects.* Reading, MA: Addison-Wesley.

Wright, B. D., & Associates. (Eds.). (1987). *Women, work and technology: Transformations.* Ann Arbor: University of Michigan Press.

Yates, D. (1977). *The ungovernable city: The politics of urban problems and policymaking.* New Haven, CT: Yale University Press.

Zimbalist, A. (Ed.). (1979). *Case studies in the labor process.* New York: Monthly Review Press.

# 25

# Engineers and the Work that People Do

## 1981

## H. H. Rosenbrock

### INTRODUCTION

The phenomenon which I wish to discuss in this chapter can be illustrated by a plant which was making electric light bulbs in 1979. Production was 800 bulbs an hour, of the type having a metallized reflector, and the components of the glass envelope were made elsewhere. They traveled on a chain conveyor around the plant, which occupied an area about 30 feet by 10 feet and was quite new. It was noisy, and the large room which housed it was drab, but conditions otherwise were not unpleasant.

The plant was almost completely automatic. Parts of the glass envelope, for example, were sealed together without any human intervention. Here and there, however, were tasks which the designer had failed to automate, and workers were employed, mostly women and mostly middle-aged. One picked up each glass envelope as it arrived, inspected it for flaws, and replaced it if it was satisfactory: once every four-and-one-half seconds. Another picked out a short length of aluminum wire from a box with tweezers, holding it by one end. Then she inserted it delicately inside a coil which would vaporize it to produce the reflector: repeating this again every four-and-one-half seconds. Because of the noise, and the isolation of the work places, and the concentration demanded by some of them, conversation was hardly possible.

This picture could be matched by countless other examples, taken from any of the industrialized countries. Beyond the comment that the jobs were obviously bad ones, and that something should have been done about them, we are not likely to be surprised or to feel that the situation was unusual. Yet, as I shall hope to show, what has been described is decidedly odd.

### A DESIGN EXERCISE

To prepare the way, let us take one of the jobs, say the second one, and suppose that in a first-year engineering degree course it was proposed, as a design exercise, to automate it. Picking up bits of wire out of a box is obviously not too difficult, but we can easily avoid it. Let the wire be taken off a reel by pinch rollers and fed through a narrow tube. At the end of the tube, let it pass through holes in two hardened steel blocks. Then we can accurately feed out the right length, and by displacing one of the steel blocks we can shear it off. If this is all made small enough, it can enter the coil, so that when the wire is cut off it falls in the right place.

So far, so good, but the coil may perhaps not be positioned quite accurately. Then, if we cannot improve the accuracy, we shall have to sense its position and move the wire feeder to suit. Perhaps we could do this by using a conical, spring-loaded plunger, which could be pushed forward by a cam and enter the end of the coil. Having found its position in this way, we could lock a floating carriage on which the plunger and wire feeding mechanism were mounted, withdraw the plunger, and advance the wire feeder.

There would be scope here for a good deal of mechanical ingenuity, but a kind which might not appeal to all of the students. "Why not," one of them might ask, "why not use a small robot with optical sensing. The wire feeder could be mounted on the robot arm, and then sensing the position of the coil and moving the arm appropriately would be a simple matter of programming."

An experienced engineer would probably not find much merit in this proposal. It would seem extravagant, using a complicated device to meet a simple need. It would offend what Veblen (1898) calls the "instinct of workmanship," the sense of economy and fitness for purpose. Yet the student might not be discouraged. "All that is true," he might say, "but the robot is still economically sound. Only a small number of these plants will be made, and they will have to bear the development costs of any special device we design. Robots are complicated, but because they are made in large numbers they are cheap, while the development costs will be much less."

After a little investigation, and some calculation, it might perhaps turn out that the student was right. A plant might even be built using a robot for this purpose. What I would like to suggest, however, is that this would not be a stable solution. It would still offend our instinct of workmanship. The robot has much greater abilities than this application demands. We should feel, like the robot specialist (George & Humphries, 1974), that "to bring in a universal robot would mean using a machine with many abilities to do a single job that may require only one ability."

As opportunity served we might pursue one of two possibilities. We might in the first place seek to find some simpler and cheaper device which would replace the robot. Alternatively, having a robot in place with capacities which had been paid for but were not being used, we might attempt to create for it a task which more nearly suited its abilities. It might, for example, be able to take over some other task on a neighboring part of the line. Or we might be able to rearrange the line to bring some other suitable task within the reach of the robot. At all events, as engineers we should not rest happy with the design while a gross mismatch existed between the means we were employing and the tasks on which they were employed.

## THE APPLICATION

The drift of this fable will have become clear. For robot, substitute man or woman, and then compare our attitudes. This I will do shortly, but first let me extend the quotation which was given above (George & Humphries, 1974): "However, it is less obvious that robots will be needed to take the place of human beings in most everyday jobs in industry . . . To bring in a universal robot would mean using a machine with many abilities to do a single job that may require only one ability." There is a curious discrepancy here between the apparent attitudes to robots and to people, and it is this which I wish to explore.

It will be readily granted that the woman whose working life was spent in picking up a piece of aluminum wire every four-and-one-half seconds had many abilities, and was doing a job which required only one ability. By analogy with the robot one would expect to find two kinds of reaction, one seeking to do the job with a "simpler device," and the other seeking to make better use of human ability. Both kinds of reaction do exist, though as will be seen, with a curious gap.

First, one cannot read the literature in this field without stumbling continually against one suggestion: that many jobs are more fitted for the mentally handicapped, and can be better done by them. The following are some examples.

"Slight mental retardation . . . often enables a person to do tedious work which would handicap a 'normal' worker because of the monotony (Swain, 1977)."

"The U.S. Rubber Company has even pushed experimentation so far as to employ young girls deficient in intelligence who, in the framework of 'scientific management' applied to this business, have given excellent results (Friedmann, 1955)."

"The tasks assigned the workers were limited and sterile . . . the worker was made to operate in an adult's body on a job that required the mentality and motivation of a child. Argyris demonstrated this by bringing in mental patients to do an extremely routine job in a factory setting. He was rewarded by the patients' increasing the production by 400 per cent (Herzberg, 1966)."

"Mike Bayless, 28 years old with a maximum intelligence level of a 12-year old, has become the company's NC-machining-center operator because his limitations afford him the level of patience and persistence to carefully watch his machine and the work that it produces (American Machinist, 1979)."

Swain (1977) remarks that "The methodological difficulties of using this . . . approach to the dehumanised job problem cannot be glossed over;" the meaning of which, one hopes, is that society would utterly reject it. Nevertheless, the quotations should alert our instinct of workmanship to the gross misalignment between human abilities and the demands of some jobs. A much more respectable response to this misalignment is the one which appears to many technologists and engineers—that is, to carry the process of automation to the point where human labor is eliminated.

This becomes easier in manual work as the robot becomes cheaper and more highly developed. So, for example, in the manufacture of automobile bodies spot-welding is now regularly done by robots, and spray-painting also will soon cease to be a human occupation. Similar possibilities for eliminating human labor in clerical work are opened up by the microprocessor.

When it is applied to jobs which are already far below any reasonable estimate of human ability, there can be no objection on our present grounds to this development. Difficulties begin when we consider jobs that demand skill and the full use of human ability. To automate these out of existence in one step is never possible. They have to go first through a long process of fragmentation and simplification, during which they become unsuitable for human performance.

The mismatch between jobs and human abilities has also been approached from the opposite side by social scientists. Seeing the underuse of human ability, they have developed their techniques (Drake & Smith, 1973) of job enlargement, job enrichment, and of autonomous groups. These take existing jobs, and redesign them in a way which makes more use of the human abilities of judgment and adaptability. For example, in an autonomous group the allocation of tasks among its members is not imposed from outside but is left to the group itself to decide. The jobs that result can be better matched to human abilities, within the usually severe constraints of the technology. As Kelly (1978) has noted, the opening which is given for the exercise of judgment and adaptability within the group may account for some of the increased productivity that been observed.

These, then, are the techniques available to us for eliminating the mismatch between jobs and human abilities. There are two which reduce the abilities deployed, one of them inadmissible and the other stemming from engineering. There is a group of techniques which seek to use the abilities of people more fully, and these stem from the social sciences. So far as I know there are no others of significance; and what is remarkable is that engineers and technologists have not produced any methodology for using to the full the abilities and skills of human beings.

The designer of the lamp plant, for example, had made its operation automatic wherever he could do so conveniently. Where he could not, he had used human beings. He might perhaps have used robots, and if so he would have been concerned to use them economically and to make full use of their abilities. He felt, it appears, no similar concern for the full use of human abilities. We may say, paradoxically, that if he had been able to conside people as though they were robots, he would have tried to provide them with less trivial and more human work.


## A PARADIGM

The conclusion we have reached discloses the oddity which was mentioned at the beginning of this paper. It is one that becomes more strange the more one considers it, and we are bound to ask how it arises.

The question has two parts: how do individual engineers come to adopt the view we have described, and how did this originate and become established in the engineering profession? As to the individual, engineers in my experience are never taught a set of rules or attitudes which would lead to this kind of view, nor do they base their actions on a set of explicit principles incorporating it. Instead, we have to imagine something like the ''paradigm'' discussed by Thomas Kuhn (1973). This is the name he gives, in the sciences, to a matrix of shared attitudes and assumptions and beliefs within a profession.

The paradigm is transmitted from one generation to another, not by explicit teaching but by shared problem-solving. Young engineers take part in design exercises, and later in real design projects as members of a team. In doing so, they learn to see the world in a special way: the way in fact which makes it amenable to the professional techniques which they have available. Paradigms differ from one specialization to another within engineering, so that a control engineer and a thermodynamicist, for example, will see a gas turbine in slightly different ways. Effective collaboration between them will then demand a process of mutual reeducation, as many will have discovered from this or other kinds of collaboration.

Seen in this way, as a paradigm which has been absorbed without ever being made fully explicit, the behavior of the lamp-plant designer becomes understandable. We still have to ask how this paradigm arose. This is a question which deserves a more extended historical study than any I have seen. Tentatively, however, I suggest the following explanation, which has been given elsewhere (*New Technology: Society, Employment and Skill,* 1981) in somewhat greater detail.

Looking back at the early stages of the industrial revolution we tend to see the early machines as part of one single evolution. Examples of the machines themselves can be found in museums, and in looking at them we see the family resemblance which they all bear, deriving from the materials what were used and the means by which they were fashioned. They were made of leather and wood, and of wrought and cast iron, and in all of them these materials were fashioned in similar ways.

What I wish to suggest is that there were in fact two quite different kinds of machine, similar only in their materials and their construction, but with opposed relationships to human abilities. One of them can be typified by Hargreaves's spinning-jenny, which he invented for his own or his family's use. It is a hand-operated machine, deriving from the spinning wheel, but allowing many threads to be spun at the same time. To use it demands a skill, which is a natural development from the skill needed to use the spinning wheel. This skill in the user is rewarded by a great increase in his productivity. Samuel Crompton's spinning-mule was a similar kind of machine, and even when it was driven mechanically it needed the skilled cooperation of the spinner.

The other type of machine can be typified by the self-acting mule which was invented by Richard Roberts in 1830. What Roberts set out to do was not, like Hargreaves or Crompton, to make skill more productive. Rather he set out to eliminate skill so that the spinner was no longer needed except to supervise a set of machines. Fragments of his job remained, such as mending broken threads, or removing thread which had been spun. These jobs were given largely to children, and they began to resemble the jobs around the lamp-making plant.

For reasons which were valid enough in the early nineteenth century, and which were well documented by Ure (1835) and Babbage (1832), the second course proved more profitable for the inventor and the manufacturer than the first. When the engineering profession arose later in the century it therefore inherited only one attitude to the relation between machines and human skill, which is essentially the one described above.

Whether this attitude is appropriate at the present time is something which I should question. In a broad economic sense, the underuse of human ability is clearly a loss. Some of the reasons which made it nevertheless profitable for an early manufacturer no longer apply with the same force. Unskilled labor is still cheaper than skilled (Babbage, 1832), but much less so than it was at an earlier period. Once only skilled workers could strike effectively (Ure, 1835), but the less-skilled now, by their numbers, may have even greater industrial strength.

Under present conditions, the motivation of workers may be a major preoccupation of managers. By "quality circles" or other means they may strive to engage the abilities of the workers outside their jobs. By the social scientists' techniques of job-redesign they may seek to make the jobs themselves less repugnant to human ability. For engineers to spend effort and money at the same time on fragmenting jobs and reducing their content seems neither rational nor efficient, if there is any alternative.

## AN ALTERNATIVE PARADIGM

If Hargreaves and Crompton could develop machines which collaborated with the skills of workers in the eighteenth century, can we not do the same in the twentieth century, using the incomparable power and flexibility of new technology? A major difficulty is that the problem is not generally posed as a choice between two alternative routes along which technology could develop. The engineering paradigm is not explicit, and it prevails not by a conscious choice, but by suppressing the ability to see an alternative.

It is therefore useful to construct an example to show how a valid choice could indeed be made. This is not easy. At least 150 years of engineering effort have been given to one alternative, while the other has been ignored. One path is therefore broad, smooth, and easy, the other narrow, difficult, and rough. The example, however, need not be taken from engineering. What has been said applies equally to all technology, and will take on a new force as the advance of the microprocessor affects ever newer and wider areas.

What proves easiest is to choose as example an area where high skill exists, and where the encroachment of technology upon skill has hardly yet begun. In this way, both possible routes which technological development could follow are placed upon an equal basis. Following an earlier account (*New Technology, op cit.*), the example of medical diagnosis will be used.

Feigenbaum (1979) has recently described a computer system called PUFF for the diagnosis of lung diseases. It uses information about patients obtained from an instrument and from their past history. The information is matched against a set of ''rules'' which have been developed by computer scientists in collaboration with medical specialists. In the rules is captured the knowledge of the physician, part of which he was explicitly aware of knowing. Another part was knowledge which he used unconsciously and which only became explicit as he compared his own response with that of the computer.

Though still in an early stage of development, the system gave agreement of 90 to 100 per cent with the physician, according to the tests which were used. There is no difficulty in supposing that this and similar systems can be improved until they are at least as good as the unaided physician.

One way in which they might be used is to make the skill in diagnosis of the physician redundant. The computer system could be operated by staff who had not received a full medical training, but only a short and intensive course in the computer system and its area of application. There might then be no difficulty in showing that the quality of diagnoses was as good as before, and possibly even better. The cost would be reduced, and a better service could be offered to the patient.

Alternatively, diagnosis might still be carried out by the physician but he could be given a computer system to assist him in his work. Much that he had carried in his mind before would now be in the computer, and he would not need to concern himself with it. The computer would aid him by relieving him of this burden, and would allow him to carry on his work more effectively.

Under this second system, the physician would usually agree with the computer's diagnosis, but he would be at liberty to reject it. He might do so if, for example, some implicit rule which he used had not yet found its way into the computer system; or if he began to suspect a side effect from some new drug.

Using the computer in this way, the physician would gradually develop a new skill, based on his previous skill but differing from it. Most of this new skill would reside in the area where he disagreed with the computer, and from time to time more of it might be captured in new rules. Yet there is no reason why the physician's skill in using the computer as a tool should not continually develop.

This is all speculation, but I believe not unreasonable speculation. Which of these two possible routes would be the better? The first leads, step by step, towards the situation typified by the lamp plant. The operators, having no extensive training, can never disagree with the computer, and become its servants. In time, the computer might be given more and more control over their work, requesting information, demanding replies, timing responses, and reporting productivity. A mismatch would again arise between the abilities of the operators, and the trivialized tasks they were asked to perform. Social scientists might then be invited to study their jobs, and to suggest some scheme of redesign which would alleviate the monotony or the pressure of the work.

The second path allows human skill to survive and evolve into something new. It cooperates with this new skill and makes it more productive, just as Hargreaves's spinning-jenny allowed the spinner's skill to evolve and become more productive. There seems no reason to believe that this second path would be less economically effective than the first.

The example can be readily transposed into engineering terms. It applies with little change to the future development of computer-aided design. It suggests also that if we rethought the problem, the operator's job on numerically controlled machine tool need not be fragmented and trivialized, to the point where "slight mental retardation" becomes an advantage. The task of making a part, from the description produced by a CAD system, could be kept entire, and could become the basis of a developing skill in the operator.

As I have said elsewhere, (Rosenbrock, 1977) the task of developing a technology which is well matched to human ability, and which fosters skill and makes it more productive, seems to me the most important and stimulating challenge which faces engineers today. If they are held back from this task, it will not be so much by its difficulty, as by the need for a new vision of the relation between engineering and the use of human skill. That I should pose such a problem to engineers will indicate, I hope, the very high position which I give to the role of engineering.

## POSTSCRIPT

My paper could end at that point, but some readers may (and I hope will) feel a sense of unease. The argument which is developed above is in essence a broadly economic one. [The skills and abilities of people are a precious resource which we are misusing, and a sense of economy and fitness for purpose, upon which we justly pride ourselves as engineers, should drive us to find a better relation between technology and human ability.]

Yet economic waste is not the truest or deepest reason which makes the lamp plant repugnant to us. It offends against strong feelings about the value of human life, and the argument surely should be on this basis.

I wish that it could be, but my belief at present is that it cannot, for the following reasons. To develop such an argument we need a set of shared beliefs upon which to build the intellectual structure. Medieval Christianity, with its superstructure of scholastic philosophy, would once have provided the framework within which a rational argument could have been developed. By the time of the Industrial Revolution, this had long decayed, and nineteenth century Christianity did not unequivocally condemn the developments I have described.

Marxism provides an alternative set of beliefs, and a philosophical superstructure, and it utterly condemns the misuse of human ability: but only when it is carried on under a capitalist system. If it is carried on under socialism then Marxism seems not to condemn it unequivocally, and those are the conditions under which Marxism can have the greatest influence. In support, it is only necessary to say that the lamp plant was in a socialist state, and is in no way anomalous there (Haraszty 1977).

Humanism might serve as another possible basis, with its demand (Maritain, 1939) ''that man make use of all the potentialities he holds within him, his creative powers and the life of the reason, and labour to make the powers of the physical world the instruments of his freedom.'' This indeed underlies much of the thought in the social sciences, yet again it seems that no conclusive argument can be based on it.

The difficulties are twofold. First, no system of beliefs is as widely disseminated as industrial society. Therefore if a conclusive argument could be based on one system of beliefs, it would have only a limited regional force. Secondly, and almost axiomatically, if there is a system of beliefs from which some of the prevalent features of industrial society can be decisively condemned, it will not be found as the dominant set of beliefs in an industrialized country.

My own conclusion is that the rejection of trivialized and dehumanized work precedes any possible rationalization. Tom Bell (Meacham) tells the following story of his mate who, day after day, sharpened needles in Singer's Clydebank works. ''Every morning there were millions of these needles on the table. As fast as he reduced the mountain of needles, a fresh load was dumped. Day in, day out, it never grew less. One morning he came in and found the table empty. He couldn't understand it. He began telling everyone excitedly that there were no needles on the table. It suddenly flashed on him how absurdly stupid it was to be spending his life like this. Without taking his jacket off, he turned on his heel and went out, to go for a ramble over the hills to Balloch.''

No very large part of the population so far has turned on its heel and gone for a ramble over the hills, though a mood akin to that does exist. If industrial society ever comes to be decisively rejected, it seems to me that it will be in this way and for these reasons, rather than as the result of a logically-argued critique. The thought, if valid, takes on a special significance at the present time, when we are engaged in determining the kind of work which men and women will do in the era of the microprocessor.

## REFERENCES

*American Machinist, 123*(7), pg. 58. (1979, July).

Babbage, C. (1832, reprinted 1963). *On the economy of machinery and manufactures.* New York: Kelly.

Drake, R. I., & Smith, P. J. (1973). *Behavioral science in industry.* New York: McGraw-Hill.

Feigenbaum, E. A. (1979). Themes and case studies of knowledge engineering. In D. Michie (Ed.), *Expert systems in the microelectronic age* (pp. 3–25). Edinburgh, Scotland: Edinburgh University Press.

Friedmann, G. (1955). *Industrial society* (p. 216). New York: The Free Press.

George, F. H., & Humphries, J. D. (Eds.). (1974). *The robots are coming.* Manchester, UK: NCC Publications.

Haraszty, M. (1977). *A worker in a worker's state.* Baltimore, MD: Penguin Books.

Herzberg, F. (1966). *Work and the nature of man.* Cleveland, OH: The World Publishing Co.

Kelly, J. E. (1978). A reappraisal of sociotechnical system theory. *Human Relations, 31,* 1069–1099.

Kuhn, T. S. (1973). *The structure of scientific revolutions.* Chicago, IL: University of Chicago Press.

Maritain, J. (1939). *True humanism.* London: Geoffrey Bles.

Meacham, S. *A life apart.* Thames and Hudson.

*New technology: Society, employment and skill* (1981). London: Council for Science and Technology.

Rosenbrock, H. H. (1977). The future of control. *Automatica, 13,* 389–392.

Swain, A. D. (1977). Design of industrial jobs a worker can and will do. In S. C. Brown & J. N. T. Martin (Eds.), *Human aspects of man-made systems* (p. 192). Open University Press.

Ure, A. (1835). *The philosophy of manufacturers.* London: Charles Knight.

Ure, A. (1836). *The cotton manufacture of Great Britain.* London: Charles Knight.

Veblen, T. (1898). The instinct of workmanship and the irksomeness of labour. *American Journal of Sociology, 4*(2), 187–201.

# Suggestions for Further Reading—Section V

It is difficult to know where to begin with suggestions for reading on such a broad topic as the relationship between technology and society. The authors and journals mentioned here provide an introduction to the issues. A number of the papers cited themselves contain extensive bibliographies for those who wish to pursue a given issue in more detail. Note also that many of the suggestions for further reading given in the previous chapter cover some of the same issues discussed here.

We first mention some books and papers that raise interesting questions about the role of technology in society. Not all of these references discuss the role of computing technology per se, but they provide valuable background to the issues raised by the papers in this section.

The four-volume work by J. D. Bernal, *Science in History,* (MIT Press, 1969) provides a fascinating account of scientific developments through the ages, from a Marxist perspective, and shows the complex interrelationships between scientific ideas and the economic and political forces of the day. The essays by Lynn White, Jr., in *Dynamo and Virgin Reconsidered* (MIT Press: Cambridge, 1968) provide some perspective on the evolution of present-day attitudes to science and technology. For a good overview of the many relevant works of such writers as Lewis Mumford, Siegfried Giedion, Jacques Ellul, Herbert Marcuse, Karl Marx, John Kenneth Galbraith, and David Landes, the reader is directed to Langdon Winner's well-written book, *Autonomous Technology—Technics-out-of-control as a Theme in Political Thought* (MIT Press: Cambridge, 1977).

An interesting collection of articles on the social determinants of technology can be found in D. MacKenzie, and J. Wacjman (Eds.), *The Social Shaping of Technology* (Milton Keynes: Open University Press, 1985).

The father of cybernetics, Norbert Wiener, was aware of the potential dangers involved in scientific advances, as illustrated in his book *The Human Use of Human Beings* (Houghton-Mifflin: New York, 1950) and in his paper "Some Moral and Technical Consequences of Automation" that appeared in *Science,* 131, 1355–1358, 1960. Howard Rosenbrock's paper "The Future of Control" *Automatica,* 13, 389–392, 1977, makes interesting companion reading. Weizenbaum has developed his ideas in the book *Computer Power and Human Reason* (Freeman: San Francisco, 1976). This book has been harshly reviewed by several scientists. Readers may also be interested in the Weizenbaum review of Feigenbaum and McCorduck's book, *The Fifth Generation: Artificial Intelligence and Japan's Computer Challenge to the World* (Addison-Wesley: Reading, MA, 1983) in *The New York Review of Books,* 16, Oct. 27, 1983.

The positive aspects of engineering and technology are stressed in two books by Samuel Florman, *The Existential Pleasures of Engineering* (St. Martin's Press: New

York, 1975) and *Blaming Technology–The Irrational Search for Scapegoats* (St. Martin's Press: New York, 1981).

Sherry Turkle's book *The Second Self: Computers and the Human Spirit* (Simon and Schuster: New York, 1984) provides a fascinating glimpse into the way computers are seen by segments of our society. Tracy Kidder's phenomenally successful book "The Soul of a New Machine" (Boston: Little, Brown, 1981) gives us an inside view on how a particular computer system was developed, and raises a number of issues about the nature of work, motivation, and industrial organization—topics of concern to several of the chapters in this section.

Much of the current impetus for studies on the social effects of technology has been provided by the dramatic breakthroughs in microelectronics technology. These developments have been viewed by some as a vital ingredient in the transformation of Western industrialized societies into "information societies." Certainly, developments in microelectronics and telecommunications technologies have led to an increasingly diverse range of applications of all spheres of activity. Not only are computers being introduced into such sectors of production as automobiles, chemicals, printing, textiles, and so on, but they are also restructuring the office environment, and affecting the "leisure" industry—e.g. video games, personal computing systems, and videodisc systems. We also see the convergence of computing and communications technologies, as indicated by the use of digital switching systems in communications networks, and electronic mail facilities with computers. The potential economic consequences of this convergence are hinted at by the reorganization of the giant U.S. telephone company, AT&T, as it prepares to provide computing-related services, and the sizeable investment of the U.S. computer corporation, IBM, in the satellite communications company, Satellite Business Systems.

Some analysts, noting the increasingly service-oriented society that is developing, have claimed that we are moving into a new "post-industrial" society, where information serves as a key resource. This viewpoint has been expounded most comprehensively by the American sociologist Daniel Bell, in his book *The Coming of Post-Industrial Society* (Basic Books, New York, 1973). A more recent statement of his views can be found in the article "The Social Framework of the Information Society" which first appeared in the collection *The Computer Age: A Twenty-Year View* (MIT Press, 1979), edited by M. L. Dertouzos and J. Moses. There are a number of articles of interest in this book, most of which are very optimistic about future societal developments. These authors espouse a position of "systems rationalism," (see the article by Rob Kling in this volume), which assumes that there exists consensus across different social groups as to the nature of desirable scenarios for society.

The book by the late Christopher Evans—*The Mighty Micro* (Gollancz: London, 1979) is an example of popular, optimistic, accounts of the effects of the new information technology. Alvin Toffler's book, *The Third Wave*, (William Morrow: New York, 1980) provides another view on our future society.

See also the two collections of readings edited by Tom Forester—*The Microelectronics Revolution.* (Basil Blackwell: Oxford, 1985) and *The Information Technology Revolution* (Basil Blackwell: Oxford, 1985). The articles are of varying quality, but cover a wide variety of topics, from office automation to robotics and industrial relations. A special issue of *Science,* 12 Feb., vol 215, 1982, focused on computing and communications.

The theme of "life in an information society" has been of concern to many groups, including management, trade unions, and the federal government. Reports on this theme have emanated from the Organisation for Economic Co-operation and Development (OECD), and various United Nations organizations. Within Europe, most countries have conducted major studies on the employment and lifestyle changes that may occur. Perhaps the most famous of these is the report to the French Government by Simon Nora and Alain Minc, which appeared in English as *The Computerisation of Society* (MIT Press: Cambridge, 1980).

A study commissioned by the British government was eventually published independently—I. Barron & R. Curnow, *The Future with Microelectronics: Forecasting the Effects of Information Technology* (Frances Pinter: London, 1979).

Yet another study was done by the Dutch government: *The Report of the Dutch Advisory Group on Microelectronics* (Government Printing Office: The Hague, 1980).

Part of a program funded by the Commission of the European Communities on *Forecasting and Assessment in Science and Technology* (FAST) had as its focus the nature of an information society, and the results of some of this work is available in the following books:

M. Godet & O. Ruyssen *The Old World and the New Technologies—Challenges to Europe in a Hostile World.* (Office for Official Publications of the European Communities: Luxembourg, 1981) This paper is a very general survey of problems facing the member countries of the European Community, and discusses the energy crisis and biotechnology trends as well as information technology issues.

The following 2 FAST Conference volumes contain useful material:

L. Bannon, U. Barry, O. Holst (Eds.) *Information Technology: Impact on the Way of Life.* (Tycooly International: Dublin, 1981)

N. Bjorn-Andersen, M. Earl, O. Holst, E. Mumford (eds.) *Information Society—For Richer, For Poorer* (North-Holland: Amsterdam, 1982)

The Club of Rome has also published a study: G. Friedrichs and A. Schaff, (Eds.) "Microelectronics and Society—For Better or Worse" (Pergamon Press: Oxford, 1982). From the labor side, two comprehensive reports on employment issues are: J. Evans, "The Impact of Microelectronics on Employment in Western Europe in the 1908s" (European Trade Union Institute: Brussels, 1980) and J. Rada, "Microelectronics: A Tentative Appraisal of the Impact of Information Technology." (International Labour Organisation: Geneva, 1980). A more general work by union officials is C. Jenkins & B. Sherman *The collapse of work* (Eyre Metheun: London, 1979).

See also the 2 books:

Gordon, R. (Ed) *Microelectronics in Transition: Industrial Transformation and Social Change* (Norwood, NJ: Ablex, 1987).

Hirschhorn, L. *Beyond Mechanization: Work and Technology in a Post-Industrial Age* (Cambridge: MIT Press, 1986).

There are several books that provide a more explicitly political framework for analyzing the relations between new technology and social issues. The book *Architect or Bee?— the human/technology relationship* (Langley Technical Services; Slough, U.K., 1980) by Mike Cooley argues that new technology will be used by management to further control and deskill workers. Further arguments on these lines can be found in the following works:

CSE Microelectronics Group. *Microelectronics: Capitalist Technology and the Working Class.* CSE Books: London, 1980.

H. Braverman. *Labor and Monopoly Capital*. Monthly Review Press: New York, 1974.

D. Noble. Social Choice in Machine Design: The case of Automatically Controlled Machine Design: The case of Automatically Controlled Machine Tools,'' in A. Zimbalist (ed.) *Case Studies in the Labour Process*, Monthly Review Press, New York, 1979.

The collection of papers by Scandinavian researchers, mentioned in the notes for Section IV, is also highly relevant: Bjerknes, G., Ehn, P. & Kyng, M. (Eds) *Computers and Democracy—A Scandinavian Challenge*. (Aldershot; Gower, 1987). Also the recent book by Pelle Ehn, *Work-Oriented Design of Computer Artifacts* (Stockholm; Arbetslivscentrum, 1988).

Finally, the following journals and reviews often contain material of interest *The Information Society, Futures, Technological Forecasting and Social Change, Technology and Culture, Technology and Society, Social Studies of Science, Computers and the Social sciences,* and *Science, Technology, and Human Values.*

# Section VI

# Epilogue

As Tzu-Gung was traveling through the regions north of the river Han, he saw an old man working in his vegetable garden. He had dug an irrigation ditch. The man would descend into the well, fetch up a vessel of water in his arms, and pour it out into the ditch. While his efforts were tremendous, the results appeared to be very meager.

Tzu-Gung said, "There is a way whereby you can irrigate a hundred ditches in one day and whereby you can do much with little effort. Would you not like to hear of it?" Then the gardener stood up, looked at him and said, "And what would that be?"

Tzu-Gung replied, "You take a wooden lever, weighted at the back and light in the front. In this way you can bring up water so quickly that it just gushes out. This is called a draw well."

Then anger rose up in the old man's face, and he said, "I have heard my teacher say that whoever uses machines does all his work like a machine. He who does his work like a machine grows a heart like a machine, and he who carries the heart of a machine in his breast loses his simplicity. He who has lost his simplicity becomes unsure in the strivings of his soul. Uncertainty in the strivings of the soul is something which does not agree with honest sense. It is not that I do not know of such things; I am ashamed to use them."

Werner Heisenberg
*The Physicist's Conception of Nature*

Every age has its myths and preoccupations. Ours is what Ellul has called technique. Our orientation is with technical means. We have an intense devotion to the mechanical steps of our games—to the pursuit of the most efficient means to unexamined and often ephemeral ends. There is a danger that our spectacular achievements in the technical sphere may blind us to the fact that the context within which we must view these achievements must be wider than the technical one alone. We need to remind ourselves that the criteria for all our efforts must ultimately be related to the quality of life and to our image of ourselves as human beings.

In this book we have attempted to show the nature of an important and far-reaching phenomenon of our time. In the selection and adaptation of essays in this book and in the commentaries and notes, we have tried to place this revolution in relation to a variety of human and technical dimensions. At a time of rapid change it is especially important for us to have a sense of perspective about the events that are taking place and our relationship to them. Without this perspective we cannot feel that we control the forces that are shaping our future. It is essential that we understand enough of the terrain so that we can learn to ask the right questions, and thus determine how best to build a technology that is ''appropriate to our needs.''

Those in our society who take such a cosmic view are often the men and women whom we describe as artists. Their concern is not with the ephemeral means, but with a vision of the eternal and the universal. It is therefore appropriate that a book aimed at establishing perspectives should end with an essay called ''The Computer and the Poet.'' This brief essay appeared as an editorial in an issue of *Saturday Review* dedicated to computer achievements.

# 26

# The Computer and the Poet

## 1966

## *Norman Cousins*

The essential problem of man in a computerized age remains the same as it has always been. That problem is not solely how to be more productive, more comfortable, more content, but how to be more sensitive, more sensible, more proportionate, more alive. The computer makes possible a phenomenal leap in human proficiency; it demolishes the fences around the practical and even the theoretical intelligence. But the question persists and indeed grows whether the computer will make it easier or harder for human beings to know who they really are, to identify their real problems, to respond more fully to beauty, to place adequate value on life, and to make their world safer than it now is.

Electronic brains can reduce the profusion of dead ends involved in vital research. But they can't eliminate the foolishness and decay that come from the unexamined life. Nor do they connect a man to the things he has to be connected to—the reality of pain in others; the possibilities of creative growth in himself; the memory of the race; and the rights of the next generation.

The reason these matters are important in a computerized age is that there may be a tendency to mistake data for wisdom, just as there has always been a tendency to confuse logic with values, and intelligence with insight. Unobstructed access to facts can produce unlimited good only if it is matched by the desire and ability to find out what they mean and where they would lead.

Facts are terrible things if left sprawling and unattended. They are too easily regarded as evaluated certainties rather than as the rawest of raw materials crying to be processed into the texture of logic. It requires a very unusual mind, Whitehead said, to undertake the analysis of a fact. The computer can provide a correct number, but it may be an irrelevant number until judgment is pronounced.

To the extent, then, that man fails to make the distinction between the intermediate operations of electronic intelligence and the ultimate responsibilities of human decision and conscience, the computer could prove a digression. It could obscure man's awareness of the need to come to terms with himself. It may foster the illusion that he is asking fundamental questions when actually he is asking only functional ones. It may be regarded as a substitute for intelligence instead of an extension of it. It may promote undue confidence in concrete answers. "If we begin with certainties," Bacon said, "we shall end in doubts; if we begin with doubts, and we are patient with them, we shall end in certainties."

The computer knows how to vanquish error, but before we lose ourselves in celebration of the victory, we might reflect on the great advances in the human situation that have come about because men were challenged by error and would not stop thinking and probing until they found better approaches for dealing with it. "Give me a good fruitful error, full of seeds, bursting with its own corrections," Ferris Greenslet wrote. "You can keep your sterile truth for yourself."

The biggest single need in computer technology is not for improved circuitry or enlarged capacity or prolonged memory or miniaturized containers, but for better questions and better use of the answers. Without taking anything away from the technicians, we think it might be fruitful to effect some sort of junction between the computer technologist and the poet. A genuine purpose may be served by turning loose the wonders of the creative imagination on the kinds of problems being put to electronic tubes and transistors. The company of poets may enable the men who tend the machines to see a larger panorama of possibilities than technology alone may inspire.

A poet, said Aristotle, has the advantage of expressing the universal; the specialist expresses only the particular. The poet, moreover, can remind us that man's greatest energy comes not from his dynamos but from his dreams. The notion of where a man ought to be instead of where he is; the liberation from cramped prospects; the intimations of immortality through art—all these proceed naturally out of dreams. But the quality of a man's dreams can only be a reflection of his subconscious. What he puts into his subconscious, therefore, is quite literally the most important nourishment in the world.

Nothing really happens to a man except as it is registered in the subconscious. This is where event and feeling become memory and where the proof of life is stored. The poet—and we use the term to include all those who have respect for and speak to the human spirit—can help to supply the subconscious with material to enhance its sensitivity, thus safeguarding it. The poet, too, can help to keep man from making himself over in the image of his electronic marvels. For the danger is not so much that man will be controlled by the computer as that he may imitate it.

The poet reminds men of their uniqueness. It is not necessary to possess the ultimate definition of this uniqueness. Even to speculate on it is a gain.

# AUTHOR INDEX

# SUBJECT INDEX